T0314198

Historical Foundations of Entrepreneurship Research

Historical Foundations of Entrepreneurship Research

Edited by

Hans Landström

Professor in Business Administration, Institute of Economic Research and CIRCLE, Lund University, Sweden

and

Franz Lohrke

Brock Family Endowed Chair in Entrepreneurship and Chair, Department of Entrepreneurship, Management and Marketing, Brock School of Business, Samford University, USA

Edward Elgar
Cheltenham, UK • Northampton, MA, USA

© Hans Landström and Franz Lohrke 2010

All rights reserved. No part of this publication may be reproduced, stored in a retrieval system or transmitted in any form or by any means, electronic, mechanical or photocopying, recording, or otherwise without the prior permission of the publisher.

Published by
Edward Elgar Publishing Limited
The Lypiatts
15 Lansdown Road
Cheltenham
Glos GL50 2JA
UK

Edward Elgar Publishing, Inc.
William Pratt House
9 Dewey Court
Northampton
Massachusetts 01060
USA

A catalogue record for this book
is available from the British Library

Library of Congress Control Number: 2010922123

Mixed Sources
Product group from well-managed
forests and other controlled sources
www.fsc.org Cert no. SA-COC-1565
© 1996 Forest Stewardship Council

FSC

ISBN 978 1 84720 919 1 (cased)

Printed and bound in Great Britain by MPG Books Group, UK

Contents

Contributors

David Ahlstrom, Department of Management, The Chinese University of Hong Kong, Hong Kong

Robert A. Baron, Spears School of Business, Oklahoma State University, USA

Mats Benner, Research Policy Institute, Lund University, Sweden

Henrik Berglund, Center for Business Innovation, Chalmers University of Technology, Sweden

Frédéric Delmar, Center for Entrepreneurship Research, EMLYON Business School, France

Verona P. Edmond, Whitman School of Management, Syracuse University, USA

Nicolai J. Foss, Center for Strategic Management and Globalization, Copenhagen Business School, Denmark

Jonas Gabrielsson, CIRCLE, Lund University, Sweden

Andrew Godley, Centre for Entrepreneurship, Henley Business School, University of Reading, UK

Morten Huse, Department of Innovation and Economic Organization, Norwegian School of Management, Norway

Sarah Jack, Institute for Entrepreneurship and Enterprise Development, Lancaster University, UK

Alan R. Johnson, Center for Entrepreneurship Research, EMLYON Business School, France

Peter G. Klein, Contracting and Organizations Research Institute, University of Missouri, USA

Patrick Kreiser, College of Business, Ohio University, USA

Hans Landström, Institute of Economic Research and CIRCLE, Lund University, Sweden

Franz Lohrke, Brock School of Business, Samford University, USA

G.T. Lumpkin, Whitman School of Management, Syracuse University, USA

Lou Marino, Culverhouse College of Commerce and Business Administration, The University of Alabama, USA

Todd W. Moss, Rawls College of Business, Texas Tech University, USA

Brian Nagy, Foster College of Business Administration, Bradley University, USA

Olle Persson, Department of Sociology, Umeå University, Sweden

Anthony Robinson, The Hull College of Business, Augusta State University, USA

Mary Rose, Institute for Entrepreneurship and Enterprise Development, Lancaster University, UK

Martin Ruef, Department of Sociology, Princeton University, USA

Saras D. Sarasvathy, Darden School of Business, University of Virginia, USA

Lennart Schön, Department of Economic History, Lund University, Sweden

Jeremy C. Short, Rawls College of Business, Texas Tech University, USA

R. Daniel Wadhwani, Eberhardt School of Business, University of the Pacific, USA

Linda C. Wang, Department of Management, Michigan State University, USA

Johan Wiklund, Whitman School of Management, Syracuse University, USA

Acknowledgements

Systematic research on entrepreneurship has now been conducted for about 40 years, emerging in the 1970s, even though pioneering contributions on entrepreneurship could be found as far back as in the seventeenth century. As we see it, it is now time to make historical reflection about and within the field, and our main argument in the book is that 'history matters in entrepreneurship research'.

The origins of this book came out of a joint discussion at the Academy of Management Meeting in Philadelphia in 2007. Because we both are interested in historical aspects of research, particularly entrepreneurship – Franz as the former Division Chair of the Management History Division and current secretary of the Entrepreneurship Division within the Academy of Management, and Hans as author of several books and articles on the intellectual roots of entrepreneurship research – our conversation obviously focused on the historical, or rather ahistorical, character of entrepreneurship research. Entrepreneurship had evolved into a rather ahistorical research field, and we were convinced that it was timely to introduce a stronger historical understanding in entrepreneurship research.

This book directly resulted from our conversations and our views about the entrepreneurship field. First, *we believe* that contemporary scholars can learn much from earlier research on entrepreneurship, which makes it unnecessary to 'reinvent the wheel' every time we start a new study (Part I). Second, *we believe* that research on entrepreneurship has become more and more theory driven, in a large part from borrowing concepts and theories from many different disciplines. In order to import these concepts and theories, however, we need to understand the assumptions on which these theories are based and the intellectual roots from which these theories have evolved (Part II). Third, *we believe* that we have a lot to learn from the knowledge achieved in the field of economic history, and from an understanding of the historical setting and institutional context in which the entrepreneur operates (Part III).

The process involved in the production of the *Historical Foundations of Entrepreneurship Research* has been long and hard, but at the same time challenging and rewarding. At the beginning of the process we selected some of the most prominent and senior researchers and asked them to write a chapter that would cover some of the most important concepts and theories in entrepreneurship research today. We were encouraged to find a very positive reaction from the authors, and it was obvious that our book proposal was timely. The writing and reviewing process has been intensive, and the chapters have gone through three rounds of reviews and revisions. A highlight in the process was the symposium that we organized at the 2008 Academy of Management Meeting in Anaheim, California. Despite the 8:00 a.m. session time, we were thrilled to see a crammed seminar room, which convinced us that interest existed in the story that we have tried to tell.

First of all, we would like to take the opportunity to thank all the authors involved in the book. We have been very critical and demanding in our reviews, but throughout the process the authors have been extremely positive, and also very professional in their revisions of the chapters. Second, we want to thank Francine O'Sullivan and her staff at Edward Elgar Publishing, who have always been very supportive and helpful. Finally, as we have been dedicated to the topic and have taken every possible occasion to talk about the book and its content, it would be impossible to mention individually the large number of people who have discussed the subject with us, but all the discussions have been fruitful and we thank everyone for giving us the opportunity to debate and reflect on this critical topic.

Hans Landström
Institute of Economic Research and CIRCLE
Lund University
Lund, Sweden

Franz Lohrke
Brock School of Business
Samford University
Birmingham, AL, USA

1. History matters in entrepreneurship research

Franz Lohrke and Hans Landström

Entrepreneurship investigates how and why some individuals (or teams) identify opportunities, evaluate them as viable, and then decide to exploit them, whereas others do not, and, in turn, how these opportunities result in product, firm, industry and wealth creation (Brush et al., 2003; Shane and Venkataraman, 2000). In a period of 'creative destruction' in society, entrepreneurship as a research field emerged in the 1970s and 1980s, paralleled and reinforced by a host of external factors (e.g. government policy-makers) around the world that supported entrepreneurship. Along with these external factors functioning as a springboard for the growth of entrepreneurship research, several intra-scientific explanations could also be found. For example the field showed increasing opportunities for empirical research and, equally important, the research field offered great opportunities in terms of research funds, endowed chairs, and publication outlets. As a result, scholars from many different disciplines rushed into this promising field of research. Since its emergence in the 1970s and 1980s research on entrepreneurship has grown tremendously (Landström, 2005), with respect to the number of researchers, published articles, conferences, and journals focused on or opening up for entrepreneurial contributions. Indeed, the growth is obvious, irrespective of the measurements employed (Katz, 2003).

We are often told that entrepreneurship is very young as a field of research, and that the field is highly ahistorical in character. The assumption underlying this statement is often that the pace of change in society today makes it necessary to constantly 're-formulate' our knowledge, and in this respect there is not much point in looking back and learning from history. New questions and topics arise all the time that attract researchers' interest and change the research agenda in entrepreneurship, and, as a consequence, the research on entrepreneurship has been regarded as highly fragmented.

In contrast to this view of entrepreneurship as a young and ahistorical field of research, in this book we argue that, although more systematic research on entrepreneurship is indeed only about 30–40 years old, we can find early contributions in the nineteenth and twentieth centuries that significantly add to our knowledge of entrepreneurship. Accordingly, we argue that 'history matters' in entrepreneurship research.

First, some of the best and most influential works on entrepreneurship were written in the early days of entrepreneurship research, and many of these contributions are high quality intellectual achievements. In addition to the high quality knowledge provided, the researchers and their writings can represent role models for other entrepreneurship researchers.

Second, an understanding of past contributions within the field can help to prevent researchers from 'reinventing the wheel' every time they start a new study. Early scholars on entrepreneurship had a close connection to real entrepreneurs and to society, and their empirical and mainly descriptive knowledge gives us a detailed understanding of the phenomenon. This deep knowledge, in turn, provides a necessary step in effectively building theory (Eisenhardt, 1989), and it improves the validity, sophistication and power of the theoretical models developed (Ghoshal, 2006).

Third, today we can see an increased interest in a theoretical development of entrepreneurship research (Brush et al., 2008; Zahra, 2005). As entrepreneurship is highly multi-disciplinary in character, we borrow concepts and theories from other research fields. In doing so, we need 'good groundwork'. When borrowing concepts and theories from other fields, however, we need to understand the roots and assumptions on which these concepts and theories are based. Otherwise we can make a lot of mistakes in our explanations and understanding of entrepreneurship as a phenomenon.

Finally, entrepreneurship research is highly related to policy and entrepreneurial practices, and many of us assume that many of the policies and practices are the best available – based on the best knowledge available today. History teaches us, however, that what is best for one place and time, for example, in one country or region at one point in time, will not always work in other contexts, and policies and practices need also to change with the times.

The conclusion that can be drawn is that history teaches us to challenge the present (Witzel, 2009), and in this book we challenge the field of entrepreneurship in three ways. Specifically, we argue that:

- Entrepreneurship research has a long history, and the phenomenon has for a long period of time attracted scholars from many different disciplines, indicating that we have a lot of high quality knowledge to draw from and to build our future research on.
- Entrepreneurship research has become more and more theory-driven, and, because the field is highly multi-disciplinary, we tend to borrow concepts and theories from mainstream disciplines such as economics, psychology, and sociology and adapt them to the study of entrepreneurship. In borrowing concepts and theories from other fields it is of vital importance for entrepreneurship researchers to understand the assumptions on which these theories are based and the intellectual roots from which these theories have evolved.
- Entrepreneurship scholars have a lot to gain from a closer collaboration with economic historians. Knowledge in economic history can significantly contribute to our understanding of entrepreneurship, and awareness of the historical setting and institutional context is necessary for scholars to draw sensible generalizations about entrepreneurial behavior.

Thus, the aims of the book are (a) to historicize the research on the entrepreneur and entrepreneurship, and (b) to stimulate a fruitful assimilation of historical concerns and reasoning in entrepreneurship research. In the book the historical aspects of entrepreneurship research are developed in three parts. Part I focuses specifically on the field's historical development, and the evolution of entrepreneurship as research field in its own right. Next, in Part II several noted authors provide an historical review of several key theories employed in entrepreneurship research. We have arranged these as chapters focusing primarily on theories related to opportunity recognition, evaluation, and exploitation, with two integrative chapters examining the entire process. Finally, in Part III, we have included chapters focusing on the links between economic history and entrepreneurship, elaborating on our belief that the historical context, i.e. the industrial, economic and societal setting, is critical for drawing sensible generalizations about entrepreneurship.

PART I: HISTORICAL DEVELOPMENT OF ENTREPRENEURSHIP AS A RESEARCH FIELD

As noted above, entrepreneurship research is often regarded as a relatively young and ahistorical field of research. More systematic research on entrepreneurship emerged in the 1970s and 1980s, and since then, with a rapidly changing society, and a general ambition among scholars interested in entrepreneurship to understand the 'entire' phenomenon, new questions have emerged all the time. One unfortunate outcome of this growth is that it tended to make earlier contributions within the field seem less important, and the field became highly fragmented. As a consequence, early contributions in entrepreneurship research tended to be forgotten rather quickly, increasing the risk of continuously 'reinventing the wheel' in entrepreneurship research and missing the possibility to use the contributions already made, thereby missing opportunities for knowledge accumulation and effective theory building.

In recent years, however, research in entrepreneurship has become increasingly self-reflective with a stronger focus on the internal knowledge development within the field, seen in such trends as an increased number of citations made to earlier entrepreneurship research (Cornelius et al., 2006). As a consequence, we find a stronger interest in earlier contributions to entrepreneurship knowledge emerging. This trend is shown not only in the number of citations, but also in an increased number of state-of-the-art books published in entrepreneurship that summarize and synthesize our knowledge within different areas of entrepreneurship research, as well as an increased number of PhD courses around the world that include historical (doctrinal) reflections of the field.

The aim of the first part of the book is to show that entrepreneurship as a phenomenon has attracted scholarly interest for a long time, and that we have a large body of knowledge on entrepreneurship to draw from and build further research on. Part I contains two chapters. In Chapter 2, Hans Landström and Mats Benner take the multidisciplinary character of entrepreneurship research as a starting point, and look particularly at the migration pattern to (and from) entrepreneurship in order to understand the historical development of entrepreneurship as an intellectual field. In this respect, they raise two questions. What was the composition of the field over time, and what main disciplines have dominated in entrepreneurship research during different time periods? They begin their review identifying three eras of entrepreneurship research anchored in different disciplines: the 'economics era' from 1870 till 1940, the 'social sciences era' from 1940 to 1970, and the 'management studies era' from 1970 to the present. Today, they conclude, the field could be regarded as 'searching for maturation' including an intense debate on the domain of entrepreneurship research, a division of the research community, and an increased interest in the theoretical development of the field.

Chapter 3, by Hans Landström and Olle Persson, examines entrepreneurship research as a 'melting pot' of concepts and theories borrowed from other disciplines. Employing bibliometric (i.e. citation-based) analyses they plot the development of research communities within the field and discuss the possibilities for cross-disciplinary entrepreneurship research. They conclude that the field has attracted a broad range of scholars from many different disciplines, but that the research is dominated by those anchored in 'management studies', and that scholars interested in entrepreneurship are divided into 'entrepreneurship researchers' and 'disciplinary researchers'. Within the former, they note that we can find an evolving knowledge platform on entrepreneurship, but as mainstream disciplines remain important, entrepreneurship as a research field can be characterized as a 'bounded' multi-disciplinary field.

PART II: INTELLECTUAL ROOTS OF ENTREPRENEURSHIP RESEARCH

Entrepreneurship research has become more and more theory driven (Brush et al., 2008; Davidsson and Wiklund, 2001; Zahra, 2005). In this respect, entrepreneurship researchers have borrowed concepts and theories from mainstream disciplines such as economics, psychology, and sociology and adapted them to the study of entrepreneurship. Importing theories from other fields of research is often a necessary first step toward a field developing unique theories of its own, but when borrowing theories from other disciplines, we need to contextualize the theories that we use (Zahra, 2007). Imported theories from other disciplines have been developed to understand fundamentally different phenomena from entrepreneurship, however, and a mismatch between theory and context can result in inconclusive or even incorrect findings.

This intellectual borrowing of concepts and theories from other fields has produced several major benefits. First, as entrepreneurship is a multifaceted phenomenon, studying it often requires multiple concepts and theories because no single theory can simultaneously maximize generalizability, simplicity, and accuracy (Weick, 1979). Second, employing well researched theories from more established disciplines such as economics, psychology, and sociology can help develop greater rigor and increase the legitimacy of relatively young fields like entrepreneurship. Third, employing these theories has strengthened the multi-disciplinary ties between entrepreneurship and other fields (see Whetten et al., 2009).

At the same time, although this multi-theoretical approach has enhanced entrepreneurship research, it has the potential to produce a cacophony within the field as different scholars investigate entrepreneurship employing different perspectives (Gartner, 2001; Herron et al., 1991). In addition, ideas, and, in turn, concepts and theories, are products of the time and place in which they develop, so each has its own history and important assumptions (Bedeian, 2004). Thus, in order to better understand important concepts and theories employed in conducting entrepreneurship research, we have to understand both the background and intellectual roots from which the theories have evolved. Failing to do so can lead contemporary scholars to both misinterpret and misapply these borrowed theories.

Thus, in Part II of the book, we extend Zahra's argument. Not only do we need to understand the context in which concepts and theories will be applied, we also need to understand the intellectual roots of the concepts and theories that we import from other fields, including the assumptions on which the concepts and theories are based, the intellectual roots from which the concepts and theories emerged, and the continued development of these theories within their base disciplines. Each theory that we use in entrepreneurship research is based on underlying assumptions and has probably been developed within a specific intellectual 'paradigm'. When entrepreneurship researchers borrow these theories, however, they may ignore these underlying assumptions and intellectual roots, which may lead to very questionable findings and even contradictory results that do not add to our knowledge base.

The aim of the second part of the book is to elaborate on the assumptions and intellectual roots on which entrepreneurship research is based. Of course, it is not possible for us to trace the intellectual roots for all theories used in entrepreneurship research, and Part II can be regarded as offering examples in which we cover several important concepts and theories related to opportunity recognition, evaluation, and exploitation, and integrative works examining the entire process.

Section II.1 Opportunity Recognition

Opportunities can arise from different sources, including exogenous shocks in the environment or the existence of asymmetric information across individuals (Eckhardt and Shane, 2003).

To examine the role of a changing environment, we begin this section with a chapter by Lou Marino, Patrick Kreiser, and Anthony Robinson (Chapter 4) focusing on the historical development of environmental uncertainty research. The authors note that, on the one hand, uncertainty plays a central role in entrepreneurship, but on the other hand, a relatively greater depth of research has been focused on the influence of 'risk-taking' while less attention has been devoted to the role of 'uncertainty' in entrepreneurship research. In the chapter the authors clearly distinguish between the concepts of risk and uncertainty, and review the historical development of the environmental uncertainty construct and the most commonly employed measures of uncertainty. Two theoretical viewpoints, the information uncertainty perspective and resource dependence theory, serve as the foundation of this analysis, and the authors develop recommendations pertaining to the use of this key concept in future entrepreneurship research.

The next three chapters continue this focus on how opportunities arise and, in turn, how entrepreneurs recognize them. In Chapter 5, Nicolai Foss and Peter Klein review the Austrian school of economics and focus, in particular, on Kirzner's concept of 'entrepreneurial alertness'. The authors argue that even though Kirzner's contribution is often thought of as *the* Austrian conception of the entrepreneur, an alternative Austrian tradition exists that emphasizes the entrepreneur as an uncertainty-bearing, asset-owning individual, and that this tradition offers some advantages over the discovery approach (represented, for example, in the Kirznerian incarnations). Foss and Klein are also critical of the way Kirzner's work has been interpreted in entrepreneurship research – this literature goes much beyond Kirzner's work, making opportunity discovery and its determinants the key feature of the theory, whereas Kirzner's real interest lies in explaining market equilibration, a higher-level phenomenon.

In Chapter 6, Robert Baron notes that the concepts 'opportunity' and 'opportunity recognition' have been central in entrepreneurship research, and that the volume of research on these topics has increased considerably in recent years. The aims of this chapter are to offer basic definitions of the concepts, and to provide an overview of theoretical perspectives on opportunity recognition within the field of entrepreneurship. Baron focuses in particular on concepts developed in cognitive psychology to discuss how potential entrepreneurs may recognize opportunities when others do not, based on differences in information access and usage.

Finally, in Chapter 7, Verona Edmond and Johan Wiklund elaborate on another central concept in the field of entrepreneurship research, namely 'entrepreneurial orientation' – a critical construct within research that may affect whether entrepreneurs recognize potential opportunities or not. The authors examine the historical development of entrepreneurial orientations, with the aim of providing an overview of the intellectual roots of the concept of 'entrepreneurial orientation' that originates in organizational and strategy theory. They first identify key thinkers of the entrepreneurial orientation construct and then highlight the most influential contributions of each researcher. In this respect, the progress and the knowledge accumulation of the research field are made visible, and as a result the gaps in the current body of literature are identified and the authors suggest several directions for future research.

Section II.2   Opportunity Evaluation

Next, we examine how entrepreneurs evaluate potential opportunities. Scholars have employed several theories to examine how entrepreneurs' evaluations may potentially differ from those of non-entrepreneurs. In Chapter 8, Saras Sarasvathy and Henrik Berglund provide a detailed review of the theory related to entrepreneurial decision making. They argue that research into entrepreneurial decision making has accomplished only a thin slice of what is possible, because, to date, little effort has been made to relate findings from entrepreneurship research back to scholarship in decision making. Sarasvathy and Berglund conclude that it is time to move from modeling entrepreneurial activity solely as 'decision' occurring within the individual–opportunity nexus to include the 'design' of opportunities, in which opportunities are not exogenous to the entrepreneurial process, but can also be its outcome or residual.

Section II.3   Opportunity Exploitation

In the next section of the book we examine several theories and frameworks examining how entrepreneurs exploit what they have decided are viable opportunities. This section includes four chapters. First, in Chapter 9, Brian Nagy and Franz Lohrke review research related to liabilities new ventures face. They note that despite more than 40 years of 'liabilities of newness' research, the construct remains somewhat ambiguous. In addition, they review related literature examining 'liabilities of adolescence' as well as the relatively new concept of 'assets of newness'. Finally, they suggest other theoretical perspectives (e.g. the resource-based view of the firm) that may help in distinguishing these overlapping constructs.

Second, Martin Ruef focuses his chapter (Chapter 10) on entrepreneurial groups (or venture 'founding teams'). For a long time entrepreneurship was regarded as an individual achievement, and it was not long ago that our view changed, and entrepreneurship was increasingly seen as a collective act. However, from Ruef's review of significant research related to entrepreneurial groups, we learn from historical evidence and frameworks that can be employed to study entrepreneurial groups, and, in turn, learn that a preoccupation with groups is far less recent than research on entrepreneurship might suggest. In the chapter, Ruef offers a selective history of entrepreneurial groups, and traces the intellectual origins of social scientific work on them, emphasizing four classical perspectives: (a) Georg Simmel's structural sociology; (b) Ronald Coase's theory of the firm; (c) the logic of collective action in entrepreneurial groups, as developed by Mancur Olson; and (d) theories of ethnic enterprise, with particular implications for the formation and persistence of entrepreneurial groups.

In the third chapter in this section, Chapter 11 by Jonas Gabrielsson and Morten Huse, the authors discuss governance theory, and give an overview of the historical and intellectual roots of both resource dependence theory and agency theory with a particular focus on how they have been applied in studies on boards of directors. The overview given in the chapter will help entrepreneurship scholars to better understand the extent to which the two theories can be used together and what might be required to make them more compatible. The authors also provide interesting implications for researching behavioral aspects of boards and governance in entrepreneurial firms.

In Chapter 12 Sarah Jack and Mary Rose conclude this section with a chapter reviewing network theory that examines how important an entrepreneur's personal and professional network can be in exploiting an opportunity. The aim of the chapter is to explore the historical and intellectual roots of social network theory, and the authors elaborate on its application within entrepreneurship research. In addition, they examine the way in which multi-disciplinary approaches linking history to network theory can enhance our understanding of the networking behavior of the entrepreneur. In conducting their review, however, the authors also take a critical view on social network theory and explore the ways in which networks may act as a constraint to entrepreneurship.

Section II.4   Integrative Works

The last two chapters in Part II provide broad, integrative views of the entrepreneurial process. In Chapter 13 Alan Johnson and Frédéric Delmar offer an historical review of psychological research in entrepreneurship, including for example the Theory of Planned Behavior and Social Cognitive Theory. In addition, they suggest integrative links between previous and future research into the psychology of entrepreneurs, and, more specifically, integrate motivation theories within a self-regulation framework, i.e. the capacity of individuals to guide their activities over time and across changing circumstances. According to the authors, using a self-regulation perspective allows for a better understanding of the function and form of the entrepreneurial mindset, and permits integration of empirical findings about the dynamic nature of the entrepreneurial process.

Part II concludes with Chapter 14, in which Todd Moss, Tom Lumpkin and Jeremy Short examine the emerging but growing research related to social entrepreneurship. To shed light on the development of social entrepreneurship as a field of research, the authors provide an analysis of earlier research within the field by applying a content analysis of Special Issues on social entrepreneurship in academic journals between 1991 and 2008. The analysis shows that initial work in social entrepreneurship research centered on change processes in the public policy sphere, moving to value creation in the nonprofit sector, and currently focuses on theory-driven research in multiple sectors. Finally, the authors use a historical perspective to identify research opportunities that may predict future conceptual and empirical efforts examining social entrepreneurship and help frame a future research agenda within the field.

PART III: ECONOMIC HISTORY AND ENTREPRENEURSHIP RESEARCH

Historical reasoning has played a profound role in the early development of entrepreneurship research; for example, economic historians made pioneering contributions in understanding the role of the entrepreneurial process in the evolution of industries and economies. One of the first to call for a more extensive collaboration between economic historians and economists around entrepreneurship was Joseph Schumpeter who repeatedly argued that 'economic historians and economic theorists can make an interesting and socially valuable journey together, if they will' (Schumpeter, 1947).

For a long time economic history has been more or less neglected in entrepreneurship research, and entrepreneurship researchers have lacked an interest in the historical and institutional contexts of entrepreneurship. In the last couple of years, however, we can find a stronger attention among entrepreneurship research towards the knowledge that can be found in economic history. This interest has re-emerged in line with the repeated argument in entrepreneurship research that we need to link our knowledge of entrepreneurial behavior on the individual and firm levels of analysis to processes of change at more aggregate levels of analysis (e.g. Davidsson et al., 2001; Low and MacMillan, 1988). For example, it is not possible to understand the entrepreneur as an individual without understanding the institutional and historical context within which the entrepreneur is operating.

The aims of Part III of the book are to re-introduce the interest in economic historical reasoning in entrepreneurial research, and to show how knowledge in economic history can contribute to our understanding of entrepreneurship. As argued by Jones and Wadhwani (2006), the understanding of the historical setting and institutional context are necessary to draw sensible generalizations about entrepreneurial behavior. The four chapters included in Part III will give examples of how we can learn from scholars in economic history, following Schumpeter's plea, with the vision of stimulating a fruitful exchange between scholars in economic history and entrepreneurship research.

In Chapter 15 Daniel Wadhwani introduces the section on economic history and entrepreneurship research by making a detailed examination of the role of historical reasoning in the development of entrepreneurship as a field of research, and gives an overview of why history matters in entrepreneurship research. Wadhwani argues that historicism, i.e. the analytical tradition of contextualizing behavior and cognition in time and place, has shaped the development of the conceptions of entrepreneurship we use today, particularly those that emphasize the role of the entrepreneurial process in explaining evolution within industries and economies. In addition, the author gives examples of how historicism has been used by a number of key entrepreneurship theorists and researchers (such as William Baumol, Joseph Schumpeter, and Alexander Gerschenkron) and shows that these scholars share an approach to exploring the past in their research on entrepreneurship that recognizes the uniqueness of historical reasoning.

Next, we have included three chapters, by Andrew Godley, Hans Landström and Lennart Schön, and David Ahlstrom and Linda Wang, examining historical contexts within Great Britain, Sweden, and East Asia, respectively. In Chapter 16 Andrew Godley demonstrates how entrepreneurial behavior in Great Britain followed a long-term secular decline and then suddenly re-emerged at the end of the twentieth century. One lesson to be learnt is that, in order to understand entrepreneurial behavior, entrepreneurship researchers ought to embrace longitudinal analysis, and Godley argues that 'Detailed reconstruction of historical entrepreneurial activity ought therefore to become ever more important not only for better economic history, but for our quest to better understand entrepreneurship itself'.

In Chapter 17 Hans Landström and Lennart Schön follow a similar vein of thought, arguing that society undergoes long-term cycles, and over the course of these cycles, the characteristics of innovation and entrepreneurial behavior will change. Based on an intellectual tradition in economic history from Schumpeter's ideas about 'business cycles' and the Swedish economist Erik Dahmén's theory on 'development blocs', the authors explain the characteristics of innovation and entrepreneurship over time. The authors use the long structural cycles identified in the Swedish economy since the mid-nineteenth century as an empirical example, show how industrial society exhibits a pattern with periods of positive transformation pressure followed by rationalization and negative pressure ending in a structural crisis, and explain the cyclic variations in innovative and entrepreneurial activities in 'transformation' and 'rationalization' periods.

Finally, in Chapter 18 David Ahlstrom and Linda Wang challenge the 'cultural argument' in explaining the rise of the economies in East Asia. The so called 'Confucian capitalism' has been a key mode of economic organization in East Asia, and is seen by many as the explanation of growth in East Asian economies. Ahlstrom and Wang, however, ask the important question: Is national culture really that important? The authors argue that history seems to tell a different and more ambiguous story about culture's contributions to the development of entrepreneurial capitalism in East Asia. Their conclusion is that researchers (and other observers) must be careful not to rush to cultural explanations before examining historical context, path dependencies, institutions, firm development and other key processes that are largely distinct from culture values. They also argue for employing a history-based, organizationally oriented level of analysis for future research to better understand the development of entrepreneurial capitalism in East Asia.

ADDITIONAL READINGS ON HISTORICAL REASONING IN ENTREPRENEURSHIP RESEARCH

In sum, we have developed this book to provide an historical grounding of entrepreneurship research. We hope you find its contents and lessons useful in enhancing your research efforts, and we believe that historical reasoning will be important in future research and understanding of entrepreneurship. As noted, the primary aims of this book are to help stimulate a 'historicizing' of entrepreneurship research and to create an increased awareness that 'history matters'.

This volume is the first in a two-volume set focusing on these issues. The current volume contains original writings by several leading entrepreneurship scholars, whereas the second volume, *Intellectual Roots of Entrepreneurship Research*, includes classic foundational works on entrepreneurship. Thus, the present volume provides broad historical reviews of key theories and concepts, and the second includes what we believe to be some of the most important seminal works in entrepreneurship. We have organized the second volume much like the first by grouping these classic works within the opportunity recognition, evaluation and exploitation framework. In tandem, the two volumes offer a comprehensive overview of the field and should provide readers with a strong historical grounding in entrepreneurship research.

For those readers interested in other historical overviews of the field, we suggest, along with *Intellectual Roots of Entrepreneurship Research*, the following additional readings:

Cassis, Y. and I. Pepelasis Minoglou (eds) (2005), *Entrepreneurship in Theory and History*, New York: Palgrave.

Hébert, R.F. and A.N. Link (2009), *A History of Entrepreneurship*, Milton Park: Routledge.

Jones, G. and R.D. Wadhwani (eds) (2007), *Entrepreneurship and Global Capitalism*, Cheltenham, UK and Northampton, MA, USA: Edward Elgar.

Landes, D.S., J. Mokyr and W.J. Baumol (eds) (2010), *The Invention of Enterprise*, Princeton, NJ: Princeton University Press.

Landström, H. (2005), *Pioneers in Entrepreneurship and Small Business Research*, New York: Springer.

REFERENCES

Bedeian, A.G. (2004), 'The gift of professional maturity', *Academy of Management Learning and Education*, **3**, 92–98.

Brush, C., I. Duhaime, W. Gartner, A. Stewart, J. Katz, M. Hitt, S. Alvarez, G. Meyer and S. Venkataraman (2003), 'Doctoral education in the field of entrepreneurship', *Journal of Management*, **29**, 309–31.

Brush, C.G., T.S. Manolova and L.F. Edelman (2008), 'Separated by common language? Entrepreneurship research across the Atlantic', *Entrepreneurship Theory and Practice*, March, 249–66.

Cornelius, B., H. Landström and O. Persson (2006), 'Entrepreneurial studies: the dynamic research front of a developing social science', *Entrepreneurship Theory and Practice*, May, 375–98.

Davidsson, P. and J. Wiklund (2001), 'Levels of analysis in entrepreneurship research: current research practice and suggestions for the future', *Entrepreneurship Theory and Practice*, **24**(4), 81–99.

Davidsson, P., M.B. Low and M. Wright (2001), 'Editor's introduction: Low and MacMillan ten years on: achievements and future directions for entrepreneurship research', *Entrepreneurship Theory and Practice*, **24**(4), 5–15.

Eckhardt, J. and S. Shane (2003), 'Opportunities and entrepreneurship', *Journal of Management*, **29**, 333–49.

Eisenhardt, K. (1989), 'Building theories from case study research', *Academy of Management Review*, **14**, 532–50.

Gartner, W. (2001), 'Is there an elephant in entrepreneurship? Blind assumptions in theory development', *Entrepreneurship Theory and Practice*, **24**(4), 27–39.

Ghoshal, S. (2006), 'Scholarship that endures', in D.J. Ketchen, Jr and D.D. Bergh (eds), *Research Methodology in Strategy and Management*, New York: Elsevier, pp. 1–10.

Herron, L., H. Sapienza and D. Smith-Cook (1991), 'Entrepreneurship theory from an interdisciplinary perspective', *Entrepreneurship Theory and Practice*, **16**(2), 7–12.

Jones, G. and R.D. Wadhwani (2006), 'Schumpeter's plea: historical methods in the study of entrepreneurship', Working Paper, Cambridge, MA: Harvard Business School.

Katz, J. (2003), 'The chronology and intellectual trajectory of American entrepreneurship education: 1876–1999', *Journal of Business Venturing*, **18**, 283–311.

Landström, H. (2005), *Pioneers in Entrepreneurship and Small Business Research*, New York: Springer.

Low, M.B. and I.C. MacMillan (1988), 'Entrepreneurship, past research and future challenges', *Journal of Management*, **14**(2), 139–61.

Schumpeter, J.A. (1947), 'The creative response in economic history', *Journal of Economic History*, **7**, 149–59.

Shane, S.A. and S. Venkataraman (2000), 'The promise of entrepreneurship as a field of research', *Academy of Management Review*, **25**(1), 217–26.

Weick, K. (1979), *The Social Psychology of Organizing*, 2nd edn, Reading, MA: Addison-Wesley.

Whetten, D.A., T. Felin and B.G. King (2009), 'The practice of theory borrowing in organizational studies', *Journal of Management*, **35**, 537–63.

Witzel, M. (2009), 'Why management history matters', EFMD Newsletter www.efmd.org/globalfocus downloaded 22 December 2009.

Zahra, S.A. (2005), 'Entrepreneurship and disciplinary scholarship: return to the fountainhead', in S.A. Alvarez, R. Agarwal and O. Sorenson (eds), *Handbook of Entrepreneurship Research. Interdisciplinary Perspectives*, New York: Springer, pp. 253–68.

Zahra, S.A. (2007), 'Contextualizing theory building in entrepreneurship research', *Journal of Business Venturing*, **22**, 443–52.

PART I

Historical Development of Entrepreneurship as a
Research Field

2. Entrepreneurship research: a history of scholarly migration

Hans Landström and Mats Benner

INTRODUCTION

This book is about the historical foundations of entrepreneurship research. Thus, it appears natural to start by stating that entrepreneurship as an intellectual field has a long history – some pioneering contributions were published as far back as the eighteenth century, although more systematic entrepreneurship research only began in the 1970s and 1980s. The aim of this chapter is to provide a historical retrospect of the development of entrepreneurship as an intellectual field. We seek to answer the following questions: 'How has the composition of the field changed over time?' and 'what main disciplines have dominated during different time periods?' We address the issue from a particular angle, in that we study migration patterns to (and from) entrepreneurship research and analyze the consequences of migration for the composition of the field over time. Thus, the main subject of this chapter is the historical formation of entrepreneurship as an intellectual field. It is important to bear in mind that history can be depicted from many different perspectives and that various aspects can be focused upon. We therefore wish to stress that this is our own subjective description of history, and we are well aware that there might be other historical foundations of entrepreneurship research.

In this chapter we argue that entrepreneurship as a phenomenon has attracted scholarly interest for a very long time. Since the early contributions in the eighteenth century, entrepreneurship has evolved through three eras in which it has been anchored in different disciplines: the economics era (1870–1940), the social sciences era (1940–1970), and the management studies era (1970–). Initially, entrepreneurship was regarded as a rather marginal research theme within mainstream disciplines such as economics, and social sciences like psychology and sociology. The research was conducted by a few individual researchers within the respective disciplines. However, since the 1980s, entrepreneurship has evolved toward a field of research in its own right. The evolution of the field was reinforced by a 'creative destruction' in society toward a focus on industrial dynamics and entrepreneurship, and as a result, entrepreneurship has become a centerpiece in the political debate in many countries around the world. The development of entrepreneurship as a research field bears the stamp of an intense immigration of scholars, not least from the broader area of management studies. After the 'take off' in the 1980s, entrepreneurship as a research field grew significantly in the 1990s, creating a strong infrastructure for research. From 2000 onwards, a 'search for maturation' within the field could be identified, including (1) an intense debate on the domain of entrepreneurship research, (2) the division of the research community into a group of 'entrepreneurship researchers' and another, rather scattered group of researchers interested in entrepreneurship within many different disciplines ('disciplinary researchers'), and (3) an increased interest in the theoretical development within the field.

The chapter contains six sections. After this introduction section, some early entrepreneurship thinking is presented. This is followed by a more detailed discussion in three separate sections on the economics, the social sciences, and the management studies eras. The chapter ends with some concluding reflections on the past and future evolution of entrepreneurship research.

Analyzing the Development of Research Fields – An Analytical Perspective

The dynamics of research fields – their rise, institutionalization and possible demise – form a central part of social scientific studies. An early example is Ludwik Fleck's study of 'styles of thought' in the institutionalization of research fields (Fleck, 1979), a theme also discussed in Thomas Kuhn's famous paradigm theory (Kuhn, 1962). Both Fleck and Kuhn stressed the collective and 'sticky' nature of knowledge production, but also how unsolved anomalies in paradigms open up new avenues of research. Kuhn and Fleck adhered to a structural understanding of scientific change and paid very little attention to the personal motivation behind migration. This was instead taken up in studies of intellectual migration and mobility patterns between disciplines, focusing on the motivation for individual researchers to move between fields and how social mechanisms thereby impacted upon research dynamics (Ben-David, 1970).

The main reasons identified for intellectual migration, and for the formation of new fields on the basis of migration, were crises and anomalies of various kinds that led to a search for new theories and methods with a better fit to observations (in line with the Kuhnian approach), a lack of opportunities within existing fields (due to intellectual rigidity), and chances to pursue lines of research in a more unrestricted manner within new fields. Hence, research dynamics may be driven by migration patterns among researchers triggered by 'a crisis' in old fields and/or new opportunities in emerging fields, and the driving forces can be found in intra-academic mechanisms in the emergence of new research fields.

Later studies focused on propelling forces beyond academia, for instance how research areas evolve in political and/or economic environments with their interests and implications. Many new – often cross-disciplinary and problem-oriented – fields have been modeled on the basis of practical knowledge interests (Elzinga, 1985), and external (i.e. non-academic) forces have shaped the re-orientation of scientific inquiries in established fields (Böhme et al., 1976). The evolution of research fields is, however, not a clear-cut linear movement from policy to research; it may also reflect researchers' resource mobilization and their manipulation of policy environments (cf. Bolin, 2007). It seems reasonable to conclude that many research fields, especially those with major political and economic interests, are shaped by 'development networks' consisting of practical and academic influences, where the content, direction and validation of research are outcomes of 'negotiations' between academic and societal interests (Blume, 1985; Funtowicz and Ravetz, 1990). Related to this argument, developments in research may also be analyzed as reflections of resource mobilization among social, political and economic interests (a resource mobilization approach), informed by the political sociology of science.

Finally, we can also look at the structure of entrepreneurship as an intellectual field of research as, for example, demonstrated by Whitley's model (2000), where the social and intellectual dimensions of different research fields could be analyzed on the basis of the extent to which the results can be predicted by a common use and understanding of theories, concepts, and methods, and by a 'mutual dependency', reflecting a social aspect by determining the extent to which scholars need to be coordinated with the intellectual goals of the field in order to obtain resources and make significant contributions. However, Whitley's typology of general research fields can be criticized for building on a discipline-based and somewhat out-of-date view of the organization of sciences. It can be argued that phenomena in the social realm are often open to interpretation and can be understood from various perspectives and increasingly addressed in a cross-disciplinary setting (Landström and Åström, 2011) and, as pointed out by Whitley (2000) himself: 'scientific fields are no longer coterminous with academic disciplines' (p. 302), i.e. today, there is an increasing variation in how scientific work is organized and carried out (see e.g. Gibbons et al., 1994; Knorr Cetina, 1999; Becher and Towler, 2001). However, irrespective of our view of the sciences, we can conclude that migration into a research field will be facilitated in fields characterized by low predictability of results and low dependency among researchers – as is the case of entrepreneurship research.

This list of sociological explanations of research dynamics is by no means exhaustive; other sociological approaches pinpoint the role of macro-actors in shaping research fields and social practices (see Hambrick and Chen, 2008). Based on this reasoning, in this chapter we discuss the historical evolution of entrepreneurship research and try to understand its development from the perspective of the migration of scholars to (and from) entrepreneurship.

EARLY THINKING IN ENTREPRENEURSHIP RESEARCH

Entrepreneurship research has a long history, and in this section we present some early thinking on entrepreneurship within the emerging fields of economics and political economics during the eighteenth and nineteenth centuries. The section ends with a discussion on the further development of the field, from the end of the nineteenth century onward, and we argue that we can identify phases during which certain specific disciplinary approaches dominated entrepreneurship research.

Pioneering Thoughts on Entrepreneurship

The function of entrepreneurship is probably as old as exchange and trade between individuals in society. However, it was not until economic markets emerged that the concept gained importance and scientists started to show an interest in the phenomenon. For a long time the European economy was locked in the feudal system with no security of property rights and local tolls hampering the free flow of products. During the Middle Ages these conditions slowly changed, and a system evolved in which entrepreneurship was primarily embodied by a class of merchants who provided raw materials to the market for finished goods. In addition, the rise of the cities created a frontier for entrepreneurship and economic dynamics. In this development, the Italian cities took the lead, and their commercial success went hand-in-hand with a Renaissance in arts and sciences. The legal framework was developed, property rights secured, economies monetized; thus, by the 1700s the legal and institutional conditions had changed considerably in favor of innovation, entrepreneurship and economic development (Wennekers and Thurik, 2001).

The first author to give entrepreneurship a more precise economic meaning was Richard Cantillon (approx. 1680–1734), an Irish-born banker and businessman who lived in Paris. In his *Essai sur la nature du commerce en general* (1755/1999) he outlined the principles of the early (emerging) market economy based on individual property rights and economic interdependency and recognized three classes of economic agents: landowners, entrepreneurs, and hirelings (van Praag, 2005; Hébert and Link, 2006; 2009). According to Cantillon, entrepreneurs were engaged in market exchanges in order to make a profit, and made business judgments in the face of uncertainty. Cantillon created a vision of how a capitalist economy works and gave the entrepreneur a pivotal role – as an arbitrager responsible for all the exchange in the economy, and who, in turn, brings about the equilibrium between supply and demand. A basic characteristic of Cantillon's analysis was the emphasis on risk and uncertainty, and he related the function of the entrepreneur to uncertainty – entrepreneurship is a matter of foresight and willingness to assume uncertainty (a thought that was later refined by American economists and not least by Frank Knight).

Cantillon's essay initiated an interest among French authors on entrepreneurship, especially among a group called 'the Physiocrats' (physiocracy meaning rule of nature), whose leader François Quesnay (1694–1774) shared Cantillon's basic economic vision and emphasized the importance of capital for economic growth. According to the physiocrats, capital comes from the landlords, and entrepreneurs are present in the economy as farmers (Grebel, 2004; Hébert and Link, 1982; 2006). Another writer who should be mentioned in the French economics tradition is Jean-Baptiste Say (1767–1832), who was himself an industrial entrepreneur as manager of a textile mill in Pas-de-Calais (Hoselitz, 1960). He employed an empirical description of what entrepreneurs actually did and analyzed their function independently of the particular social framework within which they operated (Hébert and Link, 1982; Kalantaridis, 2004). In contrast to Cantillon, Say suggested another definition of entrepreneurship, one which emphasized the coordinating role in production and distribution (i.e. a coordinator): entrepreneurship consists of combining the factors of production into an organization.

In conclusion, these early French authors considered the entrepreneur as a vital component of the market economy, but different aspects were attributed to the entrepreneur and the concept was developed in a number of different directions. The early thoughts on entrepreneurship based on French economic literature of the eighteenth and nineteenth centuries were paralleled or followed by writers in England and Germany during the classical economics period from 1770 to 1870 (see Table 2.1).

Entrepreneurship in Classical Economics and Political Economy

By the mid eighteenth century, production conditions and social relations were changing, and a new way of thinking began to emerge. These changes also affected the intellectual and academic environment. Classic economic theory was developed in the realm of economic science and is generally regarded as having its origin in Adam Smith's (1723–90) *Inquiry into the Nature and Causes of the Wealth of Nations*, published in 1776 – a work

Table 2.1   Early thinking on entrepreneurship

Early contributions (France)	Classical economists (Britain)	Political economists (Germany)
Richard Cantillon 'The Physiocrats' (e.g. Quesnay, Baudeau, and Turgot) Jean-Baptiste Say	Entrepreneurship was more or less neglected in classical economics, the exceptions being Jeremy Bentham and John Stuart Mill	J.H. von Thünen Hans von Mangoldt Gottlieb Hufeland Friedrich Hermann Adolph Riedel

that in many ways set the trend for economic theory and in which Smith laid the foundation for the analysis of the way the market economy functions. Smith's work influenced the view of the entrepreneur in economic science. His entrepreneur was essentially passive, a prudent, cautious person who adjusted to circumstances (Hébert and Link, 2006; 2009), and he did not distinguish between the capitalist as the provider of the 'stock' of the enterprise and the entrepreneur as the ultimate decision-maker – instead the capitalist became the central actor in Smith's analysis.

However, there were a number of English classical economists who maintained a certain amount of interest in entrepreneurship, including Jeremy Bentham (1748–1832), who criticized Smith for not considering the role of the entrepreneur in society, and John Stuart Mill (1806–73), who contributed very little to the theory of entrepreneurship but has been recognized as the person who gave the term 'entrepreneur' a more general meaning than that attributed to it by economists at the time. It can be concluded that the English school of thought mainly interpreted the concept of entrepreneurship as one who supplies financial capital, and the so-called Smith–Ricardo–Mill tradition that dominated English classical economics did not give the entrepreneur any nuanced meaning (Grebel, 2004). As Casson (1987) argued, the disappearance of the entrepreneur in economic theory is even more pronounced following the rise of the neoclassical school of economics. After 1870 economic theory focussed increasingly on deterministic models that emphasized perfect information and perfect markets (Baumol, 1968).

It is interesting to note that there were also some contributions to entrepreneurship theory from researchers in Germany and Austria. The analyses from these countries belonged to a tradition that emphasized administration and politics. One economist who deserves mention is von Thünen (1783–1850), who argued that there is a theoretical difference between entrepreneurship and management and who considered the entrepreneur as both an innovator and a risk bearer. Another is Mangoldt (1824–68), who regarded entrepreneurial profits as the rent for ability, indicating that the entrepreneur should be regarded as a separate factor of production. The German political economy tradition nurtured the concept of business leader, and to some extent they could be regarded as anticipators of Knight's theory of risk and uncertainty (Grebel, 2004; Hébert and Link, 1982; 2006).

Three Eras of Entrepreneurial Thinking

Since these early contributions, the research field has become highly multidisciplinary with an interest among scholars from many different disciplines. At the risk of

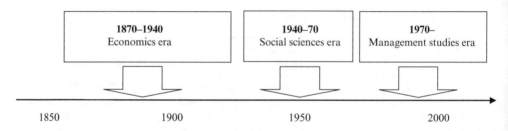

Figure 2.1   Three eras of entrepreneurial thinking

over-simplification, we argue that three different eras of entrepreneurship research can be identified, during which some specific disciplines dominated (Figure 2.1).

We hold that entrepreneurship is a complex phenomenon that requires multiple theoretical lenses to be understood. However, over time entrepreneurship research was anchored in different theories, initially in economics (1870–1940), followed by the social sciences (1940–70) and after 1970 in management studies – based primarily on migration patterns – but has now evolved as a specific research area in its own right.

In this development, the research has moved from being a (rather marginal) theme within some mainstream disciplines such as economics and social sciences like psychology and sociology, mainly based on individual achievements within the respective discipline, toward a more coherent field of research and the creation of a scholarly community of researchers. This movement from a research theme in mainstream disciplines toward a field of research in its own right is not unproblematic. Of course there are still some arguments for anchoring entrepreneurship research in mainstream disciplines. For example, it might be argued that (i) there are few contingencies of interest to entrepreneurship that are not contained in existing disciplines and therefore there is no need for entrepreneurship researchers to 'reinvent the wheel', and (ii) as a research theme within existing disciplines, entrepreneurship research is required to meet the quality criteria of the respective discipline, which is a way for the research to attain academic legitimacy (Davidsson, 2003). On the other hand, as entrepreneurship can be regarded as a rather complex phenomenon, existing theories may not always be optimal for addressing these characteristics, indicating a need to pose new questions and build concepts and models that better explain the phenomenon (Landström, 2001). Leaving entrepreneurship to mainstream disciplines may also imply the lack of a strong research community within entrepreneurship research – a community with deep knowledge and familiarity of entrepreneurship as a phenomenon (Low, 2001) – in addition to which there is no guarantee that research will focus on the most central questions of entrepreneurship (Acs and Audretsch, 2003).

ECONOMICS ERA (1870–1940)

Even though the interest in entrepreneurship among economists seemed to lose its power with the rise of the neoclassical school of economics, and most economists were working within an equilibrium tradition, we can identify a few exceptions who were mainly interested in disequilibrium processes, based on the ideas of Knight, Schumpeter, and the Austrian school of thought (Figure 2.2).

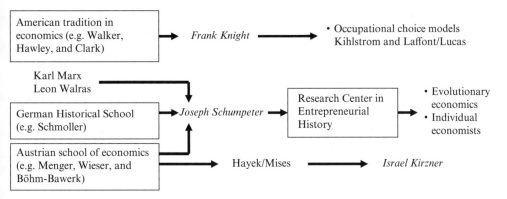

Figure 2.2   The economics era

Knightian Tradition

In the late nineteenth century, the European discussion on entrepreneurship found an audience in the United States. After the Civil War ended in 1865, the US recovered and was well on the way to becoming a major industrial power, at which point some US economists such as Amasa Walker (1799–1875), his son Francis Walker (1840–97), Frederick Hawley (1843–1929) and John Bates Clark (1847–1938) continued the discussion about entrepreneurship. Hawley established a risk theory of profit in which he equated enterprise with risk-taking and regarded risk and uncertainty as commonplace in the industrial system. This caused a dispute between Hawley and Clark, the pre-eminent American economist at that point in time, who refused to concede that risk-bearing was an entrepreneurial activity and argued, as did Schumpeter later on, that all risk is borne by the capitalist (Hébert and Link, 2006; 2009). Hawley's contributions can be regarded as limited, but his work is of interest as it constitutes an intermediate stage between Cantillon and Knight (Kalantaridis, 2004).

The risk–uncertainty theme was thus later picked up by Frank Knight (1885–1972). Within the context of the neoclassical framework, Knight considered the entrepreneur as a key figure in the economic system (Cassis and Pepelasis Minoglou, 2005). Knight's contribution to entrepreneurship theory is that he provided a distinction between insurable risks and non-insurable uncertainty and also put forward the theory of profit that related non-insurable uncertainty to rapid economic change and to differences in entrepreneurial ability. In his thesis *Risk, Uncertainty and Profit* (1916, revised 1921), Knight made a distinction between three types of future uncertainties – risk, uncertainty, and 'true' uncertainty that occurs when the future is not only unknown, but also unknowable with unclassifiable instances and a non-existing distribution of outcomes (Sarasvathy et al., 2003). Knight argued that opportunities arise out of the uncertainty surrounding change – if change is predictable there is no opportunity for profit – and the entrepreneur receives a return for making decisions under conditions of true uncertainty. Entrepreneurial return, therefore, results from the fact that individual activity cannot be predicted, and entrepreneurial competence is the individual's ability to deal with uncertainty.

The work of Frank Knight has been influential, primarily in the context of different occupational choice models, i.e. individuals' choice between becoming an entrepreneur and choosing alternative occupations. One such model was developed by Lucas (1978), who argued that individuals differ in their innate entrepreneurial ability, ranging from the most able, who choose to become entrepreneurs, all the way down to 'marginal entrepreneurs', who are indifferent to the distinction between entrepreneurship and paid employment. In addition, Kihlstrom and Laffont (1979) modeled entrepreneurial choice as a trade-off between risk and returns. In the model, individuals differ with respect to how risk averse they are, and the least risk-averse choose entrepreneurship and will also run the largest firms (Parker, 2005).

Schumpeterian Tradition

Joseph Schumpeter (1883–1950) is probably the best known of the economists with an interest in entrepreneurship at the beginning of the twentieth century. Although Schumpeter himself was a great admirer of Leon Walras, he considered Walras' equilibrium theory incomplete. He noted that some 'energy' existed within the economic system that created disequilibrium in the market. Schumpeter recognized the role of innovation in economic growth and understood that innovation had to be implemented by someone – the entrepreneur. The entrepreneur creates imperfections and growth in the market by introducing innovations.

In Schumpeter's extensive scientific production he tried to build a new economic theory based on change and innovation. In his efforts to create a theory of change he was influenced by the German Historical School – a group of economists critical of the economic doctrine of the time, especially the English tradition of economic thought – arguing that in order to understand economic behavior, economists need to comprehend human motives and behaviors in realistic psychological terms and that an understanding of historical data is a prerequisite for the proper development of economic theory (Hébert and Link, 2006). According to this tradition, the entrepreneurial process is characterized as one of breaking away from old methods of production and creating new ones. The scholars within the German History School that influenced Schumpeter included Max Weber and Gustav Schmoller (1838–1917). From Schmoller's historical and empirical data he identified a unique factor in all economic activity – the enterprising spirit, or the entrepreneur. According to Schmoller, the entrepreneur is a creative organizer whose role is innovation and the initiation of new projects. Despite the fact that Schumpeter considered Karl Marx's economic thesis of little scientific value, he regarded Marx's idea that capitalism possesses internal dynamics that transform it as a brilliant insight that merited further development (Smelser and Swedberg, 1994). Schumpeter combined ideas from Marx and the German Historical School, along with insights from his Austrian forebears, Menger, Weiser, and his teacher Böhm-Bawerk, but did not follow his predecessors and instead created something unique.

Schumpeter's production of scientific works can be regarded as rather fragmented, but throughout his career there is a very clear line of thought – to formulate a new economic theory built on change and 'newness'. Schumpeter was the first to treat innovation as an endogenous process – the entrepreneur as an innovator and prime mover of the economic system, who leads the economy away from existing equilibrium positions and forces it to a higher equilibrium position (van Praag, 2005). His thoughts are presented and analyzed in works by, for example, Swedberg (1994) and Reisman (2004) – see also Chapter 17. However, it is generally argued that Schumpeter's writings fall into two periods – until approximately 1940 he was mainly interested in developing ideas about entrepreneurship and integrating them into a new economic theory based on innovation and economic change, while in the second period, during the 1940s, he focused on the sociological aspects of entrepreneurship and also tried to sketch a research program in entrepreneurship in economic history (Swedberg, 2000).

Schumpeter's ideas stimulated a new wave of interest in the mid twentieth century. At Harvard University – Schumpeter's academic base during the 1930s and 1940s – a research program emerged, headed by the economic historian Arthur Cole (1889–1974), who established the Research Center in Entrepreneurial History in 1948, a multidisciplinary center with an interest in the entrepreneur from the standpoint of economic history. Schumpeter's insights later exerted an influence on the school of Evolutionary Economics (Nelson and Winter, 1982), which applies dynamic analysis to specific historical times and developments, although it has been argued that the link between Schumpeter's work and the new evolutionary economics is in fact rather weak (Andersen, 1994; Fagerberg, 2003). Schumpeter also influenced a few economists who have carried his heritage further, such as Erik Dahmén (1950; 1970) who formulated the concept of 'development blocs', William Baumol (1968; 1990; 1993; 2002) who argued that because entrepreneurship is present in all settings, it is the different institutional structures that generate the variances in wealth creation across societies, and Harvey Libenstein (1968), who explored the significance of entrepreneurship in economic development.

Kirznerian Tradition

Carl Menger (1840–1921) is, above all, considered to be the ideological founder of the so-called Austrian tradition of economic thought. His contribution is mainly at the methodological level. In his seminal work *Grundsätze der Volkswirtschaftslehre* (1871/1950) he introduced a subjectivistic view of the economy. He was the proponent of methodological subjectivism, where economic phenomena are perceived as relations not between objects but between people. Based on this viewpoint, in order to understand such relations, economic theory must proceed from the social, cultural and economic conceptions that govern human actions. Unlike the natural sciences, economics cannot ignore the perceptions, wishes and views of the people studied. This view is also reflected in Menger's methodological individualism. Within society and economics, the actors are individuals – not a group or social class – which means that explanations of economic phenomena have to proceed from or at least be possible to refer back to individual action (Pålsson-Syll, 1998; Koppl and Minniti, 2003). Thus, economic changes do not take place in a vacuum but are created by individuals' awareness and understanding of a given situation. This means that the entrepreneur can be considered an 'agent of change', who transforms resources into useful products and services.

The Austrian school of economic thought was further developed by Menger's disciples Friedrich von Wieser (1851–1926) and Eugen von Böhm-Bawerk (1851–1914). Wieser expanded Menger's ideas and added some dimensions to the entrepreneur, such as leadership, alertness and risk-bearing. Although Böhm-Bawerk added very little directly to the theory of entrepreneurship (Hébert and Link, 2006), one of his students, Ludwig von Mises (1881–1973), continued the ideas of the Austrian school, emphasizing that the individual is an independent economic entity and that the economic conditions in society are to a large extent influenced by his/her actions. According to Mises, economics is the study of 'human action' – people are not only calculating creatures but also alert to making use of opportunities. Like Schumpeter, Mises emigrated to the US when the Nazi party came to power in Germany, but in contrast to Schumpeter he had some difficulties finding an academic home there. Mises, who is regarded as the leader of the Austrian school from about 1920 to his death in 1973, was an important influence on the 1974 Nobel Laurate Friedrich von Hayek (1899–1992). Hayek emphasized the economic role of knowledge and the dispersion of knowledge among the various actors in society – different people know different things and the problem is how to coordinate this dispersed knowledge. He argued that the market process will solve this 'knowledge problem' through decentralized decision-making, but nobody knows in detail how the whole system works. Hayek described market competition as a 'discovery procedure' – anyone in the system may act upon new knowledge or information that allows him or her to profitably reallocate resources (Koppl and Minniti, 2003; Berglund, 2009).

Today, the most prominent disciple of the Austrian tradition is Mises's student Israel Kirzner (1930–) of New York University. In his book *Competition and Entrepreneurship* (1973), Kirzner developed the arguments presented by Mises, although he was also influenced by Hayek's ideas about the 'discovery procedure' (Koppl and Minniti, 2003). According to Kirzner, it is fundamental for an entrepreneur to be alert in identifying and dealing with profit-making opportunities ('entrepreneurial alertness'), i.e. the entrepreneur tries to discover opportunities for profit and helps to restore equilibrium to the market by acting on them. The entrepreneurial function involves the coordination of information, which implies identifying the gap between supply and demand, as well as acting as a broker between supply and demand, making it possible to earn money from the difference. Thus, the entrepreneur searches for imbalances in the system. In such situations, there is an asymmetry of information in the market, which means that resources are not coordinated in an effective way. By seeking out these imbalances and by constantly trying to coordinate the resources in a more effective way, the entrepreneur leads the process toward equilibrium. Thus, Kirzner regards the entrepreneur as a person, who is alert to imperfections in the market thanks to information about the needs and resources of the different actors and, with the help of this information, is able to coordinate resources in a more effective way, thereby creating equilibrium (see Chapter 5 for additional discussion of Kirzner's work).

An alternative conceptualization of the entrepreneur, even if the theoretical construct was only by implication, was developed by Shackle (1970), who was a student of Hayek and who argued that knowledge does not constitute the key to understanding human action, but rather 'unknowledge', or as Shackle expressed it '[economic agents] can choose only among imaginations and fictions. Imagined actions and policies can have only imagined consequences, and it follows that we can choose only an action whose consequences we can not directly know since we can not be eyewitnesses of them' (p. 106). It is the aptitude of imagination that makes individual economic agents enterprising (Kalantaridis, 2004).

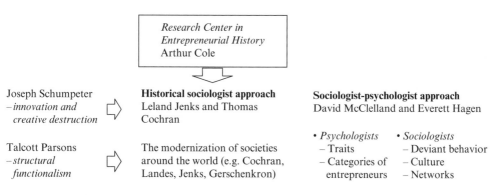

Figure 2.3   The social sciences era

SOCIAL SCIENCES ERA (1940–70)

In the mid-twentieth century the idea of the entrepreneur tended to fade away in the theory of economics (Kalantaridis, 2004), and economics as a discipline became increasingly formalized and mathematically oriented – an approach that made it difficult to include the entrepreneur in the models of economics (Hébert and Link, 2009). As a consequence, classical and early neoclassical economic theorists left the concept of entrepreneurship as a source of structural change within capitalist economies largely undeveloped. However, in the 1940s a number of social scientists, for the most part anchored in economic history and sociology, began to take an interest in entrepreneurship as an empirical phenomenon. The historical study of entrepreneurship typically employed a Schumpeterian approach and focused on the modernization process of societies around the world. By the 1960s this stream of research lost momentum, but scholars from psychology entered the field with an interest in the entrepreneur as an individual, and their works started to investigate his/her key traits and personality. The research on entrepreneurship during the social science era (1940 to 1970) is outlined in Figure 2.3.

Early Historian Sociologists' Interest in Entrepreneurship

We can find an early interest in entrepreneurship and related questions among historians. As far back as the mid nineteenth century, economic historians questioned the static theories of classical and neoclassical economics and argued for the use of historical analysis in order to understand the way in which institutions of capitalism and industries evolved (Hodgson 2001; Jones and Wadhwani, 2007).

In the early twentieth century a number of historians and historical sociologists started to emphasize the role of the entrepreneur in the process of economic change (Jones and Wadhwani, 2007). For example, some German historical sociologists including Max Weber (1864–1920) led the way to exploring the role of the entrepreneur in a changing society. His main contribution to entrepreneurship knowledge was presented in his well-known work *The Protestant Ethic and the Spirit of Capitalism* (1904/1970), in which he placed a strong emphasis on religious influences – primarily the Protestant work ethic – as a driver of entrepreneurial forces in society. Weber argued that this ethic created a positive attitude to work and to earning money, which, in turn, facilitated the development of entrepreneurship and capitalism. Weber also made some contributions to entrepreneurship in his later, more political writings during the 1910s, when he contrasted the entrepreneur with the bureaucrat, arguing that as society becomes more rationalized, bureaucracy tends to increase in importance, and the entrepreneur is the only person who can keep bureaucracy at bay (Swedberg, 1998; 2000; Martinelli, 1994).

Among the influential historical sociologists of that time were Georg Simmel (1858–1918), a contemporary of Weber with an interest in interpersonal associations and a forerunner of modern network analysis, and Werner Sombart (1863–1941), who in his six-volume magnum opus *Der moderne Kapitalismus* (Modern Capitalism, 1911), coined the concept of creative destruction, which later became a key ingredient of Schumpeter's theory of innovation.

The Historical Sociologist Approach

For many years, Schumpeter argued for empirical historical studies of entrepreneurship. In a series of articles and speeches he suggested extensive research that involved greater collaboration between economic historians and economists focusing on how entrepreneurship shaped the historical development of firms, industries, economies, and modern capitalism (Jones and Wadhwani, 2006). For example, in the article 'The creative response in economic history' (1947) Schumpeter posited that 'Economic historians and economic theorists can make an interesting and socially valuable journey together if they will' (p. 149) and called for the use of historical methods in the study of entrepreneurship (Jones and Wadhwani, 2007).

In the 1940s, a number of economic historians and sociologists began to explore entrepreneurship as an empirical historical phenomenon, and over the next few decades historians produced a large body of literature on entrepreneurship and its role in the modernization process of societies around the world, all of which was partly inspired by Schumpeter's plea to employ more elaborate historical methods in the study of entrepreneurship. Theoretically, the research drew heavily on Talcott Parsons's structural-functional theory of social roles. Over the following three decades economic historians produced a large body of research, in which the role of entrepreneurship in the historical development of countries around the world was emphasized (Sass, 1978). In addition, social scientists interested in the process of 'modernization' further built on this historical research base and used it to expand on theories of long-term economic development and historical change (Wadhwani and Jones, 2007).

The effort was led by the Harvard economic historian Arthur Cole, who in 1948 organized the Research Center in Entrepreneurial History at Harvard University, which was highly multidisciplinary in character. Several of the most influential scholars at that point in time were affiliated to the center, for example sociologists like Talcott Parsons and economic historians such as Thomas Cochran, Alexander Gerschenkron, David Landes, and Fritz Redlich, in addition to Schumpeter. The journal *Explorations in Entrepreneurial History* provided the institutional mechanism to pull the wide range of empirical studies together.

The Center adopted an eclectic view of economic history. Cole encouraged a wide range of approaches to 'entrepreneurial history', including socio-cultural studies, neo-classical economic approaches, and work that focused on the evolution of industries. Influential contributions to the intellectual milieu were made by two American historians: Leland Jenks and Thomas Cochran. In the mid-1940s Jenks presented a study in which he used Schumpeterian reasoning to examine the dynamic and disruptive entrepreneurial force in American economic development, and over the next few years Jenks and Cochran elaborated further on Parsons's structural functional theory to understand the origins of entrepreneurial 'roles' within economic development based on how social, cultural, and institutional factors promote entrepreneurship in society (Sass, 1978). Jenks and Cochran's approach rather quickly became the dominant approach to historical research on entrepreneurship (Jones and Wadhwani, 2006), and researchers tried to understand how historical context and social structure shaped the emergence, amount, and character of entrepreneurship within a particular national setting. In the 1940s and 1950s researchers anchored in economic history produced a large body of knowledge to explain how historical context and social structures shaped the rise of entrepreneurship in the transition to capitalism in countries around the world, i.e. related to the main question of why some countries had grown while others remained relatively poor over long periods (Jones and Wadhwani, 2007). By the 1950s historians were engaged in studying variation in entrepreneurship in countries around the world and linking their findings to the long-term economic development of nations (see e.g. studies by Cochran, 1950; 1960; Jenks, 1944; 1949; Landes, 1949; 1953; Sawyer, 1954; Ranis, 1955; Gerschenkron, 1962: 1966).

After a couple of decades, however, this stream of research lost momentum among economic historians. There are many potential explanations for this decline in interest. One reason might be that the structural-functional approach employed by the framework in many studies seemed to produce rather few insights beyond the observation that entrepreneurship was socially and historically embedded, and the research was criticized for providing few explanations of the great variety in development paths found in the comparative empirical studies conducted in countries around the world. As a consequence, the modernization framework came under attack for its inability to account for the tremendous variation in development paths and the diversity of conditions in developing countries (Jones and Wadwani, 2007).

Another explanation for the decline was without doubt the competition that emerged from new frameworks within economic history, not least from the new organizational approach to business history pioneered by the MIT professor Alfred Chandler. In his book *Strategy and Structure* (1962) he was mainly concerned with the growth of large professionally managed companies during the period 1850–1950. The new approach drew on a stronger focus on the organizational and managerial elements of firms in historical change, and Chandler was ambivalent regarding the role of entrepreneurship in shaping the trajectory of business development (Cassis and Pepelasis Minoglou, 2005). This new approach seemed to be tremendously promising, and a new generation of business historians started to focus their attention on building an 'organizational synthesis' of the modern, multidivisional corporation (Galambos, 1970). By the 1970s a clear shift had taken place, and researchers in economic history increasingly adopted orthodox neoclassical economic theory and quantitative methods in their research. As a manifestation of this shift in interest, the Research Center in Entrepreneurial History ran out of financial and institutional support and was forced to close down in 1958, and the journal *Explorations in Entrepreneurial History* was revived as *Explorations in Economic History* (Jones and Wadhwani, 2007).

The Psychologist and Sociologist Approach

Although social scientists remained interested in entrepreneurship, it was primarily through the works of psychologists and sociologists that entrepreneurship research continued to flourish. At the end of the 1950s and in the early 1960s, a series of large-scale studies based on a comparative-historical approach were conducted in order to understand the personal traits and characteristics of the entrepreneur. Two seminal studies are worth mentioning. The best known is David McClelland's study *The Achieving Society* (1961), in which he posed the question: Why do certain societies develop more dynamically than others? He argued that certain norms and values, particularly with regard to the 'need for achievement', are of vital importance for the development of society. The second was Everett Hagen's book *On the Theory of Social Change* (1962), in which he analyzed the emergence of innovation and technology in England, Japan, Colombia, and Burma. Whereas McClelland concentrated upon the individual, Hagen focused on the social groupings, and the question: Why do entrepreneurs more often come from certain social groupings than others? He claimed that entrepreneurs tend to come from groups that suffered from a withdrawal of status, i.e. the members of some social groups perceive that their aims and values are not respected by the groups in society that they respect and whose esteem they value (Martinelli, 1994; Kalantaridis, 2004).

McClelland and Hagen's contributions meant that the personal qualities of the entrepreneur occupied a prominent position in entrepreneurship research within the field of social sciences during the 1960s and 1970s. Many studies tried to identify the particular qualities of the entrepreneur. The number of traits identified in research has gradually increased and, with a few exceptions, it has proven difficult to link any specific traits to entrepreneurial behavior (Brockhaus, 1982; Delmar, 2000).

The interest in entrepreneurship was evident not only among psychologists but also within behavioral sciences such as sociology and social anthropology. The content of sociology as a discipline is very extensive and entrepreneurship has never been a dominant theme within the field. Entrepreneurship research conducted within the field of sociology can be related to areas such as (Martinelli, 1994; 2004; Kalantaridis, 2004):

- Entrepreneurship as deviant behavior: This research tradition dates back to the works of Sombart, who argued that the ability to break traditional values is more frequent among marginal and minority groups than the population at large – non-acceptance by society enables individuals to disregard the traditional values that regulate economic behavior (Kalantaridis, 2004). Theoretical constructs related to social marginality were introduced by Hoselitz (1963) and Young (1971), and during the 1980s and 1990s several empirical studies (for example Aldrich and Waldinger, 1990) supported their thesis.
- Entrepreneurship and culture: Following Weber's comparative analysis of religious ethics and economic development in the rise of capitalism, and Parsons's structural functional theory, scholars within economic history (e.g. Landes, 1953;

Gerschenkron, 1962) as well as sociologists (e.g. Parsons and Smelser, 1957; Lipset, 1967) continued to focus on the cultural aspects of the emergence and development of industrialization in different countries.

- Entrepreneurship and networks: The study of networks stems back to classic economics and sociology literature, in which social structure influences market processes (Veblen, 1972). Research on networks and entrepreneurship has largely concentrated on three different levels of analysis (Thornton and Flynn, 2003): network ties between individuals (e.g. Granovetter, 1973; 1985; Burt, 1992), connection of teams and groups (e.g. Aldrich and Zimmer, 1986; Ruef et al., 2003), and networks of firms and industries (e.g. Freeman, 1986).

In contrast to sociology, few studies of entrepreneurship can be found in social anthropology, but some of the most interesting pioneering work produced in entrepreneurship is by anthropologists such as Fredrik Barth (1963; 1967) and Clifford Geertz (1963). The early studies primarily concentrated on social change and economic development but also focused on the interaction between local entrepreneurship and the social pattern of the individual.

One conclusion that can be drawn is that entrepreneurship research never attracted a large number of researchers within the social sciences – the research was mainly conducted by a couple of individual researchers within the respective discipline, and the studies were strongly anchored within the discipline. The marginalization of entrepreneurship may also be explained by a limited interest in entrepreneurship and small businesses in society – economic development and dynamics were assumed to be based on mass-production, and large companies were seen as superior in efficiency as well as the driving force behind technology development. As both sociology and psychology are fairly broad yet fragmented disciplines, with different research themes competing for attention, entrepreneurship never gained a strong foothold.

MANAGEMENT STUDIES ERA (1970–)

The 1960s and 1970s were characterized by great economic and political changes in society. It was a period of 'creative destruction' in which new technologies were gaining ground, changes were taking place in the industrial structure, questions were being raised about the efficiency of larger companies, attitudes toward entrepreneurship and small businesses were emerging ('small is beautiful' became a catch phrase), and there was an increased political debate supported by politicians such as Ronald Reagan in the USA and Margaret Thatcher in the UK. In addition, entrepreneurship gained a foothold in the curriculum at US business schools and among scholars within management studies (Landström, 2005).

Against this background, entrepreneurship and industrial dynamics became a dominant theme in society. Many scholars from different areas of management studies rushed into this promising field of research. Since the 1980s the interest in entrepreneurship in society has continued, and the field has grown considerably in terms of the number of researchers but also with regard to the number of publications, journals, and conferences. The development of entrepreneurship as a research field since the 1980s can be described as three phases: (i) take-off, (ii) growth, and (iii) a search for maturation. In this section we elaborate on this development, with the focus on the migration of scholars to (and from) the entrepreneurship research field.

The 'Take-off' Phase: The Pioneers of Entrepreneurship

As society and political interest changed from large scale structures toward disintegration and new sources of economic organization and dynamics, a whole line of scholars with an emergent interest in entrepreneurship and small businesses started to conduct studies on this 'new' and important phenomenon. At first, the management scholars interested in entrepreneurship picked up where the social scientists had left off – searching for entrepreneurial traits and personalities. However, over time, the research on the individual characteristics of the entrepreneur became subject to criticism and was regarded as a 'dead end' in entrepreneurship research.

In addition, due to the newness of the field and its lack of identity in terms of concepts, theories and methods, it was easy for researchers from different fields of management studies to carry out research on entrepreneurship without experiencing obvious deficits in competence – entrepreneurship was a 'low entry' field – in which researchers could rely on concepts and theories anchored in their home field of research. As a consequence, the research on entrepreneurship became extremely diversified, and it became a question of discovering this 'new' phenomenon from many different angles. To illustrate the situation during the 1970s and 1980s, Churchill (1992) made an analogy to the story of the blind men and the elephant, where six blind men touched different parts of the elephant and gave quite different descriptions of its characteristics – and, in this relatively unstructured exploration of the 'elephant' the researchers discovered that the animal was different, composed of a number of rather unusual parts and that it was quite large.

It is obvious that this period was highly influenced by the early research on entrepreneurship, which was anchored in economics (e.g. Kirzner, Schumpeter and Knight) as well as the social sciences, i.e. contributions by economic historians, sociologists and social anthropologists (e.g. Kilby, Chandler and Cochran) and psychologists who studied the individual characteristics of the entrepreneur (e.g. McClelland, Collins et al., and Smith). In the 1980s we can find an increased number of references to management scholars with an interest in entrepreneurship, innovation, and corporate entrepreneurship such as Drucker, Burns and Stalker, and Kanter, which to some extent indicates that entrepreneurship and small businesses were seen more or less as 'small large firms' in which management models and concepts were assumed to be applicable. However, at the same time, some pioneering studies focusing on the specific characteristics of entrepreneurship and small businesses emerged among the most cited works, for example those by Birch and Storey (Landström and Åström, 2011).

This early phase of the emerging research field was characterized by enthusiasm and individualism – a group of enthusiastic scholars rooted in different fields of management studies started to take an interest in entrepreneurship and small businesses. At the same time, the research community was small and could be characterized as fragmented and individualistic, i.e. entrepreneurship research was to a high extent dependent on individual initiatives and projects. As a consequence, many initiatives were taken to stimulate communication within this fragmented and individualistic community, and in this period, we can find a great many pioneering contributions to the creation of professional organizations (e.g. International Council for Small Business, European Council for Small Business, and the Entrepreneurship Division within the Academy of Management), academic conferences (e.g. the Babson Research Conference, RENT Conference, Small Firms Policy and Research Conference in the UK, and the Nordic Conference on Small Businesses), and scientific journals (e.g. *Journal of Business Venturing*, *Entrepreneurship and Regional Development*, and *Small Business Economics*).

The 'Growth' Phase: Migration, Mobility, and Fragmentation

Entrepreneurship and small business continued to be a 'hot topic' in society, and entrepreneurship as a research field was still characterized as a 'low entry' field with a lack of strong theoretical frameworks and methodologies, but also as one with rather fuzzy definitions and unclear boundaries. As a consequence, during the 1990s migration into the field was extensive, not only from scholars within management studies but from many different disciplines in the social sciences. Entrepreneurship research grew more or less exponentially. This growth can be measured in various ways, not least in terms of the number of researchers, but also by the number of published articles, conferences and journals focusing on or opening up for entrepreneurship contributions – and the growth of the field is obvious, irrespective of the measurements employed.

There was not only large scale migration into the field, the mobility of scholars in and out of the field was equally extensive. For example, based on a citation analysis, Landström (2001) identified four categories of researchers within the field: (i) ad-hoc transients, i.e. researchers whose publication within the field of entrepreneurship was a one-off event; (ii) influential transients, i.e. researchers who publish on entrepreneurship only once, but whose work has become important for entrepreneurship research; (iii) craftsmen, i.e. researchers who frequently publish on entrepreneurship – staying within the field for a longer period of time – but whose influence is marginal; and (iv) core group, i.e. researchers who frequently publish on entrepreneurship and who are often cited by others (researchers who have a substantial impact upon the research field). During the 1990s the vast majority of researchers within the field could be regarded as transient researchers – researchers who belonged to some form of mainstream research community and who only temporarily entered the field of entrepreneurship research, whereas the 'core group' of influential entrepreneurship researchers was fairly small.

Partly as a consequence of the high migration and mobility of scholars, and partly due to a general ambition to understand the 'entire' phenomenon, i.e. to comprehend what this complex and heterogeneous phenomenon really looks like – what Davidsson (2008) calls 'phenomenon-driven research' – the research became highly fragmented, mainly atheoretical, empirical explorations of the phenomenon. Thus, we find increased fragmentation with many parallel 'conversations', and the field has been criticized for having little convergence and low knowledge accumulation. For example, Shane and Venkataraman (2000) argued that entrepreneurship research 'has become a broad label under which a "hodgepodge" of research is housed' (p. 217). Low (2001) spoke about a 'potpourri' of entrepreneurship research (pp. 20–21), Zahra (2005) described entrepreneurship research as loosely connected and with a 'mosaic of issues to be explored'

(p. 254), or as Koppl and Minniti (2003) expressed it: 'We are getting more pieces of the puzzle, but no picture is emerging' (p. 81).

The conclusion that can be drawn is that entrepreneurship research during the 1990s could be regarded as a strongly growing field with a high level of migration into it but also extensive mobility. The research was characterized by a high degree of fragmentation. It is interesting to note that the scholars interested in entrepreneurship more or less started to divide themselves into two different 'groups'. On the one hand, an increasing group of scholars that could be considered 'transient' with an anchor in different disciplines, who only occasionally performed studies on entrepreneurship and who regarded themselves as 'disciplinary' researchers. On the other, an emergent group of researchers mainly anchored in management studies who began to regard themselves as entrepreneurship scholars – thus it is perhaps not until the 1990s that we can really start talking about entrepreneurship as a research 'field'.

Among the emergent group of 'entrepreneurship scholars', there was a need to build a strong infrastructure, and the 1990s were to a very large extent characterized by the building of it, expressed in terms of an increase in organized forums for communication between researcher (e.g. conferences and scientific journals), role models (e.g. chairs in entrepreneurship), and undergraduate, master, and PhD programs and courses in entrepreneurship. A strong infrastructure is important in emerging research fields, not only in order to enhance knowledge accumulation (Cole, 1970), but also to create 'academic autonomy' (Merton, 1973), that is, emerging research fields need to legitimate themselves in the eyes of scholars from other fields, and different kinds of institutions are essential for this purpose.

A 'Search for Maturation': A Discussion on the Domain and the Division of the Research Community

During the last decade, after almost 30 years of study on entrepreneurship research, the field was searching for maturation. Some characteristics of this search can be identified, such as (i) a deeper discussion of central concepts and the delimitation of the research field, (ii) a realization that entrepreneurship is a complex, heterogeneous and multi-level phenomenon, and (iii) the return of economics and psychological aspects of entrepreneurship research. As a consequence we can identify two partly contradictory trends. On the one hand, we have had an opening-up and broadening of the field, leading to a migration of scholars from many different disciplines, who conduct studies on a broad range of entrepreneurship themes on a more or less temporary basis. On the other hand, we have witnessed the creation of a community of entrepreneurship scholars, who conduct entrepreneurship studies on a more regular basis and take part in the entrepreneurship research 'conversation', and who increasingly use a specific language and become increasingly self-reflective, makes the field less open to multi-disciplinary approaches.

Domain discussion
As in many young research fields there has been an ongoing uncertainty about and debate on the central concepts used as well as the delimitation of entrepreneurship as a research field. The seminal article by Scott Shane and Sankaran Venkataraman (2000), 'The

promise of entrepreneurship as a field of research', triggered an intense debate regarding the domain of entrepreneurship research.

First, we can find proponents who argue for a development of entrepreneurship into a distinct domain of research, i.e. a domain that predicts a set of empirical phenomena not explained in other fields of research, for example, newness, novelty and creation (Shane and Venkataraman, 2000; Davidsson et al., 2001; Bruyat and Julien, 2001; Busenitz et al., 2003; Scherdin and Zander, 2008) – what can be termed a 'domain approach'. In this respect, a narrow domain focus permits scholars to compare and contrast studies but means that the field becomes less inclusive and the breadth of the topics studied more limited. For example, Busenitz et al. (2003) argued that entrepreneurship as a research field needs to establish its 'own ontological and epistemological base' in order to define the boundaries of the field, but also to make theory building possible and create legitimacy. In addition, both Busenitz et al. (2003) and Bruyat and Julien (2001) concluded that, as a domain, entrepreneurship must develop its capacity to probe interesting and important issues from a solid foundation of entrepreneurship theory. However, there seems to be an intensive debate among the proponents of the domain approach regarding how the domain should be defined and delimited.

Second, we can find arguments that entrepreneurship should integrate with theories from other fields of research to a greater extent (Acs and Audretsch, 2003), not least with theories in the field of strategy (Meyer and Heppard, 2000; Hitt et al., 2002; Alvarez, 2003) – what can be termed an 'integrative approach'. For a long time, strategy and entrepreneurship research have overlapped intellectually as well as in social dimensions. In the Academy of Management, for example, entrepreneurship started as an interest group that emerged from the Business Policy Division in 1974. We can thus conclude that many of the pioneers of entrepreneurship research (see Landström, 2005) can also be regarded as pioneers within the field of strategic management. The argument is that the research questions addressed by strategic management and entrepreneurship researchers are inextricably interwoven. The majority of work conducted in the intersection between strategy and entrepreneurship have two strands (Alvarez, 2003): an economics approach concerned with how entrepreneurial activities can result in economic rents (e.g. Alvarez and Barney, 2004); and a management approach focusing on the design and implementation of entrepreneurial strategies in different kinds of companies (e.g. Hitt et al., 2002). Over time, strategic management has been acknowledged as one core approach within entrepreneurship research, and Grégoire et al. (2006) demonstrated that there is a stream of entrepreneurship research that focuses on entrepreneurship as a strategy, including a strong foundation in the resource based view. Today there is a strong group of scholars arguing for closer integration between strategic management and entrepreneurship, and this community of researchers has been institutionalized by the launch of a scientific journal *Strategic Entrepreneurship Journal* in 2007.

Finally, some researchers are less concerned with the distinctiveness of the domain, regarding entrepreneurship as a phenomenon 'out there' that can be studied from many different perspectives, pursuing various research interests such as innovation, nascent entrepreneurship, family business, venture capital, etc. – arguing for what we can call a 'multiple-research approach'. For example, Gartner (2001) argued that it is not possible to obtain a comprehensive theory of entrepreneurship – there is no overarching theory that can connect all the phenomena currently studied under the entrepreneurship umbrella.

As Gartner expressed it, 'there is no elephant in entrepreneurship' – meaning that the various topics do not constitute a congruous whole. As a consequence, scholars should actively separate into more homogeneous communities to study specific topic areas. Gartner et al. (2006) revealed that there seem to be a number of such distinct groups of scholars in the entrepreneurship field within topics such as venture capital, corporate entrepreneurship, 'the economists', strategic entrepreneurship and ethnic entrepreneurship (see also Brush et al., 2008). This suggests that there is an active dialogue going on around similar research interests, which supports Gartner's (2001) contention that the field of entrepreneurship may be evolving into informal homogeneous communities – or what can be termed emerging 'research circles' (Landström, 2005). In this respect the research field may move from fragmentation to specialization in which scholars will create more autonomous research areas, not only thematically but perhaps due to the methodological approaches employed. As a consequence, the development of a theory of entrepreneurship may not be possible. What we must search for is a diverse range of theories applicable to various kinds of phenomena (Gartner, 2001) – the development of 'middle range' theories that fall somewhere between grand theories and empirical findings, and that attempt to understand and explain a limited aspect of the entrepreneurship phenomenon (Blackburn and Smallbone, 2008).

The realization that entrepreneurship is a complex, heterogeneous and multi-level phenomenon

Davidsson (2008) argued that in order to understand the complexity and heterogeneity of entrepreneurship, there is a need to use knowledge from many different research fields. During the last decade we can identify a couple of (partly contradictory) trends that give expression to the characteristics of the phenomenon. These trends may not only be explained by the complexity and heterogeneity of the phenomenon but also by the divide between research traditions, academic training, and incentive structures among entrepreneurship scholars in the US and Europe, resulting in a stronger convergence around a dominant research paradigm on the part of scholars in the US and a much more diverse view on research in Europe (Edelman et al., 2009; see also Landström, 2005; Landström and Huse, 1996). However, such a statement would be an over-simplification, as many European scholars within the field are working around a similar paradigm to that of their US colleagues, and there is a strong international 'isomorphism' (Aldrich, 2000) involved, which brings researchers together through journals, conferences, cross-national projects, and international exchange of scholars.

Thus, on the one hand, there is a tendency in entrepreneurship research to open up for a broadening of entrepreneurship, viewing it not only as an economic achievement, but as a societal phenomenon (including social entrepreneurship, entrepreneurship in public organizations, etc.), and there are also scholars, particularly in Europe, who go one step further, arguing for 'recreating and recontextualizing' entrepreneurship (Hjorth et al., 2008). The arguments are based on a perceived lack of creativity and the imposition of rigid norms in the current dominant approaches in entrepreneurship research, but are also a form of criticism of the lack of contextualization of entrepreneurship in recent research. Accordingly, it is important to address the social and cultural context in which entrepreneurship operates, and this contextualization can be achieved by a closer relationship to 'the real world' and a stronger basis in the social and human sciences.

Accepting entrepreneurship's eclectic and pervasive benefits generates questions of interest to researchers from a variety of scholarly disciplines (Ireland and Webb, 2007), which means that the field has the potential to become more multi-disciplinary (Steyeart and Hjorth, 2003), leading to a migration of scholars from many different disciplines with an interest in entrepreneurship. These scholars, however, are not always a part of the 'conversation' in entrepreneurship research.

On the other hand, there is evidence that the entrepreneurship research community is evolving over time. In order to understand the complexity and heterogeneity of entrepreneurship we need specific knowledge and a special language. The trend is that entrepreneurship research has become increasingly self-reflective and more internally oriented with researchers citing the works of other entrepreneurship researchers, while the influence of 'outsiders' has decreased steadily over time (Cornelius et al., 2006) – highlighting the fact that knowledge developed within the research field has become more and more important. In addition, Karlsson (2008) revealed greater use of a specific language among entrepreneurship researchers, indicating progression along the normal science route (Aldrich and Baker, 1997). A new generation of entrepreneurship scholars is also entering the field (Hjorth, 2008). The scholars who currently dominate the field were for the most part immigrants from other fields (mainly from management studies, but also economics, economic geography, sociology, etc.), while the new generation is more strongly anchored in entrepreneurship and in the knowledge developed within the field – they have participated in PhD programs focused on entrepreneurship and written their theses on entrepreneurship research problems. Taken together, these aspects will create a community of scholars in entrepreneurship in its own right, but also make the field less open to the multi-disciplinary aspects of entrepreneurship.

The return of economics and the social sciences in entrepreneurship research
As long ago as 1968 William Baumol argued that 'The theoretical firm is entrepreneurless – the Prince of Denmark has been expunged from the discussion of Hamlet' (p. 68), pointing out that there has been little room for the entrepreneurial element in mainstream economics. He urged that serious attention should be paid to the role of entrepreneurship in economics. During recent decades Baumol's plea has been acknowledged, and several attempts have been made to include entrepreneurship in economic modeling and analysis. In the 1980s and 1990s a number of seminal contributions were presented within the field of 'small business economics', but it was not until recently that entrepreneurship has provided a fertile ground for a new generation of scholars within mainstream economics who migrated into studies on entrepreneurship and have contributed to our knowledge of it (Bianchi and Henrekson, 2005). In this respect, advances in the availability of data, lower computation costs, and new analysis techniques have contributed to the possibility of testing economic theories in the context of entrepreneurship (Minniti and Lévesque, 2008).

In recent years many aspects of entrepreneurship have been studied through the lens of economic theories. Based on theoretical frameworks such as occupational choice models (e.g. Lucas, 1978; Kihlstrom and Laffont, 1979; Holmes and Schmitz, 1990), credit rationing models (e.g. Stiglitz and Weiss, 1981; Evans and Jovanovic, 1989), entering models (e.g. Jovanovic, 1982; Klepper, 1996), etc., economists within the field of 'Economics of Entrepreneurship' have tried to answer, for example, the following questions (Parker,

2005). How many jobs do entrepreneurs create? Are small entrepreneurial ventures more innovative than large corporations? Do banks ration credits to new ventures? Do capital constraints impede entry of new ventures? Which entrepreneurial ventures are most likely to survive and grow?

New fields of economic analysis have also emerged, for example cross-disciplinary work in economics and psychology created a field of behavioral economics, whereas economics and strategy have generated a stream of work on the emergence and growth of firms. In these cross-disciplinary works, the gap between economics and other social and management sciences is declining, which indicates that economics could move from a deductive science to an open and inductive one and that a theoretical heterodoxy is emerging in economics (Minniti and Lévesque, 2008).

Over the years we have learnt that entrepreneurship is not as much about innate qualities of special individuals as the early research assumed. Personality differences do exist between 'entrepreneurs' and 'others', but such variables explain only a very low per cent of the variance. Furthermore, over the course of their lives a rather large and internally heterogeneous chunk of the human population are actively involved in business start-ups or other entrepreneurial activities (Davidsson, 2008), and therefore the focus on stable psychological characteristics of entrepreneurs is unsatisfactory. However, Steyeart (2007) argued that the field of entrepreneurship studies has done everything to draw the attention away from the individual entrepreneur in order to make space for understanding the complexity of the entrepreneurial process and that by using other methodological approaches, for example narrative approaches, we might re-introduce the individual into our analyses. 'Who is the entrepreneur?' is not the wrong question: it is a 'right' question wrongly formulated in the sense that it holds a rich set of 'right' problematizations that entrepreneurship researchers have to start addressing.

In the last decade many theories focusing on the individual have been the subject of attention in entrepreneurship research, for example, social cognition, attribution processes, attitudes, etc. (Shaver, 2003). In this respect research has taken off in different directions, opening up new possibilities of focusing on, for example, cognitive aspects of business opportunity recognition – the entrepreneur's cognitive ability to identify unsatisfied needs large enough to create profits is fundamental in the entrepreneurial process and has become significant in entrepreneurship research. Sarasvathy's (2001) view on entrepreneurial decision-making is another theme that focused on the individual and that has received a great deal of attention – the concept is based on the fact that entrepreneurs do not always think through a problem in a 'rational' way, but act in an 'effectuation' way in which s/he uses available resources and learns from failures. The research on behavioral aspects of entrepreneurs, for example habitual entrepreneurs, should also be mentioned. Entrepreneurs are expected to learn from earlier experiences, which make 'habitual' entrepreneurs behave differently from 'novice' entrepreneurs (Westhead and Wright, 1998).

SOME CONCLUDING REFLECTIONS

In this chapter we have elaborated on the historical development of entrepreneurship as a research field. We have paid particular attention to the migration of scholars into the field. In this concluding section we summarize and synthesize our discussions, but also suggest a stronger theoretical focus in entrepreneurship research as a challenge for the future.

The Evolution of Entrepreneurship as a Research Field – The Migration of Scholars

Marginal and 'disciplinary' anchored research

The (pre-) history of entrepreneurship research – until the 1970s – is one of institutional immaturity and relative marginalization, where it had not yet evolved into a field in its own right but rather figured at the margins of several disciplines. Economics is a case in point, where the entrepreneur was a centerpiece in, for example, Schumpeter's broad-ranging studies of economic dynamics and innovation. However, in the inter- and post-war periods, Schumpeter's work had a limited impact on mainstream economics, which was increasingly formalized and based on aggregate data rather than on studies of firms and actors. Such perspectives found a more congenial environment in the social sciences such as economic history, where Schumpeter's notion of the role of innovation and the entrepreneur as a source of economic dynamics was cultivated in the studies of social modernization in different societies. With an anchor in the Research Center in Entrepreneurial History at Harvard University, entrepreneurship was the subject of strong interest, and several eminent scholars from different disciplines were attracted by the topic. However, in the wake of a growing critique of the structural-functionalist paradigm and given the rather sterile results of the studies, entrepreneurship was more or less deserted by economic history and once again marginalized by the stream of literature on organizational aspects (pioneered by Alfred Chandler) from the 1960s onwards. Instead, entrepreneurship was adapted within other social sciences such as sociology and psychology, which assumed responsibility for continuing the theoretical interest in entrepreneurship, in which research on personal traits and characteristics was dominant. As other themes of inquiry became more fashionable in sociology and psychology – characterized by a pluralism of approaches and methodologies, from Marxism to hermeneutics (Gouldner, 1970) – social scientists left the scene and gave the impetus for scholars within the broader framework of management studies to enter the stage.

During the first two eras, entrepreneurship research in economics and the social sciences was mainly conducted by a few individual researchers within the respective disciplines and mainly anchored in the theories of the disciplines in question. Entrepreneurship did not attract a large number of researchers. The fact that entrepreneurship research did not become institutionalized was a reflection not only of the critical dependence on a supply of researchers within the disciplines, but also of the lack of interest in entrepreneurship in society. It was an era marked by the rise of mass-producing integrated firms in the US and later in Europe, and the key issues were primarily related to governance of large corporations in mature sectors and macro-economic stability, and there was little interest in a policy coalition for entrepreneurship research. It is therefore difficult to talk about a migration of scholars to the field of entrepreneurship – one exception might be the mobilization of researchers from different disciplines that could be found at the Research Center in Entrepreneurial History at Harvard University.

The emergence of entrepreneurship as a research field in its own right
Following the gradual decline of Fordism, the 1970s and 1980s became a turning point. The interest in entrepreneurship emerged from the changes occurring in society. A shift in focus from large companies to new and small firms could be identified, explained by factors such as intensified global competition, changes in consumer tastes and a privatization movement that swept over the world. Not least, it was a period of 'creative destruction' in which new technologies were gaining ground (Brock and Evans, 1986; 1989) – a starting point of what we would later define as the 'knowledge economy'.

The increased societal interest was paralleled and reinforced by the proliferation of policy agencies at national, regional and local level that supported entrepreneurship, i.e. entrepreneurship moved from a residual in economic and employment policies to a political centerpiece. As government labor market policies shifted from industrial and employment subsidies to firm formation and the exploration of new market opportunities, at the same time as regional policies gradually moved from industrial location to network building and the creation of new firms, entrepreneurship found itself in the midst of a broader societal reorganization. This connection with entrepreneurship policy functioned as a springboard for the growth of entrepreneurship research in the 1980s and 1990s.

Even if we can identify strong support for external factors governing the migration of scholars to the field of entrepreneurship during the 1980s and 1990s, we can also find intra-scientific explanations. The field was characterized by an 'embarras de richesses', as it offered increasing opportunities for empirical research and could be characterized as 'low entry', with highly permeable boundaries (Busenitz et al., 2003). Entrepreneurship as a research field also offered great opportunities in terms of research funds, as well as academic positions, an increased number of outlets for publication, and so on. Finally, we have to bear in mind that the field of management studies at that time was itself very young and eclectic, or what Whitley (2000) called a 'fragmented adhocracy', in which many new ideas and theories were developed (such as agency theory, transaction costs theory, industrial organization, evolutionary theory, etc.) that later formed the core of the discipline, and in management studies, that included a lot of new themes of research, entrepreneurship could easily proceed and find space for its development.

Two 'groups' of scholars in entrepreneurship research
Today, we find ambiguous, and to some extent contradictory, tendencies in entrepreneurship research, reflected in two groups of scholars. On the one hand, entrepreneurship has gradually become more institutionalized in the academic landscape, not least through the building of a strong entrepreneurship research infrastructure and an intensive debate on the boundaries of the field. Accordingly, a research community of 'entrepreneurship researchers' with a disciplinary anchor in management studies, who are a part of the 'conversation' in entrepreneurship research and who regard themselves as entrepreneurship scholars, has evolved. In this respect, the research has been increasingly self-reflective, with a stronger internal orientation and a more specific language. Interestingly, we can also find an increased conceptual traffic moving from entrepreneurship to other fields of management studies, for example a greater number of entrepreneurship articles appearing in leading (empirical) management scientific journals.

On the other hand, despite these signs of gaining academic respectability, entrepreneurship is not evolving into a coherent and closed entity. Entrepreneurship as a social practice enters into new directions, opens up for a broadening of the object of study, and creates an interest and migration of scholars from many different disciplines, paralleled by the re-emergence of entrepreneurship within economics and behavioral sciences. As a consequence, we find scattered and loosely connected researchers anchored in many different disciplines and theoretical frameworks, who now and then conduct studies on entrepreneurship. They regard themselves as 'disciplinary researchers' and do not to any great extent participate in the entrepreneurship research 'conversation'.

Entrepreneurship Research – The Next Step . . .

What will the future look like in entrepreneurship research? One main challenge for researchers in entrepreneurship will be to engage in more systematic, theory-driven efforts (Tan et al., 2009). We can see an increased interest in the theoretical development of the field (Brush et al., 2008) – entrepreneurship researchers are to a lesser extent starting from what is going on 'out there', and instead placing greater emphasis on testing theories that could help us understand the phenomenon of entrepreneurship (Davidsson, 2008). For example, theories such as the resource-based view, evolutionary perspectives, cognitive theory, etc. have been popular over the last couple of years, and Brush et al. (2008) argued that there has been an increase in the number of theory-driven articles and more rigorous inference methods in entrepreneurship research, which suggests that the study of entrepreneurship is becoming more scientific. In this respect and in line with the multi-disciplinary character of the field, entrepreneurship researchers borrow heavily from other fields, which has enhanced the rigor of the research (Zahra, 2007). According to Zahra (2005), importation of theories from other fields is a necessary first step toward developing unique theories that help us understand entrepreneurial phenomena. However, entrepreneurship researchers should not only borrow from other fields but should invent their own concepts and theories. Thus, they need both to make use of theories from other research fields and to develop specific theories and models to explain distinctive entrepreneurship phenomena that theories from other disciplines cannot explain.

It is in line with this argument that the editors have initiated this book. We believe that a necessary next step in the development of entrepreneurship research will be to focus more strongly on systematic theory-driven research, and in this respect we need to borrow concepts and theories from other disciplines. As shown in this chapter, due to the fact that entrepreneurship research has long been a multi-disciplinary field, with a far-reaching migration and mobility in and out of the field, there will be extensive possibilities for such an importation of concepts and theories from other fields that can help us understand entrepreneurship. However, in order to do this we need to know and understand the intellectual origins from which these concepts and theories have evolved, otherwise we can make many mistakes in our explanations and understandings of entrepreneurship.

REFERENCES

Acs, Z.J. and D.B. Audretsch (eds) (2003), *Handbook of Entrepreneurship Research*, Dordrecht: Kluwer Academic Publishers.

Aldrich, H.E. (2000), 'Learning together: national differences in entrepreneurship research', in D.L. Sexton and H. Landström (eds), *The Blackwell Handbook of Entrepreneurship*, Oxford: Blackwell Publishers, pp. 5–25.

Aldrich, H.E. and T. Baker (1997), 'Blinded by the cites. Has there been progress in entrepreneurship research?', in D.L. Sexton and R.W. Smilor (eds), *Entrepreneurship 2000*, Chicago, IL: Upstart, pp. 377–400.

Aldrich, H.E. and R. Waldinger (1990), 'Ethnicity and entrepreneurship', *Annual Review of Sociology*, **16**, 111–35.

Aldrich, H.E. and C. Zimmer (1986), 'Entrepreneurship through social networks', in D.L. Sexton and R. Smilor (eds), *The Art and Science of Entrepreneurship*, Cambridge, MA: Ballinger, pp. 3–23.

Alvarez, S.A. (2003), 'Resources and hierarchies: intersections between entrepreneurship and strategy', in Z.J. Acs and D.B. Audretsch (eds), *Handbook of Entrepreneurship Research*, Dordrecht: Kluwer Academic Publishers, pp. 247–63.

Alvarez, S.A. and J.B. Barney (2004), 'Organizing rent generation and appropriation. Toward a theory of the entrepreneurial firm', *Journal of Business Venturing*, **19**(5), 621–35.

Andersen, E.S. (1994), *Evolutionary Economics post-Schumpeterian Contributions*, London: Pinter.

Barth, F. (1963), *The Role of the Entrepreneur of Social Change in Northern Norway*, Oslo: Universitetsforlaget.

Barth, F. (1967), 'Economic spheres in Darfur', in R. Firth (ed.), *Themes in Economic Anthropology*, London: Tavistock, pp. 149–74.

Baumol, W.J. (1968), 'Entrepreneurship in economic theory', *American Economic Review*, **58**(2), 64–71.

Baumol, W.J. (1990), 'Entrepreneurship: productive, unproductive and destructive', *Journal of Political Economy*, **98**(5), 893–921.

Baumol, W.J. (1993), *Entrepreneurship, Management and the Structure of Pay-offs*, Cambridge, MA: MIT Press.

Baumol, W.J. (2002), *The Free-Market Innovation Machine*, Princeton, NJ: Princeton University Press.

Becher, T. and P. Towler (2001), *Academic Tribes and Territories*, 2nd edn, Buckingham: Open University Press.

Ben-David, J. (1970), *The Scientist's Role in Society*, Englewood Cliffs, NJ: Prentice Hall.

Berglund, H. (2009), 'Austrian economics and the study of entrepreneurship: concepts and contributions', 2009 Academy of Management Annual Meeting, Chicago, 7–11 August.

Bianchi, M. and M. Henrekson (2005), 'Is neoclassical economics still entrepreneurless?', *Kyklos*, **58**(3), 353–77.

Blackburn, R.A. and D. Smallbone (2008), 'Researching small firms and entrepreneurship in the UK: developments and distinctiveness', *Entrepreneurship Theory and Practice*, March, 267–88.

Blume, S. (1985), 'After the darkest hour . . .', in B. Wittrock and A. Elzinga (eds), *The University Research System*, Stockholm: Almqvist & Wiksell International, pp. 139–63.

Böhme, G., W. van Jen Daele, R. Hohlfeld, W. Krohr, W. Schäfer and T. Spengler (1976), *Die gesellschaftliche Orientierung des wissenschaftlichen Fortschritt*, Opladen: Suhrkamp.

Bolin, B. (2007), *A History of the Science and Politics of Climate Change*, Cambridge: Cambridge University Press.

Brock, W.A. and D.S. Evans (1986), *The Economics of Small Businesses: Their Role and Regulation in the US Economy*, New York: Holmes and Meier.

Brock, W.A. and D.S. Evans (1989), 'Small business economics', *Small Business Economics*, **1**, 7–20.

Brockhaus, R. (1982), 'The psychology of the entrepreneur', in C.A. Kent, D.L. Sexton and K.H. Vesper (eds), *Encyclopedia of Entrepreneurship*, Englewood Cliffs, NJ: Prentice-Hall, pp. 39–57.

Brush, C.G., T.S. Manolova and L.F. Edelman (2008), 'Separated by common language? Entrepreneurship research across the Atlantic', *Entrepreneurship Theory and Practice*, March, 249–66.

Bruyat, C. and P.A. Julien (2001), 'Defining the field of entrepreneurship', *Journal of Business Venturing*, **16**(2), 165–80.

Burt, R.S. (1992), *Structural Holes*, Cambridge, MA: Harvard University Press.

Busenitz, L.W., G.P. West III, D. Shepherd, T. Nelson, G.N. Chandler and A. Zacharakis (2003), 'Entrepreneurship research in emergence: past trends and future directions', *Journal of Management*, **29**(3), 285–308.

Cantillon, R. (1755/1999), *Essai sur la nature du commerce en général*, London: MacMillan.

Cassis, Y. and I. Pepelasis Minoglou (2005), 'Entrepreneurship in theory and history: state of the art and new perspectives', in Y. Cassis and I. Pepelasis Minoglou (eds), *Entrepreneurship in Theory and History*, New York: Palgrave, pp. 3–21.

Casson, M. (1987), 'Entrepreneur', in J. Eatwell, M. Milgate and P. Newman (eds), *The New Palgrave: A Dictionary of Economics*, Volume 2, London: Macmillan.

Chandler, A. (1962), *Strategy and Structure*, Cambridge, MA: MIT Press.

Churchill, N.C. (1992), 'Research issues in entrepreneurship', in D.L. Sexton and J.D. Kasarda (eds), *The State of the Art of Entrepreneurship*, Boston, MA: PWS-Kent Publishers, pp. 579–96.

Cochran, T. (1950), 'Entrepreneurial behavior and motivation', *Explorations in Entrepreneurial History*, **2**, 304–7.

Cochran, T. (1960), 'Cultural factors of economic growth', *Journal of Economic History*, **20**, 515–30.

Cole, S. (1970), 'Professional standing and the reception of scientific discoveries', *American Journal of Sociology*, **76**, 286–306.

Cornelius, B., H. Landström and O. Persson (2006), 'Entrepreneurial studies: the dynamic research front of a developing social science', *Entrepreneurship Theory and Practice*, May, 375–98.

Dahmén, E. (1950), *Svensk industriell företagsverksamhet*, Stockholm: Industrins Utredningsinstitut.

Dahmén, E. (1970), *Entrepreneurial Activity and the Development of Swedish Industry*, Homewood, IL: Irwin.

Davidsson, P. (2003), 'The domain of entrepreneurship research: some suggestions', in J. Katz and D. Shepherd (eds), *Advances in Entrepreneurship, Firm Emergence and Growth*, Volume 6, Greenwich, CT: JAI Press, pp. 315–72.

Davidsson, P. (2008), 'Looking back at 20 years of entrepreneurship research: what did we learn?', in H. Landström, H. Crijns, E. Laveren and D. Smallbone (eds), *Entrepreneurship, Sustainable Growth and Performance*, Cheltenham, UK, and Northampton, MA, USA: Edward Elgar, pp. 13–26.

Davidsson, P., M.B. Low and M. Wright (2001), 'Editor's introduction: Low and MacMillan ten years on: achievements and future directions for entrepreneurship research', *Entrepreneurship Theory and Practice*, **24**(4), 5–15.

Delmar, F. (2000), 'The psychology of the entrepreneur', in S. Carter and D. Jones-Evans (eds), *Enterprise and Small Business*, Harlow: Pearson Education, pp. 132–54.

Edelman, L.F., T.S. Manolova and C.G. Brush (2009), 'Still blinded by the cites: has there been progress in entrepreneurship research?', Paper at the Academy of Management Annual Meeting, Chicago, IL, 9–11 August.

Elzinga, A. (1985), 'Research, bureaucracy and the drift of epistemic criteria', in B. Wittrock and A. Elzinga (eds), *The University Research System*, Stockholm: Almqvist & Wiksell International, pp. 191–220.

Evans, D.S. and B. Jovanovic (1989), 'An estimated model of entrepreneurial choice under liquidity constraints', *Journal of Political Economy*, **97**, 808–27.

Fagerberg, J. (2003), 'Schumpeter and the revival of evolutionary economics: an appraisal of the literature', *Journal of Evolutionary Economics*, **13**, 125–59.

Fleck, L. (1979), *The Genesis and Development of a Scientific Fact*, Chicago: University of Chicago Press.

Freeman, J. (1986), 'Entrepreneurship as organizational products', *Advances in the Study of Entrepreneurship, Innovation and Economic Growth*, **1**, 33–52.

Funtowicz, S.O. and J. Ravetz (1990), 'Science for the post-normal age', *Futures*, **25**, 733–59.

Galambos, J. (1970), 'The emerging organizational synthesis in American economic history', *Business History Review*, **44**(3), 279–90.

Gartner, W.B. (2001), 'Is there an elephant in entrepreneurship? Blind assumptions in theory development', *Entrepreneurship Theory and Practice*, **24**(4), 27–39.

Gartner, W.B., P. Davidsson and S.A. Zahra (2006), 'Are you talking to me? The nature of community in entrepreneurship scholarship', *Entrepreneurship Theory and Practice*, March, 321–31.

Geertz, C. (1963), *Peddlers and Princes: Social Change and Economic Modernization in Two Indonesian Towns*, Chicago: Chicago University Press.

Gerschenkron, A. (1962), *Economic Backwardness in Historical Perspective*, Cambridge: Belknap Press.

Gerschenkron, A. (1966), 'The modernization of entrepreneurship', in M. Weiner (ed.), *Modernization: The Dynamics of Growth*, New York: Basic Books, pp. 129–39.

Gibbons, M., C. Limoges, H. Nowotny, S. Schwartzman, P. Scott and M. Trow (1994), *The New Production of Knowledge*, London: Sage.

Gouldner, A.W. (1970), *The Coming Crisis of Western Sociology*, London: Heinemann.

Granovetter, M.S. (1973), 'The strength of weak ties', *American Journal of Sociology*, **78**(6), 1360–80.

Granovetter, M.S. (1985), 'Economic action and social structure', *American Journal of Sociology*, **91**, 481–510.

Grebel, T. (2004), *Entrepreneurship – A New Perspective*, London: Routledge.

Grégoire, D.A., M.X. Noël, R. Déry and J.-P. Béchard (2006), 'Is there conceptual convergence in entrepreneurship research? A co-citation analysis of frontiers of entrepreneurship research, 1981–2004', *Entrepreneurship Theory and Practice*, May, 333–73.

Hagen, E. (1962), *On the Theory of Social Change: How Economic Growth Begins*, Homewood, IL: Dorsey.

Hambrick, D. and M.-J. Chen (2008), 'New academic fields as admittance-seeking social movements: the case of Strategic Management', *Academy of Management Review*, **33**, 32–54.

Hébert, R.F. and A.N. Link (1982), *The Entrepreneur*, New York: Praeger.

Hébert, R.F. and A.N. Link (2006), 'Historical perspectives on the entrepreneur', *Foundations and Trends in Entrepreneurship*, **2**(4), 1–152.

Hébert, R.F. and A.N. Link (2009), *A History of Entrepreneurship*, Milton Park: Routledge.

Hitt, M.A., R.D. Ireland, S.M. Camp and D.L. Sexton (2002), *Strategic Entrepreneurship. Creating a New Mindset*, Oxford: Blackwell Publishers.

Hjorth, D. (2008), 'Nordic entrepreneurship research', *Entrepreneurship Theory and Practice*, March, 313–38.

Hjorth, D., C. Jones and W.B. Gartner (2008), 'Introduction for recreating/recontextualising entrepreneurship', *Scandinavian Journal of Management*, **24**, 81–84.

Hodgson, G. (2001), *How Economics Forgot History*, London: Routledge.

Holmes, T.J. and J.A. Schmitz (1990), 'A theory of entrepreneurship and its application to the study of business transfers, *Journal of Political Economy*, **98**, 265–94.

Hoselitz, B.F. (1960), *Sociological Aspects of Economic Growth*, Glencoe, IL: Free Press.

Hoselitz, B.F. (1963), 'Entrepreneurship and traditional elites', *Explorations in Entrepreneurial History*, **2**(1), 36–49.

Ireland, R.D. and J.W. Webb (2007), 'A cross-disciplinary exploration of entrepreneurship research', *Journal of Management*, **33**(6), 891–927.

Jenks, L.H. (1944), 'Railroads as an economic force in American development', *Journal of Economic History*, **4**, 18–20.

Jenks, L.H. (1949), 'Role structure of entrepreneurial personality', in *Change and the Entrepreneur*, Research Center in Entrepreneurial History, Cambridge: Harvard University Press, pp. 108–52.

Jones, G. and R.D. Wadhwani (2006), 'Schumpeter's plea: historical methods in the study of entrepreneurship', Working Paper, Harvard Business School.

Jones, G. and R.D. Wadhwani (2007), 'Entrepreneurship', in G. Jones and J. Zeilin (eds), *The Oxford Handbook of Business History*, Oxford: Oxford University Press, pp. 501–28.

Jovanovic, B. (1982), 'Selection and the evolution of industry', *Econometrica*, **50**, 649–70.

Kalantaridis, C. (2004), *Understanding the Entrepreneur. An Institutionalist Perspective*, Aldershot: Ashgate.

Karlsson, T. (2008), 'Emergence and development of entrepreneurship research 1989–2007: key words and collocations', Babson Conference, Chapel Hill, North Carolina, 5–7 June.

Kihlstrom, R.E. and J.J. Laffont (1979), 'A general equilibrium entrepreneurial theory of firm formation based on risk', *Journal of Political Economy*, **87**, 719–49.

Kirzner, I.M. (1973), *Competition and Entrepreneurship*, Chicago: Chicago University Press.

Klepper, S. (1996), 'Entry, exit, growth and innovation over the product life cycle', *American Economic Review*, **86**, 562–83.

Knight, F.H. (1916/1921), *Risk, Uncertainty and Profit*, New York: Houghton Mifflin.

Knorr Cetina, K. (1999), *Epistemic Cultures: How the Sciences Make Knowledge*, Cambridge, MA: Harvard Business School Press.

Koppl, R. and M. Minniti (2003), 'Market processes and entrepreneurial studies', in Z.J. Acs and D.B. Audretsch (eds), *Handbook of Entrepreneurship Research*, Dordrecht: Kluwer Academic Publishers, pp. 81–102.

Kuhn, T. (1962), *The Structure of Scientific Revolutions*, Chicago: University of Chicago Press.

Landes, D. (1949), 'French entrepreneurship and industrial growth in the nineteenth century', *Journal of Economic History*, **9**, 45–61.

Landes, D. (1953), 'Social attitudes, entrepreneurship, and economic development: A comment', *Explorations in Entrepreneurial History*, **6**, 245–72.

Landström, H. (2001), 'Who loves entrepreneurship research? Knowledge accumulation within a transient field of research', Paper at the XV RENT Conference, Turku, Finland, 22–23 November.

Landström, H. (2005), *Pioneers in Entrepreneurship and Small Business Research*, New York: Springer.

Landström, H. and F. Åström (2011), 'A history of new venture creation', in K. Hindle and K. Kluver (eds), *Handbook of Research on New Venture Creation*, Cheltenham, UK, and Northampton, MA, USA: Edward Elgar.

Landström, H. and M. Huse (1996), 'Trends in european entrepreneurship and small business research: comparisons between Europe and the US', Working Paper 1996:3, Scandinavian Institute for Research on Entrepreneurship, Halmstad University, Sweden.

Libenstein, H. (1968), 'Entrepreneurship and development', *American Economic Review*, **58**(2), 72–83.

Lipset, S.M. (1967), *Revolution and Counterrevolution*, New Brunswick, NJ: Transaction Publishers.

Low, M.B. (2001), 'The adolescence of entrepreneurship research: specification of purpose', *Entrepreneurship Theory and Practice*, **24**(4), 17–39.

Lucas, R.E. (1978), 'On the size distribution of business firms', *Bell Journal of Economics*, **9**, 508–23.

Martinelli, A. (1994), 'Entrepreneurship and management', in N.J. Smelser and R. Swedberg (eds), *The Handbook of Economic Sociology*, Princeton, NJ: Princeton University Press, pp. 476–503.

Martinelli, A. (2004), 'The social and institutional context of entrepreneurship', in G. Corbetta, M. Huse and D. Ravasi (eds), *Crossroads of Entrepreneurship*, Dordrecht: Kluwer, pp. 53–73.

McClelland, D.C. (1961), *The Achieving Society*, Princeton, NJ: van Nostrand.

Menger, C. (1871/1950), *Principles of Economics*, translated by J. Dingwall and B.F. Hoselitz, Glencoe, IL: Free Press.

Merton, R.K. (1973), *The Sociology of Science: Theoretical and Empirical Investigations*, Chicago: University of Chicago Press.

Meyer, G.D. and K.A. Heppard (2000), *Entrepreneurship as Strategy*, Thousand Oaks: Sage.

Minniti, M. and M. Lévesque (2008), 'Recent developments in the economics of entrepreneurship', *Journal of Business Venturing*, **23**, 603–12.

Nelson, R. and S. Winter (1982), *An Evolutionary Theory of Economic Change*, Cambridge, MA: Harvard University Press.

Pålsson-Syll, L. (1998), *De ekonomiska teoriernas historia*, Lund: Studentlitteratur.

Parker, S.C. (2005), 'The economics of entrepreneurship: what we know and what we don't', *Foundations and Trends in Entrepreneurship*, **1**(1), 1–54.

Parsons, T. and N. Smelser (1957), *Economy and Society*, New York: Free Press.

Ranis G. (1955), 'The community-centered entrepreneur in Japanese development', *Explorations in Entrepreneurial History*, **7**, 80–98.

Reisman, D. (2004), *Schumpeter's Market: Enterprise and Evolution*, Cheltenham, UK, and Northampton, MA, USA: Edward Elgar.

Ruef, M., H. Aldrich and N. Carter (2003), 'The structure of founding teams: homophily, strong ties, and isolation among US entrepreneurs', *American Sociological Review*, **68**(2), 195–222.

Sarasvathy, S.D. (2001), 'Causation and effectuation: toward a theoretical shift from economic inevitability to entrepreneurial contingency', *Academy of Management Review*, **26**(2), 243–63.

Sarasvathy, S.D., N. Dew, S.R. Velamuri and S. Venkataraman (2003), 'Three views of entrepreneurial opportunity', in Z.J. Acs and D.B. Audretsch (eds), *Handbook of Entrepreneurship Research*, Dordrecht: Kluwer Academic Publishers, pp. 141–60.

Sass, S. (1978), 'The entrepreneurial approach to the history of business and businessmen in America', *Business and Economic History*, **7**, 83–89.

Sawyer, J. (1954), 'The social basis of the American system of manufacturing', *Journal of Economic History*, **14**, 361–79.

Scherdin, M. and I. Zander (2008), 'The roots of the domain of entrepreneurship research', paper presented at the Academy of Management Meeting, Anaheim, CA, 11–13 August.

Schumpeter, J.A. (1947), 'The creative response in economic history', *Journal of Economic History*, **7**, 149–59.

Shackle, G. (1970), *Expectation, Enterprise and Profit*, London: Allen and Unwin.

Shane, S.A. and S. Venkataraman (2000), 'The promise of entrepreneurship as a field of research', *Academy of Management Review*, **25**(1), 217–26.

Shaver, K.G. (2003), 'The social psychology of entrepreneurial behaviour', in Z.J. Acs and D.B. Audretsch (eds), *Handbook of Entrepreneurship Research*, Dordrecht: Kluwer Academic Publishers, pp. 331–57.

Smelser, N.J. and R. Swedberg (eds) (1994), *The Handbook of Economic Sociology*, Princeton, NJ: Princeton University Press.

Smith, A. (1776/1979), *An Inquiry into the Nature and Causes of the Wealth of Nations*, London: Methuen and Co.

Sombart, W. (1911), *The Jews and Modern Capitalism*, English translation 1982, New Brunswick, NJ: Transaction Books.

Steyeart, C. (2007), 'Of course that is not the whole (toy) story: entrepreneurship and the cat's cradle', *Journal of Business Venturing*, **22**, 733–51.

Steyeart, C. and D. Hjorth (eds) (2003), *New Movements in Entrepreneurship*, Cheltenham, UK, and Northampton, MA, USA: Edward Elgar.

Stiglitz, J. and A. Weiss (1981), 'Credit rationing in markets with imperfect information', *American Economic Review*, **71**, 393–410.

Swedberg, R. (1994), *Schumpeter. Om skapande förstörelse och entreprenörskap*, Stockholm: Ratio.

Swedberg, R. (1998), *Max Weber and the Idea of Economic Sociology*, Princeton, NJ: Princeton University Press.

Swedberg, R. (2000), 'The social science view of entrepreneurship', in R. Swedberg (ed.), *Entrepreneurship. The Social Science View*, Oxford: Oxford University Press, pp. 7–44.

Tan, J., E. Fischer, R. Mitchell and P. Phan (2009), 'At the center of the action: innovation and technology strategy research in the small business setting', *Journal of Small Business Management*, **47**(3), 233–62.

Thornton, P.H. and K.H. Flynn (2003), 'Entrepreneurship, networks, and geographies', in Z.J. Acs and D.B. Audretsch (eds), *Handbook of Entrepreneurship Research*, Dordrecht: Kluwer Academic Publishers, pp. 401–33.

van Praag, C.M. (2005), *Successful Entrepreneurship. Confronting Economic Theory with Empirical Practice*, Cheltenham, UK, and Northampton, MA, USA: Edward Elgar.

Veblen, T. (1972), 'Professor Clark's economics', in E.K. Hunt and J. Schwartz (eds), *A Critique of Economic Theory*, Harmondsworth, UK: Penguin.

Wadhwani, R.D. and G. Jones (2007), 'Schumpeter's plea: historical methods in the study of entrepreneurship', paper presented at Babson-Kaufmann Entrepreneurship Conference, Madrid, June.

Weber, M. (1904/1970), *The Protestant Ethic and the Spirit of Capitalism*, London: Unwin.

Wennekers, S. and R. Thurik (2001), 'Institutions, entrepreneurship and economic perform-ance', Working Paper, EIM Business and Policy Research/Erasmus University Rotterdam, The Netherlands.

Westhead, P. and M. Wright (1998), 'Novice, portfolio, and serial founders: are they different?', *Journal of Business Venturing*, **13**(3), 173–204.

Whitley, R. (2000), *The Intellectual and Social Organisation of the Sciences*, Oxford: Clarendon.

Young, F.V. (1971), 'A macro-sociological interpretation of entrepreneurship', in P. Kilby (ed.), *Entrepreneurship and Economic Development*, New York: Free Press, pp. 139–49.

Zahra, S.A. (2005), 'Entrepreneurship and disciplinary scholarship: return to the fountainhead', in S.A. Alvarez, R. Agarwal and O. Sorenson (eds), *Handbook of Entrepreneurship Research. Interdisciplinary Perspectives*, New York: Springer, pp. 253–68.

Zahra, S.A. (2007), 'Contextualize theory building in entrepreneurship research', *Journal of Business Venturing*, **22**, 443–52.

3. Entrepreneurship research: research communities and knowledge platforms

Hans Landström and Olle Persson

INTRODUCTION

In Chapter 2 we learnt, among other things, that entrepreneurship is a highly complex and heterogeneous phenomenon that needs multi-level approaches to be understood. The challenge for entrepreneurship scholars in the future will be to engage in more systematic theory-driven research. Zahra (2005) argued that the importation of theories from other fields is a necessary first step in the creation of unique theories of entrepreneurship – although the effort to invent concepts and theories of its own should not be neglected. However, the importation of theories seems to be a particularly suitable avenue in entrepreneurship research, as the immigration of scholars from other fields into entrepreneurship has for a long time been extensive. Thus, we can expect to find a great potential for the importation of concepts and theories from many different disciplines as well as a 'melting-pot' of theories flourishing in entrepreneurship research that can help us understand entrepreneurship – provided that the field is open to such cross-disciplinary efforts.

In this chapter we follow the above line of argument, which considers entrepreneurship research as a 'melting pot' of concepts and theories from many different disciplines that creates opportunities for cross-disciplinarity and the importation of theories from other fields. Based on bibliometric (i.e. citation-based) analyses, the aim is to (1) analyze the development of research communities and knowledge platforms within the field of entrepreneurship research, and (2) discuss the possibilities of creating a cross-disciplinary and theory-driven entrepreneurship research.

This chapter contributes to our understanding of the evolving entrepreneurship research field by showing that:

- Entrepreneurship has attracted a broad range of scholars from many different disciplines, but the research is dominated by those anchored in 'management studies'.
- The research community interested in entrepreneurship is divided into two parts: on the one hand a group of 'entrepreneurship researchers' who mainly have their roots in management studies, and on the other, a rather scattered group of scholars from many different disciplines who can be regarded as 'disciplinary researchers'.
- Within the group of 'entrepreneurship researchers' anchored in management studies, we can find signs of an evolving knowledge platform that increasingly integrates new literature into the field.

- The mainstream disciplines remain relevant, and although we can identify an evolving research community and knowledge platform in entrepreneurship, the 'traditional' disciplines appear to be important.

Based on our findings we conclude that the strong disciplinary boundaries may constitute an obstacle to the importation of concepts and theories from mainstream disciplines and the creation of cross-disciplinary research within the field.

In the next section we discuss bibliometric studies in general and those dealing with entrepreneurship in particular. We then describe the development of entrepreneurship research within different disciplines. After that we outline the development of evolving research communities and knowledge platforms in entrepreneurship research, indicated by a stronger 'internal' conversation within the field among 'entrepreneurship researchers' anchored in management studies. This section is followed by one in which we focus on the characteristics and content of the knowledge platforms over time in entrepreneurship research. Finally, the chapter ends with some conclusions and suggestions for the creation of a cross-disciplinary field of research.

BIBLIOMETRIC STUDIES AND ENTREPRENEURSHIP

Scientific publications play a central role in knowledge development processes, as they contribute to knowledge accumulation, guarantee quality and provide input into the ongoing dialogue between researchers and the creation of networks of researchers with similar interests. Earlier research contributions are acknowledged by citations, and the frequency of citations is often assumed to reflect the quality of the study from which they originate (Cole, 1970). In this way certain opinions are reinforced and institutionalized and, as a consequence, individual researchers end up playing a substantial role in the development of a research field (Crane, 1972). The emergent pattern of citations also introduces a control mechanism, which ensures that new ideas do not greatly diverge from the dominant research group's ontological and epistemological stance.

In addition, researchers who work with similar questions and methods tend to form networks, within which concepts and theories are developed in dialogue through mutual citations. For example, Whitley (1984) considered citations as a ritual whereby group membership is confirmed. Failure to assent to acknowledge the view of one's predecessor is tantamount to a public detachment from the group. Such behavior is especially common in a loosely structured field of research, where several different actors lay claim to territory. Entrepreneurship research is one such field, where the network of researchers is markedly decentralized (Landström and Johannisson, 2001).

Bibliometric Studies – Rationale and Limitations

Bibliometric studies, in which a given field is studied by means of quantitative analysis and statistics to describe publication patterns, have been undertaken for a variety of purposes, ranging from the evaluation of academic institutions and quality assessments of scientific journals, to analysis of the intellectual structure of a scholarly field (Brown and Gardner, 1985; Romano and Ratnatunga, 1996). Bibliometric analysis is based on the assumption that if a researcher cites a work, s/he has found it useful, and therefore the more frequently a work is cited, the greater its role in the scholarly community (Romano and Ratnatunga, 1996). This form of analysis has been used for a long time in order to increase understanding of a scientific field (the first bibliometric study dates back to the early 20th century (Gross and Gross, 1927), but the real pioneer was de Solla Price (1963/1986), who applied bibliometrics as a method for measuring scientific impact).

Bibliometric analysis and the reference to the citation behavior of published authors are not without limitations (Brown and Gardner, 1985; MacRoberts and MacRoberts, 1989). First, we have to bear in mind that bibliometric analysis is based on the assumption that research is essentially cumulative – new research is built on and cites earlier high quality foundations – i.e. a 'normal science approach' (Kuhn, 1970), but we know that this is not the only way to communicate and organize research, particularly in new and evolving fields (see e.g. Gibbons et al., 1994; Knorr Cetina, 1999).

Looking more closely at the citation behavior of scholars, it can also be argued that it is sometimes difficult to know how citations are used in the articles. Citations may, for example, be biased in favor of 'popular' authors, such as Nobel Prize winners, whose names are used by researchers anxious to legitimize their own works. Citations can also be used in a negative rather than a confirmative way, i.e. to demonstrate inadequate conceptualization and unreflected methodology (in order to pave the way for the author's own contribution). However, relatively few citations in scientific works can be characterized as negative (Moravcsik and Murugesan, 1975). In addition, it can be argued that a work that attracts many citations, negative or otherwise, makes a significant contribution because it helps to organize the research topic.

Concerns can also be raised regarding the databases used for bibliometric analysis. Firstly, citations involve an inherent delay (Watkins, 2005). The work has to be published – a process that can take several years in the social sciences – after which it has to be recognized and acknowledged in terms of inclusion in the list of cited references (included in a work that needs to be published). In addition, citation analysis requires some form of index. In practice, scholars most often use generally available databases, such as the Social Sciences Citation Index (SSCI). However, even though the SSCI is a great resource for citation analysis, it has some limitations (Watkins and Reader, 2003). For example, the database is biased toward journals of US origin, books are covered only to a limited extent, and there is but limited coverage of the total population of available journals in many fields of research (in the field of entrepreneurship, the SSCI currently fully indexes a mere five journals: *Journal of Business Venturing*, *Small Business Economics*, *Journal of Small Business Management*, *Entrepreneurship Theory and Practice* and *Entrepreneurship and Regional Development*). Thus, in general, the SSCI database has some limitations when it comes to new and evolving fields such as entrepreneurship.

A conclusion that can be drawn is that the interpretation of the results of bibliometric analysis should be applied with some caution. However, we are convinced that the choice of references in a scientific work does provide important information on the territory claimed by the author. This way of positioning oneself is not only important for knowledge accumulation and the creation of a dialogue between researchers, but also provides crucial information for our understanding of the development of the research field.

Bibliometric Studies on Entrepreneurship – A Review

Over time many bibliometric studies have been presented in order to understand the development of the field of entrepreneurship research (a summary of the studies is presented in the Appendix, Table 3A.1). Bibliometric studies on entrepreneurship are based on different databases, from broad databases like the SSCI to narrow ones such as proceedings from specific entrepreneurship conferences (Watkins, 2005). The studies cover different time periods, and focus on varying aspects of the development of the field, such as (i) the research themes and communities involved, (ii) the concepts and research paradigms used in the studies, and (iii) methodological approaches. In relation to the development of entrepreneurship as a research field discussed in Chapter 2, we can summarize the conclusions made in earlier bibliometric studies as presented in Table 3.1.

The conclusions that can be drawn from earlier bibliometric studies on entrepreneurship research are that entrepreneurship seems to be a highly mono-paradigmatic research field, dominated by a normal-science approach (Kuhn, 1970), which assumes that progress in research is achieved through an accumulation of empirically tested hypotheses and developed through quantitative studies and statistical techniques. The field also seems to be geographically dominated by scholars from the US, although the strong dominance of US scholars in bibliometric studies may be a consequence of differences in research approaches and publication traditions in different continents.

However, changes have occurred in entrepreneurship research over time. The 1980s can be called the 'take-off phase' of entrepreneurship research (see Chapter 2) due to the increased interest in entrepreneurship and small businesses in society and immigration into the field by new researchers with different disciplinary backgrounds. This phase was characterized by an interest in solving practical problems for entrepreneurs, owner-managers, and the research community, although the ideas developed were loosely connected and fragmented. As stated in Chapter 2, the 1990s was characterized by an enormous 'growth of entrepreneurship research', and the bibliometric analysis indicated that many of the researchers within the field could be regarded as 'transient' in the sense that they were only temporarily conducting studies on entrepreneurship and small businesses. The field was dominated by micro-level analysis (firm and individual level analysis), indicating that the research has a strong foothold in the field of management studies. In addition, entrepreneurship research has become methodologically more sophisticated, shifting from descriptive studies to multivariate analysis. During the 2000s, entrepreneurship research can be considered as being a phase of 'searching for maturation', reflected in, for example, increased reliance on literature within the field (internal orientation) and a sign of stabilization in terms of research themes and specialization. It is interesting to note the stronger influence of research from outside the US, a consequence of which may be that entrepreneurship research exhibits a wider range of methodological approaches (in particular the use of more longitudinal research designs).

Bibliometric Analysis in this Chapter

In this chapter we elaborate on the development of entrepreneurship research within different disciplines. In accordance with our discussion in Chapter 2, we divide our

Table 3.1   Bibliometric studies on entrepreneurship research: conclusions

	Take-off 1970–89	Growth 1990–99	Search for maturation 2000–07
Research themes and community	Practical oriented research – toward improving practice rather than theory. The ideas within the field are loosely connected and explorative, mainly based on business studies (and social sciences such as psychology and sociology). Research community fragmented and individualistic. Increased impact of entrepreneurship journal articles (*JBV* and *ETP* have the greatest impact).	Enormous growth of research, and geographical concentration to North America. Upward trend in the quality of research. Transient researchers, i.e. researchers who belong to a mainstream discipline but who temporarily conduct entrepreneurship studies, allowing scholars from other fields to apply their models and concepts to entrepreneurial settings. The importance of publications in entrepreneurship increases.	Increased reliance on literature within the field, pointing to the unique contributions of entrepreneurship research (internal orientation in citations). Still a rather fragmented research field, but there are signs of stabilization of research themes and increased specialization (with core groups of researchers). The US dominates research, but other countries present their own research traditions (national differences in topics, studies and citation patterns).
Concepts and research paradigms	Entrepreneurship research is a mono-paradigmatic research field dominated by the functionalist paradigm (Burrell and Morgan, 1979) Language specificity has increased over time; less focus on size and age and increased use of specific words such as 'opportunity' and 'nascent'.		
Methodological approaches	Diversity of research approaches (anecdotal, case studies, and so on.), but postal surveys and questionnaire-based techniques dominate. Statistical sophistication in research is low.	Mono-methodological field of research, based on postal surveys and questionnaire-based techniques. Research is becoming more sophisticated, shifting from descriptive statistics towards more rigorous and multivariate techniques.	Still a rather mono-methodological field of research, based on mail surveys and questionnaire-based techniques, i.e. in a methodological sense, there has not been any substantial change over time. However, increased use of longitudinal research designs, multi-research designs (triangulation),

Table 3.1 (continued)

	Take-off 1970–89	Growth 1990–99	Search for maturation 2000–07
		Micro-level analysis dominates (firm-level and individual-level analysis).	and more sophisticated statistical techniques. Wide variety of dependent variables in the studies, which indicates difficulties in comparability between studies.

Note: ETP: *Entrepreneurship Theory and Practice*; JBV: *Journal of Business Venturing.*

analysis into management studies, economics and 'other fields' (for example economic history, psychology, and sociology) and analyze the changes in research over time. We divide time into three periods; 1970–89, 1990–99, and 2000–07, approximately corresponding with the 'take-off phase', 'growth phase' and 'search for maturation' discussed in Chapter 2.

The data for this study is based on a topic search of the SSCI using Web of Science – covering titles, keywords, and abstracts – published between 1956 and 2007. The search resulted in 14 388 articles citing 455 950 references published between 1776 and 2007. The search terms used were: 'entrepreneur*' or 'small business*' or 'small firm*' or 'emerging business*' or 'emerging firm*' or 'new venture*' or 'emerging venture*' or 'founder*'.

The above search strategy was primarily designed to find as many papers as possible within entrepreneurship research. Thus, the recall of papers can be considered good, as not many papers will be lost. However, in terms of precision or relevance, the search will naturally identify a certain number of papers that do not belong to the study of entrepreneurship. To increase the relevance somewhat, the analysis can employ other criteria such as journal categories to include or exclude areas of less relevance. In this chapter we use journal subject categories to compare the citation behavior of different disciplines. One discipline is called 'management studies', which consists of the journal categories management, business, and business finance. The second major field is economics, which corresponds to the journal category 'economics'. All other categories are grouped in one large category labeled 'other fields'.

The focus of the paper is cited documents and as such we consider the precision and recall problems less significant. It is the knowledge base rather than a complete survey of the research field that is the subject of our attention. Another limitation is that Web of Science does not include books as citing documents; however it includes cited books. We have no indication so far that the books in the field have different citation behavior than the articles in the field. Cited references were partly standardized in order to reduce variation in spelling. In the case of books, the first year of print was generally used. To further reduce variation, only the first initial of cited first authors was used.

THE GROWTH OF ENTREPRENEURSHIP RESEARCH WITHIN DIFFERENT DISCIPLINES

Entrepreneurship is a complex, heterogeneous and multi-level phenomenon that seems to require multiple disciplinary lenses to be understood. In Chapter 2 it was argued that over time, entrepreneurship research was anchored in different disciplines, initially 'economics', followed by the 'social sciences' (e.g. economic history, psychology, and sociology), and that since the 1970s it has been rooted in the field of 'management studies'. In order to provide a picture of the development of works on entrepreneurship within different disciplines, we describe the growth of publications over time (see Figure 3.1). In the analysis we have used fraction sums of the publications, since publications can be classified within different fields. For example, the journal *Small Business Economics* is classified as being 50 per cent within the field of management studies and 50 per cent within the field of economics, whereas the *Journal of Business Venturing* is classified as 100 per cent within management studies.

The results are presented in Figure 3.1, and we can conclude that the interest among scholars within different disciplines was rather low prior to 1990. However, from 1990 onwards, and most especially since the year 2000, we can see a significant growth in the number of publications, particularly within the area of management studies, and to some extent within economics, whereas the interest among psychologists and sociologists appears stable at a rather low level.[1] It is also interesting to note that during the 1990s entrepreneurship seems to have attracted a broad range of scholars from many different disciplines (the number of publications from 'other fields' grew significantly during the 1990s and this trend continued into the 2000s). In the analysis, the category 'other fields' includes 133 different disciplines and sub-disciplines in which articles on entrepreneurship appeared, and there seems to be a special interest among disciplines with a contextual and spatial focus, such as geography, environmental studies, area studies, urban studies, and anthropology.

The results confirm our earlier argument that it was mainly scholars within the field of management studies who maintained an interest in entrepreneurship over the last decades. However, entrepreneurship has for a long time been a 'hot topic' in society, attracting a broad range of scholars from many different disciplines within the social sciences, which reinforced the fragmented character of the field that characterized the 1990s and continued during the early part of the 2000s.

The development of entrepreneurship research in different disciplines implies that we may find somewhat different research communities interested in entrepreneurship research – following the line of argument from Chapter 2. On the one hand, there is a community of 'entrepreneurship researchers' with a disciplinary anchor in management studies, who in many cases regard themselves as entrepreneurship researchers. They attend entrepreneurship conferences and publish in entrepreneurship journals, and in this way create a research community that shares a great deal of tacit knowledge of entrepreneurship and small businesses and focuses on research problems of central importance for knowledge accumulation in the field. On the other hand, there is also a loosely connected group of 'disciplinary researchers' rooted in a large variety of disciplines, who are more or less interested in entrepreneurship, but who have over time conducted studies and published works on entrepreneurship. They do not regard themselves as

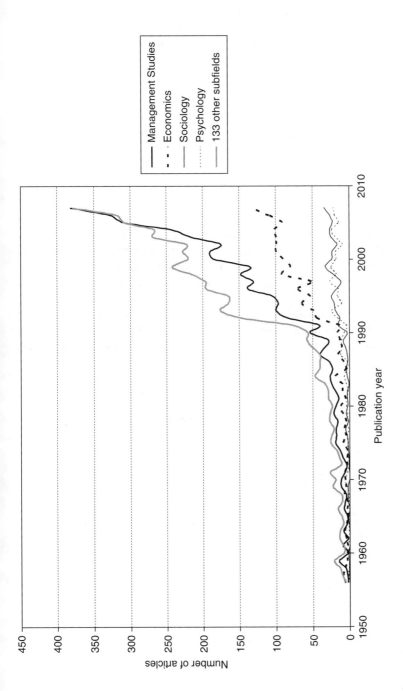

Notes:
For the whole period, the sum of paper fractions for each subfield is: Management Studies, including Business, Business Finance, Management (3577), Economics (1577), Sociology (443), Psychology (387), Planning and Development (376), Political Science (302), Geography (250), Environmental Studies (230), Public Administration (203), Social Sciences, Interdisciplinary (182), Law (179), Information Science and Library Science (150), Area Studies (148), Urban Studies (141), Operations Research, Business and Management Science (141), Education and Educational Research (136), Anthropology (123). We use paper fractions since papers may be classified into more than one subfield.

Figure 3.1   Publications by subfield and major fields

entrepreneurship researchers, nor do they participate in the entrepreneurial 'conversation'. Instead, they publish in disciplinary-based journals, and they may focus more on problems that are central to the discipline than on entrepreneurship. As a consequence, in a cognitive sense, there might be many different meanings of the phenomenon of entrepreneurship and the contexts in which it is studied – not always linked to the understanding and contexts that are reflected upon among researchers related to the community of scholars in entrepreneurship.

EVOLVING RESEARCH COMMUNITIES AND KNOWLEDGE PLATFORMS IN ENTREPRENEURSHIP RESEARCH

A young and evolving field of research like entrepreneurship always lacks a strong knowledge platform of its own – it takes some years to build such a platform that one can read and cite. However, based on the distinction between the two groups of researchers in entrepreneurship, i.e. that between 'entrepreneurship researchers' and 'disciplinary researchers', we can expect to find an evolving knowledge platform mainly developed by the group of 'entrepreneurship researchers' with their roots in management studies. In this section we elaborate on these propositions by analyzing the internal dialogue between researchers within the field of entrepreneurship.

Figure 3.2 reveals that the downloaded set of entrepreneurship publications from management studies journals has a higher share of all its citations in Web of Science from the downloaded set compared with publications in economics and 'other fields'. The share

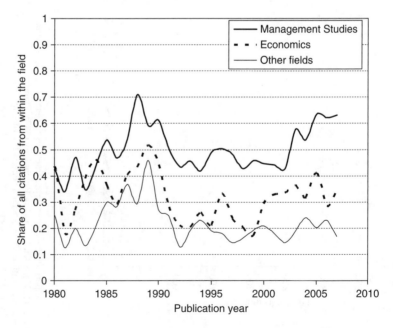

Figure 3.2   The relative share of all citations from Web of Science from the downloaded set of entrepreneurship publications between 1980 and 2007

of entrepreneurship citations varies somewhat over time, but a general impression is that it is rather stable within the respective disciplines, with an upward trend in management studies and economics since the year 2000. As a consequence, since the number of publications on entrepreneurship is increasing significantly over time, more and more citations are made to publications within the field of entrepreneurship. This is a first indication that the internal dialog between entrepreneurship researchers within 'management studies' is stronger than in 'economics' and 'other fields'. However, there are still a large number of papers in Web of Science that cite the downloaded set and could potentially be part of the field. However, they were not identified by our search strategy and are probably of less relevance.

Another indication of an evolving community of 'entrepreneurship researchers' anchored in management studies is shown in Figure 3.3. For publications in management studies journals, the mean number of citations to the field is higher and faster growing compared to economics and other fields. Thus, the growth of citations within the field of entrepreneurship has been significant in management studies during the 2000s.

A third indication of the same tendency is that entrepreneurship publications in management studies have a higher percentage of citations to their own field, i.e. publications in management studies (82 per cent), compared to economics (52 per cent) and other fields (52 per cent) (Table 3.2). It should also be noted that 'management studies' received a higher share of citations compared to 'economics' and 'other fields'. For example, publications in management studies are cited in 33 per cent of publications in economics, and 39 per cent by publications in 'other fields', whereas publications in management studies cite only 9 per cent of publications in economics, and 8 per cent in 'other fields', indicating that publications in 'management studies' constitute some form of 'core' literature in the field of entrepreneurship.

From our discussion we can conclude that the field of entrepreneurship is dominated by publications in management studies and that the interaction among the scholars in entrepreneurship is also dominated by this discipline. Furthermore, it is quite obvious

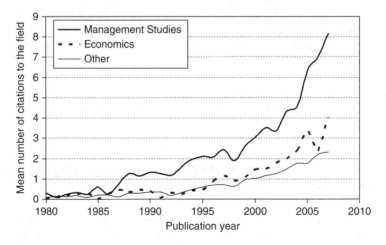

Figure 3.3   The mean number of citations to the downloaded set of entrepreneur publications by main field between 1980 and 2007

Table 3.2   Citations between main fields from 1980 to 2007 (in per cent)

Citing main field	Cited main field			
	Management studies	Economics	Other fields	Total
Management studies	82.3	9.2	8.5	100.0
Economics	33.2	52.5	14.3	100.0
Other fields	38.9	9.6	51.5	100.0
Total	68.0	13.2	18.8	100.0
Share of papers	42.4	13.6	44.0	100.0

that the field is becoming more and more self-reliant, i.e. citations are increasingly made to publications within entrepreneurship anchored in management studies, and that entrepreneurship researchers in other disciplines are citing publications on entrepreneurship in management studies. The conclusion to be drawn is that we find, in line with our assumptions, an indication of an evolving knowledge platform in entrepreneurship research, mainly developed among the group of 'entrepreneurship researchers' with their roots in management studies. The emerging knowledge platform in entrepreneurship has taken a long time to appear – about 40 years of more or less systematic research on entrepreneurship – but in this respect, entrepreneurship is not very different from any other emerging field in the social sciences.

If we take a more detailed look at the citation network among the publications, we find that the core of the network mainly consists of publications in management studies journals ('white circles' in Figure 3.4). However, the figure draws our attention to the fact that the citations seems to cluster within each discipline. Following our earlier discussion, most citations refer to management publications, but we can also find, for example in the upper right corner, an 'economics cluster' ('black circles') with publications heavily cited among economists but only partly by management scholars. The citation pattern is not evident to the same extent among publications in 'other fields' ('grey circles').

Figure 3.4 indicates that there seems to be a clear divide between scholars with roots in different disciplines – 'entrepreneurship researchers' with their roots in management tend to cite works with a basis in management studies and not rely on works outside the field, and scholars in economics follow a similar path – economists tend to cite other economists (the citation pattern of scholars in 'other fields' is not evident to the same extent). In the next section we elaborate on the emerging knowledge platforms in entrepreneurship and discuss the works that constitute them.

THE CHARACTERISTICS AND CONTENTS OF KNOWLEDGE PLATFORMS IN ENTREPRENEURSHIP RESEARCH

From the previous section we can conclude that there are signs of an evolving knowledge platform in entrepreneurship research, particularly within the group of 'entrepreneurship researchers' with roots in management. To elaborate further on the development of knowledge platforms in entrepreneurship, in this section we pose the following questions.

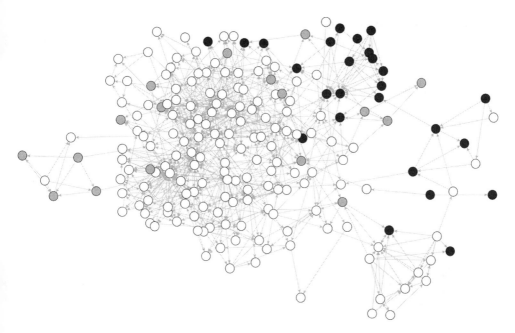

Note: Publications cited at least 25 times, with at least two connections. White circles = Management studies, Black circles = Economics, Grey circles = Other fields.

Figure 3.4   Citations among publications within the field

Which are the most cited works in each time period, irrespective of when they were published? Which are the most cited works published in each time period, and cited over all later periods? Thus, on the one hand, we are analyzing the works that are highly cited at different periods in time, i.e. the most cited works during the period 1970–89 (take-off phase), 1990–99 (growth phase), and 2000–07 (phase of searching for maturation), and in this analysis we mainly find the 'classical works' that have influenced the field, representing the 'research basis' in entrepreneurship research. On the other hand, we are analyzing the works that have been published during a certain time period and have then been influential over time, thus representing the 'core works' published in each time period.

Following our argument in the previous section indicating that the entrepreneurship research community is divided into different parts, we would expect to find fairly limited knowledge platforms shared between scholars rooted in various disciplines. If we analyze the ten most cited works within each discipline during each time period, and look for works that have been highly ranked within more than one discipline (see Tables 3.3 to 3.5), we can conclude, in line with our expectation, that there seem to be no strong shared knowledge platforms within the field of entrepreneurship, i.e. few works are highly ranked in more than one discipline (with very few exceptions such as the classic works by Schumpeter and McClelland). The conclusion that can be drawn is that the disciplinary roots seem to be more important than a general knowledge platform in entrepreneurship.

As there seems to be a strong disciplinary basis in the development of knowledge platforms in entrepreneurship, we focus our analysis of the development of such platforms on the following categories: management studies, economics, and 'other fields'.

Management Studies

By focusing on the research basis over time in management studies, we can identify (see Table 3.3) a change in the citation pattern from behavioral aspects in the period 1970–89 (with citations to McClelland, Collins et al., and Hornaday and Aboud, but also cita-

Table 3.3　Most cited works in management studies

Most cited works in each time period, irrespective of when they were published		
Ranking	1970–89 Take-off phase	1990–99 Growth phase	2000–07 Search for maturation
1	McClelland (1961)	Porter (1980)	Schumpeter (1934)
2	Chandler (1962)	Schumpeter (1934)	Barney (1991)
3	Collins et al. (1964)	Porter (1985)	Shane & Venkataraman (2000)
4	Burns & Stalker (1961)	Williamson (1975)	Cohen & Levinthal (1990)
5	Schumpeter (1934)	Williamson (1985)	Lumpkin & Dess (1996)
6	Collins & Moore (1970)	Low & MacMillan (1988)	Porter (1985)
7	Porter (1980)	Nunnally (1967)	Porter (1980)
8	Peters & Waterman (1982)	McClelland (1961)	Nelson & Winter (1982)
9	Hornaday & Aboud (1971)	Nelson & Winter (1982)	Penrose (1959)
10	Timmons (1977)	Jensen & Meckling (1976)	Stinchcombe (1965)
Most cited works published in each time period, and cited over all later periods		
1	Porter (1980)	Barney (1991)	Shane & Venkataraman (2000)
2	Porter (1985)	Cohen & Levinthal (1990)	Shane (2000)
3	Nelson & Winter (1982)	Storey (1994)	Zahra et al. (2000)
4	Jensen & Meckling (1976)	Lumpkin & Dess (1996)	Autio et al. (2000)
5	Williamson (1985)	Venkataraman (1997)	Davidsson & Honig (2003)
6	Covin & Slevin (1989)	Burt (1992)	McDougall & Oviatt (2000)
7	Pfeffer & Salancik (1978)	Petersen & Rajan (1994)	Shane & Stuart (2002)
8	Williamson (1975)	Busenitz & Barney (1997)	Adler & Kwan (2002)
9	Miller (1983)	Aldrich (1999)	Shane & Cable (2002)
10	Timmons (1977)	Eisenhardt & Schoonhoven (1990)	Baum et al. (2000)

tions to management literature such as Burns and Stalker, Porter, Peters and Waterman, and Timmons), toward a stronger interest in strategic management during the 1990s and 2000s with an anchor in Porter, and later on in the resource-based view (e.g. Barney, Cohen and Levinthal, and Penrose). Thus, looking at the citation pattern during the last period we can conclude that entrepreneurship researchers are still rooted in the discipline of management studies, and particularly in a strategic management approach. It is also interesting to note the influence of Schumpeter in all periods. Schumpeter seems to gain a high and even increasing importance over time, which may indicate that entrepreneurship research is trying to create an identity of its own.

Turning to the influential works (core works) published during each time period we can conclude that the 1970s and 1980s seem to be the decades of strong theoretical development within the discipline of management studies, which also influenced scholars with an interest in entrepreneurship. Some of the theories in management studies that have been highly influential originated in the 1970s and 1980s, for example, industrial organization (Porter, 1980; 1985), transaction costs theory (Williamson, 1975; 1985), agency theory (Jensen and Meckling, 1976), evolutionary perspective (Nelson and Winter, 1982), resource dependence (Pfeffer and Salancik, 1978), and strategic management (Miller, 1983; Covin and Slevin, 1989). Over time, these theoretical contributions from 1970 to 1989 have been frequently cited by entrepreneurship scholars, indicating that for a long time entrepreneurship researchers wanted to legitimize themselves in their own discipline and reinforce the strong theoretical anchor and tradition derived from management studies that we can find in entrepreneurship research since the 1970s.

It is more difficult to identify a particular core of works published in the 1990s that have become highly influential (cited) in management oriented entrepreneurship studies – the citations show a mix of different aspects of entrepreneurship that emerged during the 1990s and confirm our view of the decade as one of 'fragmented' entrepreneurship research (see Chapter 2). However, the importance of the resource-based view (Barney, 1991; Cohen and Levinthal, 1990) seems obvious, as it is also linked to a broader interest in strategic aspects of entrepreneurship (represented by Lumpkin and Dess, 1996; Busenitz and Barney, 1997). In the 1990s some influential works were also published in an attempt to synthesize and theorize entrepreneurship, represented by Storey (1994), Venkataraman (1997), and Aldrich (1999).

In the 2000s we can identify core works that start to build their own knowledge platforms in entrepreneurship, and these years clearly bear the stamp of Scott Shane's work on entrepreneurship – Shane has four contributions among the ten most cited works published in the 2000s. In addition, we can find three important themes based on entrepreneurship as a field in its own right: (1) the domain discussion of entrepreneurship strongly focused on in the works by Shane (Shane and Venkataraman, 2000; Shane, 2000), (2) the internationalization of entrepreneurial firms – for example in the special issue of the *Academy of Management Journal* 2000 (Zahra et al., 2000; Autio et al., 2000; McDougall and Oviatt, 2000), and (3) a strong interest in social capital and networks and their impact on start-ups, performance, and venture capital (Davidsson and Honig, 2003; Shane and Cable, 2002; Shane and Stuart, 2002; Adler and Kwan, 2002; Baum et al., 2000).

It is clear that, for a long time, entrepreneurship researchers rooted in management studies relied on mainstream management works, particularly those related to the field of strategic management. In the 2000s, however, many works with a stronger entrepreneurship focus have been emerging and have quickly become highly influential (cited), for example the works by Scott Shane, Per Davidsson and Shaker Zahra, indicating that a stronger knowledge platform of its own is emerging in entrepreneurship research.

Economics

An obvious knowledge platform in economics is represented by Schumpeter, who, over all time periods, has been frequently cited by economists interested in entrepreneurship (see Table 3.4). In the period 1970–89 economists seem to have relied heavily on classic works on entrepreneurship in economics, particularly Schumpeter (1934; 1939; 1942; 1954) but also Kirzner (1973; 1979), and Knight (1921). At the same time as the industrial landscape radically changed in the 1970s and 1980s, a number of pioneering contribu-

Table 3.4   Most cited works in economics

	Most cited works in each time period, irrespective of when they were published		
Ranking	1970–89 Take-off phase	1990–99 Growth phase	2000–07 Search for maturation
1	Schumpeter (1934)	Schumpeter (1942)	Evans & Jovanovic (1989)
2	Kirzner (1973)	Schumpeter (1934)	Evans & Leighton (1989)
3	Schumpeter (1942)	Evans & Leighton (1989)	Schumpeter (1934)
4	Knight (1921)	Williamson (1985)	Blanchflower & Oswald (1998)
5	Coase (1937)	Stiglitz & Weiss (1981)	Schumpeter (1942)
6	Schumpeter (1954)	Evans & Jovanovic (1989)	Jovanovic (1982)
7	McClelland (1961)	Jovanovic (1982)	Stiglitz & Weiss (1981)
8	Schumpeter (1939)	Williamson (1975)	Lucas (1978)
9	Kirzner (1979)	Piore & Sabel (1984)	Holtz-Eakin et al. (1994b)
10	Scherer & Ross (1980)	Nelson & Winter (1982)	Holtz-Eakin et al. (1994a)
	Most cited works published in each time period, and cited over all later periods		
1	Evans & Jovanovic (1989)	Blanchflower & Oswald (1998)	Blanchflower (2000)
2	Evans & Leighton (1989)	Holtz-Eakin et al. (1994b)	Blanchflower et al. (2001)
3	Jovanovic (1982)	Holtz-Eakin et al. (1994a)	Johnson et al. (2002)
4	Stiglitz & Weiss (1981)	Bates (1990)	Hellmann & Puri (2002)
5	Kirzner (1973)	Storey (1994)	Gompers & Lerner (2001)
6	Lucas (1978)	Saxenian (1994)	Klepper (2001)
7	Kihlstrom & Laffont (1979)	Petersen & Rajan (1994)	Cressy (2000)
8	Piore & Sabel (1984)	Baumol (1990)	Johnson et al. (2000)
9	Williamson (1985)	Audretsch (1995)	Hellmann et al. (2000)
10	Nelson & Winter (1982)	Gertler & Gilchrist (1994)	Kaplan & Strömberg (2003)

tions were published within the field of 'small business economics' – introducing a more dynamic or evolutionary framework and a stronger emphasis on the role and contributions of entrepreneurship and small businesses in society – a knowledge platform that became heavily cited among economists during the 1990s and the early part of the 2000s. For example, Richard Nelson and Sidney Winter (1982) were among the pioneers with their evolutionary model of economic development, a model that was further adapted by Jovanovic (1982). In addition, there was great interest in the question of why individuals become entrepreneurs – entrepreneurial choice models – represented by highly cited works by Evans and Jovanovic (1989) and Evans and Leighton (1989). Among seminal works frequently cited in entrepreneurship research, we can also find Robert Lucas's (1978) new growth theory, but also Piore and Sabel (1984), who provided an historical review of industrial development since the early nineteenth century.

In the 1990s and 2000s, we can identify three distinct and somewhat different areas of work that have been published as well as cited by economists. First, many works were published and frequently cited on the entry, survival and growth of new firms (e.g. Blanchflower and Oswald, 1998; Holtz-Eakin et al., 1994a; 1994b; Bates, 1990; Storey, 1994; Audretsch, 1995). In this respect, a large number of studies emphasized the importance of capital as well as the role of capital constraints in the decision to become an entrepreneur and as a determinant for the survival and growth of new firms (e.g. Petersen and Rajan, 1994; Gertler and Gilchrist, 1994). Second, probably due to the exceptional growth of the IT sector in the late 1990s and venture capitalists' involvement in the development of the sector, some of the most cited works are related to venture capital (e.g. Hellmann and Puri, 2002; Hellmann et al., 2000; Gompers and Lerner, 2001; Kaplan and Strömberg, 2003). Finally, there was a great interest in international comparisons of self-employment in different countries, and Blanchflower's studies on self-employment rates in OECD countries are among the most cited during the period 2000–07 (e.g. Blanchflower, 2000; Blanchflower et al., 2001), but the entrepreneurial development in post-communist countries also attracted attention (e.g. Johnson et al., 2000; 2002).

It appears that entrepreneurship research in economics has a rather strong theoretical anchor, which is embedded in the reasoning of Schumpeter but also in classic entrepreneurship works such as Kirzner and Knight. The pioneering studies on 'small business economics' that were mainly presented during the 1980s, have in later decades been extremely influential among entrepreneurship researchers rooted in economics. With 'small business economics' as a basis for research, entrepreneurship and small business seem to have developed in several different directions since the pioneering achievements of the 1980s and 1990s.

Other Fields

Despite the fact that the category 'other fields' represents a very heterogeneous group of research fields, there are several themes that seem to be fairly persistent with regard to both citations and publication patterns over time (Table 3.5).

The 1970s were characterized by a high level of immigration, particularly into the larger cities in the US as well as the UK, which led to social problems, unemployment, violence and race riots that triggered an increased interest in ethnic minority entrepreneurship among sociologists, with pioneering studies by Ivan Light and Edna Bonacich. Interest

Table 3.5   Most cited works in 'other fields'

	Most cited works in each time period, irrespective of when they were published		
Ranking	1970–89 Take-off phase	1990–99 Growth phase	2000–07 Search for maturation
1	McClelland (1961)	Piore & Sabel (1984)	Porter (1985)
2	Schumpeter (1934)	Light (1972)	Schumpeter (1934)
3	Storey (1982)	Light & Bonacich (1988)	Storey (1994)
4	Birch (1979)	Granovetter (1985)	Rogers (1962)
5	Bonacich & Modell (1980)	Schumpeter (1934)	Yin (1984)
6	McClelland et al. (1969)	Waldinger et al. (1990)	Saxenian (1994)
7	Weber (1908/1958)	Kingdon & Thurber (1984/1995)	Harvey (1989)
8	Collins et al. (1964)	Bonacich (1973)	Granovetter (1985)
9	Light (1972)	Portes & Bach (1985)	Penrose (1959)
10	Peters & Waterman (1982)	Williamson (1975)	Putnam et al. (1993)
	Most cited works published in each time period, and cited over all later periods		
1	Porter (1985)	Storey (1994)	Shane & Venkataraman (2000)
2	Piore & Sabel (1984)	Waldinger et al. (1990)	Light & Gold (2000)
3	Granovetter (1985)	Saxenian (1994)	Putnam (2000)
4	Light (1972)	Putnam et al. (1993)	Florida (2002)
5	Light & Bonacich (1988)	Aldrich & Waldinger (1990)	Etzkowitz & Leydesdorff (2000)
6	Harvey (1989)	Light & Rosenstein (1995)	Etzkowitz et al. (2000)
7	Yin (1984)	Osborne & Gaebler (1992)	Shane (2000)
8	Williamson (1975)	Barney (1991)	Etzkowitz (2003)
9	Portes & Bach (1985)	Portes & Sensenbrenner (1993)	Curran (2000)
10	Bonacich & Modell (1980)	Burt (1992)	Acs (2002)

in ethnic immigrant entrepreneurship has continued among sociologists, with influential contributions during the 1990s by, for example, Waldinger et al. (1990), Aldrich and Waldinger (1990), Light and Rosenstein (1995), and Portes and Sensenbrenner (1993) (see Table 3.5).

Another research theme that has persisted in 'other fields' over time concerns the changes in society and the evolution of a post-modern, knowledge-intensive society, pioneered by Michael Piore and Charles Sabel's book *The Second Industrial Divide* (1984) and David Harvey's book *The Condition of Postmodernity* (1989), followed by contributions by Robert Putnam (2000; Putnam et al., 1993). During the 2000s, there have been several publications on innovation studies, which has become a core theme among scholars anchored in 'other fields', and deals with the creation of innovations and new knowledge as well as the role of universities, regions, and societies in the new knowledge creation. The extensive number of publications during the 2000s that fairly quickly became frequently cited, not least Henry Etzkowitz's ideas about the Triple Helix model (university – industry – government), which attracted much interest, while contributions by Florida (*The Rise of the Creative Class*, 2002, and Acs (*Innovation and the Growth of Cities*, 2002) also received a great deal of attention.

Finally, the theme of social networks emerged during the 1980s, influenced by Granovetter's (1985) seminal work on strong and weak ties. Networks continued to be important in entrepreneurship research, as did Burt's work (*Structural Holes. The Social Structure of Competition*, 1992).

The 'other fields' category is strongly heterogeneous and includes many different research topics, most of which do not attract a large number of scholars. Nevertheless, some research themes stand out and have been fairly persistent over time: ethnic minority entrepreneurship, knowledge-based society, and social networks in entrepreneurship.

Knowledge Platforms in Entrepreneurship – Summary

It can be concluded that entrepreneurship as a research field lacks a strong knowledge platform, although such a platform seemed to be emerging during the 2000s among 'entrepreneurship researchers' rooted in management studies. However, in general, the 'traditional' disciplines appear to be important in the analysis of knowledge platforms in entrepreneurship. Thus, the field can be characterized as a 'bounded' multi-disciplinarity of research in which the knowledge platforms are mainly linked to the theoretical frameworks that have been developed within the respective mainstream disciplines, and there is very limited cross-fertilization between scholars interested in entrepreneurship within different disciplines.

The base disciplines matter to a great extent in entrepreneurship research. The academic system is rooted in the 'traditional' disciplinary boundaries – our theories, our academic education and careers, our social networks, and so on. There are many arguments indicating that the disciplines are the basis for understanding entrepreneurship (see Landström, 2005); for example, many concepts and theories for understanding entrepreneurship can be found in the knowledge that is rooted in the 'traditional' disciplines. It is important to take advantage of this knowledge in entrepreneurship research, despite the fact that it takes a long time to create cross-fertilization between scholars with different disciplinary backgrounds.

CONCLUSIONS

In this chapter we have demonstrated, firstly that a research community of 'entrepreneurship researchers', mainly anchored in the field of 'management studies', is evolving over time. These researchers show a stronger self-reliance in their citation pattern, in which citations are increasingly made to publications within the field of entrepreneurship. Secondly, we have demonstrated that there are signs of an emerging 'knowledge platform' in entrepreneurship research, especially within the group of 'entrepreneurship researchers'. In the 2000s, works with a strong entrepreneurship focus have become highly influential within the field.

The development of a research community and a knowledge platform has taken time, which is not unusual in new fields of research – but an obstacle has been that the mainstream disciplines matter and the strong disciplinary boundaries have made cross-disciplinary research difficult. The 'bounded' multi-disciplinarity of entrepreneurship research makes it necessary to find new ways to organize such cross-disciplinary research.

We believe that an important challenge for entrepreneurship researchers in the future will be to engage in more systematic theory driven research and, as entrepreneurship is a phenomenon characterized by high complexity, heterogeneity, and multi-level considerations, we need cross-disciplinary approaches in order to understand the phenomenon. As argued by Davidsson (2003), in the future we need to combine entrepreneurial and disciplinary knowledge, which can be achieved by (i) entrepreneurship researchers learning more about theory and method from the disciplines, (ii) disciplinary researchers focussing on entrepreneurship research, and (iii) collaboration between entrepreneurial and disciplinary researchers. According to Davidsson, all three directions are likely to be explored in the future.

NOTE

1. At the beginning of the 1990s, Web of Science introduced abstracts in their analysis, which automatically provided more hits, and could partly explain the growth trend in entrepreneurship research during the 1990s.

REFERENCES

Acs, Z.J. (2002), *Innovation and the Growth of Cities*, Cheltenham, UK, and Northampton, MA, USA: Edward Elgar.

Adler, P.S. and S.W. Kwan (2002), 'Social capital: prospects for a new concept', *Academy of Management Review*, **27**(1), 17–40.

Aldrich, H.E. (1992), 'Methods in our madness? Trends in entrepreneurship research', in D.L. Sexton and J.D. Kasarda (eds), *The State of the Art of Entrepreneurship*, Boston, MA: PWS-Kent Publishing, pp. 191–213.

Aldrich, H.E. (1999), *Organizations Evolving*, Thousand Oaks, CA: Sage.

Aldrich, H.E. and T. Baker (1997), 'Blinded by the cites? Has there been progress in entrepreneurship research?', in D.L. Sexton and R.W. Smilor (eds), *Entrepreneurship 2000*, Chicago, IL: Uppstart, pp. 377–400.

Aldrich, H.E. and R. Waldinger (1990), 'Ethnicity and entrepreneurship', *Annual Review of Sociology*, **16**, 111–35.

Audretsch, D.B. (1995), *Innovation and Industry Evolution*, Cambridge, MA: MIT Press.

Audretsch, D.B. (1997), 'Technological regimes, industrial demography, and the evolution of industrial structures', *Industrial and Corporate Change*, **6**(1), 49–82.

Autio, E., H.J. Sapienza and J.G. Almeida (2000), 'Effects of age at entry, knowledge intensity, and imitability on international growth', *Academy of Management Journal*, **43**(5), 909–24.

Barney, J.B. (1991), 'Firm resources and sustained competitive advantage', *Journal of Management*, **17**, 99–120.

Bates, T. (1990), 'Entrepreneur human capital input and small business longevity', *Review of Economics and Statistics*, **72**(4), 551–59.

Baum, J.A.C., T. Calabrese and B.S. Silverman (2000), 'Don't go it alone: alliance network composition and startups' performance in Canadian biotechnology', *Strategic Management Journal*, **21**(3), 267–94.

Baumol, W.J. (1990), 'Entrepreneurship: productive, unproductive and destructive', *Journal of Political Economy*, **98**(5), 893–921.

Birch, D.L. (1979), *The job Generation Process*, MIT Program on Neighborhood and Regional Change, Cambridge, MA: MIT.

Blanchflower, D.G. (2000), 'Self-employment in OECD countries', *Labour Economics*, **7**(5), 471–505.

Blanchflower, D.G. and A.J. Oswald (1998), 'What makes an entrepreneur?', *Journal of Labor Economics*, **16**(1), 26–60.

Blanchflower, D.G., A.J. Oswald and A. Stutzer (2001), 'Latent entrepreneurship across nations', *European Economic Review*, **45**(4–6), 680–91.

Bonacich, E. (1973), 'The theory of middleman minorities', *American Sociological Review*, **38**(5), 583–94.

Bonacich, E. and J. Modell (1980), *The Ethnic Basis of Economic Solidarity*, Berkeley, CA: California University Press.

Bouckenooghe, D., M. Buelens, D. DeClercq and A. Willem (2004), 'A review of research methodology in entrepreneurship: current practices and trends (1999–2003)', paper presented at the Research in Entrepreneurship and Small Business (RENT XVIII) Conference, 25–26 November, Copenhagen.

Brown, L.D. and J.C. Gardner (1985), 'Using citation analysis to assess the impact of journals and articles in contemporary accounting research', *Journal of Accounting Research*, **23**(1), 84–108.

Brush, C.G., T.S. Manolova and L.F. Edelman (2008), 'Separated by common language? Entrepreneurship research across the Atlantic', *Entrepreneurship Theory and Practice*, March, 249–66.

Burns, T. and G.M. Stalker (1961), *The Management of Innovation*, London: Tavistock Publications.

Burrell, G. and G. Morgan (1979), *Sociological Paradigms and Organisational Analysis*, London: Heinemann.

Burt, R.S. (1992), *Structural Holes: The Social Structure of Competition*, Cambridge, MA: Harvard University Press.

Busenitz, L.W. and J.B. Barney (1997), 'Differences between entrepreneurs and managers in large organizations', *Journal of Business Venturing*, **12**, 9–30.

Busenitz, L.W., G.P. West III, D. Shepherd, T. Nelson, G.N. Chandler and A. Zacharakis (2003), 'Entrepreneurship research in emergence: past trends and future directions', *Journal of Management*, **29**(3), 285–308.

Chandler, A.D. (1962), *Strategy and Structure*, Cambridge, MA: MIT Press.

Chandler, G.N. and D.W. Lyon (2001), 'Issues of research design and construct measurement in entrepreneurship research: the past decade', *Entrepreneurship Theory and Practice*, **24**(4), 101–13.

Churchill, N.C. and V.L. Lewis (1986), 'Entrepreneurship research: directions and methods', in D.L. Sexton and R.W. Smilor (eds), *The Art and Science of Entrepreneurship*, Cambridge, MA: Ballinger, pp. 333–65.

Coase, R.H. (1937), 'The nature of the firm', *Economica*, **4**(16), 386–405.

Cohen, W.M. and D.A. Levinthal (1990), 'Absorptive capacity: a new perspective on learning and innovation', *Administrative Science Quarterly*, **35**(1), 128–52.

Cole, S. (1970), 'Professional standing and the reception of scientific discoveries', *American Journal of Sociology*, **76**, 286–306.

Collins, O.F. and D.G. Moore (1970), *The Organization Makers*, New York: Appleton Century Crofts.

Collins, O., D. Moore and D.B. Unwalla (1964), *The Enterprising Man*, East Lansing, MI: Michigan State University.

Cornelius, B., H. Landström and O. Persson (2006), 'Entrepreneurial studies: the dynamic research front of a developing social science', *Entrepreneurship Theory and Practice*, May, 375–98.

Covin, J.G. and D.P. Slevin (1989), 'Strategic management of small firms in hostile and benign environments', *Strategic Management Journal*, **10**(1), 75–87.

Crane, D. (1972), *Invisible Colleges. Diffusion of Knowledge in Scientific Communities*, Chicago: University of Chicago Press.

Cressy, R. (2000), 'Credit rationing or entrepreneurial risk aversion?', *Economic Letters*, **66**(2), 235–40.

Crump, M.E.S., A. Abbery and X. Zu (2009), 'Rankings of top entrepreneurship researchers and affiliations: 1995 through 2006', paper at the 2009 Academy of Management Meeting, Chicago, 9–11 August.

Curran, J. (2000), 'What is small business policy in the UK for?', *International Small Business Journal*, **18**, 36–50.

Davidsson, P. (2003), 'The domain of entrepreneurship research: some suggestions', in J. Katz and D. Shepherd (eds), *Advances in Entrepreneurship, Firm Emergence and Growth*, Volume 6, Greenwich, CT: JAI Press, pp. 315–72.

Davidsson, P. and B. Honig (2003), 'The role of social and human capital among nascent entrepreneurs', *Journal of Business Venturing*, **18**(3), 301–31.

Davidsson, P. and J. Wiklund (2001), 'Levels of analysis in entrepreneurship research: current research practice and suggestions for the future', *Entrepreneurship Theory and Practice*, **24**(4), 81–99.

de Solla Price, D.J. (1963/1986), *Little Science, Big Science . . . and beyond*, Columbia: Columbia University Press.

Dean, M.A., C.L. Shook and G.T. Payne (2007), 'The past, present, and future of entrepreneurship research: data analytic trends and training', *Entrepreneurship Theory and Practice*, July, 601–18.

Déry, R. and J.-M. Toulouse (1996), 'Social structuration of the field of entrepreneurship: a case study', *Canadian Journal of Administrative Sciences*, **13**(4), 285–305.

Edelman, L.F., T.S. Manolova and C.G. Brush (2009), 'Still blinded by the cites: has there been progress in entrepreneurship research?', paper at the Academy of Management Annual Meeting, Chicago, IL, 9–11 August.

Eisenhardt, K.M. and C.B. Schoonhoven (1990), 'Organizational growth', *Administrative Science Quarterly*, **35**(3), 504–29.

Etzkowitz, H. (2003), 'Research groups as quasi-firms', *Research Policy*, **32**(1), 109–21.

Etzkowitz, H. and L. Leydesdorff (2000), 'The dynamics of innovation', *Research Policy*, **29**(2), 109–23.

Etzkowitz, H., A. Webster, C. Gebhardt and B.R.C. Terra (2000), 'The future of the university and the university of the future', *Research Policy*, **29**(2), 313–30.

Evans, D.S. and B. Jovanovic (1989), 'An estimated model of entrepreneurial choice under liquidity constraints', *Journal of Political Economics*, **97**(4), 808–27.

Evans, D.S. and L.S. Leighton (1989), 'Some empirical aspects of entrepreneurship', *American Economic Review*, **79**(3), 519–35.

Florida, R. (2002), *The Rise of the Creative Class*, New York: Basic Books.

Gertler, M. and S. Gilchrist (1994), 'Monetary policy, business cycles, and the behaviour of small manufacturing firms', **109**(2), 303–40.

Gibbons, M., C. Limoges, H. Nowotny, S. Schwartzman, P. Scott and M. Trow (1994), *The New Production of Knowledge*, London: Sage.

Gompers, P. and J. Lerner (2001), 'The venture capital revolution', *Journal of Economic Perspectives*, **15**(2), 145–68.

Granovetter, M. (1985), 'Economic action and social structure: the problem of embeddedness', *Journal of Sociology*, **91**(3), 481–99.

Grant, P. and L. Perren (2002), 'Small business and entrepreneurship research. Meta-theories, paradigms and prejudices', *International Small Business Journal*, **20**(2), 185–211.

Grégoire, D.A., M.X. Noël, R. Déry and J.-P. Béchard (2006), 'Is there conceptual convergence in entrepreneurship research? A co-citation analysis of frontiers of entrepreneurship research, 1981–2004', *Entrepreneurship Theory and Practice*, May, 333–73.

Gross, P.L. and E.M. Gross (1927), 'College libraries and chemical education', *Science*, **66**, 385–89.

Harvey, D. (1989), *The Condition of Postmodernity*, Oxford: Blackwell.

Hellmann, T. and M. Puri (2002), 'Venture capital and the professionalization of start-up firms: empirical evidence', *Journal of Finance*, **57**(1), 169–97.

Hellmann, T., L. Lindsey and M. Puri (2000), 'Building relations early. Banks in venture capital', *Review of Financial Studies*, **21**(2), 513–41.

Holtz-Eakin, D., D. Joulfaian and H.S. Rosen (1994a), 'Entrepreneurial decisions and liquidity constraints', *Rand Journal of Economics*, **25**(2), 334–47.

Holtz-Eakin, D., D. Joulfaian and H.S. Rosen (1994b), 'Sticking it out: entrepreneurial survival and liquidity constraints', *Journal of Political Economy*, **102**(1), 53–75.

Hornaday, J.A. and J. Aboud (1971), 'Characteristics of successful entrepreneurs', *Personnel Psychology*, **24**(2), 141–53.

Jensen, M.C. and W.H. Meckling (1976), 'Theory of the firm: managerial behaviour, agency costs and ownership structure', *Journal of Financial Economics*, **3**(4), 305–60.

Johnson, S., J. McMillan and C. Woodruff (2000), 'Entrepreneurs and the ordering of institutional reforms', *Economics of Transition*, **8**, 1–36.

Johnson, S., J. McMillan and C. Woodruff (2002), 'Property rights and finance', *American Economic Review*, **92**(5), 1335–56.

Jovanovic, B. (1982), 'Selection and evolution of industry', *Econometrica*, **50**, 649–70.

Kaplan, S.N. and P. Strömberg (2003), 'Financial contracting theory meets the real world', *Review of Economic Studies*, **70**, 281–315.

Karlsson, T. (2008), 'Emergence and development of entrepreneurship research 1989–2007: Key words and collocations', Babson Conference, Chapel Hill, North Carolina, 5–7 June.

Kihlstrom, R.E. and J.-J. Laffont (1979), 'A general equilibrium entrepreneurial theory of firm formation based on risk aversion', *Journal of Political Economy*, **87**(4), 719–48.

Kingdon, J.W. and J.A. Thurber (1984/1995), *Agendas, Alternatives, and Public Policies*, New York: Harper Collins.

Kirzner, I.M. (1973), *Competition and Entrepreneurship*, Chicago, IL: University of Chicago Press.

Kirzner, I.M. (1979), *Perception, Opportunity and Profit*, Chicago, IL: University of Chicago Press.

Klepper, S. (2001), 'Employee startups in high-tech industries', *Industrial and Corporate Change*, **10**(3), 639–74.

Knight, F.H. (1921), *Risk, Uncertainty and Profit*, New York: Houghton Mifflin.

Knorr Cetina, K. (1999), *Epistemic Cultures: How the Sciences Make Knowledge*, Cambridge, MA: Harvard Business School Press.

Kuhn, T. (1970), *The Structure of Scientific Revolutions*, Chicago: University of Chicago Press.

Kyrö, P. and J. Kansikas (2005), 'Current state of methodology in entrepreneurship research and some expectations for the future', in A. Fayolle, P. Kyrö and J. Ulijn (eds), *Entrepreneurship Research in Europe. Outcomes and Perspectives*, Cheltenham, UK and Northampton, MA, USA: Edward Elgar, pp. 121–49.

Landström, H. (2000), 'The institutionalization of entrepreneurship research', paper at the XI Nordic Conference on Small Business Research, Aarhus, Denmark, 18–20 June.

Landström, H. (2001), 'Who loves entrepreneurship research? Knowledge accumulation within a transient field of research', paper at the RENT XV Research in Entrepreneurship Conference, Turku, Finland, 22–23 November.

Landström, H. (2005), *Pioneers in Entrepreneurship and Small Business Research*, New York: Springer.

Landström, H. and M. Huse (1996), 'Trends in entrepreneurship and small business research', SIRE Working Paper 1996:3, Halmstad University, Sweden.

Landström, H. and B. Johannisson (2001), 'Theoretical foundations of Swedish entrepreneurship and small-business research', *Scandinavian Journal of Management*, **17**(2), 225–48.

Light, I. (1972), *Ethnic Enterprise in America*, Berkeley, CA: University of California Press.

Light, I. and E. Bonacich (1988), *Immigrant Entrepreneurs*, Berkeley, CA: University of California Press.

Light, I. and S.J. Gold (2000), *Ethnic Economies*, San Diego, CA: Academic.

Light, I. and C.N. Rosenstein (1995), *Race, Ethnicity, and Entrepreneurship in Urban America*, New York: Gruyter.

Low, M.B. and I.C. MacMillan (1988), 'Entrepreneurship, past research and future challenges', *Journal of Management*, **14**(2), 139–61.

Lucas, R.E. (1978), 'On the size distribution of business firms', *Bell Journal of Economics*, **9**(2), 508–23.

Lumpkin, G.T. and G.G. Dess (1996), 'Clarifying the entrepreneurial orientation construct and linking it to performance', *Academy of Management Review*, **21**(1), 135–72.

MacRoberts, M.H. and B.R. MacRoberts (1989), 'Problems of citation analysis. A critical review', *Journal of the American Society for Information Science*, **40**(5), 342–49.

McClelland, D.C. (1961), *The Achieving Society*, Princeton, NJ: van Nostrand.

McClelland, D.C., D.G. Winter and S.K. Winter (1969), *Motivating Economic Achievement*, New York: Free Press.

McDonald, S., B. Ching Gan and A. Anderson (2004), 'Studying entrepreneurship: a review of methods employed in entrepreneurship research 1985–2004', paper presented at the Research in Entrepreneurship and Small Business (RENT XVIII) Conference, 25–26 November, Copenhagen.

McDougall, P.P. and B.M. Oviatt (2000), 'International entrepreneurship: the intersection of two research paths', *Academy of Management Journal*, **43**(5), 902–906.

Miller, D. (1983), 'The correlates of entrepreneurship in three types of firms', *Management Science*, **29**(7), 770–91.

Moravcsik, M.J. and P. Murugesan (1975), 'Some results of the function and quality of citations', *Social Studies of Science*, **5**(1), 86–92.

Mullen, M.R., D.G. Budeva and P.M. Doney (2009), 'Research methods in the leading small business-entrepreneurship journals: a critical review with recommendations for future research', *Journal of Small Business Management*, **47**(3), 287–307.

Nelson, R.R. and S.G. Winter (1982), *An Evolutionary Theory of Economic Change*, Cambridge, MA: Harvard University Press.

Nunnally, J.C. (1967), *Psychometric Theory*, New York: McGraw-Hill.

Osborne, D. and T. Gaebler (1992), *Reinventing Government: How the Entrepreneurial Spirit is Transforming the Public Sector*, Reading, MA: Addison-Wesley.

Paulin, W.L., R.E. Coffey and M.E. Spaulding (1982), 'Entrepreneurship research: methods and directions', in C.A. Kent, D.L. Sexton and K.H. Vesper (eds), *Encyclopedia of Entrepreneurship*, Englewood Cliffs, NJ: Prentice-Hall, pp. 352–73.

Penrose, E.T. (1959), *The Theory of the Growth of the Firm*, Oxford: Blackwell.

Peters, T.J. and R.H. Waterman (1982), *In Search of Excellence*, New York: Harper and Row.

Petersen, M.A. and R.G. Rajan (1994), 'The benefits of lending relationships: evidence from small business data', *Journal of Finance*, **49**(1), 3–37.

Pfeffer, J. and G. Salancik (1978), *The External Control of Organizations*, New York: Harper and Row.

Piore, M.J. and C.F. Sabel (1984), *The Second Industrial Divide*, New York: Basic Books.

Porter, M.E. (1980), *Competitive Strategy*, New York: John Wiley.

Porter, M.E. (1985), *Competitive Advantages*, New York: Free Press.

Portes, A. and R.L. Bach (1985), *Latin Journey: Cuban and Mexican Immigrants in the United States*, Berkeley, CA: University of California Press.

Portes, A. and J. Sensenbrenner (1993), 'Embeddedness and immigration', *American Journal of Sociology*, **98**(6), 1320–50.

Putnam, R.D. (2000), *Bowling Alone: The Collapse and Revival of American Community*, New York: Simon and Schuster.

Putnam, R.D., R. Leonardi and R.Y. Nanetti (1993), *Making Democracy Work*, Princeton, NJ: Princeton University Press.

Ratnatunga, J. and C. Romano (1997), 'A citation classics analysis of articles in contemporary small enterprise research', *Journal of Business Venturing*, **12**, 197–212.

Reader, D. and D. Watkins (2006), 'The social and collaborative nature of entrepreneurship scholarship: a co-citation and perceptual analysis', *Entrepreneurship Theory and Practice*, May, 417–41.

Rogers, E.M. (1962), *Diffusion of Innovations*, New York: Free Press.

Romano, C. and J. Ratnatunga (1996), 'A citation analysis of the impact of journals on contemporary small enterprise research', *Entrepreneurship Theory and Practice*, Spring, 7–21.

Saxenian, A.L. (1994), *Regional Advantage: Culture and Competition in Silicon Valley and Route 128*, Cambridge, MA: Harvard University Press.

Scherer, F.M. and D. Ross (1980), *Industrial Market Structure and Economic Performance*, Boston, MA: Houghton Mifflin.

Schildt, H.A., S.A. Zahra and A. Sillanpää (2006), 'Scholarly communities in entrepreneurship research: a co-citation analysis', *Entrepreneurship Theory and Practice*, May, 399–415.

Schumpeter, J.A. (1934), *The Theory of Economic Development*, Cambridge, MA: Harvard University Press.

Schumpeter, J.A. (1939), *Business Cycles*, New York: McGraw-Hill.

Schumpeter, J.A. (1942), *Capitalism, Socialism and Democracy*, New York: Harper & Row.

Schumpeter, J.A. (1954), *History of Economic Analysis*, London: Allen & Unwin.

Shane, S.A. (1997), 'Who is publishing the entrepreneurship research?', *Journal of Management*, **23**, 83–95.

Shane, S.A. (2000), 'Prior knowledge and the discovery of entrepreneurial opportunities', *Organization Science*, **11**(4), 448–69.

Shane, S.A. and D. Cable (2002), 'Network ties, reputation, and the financing of new ventures', *Management Science*, **48**(3), 364–81.

Shane, S.A. and T. Stuart (2002), 'Organizational endowments and the performance of university start-ups', *Management Science*, **48**(1), 154–70.

Shane, S.A. and S. Venkataraman (2000), 'The promise of entrepreneurship as a field of research', *Academy of Management Review*, **25**(1), 217–26.

Stiglitz, J.E. and A. Weiss (1981), 'Credit rationing in markets with imperfect information', *American Economic Review*, **71**(3), 393–410.

Stinchcombe, A.L. (1965), 'Organizations and social structure', in J.G. March (ed.), *Handbook of Organizations*, Chicago, IL: Rand McNally, pp. 142–93.

Storey, D.J. (1982), *Entrepreneurship and the New Firms*, London: Routledge.

Storey, D.J. (1994), *Understanding the Small Business Sector*, London: Routledge.

Timmons, J. (1977), *New Venture Creation*, Boston, MA: Irwin.

Venkataraman, S. (1997), 'The distinctive domain of entrepreneurship research', in J.A. Katz (ed.), *Advances in Entrepreneurship, Firm Emergence, and Growth*, Volume 3, Greenwich, CT: JAI Press, pp. 119–38.

Waldinger, R.D., H.E. Aldrich and R. Ward (1990), *Ethnic Entrepreneurs: Immigrant Business in Industrial Societies*, Newbury Park, CA: Sage.

Watkins, D. (2005), 'Identifying trends in entrepreneurship research: textual analysis revisited', paper presented at the AoM Meeting, Honolulu, Hawaii, 5–10 August.

Watkins, D. and D. Reader (2003), 'Quantitative research on entrepreneurship as a field of study: what do we know? What should we know?', paper presented at the 17th RENT Conference, Lodz, Poland.

Weber, M. (1908/1958), *The Protestant Ethic and the Spirit of Capitalism*, London: Unwin.

Whitley, R. (1984), *The Intellectual and Social Organization of Science*, Oxford: Oxford University Press.

Williamson, O.E. (1975), *Markets and Hierarchies*, New York: Free Press.

Williamson, O.E. (1985), *The Economic Institutions of Capitalism*, New York: Free Press.

Yin, R.K. (1984), *Case Study Research*, Newbury Park, CA: Sage.

Zahra, S.A. (2005), 'Entrepreneurship and disciplinary scholarship: return to the fountainhead', in S.A. Alvarez, R. Agarwal and O. Sorenson (eds), *Handbook of Entrepreneurship Research. Interdisciplinary Perspectives*, New York: Springer, pp. 253–68.

Zahra, S.A., R.D. Ireland and M.A. Hitt (2000), 'International expansion by new venture firms', *Academy of Management Journal*, **43**(5), 925–50.

APPENDIX

Table 3A.1   Entrepreneurship research in bibliometric studies

Article	Time frame	Sample	Conclusions
Research themes and community			
Romano & Ratnatunga (1996)	1986–92	Small business journals (*JSBM, ISBJ, ETP, JBV, SBE*, and *API*)	An increased impact of entrepreneurship journal articles over time. *JBV* and *ETP* had the greatest impact on the advancement of small business research.
Ratnatunga & Romano (1997)	1986–92	Small business journals (*JSBM, ISBJ, ETP, JBV, SBE*, and *API*)	The research field is characterized as a loose collection of ideas rather than a coherent structure. Most of the articles were explorative in nature and attempted to rationalize concepts and variables used in small business research.
Déry & Toulouse (1996)	1986–93	Articles in *JBV*	The authors relied heavily on disciplines associated with business studies and entrepreneurship, followed by disciplines in the social sciences (psychology and sociology). The field is characterized by a fragmentation of social relations among researchers.
Shane (1997)	1987–94	Entrepreneurship articles in 19 management and entrepreneurship journals	Ranking the impact of authors and institutions in entrepreneurship research.
Landström (2000)	1987–99	*JBV, SBE, JSBM* and *Technovation*	Enormous growth of the research community (approx. 10 per cent per year during the 1990s). Geographical concentration in North America. The strength of the research community in NA is further confirmed by the fact that collaboration between researchers in NA seems to be more pronounced, and NA is an intellectual center that attracts collaboration from researchers who mainly come from countries with a less developed infrastructure within entrepreneurship research.
Landström (2001)	1987–99	*JBV, SBE, JSBM* and *Technovation*	The research community in entrepreneurship constitutes a rather heterogeneous group of researchers.

Table 3A.1   (continued)

Article	Time frame	Sample	Conclusions
			Most researchers within the field can be regarded as 'transients', i.e. researchers who belong to some mainstream discipline and who temporarily visit the field of entrepreneurship research. There are very few researchers who work in entrepreneurship on a continual basis.
Busenitz et al. (2003)	1985–99	Leading management journals (*AMJ*, *AMR*, *ASQ*, *JM*, *MS*, *OS*, and *SMJ*)	The boundaries of the entrepreneurship field are highly permeable, i.e. allowing scholars from other fields to apply their models and concepts to entrepreneurial settings. Changes have occurred: – Some evidence was found of an upward trend in the number of published entrepreneurship articles in leading management journals, but the percentage of entrepreneurship articles remains low. – Initially, exchange in entrepreneurship research published in mainstream management journals was dominated by non-entrepreneurship citation sources, but increasingly, exchange relies upon dedicated entrepreneurship journal citations (not least to *JBV*).
Grégoire et al. (2006)	1981–2004	Full papers in Frontiers of Entrepreneurship Research (Babson Conference)	Entrepreneurship research shows: – Varying levels of convergence over time as well as an evolution of the conceptual themes that have attracted scholars over the years. – The field increasingly relies on its own literature, pointing toward the unique contribution of the research to management science.
Cornelius et al. (2006)	1982–2004	SSCI of the ISI Web of Science	Entrepreneurship research exhibits increased maturation in the sense that the field shows: – An increased internal orientation in citations. – Stabilization of research themes, and increased specialization of research. – Identification of core groups of researchers.

Table 3A.1   (continued)

Article	Time frame	Sample	Conclusions
Reader & Watkins (2006)	1972–2000	Unique database	Based on 78 prominent entrepreneurship researchers, identification of nine clusters of authors within the field of entrepreneurship research. – Fragmented research that is difficult to categorize into sub-fields. – Relative paucity of citations across – as opposed to within – sub-fields as well as social networks across sub-fields. – National differences in topics studied and citation patterns. Entrepreneurship is very much a social activity.
Schildt et al. (2006)	2000–04	30 journals selected from SSCI of the ISI Web of Science	Identification of the 25 most central research streams in entrepreneurship research. – The research remains highly fragmented. – Noncumulative – limited citations of earlier research. – The US dominates but other countries employ their own research tradition. – Research is not highly cited outside the field (sense of isolation).
Crump et al. (2009)	1995–06	Entrepreneurship articles in 26 management and entrepreneurship journals, and three US annual entrepreneurship conferences	Ranking of the impact of authors and affiliations in entrepreneurship research (cf. Shane, 1997).

Concepts and research paradigms

Karlsson (2008)	1989–2007	Entrepreneurship journals (*JBV*, *ETP*, *ERD*, and *SBE*)	Language specificity has increased over time in entrepreneurship research. – A reduction of the importance of size words, stability of age words, and rapid recent expansion of the use of specific words such as opportunity, nascent, and very recently, bricolage.

Table 3A.1   (continued)

Article	Time frame	Sample	Conclusions
Grant & Perren (2002)	2000	Entrepreneurship journals (*ETP, JBV, JSBM, SBE, ISBJ,* and *ERD*)	Entrepreneurship research is a mono-paradigmatic research field. A meta-theoretical analysis reveals the dominance of the functionalist paradigm (Burell and Morgan, 1979)
Kyrö & Kansikas (2005)	1999–2000	Entrepreneurship journals (*ETP, JBV, SBE, JSBM,* and *ERD*) Management journals (*AMR, AMJ, AME, SMJ, OS, JM,* and *ASQ*)	Methodological concerns in relation to epistemological and ontological considerations are non-existent in the articles. – Quantitative research dominates and progress is concentrated on more sophisticated statistical methods. – Qualitative methods are few (but increasing). – Borrowing of methods from other fields of science is almost invisible in the articles.
Methodological approaches			
Paulin et al. (1982)	1961–80	ABI/INFORM and Management Contents	The field is evolving: earlier work tended to use non-methodological, contemplative, or anecdotal methods. A majority of studies employed a descriptive or case study design. A trend toward more systematic empirical methods can be discerned.
Churchill & Lewis (1986)	1981–84	Ten major management journals, Frontiers of Entrepreneurship Research (Babson Conference), and Harvard Symposium on Entrepreneurship 1983	Little has changed since the 1982 analysis (Paulin et al., 1982). Research on entrepreneurship is more oriented toward improving practice than theory – it is a practice-oriented field of research. – Considerable diversity in research – many different topics under study, but the category encompassing most studies is 'how to manage entrepreneurial ventures better and more effectively'. – Survey techniques and a combination of informal and reflectional observations are the most common methodologies in the studies. Available data, lack of good theory, and a 'comfortableness' with proven methodologies influence what is studied.

Table 3A.1   (continued)

Article	Time frame	Sample	Conclusions
Aldrich (1992)	1985–90	Ten major management journals, *JBV*, and Frontiers of Entrepreneurship Research (1986 and 1989)	Research approaches and methods have not changed very much since the early 1980s – entrepreneurship is still a mono-methodological field of research. However, some minor changes are apparent: – The field has continued to expand its repertoire of research approaches and analytical techniques. – Mail surveys are still common, but public and archival sources are becoming more popular. A growing minority of researchers are using multivariate statistics.
Aldrich & Baker (1997)	1981–95	Ten major management journals, *JBV*, and Frontiers of Entrepreneurship Research (1986, 1989, 1990, and 1994)	Research approaches and methods used in entrepreneurship research have not changed much over the past 15 years, other than a break with journalistic and armchair methods after 1985. Surveys have remained the dominant method, and response rates are low. Statistical sophistication has improved slightly – at least at the low end.
Landström & Huse (1996)	1994	*ETP, JBV, JSBM, ERD*, and *ISBJ*	Comparison between entrepreneurship research in North America and Europe. Despite the fact that there is a great diversity within entrepreneurship research in Europe, the research seems to be more descriptive. European scholars use a broader range of methodologies, and focus on research questions on an aggregate level of analysis compared to their colleagues in NA.
Dean et al. (2007)	1976–2004 (ETP) and 1985–2004 (JBV)	Entrepreneurship journals (*ETP* and *JBV*)	Data analysis in entrepreneurship research is becoming more sophisticated. – Over time there has been a shift from descriptive statistics and nonparametric tests for hypothesis testing to more rigorous techniques such as linear models, logistic regressions, and so on. – Entrepreneurship researchers have increasingly utilized longitudinal designs.

Table 3A.1 (continued)

Article	Time frame	Sample	Conclusions
McDonald et al. (2004)	1985–2004	Entrepreneurship journals (*ERD, ETP, ISBJ, JBV,* and *JSBM*)	Entrepreneurship research is dominated by positivist approaches and research methods. – Entrepreneurship research is a 'mono-method field' dependent on postal surveys and questionnaire-based techniques.
Davidsson & Wiklund (2001)	1988/89 and 1998	Entrepreneurship journals (*ETP, JBV,* and *ERD*)	– Entrepreneurship research is dominated by micro-level analysis, predominantly using the firm or the individual as the level of analysis. – The micro-level dominance seems to have increased over the years. – An almost complete lack of studies that combine levels.
Chandler & Lyon (2001)	1988–98 (1999)	Entrepreneurship (*ETP* and *JBV*) and management journals (*AMR, AMJ, SMJ, OS, MS, JM,* and *ASQ*)	– There has been an increase in the use of multivariate techniques and some modest but greater utilization of reliability and validity tests in the course of the decade. – Almost nine out of ten studies focus on one level of analysis, the majority being at firm (53 per cent) or individual level (35 per cent).
Bouckenooghe et al. (2004)	1999–2003	Entrepreneurship (*ETP, JBV, SBE,* and *JSBM*) and management journals (*AMJ, SMJ, ASQ, OS, MS* and *JM*)	Entrepreneurship research is dominated by non-experimental research strategies, mainly sample surveys (52 per cent) and field studies (35 per cent). As a consequence, entrepreneurship research is characterized by the use of research methods that ensure external validity but have limited internal validity. – Increased use of longitudinal data collection, multi research designs (triangulation), and more sophisticated statistical techniques.
Brush et al. (2008)	2003–05	Entrepreneurship journals (*JBV, ETP, ISBJ,* and *SBE*)	Entrepreneurship researchers are using a wide variety of dependent variables (the lack of convergence in dependent variables suggests that there is little comparability), and performance, broadly defined, is the most popular dependent variable (showing a strong

Table 3A.1   (continued)

Article	Time frame	Sample	Conclusions
			link between entrepreneurship and strategic management scholars). – The most popular unit of analysis is the firm (30 per cent) followed by the individual (11 per cent) and firm + environment (11 per cent).
Edelman et al. (2009)	2003–05 Compared with 1981–95 (Aldrich & Baker, 1997)	Entrepreneurship journals (*JBV*, *ETP*, *JSBM*, *ISBJ*, *SBE*, and *ERD*) Management journals (*ASQ* and *AMJ*)	Few changes have occurred in research methodologies over the ten years since Aldrich and Baker's study (1997), but there is a widening gap in methodologies between entrepreneurship research in the US and Europe.
Mullen et al. (2009)	2001–08	*JSBM*, *JBV*, and *ETP*	Improvements have been made regarding the use of a solid methodological base for theory development in entrepreneurship research, but the evolution has not been sufficient. For example, there is a need for improvement with regard to sampling issues (sample size and potential biases), construct validity (measures of internal consistency and reliability), and internal and external validity.

Note: *AME: Academy of Management Executive; AMJ: Academy of Management Journal; AMR: Academy of Management Review; API: Asian Pacific International Management Forum; ASQ: Administrative Science Quarterly; ERD: Entrepreneurship and Regional Development; ETP: Entrepreneurship Theory and Practice; ISBJ: International Small Business Journal; JBV: Journal of Business Venturing; JM: Journal of Management; JSBM: Journal of Small Business Management; MS: Management Science; OS: Organization Science; SBE: Small Business Economics; SMJ: Strategic Management Journal.*

PART II

Intellectual Roots of Entrepreneurship Research

Section II.1

Opportunity Recognition

4. Environmental uncertainty and firm-level entrepreneurship

Lou Marino, Patrick Kreiser and Anthony Robinson

INTRODUCTION

The concept of uncertainty has maintained a central position in the study of entrepreneurship since Cantillon first coined the term 'entrepreneur' in his *Essai sur la nature du commerce en general* (*Essay on the Nature of Commerce in General*, published 1755). In this work, Cantillon described an entrepreneur as a risk-taker who bears uncertainty in buying a fixed quantity of goods for a certain price with the intention of selling these goods at a future date in markets that have a demand and price levels that are indeterminate at the time the resources are acquired. Knight (1921) reinforced the fundamental relationship between entrepreneurship and uncertainty in his book *Risk, Uncertainty and Profit*. In this work, Knight clearly delineated between risk and uncertainty, and argued that entrepreneurs are economic actors, who earn profit from bearing uncertainty.

Acknowledging the key role that uncertainty plays in entrepreneurship, numerous researchers have examined the relationship between uncertainty and a wide variety of antecedents and consequences of entrepreneurial activities. Studies that have examined the impact of uncertainty in the entrepreneurship literature include research on varied topics such as the impact of environmental hostility on the relationship between corporate entrepreneurship and firm performance (Zahra and Garvis, 2000), the role of technological uncertainty on technology alliance formation in entrepreneurial firms (Steensma et al., 2000), the impact of environmental dynamism on the relationship between entrepreneurial leadership and new venture performance (Ensley et al., 2006), the relationship between environmental dynamism, entrepreneurial orientation and access to capital on small business performance (Wiklund and Shepherd, 2005), and the impact of environmental turbulence on the choice of governance modes in external technology sourcing arrangements (Van de Vrande et al., 2009).

Despite the empirical studies that have been conducted on the role of uncertainty in the entrepreneurship literature, a relatively greater depth of theoretical research has been focused on the influence of risk-taking, while less attention has been devoted to the role of uncertainty in this area (Alvarez, 2007). This is an especially significant issue given that risk-taking and uncertainty represent independent concepts, and both constructs represent different elements of the entrepreneurial process (Knight, 1921). In an effort to promote additional research on the theoretical impact of uncertainty on entrepreneurial activities, this chapter clearly distinguishes between the concepts of risk and uncertainty, reviews the historical development of the environmental uncertainty construct and the most commonly employed measures of uncertainty, and develops recommendations pertaining to the use of this key concept in future entrepreneurship research.

In order to achieve these objectives, the chapter is structured in the following manner. The first section explores the conceptual differences between the uncertainty and risk-taking constructs. Particular attention is devoted to the role that uncertainty plays in the entrepreneurial process. The second section provides an in-depth examination of previous research efforts examining the concept of uncertainty. Two theoretical viewpoints, the information uncertainty perspective and resource dependence theory, serve as the foundation of this analysis. We also examine the manner in which researchers from both viewpoints have operationalized the uncertainty construct in previous studies. The third section integrates these various arguments to highlight the implications of this chapter for organizations and researchers. The use of the uncertainty construct in future research efforts, as well as the importance of uncertainty to entrepreneurial firms, is considered.

DISTINCT CONSTRUCTS: EXPLORING THE DIFFERENCES BETWEEN UNCERTAINTY AND RISK

The argument that entrepreneurial firms are more willing to immerse themselves in uncertain environments than are non-entrepreneurial firms has been a central tenet of entrepreneurial theory since the earliest days of the discipline (Knight, 1921). However, there is often a lack of clarity in the entrepreneurship literature when authors discuss uncertainty and risk as they are frequently treated as synonymous concepts. Authors have recently begun to more precisely distinguish between the two concepts, with the concept of risk-taking having received a relatively disproportionate amount of scrutiny in recent entrepreneurship research (Alvarez, 2007; Alvarez and Barney, 2005; Janney and Dess, 2006). Although Knight (1921) initially suggested developing a clear, theoretical differentiation between risk and uncertainty, the call for a more precise differentiation between these concepts was not stressed in the modern entrepreneurship literature until Janney and Dess's (2006) and Alvarez's (2007) work. In defining these two key concepts, Knight differentiated between risk (which involves decision-making scenarios when the probability of an outcome is known or can be reasonably inferred) and uncertainty (which refers to decision-making contexts in which this probability can be neither known nor calculated with any reasonable degree of confidence).

In a review of the use of the concept of risk in entrepreneurship, risk-taking has been defined as the 'degree to which managers are willing to make large and risky resource commitments – i.e. those which have a reasonable cost of failure' (Miller and Friesen, 1978, p. 923). Building on this conceptualization, Miller (1983) argued that risk-taking is an essential element of entrepreneurship and that entrepreneurs engage in constructive risk-taking. Similarly, Baird and Thomas (1985) defined entrepreneurial risk-taking as the propensity of a firm's management team to engage in taking calculated business risks. In reviewing the role of risk in the entrepreneurship literature, Janney and Dess (2006) noted that three conceptualizations of risk dominate the literature: defining risk as variance, downside loss, and opportunity (or opportunity-cost). They argued that the conceptualization most salient for entrepreneurs and entrepreneurial decision-making, especially in the context of launching a new venture, is risk as downside loss. Authors who have utilized this conceptualization of risk (e.g. Lumpkin and Dess, 1996) have tended to define it as a manager's ability to assess the likelihood of experiencing loss.

This ability to assign the probability of a loss is a key distinction between risk and uncertainty. Building on the work of Knight (1921), Alvarez (2007) points out the 'growing agreement that one of the most important differences between non-entrepreneurial and entrepreneurial decision-making is that the former takes place under conditions of risk, while the latter takes place under conditions of uncertainty' (Alvarez, 2007, p. 429). This is a significant distinction given that entrepreneurs tend to be more optimistic about the business situations that they pursue than non-entrepreneurs and 'may not think of themselves as being any more likely to take risks than non-entrepreneurs' (Palich and Bagby, 1995, p. 426). Janney and Dess (2006) argued that entrepreneurs may not have a higher risk preference than the general population, but they may simply have access to specialized knowledge that allows them to assess the true nature of risk in a situation. Combining these arguments with Knight's views regarding uncertainty, it is possible to conclude that entrepreneurial firms may in fact be more willing to tolerate ambiguous and uncertain situations than non-entrepreneurial firms, but may not necessarily be any more willing to take risks.

Consistent with these arguments is the concept of the learning curve (Wiersma, 2007) and entrepreneurial learning (Hayton, 2005; Zahra et al., 1999). Organizations involved in entrepreneurial activities experience higher levels of experimental learning, which occurs internally and leads to the creation of new knowledge that is distinct to that particular organization (Zahra et al., 1999). As levels of experimental learning go up, the amount of risk inherent in future activities is reduced. However, if risk-taking is considered to be a fundamental element of firm-level entrepreneurship, then at some point an organization's level of experimental learning would cause their levels of risk-taking to fall below that 'suggested' level, thus making them less entrepreneurial by definition. Clearly in this situation, the firm is no less entrepreneurial; they have simply developed a more effective approach to create and/or exploit opportunities while utilizing a lower level of risk-taking. Further, if a learning curve exists, then the risk associated with firm-level entrepreneurship would be reduced over time as the organization learns how to reduce its probability of failure and enhance its chances of success. Again, this would imply that a particularly high level of risk-taking is not always necessary for an organization to engage in entrepreneurial activities.

Uncertainty in Entrepreneurial Firms

As previously noted, one of the first authors to assess the impact of uncertainty on entrepreneurial behaviors was Richard Cantillon (1755/1959) in his *Essai sur la nature du commerce en general*. Although Cantillon does not offer a precise definition of uncertainty in this text, it is clear that he equates uncertainty with the inability to predict a future state or condition. Consistent with Cantillon's conceptualization, Knight (1921) defines uncertainty in terms of the entrepreneur's inability to accurately predict a future situation. However, as noted, Knight makes a key distinction between risk and uncertainty. According to Knight, the term risk is properly used to refer to situations in which the possibility of potential outcomes and the probabilities of these outcomes can be expressed in terms of mathematical probabilities before a decision is made. Thus, under conditions of risk the decision-maker is able to insure against possible negative outcomes. Within Knight's context, uncertainty represents 'defects of managerial knowledge,' and it is these defects that account for profit and loss. Under conditions of uncertainty decision-makers are not able to insure against possible negative outcomes because not only are they unable to predict the probability that any specific outcome will occur, but they are unable to meaningfully foresee the true range of possible outcomes.

As the discipline of entrepreneurship gained prominence in the organizational litera-ture in the 1980s and 1990s, a number of researchers recognized that uncertainty played a significant role in the entrepreneurial process. For example, Covin and Slevin (1989) examined the relationship between environmental uncertainty (in the form of environ-mental hostility) and a firm's strategic posture. Likewise, McGrath et al. (1992) exam-ined cultural differences between entrepreneurs and non-entrepreneurs. One of the key characteristics assessed in this study was the tolerance for uncertainty. However, Knight's distinction between risk and uncertainty seems to have been largely ignored in the entrepreneurial literature until Brouwer's (2000) study of innovation, which combined Knight's concept of uncertainty with Schumpeter's (1934) model of innovation. This distinction between risk and uncertainty and their respective roles was further clarified by Alvarez and Barney (2005), who examined how entrepreneurs organize firms under con-ditions of risk and uncertainty. As interest in the impact of uncertainty on entrepreneur-ship continues to grow, it will become even more necessary for researchers to understand the historical evolution of the concept and the role it has played in the early foundations of the organizational literature.

THE HISTORICAL EVOLUTION OF THE UNCERTAINTY CONSTRUCT

The entrepreneurship literature draws its primary conceptualizations of uncertainty from the management literature, which has been predominately focused on the exogenous uncertainty that exists in the external environment. It has generally been argued that the external environment consists of all the factors outside the firm that an organization must consider when making strategic decisions (Duncan, 1972). Thus, uncertainty in the external environment, or the inability to predict the future state of these factors, is an important consideration for firms during the strategic decision-making process (Barnard, 1938). However, there has never been a consensus on a specific definition of environmen-tal uncertainty in the organizational literature and multiple conceptualizations have been explored (e.g. Barnard, 1938; Duncan, 1972; Lawrence and Lorsch, 1967; Milliken, 1987; Pfeffer and Salancik, 1978; Tan and Litschert, 1994; Thompson, 1967).

Despite the breadth of conceptualizations of uncertainty, Tan and Litschert (1994) argued that the vast majority could be categorized into one of two dominant perspec-tives: information uncertainty or resource dependence theory. The information uncer-tainty perspective is consistent with Knight's (1921) assertion that uncertainty represents a defect in managerial knowledge. Similar to Knight's arguments, Barnard (1938) argued that uncertainty arises from a lack of perfect information about the environment. A number of researchers have adopted this perspective in their theory building, including Lawrence and Lorsch (1967), Thompson (1967), Duncan (1972), and Milliken (1987).

Building on this tradition, more recent research in entrepreneurship such as Sapienza (1992), Ensley et al. (2006), Harper (2008), and McVea (2009) have conceptualized uncertainty from an information-based perspective.

Research on environmental uncertainty was largely dominated by Barnard's conceptualization until the early 1970s. At this time, researchers began to examine the impact of organizational and environmental resources on organizational processes. One of the most influential schools of thought in this area was resource dependence theory, established by Child (1972) and Pfeffer and Salancik (1978). Within this theoretical framework, environmental uncertainty is not seen as being manifested through a lack of information on the part of key managers. Rather, uncertainty is argued to be the result of organizational dependence on resources that are controlled by external constituencies and the power differentials that exist as organizations attempt to manage critical resource flows from partners (Pfeffer and Salancik, 1978). Researchers who have drawn upon this theory include Child (1972), Pfeffer and Salancik (1978), Dess and Beard (1984), and Finkelstein (1997). More recently, entrepreneurship scholars including Zahra and Garvis (2000), Specht (1993), Begley et al. (2005), and Steensma et al. (2000) have examined uncertainty utilizing conceptualizations consistent with the resource dependence theory. The following sections will explore the major tenets of these two theoretical perspectives (information uncertainty and resource dependence).

The Information Uncertainty Perspective

One of the earliest management scholars to explore the relationship between firms and their external environment was Chester Barnard (1938). He examined the impact that environmental uncertainty had on organizational strategies in *The Functions of the Executive*. A fundamental premise of this book was Barnard's belief that executives and their firms experienced strategic uncertainty due to the inherent instability of the external environment. Similar to Knight (1921), Barnard argued that the inability of managers to comprehend all the information present in a given environmental situation was the primary cause of this uncertainty. Barnard felt that 'under most ordinary conditions, even with simple purposes, not many men can see what each is doing or the whole situation' (Barnard, 1938, p. 106). This is similar to Knight's (1921) view of uncertainty arising as a result of a defect in managerial knowledge. From Barnard's perspective, the imperfect knowledge regarding the environment posed significant problems as it created ambiguity during the strategic decision-making process.

Barnard's assertions were expanded and refined by several authors including Simon (1957), March and Simon (1958), and Cyert and March (1963). One of the primary contributions of this line of research was the introduction of the concept of 'bounded rationality'. According to Thompson, bounded rationality is concerned with organizational processes related to the 'choice of courses of action in an environment which does not fully disclose the alternatives available or the consequences of those alternatives' (Thompson, 1967, p. 9). This is an important contrast to more traditional research in classical economics that assumed perfect information was available to all actors. Executives operating under bounded rationality could be expected to make rational choices, but only based on the relatively limited and incomplete information they were able to access when making strategic decisions.

The information uncertainty perspective developed by Barnard was further enhanced by Lawrence and Lorsch (1967) and Duncan (1972). In both of these works, the authors argued that imperfect knowledge about the environment created uncertainty for firms. However, these authors argued that the primary impact of uncertainty on strategic decision-making was through the interaction of the firm, its managers, and the environment. Thus, firm-level and individual-level characteristics could be expected to impact the amount of uncertainty perceived in the external environment.

An additional contribution offered by Lawrence and Lorsch (1967) was their delineation between three components of environmental uncertainty. Lawrence and Lorsch argued that the first component of uncertainty was the inability of management to consistently acquire accurate information regarding the state of the external environment. The second component focused on the challenges managers faced in determining whether an adequate fit had been achieved between the firm and its environment due to the lengthy time span required for feedback after strategic action. The final component concerned the difficulty managers faced with regard to the uncertainty inherent in causal relationships. The authors argued that it was very difficult for firms to accurately predict not only the effect that specific environmental changes would have on the firm, but also the impact that specific strategic actions would have on the external environment.

Duncan furthered clarified the importance of the interaction between managers and the environment by arguing that the degree of uncertainty is not a constant feature, but rather is 'dependent on the perceptions of organization members and thus can vary in their incidence to the extent that individuals differ in their perceptions' (Duncan, 1972, p. 325). Duncan argued that the overall amount of uncertainty present in the environment is not an objective constant, but is determined by managerial perceptions of that environment. Building on Duncan's work, Hitt et al. (1982) argued that managerial perceptions of environmental uncertainty can also be influenced by the importance managers assign to certain environmental variables and that organizations are more likely to respond to environmental factors that they judge as having a high degree of importance to firm survival.

The common theme unifying the works of Knight (1921), Barnard (1938), Lawrence and Lorsch (1967), and Duncan (1972) was the fundamental belief that it was impossible for a firm to acquire perfect knowledge about its environment. This lack of information created uncertainty for the firm and impacted strategic decision-making. Scholars in the information uncertainty perspective tended to be more interested in managerial perceptions of uncertainty in the external environment than in the objective state of the environment (Sharfman and Dean, 1991). The rationale for this was that managerial perceptions ultimately determined a firm's choice of strategic actions and influenced a firm's overall evaluation of its strategic options.

Information Uncertainty and Perceptual Measures of Uncertainty

Given the fundamental assumption within the information uncertainty perspective that managerial perceptions ultimately shaped strategy formation, researchers adhering to this perspective have typically employed perceptual measures of uncertainty (Buchko, 1994; Daft et al., 1988; Dickson and Weaver, 1997; Duncan, 1972; Hrebiniak and Snow, 1980; Miles and Snow, 1978; Milliken, 1987; Sawyerr, 1993; Tung, 1979). Researchers in this perspective argued that environmental conditions not perceived by managers are not able to have a significant impact on strategic decision-making and thus 'objected to the use of objective measures of environmental uncertainty' (Sawyerr, 1993, p. 290).

Similar to the manner in which Knight (1921) identified uncertainty as the fundamental driver of entrepreneurial profit, Thompson (1967) asserted that uncertainty was 'the fundamental problem for complex organizations and coping with uncertainty [was] the essence of the administrative process' (Thompson, 1967, p. 159). Thompson argued that uncertainty in the external environment was most properly conceptualized as being a multidimensional construct. Thompson theorized that the two primary dimensions of uncertainty were homogeneity/heterogeneity and stability/dynamism. Homogeneous environments contained very similar elements while heterogeneous environments consisted of many elements that were different in nature. Alternately, the stability/dynamism dimension focused on the rate of change present in the environment. Stable environments were thought to be more predictable as they typically remained unchanged. Dynamic environments presented significant uncertainty to managerial decision-makers as they changed at a very rapid pace.

Building on Thompson's multidimensional conceptualization, as well as the work of Emery and Trist (1965), Duncan (1972) argued that there were two main dimensions along which the environment could be measured: the simple–complex dimension and the static–dynamic dimension. The simple–complex dimension measured the number of factors that were present in the environment. A complex environment contained many different defining factors while a simple environment consisted of a small number of key factors. Similar to Thompson's dynamic environments, the static–dynamic dimension of Duncan's conceptualization of uncertainty was concerned primarily with the amount of change in these factors. A dynamic environment was in a constant state of change whereas a static environment experienced little or no change.

Further extending the multidimensional conceptualization of environmental uncertainty, Milliken (1987) distinguished between three types of uncertainty that existed in a firm's external environment: state, effect, and response uncertainty. State uncertainty was perhaps closest to Knight's and Barnard's conceptualizations of uncertainty and referred to the general unpredictability of the environment and its various components. Effect uncertainty was similar to Lawrence and Lorsch's conceptualization of causal ambiguity and captured a firm's inability to predict the effect of future environmental changes on their business operations. Finally, response uncertainty focused on the difficulty firms had in predicting the response of their competitors to a particular strategy that the firm implemented. Within Milliken's conceptualization, these three concepts acted together to determine the overall level of uncertainty present in a firm's external environment.

Numerous studies have examined how perceptual levels of environmental uncertainty impact entrepreneurial strategies. The primary argument of these studies is that strategic approaches and outcomes are both affected by environmental conditions. For instance, entrepreneurial firms that innovate in environments characterized as more dynamic tend to enjoy greater performance levels (Russell and Russell, 1992). Perceptions of opportunities associated with more uncertain environments allow entrepreneurial firms to exploit market prospects with greater amounts of risk-taking. Zahra and Bogner's (2000) study reinforced this finding. They found that introducing radical product innovations in dynamic environments positively impacted new venture performance. However, increasing patents and copyrights in these rapidly changing conditions allowed competitors to more easily imitate product introductions and were less beneficial than not protecting intellectual property in this way.

Additionally, the manner in which new ventures engage in strategic planning has been linked to levels of perceived environmental uncertainty. Uncertainty in dynamic markets requires greater amounts of planning to reduce the amount of ambiguous information and to enhance learning (Castrogiovanni, 1996). Gruber (2007) found that speeding up planning activities and engaging in high value planning in highly dynamic marketplaces can be more beneficial than doing so in slowly changing markets. Organizations tended to innovate and create more businesses in dynamic markets, particularly as their financial performance of these businesses increased (Zahra, 1993). Van de Vrande et al. (2009) found that environmental uncertainty associated with turbulence can affect governance mode choices when firms are pursuing corporate entrepreneurship. For example, managers selected less integrated modes (i.e. non-equity alliances) in turbulent environments due to the greater flexibility associated with them.

Dynamic environments also influence the linkages between the various types of entrepreneurial leadership and new venture performance. Specifically, the dynamic nature of some environments enhances benefits related to transformational leadership as opposed to transactional leadership (Ensley et al., 2006). The rapid change experienced in dynamic environments lends itself to a leadership style that is better adapted to change than those that seek to maintain current operations. Furthermore, the level of optimism entrepreneurs possess and the effect on venture performance is moderated by environmental dynamism (Hmielski and Baron, 2009). The negative relationship between managerial optimism and firm performance intensifies as dynamism increases due to more heuristic decision-making and a failure to consider all opportunities.

Finally, research regarding entrepreneurial orientation (EO) has examined the degree to which perceived environmental uncertainty affects organizations. Using a configurational approach, Wiklund and Shepherd (2005) found that the level of dynamism in a firm's environment influenced the extent to which a high EO improves performance. High EOs in more stable environments, when combined with access to capital, helped augment firm performance. Conversely, low EOs in dynamic environments, when combined with access to capital, tended to be associated with improved firm performance.

In summary, the information uncertainty perspective suggests that managerial perceptions of environmental uncertainty impact both the strategic options implemented by firms, as well as the ensuing performance associated with these strategic choices. We next examine the resource dependence theory view of uncertainty.

Resource Dependence Theory

Although the information uncertainty perspective dominated the organizational literature for the early part of the twentieth century, managerial scholars in the 1970s began to question the extent to which key decision-makers were able to accurately perceive levels of environmental uncertainty. In response to these concerns, researchers began to search for more objective methods of conceptualizing and operationalizing the environmental uncertainty construct. One of the first efforts in the management literature to focus primarily on objective conceptualizations of uncertainty was resource dependence theory

(Pfeffer and Salancik, 1978), which is predicated on the belief that organizations are dependent on scarce resources for their survival and that the firm's external environment is the source of these scarce and finite resources. Uncertainty, therefore, is created as a result of the firm's lack of control over these resources. In order to reduce uncertainty and ensure their own survival, organizations are forced to develop strategies that allow them to effectively compete for, control, and exploit these resources.

In contrast to the information uncertainty perspective, resource dependence theory posits that the lack of control over critical resources, rather than a lack of information, gives rise to environmental uncertainty. Environments that are abundant in resources are considered to be less hostile and uncertain than are environments characterized by low levels of resources in which firms must intensely compete for these scarce resources. These hostile environments are characterized by greater uncertainty as firms are able to predict neither their ability to gain access to key resources nor the potential moves of key rivals as they compete to capture resources. Within resource dependence theory, one of the key mechanisms that firms must utilize to effectively manage uncertainty is to develop relationships with key constituencies in their external environment that control scarce resources.

In a similar way to several researchers in the information uncertainty perspective, Pfeffer and Salancik (1978) proposed a multidimensional conceptualization of uncertainty that could be used to assess resource dependence theory. From this perspective, the uncertainty that firms faced was impacted by the level of conflict and interdependence among key firms. This conflict and interdependence was ultimately a function of the concentration of power and authority, munificence (the availability of resources), and the interconnectedness among firms in the external environment (Pfeffer and Salancik, 1978). Taken together, these factors determined the amount of uncertainty faced by an organization in a particular operating environment.

Within the entrepreneurship literature, scholars who have employed a resource dependence theory of uncertainty include Specht (1993), Begley et al. (2005), and Steensma et al. (2000). While conceptualizing munificence as a key aspect of environmental uncertainty, Specht (1993) proposed that the rate of new venture formation depends directly on resource munificence. He argued that the extent to which market, social, political, economic, and infrastructural resources are subjectively known to exist provides a more viable explanation for the rate of new venture formation than do the traits of individual entrepreneurs. Begley et al. (2005) utilized the resource dependence framework to test these propositions and found empirical evidence to support the notion that political-economic resource considerations influenced the entrepreneur's desire to start a new business. Using a similar framework and a slightly different approach, Steensma et al. (2000) found that the resource dependence theory offered greater explanatory power than transaction cost theory when considering how collectivist cultures influence perceived technology uncertainty and alliance formation relationships. Technology alliances were found to reduce uncertainty among small and medium-sized enterprises (SMEs) and were seen as a way to help these organizations acquire and develop key resources.

Resource Dependence and Objective Measures of Uncertainty

When examining the environmental uncertainty construct, researchers based in the resource dependence theory have employed both perceptual and objective measures of uncertainty. However, objective (archival) measures have been most commonly employed to measure the organizational dependence on resources (e.g. Boyd, 1990; Dess and Beard, 1984; Goll and Rasheed, 1997; Simerly and Li, 2000; Wiersema and Bantel, 1993; Yasai-Ardekani, 1989). Authors who have employed objective operationalizations of uncertainty argue that resource scarcity in the external environment represents an empirically verifiable condition, and thus should be measured objectively. Consistent with this perspective, Yasai-Ardekani stated that 'environmental munificence and scarcity refer to the objective condition of an environment' and should thus be measured with objective industry-level data (Yasai-Ardekani, 1989, p. 133).

One of the first authors to develop a measure that focused on the organizational dependence on resources in the external environment was Child (1972), who utilized three dimensions to conceptualize the external environment: rate of change, complexity, and illiberality. The first two dimensions were similar to those theorized by Thompson (1967) and Duncan (1972). However, Child also developed a third dimension called 'illiberality' which referred to the overall availability of resources in the external environment.

The most influential operationalization of uncertainty in the context of resource dependence theory was developed by Dess and Beard (1984). They built on the work of previous authors to develop a three-dimensional measure of uncertainty, similar to Child's conceptualization, which they termed 'dynamism', 'complexity', and 'munificence'. Taken together, these three dimensions could be utilized in order to objectively measure the level of uncertainty present in a given environment. Specifically, environments with high levels of dynamism, complexity, and hostility indicated high levels of uncertainty, whereas low levels of these three variables acted to reduce the overall amount of environmental uncertainty.

The first two dimensions were not altogether different from those posited by the information uncertainty perspective. The first dimension, dynamism, was similar to the static/dynamic element of Duncan's model, the variability dimension of Child's model, and the stability/dynamism component of Thompson's conceptualization. Specifically, dynamism referred to the 'rate of change and innovation in an industry as well as the uncertainty or predictability of the actions of competitors and customers' (Miller and Friesen, 1983, p. 222). The second component of Dess and Beard's measure was 'complexity'. This component was conceptually similar to Thompson's heterogeneity/homogeneity dimension and Duncan's simple/complex component. Within Dess and Beard's framework, complexity referred to 'the level of complex knowledge that understanding the environment requires' (Sharfman and Dean, 1991, p.683). This dimension was concerned with the overall number of factors that a firm needed to analyze in its external environment. As the number of environmental factors that must be considered by a firm increased, so did the level of uncertainty present in the environment.

In addition to the fact that their operationalization could be objectively measured, there was another important distinction between the Dess and Beard framework and the earlier frameworks developed by researchers in the information uncertainty perspective. The third component of Dess and Beard's conceptualization took into account the availability of resources in the external environment. This final component of Dess and Beard's operationalization measured 'munificence'. Munificence described the level of resources available to firms and could thus be used to assess resource dependence (Tan, 1996). The concept of munificence was included in order to account for the dependence that organizations had on resources that were often outside the firm's control. This dimension was similar to Child's 'illiberality'. The opposite of munificence, or environmental hostility, has also been utilized extensively in previous research efforts. Covin and Slevin (1989) argued that 'hostile environments are characterized by precarious industry settings, intense competition, harsh, overwhelming business climates, and the relative lack of exploitable opportunities' (Covin and Slevin, 1989, p. 75).

The concept of munificence/hostility has received considerable attention in the entrepreneurship literature. For example, Specht (1993) argued that the rate of new venture formation depends on the extent to which sufficient resources exist to support the presence of the new venture. Specht's propositions were subsequently supported by empirical evidence from Begley et al. (2005). The empirical support offered by this study regarding the role that munificence plays in the entrepreneurial setting suggested that the impact of munificence persists across various regional settings, differing stages of economic development, and a range of cultural groups. These findings strengthen the application of the munificence variable to different contexts and groups.

Although studies have shown that resource munificence increases the rate of new venture formation, it has also been argued that high levels of resource munificence improve the chances of a new venture being able to survive and maintain adequate levels of growth. Castrogiovanni (1996) posited that new venture survival was greater in highly munificent environments given the more favorable trade-offs between supply and demand. Even those firms that are poorly managed and/or poorly positioned may enjoy some level of profitability in a munificent environment. Gartner et al. (1999) provided evidence to support this notion when analyzing the environmental conditions faced by new business startups.

The dependence on resources also has consequences for corporate entrepreneurship activities. For instance, under hostile conditions when munificence is expected to be low, businesses tend to engage in strategic change or renewal activities. Efforts to reduce hostility may lead to business divestitures (Zahra, 1993). The limited availability of resources encourages firms to pursue more conservative strategies, which may include cost reductions (Zahra and Bogner, 2000). As with new ventures, corporate entrepreneurship activities under hostile conditions tend to focus on increasing the chances for survival through improved efficiencies rather than through greater exploitation efforts. Having made these assertions, it is important to note that some might argue that small firms in hostile environments tend to take more entrepreneurial postures (Covin and Slevin, 1989). Yet whichever camp one falls into with regard to the impact of hostility on entrepreneurial strategy formation, most scholars strongly believe that the objective availability of resources is an important consideration when attempting to explain and predict entrepreneurial behaviors.

IMPLICATIONS AND CONTRIBUTIONS

The preceding arguments illustrate that while risk-taking has traditionally been viewed as a central concept in the entrepreneurship literature, there is significant benefit to be gained by expanding our inquiries to also include the role of uncertainty in the entrepreneurial process. In an effort to encourage such research, this chapter has delineated the distinct concepts of risk-taking and uncertainty, while paying particular attention to the theoretical role played by uncertainty in impacting firm-level entrepreneurship. We have also included a discussion of the historical evolution of the uncertainty construct in the organizational literature to provide a more thorough understanding of how the field has moved from the early conceptualizations of uncertainty by authors such as Knight to the conceptualizations that are employed today.

In particular, we have analyzed the development of two different theoretical perspectives, the information uncertainty perspective and resource dependence theory, and assessed the role that both of these theories play in impacting entrepreneurial behavior. However, the chapter would not be complete without a discussion of the implications of these arguments for both researchers and practitioners. The following sections look at implications for managers, organizations, and future research efforts. The final section offers several concluding thoughts regarding how the uncertainty construct should be examined in future studies on the topic of firm-level entrepreneurship.

Research Implications

Future entrepreneurship research would benefit from the continued development of a clear and accurate understanding of the role of environmental uncertainty in the entrepreneurial process. In particular, researchers should be aware of the theoretical and empirical distinctions between the concepts of uncertainty and risk-taking. For instance, if risk-taking was included in a model of entrepreneurship, it would indicate that a high level of risk-taking should always be a goal of the entrepreneurial firm (as is a high level of other variables such as innovativeness). However, theoretical and empirical evidence suggests that there is not an optimum level of risk-taking that should be displayed by an entrepreneurial firm. For example, McClelland (1960) argued that entrepreneurs tend to be moderate in their willingness to engage in risk-taking behavior and that they tend to avoid excessive levels of risk-taking because such behaviors contain a high probability of failure. On the other hand, environmental uncertainty has been shown to play an important role in determining the success of entrepreneurial organizations (Covin and Slevin, 1989; Lumpkin and Dess, 1996; Miller and Friesen, 1983; Zahra, 1993).

Future research efforts should be undertaken in order to establish additional types of uncertainty that may have a specific and identifiable impact on the entrepreneurial process. For example, Dimov and Milanov (2010) identified two types of uncertainty that entrepreneurs may face in the venture capital syndication process: egocentric uncertainty, which focuses on a lack of information a focal firm may have regarding decisions that need to be made for an investment to succeed, and altercentric uncertainty, which focuses on the inability of external parties to accurately judge the quality of the entrepreneurial firm as a potential partner (Dimov and Milanov, 2010). Additionally, Van de Vrande et al. (2009) differentiated between exogenous (e.g. environmental dynamism) and endogenous (e.g. relational uncertainty) information uncertainty in examining the impact of uncertainty on governance mode decisions in external technology sourcing.

These more recent conceptualizations are important as they are indicative of two separate issues that need to be addressed to facilitate the continued development of the role played by the uncertainty construct in the entrepreneurial process. First, the vast majority of uncertainty research has focused solely on the entrepreneurial firm or the entrepreneur. However, there is a need to understand how uncertainty will impact other actors that are involved in the entrepreneurial process, such as potential investors. Second, these recent studies recognize that there are different types of uncertainty that may be either endogenous or exogenous to the entrepreneurial process. For example, Marino et al. (2008) found that when firms in developing economies face extreme levels of uncertainty from sources that are generally exogenous to the entrepreneurial process (i.e. the collapse of an economic system), entrepreneurial activities can be interrupted as firms fall victim to increases in threat rigidity.

Managerial Implications

The environmental uncertainty construct also has important ramifications for entrepreneurial organizations. For example, concepts such as environmental munificence and dynamism have a direct impact on performance levels of entrepreneurial firms (Lumpkin and Dess, 2001; Miller and Friesen, 1982; Zahra, 1996). The plentiful resources and opportunities afforded to firms in munificent environments allow them to enjoy heightened levels of performance (Dess and Beard, 1984). In such environments, the relative ease with which firms can acquire the resources necessary for the pursuit of organizational objectives and the decreased threat of competition fosters higher rates of firm survival and growth (Castrogiovanni, 1991). The constant rate of change in highly dynamic environments also creates numerous opportunities that entrepreneurial firms can exploit (Miles et al., 2000). For these reasons, it is likely that entrepreneurial firms operating in highly munificent or highly dynamic environments will achieve higher levels of performance than firms operating in more hostile or stable environments.

CONCLUDING THOUGHTS

One of the main questions implicit in previous research efforts was whether objective or perceptual measures should be utilized in order to more accurately operationalize the uncertainty construct. It is our contention that the existence of expanded research methodologies and statistical techniques make it possible for researchers to utilize both types of measures in future studies. Although multiple dimensions of uncertainty have long been included in theoretical conceptualizations of uncertainty, perhaps it is time that multiple measures of uncertainty are utilized as well. Given the complex nature of the uncertainty construct, it is likely that objective and perceptual measures both provide unique (and accurate) assessments of differing elements of the construct. Thus, we would argue that a variety of methodological techniques should be utilized in future research efforts on the topic of uncertainty.

Qualitative, survey, and archival methods can all be effectively utilized to assess the uncertainty faced by entrepreneurial firms. Interviews, case studies, and other qualitative techniques can be utilized to assess the perceptions of environmental uncertainty. For example, interviews with key decision-makers within entrepreneurial firms might provide very important insights into how these companies utilized environmental perception when formulating and implementing their strategies. Survey data can be utilized to assess perceptions of the environment, as well as the resulting impact on strategy formation and firm performance. Archival data can be utilized to examine the objective state of a firm's external environment, and when combined with performance information, can be utilized to assess the impact of these environmental conditions on firm survival and profitability. Utilizing all three of these techniques (qualitative, survey, and archival) would provide a more comprehensive and in-depth understanding of the impact of environmental uncertainty on entrepreneurial activities.

In summary, while environmental uncertainty has played a central role in the development of the entrepreneurship literature, it has received relatively less research attention than the risk-taking construct. However, in order to develop a unique theory of entrepreneurship and to legitimize entrepreneurship as a field of study, we strongly believe that it is necessary for uncertainty to be included as a fundamental element of this theory. For this to be possible, researchers must understand not only the historical foundations of the uncertainty construct, but how this concept has evolved in the entrepreneurship literature and the important role that it plays in facilitating our understanding of the entrepreneurial process.

REFERENCES

Alvarez, S. (2007), 'Entrepreneurial rents and the theory of the firm', *Journal of Business Venturing*, **22**, 427–42.

Alvarez, S.A. and J.B. Barney (2005), 'How do entrepreneurs organize firms under conditions of uncertainty?', *Journal of Management*, **31**(5), 776–93.

Baird, I.S. and H. Thomas (1985), 'Toward a contingency model of strategic risk taking', *Academy of Management Review*, **10**(2), 230–43.

Barnard, C.I. (1938), *The Functions of the Executive*, Cambridge, MA: Harvard University Press.

Begley, T.M., W.L. Tan and H. Schoch (2005), 'Politico-economic factors associated with interest in starting a business: a multi-country study', *Entrepreneurship Theory and Practice*, **29**(1), 35–55.

Boyd, B. (1990), 'Corporate linkages and organizational environment: a test of the resource dependence model', *Strategic Management Journal*, **11**, 419–30.

Brouwer, M. (2000), 'Entrepreneurship and uncertainty: innovation and competition among the many', *Small Business Economics*, **15**(2), 149–61.

Buchko, A.A. (1994), 'Conceptualization and measurement of environmental uncertainty: an assessment of the Miles and Snow perceived environmental uncertainty scale', *Academy of Management Journal*, **37**, 410–25.

Cantillon, R. (1755/1959), *Essai sur la nature du commerce en general*, by R. Cantillon, edited with an English translation and other material by H. Higgs, London: Cass.

Castrogiovanni, G.J. (1991), 'Environmental munificence: a theoretical assessment', *Academy of Management Review*, **16**(3), 542–65.

Castrogiovanni, G.J. (1996), 'Pre-startup planning and the survival of new small businesses: theoretical linkages', *Journal of Management*, **22**(6), 801–22.

Child, J. (1972), 'Organizational structure, environment, and performance: the role of strategic choice', *Sociology*, **6**, 1–22.

Covin, J.G. and D.P. Slevin (1989), 'Strategic management of small firms in hostile and benign environments', *Strategic Management Journal*, **10**, 75–87.

Cyert, R. and J.G. March (1963), *A Behavioral Theory of the Firm*, Englewood Cliffs, NJ: Prentice-Hall.

Daft, R.L., J. Sormunen and D. Parks (1988), 'Chief executive scanning, environmental characteristics, and company performance: an empirical study', *Strategic Management Journal*, **9**, 123–39.

Dess, G.G. and D.W. Beard (1984), 'Dimensions of organizational task environments', *Administrative Science Quarterly*, **29**, 52–73.

Dickson, P.H. and K.M. Weaver (1997), 'Environmental determinants and individual-level moderators of alliance use', *Academy of Management Journal*, **40**, 404–25.

Dimov, D. and D. Milanov (2010), 'The interplay of need and opportunity in venture capital investment syndication', *Journal of Business Venturing*, **25**(4), 331–48.

Duncan, R.B. (1972), 'Characteristics of organizational environments and perceived environmental uncertainty', *Administrative Science Quarterly*, **17**, 313–27.

Emery, F.E. and E.L. Trist (1965), 'The causal texture of organizational environments', *Human Relations*, **18**, 21–31.

Ensley, M.D., C.L. Pearce and K.M. Hmieleski (2006), 'The moderating effect of environmental dynamism on the relationship between entrepreneur leadership behavior and new venture performance', *Journal of Business Venturing*, **21**(2), 243–63.

Finkelstein, S. (1997), 'Interindustry merger patterns and resource dependence: a replication and extension of Pfeffer (1972)', *Strategic Management Journal*, **18**(10), 787–810.

Gartner, W.B., J.A. Starr and S. Bhat (1999), 'Predicting new venture survival: an analysis of anatomy of startup. Cases from INC. Magazine', *Journal of Business Venturing*, **14**, 215–32.

Goll, I. and A.M. Rasheed (1997), 'Rational decision-making and firm performance: the moderating role of environment', *Strategic Management Journal*, **18**, 583–91.

Gruber, M. (2007), 'Uncovering the value of planning in new venture creations: a process and contingency perspective', *Journal of Business Venturing*, **22**, 782–807.

Harper, D.A. (2008), 'Towards a theory of entrepreneurial teams', *Journal of Business Venturing*, **23**, 613–26.

Hayton, J.C. (2005), 'Promoting corporate entrepreneurship through human resource management practices: a review of empirical research', *Human Resource Management Review*, **15**, 21–41.

Hitt, M.A., R.D. Ireland and K.A. Palia (1982), 'Industrial firms' grand strategy and functional importance: moderating effects of technology and uncertainty', *Academy of Management Journal*, **25**, 265–98.

Hmieleski, K.M. and B.A. Baron (2009), 'Entrepreneurs' optimism and new venture performance: a social cognitive perspective', *Academy of Management Journal*, **52**(25), 473–88.

Hrebiniak, L.G. and C.C. Snow (1980), 'Industry differences in environmental uncertainty and organizational characteristics related to uncertainty', *Academy of Management Journal*, **23**, 750–59.

Janney, J.J. and G.G. Dess (2006), 'The risk concept for entrepreneurs reconsidered: new challenges to the conventional wisdom', *Journal of Business Venturing*, **21**(3), 385–400.

Knight, F.H. (1921), *Risk, Uncertainty and Profit*, New York: Kelly and Millman.

Lawrence, P.R. and J.W. Lorsch (1967), *Organization and Environment*, Cambridge, MA: Harvard University Press.

Lumpkin, G.T. and G.G. Dess (1996), 'Clarifying the entrepreneurial orientation construct and linking it to performance', *Academy of Management Review*, **21**(1), 135–72.

Lumpkin, G.T. and G.G. Dess (2001), 'Linking two dimensions of entrepreneurial orientation to firm performance: the moderating role of environment and industry life cycle', *Journal of Business Venturing*, **16**, 429–51.

March, J.G. and H.A. Simon (1958), *Organizations*, New York: McGraw-Hill.

Marino, L.D., F.T. Lohrke, J.S. Hill, K.M. Weaver and T. Tambunan (2008), 'Environmental shocks and SME alliance formation intentions in an emerging economy: evidence from the Asian financial crisis in Indonesia', *Entrepreneurship Theory and Practice*, **32**(1), 157–83.

McClelland, D.C. (1960), *The Achieving Society*, Princeton, NJ: Van Nostrand.

McGrath, R.G., I.C. Macmillan and S. Scheinberg (1992), 'Elitists, risk-takers, and rugged individualists? An exploratory analysis of cultural differences between entrepreneurs and non-entrepreneurs', *Journal of Business Venturing*, **7**(2), 115–35.

McVea, J.F. (2009), 'A field study of entrepreneurial decision-making and moral imagination', *Journal of Business Venturing*, **24**(5), 491–504.

Miles, R.E. and C.C. Snow (1978), *Organizational Strategy, Structure, and Process*, New York: McGraw-Hill.

Miles, M.P., J.G. Covin and M.B. Heeley (2000), 'The relationship between environmental dynamism and small firm structure, strategy, and performance', *Journal of Marketing Theory and Practice*, **8**(2), 63–78.
Miller, D. (1983), 'The correlates of entrepreneurship in three types of firms', *Management Science*, **29**(7), 770–91.
Miller, D. and P.H. Friesen (1978), 'Archetypes of strategy formulation', *Management Science*, **24**, 921–33.
Miller, D. and P.H. Friesen (1982), 'Innovation in conservative and entrepreneurial firms: two models of strategic momentum', *Strategic Management Journal*, **3**, 1–25.
Miller, D. and P.H. Friesen (1983), 'Strategy-making and environment: the third link', *Strategic Management Journal*, **4**, 221–35.
Milliken, F.J. (1987), 'Three types of perceived uncertainty about the environment: state, effect, and response uncertainty', *Academy of Management Review*, **12**, 133–43.
Palich, L. and D. Bagby (1995), 'Using cognitive theory to explain entrepreneurial risk-taking: challenging conventional wisdom', *Journal of Business Venturing*, **10**, 425–38.
Pfeffer, J. and G. Salancik (1978), *The External Control of Organizations: A Resource Dependence Perspective*, Boston, MA: Pitman Press.
Russell, R.D. and C.J. Russell (1992), 'An examination of the effects of organizational norms, organizational structure, and environmental uncertainty on entrepreneurial strategy', *Journal of Management*, **18**(4), 639–56.
Sapienza, H.J. (1992), 'When do venture capitalists add value?', *Journal of Business Venturing*, **7**(1), 9–29.
Sawyerr, O.O. (1993), 'Environmental uncertainty and environmental scanning activities of Nigerian manufacturing executives: a comparative analysis', *Strategic Management Journal*, **14**, 287–99.
Schumpeter, J.A. (1934), *The Theory of Economic Development*, Cambridge, MA: Harvard University Press.
Sharfman, M.P. and J.W. Dean (1991), 'Conceptualizing and measuring the organizational environment: a multidimensional approach', *Journal of Management*, **17**, 681–700.
Simerly, R.L. and M. Li (2000), 'Environmental dynamism, capital structure and performance: a theoretical integration and an empirical test', *Strategic Management Journal*, **21**, 31–49.
Simon, H.A. (1957), *Models of Man, Social and Rational*, New York: John Wiley.
Specht, P.H. (1993), 'Munificence and carrying capacity of the environment and organization formation', *Entrepreneurship Theory and Practice*, **17**, 77–86.
Steensma, H.K., L. Marino, K.M. Weaver and P.H. Dickson (2000), 'The influence of national culture on the formation of technology alliances by entrepreneurial firms', *Academy of Management Journal*, **43**(5), 951–73.
Tan, J. (1996), 'Regulatory environment and strategic orientations in a transitional economy: a study of Chinese private enterprise', *Entrepreneurship Theory and Practice*, **21**, 31–46.
Tan, J.J. and R.J. Litschert (1994), 'Environment-strategy relationship and its performance implications: an empirical study of the Chinese electronics industry', *Strategic Management Journal*, **15**, 1–20.
Thompson, J.D. (1967), *Organizations in Action*, New York: McGraw-Hill.
Tung, R.L. (1979), 'Dimensions of organizational environments: an exploratory study of their impact on organization structure', *Academy of Management Journal*, **22**, 672–93.
Van de Vrande, V., W. Vanhaverbeke and G. Duysters (2009), 'External technology sourcing: the effect of uncertainty on governance mode choice', *Journal of Business Venturing*, **24**, 62–80.
Wiersema, M.F. and K.A. Bantel (1993), 'Top management team turnover as an adaptation mechanism: the role of the environment', *Strategic Management Journal*, **14**, 485–504.
Wiersma, E. (2007), 'Conditions that shape the learning curve: factors that increase the ability and opportunity to learn', *Management Science*, **53**(12), 1903–15.
Wiklund, J. and D. Shepherd (2005), 'Entrepreneurial orientation and small business performance: a configurational approach', *Journal of Business Venturing*, **20**(1), 71–91.
Yasai-Ardekani, M. (1989), 'Effects of environmental scarcity and munificence on the relationship of context to organizational structure', *Academy of Management Journal*, **32**, 131–56.

Zahra, S.A. (1993), 'Environment, corporate entrepreneurship, and financial performance: a taxonomic approach', *Journal of Business Venturing*, **8**, 319–40.

Zahra, S.A. (1996), 'Technology strategy and financial performance: examining the moderating role of the firm's competitive environment', *Journal of Business Venturing*, **11**(3), 189–219.

Zahra, S.A. and W.C. Bogner (2000), 'Technology strategy and software new ventures' performance: exploring the moderating effect of the competitive environment', *Journal of Business Venturing*, **15**(2), 135–73.

Zahra, S.A. and D.M. Garvis (2000), 'International corporate entrepreneurship and firm performance: the moderating effect of international environmental hostility', *Journal of Business Venturing*, **15**, 469–92.

Zahra, S.A., A.P. Nielsen and W.C. Bogner (1999), 'Corporate entrepreneurship, knowledge, and competence development', *Entrepreneurship Theory and Practice*, **23**(3), 169–89.

5. Entrepreneurial alertness and opportunity discovery: origins, attributes, critique

Nicolai J. Foss and Peter G. Klein

INTRODUCTION

Israel Kirzner's concept of entrepreneurship as alertness to profit opportunities is one of the most influential modern interpretations of the entrepreneurial function. Shane and Venkataraman's (2000, p. 218) important assessment defines entrepreneurship research as 'the scholarly examination of how, by whom, and with what effects opportunities to create future goods and services are discovered, evaluated, and exploited.' As such, 'the field involves the study of sources of opportunities; the processes of discovery, evaluation, and exploitation of opportunities; and the set of individuals who discover, evaluate, and exploit them.' Shane's *A General Theory of Entrepreneurship* (2003) cites Kirzner more than any writer except Joseph Schumpeter. More generally, the entrepreneurial opportunity, rather than the individual entrepreneur, the startup company, or the new product, has become the centerpiece of the academic study of entrepreneurship (Gaglio and Katz, 2001; Shane, 2003; Shane and Venkataraman, 2000).

Kirzner's framework builds on the market-process approach associated with the Austrian school of economics and can trace its roots further back to Richard Cantillon, J.B. Clark, Frank A. Fetter, and other writers. Kirzner himself sees his contribution as primarily an extension of the work of Mises and F.A. Hayek, in effect bridging Mises's (1949) emphasis on the entrepreneur with Hayek's (1946; 1968) concept of market competition as an unfolding process of discovery and learning.[1] Among mainstream economists, Kirzner has been cited in the literature on occupational choice, and there have been a few attempts to formalize his model of the market process (Littlechild, 1979; Littlechild and Owen, 1980; Yates, 2000), in the context of a more general interest in equilibration processes (Fisher, 1983). Kirzner has explained the Austrian model of the entrepreneurial market process to readers of the prestigious *Journal of Economic Literature* (Kirzner, 1997a). Still, his work has been more influential among management scholars than among economists, who tend to view equilibration as a second-order phenomenon; the main focus of theoretical work in economics today (both microeconomic and macroeconomic) remains identifying and characterizing market equilibria in terms of existence, uniqueness, and stability. In this sense, the opportunity-discovery branch of the entrepreneurship literature provides an example of management scholarship that builds upon a simple, yet fundamental insight from economics, and pushes that insight in directions that economists are reluctant to go.

This chapter traces the origin and development of the concept of entrepreneurial alertness and its place as the centerpiece of the opportunity-discovery approach to entrepreneurship. In particular, we place Kirzner's contribution within the broader context of the Austrian school of economics, comparing and contrasting it with other Austrian conceptions of entrepreneurship. We argue that even though Kirzner's contribution is often thought of as *the* Austrian conception of the entrepreneur, an alternative Austrian tradition, in fact, exists that emphasizes the entrepreneur as an uncertainty-bearing, asset-owning individual and that this tradition offers some advantages over the discovery approach (whether in the Kirznerian or modern-management incarnations). We also critically discuss the way Kirzner's work has been interpreted and used in the theoretical, empirical, and experimental literatures looking into the antecedents and consequences of such opportunity discovery. As we argue, this literature goes much beyond Kirzner's work, making opportunity discovery and its determinants the key feature of the theory, whereas Kirzner's real interest lies in explaining market equilibration, a higher-level phenomenon.

THE AUSTRIAN SCHOOL OF ECONOMICS

The Austrian school of economics (Böhm-Bawerk, 1889; Hayek, 1948; 1968; Kirzner, 1973; Lachmann, 1956; Menger, 1871; Rothbard, 1962; Mises, 1949) is increasingly well known in management studies for its contributions to the theory of entrepreneurship and the complementary 'market process' account of economic activity (Chiles, 2003; Chiles and Choi, 2000; Hill and Deeds, 1996; Jacobson 1992; Langlois, 2001; Roberts and Eisenhardt, 2003). Other characteristically Austrian ideas such as the time structure of capital (Hayek, 1941) and the heterogeneity of capital goods (Lachmann, 1956) have received less attention (but see Foss et al., 2007b; Chiles et al., 2007). Like all 'heterodox' approaches, the Austrian school occupies a marginal position among contemporary, mainstream economists, though Hayek's theory of the business cycle has attracted renewed interest in the last few years (e.g. Oppers, 2002).

Here we offer a brief sketch of the history and development of the Austrian school, with particular reference to its approach to the entrepreneur. As we discuss in more detail below, the Austrian tradition is more diverse than is conventionally recognized. For example, we see important differences between Kirzner's approach to entrepreneurship and that of Menger, the early twentieth-century American representatives of the Austrian school, and Mises, Kirzner's teacher and the most important and influential of the modern Austrian economists.

Menger and the Early Austrian School

The Austrian tradition begins with Carl Menger (1871), who sought to develop a causal, realistic account of price formation (and other economic phenomena) in contrast to the inductive, historicist approach that dominated late nineteenth-century German economics. Menger's approach emphasized the subjectivity of economic value, marginal analysis, resource heterogeneity, distributed knowledge, and the time-structure of production. The entrepreneur figures prominently in Menger's account of production, though not in the sense emphasized by Kirzner. The entrepreneur is described by Menger (1871, p. 68) as a coordinating agent who is both capitalist and manager.

Entrepreneurial activity includes: (a) obtaining information about the economic situation; (b) economic calculation – all the various computations that must be made if a production process is to be efficient (provided that it is economic in other respects); (c) the act of will by which goods of higher order (or goods in general – under conditions of developed commerce, where any economic good can be exchanged for any other) are assigned to a particular production process; and finally (d) supervision of the execution of the production plan so that it may be carried through as economically as possible. This formulation emphasizes the importance of uncertainty and knowledge, and the deliberate, decisive action of the entrepreneur in arranging the productive resources at his or her disposal. Menger also makes the entrepreneur a resource owner, as do Knight (1921) and Foss et al. (2007b).

In his emphasis on uncertainty-bearing Menger picks up a theme introduced by Richard Cantillon, often considered a forerunner of the Austrian tradition (Rothbard, 1995; Thornton, 1999). Cantillon was the first economist to analyze the entrepreneur systematically. In the *Essai sur la nature du commerce en general* (1755), he described three classes of economic agents, landowners, wage workers, and entrepreneurs whose main purpose is to engage in arbitrage, motivated by the profit that may stem from 'buying at a certain price and selling at an uncertain price' (Cantillon, 1755/1931, p. 54):

> Entrepreneurs work for uncertain wages, so to speak, and all others for certain wages until they have them, although their functions and their rank are very disproportionate. The General who has a salary, the Courtier who has a pension, and the Domestic who has wages, are in the latter class. All the others are Entrepreneurs, whether they establish themselves with a capital to carry on their enterprise, or are Entrepreneurs of their own work without any capital, and they may be considered as living subject to uncertainty; even Beggars and Robbers are Entrepreneurs of this class.

Thus, Cantillon saw uncertainty as an integral part of understanding profits and emphasized that entrepreneurs, rather than being a distinct group of individuals, are all those who bear commercial risk. He also emphasized the importance of foresight and argued that entrepreneurs do not need to own capital, a characteristic of Kirzner's approach that we discuss in more detail below.

In the 1880s and 1890s, an Austrian school coalesced around Menger and his disciples, most notably Eugen von Böhm-Bawerk and Friedrich Wieser. Important British and American economists such as Philip Wicksteed, John Bates Clark, Herbert J. Davenport, and Frank A. Fetter also adopted and developed Menger's principles of pricing and his causal-realistic approach to economic theorizing. Clark, for example, developed a theory of the entrepreneur based on the distinction between the 'static state' and 'dynamic societies' (Salerno, 2008, p. 18). Under static conditions, the entrepreneur's function is 'purely passive . . . the *entrepreneur* in his capacity of buyer and seller does not even do the work which purchases and sales involve . . . Sales and purchases are made in his name, but he does none of the work that leads up to them' (Clark, 1918, p. 122). There is essentially nothing for the entrepreneur to do under static conditions because under such conditions all factors of production are already allocated to their optimal uses, so that profits and losses will be zero. However, in the 'dynamic society' profits and losses are unavoidably present, because under such conditions and the uncertainty that accompanies them, the entrepreneur 'makes the supreme decisions which now and again lead to changes in the business' (Clark, 1918, p. 124). The entrepreneur, in Clark's view, is the ultimate decision-maker, and that 'part of the management of a business which consists in making the most far-reaching decisions cannot safely be entrusted to a salaried superintendent or other paid official, and must get its returns, if at all, in the form of profits' (Clark, 1918, p. 157). This means that the entrepreneur must also be the owner of the business.

Clark's contemporary, Frank A. Fetter, known primarily for his contributions to the theory of capital and interest, also gave the entrepreneur a central role in the process of resource allocation (Fetter, 1905; 1915; 1977). Fetter's explanation of the differences between short-run and long-run profits anticipates both Knight's (1921) distinction between 'risk' and 'uncertainty' and Kirzner's concept of market equilibration. In the long run, Fetter argued, the net returns to production are determined by interest rates, themselves determined by the market's rate of 'time preference', or the relative valuation of present and future consumption. In the short run, business incomes fluctuate around these 'normal' returns because some entrepreneurs are better able than others to anticipate future prices and can thus acquire resources at prices below the present discounted values of their eventual contributions to output, leaving profit in addition to interest. In doing so, these entrepreneurs bid up the prices of the 'underpriced' factors and help bring about the long-run equilibrium in which such profits are eliminated.[2]

Fetter's (1905, pp. 286–7) description of the entrepreneur (he uses the term 'enter-priser') identifies uncertainty-bearing as the key entrepreneurial function. The entrepreneur (a) 'guarantees to the capitalist-lender a fixed return', (b) 'gives up the certain income to be got by lending his own capital, and, becoming a borrower, offers his capital as insurance to the lender', (c) 'gives to other workers a definite amount for services applied to distant ends', and (d) 'risks his own services and accepts an indefinite chance instead of a definite amount for them'. He also serves as an 'organizer' and 'director', possessing 'unusual foresight' and the 'ability to judge men and tact in relations with them' (Fetter, 1905, p. 268). In short, the entrepreneur 'is the economic buffer; economic forces are transmitted through him'.

> As the specialized risk-taker, he is the spring or buffer, which takes up and distributes the strain of industry. He feels first the influence of changing conditions. If the prices of his products fall, the first loss comes upon him, and he avoids further loss as best he can by paying less for materials and labor. At such times the wage-earners look upon him as their evil genius, and usually blame him for lowering their wages, not the public for refusing to buy the product at the former high prices. Again, if prices rise, he gains from the increased value of the stock in his hand that has been produced at low cost. If the employer often appears to be a hard man, his disposition is the result of 'natural selection'. He is placed between the powerful, selfish forces of competition, and his economic survival is conditioned on vigilance, strength, and self-assertion. Weak generosity cannot endure. (Fetter, 1905: 287–88)

As in Knight and Kirzner, the entrepreneurial role is not limited to new-venture creation or the introduction of new products, services, production methods, and the like, but lies at the heart of the everyday affairs of production and exchange.

Mises, a student of Böhm-Bawerk, and Mises's younger colleague Hayek, more a student of Wieser than of Böhm-Bawerk, would develop and extend the Austrian tradition in the early twentieth century, with Kirzner, Murray Rothbard, both Mises students, and Ludwig Lachmann, a Hayek student, making critical contributions in the 1950s, 1960s, and 1970s. Recent scholars have noted considerable variety within the Austrian school, particularly in its modern interpretations. Salerno (1993), in particular, argues that there are two distinct strands of Austrian economics, both tracing their origins to Menger. One strand, manifest in the works of Wieser, Hayek, and Kirzner, emphasizes disequilibrium, the informational role of prices, discovery of already existing opportunities, and profit-seeking behavior as an equilibrating force. Another strand, developed by Böhm-Bawerk, Mises, and Rothbard, focuses on monetary calculation and forward-looking, uncertainty-bearing, entrepreneurial appraisal and investment, rather than discovery.[3] The concept of entrepreneurship as alertness to profit opportunities created by disequilibrium comes out of the Wieser–Hayek–Kirzner strand. There are, however, important precursors to both strands.

Wieser and Hayek: The Beginnings of the 'Discovery View'

In his treatise *Social Economics* (1914) Wieser presented an eclectic definition of the entrepreneur as owner, manager, leader, innovator, organizer, and speculator. He noted that the entrepreneur 'must possess the quick perception that seizes new terms in current transactions as his affairs develop' (Wieser, 1914, p. 324), the first hint of alertness as an entrepreneurial attribute.

Wieser's student, Hayek, did not contribute to the theory of entrepreneurship *per se*, but his discovery view of competition, developed in a series of essays from the mid-1940s (notably Hayek, 1945; 1946) as a critical reaction to the perfect-competition model, is a crucial input into the opportunity discovery approach. Competition, Hayek argued, should be understood not as a static state of affairs, but as a rivalrous process that is essentially a procedure for discovering '*who* will serve us well: which grocer or travel agency, which department store or hotel, which doctor or solicitor, we can expect to provide the most satisfactory solution for whatever personal problem we may have to face' (Hayek, 1946, p. 97). The basis for this conceptualization is the characteristically Austrian emphasis on dispersed knowledge, present already in Menger, but fully articulated by Hayek. Competition, Hayek maintains, is the mechanism that makes best use of dispersed knowledge – it is an effective way to discover knowledge we do not yet know is available or indeed needed at all (Hayek, 1968/2002).

However, Hayek is not entirely forthcoming on how exactly the market performs this discovery function. Entrepreneurs are mentioned only in passing.[4] Indeed, different mechanisms underlying the market's discovery process can be imagined, depending on how much intention, rationality, and learning ability are ascribed to market participants. At one extreme lies a selection mechanism that selects effectively among various entrepreneurial ventures formed essentially in ignorance of consumer preferences (Alchian, 1950; Becker, 1962). Such a process is heavily error-prone, and, more importantly, no one learns from past errors. Although Hayek's writings may sometimes describe such processes in which the system, and not individual agents, are 'rational' (Langlois, 1985), most other Austrians have strongly emphasized the intentions of entrepreneurs in coping with uncertainty and ignorance, allowing for various degrees of error. Indeed, Kirzner has often conceptualized the market process as one of a 'systematic' elimination of errors. Interestingly, one of Kirzner's earliest papers is a strong critique of Becker's (1962) evolutionary argument that one can dispense entirely with the rationality of market participants in doing basic price theory (Kirzner, 1962). Kirzner's entrepreneur is highly rational, or perhaps more precisely, extra-rational, in going beyond the given means-ends frameworks and noticing previously undiscovered opportunities for pure profit. Kirzner, then, supplies a crucial mechanism (or micro-foundation) for the Wieser–Hayek discovery view: a competitive market is a superior setting because it generates entrepreneurial discoveries through the exercise of alertness. As Kirzner (1973, p. 14) argues, 'our confidence in the market's ability to learn and to harness the continuous flow of information to generate the market process depends crucially on our belief in the benign presence of the entrepreneurial element.' Although the entrepreneur may not search for any profit opportunity in particular, the lure of pure profit may nevertheless lead him or her to continually scan the horizon, as it were (Kirzner, 1997a, p. 72).

Böhm-Bawerk, Mises, and Rothbard

Böhm-Bawerk was one of Austria's most prominent economists, not only as a theorist but as a three-time Austrian minister of finance (whose picture still graces Austria's 100 schilling note). His work was mainly on the theory of capital and interest (Böhm-Bawerk, 1889), and his approach has largely been abandoned within mainstream macroeconomic theory. (He also authored a penetrating and original critique of Marx (Böhm-Bawerk, 1898)). Perhaps for this reason, his work is little known to contemporary management scholars.

Böhm-Bawerk's two most important students were Joseph Schumpeter and Ludwig von Mises. Mises is generally considered the most important twentieth-century representative of the Austrian school, and his work provided a main impetus to the 'Austrian revival' of the 1970s (Vaughn, 1994; Salerno, 1999). Mises became an internationally known monetary theorist with the publication of his *Theory of Money and Credit* in 1912, followed by an important 1920 article and 1922 book on the economic theory of socialism (Mises, 1920; 1922). Mises's best-known book is his 1949 treatise, *Human Action,* which continues to be a foundational text for Austrians.

Kirzner has always described his work as an extension of Mises's theory of the market process.[5] Mises, Kirzner's mentor and teacher at New York University, and Kirzner are usually lumped together as offering a unified Austrian account of the entrepreneur. However, as we clarify later, we see Mises as closer to the Cantillon–Knight position that entrepreneurship is judgment over the deployment of resources, not alertness *per se*. Kirzner (1973, pp. 39–40) agrees that in a world of uncertainty, resource owners exercise entrepreneurial judgment in allocating their resources to particular uses. But he goes on (1973, pp. 40–43) to introduce the analytical device of the pure entrepreneur, the agent who discovers profit opportunities without putting any resources at stake, and claims that this function, rather than investment under uncertainty, is the 'driving force' of the market economy. This view, we maintain, and the Wieser–Hayek–Kirzner account in general, is very different from the view found in Cantillon, Knight, and Mises.

Mises's own position is somewhat ambiguous (Salerno, 2008). The entrepreneur, Mises writes, 'shows how the activities of enterprising men, the promoters and speculators, eager to profit from discrepancies in the price structure, tend toward eradicating such discrepancies and thereby also toward blotting out the sources of entrepreneurial profit and loss.' Describing this equilibrating process 'is the task of economic theory' (Mises, 1949, pp. 352–3). Elsewhere, however, Mises describes the entrepreneur as an investor, an economic actor who bears uncertainty, rather than discovering (certain) opportunities for gain. '[T]he outcome of action is always uncertain. Action is always speculation' (Mises, 1949, p. 253). Consequently, 'the real entrepreneur is a speculator, a man eager to utilize his opinion about the future structure of the market for business operations promising profits. This specific anticipative understanding of the conditions of the uncertain future defies any rules and systematization' (Mises, 1949, p. 582).

This emphasis on action under conditions of uncertainty calls to mind Cantillon's (1755) brief account of the entrepreneurial function and Knight's (1921) concept of entrepreneurial judgment. Judgment is business decision-making when the range of possible future outcomes, let alone the likelihood of individual outcomes, is generally unknown (what Knight terms uncertainty, rather than mere probabilistic risk). Exercising judgment thus requires the investment of resources (primarily, the purchase of factors of production in the present, in anticipation of future receipts from the sale of finished goods).[6] Alertness, or awareness of particular conditions, does not itself involve judgment, and does not, in this understanding, have a direct effect on the allocation of resources.

Kirzner's contemporary Murray Rothbard, another influential contemporary Austrian economist, was among the first to question Kirzner's strict separation between the 'discovery' and 'ownership' functions of the entrepreneur (Rothbard, 1995). Rothbard argued that unless buying and selling are instantaneous, even arbitrageurs bear uncertainty, in that selling prices may change after goods and services are acquired for arbitrage. More generally, the driving force of the market economy is not Kirzner's 'pure entrepreneur', but the capitalist-entrepreneurs who invest resources in anticipation of uncertain rewards:

> Kirzner's entrepreneur is a curious formulation. He need not, apparently, risk anything. He is a free-floating wraith, disembodied from real objects. He does not, and need not, possess any assets. All he need have to earn profits is a faculty of alertness to profit opportunities. Since he need not risk any capital assets to meet the chancy fate of uncertainty, he cannot suffer any losses. But if the Kirznerian entrepreneur owns no assets, then how in the world does he earn profits? Profits, after all, are simply the other side of the coin of an increase in the value of one's capital; losses are the reflection of a loss in capital assets. The speculator who expects a stock to rise uses money to purchase that stock; a rise or fall in the price of stock will raise or lower the value of the stock assets. If the price rises, the profits are one and the same thing as the increase in capital assets. The process is more complex but similar in the purchase or hiring of factors of production, the creating of a product and then its sale on the market. In what sense can an entrepreneur ever make profits if he owns no capital to make profits on? (Rothbard, 1985, pp. 282–3)

Summary

In short, the Austrian tradition comprises a variety of diverse elements, some complementary but others distinct. Methodological individualism, subjectivism, realism, human purpose, resource heterogeneity, the division of labor and division of knowledge, dynamic processes of adjustment, and decentralized organizational structures are key elements in all strands of Austrian economics. However, there are important differences among scholars working in this tradition. In particular, we distinguish a Wieser–Hayek–Kirzner strand, emphasizing knowledge, discovery, and process, and a Böhm–Bawerk–

Mises-Rothbard strand, emphasizing monetary calculation and decision-making under uncertainty.

Management scholars, particularly those working on entrepreneurial discovery and opportunity identification, may wish to study these strands more carefully, and to consider Austrian insights that have not made appearances in contemporary management theory. For example, the Hayekian emphasis on tacit knowledge and spontaneous processes of discovery has influenced the knowledge-based view of the firm and, to a lesser degree, Williamson's transaction cost economics (Williamson, 1991). But Austrian capital theory is largely unknown among management scholars, despite its close connection to concepts of resource heterogeneity (firm-specific resources and capabilities, asset specificity, etc.) that are central to strategic management (Foss et al., 2007b). The Austrians also made important early contributions in the areas of property rights, knowledge, incentives, and institutions (Foss and Klein, 2010). We hope that interest in Austrian ideas within the opportunity-discovery tradition will lead to greater attention to Austrian contributions in these other areas as well.

KIRZNER AND ENTREPRENEURIAL ALERTNESS

We turn next to Israel Kirzner's important and influential interpretation of entrepreneurship as alertness, or discovery, of opportunities for gain. Kirzner, Mises's student and colleague at New York University and director of its graduate program in Austrian economics until his retirement in 2001, is one of the best-known and most cited Austrian economists. Here we briefly summarize Kirzner's approach to entrepreneurship and its place within the broader Austrian and mainstream entrepreneurial literatures. We then summarize some controversies surrounding Kirzner's views, both within and outside the Austrian tradition. These include disagreements about the equilibrating nature of entrepreneurial action (and the market process more generally), the relationship between entrepreneurial discovery and innovation, Kirzner's approach to entrepreneurial creativity, and the role of resource ownership in the Kirznerian system.

Kirzner's Contribution

Kirzner's *Competition and Entrepreneurship* (1973) is conventionally seen as *the* seminal modern Austrian statement on entrepreneurship. Kirzner's later work on entrepreneurship has mainly consisted in clarifying the positions in that book (Kirzner, 1979a; 1992; 1997b; 2009), as well as relating them to other theories of entrepreneurship, and applying them to, for example, regulation (e.g. Kirzner, 1984; 1985) and ethics (Kirzner, 1989).

In Kirzner's framework, profit opportunities result from prices, quantities, and qualities that diverge from their equilibrium values. Some individuals tend to notice, or be alert to, these opportunities, and their actions bring about changes in prices, quantities, and qualities. The simplest case of alertness is that of the arbitrageur, who discovers a discrepancy in present prices that can be exploited for financial gain. In a more typical case, the entrepreneur is alert to a new product or a superior production process and steps in to fill this market gap before others. Success, in this view, comes not from following a well-specified maximization problem, such as a search algorithm (High, 1980), but from having some insight that no one else has, a process that cannot be modeled as an optimization problem.[7] Entrepreneurship, in other words, is the act of grasping and responding to profit opportunities that exist in an imperfect world. Unlike other approaches in modern economics, the imperfections in question are not seen as temporary 'frictions' resulting from ill-defined property rights, transaction costs, or asymmetric information. Although those imperfections can be cast in an equilibrium mold – as in the modern economics of information – Kirzner has in mind a market in permanent and ineradicable disequilibrium.[8]

Kirzner's approach, like that of Knight, Schumpeter, and other key contributors to the economic theory of entrepreneurship, sees entrepreneurship as an economic function, not an employment category (i.e. self-employment) or type of firm (i.e. a startup company).[9] The main effect of the entrepreneurial function is market equilibration: by closing pockets of ignorance in the market, entrepreneurship always stimulates a tendency towards equilibrium (Selgin, 1987). While Kirzner's 'pure entrepreneur', an ideal type, performs *only* this function, and does not supply labor or own capital, real-world business people may be partly entrepreneurs in this sense, partly laborers, partly capitalists, and so on. As we suggested in the previous section, the relationship between entrepreneurial discovery and capital investment distinguishes Kirzner's approach sharply from Knight's (and, arguably, from that of Kirzner's mentor, Ludwig von Mises). Because Kirzner's (pure) entrepreneurs perform only a discovery function, rather than an investment function, they do not own capital; they need only be alert to profit opportunities. Kirznerian entrepreneurs need not be charismatic leaders, do not innovate, and are not necessarily creative or in possession of sound business judgment. They do not necessarily start firms, raise capital, or manage an enterprise. They perform the discovery function, and nothing else.

Key in Kirzner's work is his distinction between 'Robbinsian maximizing' and 'entrepreneurial alertness'. The first conforms to the standard picture of economic man as applying given means to best satisfy given but conflicting ends in a fundamentally mechanical way (Robbins, 1932). Because everything is given, action becomes purely a matter of calculation. Kirzner argues that this conceptualization of behavior cannot accommodate the discovery of new means, new ends, and the setting up of new means-ends structures. As a result, the dynamic market process cannot be captured by the model of Robbinsian maximizing; another behavioral quality is needed, namely the quality of entrepreneurial alertness to previously unexploited profit opportunities. Alertness ranges from the discovery of a ten dollar bill on the street to the discovery of a new, highly profitable drug. Thus, entrepreneurs are discoverers; they discover new resource uses, new products, new markets, new possibilities for arbitrage – in short, new possibilities for profitable trade. Alertness is not the same as search (Stigler, 1961), the deliberate search for new information. Rather, entrepreneurship is the act of discovering, or being alert to, information and opportunities that others fail to perceive. It is not only that entrepreneurial activity reduces our lack of knowledge about which products, processes, new organizational forms, etc. are needed; it is more fundamentally that entrepreneurial activity alleviates our ignorance about what we don't know. What Kirzner calls 'sheer ignorance' is 'necessarily accompanied by the element of surprise – one had not hitherto realized one's ignorance' (Kirzner, 1997a, p. 62).

Combining his notion of entrepreneurial behavior with Hayek's notion of the market as a dynamic process, Kirzner develops a view of the market process as a continual process of entrepreneurial discovery of previously unnoticed opportunities for pure profit. The profits earned in this process reflect the discovery and exploitation of profit opportunities that would not have been grasped in the absence of entrepreneurial activity. Thus, the entrepreneurial function is beneficial because it alleviates the problems of coordination introduced by the division of knowledge (Hayek, 1945). Here Kirzner invokes the welfare concept, borrowed from Hayek, of 'plan coordination', a concept that has generated considerable controversy within the Austrian school.[10]

Kirzner's fiction of the pure entrepreneur is introduced to elucidate the coordinating function of entrepreneurship. Although Clark and Mises introduced similar devices to emphasize selected aspects of entrepreneurship, Kirzner sees his construct as capturing its very essence. Kirzner has been insistent that the pure entrepreneur is a non-owner (Kirzner, 1975). 'An important point,' Kirzner argues (1973, p. 47), 'is that ownership and entrepreneurship are to be viewed as completely separate functions. Once we have adopted the convention of concentrating all elements of entrepreneurship into the hands of pure entrepreneurs, we have automatically excluded the asset owner from an entrepreneurial role. Purely entrepreneurial decisions are by definition reserved to decision-makers who own nothing at all.' Thus, the entrepreneur is a pure decision-maker, and nothing else. As such, anyone can be a pure entrepreneur.

The notions of decision-making in the context of entrepreneurship raise several pertinent questions. For example, the notions of 'alertness' and 'discovery' suggest that there are separate phases in the act of entrepreneurship. Similarly, Kirzner often talks about the exploitation of opportunities, which adds another possible phase (following discovery). These phases could conceivably be separated by long stretches of time. Relatedly, they could have widely different antecedents or determinants. However, Kirzner seems to treat alertness, discovery, and exploitation as parts of one *Gestalt* – inseparable parts of a whole, and does not seem interested in exploring their relationship. As we argue below, this is presumably because his explanatory concern is equilibration, not the entrepreneur as such.

However, even if entrepreneurship is ultimately a means to understanding a higher-level phenomenon, equilibration, the antecedents of entrepreneurship can still be important and worthy of academic study. The modern entrepreneurship literature in economics and management research has suggested several possible antecedents such as the personal skills (Lazear, 2004), cognitive biases (Busenitz and Barney, 1997), and prior experience (Shane, 2000), as well the characteristics of the parent company (Gompers et al., 2005), the institutional environment (Bjørnskov and Foss, 2008), and other background characteristics (Xue and Klein, 2010). However, like other contributors to the economic theory of entrepreneurship (notably Schumpeter and Knight), Kirzner is not interested in such antecedents, presumably because his aim is to construct a general theory of the equilibrating function of entrepreneurship. He does, however, argue that government interference with the price mechanism inhibits the entrepreneurial discovery process (e.g. Kirzner, 1979b).

[D]irect controls by government on prices, quantities, or qualities of output production or input employment may unintentionally block activities which have, as yet, not been specifically envisaged by anyone. Where these blocked activities turn out to be entrepreneurially profitable activities (perhaps as a result of unforeseen changes in data), the likelihood of their being discovered is then sharply diminished. Without necessarily intending it, the spontaneous discovery process of the free market has thus been, to some extent, stifled or distorted. (Kirzner, 1982a)

Debates on the Kirznerian Discovery Approach

Kirzner's approach has stimulated considerable controversy, both within and outside the Austrian school of economics. Among Austrians, debate has focused on the inherently equilibrating aspect of entrepreneurial discovery. Kirzner wants to maintain equilibrium (as understood by mainstream economists) as a meaningful and useful analytical category. The Austrian quarrel with equilibrium economics is that we are 'entitled to demand a theoretical basis for the claim that equilibrating processes systematically mold market variables in a direction consistent with the conditions postulated in the equilibrium models' (Kirzner, 1997a, p. 65). However, this 'theoretical basis' has not been offered by mainstream economists. This criticism of equilibrium economics echoes Hayek (1937), who argued that economists should devote analytical attention to understanding those learning processes that establish congruence between 'subjective data' (i.e. agents' perceptions) and 'objective data' (i.e. real scarcities and preferences). However, unlike Hayek, who argued that the 'pure logic of choice' was not helpful in this regard, Kirzner claims that entrepreneurship is a logical category that supplies the 'story' which might account for 'the economists' confidence in the special relevance of the intersection point in [the] demand and supply diagram' (Kirzner, 1997a, p. 66). This may be interpreted as implying that entrepreneurship is always and inherently equilibrating (Selgin, 1987).

However, by explicitly raising the need to theorize equilibrating processes, Kirzner may also be seen as linking up with work in mainstream economics that has dealt with the issue of how markets can converge to equilibria (cf. Selgin, 1987, p. 44), notably so-called 'stability theory' (Scarf, 1960). Also, some mainstream economists have argued that it is only meaningful to make use of the equilibrium construct if it can be theoretically demonstrated that there may exist a tendency to equilibrium (Fisher, 1983). Thus, Kirzner may be seen as forging linkages to important contributions from mainstream economics. However, overall this work demonstrates that strong assumptions must be made for convergence to take place – and no such assumptions are explicitly made in Kirzner's work.

There are several ways in which entrepreneurship may fail to equilibrate markets within Kirzner's own analytical system. First, if opportunities can be posited as existing objectively, then if entrepreneurs fail to discover all opportunities, equilibration does not take place (a possibility allowed for by Kirzner himself). Second, if by equilibrium Kirzner has in mind Hayek's sense of multi-period plan coordination, then Kirzner has introduced an inter-temporal dimension that may wreak havoc with the whole notion of entrepreneurship as equilibrating. In parts of Kirzner's early work (e.g. Kirzner, 1973), the exercise of entrepreneurship does not seem to presuppose uncertainty. If entrepreneurship means overcoming sheer ignorance by the exercise of alertness, this is a logically correct inference. However, uncertainty is clearly a fundamental aspect of action (Mises, 1949), and it is difficult to see the usefulness of a theory of entrepreneurship that abstracts from it. However, introducing uncertainty may destroy the basis for the claim that entrepreneurship is equilibrating.

In particular, Ludwig Lachmann, drawing on English economist George Shackle's work on the radically uncertain, 'kaleidic' economy, raised strong doubts in the 1970s concerning equilibration.[11] If the future is unknowable and emerges from creative acts in a kaleidic manner, current profits and losses – which are based on past actions – do not provide reliable guides to future-oriented current actions (Lachmann, 1976). Only a small subset (e.g. futures markets) of the full set of intertemporal prices exists. In other words, there is very little rational basis for entrepreneurs to form expectations of future consumer demands and resource scarcities, and such expectations are, therefore, more likely to be divergent than convergent.[12]

Selgin (1987) argues that these debates misunderstand the nature of the equilibration process. Correctly understood, 'equilibration' does not refer to coordination of plans as in Hayek (1937), mainstream stability theory, convergence to rational expectations equilibrium, and the like; it refers to entrepreneurial profits and losses. These are strictly subjective categories and have no objective basis outside the minds of entrepreneurs:

> It is necessary . . . to treat entrepreneurial profit opportunities as the unique products of the valuations and understanding (*Verstehen*) of actors who will seek their exploitation. Upon the fact of action, these 'imagined' or 'understood' (rather than 'perceived') profits are, logically and temporally, destroyed. Thus, action leads to the systematic elimination of entrepreneurial profit and loss; it is *equilibrating*. (Selgin, 1987, p. 39)

Thus, equilibration in this (Misesian) sense makes no reference to the state of knowledge of market participants and whether their plans are consistent or not. In fact, Selgin (1987) dismisses the very notion of coordination in a world in which profit opportunities cannot be thought of as 'objectively existing', in which preferences have no existence apart from actions, etc. Klein (2008b, p. 182) argues, following Salerno (1991), that Mises has in mind a concept of coordination that refers only to real-world exchanges, not the movements of prices and quantities toward some hypothetical long-run equilibrium values. In this sense, the existence or nonexistence of equilibrating tendencies in the unhampered market – the issue that divided 'Kirznerians' and 'Lachmannians', and dominated much of the Austrian discussion in the 1980s – is relatively unimportant. For Mises, the critical 'market process' is not the convergence to equilibrium, but the selection mechanism in which unsuccessful entrepreneurs – those who systematically overbid for factors, relative to eventual consumer demands – are eliminated from the market (Mises, 1951).

Other economists have emphasized the contrast between the Kirznerian and Schumpeterian entrepreneurs, asking if Kirzner's entrepreneur can also innovate, be creative, take risks, and so on. Kirzner emphasizes that his 'pure entrepreneur' performs only a discovery function and need not be an innovator in the Schumpeterian sense of disrupting an existing equilibrium allocation of resources by introducing new products, services, sources of supply, production methods, etc. Kirzner does not deny that businesspeople, resource owners, financiers, traders, and the like exercise boldness, creativity, and imagination, only that an entrepreneur *need* not exercise these functions to perform the role of alertness to previously unknown profit opportunities. 'My entrepreneurs were engaged in *arbitrage*, acting entrepreneurially even when they might *not* be seen as Schumpeterian "creators". . . . In so emphasizing the difference between Schumpeter's theory of entrepreneurship and my own, I was motivated by my primary scientific objective. This was to understand the nature of the market process – even in its *simplest* conceivable contexts' (Kirzner, 2009, p. 147).

A recent stream of management literature, discussed in more detail below, conceives the distinction between Kirznerian discovery and Schumpeterian innovation in terms of different kinds of profit opportunities. Under particular circumstances – for instance, mature industries with well-functioning product and factor markets, little technological change, a stable customer base, and so on – gains from trade may be regarded as 'discovery opportunities'. Under different circumstances, such opportunities do not exist, and entrepreneurs must 'create' their own products, markets, production methods, and so on, and these may be regarded as 'creation opportunities' (Alvarez and Barney, 2007). This perspective, we believe, takes the discovery metaphor too literally. Kirzner does not mean that opportunities literally are given, objectively, in the environment, independent of human creativity. 'Discovery' is an analytical construct, an instrumental device, not a description of behavior. As Kirzner explains in a 1997 interview:

> I do not mean to convey the idea that the future is a rolled-up tapestry, and we need only to be patient as the picture progressively unrolls itself before our eyes. In fact, the future may be a void. There may be nothing around the corner or in the tapestry. The future has to be created. Philosophically, all this may be so. But it doesn't matter for the sake of the metaphor I have chosen. Ex post we have to recognize that when an innovator has discovered something new, that something was metaphorically waiting to be discovered. But from an everyday point-of-view, when a new gadget is invented, we all say, gee, I can see we needed that. It was just waiting to be discovered. (Kirzner, 1997b)

Notice that Kirzner describes opportunities as 'metaphorically waiting to be discovered', not literally waiting to be discovered. He is not offering a particular ontology or epistemology, just proposing an analytical device, designed for a specific purpose (to understand equilibration).

We have discussed elsewhere the relationship between entrepreneurship and resource ownership (Foss and Klein, 2005: Foss et al., 2007a; Foss et al., 2007b; Klein, 2008a). Kirzner's entrepreneurs do not own capital; they need only be alert to profit opportunities. Because they own no assets, they bear no uncertainty. Critics have seized on this point as a defect in Kirzner's conception. According to this criticism, mere alertness to a profit opportunity is not sufficient for earning profits. To reap financial gain, the entrepreneur must invest resources to realize the discovered profit opportunity. 'Entrepreneurial ideas without money are mere parlor games until the money is obtained and committed to the projects' (Rothbard, 1985, p. 283). Moreover, excluding the few cases where buying low and selling high are nearly instantaneous (say, electronic trading of currencies or commodity futures), even arbitrage transactions require some time to complete. The selling price may fall before the arbitrageur has made his sale, and thus even the pure arbitrageur faces some probability of loss. In Kirzner's formulation, the worst that can happen to an entrepreneur is the failure to discover an existing profit opportunity. Entrepreneurs either earn profits or break even, but it is unclear how they suffer losses.[13]

ENTREPRENEURSHIP AS OPPORTUNITY DISCOVERY

The contemporary opportunity identification literature seeks to build a positive research program by operationalizing the concept of alertness (Busenitz, 1996; Cooper et al., 1995; Demmert and Klein, 2003; Gaglio and Katz, 2001; Kaish and Gilad, 1991; Kitzmann and Schiereck, 2005). How is alertness manifested in action? How do we recognize it, empirically? Can we distinguish 'discovery' from systematic search? What are the psychological characteristics of particularly 'alert' individuals? However, as discussed by Klein (2008a), this positive research program may miss the point of Kirzner's metaphor of entrepreneurial alertness: namely, that it is only a metaphor. Kirzner's aim is not to characterize entrepreneurship, per se, but to explain the tendency for markets to clear. In the Kirznerian system opportunities are (exogenous) arbitrage opportunities and nothing more. Entrepreneurship itself serves a purely instrumental function; it is the means by which Kirzner explains market clearing. As Kirzner (2009, pp. 145–6) explains, reviewing his main contributions and critiquing his own critics:

> [M]y own work has *nothing* to say about the secrets of successful entrepreneurship. My work has explored, not the nature of the talents needed for entrepreneurial success, not any guidelines to be followed by would-be successful entrepreneurs, but, instead, the *nature of the market process set in motion* by the entrepreneurial decisions (both successful and unsuccessful ones!). . . . This paper seeks (a) to identify more carefully the sense in which my work on entrepreneurial theory does *not* throw light on the substantive sources of successful entrepreneurship, (b) to argue that a number of (sympathetic) reviewers of my work have somehow failed to recognize this limitation in the scope of my work (and that these scholars have therefore misunderstood certain aspects of my theoretical system), (c) to show that, despite all of the above, my understanding of the market process (as set in motion by entrepreneurial decisions) *can*, in a significant sense, provide a theoretical underpinning for public policy in regard to entrepreneurship.

Of course, arbitrage opportunities cannot exist in a perfectly competitive general-equilibrium model, so Kirzner's framework assumes the presence of competitive imperfections, in the language of strategic factor markets (Alvarez and Barney, 2004; Barney, 1986). Beyond specifying general disequilibrium conditions, however, Kirzner offers no theory of how opportunities come to be identified, who identifies them, and so on; identification itself is a black box. The claim is simply that outside the Arrow–Debreu world in which all knowledge is effectively parameterized, opportunities for disequilibrium profit exist and tend to be discovered and exploited. In short, what Kirzner calls 'entrepreneurial discovery' is simply that which causes markets to equilibrate.

Contemporary entrepreneurship scholars, considering whether opportunities are objective or subjective (Companys and McMullen, 2007; McMullen and Shepherd, 2006), note that Kirzner tends to treat them as objective. Again, this is true, but misses the point. Kirzner is not making an ontological claim about the nature of profit opportunities per se – not claiming, in other words, that opportunities are, in some fundamental sense, objective – but merely using the concept of objective, exogenously given, but not-yet-discovered opportunities as a device for explaining the tendency of markets to clear. To a certain extent this confusion is caused by the different levels of analysis, Kirzner moving on the level of markets, modern entrepreneurship scholars being concerned with entrepreneurs *per se*. However, this is a case of a fruitful misunderstanding, for the basic notion that opportunity discovery may be taken as the unit of analysis, and that analytical and empirical attention may center on the antecedents to such discovery, has led to a positive research program. This program emphasizes the means by which individuals identify and react to opportunities, relying largely on survey data (Busenitz, 1996; Cooper et al., 1995; Kaish and Gilad, 1991). These studies suggest that founders of new ventures (the operational definition of entrepreneurs) spend more time gathering information, and rely more heavily on unconventional sources of information, than do managers of existing enterprises.

CRITIQUES OF THE DISCOVERY APPROACH

The alertness or discovery perspective faces several challenges, however. First, a precise definition of opportunities has remained elusive. Typically, opportunities are defined very broadly; Shane and Venkataraman's (2000, p. 220) influential paper defines entrepreneurial opportunities as 'those situations in which new goods, services, raw materials, and organizing methods can be introduced and sold at greater than their cost of production.' This involves not only technical skills like financial analysis and market research, but also less tangible forms of creativity, team building, problem solving, and leadership (Hills et al., 1997; Hindle, 2004; Long and McMullan, 1984). It can involve both the recognition of already existing opportunities and the creation, *ex nihilo*, of new opportunities (Alvarez and Barney, 2007). Although value can, of course, be created not only by starting new activities, but also by improving the operation of existing activities, research in opportunity identification tends to emphasize the launching of new ventures (firms, products, or services). As summarized by Shane (2003, pp. 4–5),

> the academic field of entrepreneurship incorporates, in its domain, explanations for why, when and how entrepreneurial opportunities exist; the sources of those opportunities and the forms that they take; the processes of opportunity discovery and evaluation; the acquisition of resources for the exploitation of these opportunities; the act of opportunity exploitation; why, when, and how some individuals and not others discover, evaluate, gather resources for and exploit opportunities; the strategies used to pursue opportunities; and the organizing efforts to exploit them.

A recent debate asks whether opportunities are 'discovered' or 'created'. Alvarez and Barney (2007) distinguish, within the applied entrepreneurship literature, a 'discovery approach', in which entrepreneurial actions are seen as responses to exogenous shocks, and a 'creation approach', in which such actions are taken as endogenous. 'Discovery entrepreneurs' focus on predicting systematic risks, formulating complete and stable strategies, and procuring capital from external sources. 'Creation entrepreneurs', by contrast, appreciate iterative, inductive, incremental decision-making, are comfortable with emergent and flexible strategies, and tend to rely on internal finance. More generally, as noted by McMullen et al. (2007, p. 273), 'some researchers argue that the subjective or socially constructed nature of opportunity makes it impossible to separate opportunity from the individual, [while] others contend that opportunity is as an objective construct visible to or created by the knowledgeable or attuned entrepreneur.'

Klein (2008a) argues that the discovery–creation distinction places too much emphasis on the ontology of the opportunity, and that opportunities should be treated instead as instrumental constructs, as metaphors useful for the economist or management theorist, rather than frameworks for entrepreneurial decision-making itself. In the Knightian approach (as developed in Foss et al., 2007b, and Foss et al., 2007a) opportunities are best characterized as neither discovered nor created, but imagined. The creation metaphor implies that profit opportunities, once the entrepreneur has conceived or established them, come into being, objectively, like a work of art. Creation implies that something is created. There is no uncertainty about its existence or characteristics (though, of course, its market value may not be known until later). By contrast, the concept of opportunity imagination emphasizes that gains (and losses) do not come into being, objectively, until entrepreneurial action is complete (i.e. until final goods and services have been produced and sold).

Another issue relates to entrepreneurial opportunities and profit opportunities more generally. Shane and Venkataraman (2000) define profit opportunities as opportunities to create value by enhancing the efficiency of producing existing goods, services, and processes, reserving the term entrepreneurial opportunities for value creation through 'the discovery of new means–ends frameworks', appealing to the Kirznerian distinction between Robbinsian maximizing and entrepreneurial alertness described above. They may misunderstand Kirzner (and the Austrians more generally) on this point, however. In a world of Knightian uncertainty, all profit opportunities involve decisions for which no well-specified maximization problem is available. Kirzner does not mean that some economic decisions really are the result of Robbinsian maximizing while others reflect discovery. Instead, Kirzner is simply contrasting two methodological constructions for the analysis of human action.

An alternative approach is to focus not on what opportunities 'are', but what opportunities 'do'. Opportunities, in this sense, are treated as a latent construct that is manifested in entrepreneurial action – investment, creating new organizations, bringing products to market, and so on. Empirically, this approach can be operationalized by treating entrepreneurship as a latent variable in a structural-equations framework (Xue and Klein, 2010). Moreover, by treating opportunities as a latent construct, this approach sidesteps the problem of defining opportunities as objective or subjective, real or imagined, and so on. The formation of entrepreneurial beliefs is treated as a potentially interesting psychological problem, but not part of the economic analysis of entrepreneurship. It also avoids thorny questions about whether alertness or judgment is simply luck (Demsetz, 1983), a kind of intuition (Dane and Pratt, 2007), or something else entirely.

If opportunities are inherently subjective, and we treat them as a black box, then the unit of analysis should not be opportunities, but rather some action – in Knightian terms, the assembly of resources in the present in anticipation of (uncertain) receipts in the future. One way to capture the Knightian concept of entrepreneurial action is Casson and Wadeson's notion of 'projects' (Casson and Wadeson, 2007). A project is a stock of resources committed to particular activities for a specified period of time. (Opportunities are defined as potential, but currently inactive, projects.) Focusing on projects, rather than opportunities, implies an emphasis not on opportunity identification, but on opportunity 'exploitation'. More generally, this perspective suggests that entrepreneurship research should focus on the execution of business plans.

Foss et al. (2007b) offer an account of opportunity exploitation that combines the Knightian concept of judgment and the Austrian approach to capital heterogeneity. In Knight's formulation, entrepreneurship represents judgment that cannot be assessed in terms of its marginal product and which cannot, accordingly, be paid a wage (Knight, 1921, p. 311). In other words, there is no market for the judgment that entrepreneurs rely on, and therefore exercising judgment requires the person with judgment to start a firm. Of course, judgmental decision-makers can hire consultants, forecasters, technical experts, and so on. However, in doing so they are exercising their own entrepreneurial judgment. Judgment thus implies asset ownership, for judgmental decision-making is ultimately decision-making about the employment of resources. The entrepreneur's role, then, is to arrange or organize the capital goods he or she owns. As Lachmann (1956, p. 16) puts it: 'We are living in a world of unexpected change; hence capital combinations . . . will be ever changing, will be dissolved and reformed. In this activity, we find the real function of the entrepreneur.'

CONCLUSIONS

The concept of entrepreneurial alertness continues to be one of the most heavily used, and potentially valuable, constructs in entrepreneurship research. It dovetails nicely with ideas from microeconomic theory about equilibration and arbitrage, and it appears to have recognizable empirical analogs in processes of decision-making, evaluation, assessment, environmental recognition, and the like. It is easy to see why the concept of alertness has become foundational in applied entrepreneurship studies.

However, as Kirzner's recent essay (2009) makes clear, the relationship between the theoretical construct of alertness and the applied study of opportunity recognition is subtle and complex. Kirzner (2009) sees his concept of the entrepreneurial market process as relevant to applied work not primarily to management research, but in public policy. After arguing that Schumpeterian creativity can, in an important sense, be subsumed as a category of alertness – even Schumpeter's innovations can, ex post, be seen as improvements that were waiting to be discovered – Kirzner (2009, p. 151) notes that 'the way in which policymakers understand the market economy is likely to carry enormously significant implications for encouragement or discouragement of entrepreneurial creativity.' Specifically, although '[w]e know very little that is systematic about what "switches on" alertness . . . it does seem intuitively obvious that alertness can be "switched off" by the conviction that external intervention will confiscate (wholly or in part) whatever one might notice.'

More generally, it suggests that we can analyze specifically the effects of the competitive, regulatory, and technological environment on entrepreneurial behavior, an approach that is not easily squared with the pure concept of alertness, as Kirzner conceives it. In essence, Kirzner wants to treat alertness as an analytical primitive, and there is indeed very little mention of antecedents to alertness in his work. However, as indicated by the above quotation Kirzner – like contemporary management scholars studying entrepreneurship – does allow antecedents to slip into the analysis. Kirzner has in mind regulation, antitrust, and other government policies that affect business decision-making. However, similar arguments could possibly also be applied to alertness within organizations: the belief that senior managers will appropriate the rent streams created by discovery or creation of new activities or uses of assets by lower-level employees will likely stifle 'entrepreneurial' activity within the firm.

Our own work on entrepreneurship and the firm (Foss and Klein, 2005; Foss et al., 2007a; Foss et al., 2007b; Klein, 2008a) suggests a different way of incorporating Austrian insights in management research, combining the Knight–Mises concept of entrepreneurship as judgment and the Austrian approach to capital heterogeneity. Austrian capital theory, we argue, provides a unique foundation for an entrepreneurial theory of economic organization. Neoclassical production theory, with its notion of capital as a permanent, homogeneous fund of value, rather than a discrete stock of heterogeneous capital goods, is of little help here. Transaction cost, resource-based, and property-rights approaches to the firm do incorporate notions of heterogeneous assets, but they tend to invoke the needed specificities in an ad hoc fashion to rationalize particular trading problems – for transaction cost economics, asset specificity; for capabilities theories, tacit knowledge; and so on. The Austrian approach, as described above, offers a more rigorous and systematic treatment of heterogeneity.

Entrepreneurs, who seek to create or discover new attributes of capital assets (in the sense of Barzel, 1997), will want ownership titles to the relevant assets, both for speculative reasons and for reasons of economizing on transaction costs. These arguments provide room for entrepreneurship that goes beyond deploying a superior combination of capital assets with 'given' attributes, acquiring the relevant assets, and deploying these to producing for a market: entrepreneurship may also be a matter of experimenting with capital assets in an attempt to discover new valued attributes. Such experimental activity may take place in the context of trying out new combinations through the acquisition of or merger with other firms, or in the form of trying out new combinations of assets already under the control of the entrepreneur. Hence we see many fruitful complementarities between the theory of economic organization and Austrian theories of capital heterogeneity and entrepreneurship.

NOTES

1. More specifically: 'The key to understanding the market process is to understand the dynamic character of market competition. But the neoclassical focus on perfect competition as an equilibrium *state of affairs* prevented appreciation of this insight. It was not until Hayek's pioneering, but insufficiently-appreciated work on the dynamically competitive market as a process of mutual discovery, that Austrian economics was able explicitly to grapple with this embarrassing hiatus. It was particularly in the work of Ludwig von Mises that this writer discovered, in the Misesian entrepreneur and in the Misesian dynamically competitive process, what he believed (and believes) to be the true solution. My 1973 work was written in order to spell out this solution' (Kirzner, 2009, p. 147).
2. As Rothbard (1977, p. 16) puts it: why does an entrepreneur borrow at all if in so doing he will bid up the loan rate of interest to the rate of time preference as reflected in his long-run normal rate of profit (or his 'natural rate of interest', to use Austrian terminology)? The reason is that superior forecasters envision making short-run profits whenever the general loan rate is lower than the return they expect to obtain. This is precisely the competitive process, which tends, in the long run, to equalize all natural and loan rates in the time market. Those entrepreneurs 'with superior knowledge and superior foresight,' wrote Fetter, 'are merchants, buying when they can in a cheaper and selling in a dearer capitalization market, acting as the equalizers of rates and prices.'
3. Schumpeter is often classified with the Austrian economists but, despite being trained by Böhm-Bawerk, was most heavily influenced by Walras and is better classified as a neoclassical equilibrium theorist. See also Klein (2008b) on these two strands within the Austrian tradition.
4. Hayek (1968/2002) mentions that competition 'is important primarily as a discovery procedure whereby entrepreneurs constantly search for unexploited opportunities that can also be taken advantage of by others. . . . [This] ability to detect certain conditions . . . can [be used] effectively only when the market tells them what kinds of goods and services are demanded, and how urgently' (Hayek, 1968/2002), that is, how effectively the price system works. Hayek also uses the term 'entrepreneur' in his earlier writings on socialist calculation and capital theory, but he seems to mean simply 'businessman', and does not distinguish sharply among entrepreneurs, managers, capitalists, and other business professionals.
5. 'I have always emphasized that my own contribution is simply an expansion and deepening of insights

articulated by my teacher, Ludwig von Mises' (Kirzner, 2009, p.146). See also Kirzner (1982b) for Kirzner's most extensive reflections on the relations between his and Mises's work.

6. Knight (1921) introduces the concept of judgment to decompose business income into two elements, interest and profit. Interest is a reward for forgoing present consumption, is determined by the relative time preferences of borrowers and lenders, and would exist even in a world of certainty. Profit, by contrast, is a reward for anticipating the uncertain future more accurately than others and exists only in a world of 'true' uncertainty. In such a world, given that production takes time, entrepreneurs will earn either profits or losses based on the differences between factor prices paid and product prices received. This understanding of entrepreneurship is central to Mises's argument that rational economic planning is 'impossible' under socialism (Mises, 1920). Entrepreneurs make production plans based on the current prices of factors of production and the anticipated future prices of consumer goods. What Mises calls 'economic calculation' is the comparison of these anticipated future receipts with present outlays, all expressed in common monetary units. Under socialism, the absence of factor markets, and the consequent lack of factor prices, renders economic calculation – and hence rational economic planning – impossible. Mises's point is that a socialist economy may assign individuals to be workers, managers, technicians, inventors, and the like, but it cannot, by definition, have entrepreneurs, because there are no money profits and losses.

7. Kirzner is careful to distinguish alertness from systematic search, as in Stigler's (1961; 1962) analysis of searching for bargains or for jobs. A nice example is provided by Ricketts (1987, p.58): 'Stigler's searcher decides how much time it is worth spending rummaging through dusty attics and untidy drawers looking for a sketch which (the family recalls) Aunt Enid thought might be by Lautrec. Kirzner's entrepreneur enters a house and glances lazily at the pictures which have been hanging in the same place for years. "Isn't that a Lautrec on the wall?"' See also Kirzner (1997a) for his most extensive discussion of the distinction between 'sheer ignorance' and asymmetric information, and the role of alertness in overcoming the former.

8. For details on Kirzner's treatment of equilibrium see Klein (2008b).

9. See Klein (2008a) for more on the distinction between occupational, structural, and functional approaches to entrepreneurship.

10. O'Driscoll and Rizzo (1985, pp.80–85) argue that plan coordination – they call it Hayekian equilibrium – is not consistently defined in the Austrian literature. On plan coordination see also Salerno (1991), Klein (2008b), and Klein and Briggeman (2009).

11. Lachmann's perspective has generated relatively little attention among management scholars. An exception is Chiles et al. (2007).

12. Note that Lachmann (1986) does allow for temporary market clearing, that is, Marshallian short run equilibria.

13. This has been a critique of Kirzner's work from the beginning (i.e. the publication of Kirzner, 1973). See Salerno (2008) for a stocktaking and assessment of Austrian views of the entrepreneurs, and a summary of some of the early (Austrian) critiques of Kirzner's work.

REFERENCES

Alchian, A. (1950), 'Uncertainty, evolution, and economic theory', *Journal of Political Economy*, **58**, 211–22.

Alvarez, S. and J. Barney (2004), 'Organizing rent generation and appropriation: toward a theory of the entrepreneurial firm', *Journal of Business Venturing*, **19**(5), 621–35.

Alvarez, S.A. and J. Barney (2007), 'Discovery and creation: alternative theories of entrepreneurial action', *Strategic Entrepreneurship Journal*, **1**(1–2), 11–26.

Barney, J. (1986), 'Strategic factor markets: expectations, luck and business strategy', *Management Science*, **42**, 1231–41.

Barzel, Y. (1997), *Economic Analysis of Property Rights*, 2nd edn, Cambridge: Cambridge University Press.

Becker, G.S. (1962), 'Irrational behavior and economic theory', *Journal of Political Economy*, **70**, 1–13.

Bjørnskov, C. and N.J. Foss (2008), 'Economic freedom and entrepreneurial activity: some cross-country evidence', *Public Choice*, **134**(3), 307–28.

Böhm-Bawerk, E. von (1889/1959), *Positive Theory of Capital*, North-Holland, IL: Libertarian Press.

Böhm-Bawerk, E. von (1898), *Karl Marx and the Close of His System*, London: T.F. Unwin.

Busenitz, L.W. (1996), 'Research on entrepreneurial alertness: sampling, measurement, and theoretical issues', *Journal of Small Business Management*, **34**(4), 35–44.

Busenitz, L. and J. Barney (1997), 'Differences between entrepreneurs and managers in large organizations: biases and heuristics in strategic decision-making', *Journal of Business Venturing*, **12**, 9–30.

Cantillon, R. (1755/1931), *Essai sur la nature du commerce en general*, edited by Henry Higgs, London: Macmillan.

Casson, M. and N. Wadeson (2007), 'The discovery of opportunities: extending the economic theory of the entrepreneur', *Small Business Economics*, **28**(4), 285–300.

Chiles, T.H. (2003), 'Process theorizing: too important to ignore in a kaleidic world', *Academy of Management Learning and Education*, **2**(3), 288–91.

Chiles, T.H. and T.Y. Choi (2000), 'Theorizing TQM: an Austrian and evolutionary economics interpretation', *Journal of Management Studies*, **37**(2), 185–212.

Chiles, T.H., A.C. Bluedorn and V.K. Gupta (2007), 'Beyond creative destruction and entrepreneurial discovery: a radical Austrian approach to entrepreneurship', *Organization Studies*, **28**(4), 467–93.

Clark, J.B. (1918), *Essentials of Economic Theory*, New York: Macmillan.

Companys, Y.E. and J.S. McMullen (2007), 'Strategic entrepreneurs at work: the nature, discovery, and exploitation of entrepreneurial opportunities', *Small Business Economics*, **28**(4), 302–22.

Cooper, A.C., T.B. Folta and C.Y. Woo (1995), 'Entrepreneurial information search', *Journal of Business Venturing*, **10**(2), 107–20.

Dane, E. and M. Pratt (2007), 'Exploring intuition and its role in managerial decision-making', *Academy of Management Review*, **32**(1), 33–54.

Demmert, H. and D.B. Klein (2003), 'Experiment on entrepreneurial discovery: an attempt to demonstrate the conjecture of Hayek and Kirzner', *Journal of Economic Behavior and Organization*, **50**(3), 295–310.

Demsetz, H. (1983), 'The structure of ownership and the theory of the firm', *Journal of Law and Economics*, **26**(2), 375–90.

Fetter, F.A. (1905), *The Principles of Economics*, New York: Century Co.

Fetter, F.A. (1915), *Economic Principles*, New York: Century Co.

Fetter, F.A. (1977), *Capital, Interest, and Rent: Essays in the Theory of Distribution* (edited by M.N. Rothbard), Kansas City: Sheed Andrews and McMeel Inc.

Fisher, F.M. (1983), *Disequilibrium Foundations of Equilibrium Economics*, Cambridge: Cambridge University Press.

Foss, N.J. and P.G. Klein (2005), 'Entrepreneurship and the economic theory of the firm: any gains from trade?', in R. Agarwal, S.A. Alvarez and O. Sorenson (eds), *Handbook of Entrepreneurship Research: Disciplinary Perspectives*, New York: Springer, pp. 55–80.

Foss, N.J. and P.G. Klein (2010), 'Austrian economics and the transaction cost approach to the firm', in P.G. Klein and M.E. Sykuta (eds), *The Elgar Companion to Transaction Cost Economics*, Cheltenham, UK and Northampton, MA, USA: Edward Elgar, forthcoming.

Foss, K., N.J. Foss and P.G. Klein (2007a), 'Original and derived judgment: an entrepreneurial theory of economic organization', *Organization Studies*, **28**(12), 1893–1912.

Foss, K., N.J. Foss, P.G. Klein and S.K. Klein (2007b), 'The entrepreneurial organization of heterogeneous capital', *Journal of Management Studies*, **44**(7), 1165–86.

Gaglio, C.M. and J. Katz (2001), 'The psychological basis of opportunity identification: entrepreneurial alertness', *Journal of Small Business Economics*, **16**, 11–95.

Gompers, P.A., J. Lerner and D.S. Scharfstein (2005), 'Entrepreneurial spawning: public corporations and the formation of new ventures, 1986–1999', *Journal of Finance*, **60**(2), 577–614.

Hayek, F.A. (1937), 'Economics and knowledge', in F.A. Hayek (1948), *Individualism and Economic Order*, Chicago: University of Chicago Press.

Hayek, F.A. (1941), *The Pure Theory of Capital*, London: George Routledge and Sons.

Hayek, F.A. (1945), 'The use of knowledge in society', in F.A. Hayek (1948), *Individualism and Economic Order*, Chicago: University of Chicago Press.

Hayek, F.A. (1946), 'The meaning of competition', in F.A. Hayek (1948), *Individualism and Economic Order*, Chicago: University of Chicago Press, pp. 92–106.

Hayek, F.A (1948), *Individualism and Economic Order*, Chicago: University of Chicago Press.

Hayek, F.A. (1968/2002), 'Competition as a discovery procedure', (translation Marcellus Snow), *Quarterly Journal of Austrian Economics*, **5**(3), 9–23.

High, J.C. (1980), 'Maximizing, action, and market adjustment: an inquiry into the theory of economic disequilibrum', PhD Thesis, University of California Los Angeles.

Hill, C.W.L and D.L. Deeds (1996), 'The importance of industry structure for the determination of firm profitability: A neo-Austrian perspective', *Journal of Management Studies*, **33**, 429–51.

Hills, G.E., G.T. Lumpkin and R.P. Singh (1997), 'Opportunity recognition: perceptions and behaviors of entrepreneurs', *Frontiers of Entrepreneurship Research*, **17**, 168–82.

Hindle, K. (2004), 'A practical strategy for discovering, evaluating, and exploiting entrepreneurial opportunities: research-based action guidelines', *Journal of Small Business and Entrepreneurship*, **17**, 267–76.

Jacobson, R. (1992), 'The "Austrian" school of strategy', *Academy of Management Review*, **17**, 782–807.

Kaish, S. and B. Gilad (1991), 'Characteristics of search of entrepreneurs versus executives: sources, interests, general alertness', *Journal of Business Venturing*, **6**(1), 45–61.

Kirzner, I.M. (1962), 'Rational action and economic theory', *Journal of Political Economy*, **70**, 380–85.

Kirzner, I.M. (1973), *Competition and Entrepreneurship*, Chicago: University of Chicago Press.

Kirzner, I.M. (1975), 'Producer, entrepreneur, and the right to property', in S.L. Blumenfeld (ed.), *Property in a Humane Economy*, LaSalle, IL: Open Court.

Kirzner, I.M. (1979a), *Discovery and the Capitalist Process*, Chicago: University of Chicago Press.

Kirzner, I.M. (1979b), 'The perils of regulation: a market process approach', Occasional Paper of the Law and Economics Center, University of Miami School of Law.

Kirzner, I.M. (1982a), 'Competition, regulation, and the market process: an "Austrian" perspective', Cato Policy Analysis No. 18, 30 September.

Kirzner, I.M. (1982b), 'Uncertainty, discovery, and human action: a study of the entrepreneurial profile in the Misesian system', in I.M. Kirzner (ed.), *Method, Process and Austrian Economics: Essays in Honor of Ludwig von Mises*, New York: Lexington Books.

Kirzner, I.M. (1984), 'Prices, the communication of knowledge, and the discovery process', in K.R. Leube and A.H. Zlabinger (eds), *The Political Economy of Freedom: Essays in Honor of F.A. Hayek*, Munich and Vienna: Philosophia Verlag.

Kirzner, I.M. (1985), *Discovery and the Capitalist Process*, Chicago and London: University of Chicago Press.

Kirzner, I.M. (1989), *Discovery, Capitalism and Distributive Justice*, Oxford: Basil Blackwell.

Kirzner, I.M. (1992), *The Meaning of Market Process: Essays in the Development of Modern Austrian Economics*, London: Routledge.

Kirzner, I.M. (1997a), 'Entrepreneurial discovery and the competitive market process: an Austrian approach', *Journal of Economic Literature*, **35**, 60–85.

Kirzner, I.M. (1997b), 'Interview with Israel M. Kirzner', *Austrian Economics Newsletter*, **17**(1).

Kirzner, I.M. (2009), 'The alert and creative entrepreneur: a clarification', *Small Business Economics*, **32**, 145–52.

Kitzmann, J. and D. Schiereck (2005), 'Entrepreneurial discovery and the Demmert/Klein experiment: another attempt at creating the proper context', *Review of Austrian Economics*, **18**(2), 169–78.

Klein, D.B. and J. Briggeman (2009), 'Israel Kirzner on coordination and discovery', *Journal of Private Enterprise*, forthcoming.

Klein, P.G. (2008a), 'Opportunity discovery, entrepreneurial action, and economic organization', *Strategic Entrepreneurship Journal*, **2**(3), 175–90.

Klein, P.G. (2008b), 'The mundane economics of the Austrian school', *Quarterly Journal of Austrian Economics*, **11**(3–4), 165–87.

Knight, F.H. (1921), *Risk, Uncertainty, and Profit*, Chicago, IL: Houghton Mifflin Company.

Lachmann, L.M. (1956), *Capital and Its Structure*, Kansas City, MO: Sheed and Ward.

Lachmann, L.M. (1976), 'On the central concept of Austrian economics: market process', in E.G. Dolan (ed.), *The Foundations of Modern Austrian Economics*, Kansas City, MO: Sheed and Ward.

Lachmann, L.M. (1986), *The Market as an Economic Process*, Oxford: Blackwell.

Langlois, R.N. (1985), 'Knowledge and rationality in the Austrian school: an analytical survey', *Eastern Economic Journal*, **9**, 309–30.

Langlois, R.N. (2001), 'Strategy and the market process: introduction to the special issue', *Managerial and Decision Economics*, **22**, 163–68.

Lazear, E.P. (2004), 'Balanced skills and entrepreneurship', *American Economic Review*, **94**(2), 208–11.

Littlechild, S.C. (1979), 'An entrepreneurial theory of games', *Metroeconomica*, **31**, 145–65.

Littlechild, S.C. and G. Owen (1980), 'An Austrian model of the entrepreneurial market process', *Journal of Economic Theory*, **23**(3), 361–79.

Long, W. and W.E. McMullan (1984), 'Mapping the new venture opportunity identification process', *Frontiers of Entrepreneurship Research*, **4**, 567–90.

McMullen, J.S. and D.A. Shepherd (2006), 'Encouraging consensus-challenging research in universities', *Journal of Management Studies*, **43**(8), 1643–69.

McMullen, J.S., L.A. Plummer and Z.J. Acs (2007), 'What is an entrepreneurial opportunity?', *Small Business Economics*, **28**(4), 273–83.

Menger, C. (1871/1985), *Principles of Economics*, New York: New York University Press.

Mises, L. von (1920/1990), 'Economic calculation in the socialist commonwealth' (translation S. Adler), Auburn, AL: Ludwig von Mises Institute.

Mises, L. von (1922/1936), *Socialism: An Economic and Sociological Analysis*, (translation J. Kahane), London: Jonathan Cape.

Mises, L. von (1949), *Human Action*, New Haven: Yale University Press.

Mises, L. von (1951/1952), 'Profit and loss', in L. von Mises, *Planning for Freedom*, South Holland, IL: Libertarian Press.

O'Driscoll, G.P. and M.J. Rizzo (1985), *The Economics of Time and Ignorance*, Oxford and New York: Basil Blackwell.

Oppers, S.E. (2002), 'The Austrian theory of business cycles: old lessons for modern economic policy?', IMF Working Paper No. 02/2.

Ricketts, M. (1987), *The New Industrial Economics: An Introduction to Modern Theories of the Firm*, New York: St. Martin's Press.

Robbins, L. (1932), *An Essay on the Nature and Significance of Economic Science*, London: Macmillan.

Roberts, P.W. and K.M. Eisenhardt (2003), 'Austrian insights on strategic organization: from market insights to implications for firms', *Strategic Organization*, **1**, 345–52.

Rothbard, M.N. (1962), *Man, Economy, and State: A Treatise on Economic Principles*, Princeton, NJ: Van Nostrand.

Rothbard, M.N. (1977), 'Introduction' to F.A. Fetter, *Capital, Interest, and Rent: Essays in the Theory of Distribution*, Kansas City: Sheed Andrews and McMeel, pp. 1–23.

Rothbard, M.N. (1985), 'Professor Hébert on entrepreneurship', *Journal of Libertarian Studies*, **7**(2), 281–6.

Rothbard, M.N. (1995), *Economic Thought Before Adam Smith. An Austrian Perspective on the History of Economic Thought*, Aldershot, UK and Brookfield, USA: Edward Elgar.

Salerno, J.T. (1991), 'The concept of coordination in Austrian macroeconomics', in R.M. Ebeling (ed.), *Austrian Economics: Perspectives on the Past and Prospects for the Future*, Hillsdale, MI: Hillsdale College Press, pp. 325–45.

Salerno, J.T. (1993), 'Mises and Hayek dehomogenized', *Review of Austrian Economics*, **6**(2), 113–46.

Salerno, J.T. (1999), 'The place of Mises's human action in the development of modern economic thought', *Quarterly Journal of Austrian Economics*, **2**(1), 35–64.

Salerno, J.T. (2008), 'The entrepreneur: real and imagined', *Quarterly Journal of Austrian Economics*, **11**(3–4), 188–207.

Scarf, H.E. (1960), 'Some examples of global instability of the competitive equilibrium', *International Economic Review*, **1**, 157–72.

Selgin, G. (1987), 'Praxeology and understanding: an analysis of the controversy in Austrian economics', *Review of Austrian Economics*, **2**, 19–58.

Shane, S. (2000), 'Prior knowledge and the discovery of entrepreneurial opportunities', *Organization Science*, **11**(4), 448–69.

Shane, S. (2003), *A General Theory of Entrepreneurship. The Individual–Opportunity Nexus*, Cheltenham, UK and Northampton, MA, USA: Edward Elgar.

Shane, S. and S. Venkataraman (2000), 'The promise of entrepreneurship as a field of research', *Academy of Management Review*, **25**(1), 217–26.

Stigler, G.J. (1961), 'The economics of information', *Journal of Political Economy*, **69**, 213–25.

Stigler, G.J. (1962), 'Information in the labor market', *Journal of Political Economy*, **70**(2), 94–105.

Thornton, M. (1999), 'Richard Cantillon: the origins of economic theory', in R.G. Holcombe (ed.), *Fifteen Great Austrian Economists*, Auburn, AL: Mises Institute.

Vaughn, K.I. (1994), *Austrian Economics in America: The Migration of a Tradition*, Cambridge: Cambridge University Press.

Wieser, F. (1914/1927), *Social Economics* (translation A.F. Hinrichs), New York: Adelphi.

Williamson, O.E. (1991), 'Economic institutions: spontaneous and intentional governance', *Journal of Law, Economics, and Organization*, **7**, 159–87.

Xue, J.-H. and P.G. Klein (2010), 'Regional determinants of technology entrepreneurship', *International Journal of Entrepreneurial Venturing*, **1**(3), 291–308.

Yates, A. (2000), 'The knowledge problem, entrepreneurial discovery, and Austrian market process', *Journal of Economic Theory*, **91**, 59–85.

6. Opportunity recognition: evolving theoretical perspectives

Robert A. Baron

INTRODUCTION

Ideas are the beginning of all achievement.

(Bruce Lee)

Every field has, at its core, a set of basic terms – concepts or ideas that play a central role in that field's key activities and in its efforts to understand the phenomena on which it focuses. In physics, such terms include 'matter' and 'energy'; in biology, 'cell' and 'reproduction'; and in psychology, terms such as 'stimulus' and 'behavior' are fundamental. Entrepreneurship, as a field of scholarly activity (Shane and Venkataraman, 2000), is no exception to this basic rule, and among its central terms or concepts are 'opportunity' and 'opportunity recognition'. The centrality of these terms is suggested by the quotation above – words to the effect that all human endeavors, including the formation of new business ventures, begin with ideas – cognitive activity in the minds of specific persons. It is also suggested by the considerably increased volume of research on these topics in recent years. That is a central assumption of the present discussion which, overall, seeks to accomplish two major tasks.

First, basic definitions for these terms will be offered – definitions that closely reflect decades of careful thought by scholars in the field of entrepreneurship. Second, the remainder of the chapter will focus on providing an overview of the development of theoretical perspectives on opportunity recognition within the field of entrepreneurship. Reflecting changes in entrepreneurship itself, these frameworks have become increasingly sophisticated and comprehensive in nature, and the present chapter describes the course of such advances, as well as their implications for ongoing research.

BASIC DEFINITIONS

Many definitions of the term 'opportunity' have been proposed (e.g. Bhave, 1994; Herron and Sapienza, 1992; Kirzner, 1979; Shane, 2003), but careful examination of these contrasting proposals suggests that most include reference to three central characteristics: (1) potential economic value (i.e. the potential to generate profit); (2) newness (i.e. some product, service, technology, etc. that did not exist previously), and (3) perceived desirability (e.g. moral and legal acceptability of the new product or service in society). For the purposes of the present discussion, therefore, a definition derived from these previous views, but also consistent with the emerging cognitive perspective on this issue, is proposed. Specifically, 'opportunity' is defined as perceived means of generating economic value (i.e. profit) that have not previously been exploited, and are not currently being exploited by others, and are perceived, in a given society, as desirable (or, at least, socially acceptable).[1] The means of generating profit include the creation of something new (e.g. new products, services, technologies, markets, or production processes) as well as utilization of existing products, services, technologies, etc. in ways that offer increased potential for generating economic value. An example of this latter form of opportunity would be identifying new uses for an existing product. Note that there is no assumption that perceived opportunities will, in fact, generate profit; rather, opportunities involve the 'perception' by one or more persons that such outcomes can be obtained by certain means.

The definition offered above also suggests that opportunities have a social or societal component: to be a bona fide opportunity, means of generating profit must not only be new, they must also be acceptable to members of the society in which the new ventures are launched and operate. This requirement is included to avoid labeling as opportunities activities that involve new products or services that can potentially generate huge profits, but are inconsistent with, or even inimical to, the norms and values of a society. Although recent evidence suggests that experience in operating ventures that violate societal norms (e.g. new ventures defined as illegal or immoral in a particular society) can contribute to entrepreneurs' human capital (Aidis and van Praag, 2007), it is important to exclude from the concept of business opportunities actions that result in actual harm to a large number of persons, or that violate a society's well-established values. Perhaps a concrete example will help clarify this point.

Imagine, for instance, that a chemist discovers a new chemical that is incredibly addictive; exposure to just a few molecules induces intense cravings for this substance in the persons who encounter it. Further, the chemical has cumulative effects that are truly harmful; over time, continued exposure to it seriously damages the nervous system. In some countries (e.g. those without strict regulation of drugs), the chemist could, if unscrupulous, produce the drug and sell it to an ever-growing number of persons who would become instantly and hopelessly addicted. The chemical would be new and perhaps the means of distributing it would also be novel (e.g. given specific properties of the chemical, it would have to be stored and transported in special ways). Moreover, the potential profits would be enormous. However, labeling this discovery an 'opportunity' would, in the opinion of the present author, render a major disservice to the vast majority of entrepreneurs who, in contrast, work diligently to bring useful and/or beneficial products and services to market.

To recap, then, for the purposes of the present discussion, 'opportunity' will be defined in terms of the three criteria noted above: potential profitability, newness, and social desirability in a given society.

If opportunity is defined in this manner, then within the present context, the term 'opportunity recognition' refers to the cognitive process (or processes) through which individuals conclude that they have identified an opportunity. The processes that lead to such cognition can be relatively automatic in nature (i.e. rapid, requiring minimal effort, difficult to express in words) or relatively controlled in nature (i.e. slower, more effortful, and readily expressed verbally; e.g. Schneider and Shiffrin, 1977). However, ultimately, the outcome of this process is the conscious thought that a specific and describable business opportunity has been identified. It is important to note, as emphasized by Ardichvili et al. (2003) and McMullen and Shepherd (2006), that opportunity recognition is only the initial step in a continuing process. As such, it is distinct both from detailed evaluation of the feasibility and potential economic value of identified opportunities and from active steps to develop these opportunities through new ventures. Further discussion of these aspects of the process are presented in a later section. Having offered these basic definitions, I turn next to an overview of theoretical development with respect to the process of opportunity recognition.

THEORIES OF OPPORTUNITY RECOGNITION: FROM ALERTNESS AND EXPERIENCE TO UNDERLYING COGNITIVE PROCESSES

If opportunities involve ideas (e.g. conceptions of potentially valuable new products or services), then the words of Bruce Lee (presented at the start of this chapter) do ring true: in a sense, everything else in the new venture creation process derives from this beginning. In other words, entrepreneurs' decisions to found new ventures often stem from their belief that they have identified an opportunity no one else has yet recognized, and can benefit from being first to enter the marketplace with this new product or service (Durand and Courerderoy, 2001). Because opportunity recognition is often the start of the entrepreneurial process, it is not at all surprising that it has long been a central concept in the field of entrepreneurship. Until recently, however, little effort was made to examine it as a 'process' – a series of events or occurrences that, ultimately, generate identification of specific business opportunities. Rather, opportunities were defined largely in economic terms: any idea for a new product, service, raw material, market, or production process that can be successfully exploited so as to generate economic benefits for stakeholders was viewed as constituting an opportunity. Further, the approach to understanding opportunity recognition was, to some extent, purely empirical in nature. Often, research on this topic simply sought to establish that, for instance, individuals with a broad range of work experience, or those with a high level of technical expertise, are more likely to recognize opportunities in certain domains than persons lower on these dimensions (see e.g. Shane, 2003). Efforts to understand the processes involved – cognitive or otherwise – that underlie these relationships were relatively rare (e.g. Gaglio and Katz, 2001 provides one notable exception). In other words, an over-arching theoretical framework was not an integral part of this early research. This changed when, primarily in work by Shane (2000; 2003) a basic unifying principle was identified: information. In essence, it was suggested that having more information or better access to information than other persons, was a key foundation of opportunity recognition. This focus on information developed in several different directions, including the role of active search for information, being particularly alert to specific kinds of information, and having extensive knowledge in a field or industry – knowledge that provided entrepreneurs with an initial 'edge' they use in recognizing potentially valuable opportunities (e.g. Ardichvili et al., 2003; McMullen and Shepherd, 2006). It is discussed in detail here because in an important sense, it paved the way for efforts to apply the findings and principles of cognitive science to the task of understanding the essence of opportunity identification (see below).

Access to Information and its Effective Use as the Basis for Opportunity Recognition

A key question that has emerged and re-emerged in efforts to understand opportunity recognition is this: why are some people and not others able to discover specific opportunities? If we can understand why certain people recognize opportunities that others overlook, it can be reasoned, this will potentially provide key insights into how this process takes place – and how, perhaps, it can be enhanced. A focus on information, both access to it and its effective use, provides important insights into this question, but only, as will be noted below, initial insights of this type.

Greater access to information
With respect to greater access to information, it has been suggested – and confirmed in many studies – that specific persons gain an advantage with respect to opportunity recognition by having enhanced access to relevant information. They gain this edge in several different ways. For example, they may have jobs that provide them with information 'on the cutting edge' that is not widely available to others. Jobs in research and development or marketing appear to be especially valuable in this respect.

Another way in which individuals gain superior access to information is through varied work and life experience – factors that, because they contribute to individuals' knowledge base, also increase their creativity (Blanchflower and Oswald, 1998). Finally, entrepreneurs often gain enhanced access to information through a large social network (Ozgen and Baron, 2007). Other people often serve as a valuable source of information, and frequently the information they provide cannot be acquired easily in any other way.

Superior utilization of information
Greater access to valuable information is only the beginning of the process, however. It was further suggested, in early theorizing, that entrepreneurs who recognize opportunities not only have greater access to information than other persons, they are also better at 'using' such information. In other words, cognitive skills or abilities also enter the picture. As a result of having greater access to information, some persons have richer and better-integrated stores of knowledge than other persons – for instance, more information (retained in memory) about markets and how to serve them. This, in turn, enhances their ability to interpret and use new information because, not only do they have more information at their disposal, it is also better organized, too. Large quantities of well-organized information play a key role in creativity, so it is not at all surprising that persons who identify opportunities have also been found to possess richer and better organized stores of information (e.g. Sternberg, 2004).

Other aspects of cognition relating to the effective utilization of information play a role. For instance, persons who found new ventures tend to be higher in intelligence than persons who do not, for example managers (Shane, 2003). Moreover, entrepreneurs have been found to be higher in intelligence even when this was measured many years in the past – when they were, on average, 12 years old (Van Praag and Cramer, 2001) Additional evidence suggests that entrepreneurs are especially likely to be higher than other persons in 'practical intelligence' – the ability to solve the varied problems of everyday life (Sternberg, 2004). Finally, and again, far from surprising, entrepreneurs are higher in creativity than other persons (Baron and Shane, 2008). In other words, they are more adept at combining the information at their disposal into something new.

In sum, it seems clear that a key component in opportunity recognition is 'information' – greater access to it, and better cognitive tools for putting it to good use.

The Search for Information: Active Searches, Alertness, Prior Knowledge, and Social Networks

Although access to information plays a key role in opportunity recognition, three other factors were soon identified as important in theoretical proposals concerning the nature of opportunity identification. These included engaging in an 'active search' for, 'alertness' to opportunities (i.e. the capacity to recognize them when they emerge), and 'prior knowledge' of a market, industry, or customers, and information provided by social networks, as foundations for recognizing new opportunities in these areas. Although at first glance these factors are diverse, they are related by common interest in the search for information. Research findings have provided support for the importance of all three factors. For instance, with respect to an active search for opportunities, many studies indicate that entrepreneurs are more likely than other persons (e.g. managers) to engage in such activities (Kaish and Gilad, 1991). Additional evidence for the importance of active search is provided by an intriguing study in which a group of highly successful entrepreneurs (all belonging to the Chicago area Entrepreneurship Hall of Fame) were compared with other entrepreneurs who were not so eminent (Hills and Shrader, 1998). The highly successful entrepreneurs were found to be less likely to identify their opportunities from public information such as magazines, newspapers, and trade publications, and more likely to seek opportunities in more exclusive sources, such as personal contacts and specialized publications. These and other findings indicate that actively searching for information is an important factor in the recognition of many opportunities by entrepreneurs, although, as noted by several authors, such searches must be carefully directed to succeed (Fiet et al., 2004). In some cases, these searches can proceed in a relatively 'automatic' manner rather than in a conscious and carefully directed one.

Alertness, in contrast, emphasizes the fact that opportunities can sometimes be recognized by individuals who are *not* actively searching for them, but who possess 'a unique preparedness to identify them . . .' when they appear (Kirzner, 1985, p. 48). Kirzner, who first introduced this term into the entrepreneurship literature, defined it as referring to 'alertness to changed conditions or to overlooked possibilities.' What are the foundations of entrepreneurial alertness? It has been suggested that alertness rests, at least in part, on cognitive capacities possessed by individuals – capacities such as high intelligence and creativity (Shane, 2003). These capacities help entrepreneurs to identify new solutions to market and customer needs in existing information, and to imagine new products and services that do not currently exist.

Systematic evidence for the importance of cognitive processes in entrepreneurial alertness has been obtained in several studies. For instance, as noted earlier, intelligence has been found to be linked to founding new ventures (De Wit, 1993). Creativity, another aspect of cognition, has also been found to play a role in alertness; entrepreneurs tend to score higher on various tests of creativity than other persons (Fraboni and Saltstone, 1990). Additional findings indicate that other personal characteristics, too, promote alertness. Optimism – the belief that events will generally result in favorable outcomes – has been found to be positively linked to opportunity recognition (Krueger and Brazael, 1994), and, more recently, to actual performance of new ventures (Hmieleski and Baron, in press). Perceptions of risk, too, may be important, because individuals who perceive high levels of risk in many situations may be reluctant to view almost any idea as a bona fide opportunity (Stewart and Roth, 2001).

A third factor that was suggested as important in theoretical perspectives that emphasized the role of information in opportunity recognition is prior knowledge of a market or industry. Much evidence offered support for this view, suggesting that information gathered through rich and varied life experience (especially, through varied business and work experience) can be a major 'plus' for entrepreneurs in terms of recognizing potentially profitable opportunities. For example, it has been found that prior knowledge of customer needs and ways to meet them greatly enhances entrepreneurs' ability to provide innovative solutions to these problems – in other words, to identify potentially valuable business opportunities (Shane, 2000).

Finally, a very different type of factor, the breadth of entrepreneurs' social networks, was also included in theoretical frameworks emphasizing the importance of information in opportunity recognition. Specifically, it was suggested that the broader the entrepreneurs' social networks (i.e. the more people they know and with whom they have relationships), and the more conferences and professional meetings they attend, the more opportunities they would identify. This suggestion, too, has been confirmed by many studies (e.g. Aldrich and Kim, 2007; Ozgen and Baron, 2007). Social networks are an important source of information for entrepreneurs, and as such, often provide the 'raw materials' on which opportunity recognition rests.

In sum, considerable evidence suggested that a theoretical perspective on opportunity recognition that emphasized the importance of information – both access to it and its effective use – was both useful and accurate. As useful as it is, however, this perspective generally devotes very little attention to the key question of how opportunity recognition actually occurs – what cognitive processes underlie the emergence, in the minds of specific entrepreneurs, of ideas for new products or services? This question, in turn, derives from the basic assumption that recognition of specific opportunities is an event that occurs primarily in the minds of individual entrepreneurs. Although information can – and often is – shared or exchanged, and various events and trends in markets, technology, and government policies (to mention just a few variables) can be readily observed by many persons, it is often just one or a few individuals who move from these external conditions and changes to the formulation of cognitive representations that constitute recognized opportunities. If this perspective is adopted, an important route for enriching and expanding theoretical frameworks concerning opportunity recognition becomes available: adaptation of existing, and often well-validated theories of human cognition to the task of understanding opportunity recognition. It is to these recent developments that we turn next. Before doing so, however, the historical foundations of the cognitive perspective will be briefly reviewed.

Historical Roots of the Cognitive Perspective

Before considering applications of cognitive theory to understanding opportunity recognition, it is useful, given the focus of this volume, to briefly consider the historical roots of this theory. In fact, the term 'cognitive perspective' is more appropriate to the present discussion than 'cognitive theory', because this perspective actually encompasses many different theories, most of them focused on specific aspects of human cognition such as memory, information processing, decision making, and problem solving, to name just a few (e.g. Matlin, 2004). Notably, the pendulum of scientific opinion concerning the usefulness or appropriateness of efforts to understand human cognition has swung widely – one might say 'wildly' – in the development of psychology and other disciplines that focus on human behavior and the human mind (Schultz and Schultz, 2007).

Initially, the field of psychology was identified largely with efforts to understand human cognition. More specifically, one group of early psychologists, the 'structuralists' (e.g. Wilhelm Wundt), suggested that the newly emerging field of psychology should focus on efforts to understand the structure of the human mind – the basic components of which consciousness is constructed. They argued that even complex cognitive phenomena such as problem solving and creativity are based on 'mental structures' composed of simpler cognitive elements – for instance, sensations, associations, and volitions. In order to identify these components and develop a broad 'roadmap' of the human mind, structuralists often used the method of introspection, careful self-examination of conscious experience by objective observation, often performed by individuals trained in this method.

Unfortunately, despite amazing diligence in their pursuit of these goals, the structuralists' approach ultimately seemed, to most psychologists, to be a dead-end, producing nothing of concrete or lasting value. This set the stage for what is now known as 'radical behaviorism', the most famous proponent of which was John B. Watson. Watson and other behaviorists concluded that because cognitive events are hidden from direct view, they can never form the basis for a scientific field of psychology. Thus, they totally rejected the structuralists' conception of the nature of psychology as an independent discipline. Rather, behaviorists contended, overt behavior – which can be seen and, even more importantly, precisely measured – is the appropriate focus of a scientific field of psychology. The behaviorist view became tremendously popular, and prevailed in the young field of psychology for several decades – until, in fact, the 1950s. During this period, psychologists directed little, if any, attention to cognitive processes we now recognize as crucial to all aspects of human existence – memory, judgment, reasoning, problem-solving, and language.

It became increasingly clear, however, that although cognitive processes and events could not be observed directly, they could be studied objectively and systematically. What was required was the development of indirect measures of these events. For example, the basic nature of memory could be investigated by exposing individuals to verbal information they had never encountered previously (e.g. nonsense syllables). Further, measures such as reaction time (e.g. the time required to respond to various stimuli) could, especially with advances in electronics that made it possible to measure this in milliseconds, provide the external indices of internal cognitive processes that behaviorists demanded. The result of these changes was growing interest, in psychology and other fields, in key aspects of human cognition. In fact, progress in understanding such central topics as memory and language development proceeded so rapidly, that by the 1970s, psychology and other fields were experiencing a 'cognitive revolution' – an expansion of a cognitive perspective to encompass virtually all aspects of human behavior. For instance, in social psychology (and soon afterwards, in the management fields of organizational behavior and human resource management), a cognitive perspective strongly influenced – and added to – knowledge concerning social perception (for example how we perceive and seek to understand other persons), attitude change and persuasion, group processes (such as group decision making), and even human aggression (as in attributions concerning provocations from others) (Baron et al., 2009).

Further rapid progress in converting inner cognitive processes into events that can be observed and measured has come, in recent years, as a result of the development of techniques for measuring neural activity in human brains as individuals engage in various cognitive tasks. PET scans, MRI, and other techniques developed initially for medical uses were soon pressed into service in research designed to reveal the physiological and neural foundations of cognition.

The ultimate result of all these historical trends and developments is that at present, the cognitive perspective is being applied to a very wide range of phenomena, including, as described in more detail in the next section, opportunity recognition. As such, its value is so widely recognized that this issue is no longer a topic of debate. Indeed, at present, researchers and theorists in many different fields, from psychology, cognitive science and other social sciences (e.g. economics and sociology), through many branches of management, could no more imagine eliminating this perspective from their work than they could imagine deleting statistical procedures from their efforts to interpret their data. Given this current state of affairs, it is not at all surprising that a cognitive perspective has been widely adopted in entrepreneurship theory and research (e.g. Mitchell et al., 2007). The next section describes how this perspective – and specific aspects of it – can add to our understanding of one central aspect of entrepreneurship: the identification of new business opportunities.

APPLYING COGNITIVE THEORIES TO THE PROCESS OF OPPORTUNITY RECOGNITION

If opportunity recognition is viewed primarily as a cognitive process, then three key questions arise. (1) What is the process (or processes) through which opportunities are initially identified? (2) Once individuals have perceived what they believe to be an opportunity, how do they decide whether this opportunity is real – a bona fide business opportunity worthy of further consideration – or a potential 'dead-end' that will not yield projected economic benefits? (3) What skills or cognitive frameworks play a role in opportunity recognition? In other words, what frameworks, acquired through experience, contribute to the capacity to perceive connections among highly diverse conditions and changes?

These questions will now be considered in the context of major cognitive theories: models of pattern recognition, which relate closely to the issue of how information is organized in semantic memory, the memory system that retains general information about the world, and theories concerning the decision mechanisms through which individuals conclude that the patterns they have perceived are, or are not, sufficiently clear to be viewed as actual opportunities. In discussing these decision mechanisms, the relevance of signal detection theory (e.g. Swets, 1992) and regulatory focus theory (e.g. Higgins, 2006) will be explored in more detail.

Pattern Recognition: Opportunities as Complex, Discernible Patterns

In cognitive science, 'perception' refers to the complex process through which we interpret information brought to us by our senses and integrate it with information already stored in memory (e.g. Baddeley, 1997). To the extent that opportunities exist in the external world as complex patterns of observable stimuli, perception must, logically, play a role in opportunity recognition. Presumably, there is a pattern of observable events or stimuli in the external world that entrepreneurs can notice or perceive; whether this pattern is or is not recognized is, in a sense, the central question of opportunity recognition. Basic research on perception refers to this task as 'object' or 'pattern recognition' (e.g. Matlin, 2004), and it involves a process through which specific persons perceive complex and seemingly unrelated events or stimuli as constituting 'identifiable patterns'. In essence, it involves recognizing links between apparently unrelated trends, changes, and events – links suggestive of patterns that connect them together. The patterns suggested by these links or connections then become 'figure' instead of undifferentiated (and often overlooked) 'ground' (i.e. background). As applied to opportunity recognition, then, pattern recognition involves instances in which specific individuals 'connect the dots' – perceive links between seemingly unrelated events and changes. The patterns they perceive then become the basis for identifying new business opportunities. In the discussion that follows, the potentially important role of pattern recognition in opportunity identification will be described. Before turning to that task, however, it is useful to pause to briefly consider the origins of this particular cognitive theory.

Historical Foundations of Modern Pattern Recognition Theories

Early research on perception was focused on determining the limits and parameters of 'sensation' – the sensitivity of our various senses (vision, hearing, touch, etc.) to physical energy in the external world (Schultz and Schultz, 2007). Thus, most early research was focused on establishing 'thresholds' in each sensory modality. In other words, initial research focused on such questions as, 'How much physical energy is required for individuals to accurately report the presence of some stimulus – a light, a sound, an odor, etc?' and then, somewhat later, 'How large a difference, physically, must exist between two stimuli in order for them to be perceived as different?' These were important questions, but they did not address the question of how we interpret such sensory input in order to construct a complex and sophisticated view of the world. We do not, in general, perceive the external environment as consisting of discrete stimuli (or packets of energy). Rather, we perceive it as organized and meaningful, and the process through which we combine sensory input into such interpretations is generally termed 'perception' (e.g. Wolfe et al., 2008).

Growing recognition that perception involves active cognitive processes was advanced eloquently by a group of German psychologists known, collectively, as the 'Gestalt psychologists'. As the word 'gestalt', a German word that means a set of items perceived as a whole, suggests, these psychologists noted that our perceptions of the external world do not consist of individual sensations, but rather, reflect complex combinations of such sensory input. Thus, the 'whole' – our understanding of the world around us – is indeed greater than the sum of its sensory parts. The Gestalt psychologists also called attention to the fact that perceptions are organized – they follow basic principles that, in a sense, make the task of understanding the environments in which we live, more efficient. This is certainly not the place to examine all the principles or organization Gestalt psychologists established, but perhaps it is useful to briefly mention just a few of these principles, which were carefully confirmed in extensive research: the law of similarity – the more similar stimuli are, the more likely they are to be grouped together in our perceptions; nearness – the closer, physically, stimuli are, the more likely they are to be grouped together; and the law of closure – in our minds, we tend to 'complete' incomplete patterns, sometimes 'seeing' stimuli that are not objectively present. In other words, we fill in missing parts in order to create unified, interpretable perceptions. In addition, the Gestalt movement called attention to the important distinction between figure and ground – distinct shapes or patterns which stand out against less differentiated background.

The principles established by Gestalt psychologists (especially figure/ground relationships) led logically to another historical development: efforts to understand precisely how distinct events, objects, or stimuli are cognitively linked together into 'emergent patterns'. Several different models of this process of pattern recognition have been suggested, and as noted below, they are directly relevant to the process of opportunity recognition. The two models of pattern recognition for which there is currently most evidence will now be described.

Theories of Pattern Recognition

How, precisely, does pattern recognition occur? Many different models of this process exist, but all agree on the following basic point: individuals notice various events in the external world (e.g. changes in technology, markets, and government policies) and then utilize cognitive frameworks they have acquired through past experience to determine whether these events are related in any way – whether, in short, they form a discernible pattern. Different models focus on contrasting kinds of cognitive frameworks, but the process is much the same in all of them.

Prototype models

One widely accepted model of pattern recognition suggests that individuals employ 'prototypes' as a basis for recognizing patterns. Prototypes are idealized representations of the most typical member of a category (i.e. a class of objects or events that seem to belong together). Basically, newly encountered events or trends are compared with existing prototypes to determine whether they belong to specific categories or can be seen as connected in some manner. For instance, most people possess a prototype for 'vehicle'. This mental framework is broad enough so that everything from a huge truck to a bicycle or even an elevator can be recognized as a vehicle, while other objects that do not match this prototype well (e.g. stairs or roller skates) are excluded. Prototypes seem to represent the modal or most frequently experienced combination of attributes associated with an object or pattern. So, for example, the prototype of 'vehicle' would probably include such attributes as a mechanism for achieving movement, some kind of control gear, some means of holding or securing passengers, and so on.

Applying prototype models to opportunity recognition, entrepreneurs may use prototypes as a means for identifying patterns among seemingly unrelated events or trends. For instance, consider a physician engaged in medical research. Because of extensive on-the-job experience, this individual has a clearly developed prototype for 'effective treatment' of various diseases (e.g. the treatment is safe, it can be used ethically with patients, and it enhances recovery from the illness). Further, this prototype may be especially clear for illnesses in which the physician specializes – ones with which she or he has had considerable experience. Now, imagine that this physician reads an article about a new advance in scientific knowledge concerning a basic physiological process – a process that is suspected to play a role in certain diseases. In addition, the physician knows, from actual experience, that existing treatments for these diseases have major side effects. Using her prototype of 'effective treatment' and perhaps other prototypes as well (e.g. prototypes concerning the nature of a given disease and how it develops), she now recognizes potential links between the new scientific advance and potential treatments for a specific illness. In other words, her prototypes help her to perceive an emergent pattern in these diverse events. She also realizes that if these perceived links are confirmed, this will suggest ways of developing new drugs effective in treating this illness. In short, she has noticed this possibility (i.e. opportunity) because prototypes she possesses have helped her to do so – to notice an emergent pattern among seemingly diverse and independent events.

Much evidence suggests that individuals do indeed form prototypes and that once they exist, these cognitive frameworks are employed in many ways. For instance, individuals often use them for perceiving patterns in diverse and seemingly unrelated events or trends. Used in this manner, prototypes may well play an important role in the process of opportunity recognition.

Exemplar models

A very different model of pattern recognition emphasizes the importance of specific knowledge rather than idealized prototypes. Such 'exemplar models' (Hahn and Chater, 1997) suggest that as individuals encounter new events or stimuli, they compare them with specific examples (i.e. exemplars) of relevant concepts already stored in memory. For instance, a physician's concept of 'effective treatment' for a given kind of disease would not consist solely of an idealized representation of the most typical 'effective treatment' she or he can imagine (a prototype); rather, it would also include numerous examples of 'effective treatments' the physician has actually encountered, exemplars that vary in many respects (e.g. exemplars of excellent treatments with few negative side effects as well as very poor ones that are not highly effective and that do involve negative side effects). Exemplar models seem especially relevant to opportunity recognition because they do not require the construction of prototypes. Rather, individuals simply compare newly encountered events or stimuli with examples of a given concept already present in memory.

Overall, research in cognitive science suggests that both prototype and exemplar models may be necessary to fully understand how individuals notice emergent patterns in diverse and apparently unrelated events or changes (Nosofsky and Palmieri, 1998), but further, detailed examination of the evidence pointing to this conclusion is beyond the scope of the present discussion. Suffice it to say, therefore, that given the powerful and pervasive role of pattern recognition in many aspects of perception and cognition, it seems reasonable to suggest that this process plays an important role in opportunity recognition too (Baron, 2006). Overall, the cognitive frameworks individuals construct through experience (e.g. prototypes and exemplars) may provide the basis for identifying emergent patterns, and in at least some instances, these patterns then suggest new business opportunities.

Theories of pattern recognition are elegant and offer important insights into a basic perceptual process. But are they directly applicable to understanding the nature of opportunity recognition? Several lines of evidence suggest such relevance, and it is to this information that we turn next.

Evidence that Pattern Recognition Plays a Role in Opportunity Identification

Several lines of evidence suggest that pattern recognition may indeed play a key role in opportunity recognition. First, it is clear that many opportunities exist for years before they are noticed and developed. For instance, consider wheeled luggage of the type that is now used by a large majority of all air travelers. Such luggage was used for decades by air flight crews before it was introduced into the market for general sale. Why? Perhaps because no one 'connected the dots' between several seemingly unrelated, but pertinent trends: a large increase in the number of passengers, growing problems with checked luggage, expansion in the size of airports, and so on. Once these trends were linked into a unified pattern within the minds of several different entrepreneurs, a product that would help meet the needs of a large and growing market was suggested. Once it appeared, it quickly dominated the market for luggage and drove earlier models to extinction.

Similarly, there is a large body of evidence in cognitive science suggesting that pattern recognition is a basic aspect of our efforts to understand the world around us. That is, we do indeed expend considerable effort searching for patterns among various events or trends in the external world. To the extent that opportunity recognition also involves perceiving links or connections between seemingly independent events or trends, it may be closely related to this basic perceptual process.

Third, empirical evidence exists indicating that predictions derived from models of pattern recognition are accurate and that, therefore, such models offer important insights into the nature of this process (e.g. Baron, 2006; Baron and Ensley, 2006). This evidence will be reviewed below, but before describing it, another important issue relating to opportunity identification will be examined.

Opportunities: Discovered or Created?

Throughout this discussion, it has been assumed that opportunities exist in the external world and are recognized or discovered by entrepreneurs who have the cognitive equipment (i.e. the experience-based cognitive frameworks) needed to accomplish this task. Although existing theories differ on the mechanisms that play a role in this process, most agree that it is one of 'discovery' or 'identification', and this, of course, is the guiding principle in efforts to apply theories of pattern recognition to this task. It is important to note, however, that a sharply contrasting view also exists. Several scholars (e.g. Alvarez and Barney, 2005; 2007) have proposed that opportunities are not so much discovered as created. They contend that entrepreneurs, by their actions, actually 'build the mountains' – create the opportunities they then exploit. In other words, opportunities do not exist independent of entrepreneurs (as, for instance, mountains do); rather they emerge as entrepreneurs begin to act on, and within, their environments.

This perspective certainly has appeal; growing evidence indicates that only rarely do entrepreneurs discover an opportunity and proceed to develop or exploit it in the ways they initially plan. Rather, the process is often one that evolves as the nature of the opportunities in question become clear, and sometimes change radically over time (e.g. as a result of the actions of competitors or shifts in markets, demographics or technology). Recognizing this fact, many entrepreneurs report that they truly 'make it up as they go along'. Although they begin with relatively clear ideas about what they want to accomplish and the kind of products or services they wish to bring to market, they soon change their goals, business models, and strategies in response to an ever-changing and always complex environment.

The fact that these changes occur does not, however, offer a compelling case for the view that opportunities are created rather than discovered. In most instances, entrepreneurs do not begin the process until they have some idea of the products or services they believe to be new and potentially profitable. Certainly, their ideas about the nature of these new products and services do change, and the new ventures they launch, too, are often transformed as entrepreneurs adapt to ever-changing circumstances. Still, it appears that there is at least some initial act of discovery or identification – some kind of 'connect the dots' phenomenon – that underlies the entire process.

Overall, it is suggested here that there may not be a strong or rigid line between 'discovery' and 'creation', where opportunities are concerned. One can argue that even if opportunities exist in the external world as something to be discovered, they do not really take form until one or more persons perceive their existence – until entrepreneurs connect or link seemingly disparate and unrelated events into meaningful patterns that then suggest new products or services. So, in essence, opportunities are both 'discovered' to the extent that the potential for them is generated by changes in the external environment, and 'created', because it is only when these trends and changes coalesce within the minds of individual entrepreneurs that concrete ideas, worthy of overt action, emerge. Hence, for the remainder of this discussion, I will assume that opportunities are both discovered and created, and will move forward from that assumption.

We turn next, therefore, to another important question. Once entrepreneurs conclude that they have identified an opportunity, how do they then decide whether this opportunity is real – that is, worth pursuing or exploiting?

Pattern Verification: Are the Perceived Patterns Real?

As anyone who has ever failed to notice a stop sign or another vehicle while driving can attest, perception is a probabilistic process. Although some stimuli in the external world are so clear or strong that they will be recognized by virtually everyone, many others are weaker and less distinct, so that recognizing them is far less certain. Moreover, as a result of underlying biological processes, sensitivity to external stimuli varies over time, so that a specific individual may perceive a given stimulus at one time, but fail to perceive the same stimulus at another time. These principles also apply to pattern recognition. Although some patterns are so clear as to leave little room for error, many others are far more subtle and difficult to observe. This suggests that in many instances, individuals will be uncertain as to whether they have, or have not, perceived a pattern constituting a business opportunity. How do they then decide whether the pattern they have tentatively identified is indeed real – close enough to their concept of 'business opportunity' to warrant further consideration? In other words, how do they then verify the patterns they think they have observed? Several cognitive theories are directly relevant to this task.

One such theory, signal detection theory (Swets, 1992), takes careful account of the fact that whenever individuals attempt to determine whether a stimulus is present or absent, four possible outcomes exist: (1) the stimulus is actually present and the perceiver recognizes this fact (a 'hit' or correct identification); (2) the stimulus is present but the perceiver fails to recognize it (a 'miss'); (3) the stimulus is absent and the perceiver concludes, erroneously, that it is present (a 'false alarm'); and (4) the stimulus is absent and the perceiver correctly concludes that it is absent (a 'correct negative' or 'correct rejection').

The theory further notes that many factors determine the relative rate at which individuals experience hits, misses, false alarms, and correct rejections in any given situation. Some of these relate to the properties of the stimuli themselves (e.g. the stronger the stimulus, in physical terms, the easier it is to be certain that it is present). Additional factors, in contrast, relate to the current state of the perceiver (e.g. is this person fatigued? highly or weakly motivated to be alert?).

Still other factors involve the subjective criteria perceivers apply to the task. Consider the situation faced by an entrepreneur, who believes that she has identified an opportunity for a profitable new venture. The venture is one that she can start in her spare time and for which little or no capital is needed. As a result, she may set her subjective criterion for concluding 'This is a good business opportunity' quite low: the costs of a false alarm are minimal (a little wasted time and effort) relative to the potential gains of a hit.

In contrast, consider another entrepreneur who has recognized an opportunity that cannot be pursued on a part-time basis and for which large amounts of start-up capital are required. Under these circumstances, the entrepreneur will probably set her criterion for concluding 'This is a good opportunity' somewhat higher. The costs of a false alarm are potentially very high and potential rewards are reduced by the large proportion of the business that will be owned by investors. In short, potential costs and benefits of starting a new venture determine where prospective entrepreneurs will set their criteria for concluding that an opportunity they have perceived is real and therefore worthy of further consideration.

Signal detection theory also offers additional insights into the nature of this process. For example, it suggests that individuals may differ greatly with respect to sensitivity – the ability to distinguish between situations in which the crucial stimulus (i.e. a pattern suggesting existence of an opportunity) is present and ones in which it is not. What are the origins of such differences? A cognitive perspective suggests that they may involve the knowledge structures on which individuals rely in identifying the complex patterns that constitute opportunities: the accuracy and clarity of their prototypes or the range and content of their exemplars for the concept 'business opportunity'. If this is indeed so, then research designed to compare the prototypes and exemplars of highly experienced entrepreneurs with those of less experienced ones might well reveal intriguing differences.

Applied to entrepreneurship, and the process of opportunity recognition, signal detection theory further suggests that whether entrepreneurs set their subjective criteria for concluding 'This is a real opportunity' relatively low or relatively high may also be influenced by other factors, such as their motives (Baron, 2002). For example, entrepreneurs who are strongly motivated to minimize risks, and to avoid pursuing false alarms, may set their subjective criteria relatively high, whereas those who are relatively tolerant of risk and more concerned about overlooking bona fide opportunities may set their criteria somewhat lower (see e.g. Busenitz and Barney, 1997; Krueger and Dickson, 1994; Stewart and Roth, 2001). Similarly, entrepreneurs who are high in certain personal characteristics (e.g. optimism) may set their subjective criteria low, with the result that they experience many false alarms. Interestingly, research findings suggest that entrepreneurs are generally more subject to an optimistic bias than other persons (e.g. Busenitz and Arthurs, 2006); this leads to the prediction that they tend to set their subjective criteria for identifying business opportunities relatively low – unless other factors counter or reverse this tendency.

Another cognitive theory that has recently received much attention, regulatory focus theory (Higgins, 1998), calls attention to additional factors that may influence individuals' decisions concerning whether they have or have not perceived an opportunity. In other words, it, too, is relevant to the task of pattern verification. Briefly, this theory suggests that in regulating their own behavior to achieve desired ends, individuals adopt either a 'promotion focus', in which they focus primarily on attaining positive outcomes, or a 'prevention focus', in which they focus primarily on avoiding negative outcomes (Higgins, 2006).

When combined with signal detection theory (Baron, 2004), regulatory focus theory suggests that when individuals adopt a promotion focus (an emphasis on positive outcomes), they will tend to concentrate on attaining hits (on recognizing a stimulus when it is present) and on avoiding misses (failing to recognize a stimulus that is in fact present). In contrast, when they adopt a prevention focus (an emphasis on avoiding negative outcomes), they will concentrate on avoiding errors; thus, they will be especially careful to attain correct rejections and to avoid false alarms. In other words, together, signal detection theory and regulatory focus theory suggest that entrepreneurs who focus on obtaining positive outcomes will set their subjective criteria for concluding that they have recognized opportunities relatively low: they will identify many opportunities and avoid misses, but will also experience many false alarms. In contrast, entrepreneurs who focus primarily on avoiding negative outcomes will set their subjective criteria relatively high, thus experiencing few false alarms but a larger number of misses (failing to notice opportunities that exist). Reliable measures of these two self-regulatory foci exist (e.g. Brockner et al., 2004), so these predictions can be readily investigated in future research.

How Some Entrepreneurs Become Exceptionally Adept at Recognizing Opportunities: The Role of Expertise and Expert Performance

It has long been observed that some entrepreneurs are much better at identifying potentially profitable opportunities than others. A pattern recognition perspective suggests that one source of such differences is straightforward: some entrepreneurs have 'better' (i.e. broader, more fully-developed, and more interconnected) cognitive frameworks than others, and so are more successful at 'connecting the dots' – noticing patterns that suggest new products or services (Baron, 2006). However, a large literature on the nature of expertise and expert performance points to another possibility as well: perhaps, as a result of years of experience in searching for, recognizing, and evaluating opportunities, some entrepreneurs become true experts in this task. This is certainly not the place to discuss the vast literature on expert performance in detail; however, several key findings of that research (conducted mainly in the field of cognitive science), suggest that long-term, effortful processing of information relating to opportunities may provide entrepreneurs with major advantages with respect to opportunity recognition.

First, it is important to note that existing literature on expert performance – generally defined as consistently superior, reproducible performance on tasks that are representative of a particular domain or activity (e.g. Ericsson, 2006) – indicates that such performance does not stem from innate talents or sheer amount of time spent in a given domain of performing a specific activity. On the contrary, in many fields, ranging from sports and medicine to science and music, most people do *not* continue to show improved performance as their time in the domain increases. Rather, most reach a plateau in the 'ordinary' range, and only a few individuals surpass this level and demonstrate truly exceptional performance. Systematic research suggests that a key reason why a few individuals do attain truly superior performance is that they engage in what is known as 'deliberate practice' – practice that continues on a regular basis for many hours and is highly focused on attaining specific, task-related goals (e.g. Hodges and Starkes, 1996). Such training has been found to be a key ingredient in the development of exceptional performance in many different fields (e.g. Ericsson et al., 1993). Indeed, it appears that even if individuals do possess exceptionally high levels of talent, deliberate practice is still required to translate this talent into high levels of performance.

Engaging in deliberate practice provides the persons who perform it with several key benefits. First, they gain increased stores of domain-specific information and enhanced cognitive frameworks for storing and processing such information. The value of such information has been well documented in past research in the field of entrepreneurship, where many studies indicate that the greater an entrepreneur's knowledge of a given field or industry, the greater the likelihood that the new ventures he or she launches will be successful (e.g. Fiet, 1996; Fiet and Patel, 2006). Further, as noted earlier, research findings also indicate that the more fully developed an entrepreneur's cognitive frameworks for organizing and processing such information, the greater his or her effectiveness in identifying potentially profitable business opportunities (Baron and Ensley, 2006).

Second, deliberate practice provides individuals who perform it with enhanced 'self-regulatory' and 'metacognitive' mechanisms. Self-regulatory mechanisms are aspects of cognition that assist individuals in monitoring, regulating, and enhancing their own performance. These skills are useful in a wide range of contexts.

Third, and perhaps most dramatic, deliberate practice provides individuals with actual enhancements to basic cognitive processes. For example, persons who engage in focused, effortful cognitive activity in a given domain may develop improved perceptual skills in that domain: they can often make finer discriminations than novices, and are generally superior at recognizing complex patterns than novices (e.g. Baron, 2006; Ericsson, 2004). Further, participation in extensive deliberate practice may also produce changes in 'working memory', the memory system that provides temporary storage of information currently being processed as individuals perform various cognitive tasks (e.g. Ericsson, 2005). Such memory, which is widely viewed as the system underlying consciousness, is known to have severely limited capacity: it can retain and process only small amounts of information at any given time. However, a growing body of evidence suggests that as a result of engaging in deliberate practice, individuals experience significant increases in the 'effective capacity' of their working memory. They do this by forming stronger and more numerous links between working memory and long-term memory – the memory system that holds large amounts of information for long periods of time (years or even decades). As these connections are forged, persons gaining expertise in a given domain acquire enhanced capacity to retrieve information stored in long-term memory. This means that they gain enhanced access to large amounts of information relevant to the tasks they are performing – information that is not present in working memory, but can readily be 'imported' into it from long-term memory. This enhanced access, in turn, can greatly improve performance by permitting experts in a given domain to use this information to guide their current performance and to better anticipate future events. In a sense, it effectively increases the capacity of working memory beyond what it was prior to deliberate practice. The end result is the development of what some researchers describe as 'long-term working memory' – working memory that is so intimately linked with long-term memory, that persons who have developed it possess a greatly expanded capacity for processing information relevant to the domain in which they are expert (Ericsson and Kintsch, 1995).

As a concrete example, consider an entrepreneur known to the author who has started and successfully run many new ventures. When asked how he managed to identify one highly profitable business opportunity after another, this entrepreneur made the following comment: 'I just know. When I consider an opportunity, I can see hundreds or thousands of others in my mind's eye . . . And when I see how this idea compares with those, I know instantly whether it will work . . .' These words are consistent with the findings of basic research suggesting that experts in many fields acquire enhanced working memory, a cognitive capacity that provides them with augmented access to vast stores of information acquired through past experience.

Together, the benefits provided by deliberate practice may enhance entrepreneurs' ability to recognize opportunities, to accomplish this task quickly and efficiently, and to choose, from among potential opportunities, those that offer the greatest actual economic potential. Of course, entrepreneurs cannot ordinarily engage in deliberate practice in the same way that it occurs in many other domains. Given the rapidly changing, time-urgent environments in which they function, they simply do not have the opportunity to engage in long periods of uninterrupted, highly focused deliberate practice. Similarly, it can be argued that even if they have such opportunities, it is unclear what specific tasks or skills they would practice. Entrepreneurs focus on somewhat different activities and tasks during different phases of new venture creation. However, as suggested by Baron and Henry (2010), entrepreneurs may still reap at least some benefits of deliberate practice merely as a result of focusing intently and persistently on key aspects of the process of starting and running new ventures. In other words, just as world-class chess champions spend many hours each day examining the moves and countermoves in previous games, and so sharpen their own playing skills, entrepreneurs can acquire enhanced skill at opportunity recognition and other tasks by carefully examining large numbers of cases involving opportunity identification and related processes. As a result of such activity, they may acquire well-developed cognitive frameworks, improved self-regulatory mechanisms, and enhanced access to information stored in long-term memory – and do so vicariously, without engaging in overt deliberate practice. These enhanced cognitive capacities, in turn, may help them to perform several tasks that play an important role in shaping new venture performance, including recognizing and evaluating business opportunities.

In sum, it seems possible that the cognitive processes that contribute to expertise in many other fields may also be at work in the domain of entrepreneurship, and that those entrepreneurs who – perhaps because they possess certain characteristics, such as high levels of self-control, conscientiousness and self-efficacy (Tice et al., 2007) – are able to engage in deliberate, highly focused processing of opportunity-relevant information, may acquire enhanced capacity to accomplish this crucial task.

CONCLUDING COMMENTS

Cognitive theories such as the ones described here have greatly enriched current understanding of the process of opportunity identification. For this reason, it seems desirable for the field of entrepreneurship to continue to expand its store of useful conceptual and theoretical tools by 'importing' additional frameworks from cognitive science and other fields. Needless to say, adapting these frameworks, which are often highly sophisticated and employ highly developed (and narrow) research methodologies, is far from a simple task. However, doing so may help the field of entrepreneurship answer important questions such as these:

1. What, specifically, is alertness? Does it relate to differences in thresholds for 'noticing' patterns or specific events or trends? Can it be understood within the context of signal detection theory?
2. How do entrepreneurs acquire expertise? How do they manage to reap the cognitive benefits of traditional deliberate practice, even though they cannot engage in such activity? Is it through vicarious experiences, in which they benefit from the experience – and errors – of others?
3. What individual-level factors (skills, characteristics, motives, values) play a role in opportunity recognition? Such factors may be an important reason why entrepreneurs differ greatly with respect to their skill in this.
4. Can individuals be trained to be more proficient at opportunity recognition? How?
5. How does the overall quality of opportunities identified by entrepreneurs shape the later development of their new ventures?
6. What is the role of 'affect opportunity recognition'? A vast body of evidence indicates that affect and cognition interact continuously and in complex ways. Does positive affect, for example, enhance entrepreneurs' capacity to identify potentially valuable opportunities? Or does it send them down the path of 'false alarms'?

Further investigations designed to gather evidence on these and many related questions will assist the field of entrepreneurship in making further progress toward its central, overarching goal: acquiring full understanding of the complex process through which entrepreneurs convert their ideas, visions, and dreams into successful operating companies – and so create wealth not only for themselves, but for their communities and societies as well.

NOTE

1. This definition focuses primarily on 'traditional' entrepreneurship, where entrepreneurs form new ventures with a profit motive. The growing literature on 'social entrepreneurship', however, expands this view to include creating 'societal' along with 'economic' value. See, for example, Moss et al., Chapter 14 in this volume.

REFERENCES

Aidis, R. and M. van Praag (2007), 'Illegal entrepreneurship experience: does it make a difference for business performance and motivation?', *Journal of Business Venturing*, **22**, 283–310.

Aldrich, H. and P.H. Kim (2007), 'Small worlds, infinite possibilities? How social networks affect entrepreneurial team formation and search', *Strategic Entrepreneurship Journal*, **1**, 147–66.

Alvarez, S.A. and J.B. Barney (2005), 'How entrepreneurs organize firms under conditions of uncertainty', *Journal of Management*, **31**, 776–93.

Alvarez, S.A. and J.B. Barney (2007), 'Discovery and creation: alternative theories of entrepreneurial action', *Strategic Entrepreneurship Journal*, **1**, 11–26.

Ardichvili, A., R. Cardozo and S. Ray (2003), 'A theory of entrepreneurial opportunity identification and development', *Journal of Business Venturing*, **18**, 105–24.

Baddeley, A. (1997), *Human Memory*, New York: Psychology Press.

Baron, R.A. (2002), 'OB and entrepreneurship: the reciprocal benefits of closer conceptual links', in B.M. Staw and R. Kramer (eds), *Research in Organizational Behavior*, Greenwich, CT: JAI Press, pp. 225–69.

Baron, R.A. (2004), 'The cognitive perspective: a valuable tool for answering entrepreneurship's basic "why?" questions', *Journal of Business Venturing*, **19**, 221–40.

Baron, R.A. (2006), 'Opportunity recognition as pattern recognition: how entrepreneurs "connect the dots" to identify new business opportunities', *Academy of Management Perspective*, **20**, 104–19.

Baron, R.A. and M.D. Ensley (2006), 'Opportunity recognition as the detection of meaningful patterns: evidence from comparisons of novice and experienced entrepreneurs', *Management Science*, **52**, 1331–44.

Baron, R.A. and R.A. Henry (2010), 'How entrepreneurs acquire the capacity to excel: insights from basic research on expert performance', *Strategic Entrepreneurship Journal*, **4**, 49–65.

Baron, R.A. and S.A. Shane (2008), *Entrepreneurship: A Process Perspective*, 2nd edn, Cincinnati: Thompson-Southwestern.

Baron, R.A., N.R. Branscombe and D. Byrne (2009), *Social Psychology*, 12th edn, Boston, MA: Allyn and Bacon.

Bhave, M.P. (1994), 'A process model of entrepreneurial venture creation', *Journal of Business Venturing*, **9**, 223–42.

Blanchflower, D. and A. Oswald (1998), 'What makes an entrepreneur?', *Journal of Labor Economics*, **16**, 26–60.

Brockner, J., E.T. Higgens and M.B. Low (2004), 'Regulatory focus theory and the entrepreneurial process', *Journal of Business Venturing*, **19**, 203–20.

Busenitz, L.W. and J.D. Arthurs (2006), 'Cognition and capabilities in entrepreneurial ventures', in R. Baum, M. Frese and R.A. Baron (eds), *The Psychology of Entrepreneurship*, Mahwah, NJ: Erlbaum, pp. 31–50.

Busenitz, L.W. and J.B. Barney (1997), 'Differences between entrepreneurs and managers in large organizations: biases and heuristics in strategic decision-making', *Journal of Business Venturing*, **12**, 9–30.

De Wit, G. (1993), 'Models of self-employment in a competitive market', *Journal of Economic Surveys*, **7**, 367–97.
Durand, R. and R. Courerderoy (2001), 'Age, order of entry, strategic orientation, and organizational performance', *Journal of Business Venturing*, **16**, 471–94.
Ericsson, K.A. (2004), 'Deliberate practice and the acquisition and maintenance of expert performance in medicine and related domains', *Academic Medicine*, **79**, S70–S81.
Ericsson, K.A. (2005), 'Recent advances in expertise research: a commentary on the contributions to the special issues', *Applied Cognitive Psychology*, **19**, 233–41.
Ericsson, K.A. (2006), 'The influence of experience and deliberate practice on the development of superior expert performance', in K.A. Ericsson, N. Charness, P.J. Feltovich and R.R. Hoffman (eds), *The Cambridge Handbook of Expertise and Expert Performance*, New York: Cambridge University Press, pp. 683–703.
Ericsson, K.A. and W. Kintsch (1995), 'Long-term working memory', *Psychological Review*, **102**, 211–45.
Ericsson, K.A., R.T. Krampe and C. Tesch-Romer (1993), 'The role of deliberate practice in the acquisition of expert performance', *Psychological Review*, **100**, 363–406.
Fiet, J.O. (1996), 'The informational basis of entrepreneurial discovery', *Small Business Economics*, **8**, 419–30.
Fiet, J.O. and P.C. Patel (2006), 'Evaluating the wealth creating potential of business plans', *Journal of Private Equity*, **10**, 18–32.
Fiet, J.O., V.G. Clouse and W.I. Norton Jr (2004), 'Systematic search by repeat entrepreneurs', in J. Butler (ed.), *Research in Entrepreneurship and Management*, Vol. 4, Greenwich, CT: Information Age Publishing, pp. 1–27.
Fraboni, M. and R. Saltstone (1990), 'The entrepreneurial personality in relation to Hollands' occupational types', *Journal of Small Business and Entrepreneurship*, **7**, 23–28.
Gaglio, C.M. and J. Katz (2001), 'The psychological basis of opportunity identification: entrepreneurial alertness', *Small Business Economics*, **16**, 95–111.
Hahn, U. and N. Chater (1997), 'Concepts and similarity', in K. Lamberts and D. Shanks (eds), *Knowledge Concepts and Categories*, Cambridge, MA: MIT Press, pp. 43–92.
Herron, L. and H.J. Sapienza (1992), 'The entrepreneur and the initiation of new venture launch activities', *Entrepreneurship Theory and Practice*, **16**, 49–55.
Higgins, E.T. (1998), 'Promotion and prevention: regulatory focus as a motivational principle', in M.P. Zanna (ed.), *Advances in Experimental Social Psychology*, Vol. 30, New York: Academic Press, pp. 1–46.
Higgins, E.T. (2006), 'Value from hedonic experience and engagement', *Psychological Review*, **113**, 439–60.
Hills, G.E. and R.C. Shrader (1998), 'Successful entrepreneurs' insights into opportunity recognition', *Frontiers of Entrepreneurship Research*, 30–43.
Hmieleski, K. and R.A. Baron (in press), 'A contextual study of entrepreneurial self-efficacy', *Strategic Entrepreneurship Journal* (forthcoming).
Hodges, N.J. and J.L. Starkes (1996), 'Wrestling with the nature of expertise: a sport-specific test of Ericsson, Krampe and Tesch-Romer's (1993) theory of deliberate practice', *International Journal of Sport Psychology*, **27**, 400–24.
Kaish, S. and B. Gilad (1991), 'Characteristics of opportunities search of entrepreneurs versus executives: sources, interests, general alertness', *Journal of Business Venturing*, **6**, 45–61.
Kirzner, I.M. (1979), *Perception, Opportunity, and Profit*, Chicago, IL: University of Chicago Press.
Kirzner, I.M. (1985), *Discovery and the Capitalist Process*, Chicago, IL: University of Chicago Press.
Krueger, N.J. and D.H. Brazeal (1994), 'Entrepreneurial potential and potential entrepreneurs', *Entrepreneurship Theory and Practice*, **19**, 91–104.
Krueger, N.J. and P.R. Dickson (1994), 'How believing in ourselves increases risk taking: perceived self-efficacy and opportunity recognition', *Decision Sciences*, **25**, 385–400.
Matlin, M.W. (2004), *Cognition*, 6th edn, Fort Worth, TX: Harcourt College Publishers.
McMullen, J.S. and D.A. Shepherd (2006), 'Entrepreneurial action and the role of uncertainty in the theory of the entrepreneur', *Academy of Management Review*, **31**, 132–52.

Mitchell, R.K., L.W. Busenitz, B. Bird, C.M. Gaglio, J.S. McMullen, E.A. Morse and J.B. Smith (2007), 'The central question in entrepreneurial cognition research', *Entrepreneurship Theory and Practice*, **31**, 1–28.

Nosofsky, R.M. and T.J. Palmieri (1998), 'A rule-plus-exception model for classifying objects in continuous-dimension spaces', *Psychonomic Bulletin and Review*, **5**, 345–69.

Ozgen, E. and R.A. Baron (2007), 'Social sources of information in opportunity recognition: effects of mentors, industry networks, and professional forums', *Journal of Business Venturing*, **22**, 174–92.

Schneider, W. and R.M. Shiffrin (1977), 'Controlled and automatic human information processing: detection, search, and attention', *Psychological Review*, **84**, 1–66.

Schultz, D.P. and S.E. Schultz (2007), *A History of Psychology*, 2nd edn, New York: Harcourt College Publishers.

Shane, S. (2000), 'Prior knowledge and the discovery of entrepreneurial opportunities', *Organization Science*, **11**, 448–69.

Shane, S. (2003), *A General Theory of Entrepreneurship: The Individual-Opportunity Nexus*, Cheltenham, UK and Northampton, MA, USA: Edward Elgar.

Shane, S. and S. Venkataraman (2000), 'The promise of entrepreneurship as a field of research', *Academy of Management Review*, **25**, 217–26.

Sternberg, R.J. (2004), 'Successful intelligence as a basis for entrepreneurship', *Journal of Business Venturing*, **19**, 189–202.

Stewart, W.H. and P.L. Roth (2001), 'Risk propensity differences between entrepreneurs and managers: a meta-analytic review', *Journal of Applied Psychology*, **86**, 145–53.

Swets, J.A. (1992), 'The science of choosing the right decision threshold in high-stakes diagnostics', *American Psychologist*, **47**, 522–32.

Tice, D.M., R.F. Baumeister, D. Shmueli and M. Muraven (2007), 'Restoring the self: positive affect helps improve self-regulation following ego depletion', *Journal of Experimental Social Psychology*, **43**, 379–84.

Van Praag, C.M. and J.S. Cramer (2001), 'The roots of entrepreneurship and labour demand: individual ability and low risk aversion', *Economica*, **68**, 45–62.

Wolfe, J.M., K.R. Kluender, D.M. Levi, L.M. Bartoshuk, R.L. Klatzky, S.J. Lederman and D.M. Merfeld (2008), *Sensation and Perception*, 2nd edn, Sunderland, MA: Sinauer Associates.

7. The historic roots of entrepreneurial orientation research

Verona P. Edmond and Johan Wiklund

INTRODUCTION

Entrepreneurship is an ever evolving and maturing discipline within the organizational research family. Although the area of entrepreneurship is still relatively young in terms of empirical research, significant efforts have been made to develop the empirical grounding of the entrepreneurship field. One area of research in the field, entrepreneurial orientation (EO), has perhaps made the most significant empirical advances and has developed into a well-established construct within entrepreneurship research. EO and its intellectual roots constitute the focus of this chapter.

Originating from the work of organizational and strategy scholars, EO refers to the strategy making processes of firms, processes which have been shown to lead to new entry (Lumpkin and Dess, 1996) and to enhance the performance of firms (Wiklund and Shepherd, 2005). EO has become a central concept in the domain of entrepreneurship and has received a substantial amount of theoretical and empirical attention (Covin et al., 2006). More than 100 empirical studies of EO have been conducted, including a recent meta-analysis of the relationship between EO and performance (Rauch et al., 2009). Viewed collectively, these studies point to at least three areas of agreement: (1) EO typically has positive effects on firm performance; (2) the measurement of EO is typically carried out using a scale developed by Danny Miller in 1983 and later refined by Covin and Slevin in their 1986 and 1989 works; and (3) the measurement instrument is technically sound and has predictive, discriminant, and convergent validity. Several issues, however, are still under examination and debate including antecedents and dimensionality of EO as well as factors that may moderate the EO–performance relationship. Therefore, given the stage of current research on EO, this is a suitable time for more closely examining where EO research comes from and where it is heading.

The purpose of this chapter is to provide an overview of the intellectual roots and development of entrepreneurial orientation. To do this, we identify key thinkers of the EO construct, highlighting the most influential contributions of each. We endeavor to highlight the systematic manner in which the research has progressed, showing how scholars have effectively built on the work of those before them. We also expose the gaps in the current body of EO literature and propose directions for future study.

This chapter, which is divided into five major sections and an appendix, proceeds as follows. The first two sections discuss the intellectual beginnings of EO and the subsequent conceptual and empirical developments of the construct. The third section on 'EO empirical works' provides information on what we believe are very influential studies in

EO research, specifically those which have served to stimulate interest in and to push forward research in this area. The fourth section 'Debates in EO research' outlines areas of contentious discourse in the EO stream of research. The fifth section reports theoretical and methodological issues associated with EO research and provides suggestions for future investigation. Finally, the Appendix (Figure 7A.1) is a timeline of the key thinkers in entrepreneurship orientation research identified and discussed in this chapter.

THE CONCEPTUAL ROOTS

The conceptual roots of EO can be traced to an approximately 20-year period, starting in the early 1960s with the work of the Aston Group and ending in 1983 with the work of Danny Miller (see Appendix). This period of time begins with a paradigmatic shift in how researchers examine organizations and concludes with the development of a measurement scale for studying firm level entrepreneurship.

The Aston Group

The initial intellectual roots of EO research can be traced back to the Aston group of organization scholars in the UK. During the 1960s they published a series of papers in *Administrative Science Quarterly* (ASQ), stemming from a discontent because:

> There has been almost no systematic exploration of the causal connection between contextual factors and certain administrative systems rather than others, or certain group and individual behaviors rather than others. . . . In our view, the present study of work organization and behavior can no longer be content with a priori postulations or a continuing succession of one-case studies. (Pugh et al., 1963, p. 291)

More precisely, these scholars set out to examine systematically the structure and functioning of organizations and to relate those variables to other variables of the organizations, such as behavior, performance, and context – the latter dimension including size, technology, history and ownership. One important aim of this work was to develop standardized measurement scales for organizational structure that could be broadly used across a wide variety of organizations. The other purpose was to use these measurement scales to generate empirically derived typologies of organizations, which the scholars did in a number of writings. The work of these scholars, therefore, can be viewed as the genesis to contemporary empirical research on organizations as they shifted the research focus from descriptive social science methodologies to more of a natural science focus – one that calls for the definition, operationalization and empirical testing of variables. The pervading thought was that this new focus would facilitate comparative and generalizable studies.

The McGill Group

This approach to the study of organizations was adopted by a research group at McGill University in Montreal, Canada. In particular, this group further developed the ideas of organizational typologies as well as refined ways of measuring organizations and their environments. Important for the context of this chapter, the people at McGill started taking an interest in entrepreneurial aspects of firms. One early publication was penned by Henry Mintzberg, a McGill scholar of business policy and organization studies. Mintzberg, up to the time of the publication of 'Strategy-making in three modes' (1973), had focused his work on managerial and organizational issues, particularly emphasizing structure, power, and forms of organizations. It was in the 1973 article that he generated a typology consisting of three modes of strategy making, one of them being the entrepreneurial mode, which was characterized as having four major characteristics: (1) an active search for new opportunities, (2) power which is centralized in the hands of the chief executive, (3) dramatic leaps forward in the face of uncertainty, and (4) growth as the dominant goal (Mintzberg, 1973). Likewise, Mintzberg's colleague Pradip N. Khandwalla in 'Some top management styles, their context and performance' (1976) identified seven management styles, capturing the beliefs and norms about management held by key decision makers. Again, one of these styles was entrepreneurial management style, characterized among other things by a high level of risk-taking.

The Contributions of Danny Miller

Danny Miller, a protégé of Henry Mintzberg and also a scholar of business policy and organization studies, continued the work on business organizations. It was with his 1983 publication of 'The correlates of entrepreneurship in three types of firms' that the research on EO really started. The paper fits well within the McGill tradition of empirically studying different types of firms, quantifying environment, strategy and structure to derive a typology. With regard to the current EO research, its main contributions, however, are somewhat different from those probably intended by the author – predicting entrepreneurship in different types of firms had not yet become a major concern.

We would argue that the main contributions were, first, that the paper shifts the focus from the individual to the organization as the actor of entrepreneurship. This is succinctly captured in the statement that: 'There has been a strong tendency to identify entrepreneurship with a dominant organizational personality, generally an independent-minded owner-manager who makes the strategic decisions for his firm. . . . This paper shifts the emphasis somewhat, looking at the entrepreneurial activity of the *firm*' (Miller, 1983, p. 770, emphasis in original).

The second main contribution was that it clearly defined what characterized the entrepreneurial firm: 'An entrepreneurial firm is one that engages in product-market innovation, undertakes somewhat risky ventures, and is *first* to come up with "proactive" innovations, beating competitors to the punch' (Miller, 1983, p. 771, emphasis in original). Innovativeness refers to 'a firm's propensity to engage in and support new ideas, novelty, experimentation, and creative processes that may result in new products, services, or processes' (Lumpkin and Dess, 1996). Risk-taking relates to 'the degree in which managers are willing to make large and risky resource commitments' (Miller and Friesen, 1978). Proactiveness is defined as 'taking initiative by anticipating and pursuing new opportunities and by participating in emerging markets' (Lumpkin and Dess, 1996). Notably, this view of entrepreneurship was not rooted in any theory or based on previous empirical or conceptual work. The definition is instead rather commonsensical. Perhaps

Miller defined entrepreneurship in this way with one eye towards the measurement scales to which he had access.

The third contribution of Miller's 1983 paper, which is probably the main one, is that, based on previous McGill research, it provided a measurement scale for tapping firm-level entrepreneurship. The origins of this scale can be traced to Khandwalla (1976), who developed a measurement scale to gauge the relationship between a firm's performance, structure, and environmental context. Together with Peter Friesen, Miller built on Khandwalla's work to separately examine risk taking and innovation at the firm level (Miller and Friesen, 1978; 1982). But it was in his 1983 article that Miller added the dimension of proactiveness and also combined these three dimensions into a unified way of measuring firm-level entrepreneurship, or EO. To our knowledge, this was the first time such a measurement scale was developed.

EO FRAMEWORK AND DEVELOPMENTS

Covering a decade, the years between 1986 and 1996 (see Appendix) unveiled critical developments to the EO measurement scale and the EO conceptual model. This period birthed the term 'entrepreneurial orientation', and also ushered in fresh discussions on research methodology related to EO.

Covin and Slevin's Conceptual Model of EO

The work of Miller was extended by Jeffrey Covin and Dennis Slevin (1986; 1989). Slevin, an organizational behavior scholar, had conducted prior research on organizational innovation and the role that individuals play in establishing environments conducive for organizational performance. Covin, at the time a newly minted professor and strategic management scholar, had an interest in factors that affect firm performance. The two combined their interests and expertise to further develop, validate, and refine the measurement scale for firm-level entrepreneurship.

In the revised scale, nine items make up this measurement instrument – three items each for innovativeness, risk-taking and proactiveness. Most EO empirical work to date has been based on this scale as designed or on some modification of it. Covin and Slevin also conceptualized and hypothesized how the EO construct was related to performance (1989) and carried out a number of empirical studies. Consistent with strategic management research (and subsequent EO research), they mainly focused on the link between the construct and performance, as opposed to Miller (1983), who studied its antecedents.

Recognizing the expansion of entrepreneurial thought into the corporate ranks, Covin and Slevin (1991) proposed a sophisticated conceptual model of firm EO. This model was developed to identify EO antecedents and consequences as well as the moderating variables of the EO–performance relationship.

Their EO model (see Figure 7.1) consisted of the following elements: dependent variable – performance; independent variable – EO; external variables – environmental technological sophistication dynamism and hostility, and industry life cycle; strategic variables – firm's mission strategy, business practices and competitive tactics; and internal variables – top management values/philosophies, organizational resources/competencies,

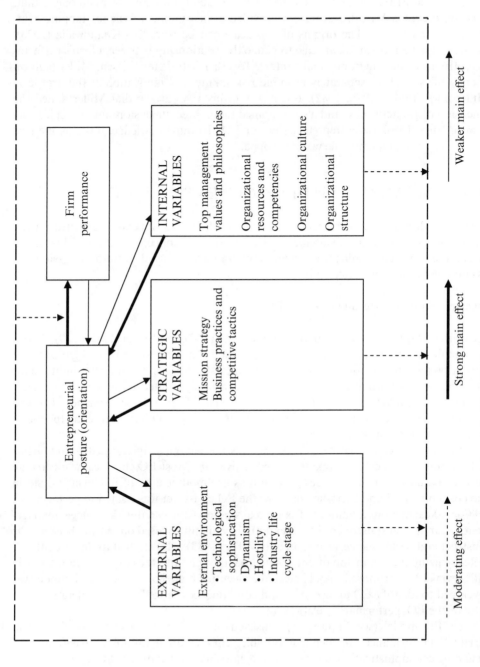

Figure 7.1 Covin and Slevin's conceptual model of EO (1991)

and organizational culture. The external variables, strategic variables and internal variables were all depicted as factors which could affect the EO–performance relationship.

A benefit of this model, as proposed by the authors, is that it captures more variables than previous models have. They argued that even though the prior models had a high degree of face validity (i.e. they appeared to measure the EO–performance relationship), these relationships tended to be modeled in an oversimplified way. Among other things, this model provides a framework to guide researchers away from simple direct effects testing of the EO–performance relationship and toward more comprehensive studies that would look at moderator effects. The Covin and Slevin (1991) model has been very influential in the study of EO, which has accelerated since the model's development. As discussed in the following sections, scholars began to investigate many of the questions proposed by Covin and Slevin (1991). Some scholars have explored the moderators of the EO–performance relationships suggested in the model (e.g. Barrett and Weinstein, 1999; Dimitratos et al., 2004; Marino et al., 2002), whereas others have examined EO's dimensionality (Lumpkin and Dess, 1996; Rauch et al., 2009), the cultural validity of the EO measurement scale (Knight, 1997; Kreiser et al., 2002; Rauch et al., 2009), methodological approaches (Wiklund, 1999), the potential effects of time on EO (Wiklund, 1999), and the theoretical grounding of the construct (Wiklund and Shepherd, 2003). It seems that the era for developing the EO framework was successful because it ushered in a new period – a period of empirical activity.

Zahra's Critique

Shaker A. Zahra (1993) presented a critique of the Covin and Slevin (1991) model of EO. Acknowledging the numerous advantages of the model (e.g. it presented a clear framework, integrated research findings to date, offered theories regarding the EO–performance relationship, provided future research questions), Zahra (1993) offered suggestions to revise and extend the model. These included: (1) to specify the nature of entrepreneurship (intensity, formality and type of behavior); (2) to include dimensions of EO other than innovativeness, risk-taking and proactiveness; (3) to account for multiple levels of analysis (corporate, business strategic unit and functional levels); (4) to distinguish between domestic and international ventures; and (5) to eliminate the technological sophistication variable as it seemed to be redundant with environmental dynamism.

Based on a review of citations for each of these two articles, it appears that the original model offered by Covin and Slevin (1991) has received substantial scholarly attention whereas the modifications suggested by Zahra (1993) have received a more modest following. This possibly could be attributed to the fact that the proposed modifications by Zahra (1993) did not change the logic or the usefulness of the original model, and to the 'first mover advantage' held by Covin and Slevin (1991).

Clarifications by Lumpkin and Dess

The work of Tom Lumpkin and Gregory Dess, both strategic management scholars, extended the discussion on EO in several ways. First, they are credited with coining the term 'entrepreneurial orientation.' Next, they introduced two additional dimensions – autonomy and competitive aggressiveness – as salient dimensions of EO, challenging the thought on the three-dimensional depiction as introduced by Danny Miller in 1983. These scholars argued for increased research examining the moderating effects of certain factors on the EO–performance relationship and also challenged the dominant uni-dimensional perspective on the dimensionality of EO.

Lumpkin and Dess's seminal article 'Clarifying the entrepreneurial orientation construct and linking it to performance' (1996) built on Covin and Slevin's (1991) model and incorporated some of the suggestions made by Zahra (1993), in particular his notion that entrepreneurship extended beyond the three dimensions suggested by Miller (1983) and used by Covin and Slevin. Importantly, the actual term entrepreneurial orientation (EO) was coined by these authors, who made a clever distinction between entrepreneurship on the one hand and EO on the other, building on the simple distinction between 'what' and 'how'. Noting the practice of borrowing concepts from strategy and applying them to firm-level entrepreneurship, the authors indicated that the term 'entrepreneurship' in the early strategic management literature signified 'going into business.' However, as the strategic management field matured, a focus on the methods, practices, and decision making styles of managers surfaced. As such, Lumpkin and Dess (1996) acknowledged the major entrepreneurial processes and labeled these 'entrepreneurial orientation' (EO). In other words, they connected entrepreneurship with *what* (as opposed to *how*), which they defined as new entry. Although appearing consistent with William Gartner's (1988) conceptualization of entrepreneurship as 'new venture', the authors argued that their perspective was broader than that of Gartner. Specifically, they argued that Gartner's conceptualization related only to the new creation of organizations, that the concept of 'new entry' included the activities of individuals and firms alike, and that the process did not necessarily include creating a new organization. EO was associated with the *how* of this behavior, suggesting that new entry is accomplished through actions that are autonomous, innovative, risky, proactive and competitively aggressive.

Additions to the Covin and Slevin Model

Lumpkin and Dess (1996) also proposed modifications to the EO concept as presented by Miller (1983). Specifically, the authors challenged Miller's (1983) tri-dimensional depiction of EO by adding two additional dimensions, autonomy and competitive aggressiveness, and proposing that the EO construct was not uni-, but multi-dimensional. The additions could be viewed as a response to Zahra's (1993) suggestion that the '. . . Covin and Slevin model (and research in this area) would benefit from recognizing other dimensions of firm-level entrepreneurship' (p. 6). Interestingly, autonomy was specifically mentioned by Zahra – '. . . Burgelman's [1983, 1991] work has established the need for differentiating formal ("induced") and informal ("autonomous") entrepreneurship activities. . . . Informal activities reflect the autonomous efforts undertaken by individual members of an organization' (Zahra, 1993, p. 6). The addition of the competitive aggressiveness dimension was probably a result of empirical analyses, which showed that one item of the proactiveness dimension of Covin and Slevin's scale tended to load on its own factor in factor analysis. This item explicitly captures 'undoing the competitor', which arguably relates more closely to competitive aggressiveness than to proactiveness.

Lumpkin and Dess (1996) defined autonomy as the 'ability and will to be self-directed in the pursuit of opportunities' (p. 140). To support the inclusion of this dimension, the authors cited the independent spirits of those who historically have sacrificed security in the pursuit of freedom and creativity and the role of autonomous behavior in the entrepreneurship literature. Beginning with the work of Mintzberg (1973), the entrepreneurial strategy-making mode was characterized by the strong, decisive and powerful leader. This mode, along with the command mode of strategy-making (Hart, 1992) and the commander mode (Bourgeois and Brodwin, 1984) were cited as examples of the autonomous leadership in small firms in which the leader's visions and actions drive the activities of the organization. Likewise, the authors spoke of the individuals in large firms who serve as resource gatherers, rule benders, and risk-takers in their attempt to drive firm innovation. Lumpkin and Dess (1996) thus viewed autonomy as a defining characteristic of entrepreneurship – one that was a salient dimension of EO to be included.

Based on previous studies, the authors also proposed the addition of competitive aggressiveness as a dimension of EO. Competitive aggressiveness is defined as a firm's propensity to challenge and outperform its competitors (Lumpkin and Dess, 1996). The authors argued that this concept's undeniable presence in the literature – the adoption of unconventional tactics (Cooper et al., 1986), targeting competitors' weaknesses (MacMillan and Jones, 1984), adopting a strategy that focuses on value added products and cost reductions (Woo and Cooper, 1981), and developing scales that measured the competitiveness and aggressiveness of processes used by managers (Ginsberg, 1985; Khandwalla, 1976) – supported its inclusion as an EO dimension.

The Contingency Approach

Lumpkin and Dess (1996) also present a set of contingency relationships to explain how EO enhances performance. This approach follows the earlier suggestions of Covin and Slevin (1991) which urged scholars to investigate factors that might moderate the EO–performance relationship. The contingency approach, as outlined by Lumpkin and Dess (1996), suggests that many (e.g. environmental, managerial, and industrial) factors influence how the dimensions of EO are configured in order to promote enhanced performance of a firm. These authors identified several contingency variables on which the EO–performance relationship could depend. These variables fall into two categories – organizational factors and environmental factors. The organizational factors include structure, strategy, strategy-making processes, firm resources, culture, and top management team characteristics. The environmental factors include environmental and industry characteristics. These organizational and environmental factors were all outlined in the earlier work of Covin and Slevin (1991). In addition, it was proposed that scholars take a closer look at how performance is operationalized in empirical studies and consider using non-financial, as well as financial, measures of a firm's performance.

EO as a Multi-dimensional Construct

Lumpkin and Dess (1996) also proposed that EO should be viewed as a multi-dimensional construct. Opposing the original conceptualization of EO as uni-dimensional (Covin and Slevin, 1989; Miller, 1983), they suggested that EO's dimensions could vary independently of each other; thus, a firm could be entrepreneurial without having high levels of every EO dimension. It could have high levels of one dimension, but lower levels of another. They also hypothesized that the level of a certain EO dimension exhibited by a firm is determined by the type of opportunity being pursued and the environmental setting of the firm. As such, EO dimensions could have a unique configuration for each opportunity and/or each setting.

The work of Lumpkin and Dess (1996) has provided fertile ground for debate. In particular, scholarly discussions on EO dimensionality have created interesting dialogue. The majority of empirical work relies on EO as defined by the three dimensions of innovativeness, risk-taking and proactiveness, whereas others have adopted the usage of the additional dimensions of autonomy and competitive aggressiveness. Regarding the issue of uni-dimensionality and multi-dimensionality, both approaches are still being used in parallel. Some favor the uni-dimensional approach whereas others have heeded the call of Lumpkin and Dess and view EO as consisting of separate dimensions. These issues on dimensionality will be explored in further depth later in this chapter.

The work of Lumpkin and Dess has had considerable impact on the progression of EO research. In particular, the conceptual and methodological frameworks introduced by these scholars have spurred many researchers to question the prior trend of viewing EO as a construct consisting of only three dimensions which co-vary. As such, the field is currently charged with providing empirical evidence which will either substantiate or refute these assertions.

EO EMPIRICAL WORKS

It is impossible to give credit to all important contributions in the EO literature, so in this section we limit ourselves to works that we feel have been influential in moving the field in new directions. We make no claim that we treat the topic exhaustively or that we have necessarily included all the most important pieces. We do believe, however, that the works we mention have played a role in guiding the direction of EO research. Spanning a six-year period (see Appendix), we begin with the contributions of Knight (1997), which highlighted cross-cultural issues regarding the measurement of EO. We end our discussion with the work of Wiklund and Shepherd (2003), which gave a novel theoretical grounding for EO.

Cross-cultural Scale Validity

Extending the influence of Miller (1983) and Covin and Slevin (1986; 1989) and facilitating the emerging interest in international business, Gary Knight (1997) recognized the lack of cross-cultural validity and reliability in scales designed to measure EO. This situation was attributable to the fact that the widely adopted EO measurement scale (Covin and Slevin, 1989; Miller, 1983) was developed in North America, and its validity and reliability had been established only in the English-speaking areas of North America. To address this international measurement issue, Knight (1997) conducted an assessment of the cross-cultural validity and reliability of this EO measurement scale using English and French managers in Quebec, Canada. This assessment confirmed that the scale was reliable and valid in the French Canadian context, in addition to an English-speaking population.

Knight also noted that there were some interesting differences between the English-speaking and the French-speaking respondents related to the confirmatory factor analysis and Cronbach Alpha tests performed to assess the reliability of the scale. For example, the variable 'new techniques' loaded on 'proactiveness' on the French questionnaire, but loaded on both 'innovativeness' and 'proactiveness' on the English questionnaire. Also, in the test of internal consistency, the variable 'R & D leadership' exhibited a low correlation (.245) on the French questionnaire. These occurrences represented the exception in Knight's (1997) study, and did not adversely affect the overall reliability of the scale. However, the reasons for the noted exceptions were not explored, and we suggest that they could be attributable to cultural influences on EO. In other words, some nuance in the translation of the scale from English to French or some connotation inherent in the English version of the scale could exist that did not translate into the French version.

The findings of this cross-cultural validity of the scale likely spurred increased international research on EO (Low et al., 2007; Real et al., 2006) and its measurement in different contexts (Antoncic and Hisrich, 2001). This is supported by the findings of Rauch et al. (2009), who noted rapid expansion of EO research, in particular outside North America. They found that in the 1980s, three studies were published – all from North America. The 1990s saw fourteen studies, twelve from the USA, one from Europe and one from Australia. Between the years 2000 and 2006, no less than 34 studies were published. Twenty-two of these used data from outside the USA, with seven from Asia, eight from Europe, two from Australia and five utilizing data from more than one continent. The remaining twelve studies were carried out in the USA. These findings suggest that EO research is becoming increasingly popular around the globe.

Methodological Issues

Acknowledging prior research, which suggested that national culture could have significant influence on a firm's entrepreneurial orientation, and seeking to facilitate increased cross-cultural studies of EO, Kreiser et al. (2002) conducted a study on the psychometric properties of the Covin and Slevin EO scale. Their goal was to test the validity of this scale in cultural settings located outside North America and to assess the dimensionality of EO. Based on a sample of firms from Australia, Finland, Mexico, the Netherlands, Norway and Sweden, findings of this study supported the cross-cultural validity of the scale. This study, therefore, extended and provided support for the work of Knight (1997). In addition, this research examined the dimensionality of EO and supported the Miller/Covin and Slevin concept of a three-dimensional structure consisting of innovativeness, risk-taking and proactiveness. The question of whether the dimensions of EO could co-vary was also addressed by these scholars. The results of this examination contested the assertions of Covin and Slevin and supported Lumpkin and Dess's view that the dimensions of the EO construct could vary independently of each other. This study also highlighted the fact that even though our knowledge of EO, its character, and its effects on performance has vastly increased over the last few decades, our understanding is still very much incomplete.

As a group, these studies point to the need to further investigate the dominant perception that an entrepreneurial firm has to have high levels of innovativeness, risk-taking and proactiveness. For example, can firms, such as those classified as imitators, be considered entrepreneurial even if they have high levels of only one or two of these dimensions? Continued study is needed to clarify this and other questions related to the dimensionality of EO.

The effects of EO on performance have traditionally been tested in cross-sectional studies. As such, for years the temporal dimension of this relationship remained untested. Johan Wiklund (1999) explored the sustainability of the EO–performance relationship in a two-year longitudinal study of small firms. His results revealed that the positive effects of EO on performance were not only maintained over the period of the study, but that the effects increased with time. Importantly, although the study did not test causality in any strict sense, it had a time lag between measuring EO and performance outcomes, which was suggestive of causality. In addition, the results suggested that investments in EO seem to provide long-term benefit, which has important practical implications.

Theoretical Grounding of the EO Construct

Johan Wiklund and Dean Shepherd (2003) took a novel perspective on EO by building on the logic of the resource based view (RBV). They argued that competitive advantage resides in resources that are valuable, rare, inimitable, and organized, suggesting that EO could reflect the 'organized' aspect. This approach also heeds the call of Lumpkin and Dess (1996) to investigate the contingency effects of a firm's internal characteristics on the EO–performance relationship. The findings showed that EO serves as a positive moderating factor between a firm's knowledge-based resources and performance. Perhaps more importantly, however, this study took a novel perspective on EO by providing a solid theoretical grounding for the concept and the construct, placing it firmly within RBV. This action pointed EO research into a direction that, until that time, had been rather elusive, because although EO research has enjoyed a fruitful tradition of empirical investigation, the concept had yet to find a theoretical base. Notably, EO studies have tended to build on previous conceptual and empirical works, but have not endeavored to explain the 'why' of the findings. We believe that this chapter should present an 'aha' moment for researchers, one that will motivate them to focus more work on the theoretical development of EO.

DEBATES IN EO RESEARCH

Certain areas of EO research remain open for clarification despite the significant growth in this line of inquiry. Two such areas, dimensionality and the relationship of EO to performance, are discussed in this section.

Dimensionality

A review of past EO research unveils some interesting research debates. One relates to measurement of EO and more specifically the appropriateness of the original three dimensions of EO, innovativeness, risk-taking and proactiveness, as proposed by Miller (1983). As discussed earlier, Lumpkin and Dess (1996) argued for the inclusion of five dimensions in the EO construct – adding autonomy and competitive aggressiveness to the original trio of dimensions. Although this conceptualization has been adopted by a few authors (e.g. Frese et al., 2002) this has not been the common practice of entrepreneurship scholars. Critics hold that autonomy may be more of an individual-level characteristic and therefore difficult to create and maintain at a firm level, or that autonomy is an antecedent of EO rather than a separate dimension. The major criticism against competitive aggressiveness is that it simply does not relate to entrepreneurship, at least not in all cultural contexts. Thus, although competitive aggressiveness may be important to performance, it may fall outside of the entrepreneurship domain.

A review of the literature also shows that other dimensions have been included in the EO construct. Some of these are: analysis, defensiveness and futurity (Morgan and Strong, 2003; Venkatraman, 1989); strategic planning activities, customer needs and wants identification, vision to reality, identification of opportunities (Smart and Conant, 1994); strategic renewal (Zahra, 1996); futurity, risk affinity, analysis, and defensiveness (Tan and Tan, 2005); and assertiveness (Walter et al., 2006). These and other dimensions have not received any significant following among researchers.

We believe that the reason why the dimensionality of EO is still debated and remains unresolved is that the construct was initiated without any solid theoretical grounding. Using logic, examples, and rhetorical skill, it is probably possible to argue for any number of dimensions of the EO construct. Our review indicates that rather than worrying too much about conceptual issues, EO researchers have been very pragmatic in their approach to the issue of the number of EO dimensions. They have typically utilized measurement scales that are available, and that have seemed to work empirically based on previous research. A three-dimensional version of the instrument consisting of nine well-established items is, of course, easier to use than a longer five-dimensional version where not all items have been developed and validated. Such practical issues are probably a reason why the three-dimensional instrument developed by Covin and Slevin (1986; 1989) still dominates. Given the origin of EO research in the ambitions of the Aston group to weigh and measure organizations, this approach is true, in a way, to the origins of the research.

The second debate in the study of EO is about the uni- or multi-dimensionality of EO. Uni-dimensionality refers to the tendency of all variables in question to co-vary, that is, when a firm scores high on one variable, it will also score high on the others. Miller (1983) proposed that the EO construct was uni-dimensional based on the 'intuitive' reasoning that an entrepreneurial firm would exhibit innovativeness, risk-taking and proactiveness. This position was adopted by Covin and Slevin (1989), who further developed the EO measurement scale as designed by Miller. In a recent meta-analysis, the uni-dimensional nature of EO could not be rejected (Rauch et al., 2009).

The uni-dimensionality of EO was challenged by Lumpkin and Dess (1996), who argued that the dimensions of EO need not co-vary, but that based on a particular context, each could vary independently of the others. These authors suggested that the uni-dimensional measure of EO would not fully capture the distinct contribution of each dimension and suggested a multi-dimensional conceptualization of the construct. This position has also found some empirical support (e.g. Kreiser et al., 2002).

It appears, however, that researchers have primarily investigated EO as a uni-dimensional construct (e.g. Becherer and Maurer, 1999; Covin et al., 2006; Lee et al.,

2001; Miller and Toulouse, 1986; Smart and Conant, 1994). Again, we attribute this to pragmatism because it is analytically easier to deal with a uni-dimensional than a multi-dimensional construct. It is also clear that in the vast majority of studies, the dimensions of EO correlate positively to such an extent that combining all items into one variable does not violate measurement conventions. Interestingly, a recent paper addressing EO dimensionality showed that this issue is much more complex analytically than previously assumed (George, 2006). Much more likely remains to be said on this issue. Our prediction, however, is that for practical reasons, scholars will predominantly rely on the uni-dimensional approach.

EO and Performance

The dominant focus of entrepreneurial orientation research has been on the construct's relationship to performance, with most scholars assuming a positive relationship. This hypothesis has been consistently supported in empirical tests (e.g. Covin and Slevin, 1986; Lumpkin and Dess, 2001; Wiklund, 1999; Zahra and Covin, 1995), suggesting that EO enhances performance. Building on this consistency of results, empirical work began to investigate those factors that might moderate the EO–performance relationship.

Although the early research on EO focused largely on the direct effect of this construct on a firm's performance, a stream of research has emerged which uses the contingency approach to studying the EO–performance relationship. The use of this approach, as promoted by several scholars (e.g. Covin and Slevin, 1991; Lumpkin and Dess, 1996), has shown that the EO–performance relationship can be affected by other variables. For example, uncertainty in a firm's home country was found to have a positive and moderate effect on the firm's international EO–performance relationship (Dimitratos et al., 2004). Other factors have also been found to exercise moderating effects in EO studies, including a firm's life cycle stage (Lumpkin and Dess, 2001), national culture (Marino et al., 2002), network capabilities (Walter et al., 2006), and strategic decision making participativeness, strategy formation mode, and strategic learning from failure (Covin et al., 2006).

A configurational approach can also produce richer results than those obtained through bivariate correlations. The significance of using this approach in EO research was demonstrated by Wiklund and Shepherd (2005). They tested the three-way interaction of EO, access to capital, environmental dynamism and its influence on performance. Comparing the results of main effect, contingency and configurational models, they found that the configurational model yielded the most informative findings. This study also suggested that researchers extend this approach to include additional variables for configurational analysis.

FUTURE CHALLENGES AND DIRECTIONS FOR EO RESEARCH

On the basis of our documenting EO research to date, some future challenges and opportunities for research become clear. In the sections below, we identify areas that we believe hold significant promise for future investigation. We begin with a discussion on the theoretical grounding for EO research, followed by a discussion on measurement issues. We then provide thoughts on the potential relationship between EO and failure as well as levels of analysis used in EO research. We conclude with a discussion on antecedents and causal mechanisms of EO.

Theoretical Grounding

Research has developed substantially since the 1960s when the Aston group first started its attempts to measure organizational characteristics. Likewise, entrepreneurship research was in its infancy when Miller developed his approach and measurement scale in the early 1980s. As a result, EO research has a very empirically driven origin, and research has largely remained empirical. Today, however, management and entrepreneurship research is theory driven to a much larger extent. A major challenge for EO research, therefore, is to provide the construct and research with a solid theoretical grounding.

This is not the place to make suggestions as to exactly how this should be done. We do note, however, that strategy research increasingly deals with dynamic issues that are largely entrepreneurial in nature. Potentially, EO research can find a theoretical habitat within these dynamic approaches in strategy research. One such approach is to view EO through the lens of absorptive capacity theory. According to this theory, 'the ability of a firm to recognize the value of new, external information, assimilate it, and apply it to commercial ends is critical to its innovative capabilities' (Cohen and Levinthal, 1990). If we remember Covin and Slevin's conceptual model of EO (Figure 7.1), we could be led to examine an organization's absorptive capacity (internal variable) as a moderator in the EO–performance relationship.

We also believe that it is probably less fruitful to try to develop a unique EO theory separate from other theories in entrepreneurship or strategy research. An added benefit of a solid theoretical grounding is that it may be easier for EO scholars to publish their work in the kind of high quality journals that favor theory-driven research.

Measurement

In terms of empirical issues, despite substantial efforts in the past, a concern remains with EO measurement; thus, there remains opportunity to improve the EO measurement scale, particularly in non-US contexts. Although notable advances have been made in this arena (Knight, 1997; Kreiser et al., 2002), the scale still has not been validated for universal usage. Additional validation, and even the development of new measurement scales, would facilitate the growing body of international EO research.

In addition, although the majority of the current research uses the dimensions of innovativeness, risk-taking and proactiveness in measuring EO, Rauch et al. (2009) noted that due to the paucity of studies that had been conducted using additional dimensions of EO, the impact of additional dimensions on performance has not yet been adequately determined. Thus, this remains a rich area for further inquiry. For example, Brown et al. (2001) operationalized and validated a firm-level entrepreneurship construct labeled 'Entrepreneurial Management' as an alternative to EO. They showed that their six dimensions of this construct were positively associated with each of the EO dimensions, so some or all of these dimensions could potentially be integrated into the EO construct to arrive at a more complete measurement scale.

Researchers may also want to consider the suggestions of Zahra (1993) that have not yet been incorporated into EO research. These ideas include considering non-financial outcomes (e.g. retention of the best employees or the creation of a positive organizational environment) in addition to the financial outcomes of entrepreneurial activity.

EO and Failure

The relationship between performance and EO continues to be a fertile area of research. Although prior studies have firmly established the relationship of EO and performance in surviving firms, little (if any) of the prior work has examined the role of EO on firm failure (Rauch et al., 2009). Extant literature implies that firms can be 'too' entrepreneurial, and that this behavior can lead to failure. For example, Rauch et al. (2009) suggested that a firm's propensity for risk taking can not only lead to improvements in performance, but also to higher incidence of failure. Additional research in this area could help to determine whether, in fact, EO can have opposite effects on performance, and to determine which characteristics of this construct (such as degree or level of EO exhibited) facilitates positive or negative outcomes.

Levels of Analysis

Future work could also focus on clarifying the levels of analysis (Davidsson and Wiklund, 2001) and integrating the findings of EO research into a single framework. To date, various studies have investigated this phenomenon at the firm, business unit, or functional level, but a framework is also needed, that facilitates an understanding of how findings from these studies relate to each other.

Antecedents of EO

Miller started out by examining the antecedents of EO, but most research since then has looked at the consequences. We feel, however, that there is still plenty of opportunity for making a contribution to the EO literature by further examining its antecedents. For example, why do some firms become entrepreneurial, whereas others refrain from doing so? The variables included in Covin and Slevin's model of entrepreneurship (1991) might be investigated as possible antecedents. As such, one might consider examining whether the degree of technological sophistication, environmental dynamism or hostility, life cycle stage, certain business practices, or top management values/philosophies act as antecedents to firm entrepreneurial behavior. Although not intended to be exhaustive, this list provides a good starting point for identifying possible antecedents to EO. Investigators may obtain the most revealing results by testing the direct effects of possible antecedents of EO as well as testing configurational relationships between various antecedents, EO, and performance.

Performance and Causal Mechanisms

Finally, the recommendations for the future listed above clearly point out that the causal mechanisms underlying the positive performance implications of EO are still not well understood. There is, however, a general movement in the literature towards explicating the mechanisms of phenomena. As stated by Davis and Marquis (2005, p. 340): 'The most productive theoretical work going forward will be in the cataloging and developing organizational mechanisms,' and in-depth case studies are ideal for explicating such mechanisms. A fruitful research design would likely be to select some cases that score high on the EO scale and some that score low, and documenting in detail the reasons for and consequences of these differences in behavior, as well as what kinds of entrepreneurial behaviors tend to cluster together. Such research could likely serve to illuminate (but not provide definite answers to) many of the remaining challenges that we have just discussed.

Given that the EO research has been so successful at developing measurement scales, showing relationships with other important variables and building a cumulative body of research in entrepreneurship, this call for case studies may appear out of date. As we mentioned in the beginning of this chapter, however, we should keep in mind that EO research builds on the work of the Aston group conducted in the early 1960s. These researchers set out to measure organizations using an approach inspired by the natural sciences. In the cataloguing and measurement of important aspects of organizations, they built on extensive field work and case studies. Returning to such methods almost 50 years later would likely reveal many new and exciting aspects of EO.

REFERENCES

Antoncic, B. and R.D. Hisrich (2001), 'Intrapreneurship: construct refinement and cross-cultural validation', *Journal of Business Venturing*, **16**, 495–527.

Barrett, H. and A. Weinstein (1999), 'The effects of market orientation and organizational flexibility on corporate entrepreneurship', *Entrepreneurship Theory and Practice*, **23**(1), 57–70.

Becherer, R.C. and J.G. Maurer (1999), 'The proactive personality disposition and entrepreneurial behavior among small company presidents', *Journal of Small Business Management*, January, 28–36.

Bourgeois, L. and D. Brodwin (1984), 'Strategic implementation: five approaches to an elusive phenomenon', *Strategic Management Journal*, **5**, 241–64.

Brown, T.E., P. Davidsson and J. Wiklund (2001), 'An operationalization of Stevenson's conceptualization of entrepreneurship as opportunity-based firm behavior', *Strategic Management Journal*, **22**(10), 953–68.

Burgelman, R.A. (1983), 'A model of the interaction of strategic behavior, corporate context and the concept of strategy', *Academy of Management Review*, **8**(1), 61–70.

Burgelman, R.A. (1991), 'Intraorganizational ecology of strategy making and organizational adaptation: theory and field research', *Organizational Science*, **2**(3), 239–62.

Cohen, W.M. and D.A. Levinthal (1990), 'Absorptive capacity: a new perspective on learning and innovation', *Administrative Science Quarterly*, **35**(1), 128–52.

Cooper, A.C., G.E. Willard and C.W. Woo (1986), 'Strategies of high-performing new and small firms: a re-examination of the niche concept', *Journal of Business Venturing*, **1**, 247–60.

Covin, J.G., K.M. Green and D.P. Slevin (2006), 'Strategic process effects on the entrepreneurial orientation–sales growth rate relationship', *Entrepreneurship Theory and Practice*, **30**(1), 57–81.

Covin, J.G. and D.P. Slevin (1986), 'The development and testing of an organizational-level entrepreneurship scale', in R. Ronstadt, J.A. Hornaday, R. Peterson and K.H. Vesper (eds), *Frontiers of Entrepreneurship Research*, Wellesley, MA: Babson College, pp. 628–39.

Covin, J.G. and D.P. Slevin (1989), 'Strategic management of small firms in hostile and benign environments', *Strategic Management Journal*, **10**, 78–87.

Covin, J.G. and D.P. Slevin (1991), 'A conceptual model of entrepreneurship as firm behavior', *Entrepreneurship Theory and Practice*, **16**(1), 7–24.

Davidsson, P. and J. Wiklund (2001), 'Levels of analysis in entrepreneurship research: current research practice and suggestions for the future', *Entrepreneurship Theory and Practice*, **25**(4), 81–100.

Davis, G.F. and C. Marquis (2005), 'Prospects for organization theory in the early twenty-first century: institutional fields and mechanisms', *Organization Science*, **16**(4), 332–43.

Dimitratos, P., S. Lioukas and S. Carter (2004), 'The relationship between entrepreneurship and international performance: the importance of domestic environment', *International Business Review*, **13**, 19–41.

Frese, M., A. Brantjes and R. Hoorn (2002), 'Psychological success factors of small scale businesses in Namibia: the roles of strategy process, entrepreneurial orientation and the environment', *Journal of Developmental Entrepreneurship*, **7**(3), 259–82.

Gartner, W.B. (1988), 'Who is the entrepreneur? is the wrong question', *American Journal of Small Business*, **12**(4), 11–32.

George, B.A. (2006), 'Entrepreneurial orientation: A theoretical and empirical examination of the consequences of differing construct representations', paper presented at the Babson conference, Bloomington, IA.

Ginsberg, A. (1985), 'Measuring changes in entrepreneurial orientation following industry deregulation – the development of a diagnostic instrument', in G.B. Roberts (ed.), *Proceedings: Discovering Entrepreneurship*, US Affiliate of the International Council for Small Business, Marietta, GA.

Hart, S.L. (1992), 'An integrative framework for strategy-making processes', *Academy of Management Review*, **17**, 327–51.

Khandwalla, P.N. (1976), 'Some top management styles, their context and performance', *Organization and Administrative Sciences*, **7**(4), 21–51.

Knight, G.A. (1997), 'Cross-cultural reliability and validity of a scale to measure firm entrepreneurial orientation', *Journal of Business Venturing*, **12**, 213–25.

Kreiser, P.M., L.D. Marino and K.M. Weaver (2002), 'Assessing the psychometric properties of the entrepreneurial orientation scale: a multi-country analysis', *Entrepreneurship Theory and Practice*, **26**(4), 71–94.

Lee, C., K. Lee and J.M. Pennings (2001), 'Internal capabilities, external networks, and performance: a study of technology based ventures', *Strategic Management Journal*, **22**, 615–40.

Low, D.R., R.L. Chapman and T.R. Sloan (2007), 'Inter-relationships between innovation and market orientation in SMEs', *Management Review News*, **30**(12), 878–91.

Lumpkin, G.T. and G.G. Dess (1996), 'Clarifying the entrepreneurial orientation construct and linking it to performance', *Academy of Management Review*, **21**(1), 135–72.

Lumpkin, G.T. and G.G. Dess (2001), 'Linking two dimensions of entrepreneurial orientation to firm performance: the moderating role of environment and industry life cycle', *Journal of Business Venturing*, **16**, 429–51.

MacMillan, I.C. and P.E. Jones (1984), 'Designing organizations to compete', *Journal of Business Strategy*, **4**, 11–26.

Marino, L., K. Strandholm, H.K. Steensma and K.M. Weaver (2002), 'The moderating effect of national culture on the relationship between entrepreneurial orientation and strategic alliance portfolio extensiveness', *Entrepreneurship Theory and Practice*, **26**(4), 145–60.

Miller, D. (1983), 'The correlates of entrepreneurship in three types of firms', *Management Science*, **29**(7), 770–91.

Miller, D. and P.H. Friesen (1978), 'Archetypes of strategy formulation', *Management Science*, **24**(9), 921–33.

Miller, D. and P.H. Friesen (1982), 'Innovation in conservative and entrepreneurial firms: two models of strategic momentum', *Strategic Management Journal*, **3**(1), 1–25.

Miller, D. and J.M. Toulouse (1986), 'Chief executive personality and corporate strategy and structure in small firms', *Management Science*, **32**(11), 1389–409.

Mintzberg, H. (1973), 'Strategy-making in three modes', *California Management Review*, **16**, 44–53.

Morgan, R.E. and C.A. Strong (2003), 'Business performance and dimensions of strategic orientation', *Journal of Business Research*, **56**(3), 163–76.

Pugh, D.S., D.J. Hickson, C.R. Hinings, K.M. Mcdonald, C. Turner and T. Lupton (1963), 'A conceptual scheme for organizational analysis', *Administrative Science Quarterly*, **8**(3), 289–315.

Rauch, A., J. Wiklund, G.T. Lumpkin and M. Frese (2009), 'Entrepreneurial orientation and business performance: an assessment of past research and suggestions for the future', *Entrepreneurship Theory and Practice*, **33**(3), 761–87.

Real, J.C., A. Leal and J.L. Roldan (2006), 'Determinants of organizational learning in the generation of technological distinctive competencies', *International Journal of Technology Management*, **35**(1–4), 284–307.

Smart, D.T. and J.S. Conant (1994), 'Entrepreneurial orientation distinctive marketing competencies and organizational performance', *Journal of Applied Business Research*, **10**(3), 28–39.

Tan, J. and D. Tan (2005), 'Environment-strategy coevolution and coalignment: a staged-model of chinese SOEs under transition', *Strategic Management Journal*, **26**(2), 141–57.

Venkatraman, N. (1989), 'Strategic orientation of business enterprises: the construct, dimensionality and measurement', *Management Science*, **35**(8), 942–62.

Walter, A., M. Auer and T. Ritter (2006), 'The impact of network capabilities and entrepreneurial orientation on university spin-off performance', *Journal of Business Venturing*, **21**, 541–67.

Wiklund, J. (1999), 'The sustainability of the entrepreneurial orientation – performance relationship', *Entrepreneurship Theory and Practice*, **24**, 37–48.

Wiklund, J. and D. Shepherd (2003), 'Knowledge-based resources, entrepreneurial orientation, and the performance of small and medium sized businesses', *Strategic Management Journal*, **24**(13), 1307–14.

Wiklund, J. and D. Shepherd (2005), 'Entrepreneurial orientation and small business performance: a configurational approach', *Journal of Business Venturing*, **20**, 71–91.

Woo, C.Y. and A.C. Cooper (1981), 'Strategies of effective low share business', *Strategic Management Journal*, **2**, 301–18.

Zahra, S.A. (1993), 'A conceptual model of entrepreneurship as firm behavior: a critique and extension', *Entrepreneurship Theory and Practice*, **17**, 5–21.

Zahra, S.A. (1996), 'Governance, ownership, and corporate entrepreneurship: the moderating impact of industry technological opportunities', *Academy of Management Journal*, **39**(6), 1713–35.

Zahra, S.A. and J.G. Covin (1995), 'Contextual influences on the corporate entrepreneurship performance relationship: a longitudinal analysis', *Journal of Business Venturing*, **10**(3), 43–58.

APPENDIX

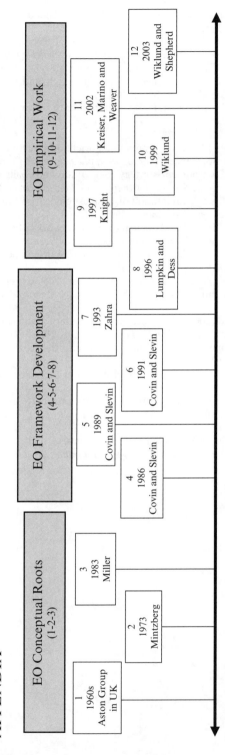

Figure 7A.1   Timeline: key thinkers in EO research

Section II.2

Opportunity Evaluation

8. On the relevance of decision-making in entrepreneurial decision-making

Saras D. Sarasvathy and Henrik Berglund

INTRODUCTION: ENTREPRENEURSHIP AS DECISION-MAKING

The very first Frontiers of Entrepreneurship Research, published in 1981, included an article on venture capital decision-making. Mostly atheoretical, it just mapped out the process of decision-making.

Thereafter, Olson defined entrepreneurs as decision makers:

> This paper has characterized entrepreneurs as decision makers who identify and capitalize on opportunities through approaches that emphasize innovation, profitable venture identification, effectiveness rather than efficiency, and nonprogrammed or ambiguous situations. (Olson, 1986)

The link between decision theory and entrepreneurs was noted as early as 1959, however, in *Administrative Science Quarterly*. In a paper entitled 'Managers and entrepreneurs: a useful distinction?', Heinz Hartmann argued for decision-making as a basic and useful differentiator between managers and entrepreneurs.

More recently, however, scholars are beginning to include affect and even biological and neurological processes in determining entrepreneurial behavior. Yet, when we examine the actual use of decision-making research in our scholarship, it is clear that only a thin slice of what is possible has been accomplished, to date. Even more importantly, hardly any efforts have been made to take results from entrepreneurship back to scholarship in decision-making – whether to cumulate overlapping findings or to challenge assumptions and claims.

Accordingly, in this chapter, we hope to highlight both the untapped possibilities from decision-making to entrepreneurship and the opportunities for dialog back from entrepreneurship to decision-making. We begin with a brief overview of the history of decision-making, which turns out to be a tapestry of arguments around the notion of 'rationality'.

A HISTORY OF DECISION-MAKING: FROM RATIONALITY TO DEVIATIONS TO PLURAL VIEWS

Most theories used in entrepreneurship research consist as variations of classical models examining economic rationality. In recent times, the trend has been to look at research from cognitive psychology, with a particular emphasis on deviations from classical rationality – such as heuristics and biases (Baron, 1998). Formal models of decision-making under risk (Douglas and Shepherd, 2002) and uncertainty (Fiet et al., 2005) have also been used.

The history and theory of rationality, however, has a lot more to offer than classical economic rationality and its deviations. In *The Nature of Rationality*, philosopher Robert Nozick (1993) argued for the importance of acknowledging modes of rationality that go beyond expected utility maximization. In social settings it is, for instance, important to embrace the symbolic utilities of acts themselves, and more generally it is important to recognize the rationality of producing novel outcomes and new ideas. Along the same lines, Jim March (1978) had earlier observed a range of human behaviors that are in open conflict with the canons of classical rationality: e.g. choices based on inconsistent, vague, fleeting or ostensibly unimportant preferences. While acknowledging that such behaviors are often irrational, March, like Nozick, also argued that it is quite possible that in some situations – especially situations characterized by uncertainty and ambiguity – such behaviors are highly appropriate and that they represent 'not necessarily a fault in human choice to be corrected but often a form of intelligence to be refined by the technology of choice rather than ignored by it' (March, 1978, p. 598).

Clearly, both philosophical and organizational understandings of rationality are open to a much broader spectrum of explanations than those traditionally included in models of rational decision-making. Moreover, because many interesting entrepreneurial activities take place in uncertain and ambiguous situations, the field probably has much to gain from embracing such broadened conceptions of rationality and decision-making.

A Historical Review of Rationality

The sheer volume of work related to rationality and the diversity of fields that build upon various conceptions of it preclude any attempt at a comprehensive review, short of a complete encyclopedia. Therefore, we limit ourselves here to a simple chronological listing of several different types of rationality and then move toward a framework relevant to entrepreneurship research.

Decision-making under certainty

While assuming a certain level of rationality, many classical economists, including Adam Smith, also speculated about the psychological make-up of the individual agents populating their theories. However, in the 1930s a group of economists started to build strictly mathematical models of the economy, based on a few simple axioms including complete and transitive preferences and rational choice (e.g. Samuelson, 1938). In these models, environmental constraints and possible outcomes are assumed to be known and stable. Decision-making is then a matter of calculating the optimal alternative. With some modifications (discussed next), this is the type of rationality that the bulk of mainstream economics is based on.

Decision-making under risk and uncertainty

Although nowadays considered fundamental to economic theorizing, risk was not formally incorporated into the discipline until fairly late. In more colloquial terms, risk and uncertainty had been part of economic discourse for quite some time (cf. the discussion of judgmental decision-making under true uncertainty below), but it was only when precise mathematical models were extended to also include risky choices – i.e. where all outcomes and their respective probabilities are treated as objectively known – that risk truly became central to economic theory (von Neumann and Morgenstern, 1944). Even with risk present, however, choices are still a matter of rationally maximizing expected utility within a given decision framework. Consequently, although there are choices to be made, little room for the type of creativity commonly associated with entrepreneurship exists because changes in the decision environment always come from the outside. In the words of Baumol, 'until exogenous forces lead to an autonomous change in the environment . . . the firm is taken to replicate precisely its previous decisions, day after day, year after year' (Baumol, 1968 p. 67). Many economists have therefore sought to explain entrepreneurship by focusing on certain individuals' extraordinary capabilities (e.g. Caplan, 1999; Demsetz, 1983) or risk-propensities (e.g. Kihlstrom and Laffont, 1979) when facing a given decision-environment.

In the entrepreneurship field, studies of how entrepreneurs make risky decisions abound. In line with the economists just cited, the assumption in many of these studies is that risks can be accurately evaluated and that entrepreneurs tend to either underestimate these risks or overestimate their own ability to avoid or overcome them (Camerer and Lovallo, 1999; Forbes, 2005; Koellinger et al., 2007). Empirically, however, the issue of whether entrepreneurs are indeed risk takers is mixed. In two meta-reviews of this rather vast and robust literature, one found that entrepreneurs were risk averse (with a small effect size; Miner and Raju, 2004) and the other found the opposite (also with small effect size; Stewart and Roth, 2001). Other studies have focused on the decision to enter into self employment, which is modeled as a matter of individuals maximizing their expected utility given a known decision framework that includes individual ability and potential incomes, combined with constraints such as attitudes toward risk, independence and work effort (cf. Douglas and Shepherd, 2000; 2002; Lévesque et al., 2002). When the expected utility from self employment outweighs that of employment, the rational individual decides to become an entrepreneur.

When decisions are made under conditions of uncertainty – where outcomes are known but their probabilities are not – it is impossible to rationally calculate expected utilities, something which is possible when probability sets are known objectively (i.e. decision-making under risk) or subjectively (see Bayesian rationality below). This lack of information makes the definition of rationality problematic because it forces the decision-maker to rely on more or less arbitrary decision-making strategies such as: choose the alternative where the worst possible outcome is as good as possible (maximin), or choose the alternative where the best possible expected utility is as good as possible (maximax) (Pearman, 1977). Adoption of strategies such as these reflects either a pessimistic or an optimistic outlook. Thus it appears that accounts of entrepreneurial decision-making under uncertain conditions – much as decision-making under risk – boil down to individual risk-propensities or attitudes.

Bayesian rationality
Bayesian, or subjective expected utility, models of decision-making are quite similar to models of decision-making under risk. Instead of assuming that the probabilities of

outcomes refer to likelihoods in the physical world, however, Bayesian models assume that such probability sets are subjective, i.e. that they are based on the limited information about the world that the agent currently has available (Savage, 1954). Agents are still assumed to maximize their expected utility, but based on both a subjective utility function and a subjective probability set. A key feature of Bayesian rationality is that decision makers update their subjective probability sets with experience (Oaksford and Chater, 2009). As a result, the Bayesian decision maker will gradually make more qualified decisions based on more and more information about the world.

Fiet and colleagues have developed a normative Bayesian model of entrepreneurial decision-making, in which individuals plan and search systematically for pre-existing opportunities. This is achieved as individuals restrict their search to a limited domain of inquiry – in which the subjective probabilities of all alternative outcomes are known – and within this domain make optimal decisions, e.g. investments in new information signals (Fiet, 2002; Fiet et al., 2005).

Bounded and procedural rationality

The notion of judgment has also been the focus of attention of a large body of research in behavioral decision theory that was originally motivated by Herbert Simon's work on bounded rationality. Models of bounded rationality embrace much of the classical model of rational decision-making (Simon, 1955; 1977). Individuals still seek to maximize their expected utility in a known decision environment, but with some added constraints on information processing capacity, problem solving skills, and memory usage. Because these limitations make the task of maximizing expected utility overwhelming, the decision-making process is brought into sharper focus as people are forced to rely on 'satisficing' decision-making procedures.

Much of the work on entrepreneurial cognition can be seen as explorations of bounded rationality in the context of entrepreneurial decision-making. Often these studies focus on how certain cognitive heuristics and biases produce decisions that deviate from the precepts of classical rationality. Drawing on these insights, entrepreneurship scholars have found evidence that entrepreneurs are more prone than others to certain biases such as overconfidence, belief in the law of small numbers and illusion of control (Busenitz and Barney, 1997; Camerer and Lovallo, 1999; Simon et al., 2000), and less prone than bankers to certain biases such as status quo bias (Burmeister and Schade, 2007). Although such biases can clearly be both harmful and beneficial to entrepreneurship, the goal is often to help entrepreneurs identify their flawed modes of reasoning and help them behave more in accord with classical rationality (e.g. Baron, 1998).

Other proponents of process rationality downplay outcomes and expected utilities even more – partly because the uncertainty of future preferences make expected utility calculations problematic (March, 1978) – and instead highlight salient attributes of the decision-making process as such. The argument is that outcomes can often be seen as ancillary end-results of processes that are halted, redirected and driven forward by the pleasures and pains of the process itself, including wishes to avoid discomfort or embarrassment (March, 1978), or ambitions to signal legitimacy or creativity (Nozick, 1993). In an example from the entrepreneurship field, Honig and Karlsson (2004) found that the decision to write a business plan could be better explained as the result of coercive and mimetic forces than as a consequence of rational considerations.

Prospect theory and regret theory

Clearly acknowledging the bounds on human rationality, prospect theory is an empirically grounded model of decision-making that accounts for a number of empirically identified violations of the axioms of rational decision-making (i.e. axioms that are common to decision-making under risk and Bayesian decision-making; Kahneman and Tversky, 1979). Prospect theory divides decision-making procedure into two phases: editing and evaluation. During the editing phase, the agent analyzes the problem's 'prospects' (i.e. its outcomes and probabilities) in a way that yields a simpler representation of the problem, for example by reducing, combining or simplifying prospects. The most important editing, however, consists in determining a reference point that marks the border between what is considered a loss or a gain. During the evaluation phase, the agent chooses the prospect with the highest utility. When doing so, however, people tend to: (1) value similar sized losses higher than gains, (2) overvalue small probability events and undervalue medium and high probability events and, (3) most importantly, be risk-averse in gain situations and risk-prone when facing losses.

A number of authors have suggested prospect theory as a useful framework for understanding how entrepreneurs decide to take, what appear to be, extraordinary risks when developing their companies (Busenitz et al., 2003). Prospect theory has also been used to explain the decision to become an entrepreneur. Baron thus suggests that: 'persons who choose to become entrepreneurs tend to frame many situations in terms of losses; that is, they focus on the possibilities for economic gains they will forfeit if they ignore or overlook an opportunity and continue to work for an existing organization' (Baron, 2004, p. 225).

Similarly, regret theory seeks to improve on the classical model of rationality by incorporating behavioral evidence. This is done by including the feelings of regret (or rejoicing) that subjects anticipate, should a better (worse) outcome than the one chosen materialize. The result is a two dimensional utility function U(X, Y), where X represents the traditional expected utility and Y denotes the difference in utility between actual outcomes and best (worst) alternatives (Sugden, 1986). Although regret theory has, to the best of our knowledge, not been used by entrepreneurship researchers, it is a parsimonious theory that can explain decision paradoxes such as how the same person can be both risk-prone and risk-averse (see Markham et al. (2002) for related literature on regretful thinking). For example, if you consider betting on a particular horse for the next race and then decide not to, it would be awful to see it win at long odds, making you more likely to actually bet. In the same way, seeing your house burn down after you have decided not to insure it would be an occasion for strongly felt regret, making you more likely to buy insurance.

Judgmental decision-making under true uncertainty

Many economists of entrepreneurship highlight the need to clearly separate the notion of probabilistic risk from true uncertainty. True uncertainty here refers to situations where both potential outcomes and their probabilities are unknown, in part because the situations in question are unique and unrepeatable (Cantillon, 1755, p. 54; Knight, 1921, p. 227; Mises, 1949, p. 110). Consequently, decision-making under uncertainty has to rely on some form of qualitative judgment or intuition rather than on quantitative calculations. In his well known discussion on judgmental decision-making under true uncertainty, Frank Knight did not specify the content of 'judgment' but simply assumed that this capacity existed in humans; that evolution has brought about something in our relationship with the world that allows us to make sound decisions even in the face of a radically uncertain future:

> The ultimate logic, or psychology, of these deliberations is obscure, a part of the scientifically unfathomable mystery of life and mind. We must simply fall back upon a 'capacity' in the intelligent animal to form more or less correct judgments about things, an intuitive sense of values. We are so built that what seems to us reasonable is likely to be confirmed by experience, or we could not live in the world at all. (Knight, 1921, p. 228)

The issue of what constitutes judgment is an intriguing one. As discussed above, behavioral decision theorists have identified a variety of heuristics and biases to which human beings in general are prone. Proponents of ecological rationality, however, argue that seeing heuristics as imperfect versions of optimal statistical procedures may tell the wrong story (Bullock and Todd, 1999; Gigerenzer and Todd, 1999). These authors argue that human beings have evolved to use fast and frugal heuristics that help them adapt to and survive in changing environments. Consequently, environmental fit and functionality, not the internal properties of the problem solving process, provides the key to understanding human cognition. Also, in certain cases, with some interesting corrective procedures such as alternative presentations of the same data – frequencies versus point estimates in probability problems, for example – the so-called 'biases' disappear (Gigerenzer et al., 1988).

Like Knight, many recent entrepreneurship researchers continue to simply assume that there exists such a thing as good judgment and that some people have it and others do not. Casson (2005, p. 329) makes the case for entrepreneurial judgment as follows:

> Judgemental decision-making involves an element of improvisation rather than exclusive reliance on routines. It makes use not only of publicly available information but also of private information available only to a few. The exercise of judgment involves a synthesis of all this information, for it is rarely the case that a single item of information is sufficient for taking an important business decision. Although everyone makes judgmental decisions from time to time, only the entrepreneur specializes in this activity.

Langlois (2007, p. 1112) uses a definition much closer to Knight:

> Judgment is the (largely tacit) ability to make, under conditions of structural uncertainty, decisions that turn out to be reasonable or successful *ex post*.

By black-boxing the specifics of the entrepreneurial decision-making process, these authors seek to draw out the implications of true uncertainty for aspects of entrepreneurial organization and behavior. One way this is done is to make judgmental decision-making the basis of a theory of the firm (Langlois, 2007). Because qualitative judgments about uncertain outcomes cannot be bought and sold on a market – for reasons that also include moral hazard and the general problem of buying and selling information (Arrow, 1962) – the argument is that entrepreneurs must capitalize their judgments themselves (Foss et al., 2007; Langlois, 2007). Others relate judgmental decision-making under true uncertainty to charismatic leadership. Because judgments are highly subjective and hence difficult to communicate, it is difficult for entrepreneurs to use rational arguments when persuading employees or partners as to why the formers' visions of the future are plausible and worthy of allegiance. Therefore, entrepreneurs must rely on other ways of ensuring that goals and efforts are aligned. In this context, Witt (1998) speaks of the need for cognitive leadership and Langlois (1998), drawing on Weber, sees the entrepreneur as displaying charismatic authority.

Vickers (1965) takes a more normative view and urges humans to develop good judgment almost as an imperative for the future. His focus is thus on the particularities of important human situations and the impossibility of simply extrapolating from the past or following so-called 'general laws' in making decisions involving complex policy matters. At the end of his seminal compilation of detailed case studies that illustrate the particularities that necessitate judgment as opposed to mere rationality, Vickers (1965, p. 261) concludes:

> For if my analysis is remotely right, the future of our society depends on the speed with which it can *learn* – learn not primarily new ways of responding, though these are needed, but primarily new ways of appreciating a situation that is new and new through our own making . . .

A recent stream of research in entrepreneurship has begun looking into the black-box of entrepreneurial judgment under true uncertainty, codifying an internally consistent set of heuristics used by expert entrepreneurs called 'effectual logic'. (See our outline of effectual rationality below.)

Post-hoc rationality

Most temporally oriented decision-making models assert that actions follow from and conform to given preferences (e.g. a utility function). People are assumed to start with a given set of preferences and, based on this, arrive at some form of decision regarding how to behave in given situations (e.g. maximize expected utility). Models of post-hoc rationality reverse this sequence. Actions are still seen as consistent with preferences, but this consistency is brought about by individuals acting first and only later, when the outcomes can be observed, forming preferences (Weick, 1995).

Hill and Levenhagen (1995) argue that successful entrepreneurs must be able to deal with substantial uncertainty and ambiguity. This is in part accomplished through the retrospective development of plausible visions of the venture's future. Besides being critical as a way to reflexively establish order in the face of uncertainty and ambiguity, vivid post-hoc rationalizations also enable entrepreneurs to more effectively communicate broad and abstract concepts.

Creative and phenomenological rationality

In a major assault on the limitations of the notion of rationality, Hans Joas (1996) painstakingly pointed out that most models of rationality ignore at least three important aspects of decision-making, namely: 'corporeality', the fact that decision makers only have imperfect control over their bodies; 'situatedness', the fact that decision makers are situated in particular circumstances and those circumstances often are inextricable from the decision parameters; and 'sociality', the fact that decision makers are social beings who operate within the context of and interact with other human beings in important ways that make a difference to the way they make decisions.

In effect, Joas's argument boils down to the conclusion that most familiar models of rationality are actually special cases where corporeality, situatedness and sociality do not matter or are deemed not to matter. The moment we become more realistic about these three 'assumed away' aspects of real decision-making, everything changes. In particular, when we open up the decision space to these three dimensions of reality, the creativity of *all* action becomes inescapable and obvious. For the most part, creative action is not the exception but the norm in the human realm. In particular, the usual utilitarian calculus of rational decision-making ought to be relegated to those few specialized instances when we can assume away corporeality, situation and sociality. For most real world decisions and actions, it is better and more useful to use a Pragmatist philosophical basis than a Utilitarian one.

Similarly, Spinosa et al. (1997) draw on the phenomenological tradition to argue that the root source of innovative, or 'history-making', entrepreneurship cannot be explained in terms of abstract rational analyses. Grounded in an ontology that sees individuals as inseparable from the world, i.e. as 'being-in-the-world' (Dreyfus, 1991), such entrepreneurship must instead be understood in terms of individuals who sense, hold on to and engage with anomalies that they perceive in their everyday social and cultural practices. The results of such 'disclosive' activities are inconceivable in advance. Moreover, echoing March's admonition to treat future preferences as unknown, such activities are also seen to fundamentally change the worldview of the entrepreneur. This is elegantly illustrated with the example of falling in love:

> When a man falls in love, he loves a particular woman, but it is not that particular woman he needed *before* he fell in love. However, after he is in love, that is after he has found that this particular relationship is gratifying, the need becomes specific as the need for that particular woman, and the man has made a creative discovery about himself. He has become the sort of person that needs that specific relationship and must view himself as having lacked and needed this relationship all along. In such a creative discovery the world reveals a new order of significa-tion that is neither simply discovered nor arbitrarily chosen. (Dreyfus, 1979, p. 277)

Both Joas's exposition of creative rationality and Dreyfus's phenomenological account argue for a 'made' rather than a 'found' worldview. This is very much in line with both effectual rationality, described below, and the notion of moving from decision-making to design that we urge at the end of this chapter.

Recent developments directly related to entrepreneurship
More recently, researchers more directly involved in entrepreneurial decision-making have begun to realize that new conceptions of rationality may be required to describe what entrepreneurs do in building new ventures and creating innovations in the market-place. Some noteworthy developments include:

Practical intelligence   In the preface to his seminal book on the topic, Sternberg (2000, p. xi) describes practical intelligence as follows:

> Practical intelligence is what most people call common sense. It is the ability to adapt to, shape and select everyday environments. Intelligence as conventionally defined may be useful in eve-ryday life, but practical intelligence is indispensable. Without some measure of it, one cannot survive in a cultural milieu or even in the natural environment. In our work, we have studied

many aspects of practical intelligence, although we have concentrated on one particularly important aspect of it, *tacit knowledge,* namely the procedural knowledge one learns in everyday life that usually is not taught and often is not even verbalized.

Sternberg and colleagues have developed metrics, designed experiments and carried out fieldwork on the use of practical intelligence in a variety of different domains including entrepreneurship. In an article in the *Journal of Business Venturing,* Sternberg (2004) explains how practical intelligence may be combined with creative intelligence to generate and implement valuable new ideas in entrepreneurship:

> The most important kind of intelligence for an entrepreneur, or really anyone else, is successful intelligence, which involves a balance of analytical (IQ-based), creative, and practical intelligence. (Sternberg, 2004, p. 196)

Although research on practical intelligence is at the level of the individual, tacit knowledge in the form of successful routines and capabilities is important in the case of firms, especially the type of high-technology, high-growth firms that policy makers everywhere want to foster. Eisenhardt (1989) studied decision-making in high-velocity environments and has since connected her findings with the literature on dynamic capabilities in the strategic management literature (Eisenhardt and Martin, 2000).

Ad-hoc rationality   Winter (2003) examined the notion of 'dynamic capabilities' to argue that there are more ways for an organization to change than through the use of dynamic capabilities. Broadly speaking, dynamic capabilities involve the ability of organizations to change their capabilities in response to changing environments. As Teece et al. (1997, p. 526) define the term, dynamic capabilities are the capabilities by which firm managers 'integrate, build, and reconfigure internal and external competencies to address rapidly changing environments' (Teece et al., 1997, p. 516) in order to achieve sustained competitive advantage.

Winter cites Collis (1994) to observe that one could define an infinite regression of such capabilities – with normal operational capabilities at the zero-order, dynamic capabilities as first-order capabilities, and the ability to know when to change those being second-order and so on *ad infinitum*. In an important sense then, Winter argues, such higher order capabilities are unlikely to exist, simply because higher order changes in the environment most probably are highly unpredictable and simply cannot be 'prepared for' in any meaningful sense. Instead, Winter (2003, pp. 992–3) proposes the notion of ad-hoc problem solving:

> Whether it is because such an external challenge arrives or because an autonomous decision to change is made at a high level, organizations often have to cope with problems they are not well prepared for. They may be pushed into 'firefighting' mode, a high-paced, contingent, opportunistic and perhaps creative search for satisfactory alternative behaviors. It is useful to have a name for the category of such change behaviors that do not depend on dynamic capabilities – behaviors that are largely non-repetitive and at least 'intendedly rational' and not merely reactive or passive. I propose 'ad hoc problem solving'. Ad hoc problem solving is not routine; in particular, not highly patterned and not repetitive. As suggested above, it typically appears as a response to novel challenges from the environment or other relatively unpredictable events. Thus, ad hoc problem solving and the exercise of dynamic capabilities are two different ways to change – or two categories comprising numerous different ways to change.

But then Winter goes on to admit that there may be patterns and learnable heuristics within ad-hoc problem solving, especially with long practice and experience such as in the case of jazz musicians:

> Of course, close study of a series of 'fires' may well reveal that there is pattern even in 'firefighting.' Some of the pattern may be learned and contribute positively to effectiveness, and in that sense be akin to a skill or routine. (Winter, 2003, p. 993)

At least one such discernible pattern of internally consistent heuristics is what constitutes effectual logic, the decision–action framework by which expert entrepreneurs transform extant realities into new ventures and new markets.

Effectual rationality   Through a series of studies that compared expert entrepreneurs with novices and expert corporate executives, elements of effectual rationality have been identified and related to new market creation (Sarasvathy and Dew, 2005), marketing (Read et al., 2009), private equity investing (Wiltbank et al., 2009), as well as Austrian (Sarasvathy and Dew, 2010) and behavioral (Dew et al., 2008) and evolutionary economics (Sarasvathy et al., 2010a). Effectual logic is means-driven, driven by affordable loss rather than expected return as the criterion for investment, and focused on co-creating new ventures and markets through stakeholder self-selection processes aimed at both shaping the environment and making the future rather than predicting and adapting to them. Effectual logic is pragmatist at its core and takes a creative rather than a search-and-select stance toward decision-making. It is also action-oriented and explicitly incorporates ad-hoc or serendipitous problem solving by leveraging rather than avoiding unexpected contingencies.

Several of these recent developments in decision-making approaches listed above have not yet been fully developed in entrepreneurship research. We believe that the work to date has barely scratched the surface of what is possible, simply because entrepreneurship is a particularly rich domain for a pluralistic view of rationality and also a rather unique domain that encompasses a multi-dimensional decision space – a Galapagos island of human problem solving, as it were. In the next section, we provide an outline of the space through practical examples attached to key theoretical concepts, some of which have not yet been introduced to entrepreneurship research or even to the scholarship in decision-making in general.

THE PROBLEM SPACE FOR DECISION-MAKING IN ENTREPRENEURSHIP: FROM UNCERTAINTY TO OPENNESS

An interesting trend that emerges through a historical analysis of conceptions of rationality is the increasing entanglement of the decision maker with other decision makers as well as with the environment in which decisions occur and decision makers operate. Indeed, it is this entanglement that is of particular interest to entrepreneurship research.

In order to understand the role of decision-making in entrepreneurship research, per se, it is good to begin with Knight's typology of risk and uncertainty. This typology classifies temporal uncertainties exogenous to the decision maker's actions and unhooked from issues of interaction – between decision makers, between decision makers and their

Table 8.1 *Elements of the entrepreneurial decision space and relevant tools to tackle them*

Element of decision space		Relevant rationality/ tools	Key scholarly work
Uncertainty	*Risk*: known distribution, unknown draw	Classical rationality	Arrow (1962), von Neumann and Morgenstern (1944)
	Uncertainty: unknown distribution, unknown draw	Bayesian rationality	Oaksford and Chater (2009)
	True uncertainty/ ignorance: unknowable distribution	Judgment Ad-hoc rationality Effectual logic	Vickers (1965), Boettke (2002), Winter (2003), Sarasvathy (2008)
Openness	*Ambiguity*: preferences and goals unknown and/or conflicting	Behavioral decision theory Ecological rationality Creative rationality	Simon (1977), March (1978), Kahneman and Tversky (1979), Gigerenzer and Todd (1999), Joas (1996)
	Isotropy: what counts as data is unknown	Relevance logic	Fodor (1983)
	Causality: distribution depends on human action	Causal surgery diagrams	Pearl (2000)

environments and of course, between and within the same decision maker's preferences, tastes and values. If we bring these exogenous issues into the decision-making process, we begin to work with a space that is more characteristic of entrepreneurial decisions. In other words, entrepreneurship highlights problems not only of uncertainty, but also of ambiguity, isotropy and causality – all indicative of openness or too much information rather than too little as in the case of Knight's typology. Briefly, ambiguity refers to unpredictable changes and conflicts in entrepreneurs' own preferences and goals; isotropy refers to the problem of knowing what information is relevant to the decision under consideration and what needs to be ignored as irrelevant; and causality refers to possible changes in the environment caused by human action. See Table 8.1 for a summary of these and how each relates (approximately) to different types of rationality discussed in the previous section as well as certain new tools emerging in literatures both within and outside of entrepreneurship.

In the rest of this section we elaborate on each of these using practical examples. The point here is not to suggest solutions to these problems but to clarify the decision space so we can get a feel for new possibilities for research at the interface of decision-making and entrepreneurship.

In the previous section, we have already examined issues connected with uncertainty. It might be useful, however, to exemplify them in at least one particular context of entrepreneurship, namely, new venture creation. The canonical example of entrepreneurial opportunity in the neo-classical mold is arbitrage – or the $500 bill left on the sidewalk. In this world of perfect information, all that the entrepreneur has to do is pick up the $500. When we move from this skeletal example to a more realistic one, we can see the role of risk (namely, known distribution, unknown draw) in the case of franchise opportunities. When an entrepreneur seeks to open a new McDonald's franchise, for example, he or she faces risk that is mostly calculable and predictable. Yet, unlike the arbitrage example, the skills, experience and other resources of the entrepreneur do matter in terms of the eventual shape and performance of the particular franchise any given entrepreneur ends up developing.

We can contrast that type of risk with uncertainty, which requires a certain amount of trial and error with systematic updating of beliefs through experimental learning. Take the case of Ecotricity:

> Committed to a low-impact lifestyle, Vince began his journey into business by building small-scale windmills to serve his personal energy needs and limit his dependency on commercial power. One of the most complex pieces of the puzzle was finding out how to assess environments in order to identify a location providing the kind of consistent wind needed to drive turbines. Not finding adequate solutions on the market, Vince started crafting wind-monitoring towers in 1991 and in 1992 he founded Western Windpower. Western attracted large orders from clients such as Scottish Power, and is now Nexgen Wind, the UK's market leader in wind monitoring equipment.

> ... Armed with more knowledge of wind measurement and power generation, Vince gained permission to establish a wind farm in the UK in 1992. Just three years later, he founded Ecotricity (originally the Renewable Energy Company), offering the radical alternative of 'green' electricity to both household and business customers. The firm operates 12 wind farms today, representing 10 per cent of England's wind energy, 46GWh/year of renewable electricity (at the end of 2007), and a saving of around 46000 tonnes of CO_2 emissions a year as compared with the same amount of 'brown' energy. (Read and Sarasvathy, 2008, p. 16)

Contrast this with the development of something like the commercialization of the Internet, where at any given point in time, it was never clear what would be the next application that would show up and work well – or not. Similar uncertainties and consequently a plethora of possible, but highly uncertain, opportunities abound in the case of iPhone, Facebook and Twitter applications. Here it is not only a matter of experimentation of what might work that contributes to the uncertainty, but the thrill of a whole new industry-changing application that might develop overnight that adds to the overall volatility. In fact, in a profound philosophical sense, one could argue that Knightian true uncertainty characterizes the problem space for *all* entrepreneurship, especially at the earliest stages of firm founding – simply because a potential infinity of factors may impact decisions such as whether to start a venture at all, which venture to start, which ventures *not* to start and whether and with whom to co-found, and so on and on.

As mentioned above, however, the frayed edges of the decision space for entrepreneurship does not stop at Knightian uncertainty. There is the added issue of openness, starting with the preferences of the entrepreneur himself or herself. Here the case of Kaarma is illustrative:

> What do you do when you wake up in a lather one day in San Francisco and realise you actually want to be living on a sparsely populated Estonian island in the middle of the Baltic Sea? You make sure that you will be able to support yourself by starting a company there, of course. That

is what Stephen and Ea Greenwood did when they moved to the island of Saaremaa in 2004. But then come the details – what kind of company, where to start, and how to make it work? (Read and Wiltbank, 2009)

Sometimes, even if the entrepreneur clearly knows what he or she wants to accomplish and several parameters of the potential market are known, the decision space for particular implementations might remain open-ended due to a number of equally attractive options or alternatives that contradict each other in ways that make it impossible to choose using traditional decision criteria. Starbucks is a famous case in point. In the early days when Howard Schultz was still trying to perfect the coffee shop of his dreams through *Il Giornale,* he was flooded with input from customers on the ambiance of the place – be it the color on the walls and furniture, the background music, menu format, or the notion of the barista. Schultz's problem is not unique in this regard. Every entrepreneur faces a plethora of implementation decisions – such as name, logo, whether or not to create a Twitter account, office space, whether, when, how and how many meetings, and so on – several of which might turn out to be more or less important in hindsight. Add to this list, conflicting advice from well-wishers and mentors, exciting ideas from almost everyone the entrepreneur talks to, and information pouring from every communication medium encountered during each day – and very soon the environment gets so isotropic that the entrepreneur sometimes simply gives up.

Isotropy refers to the inability to clearly distinguish ex ante what information may or may not turn out to be relevant ex post. The word *isotropy* is made up from Greek iso (equal) and tropos (direction) and literally signifies uniformity in all directions. The conceptual notion of isotropy has been identified by philosophers and roboticists under different rubrics such as the frame problem and the relevance problem. Fodor (1983) studied it in some depth in the context of scientific discovery, for example, and used it in constructing a taxonomy of cognitive systems. For our purposes, it is important to note only that the problem of isotropy exists regardless of the truth (or probability of truth) of the facts, i.e. regardless of actors' ability to predict. In fact isotropy is not limited to the unknown aspects of a given problem, but arises from what is known and the relative relevance of different aspects of the known. Thus isotropy is different from Knightian uncertainty where the problem is one of classification and prediction; it is also different from Bayesian updating where the issue concerns how one interprets additional data; in isotropy the problem is one of what counts as data in the first place – before it can be classified or used to update one's expectations.

The final aspect of openness in the entrepreneurial decision space that we need to come to grips with consists in the fact that not only do entrepreneurs actively change, transform and reshape the environments in which they operate, the more experienced ones actively believe that the environment is not exogenous to their actions. This means that even ex ante the choice set they perceive as available is different from the choice set others might see if they believed the environment to be mostly exogenous. An actual classroom example might help us see the intuition here. Conventional wisdom takes the position that the future comes from the past. Entrepreneurs invert this paradigm to argue that the past is a reliable predictor of the future *only to the extent* the entrepreneur is *not* taken into account. Eminent probability theorists have also begun taking human agency seriously in studies of causality. Pearl (2000), for example, has invented a 'do' operator in a new kind of probability calculus where human agency is modeled through causal diagrams.

It is tempting to argue that every company that exists would have come into existence in one form or another – and hence the role of any particular entrepreneur is irrelevant to our understanding of the phenomenon. This Panglossian attitude does not help the entrepreneur in the trenches who is striving to make good decisions nor is it of any use to the development of normative approaches to point out better and worse ways to make those decisions. Moreover, Panglossian explanations fail to address the issue of time lags in the development of key ventures such as those that helped commercialize the Internet. Take, for example, a successful restaurant called 'Unsicht' in Germany. It is a restaurant where dinner is served in pitch darkness by blind waiters. It is interesting to ask whether the market for such a restaurant arose exogenously and an alert entrepreneur responded to the demand, or whether demand for such a restaurant was created through the fact of an entrepreneur creating the concept. If the latter, in what way can we argue that such a restaurant would have come to be, one way or another? And if so, why did it not happen sooner than the twenty-first century? Would it not have been more likely in an age without electricity or in a place without electricity today? Counterfactuals aside, one can find hundreds of examples of ventures that created their own markets and came to be simply because someone decided to make it happen. Faddoctor.com provides a long and lively list of ventures that created fads ranging from Rubik's cube to the wackywallwalker rubber octopus.

In sum, when we move from the history of decision-making theories to the reality of practical entrepreneuring, it is clear that an almost unlimited scope exists for profitable research in the future. An enumeration of these possibilities would be too far outside the scope of this chapter. Instead we point out just two jumping off points – one involving the future of a key issue in current entrepreneurship research (namely the individual–opportunity nexus), and the other having to do with the very role of decision-making in future entrepreneurship research.

IMPLICATIONS FOR THE INDIVIDUAL–OPPORTUNITY NEXUS: QUESTIONING THE QUESTION

Few would dispute that both (a) modes of decision-making rationality and (b) aspects of decision environments are necessary to fully understand entrepreneurial decision-making. Indeed, the widespread idea that entrepreneurship, generally, comprises a 'nexus of individuals and opportunities' (Venkataraman, 1997; Shane, 2003) is based on this very premise. The nexus view constitutes a considerable improvement over older, individual-centered, theories of entrepreneurship. Nevertheless, the preceding reviews make clear some of its limitations by showing how it fails to incorporate two very important aspects of entrepreneurship.

First, it focuses exclusively on the 'lower' levels of decision-maker rationality and decision environments, i.e. those where individuals make decisions by performing rational (or biased) calculations or somehow forming intuitive judgments regarding the state of an independent (albeit sometimes poorly known) decision environment. Focus is squarely on individuals who discover (or believe that they discover) objectively existing opportunities and act to exploit these (Shane and Venkataraman, 2000). The 'higher' level modes of rationality and decision environment discussed above do not enter into the nexus theory.

In response to such charges, it is sometimes pointed out that these lower-level nexuses (e.g. rational choice or alert discovery of existing opportunities) describe the majority of start-ups, which are neither innovative nor growth-oriented (Shane, 2008, p. 64) but quite mundane (Aldrich, 2009, p. 30). However, as Per Davidsson has repeatedly pointed out, entrepreneurship theories should not be built by democratic vote: 'it is not a given that every empirical case should be deemed equally important for our theory building and theory testing' (Davidsson, 2004, p. 68, cf. Davidsson, 2005, p. 46; 2008, p. 137). Quite to the contrary, because neither the impact nor the workings of all 'entrepreneurial' activities are equal, it is critical to pay special attention to the theoretically more interesting modes of entrepreneurship. Thus, while the nexus theory may be representative in some quantitative sense, it fails to describe what are arguably the most important and theoretically interesting forms of entrepreneurship.

This leads to the second, and related, limitation of the nexus view. It assumes that individuals and opportunities exist independently of each other; an assumption that implies that they can also be treated in isolation. For instance, it is assumed that the characteristics of individuals and opportunities can be gauged separately and thereafter 'added up' to establish their total impact as causes of entrepreneurial behavior. Shane et al. (2003, p. 269) thus write that: 'Researchers need to know the magnitude of the force exerted by the opportunities themselves to accurately estimate the effect of the individual motivations.' However, as we move up the two taxonomies and embrace more and more innovative modes of entrepreneurship, we see that it becomes more and more difficult to keep decision maker and decision environment analytically, indeed ontologically, separate.

In sum, the nexus idea constitutes an improvement over individual-centered theories by regarding entrepreneurship as comprising both individuals and opportunities. However, as shown by Joas (1996) and Spinosa et al. (1997), in order to grasp the nature of truly creative modes of entrepreneurship, the relation between individual and opportunity (or agent and structure, if you will) can probably no longer be thought of as a detached *dualism* but needs to be treated as an integrated *duality* where the development of each is inseparable from the development of the other (cf. Giddens, 1984). This brings us to the most important issue for research into entrepreneurial decision-making: how relevant is the notion of 'decision-making' per se?

CONCLUSION: FROM DECISION TO DESIGN

Perhaps it is time we moved from modeling entrepreneurial activity as 'decisions' occurring within the individual-opportunity nexus to expanding the domain of our questions to include the 'design' of opportunities. In this view, opportunities are not exogenous to the entrepreneurial process, but can also be its outcome or residual. Opportunities, as well as ventures and markets and even institutions, may at times be initiated and propelled by individual and collective action while simultaneously being structured by those constraining elements of the decision space that are harder to transform or at least are deemed stable during the design process.

Decision theories mostly ignore design. In modeling the choice between A and B, they take A and B as outside the scope of decision analysis. In contrast, design is interested in how A and B come to be in the first place. A brief examination of the etymology of the two words might be useful here:

c. 1380, from O.Fr. *decider*, from L. *decidere* 'to decide', lit. 'to cut off', from *de-* 'off' + *cædere* 'to cut'

c. 1548, from L. *designare* 'mark out, devise', from *de-* 'out' + *signare* 'to mark', from *signum* 'a mark, sign'.[1]

The quintessential symbol of decision is the decision tree with forking branches and nodes at which reality is cut into paths taken and paths forgone. The potter's wheel serves as the symbol for design, evoking images of clay being molded into an infinite variety of shapes and sizes. Both are part of the entrepreneurial process. But focusing exclusively on one without the other cuts us off from coming to grips with the phenomenon in more useful ways.

Of course, some models of the decision-making process, such as the one illustrated in Mintzberg et al. (1976), do incorporate design as a key element. Design, however, in the sense in which Herbert Simon (1996) used it in *The Sciences of the Artificial,* is a domain worthy of study in itself. Entrepreneurship, in our opinion, ought to be as much, if not more, a phenomenon of design as of decision. Moreover, the study of design is bound to have much to offer the study of decisions. For example, consider the well-studied decision between working for a wage versus starting a venture. If looked at as a decision problem, the choice is modeled as an either-or – evoking the etymology of 'cutting' the world into two separate pathways. If looked at as a design problem, it is possible to think through a combination (continuing to work while building the venture on the weekends or through a spouse) or a third or fourth path such as getting one's company to fund a spin off or taking a sabbatical and so on. Although decisions often force a choice between alternatives, design includes the creation of new alternatives, and the latter is particularly important not only for scholarship, but for the practice, pedagogy and policy of entrepreneurship.

Scholars in entrepreneurship have begun to take notice of this importance. Take for example recent work arguing for a more 'creative' view of opportunities (Alvarez and Barney, 2007; Berglund, 2007; Sarasvathy et al., 2003) in addition to calls for the study of the creation of new networks (Aldrich and Kim, 2007) and new institutions (Battilana, 2009). In a series of five essays under the rubric, 'Made as well as found', Sarasvathy et al. (2010b) have outlined several key ideas from disciplines such as economics, sociology, psychology and philosophy that can be used to begin the study of entrepreneurship as a science of the artificial. The essays suggest methods and theoretical lenses for studying individual entrepreneurs and their stakeholders as makers of opportunities, ventures, markets and institutions as well as seekers of the same. They also urge ways to focus on fabrication processes in addition to discovery processes and examine the outcomes of entrepreneurship as artifacts and not only as unexplored landscapes mapped out through the pursuit of pre-existing opportunities. In all of these, and in new methods and tools that we can bring to bear on these, the key unit of analysis is *interaction* – interaction between entrepreneurs and their stakeholders, entrepreneurs and their external environment, and between entrepreneurs' own preferences, tastes and values.

Armed with a view of entrepreneurship as a domain of design, we believe that in the near future when our students come asking us about the fork in the road ahead in their lives, we can, like Yogi Berra, advise them to take it.

NOTE

1. http://www.etymouline.com, accessed 1 June 2009.

REFERENCES

Aldrich, H. (2009), 'Lost in space, out of time: why and how we should study organizations comparatively', in B.G. King, T. Felin and D.A. Whetten (eds), *Research in the Sociology of Organizations*, pp. 21–44.

Aldrich, H.E. and P.H. Kim (2007), 'Small worlds, infinite possibilities? How social networks affect entrepreneurial team formation and search', *Strategic Entrepreneurship Journal*, 1, 147–65.

Alvarez, S.A. and J.B. Barney (2007), 'Discovery and creation: alternative theories of entrepreneurial action', *Strategic Entrepreneurship Journal*, 1, 11–26.

Arrow, K.J. (1962), 'Economic welfare and the allocation of resources for invention', in R.R. Nelson (ed.), *The Rate and Direction of Inventive Activity: Economic and Social Factors*, Princeton, NJ: Princeton University Press.

Baron, R. (1998), 'Cognitive mechanisms in entrepreneurship: why and when entrepreneurs think differently than other people', *Journal of Business Venturing*, 13, 275–94.

Baron, R. (2004), 'The cognitive perspective: a valuable tool for answering entrepreneurship's basic "why" questions', *Journal of Business Venturing*, 19, 221–39.

Battilana, J., B. Leca and E. Bexenbaum (2009), 'How actors change institutions: towards a theory of institutional entrepreneurship', *Academy of Management Annals*, 3, 65–107.

Baumol, W. (1968), 'Entrepreneurship in economic theory', *American Economic Review*, 58(2), 64–71.

Berglund, H. (2007), 'Opportunities as existing and created: a study of entrepreneurs in the Swedish mobile internet industry', *Journal of Enterprising Culture*, 15(3), 243–73.

Boettke, P.J. (2002), 'Information and knowledge: Austrian economics in search of its uniqueness', *Review of Austrian Economics*, 15(4), 263–74.

Bullock, S. and P. Todd (1999), 'Made to measure: ecological rationality in structured environments', *Minds and Machines*, 9(4), 497–541.

Burmeister, K. and C. Schade (2007), 'Are entrepreneurs' decisions more biased? An experimental investigation of the susceptibility to status quo bias', *Journal of Business Venturing*, 22(3), 340–62.

Busenitz, L. and J. Barney (1997), 'Differences between entrepreneurs and managers in large organizations: biases and heuristics in strategic decision-making', *Journal of Business Venturing*, 12, 9–30.

Busenitz, L.W., P. West, D. Shepherd, T. Nelson, A. Zacharakis and G. Chandler (2003), 'Entrepreneurship in emergence: past trends and future directions', *Journal of Management*, 29(3), 285–308.

Camerer, C.F. and D. Lovallo (1999), 'Overconfidence and excess entry: an experimental approach', *American Economic Review*, 89(1), 306–18.

Cantillon, R. (1755/1931), *Essai sur la Nature du Commerce en Général*, London: MacMillan.

Caplan, R. (1999), 'The Austrian search for realistic foundations', *Southern Economic Journal*, 65(4), 823–38.

Casson, M.C. (2005), 'Entrepreneurship and the theory of the firm', *Journal of Economic Behaviour and Organization*, 58, 327–48.

Collis, D.J. (1994), 'Research note: how valuable are organizational capabilities?', *Strategic Management Journal*, Winter Special Issue, **15**, 143–52.

Davidsson, P. (2004), *Researching Entrepreneurship*, New York: Springer.

Davidsson, P. (2005), 'Method issues in the study of venture start-up processes', in A. Fayolle, P. Kyrö and J. Ulijn (eds), *Entrepreneurship Research in Europe: Outcomes and Perspectives*, Cheltenham: UK and Northampton, MA, USA, Edward Elgar, pp. 35–54.

Davidsson, P. (2008), *The Entrepreneurship Research Challenge*, Cheltenham, UK and Northampton, MA, USA: Edward Elgar.

Demsetz, H. (1983), 'The neglect of the entrepreneur', in J. Ronen (ed.), *Entrepreneurship*, Lexington: Lexington Books, pp. 271–80.

Dew, N., S. Read, S.D. Sarasvathy and R. Wiltbank (2008), 'A behavioral theory of the entrepreneurial firm', *Journal of Economic Behavior and Organization*, **66**(1), 37–59.

Douglas, E.J. and D.A. Shepherd (2000), 'Entrepreneurship as a utility-maximizing response', *Journal of Business Venturing*, **15**(3), 231–52.

Douglas, E.J. and D.A. Shepherd (2002), 'Self-employment as a career choice: attitudes, entrepreneurial intentions, and utility maximization', *Entrepreneurial Theory and Practice*, **26**(3), 81–90.

Dreyfus, H.L. (1979), *What Computers Can't Do*, New York: Harper and Row.

Dreyfus, H.L. (1991), *Being-in-the-World: A Commentary on Heidegger's 'Being and Time'*, *Division I*, Cambridge, MA: MIT Press.

Eisenhardt, K.M. (1989), 'Making fast strategic decisions in high-velocity environments', *Academy of Management Journal*, **12**, 543–76.

Eisenhardt, K.M. and J.A. Martin (2000), 'Dynamic capabilities: what are they?', *Strategic Management Journal*, **21**(10/11), 1105–12.

Fiet, J. (2002), *The Systematic Search for Entrepreneurial Discoveries*, Westport, CT: Quorum Books.

Fiet, J., O. Piskounov and P.C. Patel (2005), 'Still searching (systematically) for entrepreneurial discoveries', *Small Business Economics*, **25**(5), 489–504.

Fodor, J.A. (1983), *The Modularity of Mind*, Cambridge, MA: MIT Press.

Forbes, D. (2005), 'Are some entrepreneurs more overconfident than others?', *Journal of Business Venturing*, **20**(5), 623–40.

Foss, K., N.J. Foss and P.G. Klein (2007), 'Original and derived judgement: an entrepreneurial theory of economic organization', *Organization Studies*, **28**(6), 1–20.

Giddens, A. (1984), *The Constitution of Society, Outline of the Theory of Structuration*, Cambridge: Polity Press.

Gigerenzer, G. and P.M. Todd (1999), 'Fast and frugal heuristics: the adaptive toolbox', in G. Gigerenzer, P.M. Todd and the ABC Research Group (eds), *Simple Heuristics that Make Us Smart*, New York: Oxford University Press, pp. 3–34.

Gigerenzer, G., W. Hell and H. Blank (1988), 'Presentation and content: the use of base rates as a continous variable', *Journal of Experimental Psychology*, **14**(3), 513–25.

Hartmann, H. (1959), 'Managers and entrepreneurs: a useful distinction?', *Administrative Science Quarterly*, **3**(4), 429–51.

Hill, R.C. and M. Levenhagen (1995), 'Metaphors and mental models: sensemaking and sensegiving in innovative and entrepreneurial activities', *Journal of Management*, **21**(6), 1057–74.

Honig, B. and T. Karlsson (2004), 'Institutional forces and the written business plan', *Journal of Management*, **30**(1), 29–48.

Joas, H. (1996), *The Creativity of Action*, Chicago: University Press.

Kahneman, D. and A. Tversky (1979), 'Prospect theory: an analysis of decisions under risk', *Econometrica*, **47**, 313–27.

Kihlstrom, R. and J. Laffont (1979), 'A general equilibrium entrepreneurial theory of firm formation based on risk aversion', *Journal of Political Economy*, **87**(4), 719–48.

Knight, F.H. (1921), *Risk, Uncertainty and Profit*, Chicago: University of Chicago Press.

Koellinger, P., M. Minniti and C. Schade (2007), 'I think I can, I think I can: overconfidence and entrepreneurial behavior', *Journal of Economic Psychology*, **28**, 502–27.

Langlois, R. (1998), 'Personal capitalism as charismatic authority: the organizational economics of a Weberian concept', *Industrial and Corporate Change*, **7**(1), 195–213.

Langlois, R.N. (2007), 'The entrepreneurial theory of the firm and the theory of the entrepreneurial firm', *Journal of Management Studies*, **44**, 1107–24.

Lévesque M., D.A. Shepherd and E.J. Douglas (2002), 'Employment or self-employment: a dynamic utility-maximizing model', *Journal of Business Venturing*, **17**(3), 189–210.

March, J. (1978), 'Bounded rationality, ambiguity, and the engineering of choice', *Bell Journal of Economics*, **9**(2), 587–608.

Markham, G., D. Balkin and R. Baron (2002), 'Inventors and new venture formation: the effects of general self-efficacy and regretful thinking', *Entrepreneurship Theory and Practice*, **27**(2), 149–66.

Miner, J.B and N.S. Raju (2004), 'When science divests itself of its conservative stance: the case of risk propensity difference between entrepreneurs and managers', *Journal of Applied Psychology*, **89**(1), 14–21.

Miner, J.B., N.S. Raju and S. Nambury (2004), 'Risk propensity differences between managers and entrepreneurs and between low- and high-growth entrepreneurs: a reply in a more conservative vein', *Journal of Applied Psychology*, **89**(1), 3–13.

Mintzberg, H., D. Raisinghani and A. Theoret (1976), 'The structure of "unstructured" decision processes', *Administrative Science Quarterly*, **21**(2), 246–75.

Mises, L. (1949/1996), *Human Action: A Treatise on Economics*, 4th edition, San Francisco: Fox and Wilkes.

Nozick, R. (1993), *The Nature of Rationality*, Princeton: Princeton University Press.

Oaksford, M. and N. Chater (2009), 'Précis of Bayesian rationality: the probabilistic approach to human reasoning', *Behavioral and Brain Sciences*, **32**, 69–84.

Olson, P. (1986), 'Entrepreneurs: opportunistic decision makers', *Journal of Small Business Management*, **24**, 29–35.

Pearl, J. (2000), *Causality: Models, Reasoning, and Inference*, Toronto: Cambridge University Press.

Pearman, A.D. (1977), 'A weighted maximin and maximax approach to multiple criteria decision making', *Operational Research Quarterly*, **28**, 584–87.

Read, S. and S.D. Sarasvathy (2008), 'Winds of change', Lessons in Entrepreneurship series, *British Airways In-flight Magazine*, December.

Read, S. and R.E. Wiltbank (2009), 'Making a clean start', Lessons in Entrepreneurship series, *British Airways In-flight Magazine*, November.

Read, S., N. Dew, S.D. Sarasvathy and R. Wiltbank (2009), 'Marketing under uncertainty: the logic of an effectual approach', *Journal of Marketing*, **73**, 1–18.

Samuelson, P. (1938), 'A note on the pure theory of consumers' behaviour', *Economica*, **5**, 61–71.

Sarasvathy, S.D. (2008), *Effectuation: Elements of Entrepreneurial Expertise*, Cheltenham, UK and Northampton, MA, USA: Edward Elgar.

Sarasvathy, S.D. and N. Dew (2005), 'New market creation as transformation', *Journal of Evolutionary Economics*, **15**(5), 533–65.

Sarasvathy, S.D. and N. Dew (2010), 'Without judgment: an empirically-based entrepreneurial theory of the firm', *Review of Austrian Economics* (forthcoming).

Sarasvathy, S.D., N. Dew, S. Read and R. Wiltbank (2010a), 'On the entrepreneurial genesis of new markets: effectual transformations versus causal search and selection', *Journal of Evolutionary Economics* (forthcoming).

Sarasvathy, S.D., N. Dew, S.R. Velamuri and S. Venkataraman (2003), 'Three views of entrepreneurial opportunity', in Z.J. Acs and D.B. Audretsch (eds), *Handbook of Entrepreneurship*, Berlin: Springer, pp. 141–60.

Sarasvathy, S.D., N. Dew and S. Venkataraman (2010b), *Made, As Well As found: Researching Entrepreneurship as a Science of the Artificial*, Yale University Press (forthcoming).

Savage, L.J. (1954), *The Foundations of Statistics*, New York: Wiley.

Shane, S. (2003), *A General Theory of Entrepreneurship: The Individual-Opportunity Nexus*, Cheltenham, UK and Northampton, MA, USA: Edward Elgar.

Shane, S.A. (2008), *The Illusions of Entrepreneurship: the Costly Myths that Entrepreneurs, Investors, and Policy Makers Live By*, New Haven, CT: Yale University Press.

Shane, S. and S. Venkataraman (2000), 'The promise of entrepreneurship as a field of research', *Academy of Management Review*, **25**(1), 217–26.

Shane, S., E. Locke and C. Collins (2003), 'Entrepreneurial motivation', *Human Resource Management Review*, **13**(2), 257–79.

Simon, H.A. (1955), 'A behavioral model of rational choice', *Quarterly Journal of Economics*, **69**, 99–118.

Simon, H.A. (1977), *The New Science of Management Decision*, Englewood Cliffs, NJ: Prentice Hall.

Simon, H.A. (1996), *The Sciences of the Artificial*, 3rd edition, Cambridge, MA: MIT Press.

Simon, M., S. Houghton and K. Aquino (2000), 'Cognitive biases, risk perception, and venture performance: how individuals decide to start companies', *Journal of Business Venturing*, **15**(2), 113–34.

Spinosa, C., F. Flores and H. Dreyfus (1997), *Disclosing New Worlds: Entrepreneurship, Democratic Action, and the Cultivation of Solidarity*, Cambridge, MA: MIT Press.

Sternberg, R.J. (2000), *Practical Intelligence in Everyday Life*, Cambridge: Cambridge University Press.

Sternberg, R.J. (2004), 'Successful intelligence as a basis for entrepreneurship', *Journal of Business Venturing*, **19**(2), 189–201.

Sternberg, R.J., G.B. Forsythe, J. Hedlund, J.A. Horvath, R.K. Wagner, W.M. Williams, S.A. Snook and E.L. Grigorenko (2000), *Practical Intelligence in Everyday Life*, New York: Cambridge University Press.

Stewart Jr., W.H. and P.L. Roth (2001), 'Risk propensity differences between entrepreneurs and managers: a meta-analytic review', *Journal of Applied Psychology*, **86**(1), 145–53.

Sugden, R. (1986), 'Regret, recrimination and rationality', in L. Daboni et al. (eds), *Recent Developments in the Foundations of Utility and Risk Theory*, Theory and Decision Library Series, vol. 47, pp. 67–80.

Teece, D.J., G. Pisano and A. Shuen (1997), 'Dynamic capabilities and strategic management', *Strategic Management Journal*, **18**, 509–33.

Venkataraman, S. (1997), 'The distinctive domain of entrepreneurship research', in J. Katz (ed.), *Advances in Entrepreneurship, Firm Emergence and Growth*, Volume III, New York: JAI Press, pp. 119–38.

Vickers, G. (1965), *The Art of Judgment: A Study of Policy Making*, New York: Basic Books.

von Neumann, J. and O. Morgenstern (1944), *Theory of Games and Economic Behavior*, Princeton, NJ: Princeton University Press.

Weick, K. (1995), *Sensemaking in Organizations*, Thousand Oaks, CA: Sage.

Wiltbank, R., S. Read, N. Dew and S.D. Sarasvathy (2009), 'Prediction and control under uncertainty: outcomes in angel investing', *Journal of Business Venturing*, **24**(2), 116–33.

Winter, S. (2003), 'Understanding dynamic capabilities', *Strategic Management Journal*, **24**(10), 991–95.

Witt, U. (1998), 'Imagination and leadership: the neglected dimension of an evolutionary theory of the firm', *Journal of Economic Behavior and Organization*, **35**(2), 161–77.

Section II.3

Opportunity Exploitation

9. Only the good die young? A review of liability of newness and related new venture mortality research

Brian Nagy and Franz Lohrke

INTRODUCTION

New ventures often face discouraging odds in terms of their potential long-term survival. For example, both organizational studies and entrepreneurship textbooks frequently cite new venture failure statistics that suggest over half of all new ventures will fail within their first four years of existence. Although these high rates may result, in part, from how 'failure' is defined (e.g. selling a successful new venture would be classified as having 'failed' in some governmental surveys, see Headd, 2003), organizational researchers have frequently suggested these high mortality rates occur because most new ventures face a 'liability of newness'. This liability results from a new venture's lack of an established track record, which, in turn, makes it difficult for its managers to convince potential resource providers (e.g. investors, suppliers, and customers) to conduct business with the firm (Singh et al., 1986). Without these resources (e.g. capital, raw materials, and continuing sales), however, a new venture often faces dim survival chances. In addition, a new venture can initially lack internal efficiencies (e.g. established organizational routines), which can also create significant operational (e.g. cost) disadvantages relative to its more established competitors (Stinchcombe, 1965).

Given these high mortality rates among new ventures, numerous organizational studies have examined liability of newness (LoN) issues. Stinchcombe (1965) introduced the construct, and researchers have since examined it in several conceptual (e.g. Shepherd et al., 2000) and empirical (e.g. Singh et al., 1986) studies. Many of these works have framed LoN as a legitimacy issue; that is, managers need to obtain favorable judgments of acceptance, appropriateness, and worthiness for both themselves and the ventures they lead (Zimmerman and Zeitz, 2002). In short, the granting of legitimacy by organizational stakeholders serves as a precursor to subsequent investments and economic transactions, and, therefore, serves to mitigate LoN threats (Shepherd et al., 2000). Along with legitimacy, studies have also suggested and tested other related theoretically linked conditions such as lack of perceived reputation, reliability, accountability, and trustworthiness as contributors to the malevolent condition of newness (e.g. Choi and Shepherd, 2005; Delmar and Shane, 2004).

Despite this established body of research, consensus on both how to define the LoN construct and its overall impact on new ventures is far from universal. For example, along with investigating LoN in new ventures, researchers have employed it at different levels of analysis including industry (Aldrich and Fiol, 1994), and organizational type or 'form' (e.g. Hannan and Freeman, 1977) as well as to investigate different organizational types including those undergoing significant strategic change (e.g. Amburgey et al.,1993) or entering overseas markets (Zaheer, 1995).

On the other hand, other scholars have suggested that new ventures may actually enjoy a 'honeymoon' period, including initial acceptance by key stakeholders, which eventually diminishes, resulting in a 'liability of adolescence' rather than 'newness' (Brüderl and Schüssler, 1990). In a related vein, Choi and Shepherd (2005) recently introduced the construct 'assets of newness', suggesting that ventures, in some circumstances, can actually gain advantages based on their 'newness' that may at least partially counteract liabilities associated with a firm's newness. Other recent theoretical work has examined benefits related to newness in specific industries that thrive on innovation and dominant design changes (e.g. Carayannopoulos, 2009). Consequently, despite the oft cited daunting odds of new venture survival noted above, the extent to which new ventures face LoN and what boundary conditions exist between LoN and other related constructs, such as liability of adolescence (LoA) and assets of newness (AoN), remain somewhat ambiguous.

Accordingly, in this chapter, we endeavor to sort through these disparate new venture concepts. We begin our discussion by reviewing both theoretical developments and extant empirical efforts examining LoN. Specifically, we discuss, in detail, the conditions and dimensions associated with the construct, focusing on the likely impacts these conditions and dimensions have on new venture success or failure. As expected, most conditions tied to newness seem to have malevolent effects on start-up viability. We also discuss the original and seminal theoretical writings of Stinchcombe (1965) and then employ the theoretical lenses of institutional theory, strategic theory, and stakeholder theory to both categorize and summarize extant empirical works related to LoN. In doing so, we review several empirical works that examine dimensions of this multi-faceted construct, focusing primarily on issues related to new venture legitimacy. Next, we review studies examining LoA and AoN. Finally, we highlight two other theoretical perspectives, the resource-based view of the firm and trust, that may provide fruitful avenues for future LoN studies to help better circumscribe the boundaries of the LoN, LoA, and AoN, and, thus, provide important avenues for future new venture research.

THE EVOLUTION OF THE LIABILITY OF NEWNESS CONSTRUCT

A critical topic of many theoretical and empirical efforts in the organization research has been the disparity in mortality rates between newer, start-up firms and older, more established firms (Hannan and Carroll, 1995; Hannan and Freeman, 1989). Entrepreneurship researchers have long noted the significant differences in survival probabilities between established and new firms and have investigated several issues associated with new ventures' high failure rates (Delmar and Shane, 2004; Shepherd et al., 2000; Thornhill and Amit, 2003).

Organizational researchers have often assumed an inverse relationship exists between firm age and firm failure (although, as we have already noted, this view is not universal). According to this view, the greater the age of an organization, the less likely it is to fail, *ceteris paribus* (Carroll, 1983; Freeman et al., 1983; Thornhill and Amit, 2003). In most cases, firm newness hampers start-ups' abilities to thrive in their environments, given the time and continuous effort required to attain legitimacy, to be perceived as reliable, and to establish a verifiable history of serving the needs of stakeholders (Aldrich and Auster, 1986; Choi and Shepherd, 2005; Hannan and Freeman, 1984; Zimmerman and Zeitz, 2002). These disadvantages associated with newness can become particularly problematic as firms enter the commercialization stage of new venture growth (Kazanjian, 1988).

Stinchcombe (1965) identified four conditions that affect the degree to which a new venture will face LoN issues (see Table 9.1). First, organizational members newly assembled to act as a unit often have little in common with one another, other than a general knowledge of business practices and norms. Thus, they face many challenges related to learning new roles and performing in new ways within a new venture. Unlike established organizations that often have succession plans in place and employ those plans to ensure knowledge is passed from one generation of organizational members to the next, newly hired individuals working within new ventures often must learn new behaviors and norms associated with their new and heretofore unestablished roles. The general 'outside' knowledge that accompanies hiring an organizational member at times will provide a partial foundation for learning new skills and attaining new knowledge; the lack of extant 'inside' knowledge, however, often proves problematic and results in internal inefficiencies. The inside knowledge that is passed down and disseminated through organizational members within established organizations tends to be far more detailed, direct, and understandable, given the ability of seasoned organizational members to support the passing on of this information by relating it to actual experiences they have had in the organization.

Second, Stinchcombe discusses the liability new ventures face while seeking to achieve consistency in day-to-day performances without the appropriate routines in place to do so. In order to achieve acceptable organizational performance, new venture leaders must define roles, set routines, and develop standardized operating procedures that are tested at a time when new members of the organization are uncertain about their roles in the organization. When large organizational performance variance results from this uncertainty, bottlenecks, unnecessary costs and interpersonal conflicts are likely to occur (Nelson and Winter, 1982). Recurring organizational performance issues will lead to a 'perpetual psychology of crisis' prevailing within organizations lacking routines and standard practices.

The third condition plaguing new ventures, as noted by Stinchcombe, is the lack of trust among new venture employees. Indeed, he noted that, in some cases, groups inside a new venture (e.g. founding teams) can have interactions that resemble those among strangers. Although founding team members may heavily depend on one another and one another's capabilities, uncertainty about members' knowledge and capabilities may raise doubt related to whether organizational tasks are being completed correctly and in line with organizational visions and goals.

Fourth, Stinchcombe noted that new ventures lack critical external ties. Further, the probability stakeholders will significantly rely on new ventures is likely very low due to lack of social ties. He discussed this stakeholder reliance as an asset that new ventures must sometimes purloin from their more established competition if they themselves are to become established in a particular marketplace. As long as a sense of reliance serves to bond the new venture and its customers, the ties that bind the constituents to the venture

Table 9.1   Examples of research examining LoN, LoA, and AoN issues

Topic/Authors	Level of analysis	Conceptual dimensions	Independent variable operationalizations
Liability of Newness			
Stinchcombe (1965)	Organizational form or firm	New roles that must be established. Bottlenecks that must be solved by 'perpetual psychology of crisis', 'social relations among strangers within the firm', 'lack of stable external ties'	Conceptual
Carroll and Delacroix (1982)	Organizational population	Relationship between firm age and new venture failure	Economic indicators such as imports and exports
Freeman, Carroll and Hannan (1983)	Organizational population	Relationship between firm age and new venture failure	Organizational age, dissolution versus merger
Hannan and Freeman (1984)	Organizational form	Role of the selection process in generating structural inertia	Conceptual
Aldrich and Fiol (1994)	Industry	Cognitive and sociopolitical legitimacy in emerging industries	Conceptual
Thornhill and Amit (2003)	Firm	Firm resource endowments or deficiencies, based on the RBV, that relate to new venture failure	Changing industry conditions, managerial knowledge, financial management, market development
Liability of Adolescence			
Levinthal and Fichman (1988)	Interorganizational relationships	Relationship-specific asset development effects on continued relationships	Firm size, firm diversification, task difficulty, qualified auditor opinion
Brüderl and Schüssler (1990)	Organizational population	Initial resource and organizational legal form effects on new venture failure	Firm size, firm legal form
Preisendörfer and Voss (1990)	Organizational population	Human capital effects on new venture failure	Founder age, founder industry experience
Henderson (1999)	Firm	Competitive strategy effects on LoA	Age, technology strategy
Thornhill and Amit (2003)	Firm	Firm resource endowments or deficiencies, based on the RBV, that relate to new venture failure	Changing industry conditions, managerial knowledge, financial management, market development

Table 9.1   (continued)

Topic/Authors	Level of analysis	Conceptual dimensions	Independent variable operationalizations
Strotman (2007)	Firm	Firm- and industry-level characteristics that impact new venture failure	Firm size, industry growth, size, concentration, rate of entry economies of scale, technological regime
Assets of Newness			
Choi and Shepherd (2005)	Firm	Role of age and other dimensions of newness that impact stakeholder support	Organizational age, cognitive legitimacy, product/ service reliability, accountability, affective congruence, strategic flexibility

can be managed and a continuous stream of revenues will likely increase the probability the new venture will survive and prosper.

Following Stinchcombe, subsequent research has studied several issues related to LoN. We briefly review three of these, focussing on external and internal obstacles to survival, specific different forms of novelty, and other general organizational challenges related to newness.

External and Internal Obstacles to Survival

Subsequent research has built on Stinchcombe's classification by examining LoN issues arising from obstacles present both within and outside a new venture. Aldrich and Auster (1986) noted that externally, environments characterized as highly dynamic and competitive often create several barriers that keep these ventures from prospering. High levels of product differentiation and significant barriers associated with technological developments, regulations, licensing, vertical integration, retaliatory competitive actions, and experiential effects tied to tactic knowledge often thwart new firms' efforts to execute strategic actions. Many of these externally derived obstacles make acquiring resources and cultivating capabilities very difficult, especially for start-up firms.

Internal obstacles to survival primarily result from new venture leaders' inabilities to create roles and structure in their organizations, as well as the failure to communicate the need for roles and structure among organizational members. According to Aldrich and Auster (1986), new venture leaders must discover cost-effective methods of structuring and managing internal operations if their firms are to survive. Internally derived obstacles of newness relate to a large number of organizational challenges, including those associated with training, establishing new routines, structuring governance mechanisms, and operating at optimal levels of efficiency. These operational obstacles stem from the challenges organizational leaders face when planning, organizing, commanding, coordinating, and controlling begin in the organization (Fayol, 1949). Given the lack of experience in most new ventures associated with these vital managerial functions, methods for their execution and completion often must be borrowed from more established organizations with histories of operating effectively (DiMaggio and Powell, 1983).

Novelties Related to Newness

Similar to Aldrich and Auster (1986), Shepherd et al. (2000) posited that constraints and novelties associated with LoN can be either externally or internally rooted. They note that from the outset, new ventures face liabilities in many forms, primarily (1) differences between new venture managers' and potential stakeholders' knowledge of the new venture (i.e. 'information asymmetry') and (2) a general lack of knowledge, or, alternatively, the existence of ignorance, within and outside the new venture. These shortfalls are at the root of three novelties that must be quickly minimized if a new venture is to survive.

The first is 'novelty to the market', which is tied to a new venture's lack of legitimacy and its need to institutionalize processes and offerings. Another, 'novelty to management' is linked to the social relationships inside and outside the firm, including a start-up team's reputation and collective social ties that link the firm to its potential stakeholders. Finally, because new ventures often lack the routines and knowledge necessary to effectively produce their products and services from their available resources, the 'novelty in production' also impedes their early operations. We next examine each of these in turn.

Novelty to the market   Firm survival is enhanced by the products and activities that to observers seem recognizable and familiar (Delmar and Shane, 2004; Hannan and Freeman, 1984; Meyer and Rowan, 1977). Because a new venture may offer innovative products or services, potential stakeholders are not immediately familiar with the firm and its offerings.

'Novelty to the market' is defined as key stakeholders' general lack of knowledge related to a new venture and that venture's products and services. Shepherd et al. (2000) relate this inherent liability to the amount of information about the new venture available to key stakeholders such as customers and investors. Specifically, in contrast to information related to established and well-known firms in a market, the awareness of a new venture as well as the amount of important information about it is often, and sometimes purposely, quite limited. As a result, new firms can lack the legitimacy needed to be perceived as effective and reliable (Hannan and Freeman, 1984). Specifically, in order to compete in most industries, new venture managers must strive to simultaneously create the perception that their organizations are legitimate and trustworthy by disseminating information related to their venture's competencies and affable qualities. In addition, in attempting to manage stakeholder perceptions and demands, new firms create the external routines needed to minimize the uncertainty shrouding their firms by fostering awareness among stakeholders and continuously servicing them, thereby becoming viewed or rated as reliable and competent (Delmar and Shane, 2004; Singh et al., 1986; Zimmerman and Zeitz, 2002). At the same time, new venture managers must guard against revealing too much information about the firm, particularly proprietary information that may compromise key organizational knowledge vital to creating and sustaining the venture's competitive advantage.

Novelty to management A second type of novelty relates to stakeholders' perceptions of a new venture's top management team. 'Novelty to management' is defined as uncertainty stemming from stakeholders' lack of knowledge about a team's competency, experience, and skills. A proven record of managing projects or ventures in environments characterized as uncertain and ambiguous, coupled with beneficial relationships with stakeholders, will aid new venture managers' efforts to minimize this particular novelty. The focal stakeholder related to this type of novelty is most often the financial investor (Evans and Leighton, 1989; Shane and Cable, 2002), but it might also relate to stakeholders residing in the broader environment, such as the media and governmental agencies.

If knowledge and a general understanding of the successes and potential of the leadership team can be relayed to potential stakeholders, social ties may be established. These bonds, in turn, increase the probability the two parties will engage in transactions that bind stakeholders and new venture managers if the former are eventually convinced that the latter are qualified (Fried and Hisrich, 1994; Shane and Cable, 2002).

Novelty in production New ventures may rely on both innovation and novel resource transformation methods to produce goods and services that will be valued by market constituents. Paradigm shifts as well as systematic innovations to production processes with the use of new technologies can be troublesome to manage, however, especially when all other facets of the organization are new as well (Teece, 1996). Uncertainty and complexity associated with production technologies used by new ventures are often linked to difficulties related to the production of goods and services (Schumpeter, 1934; Thompson, 1967).

Novelty as it relates to the production process is viewed as problematic whenever new technology is introduced into an organizational setting in an effort to spur innovation and create competitive advantage. Thus, 'novelty in production' is defined as new venture managers' lack of knowledge pertaining to the production technology used by a new firm. The common effect of novelty in production is difficulty in manufacturing a new product or rendering a new service given the lack of knowledge and experience among the firm's production team members (Shepherd et al., 2000).

This novelty actually may be internally rooted in two features of new venture work groups. First, because the firm is new, the assembly of the production group is very recent and untested. As Stinchcombe (1965) noted, this may lead to uncertainty related to work roles, duties and responsibilities within the entire organization, especially those functions directly tied to the production department. In a firm's infancy, formal structures and standard operating procedures often do not exist, and much knowledge must be gained via experiential learning. Second, because new venture production team members may also be working with new technologies, uncertainties related to the technologies will often negatively affect production, and, in turn, many other facets of the organization.

Other Challenges Associated with Firm Newness

As noted, internally derived conditions of newness are often related to learning efforts, establishing new routines, structuring governance mechanisms, and developing various other internal processes in a new venture. Failure to manage these functions sometimes results in new ventures lacking reliability, accountability, inventory, information, parts, and services requested or required by customers and other stakeholders (Aldrich and Auster, 1986; Choi and Shepherd, 2005). New ventures may face additional challenges, however.

Other potential external liabilities include experiential barriers, licensing and regulatory barriers, and barriers associated with brand recognition and market acceptance (Aldrich and Auster, 1986; Choi and Shepherd, 2005). The degree to which these external factors manifest themselves is, therefore, highly dependent on how well new ventures attract and manage stakeholders in their task and broad environments. By properly managing stakeholder perceptions and demands new ventures can minimize LoN by creating the social ties and external routines needed in order to attain legitimacy and be viewed as reliable, accountable and available (Choi and Shepherd, 2005; Delmar and Shane, 2004; Zimmerman and Zeitz, 2002).

Legitimacy   While formulating new strategic initiatives and business models, new venture managers must consider the environments in which their firms compete (Aldrich, 1995). New firms must develop relationships with environmental constituents before and after they bring products to market. From the perspective of a new venture, legitimacy is one of the assets that it must develop if it is to prosper. Legitimacy is an opportunity-enhancing characteristic that results from customers perceiving firms as competent, effective, and worthy. It has been defined as a condition of low-level acceptability that is bestowed upon new venture firms after expectations and claims based on stakeholder norms and values have been met (Ashforth and Gibbs, 1990; Brown, 1997). Thus, ultimately, legitimacy, like beauty, exists in the eyes and perceptions of the beholder.

Legitimacy involves favorable judgments of acceptance, appropriateness, and worthiness made about individuals and the organizations they lead (Zimmerman and Zeitz, 2002). The granting of legitimacy by organizational stakeholders serves as a precursor to subsequent investments and economic transactions (Shepherd et al., 2000). Extant research has posited that attaining legitimacy facilitates new firm survival by providing firms with access to resources such as capital, employees, and ties to customers that they otherwise would not be able to obtain (Aldrich and Fiol, 1994; Meyer and Rowan, 1977; Zucker, 1987). In addition, legitimacy may be a 'threshold' variable – below some minimum level, a new venture will struggle for survival, but once obtained, it gains greater access to resources (Zimmerman and Zeitz, 2002).

Reliability   Inconsistencies hinder new venture performance, and, in turn, negatively skew customer perceptions. Reliability is defined as the ability to produce the same or compatible goods or services in various settings at different times. Measurements of product attributes, service time, and information correctness are just a few of the important determinants that will contribute to stakeholders' perceptions and judgments of a venture's reliability. Uncertainty in the minds of key customers related to the ability of new ventures to produce consistent products or services is the essence of this LoN dimension (Choi and Shepherd, 2005).

Accountability   Accountability is defined as the extent to which responsibility has been assigned for operational activities as well as for the outputs of those activities within an organizational context. A common precursor to accountability is documentation of how an organization transforms inputs into outputs (Hannan and Freeman, 1984). The inherent problem for new ventures is their lack of established and documented processes for production and servicing stakeholders.

Sometimes potential investors and key customers assess accountability levels through signaling methods employed by organizations. The ISO 9000 and QS 9000 standardization and quality certifications are two examples of such signals, which signify that accountability levels within organizations are high. Through detailed documentation of procedures and practices a firm often can assure customers that its manufacturing and quality systems are capable of identifying inconsistencies in processes, products and services, and that the firm has established who is responsible for correcting problems (Briscoe et al., 2005).

Accountability levels, however, are not only derived from globally recognized certification programs. Evidence of well-honed organizational routines and dynamic capabilities can also indicate firms have high levels of accountability within their organizations (Nelson and Winter, 1982; Pisano, 1994).

Availability   Availability is defined as the condition of possessing desired information and resources at the times they are requested or required (Choi and Shepherd, 2005). Organizational size and newness play roles in hampering the ability to provide products and information to market as the market demands them (Aldrich and Auster, 1986). When firms are new to the market, they often attempt to stay as lean as possible with regard to capital expenditures, staff payrolls, and inventories in efforts to control costs. These efforts are economically correct (Barnard, 1938), but by attempting to stay small in the early stage of development, new ventures often lack the information, the employees, and the inventories to satisfy customer needs (Aldrich and Auster, 1986). Information and resources might be requested by customers so they can develop answers to product-related questions (e.g. origins of components). Information and resources to fulfill these requests, however, are often not available in new ventures due to lack of experience and size.

EMPIRICAL STUDIES RELATED TO LIABILITY OF NEWNESS

The need to empirically investigate and understand LoN has prompted a progressive stream of discussion and empirical research that has resulted in some understanding of who new venture constituents are and why they maintain their conservative postures relative to new ventures (Aldrich and Fiol, 1994; Choi and Shepherd, 2005; Delmar and Shane, 2004; Shepherd et al., 2000). A considerable amount of work remains to be done on methods for minimizing the uncertainty among the many relationships new ventures have with their constituents (Choi and Shepherd, 2005; Shepherd and Zacharakis, 2003).

Extant research suggests three different approaches to minimizing LoN: the institutional, strategic, and social approaches. The theoretical and empirical works that have adopted these approaches have received significant attention in entrepreneurship and management journals, and each has been employed, often in isolation from the other perspectives, to examine LoN issues. We next examine each approach in turn, and discuss its central tenets as they relate to organizational newness.

Institutional Approach

The institutional theoretical strand of evolutionary theory is the most widely established approach used to describe how firms manage LoN. This approach combines elements of institutional theory (DiMaggio and Powell, 1983) with the entrepreneurship context and assumes that because a new venture is most often unique in appearance and operating in unfamiliar fashions, its products and services are often immediately regarded as both unreliable and unaccountable. A new venture, therefore, must add more common and familiar activities, resources, and firm attributes to increase the probability it will be perceived as legitimate in the industry (Choi and Shepherd, 2005; Hannan and Freeman, 1984; Meyer and Rowan, 1977).

Successful efforts to minimize the malevolent properties tied to newness are often made through 'isomorphic' means that hinge on the existence of institutionalized norms and standards in existing industries. Unfortunately for many start-ups, a newly formed industry might provide its component organizations little hope for legitimacy attainment and the establishment of trust and routines, due to lack of history, established standards, and institutionalized norms (Aldrich, 1995). For example, firms founded in the earliest stages of an industry's development might not be able to understand and mimic what external stakeholders view as acceptable and legitimate, because of the lack of information available about their constituents' dealings in other more established industries.

Researchers have empirically tested the importance of new ventures adhering to industry norms, thereby gaining the acceptance they need in order to acquire needed resources from environmental constituents. For example, Singh et al. (1986) examined how new ventures establish legitimacy through listing their ventures in community directories, obtaining charitable registration numbers, and forming a board of directors. Their results revealed that all three factors leading to legitimacy significantly reduced death rates among those firms sampled. In the same vein, Delmar and Shane (2004) empirically tested whether the occurrence and timing of founders' organization activities influence survival rates. Results related to their tests of the importance of establishing a legal entity and the completion of a business plan suggest these organizational actions are significantly related to reducing LoN.

Strategic Approach

The second approach to minimizing LoN relates to the Schumpeterian strand of evolutionary economic theory. This approach argues that new firm survival is enhanced by obtaining, controlling, and recombining resources in ways superior to those of established firms (Schumpeter, 1934). By virtue of their newness, start-ups lack routines necessary to effectively transform resources into finished products or services. Thus, to compete with more operationally advanced firms, new ventures must establish and foster routines that enhance stakeholder perceptions of reliability, consistency and appropriateness. If the methods for resource transformation prove beneficial to environmental constituents and competitors, dissemination of those methods can serve to diminish the detrimental effects of utilizing unrecognized processes and thereby minimize LoN.

This approach borrows heavily from strategic choice theory in highlighting potential ways to minimize LoN. Specifically, the approach contends that both established and new organizations' successful operations depend on the strategic choices managers make concerning the manipulation of firms' environments, and the competitive advances organizations make while operating in their environments (Child, 1972). An example of this approach to combat LoN is the situation where a new venture operating in the technology sector attempts to change a dominant design in its industry. By imparting highly effective and highly regarded processes and methods, its managers hope to proactively acquire societal support and legitimacy (Suchman, 1995). The effectiveness of this approach is highly contingent on both the capabilities of the new venture's management and the nature of its operating environment. For example, this approach may be most useful in establishing legitimacy among stakeholders befuddled by uncertainty in highly dynamic environments (Borum and Westenholz, 1995; Oliver, 1991).

Two empirical works stress the potential of enacting sound firm strategy while vying for acceptance in a particular environment. Henderson (1999) studied failure rates among United States personal computer firms. Her results suggest that firms in the adolescent stage of growth should formulate and enact unique, firm-specific strategies rather than adopt recognizable industry standard offerings. The results may be industry-specific; however, the value of proprietary offerings in many other industries seems quite salient. Tornikoski and Newbert (2007) provide further evidence that deviating from industry norms might also prove beneficial when certain nascent organizations seek legitimacy and funding. In their empirical study, the researchers tested whether promotional efforts, applying for a patent or trademark, and projecting financial statements is positively related to legitimacy attainment. They conclude that efforts made to frame and characterize a firm as decidedly differentiated from other resident organizations in an industry significantly increase the firm's chances of attaining legitimacy.

Stakeholder Approach

The third approach to understanding and describing how new ventures minimize LoN draws from the social relationship school of evolutionary theory, which contends that venture survival hinges on establishing and managing social relationships between the entrepreneur and the outside stakeholders (Stinchcombe, 1965; Stuart et al., 1999). Given both a new venture's limited track record and the difficulty associated with thoroughly disseminating organizational information into the firm's environment, potential stakeholders often face a high 'adverse selection' risk when considering whether to do business with a new venture (Akerlof, 1970). Consequently, they often have very few incentives to break ties with their current, more established partners and customers and foster new social relationships with new venture leaders with whom they have little acquaintance (Stinchcombe, 1965).

When stakeholder knowledge pertaining to the founding team and new venture proves deficient, market, production, and/or management novelty is often present. As previously mentioned, these novelties can significantly reduce the probability that the new venture will survive or even be founded (Shepherd and Shanley, 1998; Shepherd et al., 2000). It is, therefore, necessary for entrepreneurs to seek social ties and employ them to amass resources and compete in their chosen markets (Aldrich and Zimmer, 1986). Social ties are considered among the most important catalysts for many types of economic transactions (Arrow, 1974), making those who are able to establish and use social ties often far more successful than those who cannot (Granovetter, 1985).

Organizational managers, in general, must strive to properly manage customer relationships and expectations so as to achieve acceptance and recognition among market competitors (Donaldson and Preston, 1995; Freeman, 1984). Thus, they must usually spend large amounts of valuable time and energy to discern and manage key stakeholders' needs and desires, as their firms' resources, reputation and power are derived from these particular stakeholder relationships (Frooman, 1999; Jahwahar and McLaughlin, 2001; Scott and Lane, 2000). For new venture managers, in particular, the amount of attention specifically paid to key stakeholders like customers, investors, and other constituents is an especially salient concern because their actions have profound effects on new ventures in the early stages of operation (Schroeder et al., 2002; Yli-Renko et al., 2001).

A number of empirical inquiries have underscored the necessary nature of managing stakeholder relationships while firms are in their earliest stages of growth. In terms of cognitive legitimacy – that is, the legitimacy that is attained through the ability to disseminate knowledge about the entrepreneurial founding team members, the new venture, and the new venture's offerings to key stakeholders – what seems to be most important is the quantity of information available to stakeholders to reduce the concerns associated with newness (Shepherd and Zacharakis, 2003). Shane and Cable (2002) found that establishing strong network ties to potential financiers has a positive impact on gaining the funding necessary to found a venture. Calling it the 'social embeddedness solution', the researchers reveal evidence suggesting that the most important reason why nascent entrepreneurs are able to obtain funding whereas others cannot is new ventures' ability to transfer information to potential financiers. These transfers can stem from the petitioning entrepreneurs as well as the entrepreneurs' referrals, and both can provide social ties and reliable sources of information and recommendations. In addition, Shepherd and Zacharakis (2003) reported that the more information is available to consumers about the new venture's products, organization, and management, the higher the propensity for customers to deem the venture legitimate.

LIABILITIES OF ADOLESCENCE

In contrast to LoN, which posits high initial new venture mortality followed by declining failure rates, the liability of adolescence (LoA) perspective posits that new ventures may enjoy a 'honeymoon' period early on, followed by increasing venture failure (Levinthal and Fichman, 1988). Organizational researchers embracing the LoA perspective contend that managers may navigate new ventures through their initial LoN challenges based on their abilities both to draw from their ventures' initial resource stocks (e.g. financial, goodwill, and psychological commitment by both new venture owners and key stakeholders), and to capitalize on their stakeholders withholding judgment until after the start-up phase when they can better assess performance (Fichman and Levinthal, 1991). Thus, rather than failure risks starting out high in a new venture's existence and declining monotonically, as is typically posited in LoN research, LoA studies typically hypothesize that failure risks may start low, increase, and then decline, resulting in an inverted-U shape relationship (Brüderl and Schüssler, 1990). Once they have passed successfully through the start-up phase, the major threat facing these adolescent firms arises from routines they have developed that may have aided their survival initially, but which soon after lock them in to inertial actions that ultimately prove fatal, especially in dynamic environments (Thornhill and Amit, 2003).

Empirical results lend some support to this LoA hypothesis. For example, in an early ecological study, Preisendörfer and Voss (1990) found that mortality rates of (West) German firms, rather than starting out high and declining, as is suggested by LoN, actually started low, increased, and then later began to decline. They attributed this trend to an initial 'honeymoon' or 'probationary' period in which the founder exerts significant effort and customers may give some initial support to the company. Closer examination of their data, however, reveals that new venture mortality tended to peak around 10 months after founding, then declined, suggesting that they adopted a much shorter view of venture 'newness' than the typical five to seven years employed in many entrepreneurial studies (e.g. Shrader and Simon, 1997). This issue notwithstanding, their findings provided early evidence that (1) key contingencies (e.g. human capital based on founder age and industry-specific experience) can impact LoN, and (2) LoN may not monotonically decline as age increases.

Employing similar methods, Brüderl and Schüssler (1990) employed a resource-dependency perspective to posit that new ventures would exhibit different mortality patterns, but these patterns, in general, would follow an inverted-U shape track, as posited by LoA. Their results supported their hypothesis, with mortality rates peaking between one and fifteen years after founding, depending on a firm's initial size, legal form, and industry.

More recent studies have begun directly comparing and contrasting LoN with LoA by examining critical contingency variables that might affect a new venture's early or delayed mortality (Hannan, 1998). For example, Henderson (1999) employed a sample from the US computer industry to examine whether new ventures that relied on internally developed, proprietary technology exhibited different mortality rates than those that employed technology based on prevailing industry standards. She found that the latter were more likely to suffer from LoA, suggesting that different mortality patterns can exist within the same population depending on a firm's competitive strategy. In addition, Thornhill and Amit (2003) employed the resource-based view of the firm (RBV) to examine whether different explanations account for firm failures at different stages of development. They found that ventures that succumbed to LoN tended to lack managerial resources and financial management capabilities, whereas those that capitulated to LoA were often unable to adjust to a changing environment. Strotman (2007) also found that industry characteristics (e.g. minimum efficient scale and dynamism) related to new venture mortality in a pattern consistent with the LoA hypothesis.

ASSETS OF NEWNESS

Benevolent properties associated with newness, referred to as assets of newness (AoN), are time-specific characteristics of start-ups that have the potential to aid teams in their quests for new venture viability and profitability. Instead of hindering new venture success and survival, AoN are viewed as stocks of intangible distinctions that cast the new venture as fresh, amicable and malleable in the eyes of customers and other key stakeholders, thereby aiding or buffering the firms in their start-up stage (Fichman and Levinthal, 1991). Stakeholders who perceive innovation, new orientations, and change as key elements to the progression of technological and societal advancement may view these distinctions as very desirable. As new ventures age and become engrained in their internal and external processes and relationships, however, their novelty may fade. Therefore, exploiting these early attractive distinctions is a vital step in the commercialization stage of new venture development. Two salient distinctions, affect and organizational flexibility, represent two critical AoNs, which facilitate the interaction between new firms and their constituents (Choi and Shepherd, 2005).

Affect congruence Affect congruence is the level of consistency between the needs and desires of a particular customer and the goals, values and aspirations of a new venture (Choi and Shepherd, 2005). Stakeholders may support new ventures because they value innovative products (Carayannopoulos, 2009) or perceive the new venture team as affable, eager, and youthful (Lutz, 1982). So long as the firms are viewed as new to the market and offering innovative products and services, influential stakeholders (e.g. 'early adopter' customer groups) may view them in a positive light. These cognitions, thus, can be regarded as an asset associated with being new.

Flexibility New venture firms may also develop competitive advantages by demonstrating the ability to quickly respond to changing competitive conditions and dynamism in the marketplace (Hitt et al., 1991). As firms age and become entrenched in their markets, the relationship between flexibility and competitive advantage often becomes inverse in nature because structural inertia provides benefits, including economies of scale (Aldrich and Auster, 1986; Hannan and Freeman, 1984). Therefore, the asset may often times be short-lived.

Flexibility is measured in three forms: operational, tactical, and strategic. Operational flexibility is the ability to conform endogenous processes to exogenous changes (Galbraith, 1990; Suarez et al., 1995), tactical flexibility refers to a firm's capability to exploit opportunities stemming from the environment (Johnson et al., 2003), and strategic flexibility refers to its capability to generate firm-specific options in an effort to align itself with customer needs and proposals (Hitt et al., 1998; Johnson et al., 2003). These strategic options are formulated in response to market uncertainty and pressures to adopt new technology, innovations and standards, and each is considered a beneficial property of new ventures lacking structure and routine (Carayannopoulos, 2009; Choi and Shepherd, 2005).

FUTURE RESEARCH

Our review suggests that organizational research has made tremendous progress in examining the issues new ventures face that can impact survival, particularly in terms of how they can attain legitimacy. At the same time, some issues that Stinchcombe (1965) and others have proposed remain under-researched. In particular, most research, to date, has focused on external issues (e.g. stakeholder perceptions) related to LoN rather than several internal issues that may also imperil new ventures (studies focusing on initial resource endowments represent an exception). Thus, to conclude our review, we highlight two other theoretical perspectives – the resource-based view of the firm (RBV) and trust – that may prove critical in future research efforts to circumscribe the boundaries of LoN, LoA, and AoN.

First, according to the RBV, a firm's competitiveness is enhanced by the extent to which it can develop and maintain control over resources (e.g. brand name or reputation) or capabilities (e.g. workforce creativity or flexibility) that are valuable, rare, imperfectly inimitable, and lacking strategically equivalent substitutes (Barney, 1991). Some resources could contribute to a new venture's AoN (e.g. affect congruence), and, in turn, mitigate some of the LoN issues it faces. In addition, LoA studies have also cited the importance of initial resource endowments (Hannan, 1998), including some (e.g. goodwill and top management social capital) that would qualify as resources based on the RBV definition (Fichman and Levinthal, 1991; Packalen, 2007).

At the same time, depending on the resource or capability, some interesting future research questions arise. For example, as noted above, a firm's legitimacy often depends on its ability to conform to widely accepted norms related to organizational characteristics (DiMaggio and Powell, 1983). Conversely, employing the RBV, a firm's competitive advantage is predicated on its ability to differentiate itself from competitors. In a new venture context, conformity could result in a new venture failing to 'stand out' or attract attention in a crowded competitive landscape. Thus, one critical future research question for LoN research involves the extent to which a new venture must balance conformity with differentiation as it moves through the different phases of the start-up process (cf. Deephouse, 1999).

On a related note, many resources and capabilities result from establishing firm routines (Nelson and Winter, 1982), which, as Stinchcombe (1965) notes, represents a critical step in overcoming LoN. At the same time, however, establishing these routines can also decrease a new venture's future ability to adapt, which may be critical when operating in dynamic environments. Indeed, routines that have survival value early in a new venture's life may become 'core rigidities' later in life (Leonard-Barton, 1992), contributing to a potential LoA (Thornhill and Amit, 2003). Consequently, examining the role of routines, as well as how different types of routines contribute to early versus later venture survival, is an important future research issue.

Second, how new ventures establish stakeholder trust also warrants close examination. Trust represents an important, multifaceted construct in organizational research, and Stinchcombe (1965) notes that a lack of trust among new venture employees represents a critical issue contributing to a new venture's LoN. In addition, lack of external ties, which represents another key issue, can include an external trust dimension. For example, Aldrich and Fiol note that '[t]rust is a critical first-level determinant of the success of founding entrepreneurs because, by definition, there is an absence of information and evidence regarding their new activity' (1994, p. 650).

The role of trust within organizations, in general, and new ventures, in particular, has received increasing attention. To date, however, most trust research has adopted either agency or social exchange theory (Whitener et al., 1998). Employing the former, studies have examined how external agents (e.g. venture capitalists) structure contracts with a new venture to overcome problems related to potential information asymmetry and goal incongruence with founding teams (Batjargal and Liu, 2004). This research has focused primarily on the economic side of the relationship and has often dealt with issues arising after a new venture has become more established (e.g. its initial public offering). Employing the latter, studies have examined the evolution of trust over time (Dibben, 2000). New ventures, however, may not have sufficient history to have exhibited trustworthy behavior, and some forms of trust can be exceedingly difficult for a person or organization to create in the short run (Blois, 1999). Consequently, studies examining how founding teams develop trust among themselves and how external stakeholders initially come to trust both founding teams and a new venture represent important future issues for LoN research (Smith and Lohrke, 2008).

CONCLUSION

Entrepreneurship researchers often portray potential new venture stakeholders as untrusting and skeptical constituents, sometimes responsible for the demise of a new venture if their inquiries and concerns are not acknowledged and managed. This portrayal is somewhat valid given the high failure rates of most start-ups which can be largely attributed to stakeholder relations. Researchers have acknowledged that both stakeholders' lack of trust and their general skepticism often stem from the novelty of new ventures, and both are manifested in the uncertainties associated within new venture–stakeholder relationships and the novelty of internal processes of new firms at start-up (Hannan and Freeman, 1984; Schumpeter, 1934; Stinchcombe, 1965). New venture leaders must grapple with these uncertainties and manage them effectively from the outset of the venture if it is to succeed (Delmar and Shane, 2004; Shane and Cable, 2002).

In an effort to provide additional insight into these issues, we first reviewed extant LoN research and discussed how new ventures can gain legitimacy with external stakeholders. We then examined the related constructs, LoA and AoN, as well as extant research comparing these constructs with LoN. In doing so, we note that additional research is needed to circumscribe the boundaries of these distinct, but overlapping, constructs. To help guide future research, we discussed key issues and presented two other theoretical perspectives that may be useful. Based on our review, it would seem promising for future studies to specifically examine the role that different industry, firm, and top management characteristics play in the extent to which a new venture encounters LoN, LoA or AoN. Some of these characteristics include:

- Industry – new or established, segmented or homogenous.
- Firm – differentiation or cost-based strategy, broad or early-adopter target market.
- Top management – overall industry experience, experience working together in previous start-ups.

We hope these suggestions will provide guidance to future research endeavors focusing on LoN and related new venture mortality research topics.

REFERENCES

Akerlof, G. (1970), 'The market for lemons: quality uncertainty and the market mechanism', *Quarterly Journal of Economics*, **84**, 488–500.

Aldrich, H. (1995), 'Entrepreneurial strategies in new organizational populations', in I. Bull, H. Thomas and G. Willard (eds), *Entrepreneurship: Perspectives on Theory Building*, New York: Elsevier, pp. 91–108.

Aldrich, H. and E. Auster (1986), 'Even dwarfs started small: liabilities of age and size and their strategic implications', in B. Staw and L. Cummings (eds), *Research in Organizational Behavior*, vol. 8, New York: JAI Press, pp. 165–98.

Aldrich, H. and C. Fiol (1994), 'Fools rush in: the institutional context of industry creation', *Academy of Management Review*, **19**, 645–67.

Aldrich, H. and C. Zimmer (1986), 'Entrepreneurship through social networks', in D.L. Sexton and R.W. Smilor (eds), *The Art and Science of Entrepreneurship*, Cambridge, MA: Ballinger, pp. 3–23.

Amburgey, T., D. Kelly and W. Barnett (1993), 'Resetting the clock: the dynamics of organizational change and failure', *Administrative Science Quarterly*, **38**, 51–73.

Arrow, K. (1974), *The Limits of Organization*, New York: Norton.

Ashforth, B. and B. Gibbs (1990), 'The double-edge of organizational legitimization', *Organization Science*, **1**, 177–94.

Barnard, C. (1938), *The Functions of the Executive*, Cambridge, MA: Harvard University Press.

Barney, J. (1991), 'Firm resources and sustained competitive advantage', *Journal of Management*, **17**, 99–120.

Batjargal, B. and M. Liu (2004), 'Entrepreneurs' access to private equity in China: the role of social capital', *Organization Science*, **15**, 159–72.

Blois, K. (1999), 'Trust in business to business relationships: an evaluation of its status', *Journal of Management Studies*, **36**, 197–215.

Borum, F. and A. Westenholz (1995), 'An organization's incorporation of institutional models: actors and institutional ambiguity', in W. Scott, W. Richard and S. Christensen (eds), *The Institutional Construction of Organizations*, Thousand Oaks, CA: Sage, pp. 113–31.

Briscoe, J., S. Fawcett and R. Todd (2005), 'The implementation and impact of ISO 9000 among small manufacturing enterprises', *Journal of Small Business Management*, **43**, 309–30.

Brown, A.D. (1997), 'Narcissism, identity, and legitimacy', *Academy of Management Review*, **22**, 643–86.

Brüderl, J. and R. Schüssler (1990), 'Organizational mortality: the liability of newness and adolescence', *Administrative Science Quarterly*, **35**, 530–47.

Carayannopoulos, S. (2009), 'How technology-based new firms leverage newness and smallness to commercialize disruptive technologies', *Entrepreneurship Theory and Practice*, **33**, 419–38.

Carroll, G. (1983), 'A stochastic model of organizational mortality: review and reanalysis', *Social Science Research*, **12**, 303–29.

Carroll, G. and J. Delacroix (1982), 'Organizational mortality in the newspaper industries of Argentina and Ireland: an ecological approach', *Administrative Science Quarterly*, **27**, 169–98.

Child, J. (1972), 'Organizational structure, environment and performance: the role of strategic choice', *Sociology*, **6**, 1–22.

Choi, Y. and D. Shepherd (2005), 'Stakeholder perceptions of age and other dimensions of newness', *Journal of Management*, **31**, 573–96.

Deephouse, D. (1999), 'To be different, or to be the same? It's a question and theory of strategic balance', *Strategic Management Journal*, **20**, 147–66.

Delmar, F. and S. Shane (2004), 'Legitimating first: organizing activities and the survival of new ventures', *Journal of Business Venturing*, **19**, 385–410.

Dibben, M. (2000), *Exploring Interpersonal Trust in the Entrepreneurial Venture*, London: MacMillan Press.

DiMaggio, P. and W. Powell (1983), 'The iron cage revisited: institutional isomorphism and collective rationality in organizational fields', *American Sociological Review*, **48**, 147–60.

Donaldson, T. and L. Preston (1995), 'The stakeholder theory of the corporation: concepts, evidence, and implications', *Academy of Management Review*, **20**, 65–91.

Evans, D. and L. Leighton (1989), 'Some empirical aspects of entrepreneurship', *American Economic Review*, **79**, 519–35.

Fayol, H. (1949), *General and Industrial Management*, London: Pitman and Sons.

Fichman, M. and D. Levinthal (1991), 'Honeymoons and the liability of adolescence: a new perspective on duration dependence in social and organizational relationships', *Academy of Management Review*, **16**, 442–68.

Foss, N. (1996), 'Research in strategy, economics, and Michael Porter', *Journal of Management Studies*, **33**, 1–24.

Freeman, J., G. Carroll and M. Hannan (1983), 'The liability of newness: age dependence in organizational death rates', *American Sociological Review*, **48**, 692–710.

Freeman, R. (1984), *Strategic Management: A Stakeholder Approach*, Boston, MA: Pitman.

Fried, V. and R. Hisrich (1994), 'Towards a model of venture capital investment decision making', *Financial Management*, **23**, 28–37.

Frooman, J. (1999), 'Stakeholder influence strategies', *Academy of Management Review*, **24**, 191–205.

Galbraith, C. (1990), 'Transferring core manufacturing technologies in high-technology firms', *California Management Review*, **32**, 56–70.

Granovetter, M. (1985), 'Economic action and social structure: the problem of embeddedness', *American Journal of Sociology*, **91**, 481–510.

Hannan, M. (1998), 'Rethinking age dependence in organizational mortality: logical formalizations', *American Journal of Sociology*, **104**, 126–64.

Hannan, M. and G. Carroll (1995), 'The introduction of organizational ecology', in G.R. Carroll and M.T. Hannan (eds), *Organizations in Industry*, New York: Oxford University Press, pp. 17–31.

Hannan, M. and J. Freeman (1977), 'The population ecology of organizations', *American Journal of Sociology*, **82**, 929–64.

Hannan, M. and J. Freeman (1984), 'Structural inertia and organizational change', *American Sociological Review*, **49**, 149–64.

Hannan, M. and J. Freeman (1989), *Organizational Ecology*, Cambridge, MA: Harvard University Press.

Headd, B. (2003), 'Redefining business success: distinguishing between closure and failure', *Small Business Economics*, **21**, 51–61.

Henderson, A. (1999), 'Firm strategy and age dependence: a contingency view of liabilities of newness, adolescence, and obsolescence', *Administrative Science Quarterly*, **44**, 281–314.

Hitt, M., R. Hoskisson and J. Harrison (1991), 'Strategic competitiveness in the 1990's for US executives', *Academy of Management Executive*, **5**, 7–23.

Hitt, M., B. Keats and S. DeMarie (1998), 'Navigating in the new competitive landscape: building strategic flexibility and competitive advantage in the 21st century', *Academy of Management Executive*, **12**, 22–42.

Jahwahar, I. and G. McLaughlin (2001), 'Toward a descriptive stakeholder theory: an organizational life cycle approach', *Academy of Management Review*, **26**, 397–414.

Johnson, J., R. Lee, A. Saini and B. Grohmann (2003), 'Market focused strategic flexibility: conceptual advances and an integrative model', *Academy of Marketing Science Journal*, **31**, 74–90.

Kazanjian, R. (1988), 'Relation of dominant problems to stages of growth in technology-based new ventures', *Academy of Management Journal*, **31**, 257–79.

Leonard-Barton, D. (1992), 'Core capabilities and core rigidities: a paradox of managing new product development', *Strategic Management Journal*, **13**, 111–25.

Levinthal, D. and M. Fichman (1988), 'Dynamics of interorganizational attachments', *Administrative Science Quarterly*, **22**, 345–69.

Lutz, F. (1982), 'Tightening up loose coupling in organizations of higher education', *Administrative Science Quarterly*, **27**, 653–69.

Meyer, J. and B. Rowan (1977), 'Institutionalized organizations: formal structure as myth and ceremony', *American Journal of Sociology*, **83**, 340–63.

Nelson, R. and S. Winter (1982), *An Evolutionary Theory of Economic Change*, Cambridge, MA: Belknap Press of Harvard University Press.

Oliver, C. (1991), 'Strategic responses to institutional processes', *Academy of Management Review*, **16**, 145–79.

Packalen, K. (2007), 'Complementing capital: the role of status, demographic features, and social capital on found teams' abilities to obtain resources', *Entrepreneurship Theory and Practice*, **31**, 873–91.

Pisano, G. (1994), 'Knowledge, integration, and the locus of learning: an empirical analysis of process development', *Strategic Management Journal*, **15**, 85–100.

Preisendörfer, P. and T. Voss (1990), 'Organizational mortality of small firms: the effects of entrepreneurial age and human capital', *Organization Studies*, **11**, 107–29.

Schroeder, R., K. Bates and M. Junttila (2002), 'A resource-based view of manufacturing strategy and the relationship to manufacturing performance', *Strategic Management Journal*, **23**, 105–14.

Schumpeter, J. (1934), *The Theory of Economic Development*, Cambridge, MA: Harvard University Press.

Scott, S. and V. Lane (2000), 'A stakeholder approach to organizational identity', *Academy of Management Review*, **25**, 43–62.

Shane, S. and C. Cable (2002), 'Network ties, reputation, and the financing of new ventures', *Management Science*, **48**, 364–81.

Shepherd, D. and M. Shanley (1998), *New Venture Strategy*, London: Sage Publications.

Shepherd, D. and A. Zacharakis (2003), 'A new venture's cognitive legitimacy: an assessment by customers', *Journal of Small Business Management*, **41**, 148–67.

Shepherd, D., E. Douglas and M. Shanley (2000), 'New venture survival: ignorance, external shocks, and risk reduction strategies', *Journal of Business Venturing*, **15**, 393–410.

Shrader R. and M. Simon (1997), 'Corporate versus independent new ventures: resource, strategy and performance differences', *Journal of Business Venturing*, **12**, 47–66.

Singh, J., D. Tucker and R. House (1986), 'Organizational legitimacy and the liability of newness', *Administrative Science Quarterly*, **31**, 171–93.

Smith, D. and F. Lohrke (2008), 'Entrepreneurial network development: trusting in the process', *Journal of Business Research*, **61**, 315–22.

Stinchcombe, A. (1965), 'Social structure and organizations', in J.G. March (ed.), *Handbook of Organizations*, Chicago, IL: Rand McNally, pp. 142–93.

Strotman, H. (2007), 'Entrepreneurial survival', *Small Business Economics*, **28**, 84–101.

Stuart, T., H. Huang and R. Hybels (1999), 'Interorganizational endorsements and the performance of entrepreneurial ventures', *Administrative Science Quarterly*, **44**, 315–49.

Suarez, F., M. Cusumano and C. Fine (1995), 'An empirical study of flexibility in manufacturing', *Sloan Management Review*, **37**, 25–32.

Suchman, M. (1995), 'Managing legitimacy: strategic and institutional approaches', *Academy of Management Journal*, **20**, 571–610.

Teece, D. (1996), 'Firm organization, industrial structure, and technological innovation', *Journal of Economic Behavior and Organization*, **31**, 193–224.

Thompson, J. (1967), *Organizations in Action*, New York: McGraw-Hill.

Thornhill, S. and R. Amit (2003), 'Learning about failure: bankruptcy, firm age, and the resource-based view', *Organizational Science*, **14**, 497–509.

Tornikoski, E. and S. Newbert (2007), 'Exploring the determinants of organizational emergence: a legitimacy perspective', *Journal of Business Venturing*, **22**, 311–35.

Whitener, E., S. Brodt, M. Korsgaard and J. Werner (1998), 'Managers as initiators of trust: an exchange relationship framework for understanding managerial trustworthy behavior', *Academy of Management Review*, **23**, 513–30.

Yli-Renko, H., E. Autio and H. Sapienza (2001), 'Social capital, knowledge acquisition, and knowledge exploitation in young technology-based firms', *Strategic Management Journal*, **22**, 587–613.

Zaheer, S. (1995), 'Overcoming the liability of foreignness', *Academy of Management Journal*, **38**, 341–63.

Zimmerman, M. and G. Zeitz (2002), 'Beyond survival: achieving new venture growth by building legitimacy', *Academy of Management Review*, **27**, 414–31.
Zucker, L. (1987), 'Institutional theories of organization', *Annual Review of Sociology*, **13**, 443–64.

10. Entrepreneurial groups

Martin Ruef

INTRODUCTION

To many observers, a focus on entrepreneurial groups – or, more colloquially, venture 'founding teams' – is a thoroughly modern pre-occupation. It was only in the late 1980s and early 1990s that scholars in business management and policy began to question the image of the heroic individual found in traditional treatments of entrepreneurship. Writing in the *Harvard Business Review*, the economist Robert Reich (who would become Bill Clinton's Secretary of Labor six years later) argued that 'to compete effectively in today's world, we must begin to celebrate collective entrepreneurship' rather than 'the traditional myth of the entrepreneurial hero' (1987, p. 78). Some management thinkers had touted the importance of 'team entrepreneurship' as much as a decade earlier (e.g. Timmons, 1975; 1979), but a new generation of scholars were the first to call for a systematic program of research that would document the prevalence of entrepreneurial groups, describe their properties, and assess their impact on business performance (e.g. Kamm et al., 1990; Gartner et al., 1994). In a review of developments in entrepreneur research and theory, Gartner and colleagues (1994, p. 6) noted that 'the "entrepreneur" in entrepreneurship is more likely to be plural, rather than singular'. They offered an expansive definition of the entrepreneurial group, which included owner-managers, investors, organizational decision-makers, family members, advisors, critical suppliers and buyers as possible candidates in the entrepreneur role.

Contributors to the management literature have primarily displayed an interest in teams as a contemporary phenomenon. In this chapter, I suggest that the historical evidence and frameworks that can be deployed to study entrepreneurial groups are far less recent than this literature might seem to suggest. Indeed, the social sciences evidence a long pedigree of research devoted to entrepreneurs and the collective nature of activities surrounding the creation of new organizations (Ruef and Lounsbury, 2007). The goals of the chapter are twofold. First, the chapter offers a selective history of entrepreneurial groups, addressing the legal origins of commercial partnerships in Roman and medieval law, the elaboration of partnership systems in the Mediterranean region during the Renaissance, and the evolution of entrepreneurial groups during the Industrial Revolution. Second, it traces the intellectual origins of social scientific work on entrepreneurial groups. I emphasize four classical perspectives, in particular: (a) Georg Simmel's structural sociology; (b) Ronald Coase's theory of the firm; (c) the logic of collective action in entrepreneurial groups, as developed by Mancur Olson; and (d) theories of ethnic enterprise, with particular implications for the formation and persistence of entrepreneurial groups.[1] In designating these as 'classical' perspectives, I apply the informal criterion of emphasizing contributions that were published by the mid-1970s, a time when a number of new organizational theories with broad implications for entre-preneurial studies (including organizational ecology, institutional theory, and transaction cost economics) first emerged.

My review of the historical literature is necessarily selective. It is fairly easy to locate work on entrepreneurial groups that has intellectual roots aside from the classical perspectives discussed in this chapter. For instance, in a study of the decision-making biases of venture capitalists who are evaluating entrepreneurial teams, Franke and his colleagues (2006) employ social identity theory, a perspective developed by Henri Tajfel in the late 1970s (Tajfel and Turner, 1979), which also draws on earlier research on in-group and out-group comparisons (e.g. Bass and Duntemann, 1963). Despite the utility of social identity theory for understanding group dynamics, I restrict my attention to historical social science perspectives that sought to address the process of entrepreneurial association *even when those perspectives were first formulated*. That is, I focus on schol-ars who discuss entrepreneurial partnership *per se*, not simply generic aspects of group formation and functioning. In the concluding section of the chapter, I suggest how the classical perspectives continue to raise questions that animate contemporary research on entrepreneurial groups.

HISTORICAL EVIDENCE

Many of us – especially those raised in an Anglo-American context – take it for granted that individuals can readily construct autonomous, organizational entities to act on their behalf. However, even a cursory review of the historical record suggests that societies differ greatly in the amount of agency they accord to entrepreneurs and their organi-zational ventures (Hwang and Powell, 2005; Meyer and Jepperson, 2000). Institutional frameworks strongly influence whether entrepreneurial groups are short-lived affairs that are tied closely to the fates of their creators, or whether they are able to develop as inde-pendent and, potentially, perpetual legal fictions. Between the late Middle Ages and the nineteenth century, the understanding of entrepreneurial groups in Western civilization displayed considerable stability for four or five centuries, only to be disrupted by rapid social and legal changes during the era of industrialization.

From the Middle Ages to the Industrial Revolution

The German sociologist Max Weber (1864–1920) offered one of the earliest, and most prescient, treatments of the historical origins of entrepreneurial groups. In his J.D. dissertation on the *History of Commercial Partnerships* (hereafter, HCP), Weber (1889/2003) compared the influence of Roman and Germanic commercial laws on partnerships among medieval entrepreneurs. He based his analysis on a systematic review of Italian and Spanish legal charters and statutes from the eleventh through the sixteenth centuries, with detailed case studies of commercial law in Florence and Pisa's *Constitutum Usus*. Beginning with a discussion of Roman property law, Weber (Chapter 1) argued that the legal differentiation of partnerships (*societas*) from indi-vidual entrepreneurs participating in them (*socius*) was largely nominal in this legal form: 'the partnership, as merely a complex of obligatory relations among the *socii*, is of no concern to third parties; in its legal consequences, a transaction a *socius* makes on the account of the partnership is no different from any transaction made on a personal account' (1889/2003, p. 54). The differentiation between individual and group strengthened, however, with the growing needs of maritime and overland trade during the Middle Ages. Two new organizational forms – the *societas maris* and *societas terrae* – relied increasingly on a cash fund that was separate from the assets of entrepreneurs participating in the venture (1889/2003, Chapter 2). A further development was the emergence of the joint household in Germanic law. This organizational form introduced the concept of solidary liability, whereby the debt of a family or community member 'encumbers the joint assets' of that community (1889/2003, p. 98). The concept was quickly generalized in the Middle Ages to commercial partnerships, as joint households were not only defined in terms of kinship ties, but also in terms of cohabitation and 'communities of labor' (e.g. craft guilds).

In broad strokes, what Weber was identifying theoretically in the HCP were a set of institutional conditions that would allow for the social construction of entrepreneurial groups: partnerships that had a legal, economic, and social existence apart from the entrepreneurs that constituted them. A concrete example in this respect involves his comparison of medieval *commendas*, or trade associations (see Lutz, pp. 22–7, in Weber 1889/2003). In the unilateral commenda, investment capital was provided by only a single party, while in the bilateral commenda, investment came from (at least) two parties (see Figure 10.1). Each organizational form involved both a *commendator* (or passive investor) and an entrepreneur known as a *tractator*. The unilateral commenda differed, however, in that all of the financial risk was borne on the part of the passive investor, who contributed to a fund that would be managed by the *tractator*, serving as his or her agent. In contrast to prevailing legal wisdom, Weber (1889/2003, pp. 135–6) argued that the lack of a separate fund in the unilateral commenda meant that it was not an institutional precursor of modern partnerships. Indeed, the weak organizational foundation that the unilateral commenda provided for entrepreneurial ventures led to its eventual replacement by simpler financing arrangements, such as commercial loans. The bilateral commenda, by contrast, specified the existence of a fund that was separate from the assets of investors and entrepreneurs and, in Weber's account, served as a legal template for modern partnership forms.[2]

As Weber's legal history of partnerships attests, entrepreneurial groups have been a prominent feature of Western capitalism since its origins, even predating it according to some definitions. During the late Middle Ages, associations of businessmen already thrived in the Mediterranean region. These groups were not simply a reflection of economic growth, but an important catalyst as well. In thirteenth-century Italy, the historian Thomas Blomquist (1971, pp. 157–8) has argued, 'the favored method of doing business . . . was through association: at all levels of business, capital and/or labor were pooled in order to realize a maximum economic potential'. Whether the primary purpose of such associations was to achieve 'maximum economic potential' is a debatable empirical point, but the prevalence of entrepreneurial groups is not. For example, the northern Italian city of Lucca, a center of the silk trade, featured at least 22 large-scale (international) business partnerships by the late 1200s, some with as many as 19 partners (ibid, pp. 159–60). Through associates in Flanders, Champagne, Paris, and England, these groups penetrated

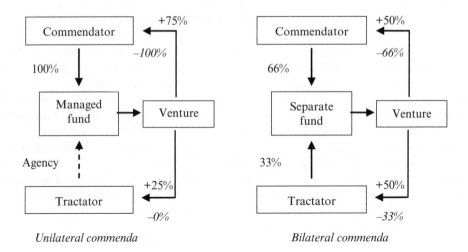

Unilateral commenda   *Bilateral commenda*

Note: Positive percentages correspond to financial contributions and shares of profit. Negative percentages correspond to losses borne by each partner.

Source: Ruef and Lounsbury (2007, p. 8); based on Weber (1889/2003).

Figure 10.1 *The organizational structure of two medieval forms of entrepreneurial partnership*

markets in Northern Europe and contributed to the widespread influence of the Italian associational business model.

By the time of the Renaissance, Europe witnessed not just the emergence of a precursor of modern partnerships, but also of 'partnership systems': autonomous firms (either sole proprietorships or partnerships) that were connected together through a single or small group of entrepreneurs. As Padgett and McLean (2006) document, the new organizational form was first developed in Florence during the late 1300s to encourage diversification and protect entrepreneurs against the risk of unlimited liability. Prominent adopters included Francesco Datini, the merchant of Prato, who between 1382 and 1410 participated in one of the first partnership systems (Origo, 1957/1992), as well as the banker Giovanni di Bicci de Medici and his descendents, Cosimo and Lorenzo 'the Magnificent' de Medici (de Roover, 1966). The birth of partnership systems was a major organizational innovation at the time, predating other forms of entrepreneurial groups such as the limited liability partnership, which was not developed until 1408 in Florence and not widely adopted until the 1500s (Padget and McLean, 2006, p. 1466).

During the early stages of the Industrial Revolution, business partnerships evidenced little change from their medieval and Renaissance forebears. Considering partnership agreements (*actes de société*) in Lyon between 1783 and 1793, Taylor (1963, p. 49) commented that 'as an entrepreneurial form the partnership met all the needs of business practice . . . before the [French] Revolution and . . . differed in no important way from partnerships of the Renaissance. On the other hand, it was far removed from the 19th century corporate or joint-stock institution . . . [The partnership] had more in common with the remote past than with the organizational forms that appeared some seven decades later'. The Lyonnaise partnership agreements, which were typical of much of late eighteenth-century Europe, ran for short terms (three to eight years), established fixed financial relationships, and defined a line of specialized trade among partners. But the content of the agreements also suggests that these businesses were more than economic units. Highlighting their character as 'households', Taylor notes that 'partners and employees often lived in the buildings that the companies rented[;] clerks got meals and rooms in addition to salaries, and servants, warehouse workers, and artisans lived and worked in the house' (1963, p. 53). The combination of business partners and workers from different status ranks at the same physical site led to 'a curious mixture of commerce and gentility' in these enterprises (p. 54).

The legal forms available to entrepreneurial teams evolved considerably during the nineteenth century. At the beginning of the century, entrepreneurs who sought to found a venture together had little choice but to create a business partnership – or to seek a special charter from a legislature that would allow them to incorporate their enterprise under public auspices (Lamoreaux, 1998). Over the course of the succeeding decades, the diffusion of general laws of incorporation in the United States and Europe greatly simplified the chartering of corporate entities.

Aside from the obvious implications of the corporate form for the liability of business owners (which was far more limited than in commercial partnerships), it also had crucial implications for the longevity and governance of entrepreneurial ventures. As suggested by Taylor's Lyonnaise example, partnership agreements tended to end after a fixed period of time, and they also tended to be dissolved by the death of one of their members. The corporation, by contrast, was 'more commonly chartered in perpetuity' and its life 'was independent of that of any of its stockholders' (Lamoreaux 1998, p. 66). In terms of governance, the autonomy of an owner of the corporate venture to act on behalf of the organization was also severely limited compared to the simpler business partnership. The legal view of these entrepreneurial groups evolved only gradually over the century: at the beginning of the 1800s, 'the view that corporations were artificial creatures of the state held sway; by the middle it was increasingly common to view corporations as private contracts made by "aggregations" of businessmen; by the end, the courts were moving toward the view that corporations were legal persons in the eye of the law' (p. 67). These institutional developments represented a culmination of the evolutionary process whose legal origins were already identified by Weber in the late medieval period.

Historical Diversity in Entrepreneurial Groups

Although much of the historical literature on commercial partnerships has emphasized associations among male participants, entrepreneurial groups have likewise played an important role for women. In nineteenth-century Britain, women comprised roughly a fifth of all entrepreneurs, with a particularly strong concentration in the garment trades (Nenadic, 1998). Because these businesses often relied on 'the cultivation of "dovetailed" effort whereby the income-producing activities of one related woman reinforced and supplemented those of another' (ibid, p. 633), kinship-based co-partnerships represented the dominant form of organization. For instance, in Stana Nenadic's sample of 53 female-run Edinburgh garment firms, more than 80 per cent depended on kin co-partnerships, most commonly sibling or mother-daughter teams.[3] Owing to family law at the time, these 'co-partneries' became associated with separate funds that resembled the more formal arrangements found among male entrepreneurs in other contexts. As Nenadic suggests, 'in family financial affairs, sisters were treated as a package, bound together for life – or until they married – the individualised interests of each sister subordinated to those of the family as a whole' (1998, p. 635). Moreover, in contrast to some of their male counterparts, 'the non-individualised character of women's capital and women's business . . . probably negated any imperative to maximize profits in the interests of self' (ibid.). In Victorian Britain, then, one could argue that entrepreneurial groups were even more critical to business development among women than among male entrepreneurs.

Considering the importance of entrepreneurial groups in the West, one might also ask whether a similar influence can be identified during the emergence of Asian capitalism. Here the historical evidence is more difficult to interpret, given the unique pathway taken by these economies vis-à-vis the Occident. In Japan, entrepreneurial activity in the medieval Buddhist economy was undertaken by monasteries and temples (Collins, 1997), whereas secular capitalism was generally unknown before the Muromachi period (1333–1460). On the surface, the monastic enterprises appear quite different than the business partnerships that formed in the Mediterranean basin around the same time period. As the sociologist Randy Collins suggests, however, insightful parallels can be drawn with respect to the organizational preconditions of capitalist development. Monastic culture encouraged an ethos of asceticism and investment, much as entrepreneurial groups did in the West. Similar to the 'separate fund' that appeared in the European partnership forms, the collective nature of monastic entrepreneurship was critical to capital accumulation: 'Because celibate monks could not siphon [material capital] off to family consumption, it was the monastic corporation that grew rich' (ibid., p. 848). Some monasteries even recruited bands of wandering ascetics (*hijiri*), who had existing entrepreneurial skills as itinerant merchants and artisans. During the Kamakura period (1185–1333), monastic enterprises gained in political and economic status and subsequently served as the dominant institution in Japanese society for nearly two-and-a-half centuries (Collins, 1997).

Summary

The historical record suggests, therefore, that the concept of the entrepreneurial group is neither distinctively modern nor distinctively Western. From its origins, capitalist development has relied on groups of entrepreneurs to pool resources and competencies, manage risk, expand into new territories, offer social support, and share responsibility for undertakings, both large and small. The legal evolution of these groups can be characterized broadly in three phases: (a) cases where the distinction of individual entrepreneurs and groups is largely nominal (e.g. Roman *societas*); (b) cases where the group maintains a separate fund from its members (communities of labor, joint households, Japanese monastic enterprise); and (c) cases where the responsibilities (debts and obligations) of the group are separated from the personal responsibility of the participating entrepreneurs (joint stock corporations). Over time, these legal conditions allowed for the emergence of entrepreneurial groups that were fully independent from the 'natural' persons that created them (Coleman, 1974; Ruef and Lounsbury, 2007).

HISTORICAL PERSPECTIVES

Now let us turn to the historical frameworks that have been used to study entrepreneurial groups. Who are their progenitors, and what is their impact on the contemporary social sciences? Over the course of the century following Weber's treatment of commercial partnerships, a number of sociologists and economists tackled the functions and dysfunctions of entrepreneurial groups. Arguably, the most enduring of these contributions can be found in four intellectual traditions, including the structural sociology of Georg Simmel, Ronald Coase's theory of the firm, Mancur Olson's logic of collective action, and sociological theories of ethnic enterprise.

Simmel's Structural Sociology

Georg Simmel (1858–1918) was a contemporary of Weber and early proponent of structural sociology, a forerunner of modern network analysis.[4] He had a particular interest in interpersonal associations, which he described as the 'form (realized in innumerable, different ways) in which individuals grow together into units that satisfy their interests' (1917/1950, p. 41). These units comprised a diverse set of groups, including social gatherings, religious sects, military alliances, extended families and (most notably for our purposes) business partnerships. While Simmel devoted considerable attention to the simplest structural arrangements – dyads and triads – he also maintained that structural sociology should account for the origin and composition of larger groups. It was in these settings, he maintained, that an 'autonomous, super-individual unit' (Simmel, 1908a/1950) transcends the individual personalities involved and confronts members as an objective structure. Like Weber, Simmel was thus intrigued by groups as an intermediate building block between individual persons and formal organizations.

In Simmel's work, a tension between autonomy and constraint is evident even in the simplest of entrepreneurial partnerships. Considering dyads of business partners, he noted that:

> The formation and operation of the business rests, exclusively perhaps, on the cooperation of these two personalities, nevertheless the subject matter of the cooperation, the business or firm, is an objective structure. Each of the two [entrepreneurs] has rights and duties toward it that in many respects are not different from those of any third party. And yet this fact here has another sociological significance . . . Because of the objective character of the economic system, business is intrinsically separate from the person of the owner, whether he be one or two, or more persons. (Simmel, 1908a/1950, p. 132)

The question of the legal separation of a business from the entrepreneurs that create it – the central concern for Weber's historical analysis of entrepreneurial partnerships – was taken for granted in Simmel's structural sociology. In Simmel's mind, this fact alone was enough to fundamentally differentiate the social psychological dynamics of entrepreneurial dyads from other dyadic relationships, such as monogamous marriage.

Elaborating on this perspective, Simmel suggested that the addition of a third participant in a group created new tensions and opportunities. When the other two participants had limited prior affiliation or interpersonal trust, an individual who comprised the third element of the triad could assume the role of a broker or intermediary. A broker with self-serving motivations was identified by Simmel as the *tertius gaudens* (or the 'third who enjoys'), because s/he could derive benefit from potential conflict between the other two members of the group (Simmel, 1908a/1950, pp. 154–5). In contemporary structural sociology, this arrangement is seen by Ronald Burt as a defining characteristic of entrepreneurial activity: 'when you take the opportunity to be the *tertius*, you are an entrepreneur in the literal sense of the word – a person who generates profit from being between others . . . [E]ntrepreneur refers to a kind of behavior, the *tertius* is a successful entrepreneur' (Burt, 1992, p. 34).

Recent work on entrepreneurial groups has documented the impact of the *tertius* role on economic inequality within business partnerships. In one nationally representative sample of US founding teams, the equity share held by participating entrepreneurs was significantly higher when they assumed brokerage positions, mediating between weakly connected partners (Ruef, 2009). Consistent as well with Simmel's intuitions, however, the exercise of the *tertius* strategy was not appropriate in all contexts. As he (Simmel, 1908a/1950, p. 159) argued, 'the advantage accruing to the *tertius* derives from the fact that he has an equal, *equally independent*, and for this reason decisive relation to two others' (italics added). Where entrepreneurs serve in a mediating position between their spouses or kin, who are co-owners in a startup business, and other partners, their lack of independence can lead to strong norms against the 'divide and conquer' strategy of the *tertius gaudens*. Consequently, the empirical evidence for the US suggests that entrepreneurs do not derive a greater equity stake in such contexts than would be expected in the absence of brokerage opportunities (Ruef, 2009). By the same token, David Obstfeld (2005) has found that an alternative strategy – the *tertius iungens* (or 'third who joins') – may apply when an entrepreneur seeks to act as a non-partisan mediator between two disconnected parties.

Aside from his analysis of the *tertius gaudens*, Simmel's work has other implications for contemporary work on entrepreneurial groups. His essay on 'the stranger', for instance, highlighted the relationship between outsider status and middleman entrepreneurs, who make a living from intermediate trade between otherwise closed societies (Simmel, 1908b/1950). These middleman entrepreneurs are distinguished by their contact with diverse segments of society, but they lack an 'organic' connection, 'through ties of kinship, locality, and occupation, with any single one' (ibid., p. 404). A theoretical implication that follows from this claim is that an in-group affiliation bias should be sustained among middleman minorities, despite their regular contact with out-group members (typically, in the role of customers or suppliers). Recent statistics on homophilous (in-group) affiliations in entrepreneurial partnerships tend to support this contention. Among US startups in 1998, for instance, the rate at which minority entrepreneurs formed new businesses with members of their own ethnic group was over 800 times the rate expected under a model of random mixing, while the comparable rate for white entrepreneurs was over 100 times random expectations (Ruef et al., 2003, Table 9, Model 3).

In other work, Simmel highlighted the effect of group size and composition on cohesiveness. He argued that group 'solidarity decreases in the measure in which numerical increase involves the admission of heterogeneous individual elements' (1908a/1950, p. 95). Again, his theory bears directly on modern conceptions of entrepreneurial groups, particularly the tension between a desire for functional diversification and the interpersonal conflict that may result from team heterogeneity (Ensley, 1999). This paradox – which also pertains to top management teams more generally (Amason, 1996) – was anticipated by Simmel in terms of 'the disadvantages for cohesion and unity' following from increases in group size, coupled with the 'advantages of nearing [functional] completeness' (1908a/1950, p. 95).

Following Simmel, structural sociology moved in two (quite distinctive) directions, each of which bears on the analysis of entrepreneurial groups. One direction involved the post-World War II development of *sociometry*, the formal methodological toolkit for collecting data on and analyzing social networks (see Wasserman and Faust (1994) for a systematic overview). While network analysts, on the whole, only gradually recognized the relevance of their framework for entrepreneurial behavior, it is now well established that 'most forms of entrepreneurship are centered around firms and interaction rather than around the activities of a single, heroic actor' (Swedberg and Granovetter, 2001, pp. 12–13). Some crucial theoretical milestones in the development of this relational view of entrepreneurial groups have been Mark Granovetter's (1985) influential statement on the 'embeddedness' of economic life and Burt's (1992) conceptualization of the 'network entrepreneur', both of which exhibit a strong Simmelian pedigree.

The other direction is the relationship of social structure outside of the organization to the internal dynamics of the entrepreneurial venture (Aldrich, 1979/2007). Arthur Stinchcombe's path-breaking (1965) essay re-ignited sociological interest in this topic, emphasizing the fragility of entrepreneurial groups that formed without the benefit of pre-existing relationships that could be imported into startup enterprises. For entrepreneurial teams, 'the process of inventing new roles, the determination of their mutual relations and of structuring the field of rewards and sanctions . . . have high costs in time, worry, conflict, and temporary inefficiency' (1965, p. 148). These problems of organizational learning are compounded because 'new organizations must rely heavily on social relations among strangers' (p. 149), producing networks within the group that may be threatened by a lack of interpersonal trust. Stinchcombe argued that the problems could be mitigated by institutions – such as universalistic laws, religious norms, and contractual instruments – that enforce agreements developed among strangers.[5] These institutions seem to figure prominently in the history of entrepreneurial groups discussed in the previous section, with the bilateral commenda, for instance, providing a legal foundation for agency relationships in late medieval trade in the Mediterranean, and Buddhist oaths serving a similar function among entrepreneurial *hijiri* in Japan.

In both the modern network and macro-structural treatments of entrepreneurship, we continue to see the sociological concepts (e.g. the 'tertius gaudens', the 'stranger') introduced by Georg Simmel. His legacy has had a far-reaching effect on the structural analysis of entrepreneurs and groups. Some contemporary analysts of entrepreneurial phenomena frame their analysis explicitly in Simmelian terms (Aldrich and Kim, 2007; Burt, 1992, 2000; Obstfeld, 2005; Ruef, 2002). In other cases, such as the wide-ranging literature on social networks and business founding (e.g. Baker and Nelson, 2005; Renzulli et al., 2000), the intellectual debt is palpable yet unstated. What seems clear is that our understanding of the structural features of entrepreneurial groups – including size, diversity, in-group bias, brokerage, and potential for conflict – would be diminished without Simmel's pioneering work.

Coase's Theory of the Firm

The theory of the firm developed by the British economist Ronald Coase (1910–) is widely recognized as a cornerstone of modern institutional economics. Nevertheless, at first glance, its implications for entrepreneurial groups may seem far from obvious. Oliver Williamson, Coase's most influential and active proponent, writes that the theory of the firm highlighted the fact that, in addition to the price mechanism of the market, the 'economic system is also made up of subsystems, of which the *large corporation* is a conspicuous member' (Williamson and Winter, 1993, p. 3, italics added). When we survey the contemporary literature on the governance of firms, much of it is devoted to the analysis of large and mature enterprises (see David and Han (2004) for a review). Closer scrutiny of Coase's seminal work suggests, however, that in both terminology and content, there is much effort to address the nature of the entrepreneurial firm. Moreover, contemporary economic work on the formation of entrepreneurial partnerships has drawn extensively from Coase's inspiration.

'The nature of the firm' (1937) considers two 'co-ordinating instruments' in the economy – one being the price mechanism and the other being the 'co-ordinating function of the "entrepreneur"' – and asks 'why co-ordination is the work of the price mechanism in one case and of the entrepreneur in another' (p. 389). The central feature of Coase's response, now well rehearsed by students of transaction cost economics, is that the price mechanism imposes costs on market exchange (through problems of contract enforcement, monitoring, and the like) that can be alleviated by the entrepreneur who is coordinating similar transactions within the business firm. The 'transactional' view, in turn, leads Coase to his definition of the firm, which 'consists of the system of relationships which comes into existence when the direction of resources is dependent on an entrepreneur' (Coase, 1937, p. 393).

When this system of relationships involves a set of other entrepreneurs, then Coase's definition circumscribes the boundaries of the entrepreneurial group. The size of the group 'becomes larger as additional transactions (which could be exchange transactions co-ordinated through the price mechanism) are organised by the [focal] entrepreneur and becomes smaller as he [*sic*] abandons the organisation of such transactions' (ibid.). Coase defines the process of *combination* as an event 'when transactions which were previously organised by two or more entrepreneurs become organised by one' and contrasts this with *integration*, which 'involves the organisation of transactions which were previously carried out between the entrepreneurs on a market' (pp. 397–8). As in all facets of the theory of the firm, the decision as to when an entrepreneur should seek out combination or integration (and, thus, form a venture with greater transactional scope) depends on the costs of organizing, the likelihood that the entrepreneur will make 'mistakes' that would otherwise be corrected in the market, and the economies of scale that accrue to the entrepreneurial group.

By most accounts, Ronald Coase's article only exercised a limited influence in the decades after it was published (see Coase (1988) for a retrospective). Even after its resuscitation by Williamson in the 1970s, the initial impetus of transaction economics steered the theory of the firm away from small, entrepreneurial ventures (Williamson, 1975, 1985). Nevertheless, recent applications have highlighted the relevance of Coase's ideas for entrepreneurial groups. In a model of the allocation of rights in venture capital contracts, for instance, Thomas Hellmann (1998) proposes that the willingness of an entrepreneur to give up control rights to an outside investor (e.g. permitting the replacement of the entrepreneur by a professional manager) is partially a function of the entrepreneur's wealth constraints and equity stake. As in Coase's formulation, the decision also hinges on the relative productivity of entrepreneurs (e.g. ability to achieve low organizing costs) compared to professional management (Hellmann, 1998, p. 60). Similarly, in a study of joint ventures between Chinese and foreign partners, Chong-En Bai and his colleagues (2004) offer a theoretical model that emphasizes the private economic benefits and verifiable payoff to both partners as influencing the character of control-right and revenue sharing arrangements. Both Bai and colleagues and Hellmann build on the transaction cost economics (TCE) of Williamson (1985), which addresses the implications of opportunism, bounded rationality, and incomplete contracting for the allocation of control rights in business firms. Their approaches differ from TCE insofar as they consider features of entrepreneurial groups (e.g. founder replacement, revenue sharing) that tend to be ignored in Williamson's focus on mature businesses.

One of the most explicitly historical efforts to develop Coase's ideas in order to understand entrepreneurial partnerships can be found in Avner Greif's (2006) influential text on medieval trade. As Greif points out, a central problem in long distance mercantile exchange at the time was the reliance of entrepreneurs on overseas agents, a contractual partnership fraught with uncertainty and potential for theft or malfeasance. One possible solution – emphasized in other treatments of these partnerships (e.g. Rosenberg and Birdzell, 1986) – is that these mercantile relationships would only be reliable if they were constructed on the basis of a 'natural group', the family. Like Coase, Greif sought to identify other institutions and organizational arrangements that were able to reduce the transaction costs inherent in these affiliations.

A response that arose serendipitously among the (Jewish) Maghribi traders in the eleventh century was the creation of a reputational mechanism that reflected past mercantile conduct. As Greif writes (1989, p. 862), 'the Maghribi traders did not establish a separate religious-ethnic community . . . nor did they represent a "natural" group, which binds together individuals in all (or at least most) important aspects of their lives.' But these traders did operate on a repeated basis through business associates and, in that process, constituted an informal entrepreneurial group – which Greif terms a 'coalition'. The Maghribi coalition was sustained by several institutional mechanisms, few of them sanctioned formally by law in the medieval states of the Mediterranean basin. Perhaps foremost among these, according to Greif, was an implicit contract that governed the relationships among coalition members. Maghribi traders agreed to employ only other coalition members as agents and to pay them a premium for their mercantile services. In addition, 'all coalition merchants agree[d] never to employ an agent who cheated while operating for a coalition member' and were permitted to cheat any trader who had previously cheated a member of the coalition (Greif, 1989, p. 868). Like Coase's 'firm', then, Greif's Maghribi coalition offered an organizational solution to the problem of rampant transaction costs in the open market.

Greif's research demonstrates that the concept of transaction costs can have wide-ranging implications for our understanding of entrepreneurial coordination in social groups. The Maghribi coalition represents a relatively informal organizational arrangement for managing these costs. Another – more formalized – arrangement identified by

Greif was the merchant's guild, which was especially prevalent among the traders of the German *Hansestädte* (2006, Chapter 4). These exemplars flesh out the abstract features of the Coasian firm and illustrate how transactions costs may affect the nature of organizational activities among entrepreneurs. By cataloguing other organizational arrangements and the solutions they offer to instances of market (or state) failure, institutional economists can fruitfully extend Coase's approach to a variety of historical cases of entrepreneurial groups.

Olson's Theory of Collective Action

Mancur Olson (1932–98) is often credited with introducing the analysis of groups with shared interests into economics. In his classic book *The Logic of Collective Action* (1965, revised 1971), Olson addressed the 'free rider' problem, whereby the contributions offered by group members toward collective goals decline with increases in group size.[6] The free rider problem tends to arise in groups, such as entrepreneurial teams, where access to collective rewards (e.g. startup profits) is defined in advance and, for any given group member, is not contingent on their subsequent effort. A strong version of this dilemma applies when entrepreneurial groups formally specify ownership shares (and other benefits) early in the startup process based only on the ostensible competencies and traits of owner-managers, with little provision for sanctioning entrepreneurs whose subsequent investment of time, ideas, or other resources falls short of expectations. More commonly, there is not a complete 'impossibility of exclusion' from collective goods (Hardin, 1982; Oliver, 1993), since business partnerships retain some ability to remove lackadaisical participants from the group. Still, the process of exclusion from the group imposes sufficient burden and turmoil that the free rider problem remains highly salient even in these contexts.

Given the assumptions that (a) group members cannot be excluded from collective benefits (at least not without burden) and that (b) those benefits are produced jointly through the actions of group members, Olson argued that rational individuals would engage in shirking behavior, especially within larger groups where the link between individual effort and collective outcomes was less tangible. Applying his theory to business partnerships, Olson wrote:

> The fact that the [business] partnership can be a workable institutional form when the number of partners is quite small, but is generally unsuccessful when the number of partners is very large, may provide another illustration of the advantages of smaller groups. When a partnership has many members, the individual partner observes that his [*sic*] own effort or contribution will not greatly affect the performance of the enterprise, and expects that he will get his prearranged share of the earnings whether or not he contributes as much as he could have done. The earnings of a partnership, in which each partner gets a prearranged percentage of the return, are a collective good to the partners, and when the number of partners increases, the incentive for each partner to work for the welfare of the enterprise lessens. (Olson, 1971, p. 55)

In Olson's perspective, there are compositional features of social groups that serve to mitigate the free rider problem. Particularly important, in this respect, are social incentives that encourage individuals to contribute, even when they might otherwise be inclined toward free riding. Olson distinguishes between groups bound by strong pre-existing social relationships and those that lack such interpersonal ties: 'if a small group of people who had an interest in a collective good happened also to be personal friends . . . and some of the group left the burden of providing that collective good on others, they might, even if they gained economically by this course of action, lose socially by it, and the social loss might outweigh the economic gain' (ibid., p. 60). Part of the reason that strong social networks are crucial to mitigating free riding is that they offer selective incentives to individuals that must not be explicitly agreed upon or paid for by other members of the group. As a consequence, these social incentives avoid the circularity inherent in the provision of private economic incentives to resolve the collective action problem, in which one collective action problem (the provision of collective goods) begets another (the creation of a system of selective incentives to resolve that problem).

During the late 1960s, the impact of Olson's monograph on the study of entrepreneurship was immediate, especially when 'entrepreneurs' are defined broadly to include actors in the political as well as the business realm. In the revised edition of the book, in 1971, Olson wrote that 'some recent writers, in discussions of the difficulty of providing collective goods for unorganized groups, have introduced the idea of the entrepreneur who might help a group obtain a collective good it lacked' (1971, p. 173). Frohlich and Oppenheimer (1970; 1972), for instance, advocated an entrepreneurial theory of political behavior that was developed explicitly based on Olson's ideas. The earliest formulation of such a theory was advanced by Robert Salisbury (1969), distinguishing between lead entrepreneurs, who develop an incentive structure for a new organization, and mere supporters, who are offered these incentives at the opportunity cost of organizational membership. In Salisbury's framing, the successful emergence of new organizations hinges on the particular mix of benefits – material, solidary, and expressive – between lead entrepreneurs and supporters. Olson's problem of collective action was thus re-formulated as a problem of exchange within a group.[7]

Despite its origin as a theory of economic groups, Olson's theory has since been applied almost exclusively to the formation of groups outside the world of business.[8] As Nownes and Neeley (1996, p. 122) write, 'Olson's logic remains the dominant paradigm for explaining the formation (or lack of formation) of non-economic and public interest groups'. In their own study of public interest group founders, Nownes and Neeley identified only partial support for an exchange-theoretic formulation of Olson's thesis: 'virtually all entrepreneurs noted that they [could] offer charter members nothing in return for their support . . . a member responding to initial entrepreneurial pleas has little or no prospect of personal or collective gain' (p. 137). Still, political scientists have routinely invoked Olson in drawing a link between entrepreneurs and political groups (e.g. Ainsworth and Sened, 1993; Moe, 1988; Schneider and Teske, 1992).

Some of these contributors have also raised questions about the relevance of Olson's theory of collective action for new business partnerships. Owing to the free rider problem, Schneider and Teske (1992, p. 741) suggest that the 'stereotypical private sector entrepreneur works alone or in a small organization, thus solving collective action problems by avoiding collectivities'. By contrast, 'a public sector entrepreneur is much more likely to need a collective *group* foundation to survive and prosper in the political marketplace.' Nownes and Neeley (1996) approach the issue from a different angle, suggesting that the free rider thesis may apply to the maintenance of effort in established groups, rather than the elicitation of effort in new ones. This will be true, in particular, if newly formed organizations tend to receive substantial support from specific patrons, while older organizations rely on the incremental support of a broader set of supporters.[9]

To test the applicability of the theory of collective action to business partnerships, I conducted an empirical study of entrepreneurial effort (hours worked and additional funds invested) among a nationally representative sample of startups (Ruef, 2010, Chapter 7). As anticipated by Olson's thesis, effort decreased substantially as the number of owners in an entrepreneurial group grew larger. Olson also argued that the free rider problem could be resolved in face-to-face groups through social pressures created by intimate bonds among participants. In an entrepreneurial context, a particularly important source of such pressure involves the substantial number of ties between spouses and cohabiting (intimate) partners. Where such ties exist, we expect little free riding among entrepreneurs, since shirking in the amount of time and money devoted to the venture has immediate repercussions in the domestic realm. Consistent with these intuitions, I found that the free rider problem, i.e. the covariation of group size and level of entrepreneurial effort, was absent when a group of business startup owners included intimate partners.

The importance of Olson's theory for the formation of political groups is widely acknowledged, but its implications for entrepreneurial activity in other sectors (e.g. business or social entrepreneurship) would benefit from further attention. Olson's entrepreneur also retains an unusually heroic persona, often serving as a *deus ex machina* to resolve the (otherwise) unsolvable problem of collective action. This heroic attribution was pursued by Olson himself, when he wrote that the:

> [E]ntrepreneur, who is generally trusted (or feared), or who can guess who is bluffing in the bargaining, or who can simply save bargaining time, can sometimes work out an arrangement that is better for all concerned than any outcome that could emerge without entrepreneurial leadership or organization. (1971, p. 175)

As Olson acknowledged, such heroic visions must be tempered by the constraints on entrepreneurial groups: entrepreneurs 'strive mightily to organize large groups . . . [but] many of [these efforts] will come to naught' (p. 176).[10] The puzzle for a theory of collective action is identifying the social conditions and incentives under which entrepreneurs can develop stable and successful groups that produce collective goods.

Theories of Ethnic Enterprise

The last classical theory of entrepreneurial groups that I review does not derive from the work of a single scholar, but, rather, from the work of a set of sociologists who reinvigorated interest in ethnic enterprise during the early 1970s. On a sporadic basis, one can readily locate earlier articles and monographs on ethnicity and entrepreneurship, such as Rose Lee's (1949) research on the changing organizational structure of Chinatown businesses. In the United States, there was also a sustained intellectual tradition that addressed entrepreneurial activity among African-Americans, including such influential works as E. Franklin Frazier's (1957) *Black Bourgeoisie* and W.E.B. DuBois's (1899) *The Negro in Business*. Arguably, however, it was not until the 1970s that sociologists developed a general *theory* of ethnic enterprise, as opposed to the empirical generalizations that were found in much of the preceding scholarship.[11]

Three scholars – Ivan Light, Edna Bonacich, and Howard Aldrich – were especially influential in developing the theory of ethnic enterprise and cultivating its implications for entrepreneurial groups. Light's (1972) *Ethnic Enterprise in America* offered one of the first comparative examinations of entrepreneurial activity across a number of ethnic categories, including Chinese, Japanese, and African-Americans. The puzzle identified by Light was that the Chinese and Japanese immigrants were historically 'poor and visibly non-European and were subject to racial discrimination on that account . . . [the] very qualities [that] tended to force [them] into the classic small business occupations with which they have now become identified in the popular mind' (1972, pp. 5–6). At the same time, African-Americans, who were located in a similarly disadvantaged social location, lacked a corresponding level of prevalence among small business owners. Quoting Nathan Glazer and Daniel Moynihan on the same point, Light noted that the 'complete absence of a business class' among African-Americans was 'especially perplexing' (p. 4).[12]

According to Light, the theoretical solution to this puzzle lay in group processes. Descriptively, this could already be seen to some extent in the comparative propensity of Asians and African-Americans to form entrepreneurial groups: 'there was a noteworthy tendency of Chinese and Japanese to operate partnerships with more than one owner . . . while most of the black stores were solo proprietorships employing no hired labor' (p. 11). This difference in associational propensity may have proven to be minor, had it not also reflected on the ability of entrepreneurs from these different ethnic categories to secure business financing. Light suggested that the Chinese and Japanese had imported institutions – such as rotating credit associations (*hu* in China and *ko* in Japan) – which made it easier to capitalize small businesses, while similar institutional traditions from Africa and the Carribean (e.g. the West African *esusu*) 'vanished from [the] cultural repertoire' (p. 36) of African-Americans during slavery and beyond. The rotating credit associations were essential, not only as a means of distributing capital, but as a system of mutual trust among Chinese and Japanese immigrants. In Light's theory, it was the absence of group generalized exchange that accounted for the dampened entrepreneurial activity among African-Americans.

Extending Light's insights, Edna Bonacich (1973) developed a theory of 'middleman minorities', entrepreneurs from minority ethnic groups who assume an intermediary mercantile position between producer and consumer.[13] Internationally, a variety of ethnic minorities, such as the Chinese of Southeast Asia, Indians in East Africa, Jews in Europe, or Armenians in Turkey, have taken on this role in host societies outside of their own. Like Light, Bonacich acknowledged that part of the catalyst for entrepreneurship among these minorities was the hostility of the host society and the effects of 'sojourning', a form of temporary migration in which individuals plan to return to their homeland once their economic or political prospects have improved. But these are merely necessary, not sufficient conditions for middleman entrepreneurship. The missing variable, according to Bonacich's theory, was the appearance of 'a general "group" orientation', which is 'undoubtedly a product of conditions in the country of emigration' (1973, p. 584). This group orientation yields an unusually high level of solidarity among middleman minorities, marked by features such as marital homogamy, residential self-segregation, the perpetuation of a distinct language and education, and an avoidance of political activism in the host society (except when the minority group itself is threatened). For middleman entrepreneurs, in turn, this communal solidarity reinforces 'family, regional, dialect, sect, and ultimately ethnic ties' that distribute business credit and information, allow for the recruitment of inexpensive labor, and place informal limits on business competition with co-ethnics (p. 586).

A third component of the classical perspective on ethnic enterprise involves the ecological succession of neighborhoods and how it impacts startup opportunities for entrepreneurs and their co-ethnic partners. Theories of 'ecological succession' – how one ethnic population in a neighborhood (or other urban region) replaces another – could be traced back to the Chicago School of Robert Park, Ernest Burgess, and their collaborators in the 1920s and 1930s (Aldrich, 1975). Although subsequent investigators also hypothesized that these residential changes would be associated with changes in the ecology of businesses, the thesis received little empirical attention until the 1970s. Howard Aldrich, along with his long-time collaborator Albert Reiss, proposed a number of parallels between residential turnover and the character of ethnic enterprise. Among black-owned business, for instance, the 'removal of white-owned competition allows black businessmen to occupy types of businesses previously closed to them[;] as white businessmen leave the more desirable niches in the business structure, we would expect black and Puerto Rican entrepreneurs to move quickly to fill them' (1976, p. 848). These succession dynamics occur not just because of commercial vacancies in a neighborhood, but because ethnic enterprise has a 'group' orientation. The mix of businesses in a neighborhood must be responsive to the fact that a 'new [ethnic] population [often] has different tastes and lower income' (Aldrich, 1975, p. 339). Ethnic business enterprises may also be dependent on other 'new' ethnic organizations – newspapers, churches, and voluntary associations – to attract business partners, workers, and customers or, more generally, to promote their efforts within the local community.

Pioneered over 30 years ago, theories of ethnic enterprise have inspired a rich and cumulative body of scholarship. It is not possible in the remainder of this section to review the numerous branches of this literature exhaustively (see Aldrich and Waldinger (1990) and Light (2005) for useful summaries), though several strands of research stand out. One area of intense empirical and theoretical attention has involved the entrepreneurial groups that arise from ethnic enclaves. Empirical debates in this area have often centered on the question as to whether the segregation and solidarity associated with ethnic enclaves generates economic benefits for immigrants; and, in particular, whether these benefits differ between entrepreneurs and non-entrepreneurs (Portes and Jensen, 1989; Portes and Zhou, 1996; Sanders and Nee, 1987). Theoretical refinement of the enclave concept has emphasized the co-occurrence of ethnic enterprises in a given geographic locale and the implications this generates for social networks among entrepreneurs and their co-ethnic employees (Portes and Shafer, 2007).

A related development has been the testing of theories bearing on ethnic enclaves and ecological succession in countries aside from the United States. Aldrich and colleagues (1985) found that segregation and social distance explained much of the contact between shopkeepers and customers in three urban areas of England. A follow-up study in the same region detailed the social networks of Asian and white shopkeepers, finding that both ethnic groups relied heavily on kin and friends in starting and sustaining new businesses, with some variation in capitalization and parental background (Zimmer and Aldrich, 1987). Despite considerable differences in migration histories and political systems, the ecological succession of small Asian-owned businesses in the English context closely resembled the pattern found among black and Puerto Rican entrepreneurs in the United States (Aldrich, et al., 1989; Aldrich and Reiss, 1976).

Recent work on ethnic identity and social networks has also considered the cross-national character of many ethnic entrepreneurial groups themselves. As Alejandro Portes and his colleagues note, 'instead of focusing on traditional concerns about [the] origins of immigrants and their adaptation to receiving societies, this emerging perspective concentrates on the continuing relations between immigrants and their places of origin' (2002, p. 279). Using data on respondents who had migrated to the United States from Colombia, the Dominican Republic, or El Salvador, Portes and his co-authors found that the social networks of Latino immigrant entrepreneurs contained a large number of non-local ties, with the ratio of non-local to local ties averaging 0.77 to 1. The prevalence of a transnational orientation among immigrant entrepreneurs has likewise received extensive qualitative attention, including Annalee Saxenian's (2006) monograph on Indian, Chinese, and Israeli entrepreneurs in Silicon Valley, which documents the ability of entrepreneurial groups to overcome international trade barriers and connect regional economies.

Research on ethnic enterprise has thus sustained several insights from the pioneering work of Light, Bonacich, and Aldrich. First, there is an understanding that ethnic identity, apart from the economic circumstances of the entrepreneur, produces both opportunities and constraints in the creation of new organizations. Second, the reason for the pervasive effect of ethnic identity is the 'group orientation' it entails; as Aldrich and Waldinger (1990, p. 112) note, 'what is "ethnic" about ethnic enterprise may be no more than a set of connections and regular patterns of interaction among people sharing common national background or migratory experiences.' Finally, there is an inherently comparative aspect to the study of these entrepreneurial groups – contrasting their activities and performance across ethnic enclaves, across generations, and across locales (Granovetter, 1995).

CONCLUSION

If the classical perspectives on entrepreneurial groups had fallen into disuse, then this review would be largely of historical interest. But, as the preceding discussion has suggested, contemporary observers of new business and political ventures continue to draw extensively on the legacy of Simmel, Coase, and Olson, as well as the theories of ethnic enterprise developed by sociologists in the 1970s. In this concluding section, I seek to identify the central questions that animate these perspectives and how they relate to one another. I also address some respects in which the classical perspectives are underutilized by research on 'founding teams' that appears in specialized entrepreneurship journals.

Figure 10.2 offers a basic typology of the classical perspectives and the central research questions they pose. One obvious distinction among the perspectives is disciplinary. The work of Georg Simmel and the scholarship on ethnic enterprise is rooted in sociology, and thus has a stronger emphasis on the identity and informal relationships among participants in entrepreneurial groups. By contrast, the work of Ronald Coase and Mancur Olson is rooted in economics (or, in the latter case, perhaps political economy), and thus has a stronger emphasis on the incentives and costs incurred among participants, as well as the 'productivity' of entrepreneurial groups as a whole. While these disciplines sometimes share explanatory variables, the outcomes they highlight tend to be distinctive. For

Disciplinary Orientation

	Sociology	Economics
Conceptual emphasis		
Group structure (Size, relationships, heterogeneity, etc.)	Classical antecedent: Georg Simmel Question: How does the structure of a group generate potential for conflict, cohesion, or opportunity? Contemporary example: Burt (2004)	Classical antecedent: Mancur Olson Question: How does the structure of a group impact individual effort and the potential for collective action? Contemporary Example: Nownes and Neeley (1996)
Characteristics of members/ transactions (Demography, benefits, costs)	Classical antecedent: Theories of ethnic enterprise Question: How does membership in an (ethnic) group yield access to capital, information, and other support? Contemporary example: Portes, Haller and Guarnizo (2002)	Classical antecedent: Ronald Coase Question: How does membership in a group reduce costs that would be incurred in an open market? Contemporary example: Greif (2006)

Figure 10.2   Classical perspectives on entrepreneurial groups in the social sciences

instance, both Simmel and Olson consider size to be a crucial feature of entrepreneurial groups. In Simmel's structural sociology, the question is how the increasing size of a group will affect its level of internal cohesion and conflict. In Olson's logic of collective action, the question is how the increasing size of a group will affect the level of entrepreneurial effort on the part of each participant.

The other distinction among the classical perspectives is more subtle, pertaining to their tendency to address features of group structure *as a whole* (e.g. size, heterogeneity, relational composition) or features of the individual members or transactions *that constitute a group* (demography, benefits, costs). Applying this standard, the explanations of Simmel and Olson are both structural in nature. By contrast, theories of ethnic enterprise tend to infer that entrepreneurs have access to supportive institutions in an ethnic community – such as rotating credit associations – by virtue of their individual demographic characteristics. Similarly, Coase's theory of the firm argues that individual transactions are the appropriate units of analysis in judging what exchanges should be internal to the entrepreneurial firm and what exchanges should occur on the open market. The structure of the entrepreneurial group, as a whole, is somewhat ancillary to these concerns.

The classical perspectives on entrepreneurial groups thus offer variation in both their units of analysis and disciplinary orientation, features that – in turn – allow these perspectives to pose a rich array of research questions concerning entrepreneurial outcomes. Despite their impact on disciplinary research, what remains remarkable is that little of the literature in business management (and, particularly, in specialized journals on entrepreneurship) makes much use of the classical perspectives. Even early contributions in business management that examined the effects of founding team composition (e.g. Eisenhardt and Schoonhoven, 1990) were relatively selective in their references, often emphasizing highly cited precursors (such as Stinchcombe, 1965) while ignoring the broader historical body of work on entrepreneurial groups. Considering our understanding of entrepreneurial groups, the consequences of this elision are not merely ones of historical myopia. Many of the questions posed by the classical perspectives have received only partial answers in contemporary empirical research.

It is hoped that this review will help stimulate entrepreneurship scholars to think further about the issues of group conflict and cohesion as raised by Simmel, transaction costs as raised by Coase, free-riding as raised by Olson, and ethnic solidarity as raised by scholars of ethnic enterprise. What may be especially promising are analyses of entrepreneurial groups that employ more than one of these classical perspectives simultaneously. How do brokerage opportunities and ethnic identities combine, for instance, to affect the distribution of rewards in business partnerships? Can the loss of entrepreneurial effort due to free-riding in large startup teams be offset by reductions in transaction costs? Scholars who draw on several of the classical perspectives will be well positioned to answer such questions about the structure and effects of entrepreneurial groups.

ACKNOWLEDGEMENTS

The initial inspiration for this historical review arose during a professional development workshop at the 2007 Academy of Management (AOM) conference in Philadelphia, in which I addressed the past and future of research on entrepreneurial teams. I would like to thank Howard Aldrich, Mark Granovetter, Hans Landström, and Franz Lohrke for their helpful feedback on an earlier draft of this chapter. As always, any errors of fact or interpretation remain those of the author.

NOTES

1. A fifth classical perspective, Max Weber's ideal-types of commercial partnerships, will be addressed in my review of historical evidence on entrepreneurial groups.
2. Using his case study of commercial law in Pisa, Weber also examines partnerships that lacked a separate fund, but treats them as peripheral to the institutional evolution of this organizational form (see discussion by Lutz in Weber 1889/2003, p. 25).
3. Partnerships among male entrepreneurs in the same city were less common.
4. Broadly construed, *structural sociology* entails the assumption that ongoing social relationships are critical to the explanation of individual identities, attitudes, and actions. It can be contrasted with 'undersocialized' conceptions of actors (which presume that individuals follow a utilitarian model of action, apart from their social context) and 'oversocialized' conceptions (which presume that individuals answer to internalized norms or beliefs, again apart from their present social context) (Granovetter, 1985).
5. The severity of these problems also depends on the culture that is adopted by entrepreneurial groups from the broader community, including 'norms concerning the extent of solidarity, norms about whose troubles one has to worry about and to contribute to alleviate' (Stinchcombe, 1965, p. 187).
6. The 'free rider' problem, *per se*, did not originate with Olson, but enjoys a long scholarly pedigree extending back to Hume and Rousseau, among others (see Frohlich and Oppenheimer, 1970, pp. 104–6). Paul Samuelson first formulated the problem in economic terms.
7. Salisbury's formulation owes an obvious (and acknowledged) debt to two previous intellectual traditions in the social sciences, one being the exchange theory framework in sociology, as advanced by George Homans (1961) and Peter Blau (1964); the other being the theory of incentives in organizations, first put forward by Chester Barnard (1938) and subsequently advanced by Clark and Wilson (1961). What appears novel about Salisbury's treatment is that he explicitly ties exchange theory and the balance of incentives among members to the creation of new organizations, rather than the survival of existing ones.
8. This coincides with the welcoming reception accorded to Olson's theory of collective action among political scientists and comparatively luke-warm reaction in contemporary economic theories of organizations.
9. There are other well-known critiques of Olson's argument that will not be reviewed here. Useful overviews can be found in Hardin (1982) and Oliver (1993).
10. Consequently, the entrepreneurial partnerships in representative samples tend to be small. In the contemporary United States, most business startups involve one or two founders, occasionally three or four, and seldom five or more (Ruef et al., 2003).
11. Given a sufficiently generous interpretation, a research interest in ethnic enterprise can also be traced back to Weber and Simmel, who noted the propensity of individuals assuming a marginalized identity in a society to band together for economic survival.
12. To a large extent, this empirical generalization is historically contingent. Between the late 1990s and the present, rates of entrepreneurship among African-Americans have tended to be higher than those among whites in the United States (Ruef, 2010).
13. Unlike Burt's (2000) 'network entrepreneur', this conceptualization does not automatically equate entrepreneurship with the act of brokerage. Bonacich notes that many forms of entrepreneurship – such as those found in the agricultural or industrial sectors – tend to be excluded from the occupational repertoire of middleman minorities.

REFERENCES

Ainsworth, S. and I. Sened (1993), 'The role of lobbyists: entrepreneurs with two audiences', *American Journal of Political Science*, **37**(3), 834–66.
Aldrich, H. (1975), 'Ecological succession in racially changing neighborhoods: a review of the literature', *Urban Affairs Quarterly*, **10**(3), 327–48.

Aldrich, H. (1979/2007), *Organizations and Environments*, Stanford, CA: Stanford University Press.

Aldrich, H. and P. Kim (2007), 'Small worlds, infinite possibilities? How social networks affect entrepreneurial team formation and search', *Strategic Entrepreneurship Journal*, **1**(1), 147–65.

Aldrich, H. and A. Reiss (1976), 'Continuities in the study of ecological succession: changes in the race composition of neighborhoods and their businesses', *American Journal of Sociology*, **81**(4), 846–66.

Aldrich, H. and R. Waldinger (1990), 'Ethnicity and entrepreneurship', *Annual Review of Sociology*, **16**, 111–35.

Aldrich, H., J. Cater, T. Jones, D. McEvoy and P. Velleman (1985), 'Ethnic residential concentration and the protected market hypothesis', *Social Forces*, **63**(4), 996–1009.

Aldrich, H., C. Zimmer and D. McEvoy (1989), 'Continuities in the study of ecological succession: Asian businesses in three English cities', *Social Forces*, **67**(4), 920–44.

Amason, A. (1996), 'Distinguishing the effects of functional and dysfunctional conflict in strategic decision making: resolving a paradox for top management teams', *Academy of Management Journal*, **39**(1), 123–48.

Bai, C., Z. Tao and C. Wu (2004), 'Revenue sharing and control rights in team production: theories and evidence from joint ventures', *RAND Journal of Economics*, **35**(2), 277–305.

Baker, T. and R. Nelson (2005), 'Creating something from nothing: resource construction through entrepreneurial bricolage', *Administrative Science Quarterly*, **50**(3), 329–66.

Barnard, C. (1938), *The Functions of the Executive*, Cambridge, MA: Harvard University Press.

Bass, B. and G. Duntemann (1963), 'Biases in the evaluation of one's own group, its allies, and opponents', *Journal of Conflict Resolution*, **7**(1), 16–20.

Blau, P. (1964), *Exchange and Power in Social Life*, New York: Wiley.

Blomquist, T. (1971), 'Commercial association in thirteenth-century Lucca', *Business History Review*, **45**(2), 157–78.

Bonacich, E. (1973), 'A theory of middleman minorities', *American Sociological Review*, **38**(5), 583–94.

Burt, R. (1992), *Structural Holes: The Social Structure of Competition*, Cambridge, MA: Harvard University Press.

Burt, R. (2000), 'The network entrepreneur', in R. Swedberg (ed.), *Entrepreneurship: The Social Science View*, Oxford: Oxford University Press, pp. 281–307.

Burt, R. (2004), 'Structural holes and good ideas', *American Journal of Sociology*, **110**(2), 349–99.

Clark, P. and J. Wilson (1961), 'Incentive systems: a theory of organizations', *Administrative Science Quarterly*, **6**(2), 129–66.

Coase, R. (1937), 'The nature of the firm', *Economica*, **4**(16), 386–405.

Coase, R. (1988), 'The nature of the firm: influence', *Journal of Law, Economics, and Organization*, **4**(1), 33–47.

Coleman, J. (1974), *Power and the Structure of Society*, New York: W.W. Norton.

Collins, R. (1997), 'An Asian route to capitalism: religious economy and the origins of self-transforming growth in Japan', *American Sociological Review*, **62**(6), 843–65.

David, R. and S. Han (2004), 'A systematic assessment of the empirical support for transaction cost economics', *Strategic Management Journal*, **25**(1), 39–58.

De Roover, R. (1966), *The Rise and Decline of the Medici Bank, 1397–1494*, New York: W.W. Norton.

DuBois, W.E.B. (1899), *The Negro in Business*, Atlanta, GA: Atlanta University.

Eisenhardt, K. and C. Schoonhoven (1990), 'Organizational growth: linking founding team, strategy, environment, and growth among US semiconductor ventures, 1978–1988', *Administrative Science Quarterly*, **35**(3), 504–29.

Ensley, M. (1999), *Entrepreneurial Teams as Determinants of New Venture Performance*, New York: Garland.

Franke, N., M. Gruber, D. Harhoff and J. Henkel (2006), 'What you are is what you like – similarity biases in venture capitalists' evaluations of start-up teams', *Journal of Business Venturing*, **21**(6), 802–26.

Frazier, E.F. (1957), *Black Bourgeoisie*, Glencoe, IL: Free Press.

Frohlich, N. and J. Oppenheimer (1970), 'I get by with a little help from my friends', *World Politics*, **23**(1), 104–20.
Frohlich, N. and J. Oppenheimer (1972), 'Entrepreneurial politics and foreign policy', *World Politics*, **24** (Spring Supplement), 151–78.
Gartner, W., K. Shaver, E. Gatewood and J. Katz (1994), 'Finding the entrepreneur in entrepreneurship', *Entrepreneurship Theory and Practice*, **18**(3), 5–9.
Granovetter, M. (1985), 'Economic action and social structure: the problem of embeddedness', *American Journal of Sociology*, **91**(3), 481–510.
Granovetter, M. (1995), 'The economic sociology of firms and entrepreneurs', in A. Portes (ed.), *The Economic Sociology of Immigration: Essays on Networks, Ethnicity and Entrepreneurship*, New York: Russell Sage Foundation, pp. 128–65.
Greif, A. (1989), 'Reputations and coalitions in medieval trade: evidence on the Maghribi traders', *Journal of Economic History*, **49**(4), 857–82.
Greif, A. (2006), *Institutions and the Path to the Modern Economy: Lessons from Medieval Trade*, Cambridge: Cambridge University Press.
Hardin, R. (1982), *Collective Action*, Baltimore, MD: Johns Hopkins University Press.
Hellmann, T. (1998), 'The allocation of control rights in venture capital contracts', *RAND Journal of Economics*, **29**(1), 57–76.
Homans, G. (1961), *Social Behavior: Its Elementary Forms*, New York: Harcourt, Brace and World.
Hwang, H. and W.W. Powell (2005), 'Institutions and entrepreneurship', in S. Alvarez, R. Agarwal and O. Sorenson (eds), *Handbook of Entrepreneurship Research: Disciplinary Perspectives*, New York: Springer, pp. 179–210.
Kamm, J., J. Shuman, J. Seeger and A. Nurick (1990), 'Entrepreneurial teams in new venture creation: a research agenda', *Entrepreneurship Theory and Practice*, **14**(4), 7–17.
Lamoreaux, N. (1998), 'Partnerships, corporations, and the theory of the firm', *American Economic Review*, **88**(2), 66–71.
Lee, R. (1949), 'Occupational invasion, succession, and accommodation of the Chinese of Butte, Montana', *American Journal of Sociology*, **55**(1), 50–58.
Light, I. (1972), *Ethnic Enterprise in America: Business and Welfare among Chinese, Japanese, and Blacks*, Berkeley, CA: University of California Press.
Light, I. (2005), 'The ethnic economy', in N. Smelser and R. Swedberg (eds), *Handbook of Economic Sociology*, Princeton, NJ: Princeton University Press, pp. 650–77.
Meyer, J. and R. Jepperson (2000), 'The actors of modern society: the cultural construction of social agency', *Sociological Theory*, **18**(1), 100–120.
Moe, T. (1988), *The Organization of Interests: Incentives and the Internal Dynamics of Political Interest Groups*, Chicago, IL: University of Chicago Press.
Nenadic, S. (1998), 'The social shaping of business behavior in the nineteenth-century women's garment trades', *Journal of Social History*, **31**(3), 625–45.
Nownes, A. and G. Neeley (1996), 'Public interest group entrepreneurship and theories of group mobilization', *Political Research Quarterly*, **49**(1), 119–46.
Obstfeld, D. (2005), 'Social networks, the *tertius iungens* orientation, and involvement in innovation', *Administrative Science Quarterly*, **50**(1), 100–130.
Oliver, P. (1993), 'Formal models of collective action', *Annual Review of Sociology*, **19**, 271–300.
Olson, M. (1971), *The Logic of Collective Action: Public Goods and the Theory of Groups*, revised edition, New York: Schocken Books.
Origo, I. (1957/1992), *The Merchant of Prato: Francesco di Marco Datini*, New York: Penguin.
Padgett, J. and P. McLean (2006), 'Organizational invention and elite transformation: the birth of partnership systems in Renaissance Florence', *American Journal of Sociology*, **111**(5), 1463–568.
Portes, A. and L. Jensen (1989), 'The enclave and the entrants: patterns of ethnic enterprise in Miami before and after Mariel', *American Sociological Review*, **54**(6), 929–49.
Portes, A. and S. Shafer (2007), 'Revisiting the enclave hypothesis: Miami twenty-five years later', *Research in the Sociology of Organizations*, **25**, 157–90.
Portes, A. and M. Zhou (1996), 'Self-employment and the earnings of immigrants', *American Sociological Review*, **61**(2), 219–30.

Portes, A., W. Haller and L. Guarnizo (2002), 'Transnational entrepreneurs: an alternative form of immigrant economic adaptation', *American Sociological Review*, **67**(2), 278–98.

Reich, R. (1987), 'Entrepreneurship reconsidered: the team as hero', *Harvard Business Review*, **65** (May), 77–83.

Renzulli, L., H. Aldrich and J. Moody (2000), 'Family matters: gender, networks, and entrepreneurial outcomes', *Social Forces*, **79**(2), 523–46.

Rosenberg, N. and L.E. Birdzell (1986), *How the West Grew Rich: The Economic Transformation of the Industrial World*, New York: Basic Books.

Ruef, M. (2002), 'A structural event approach to the analysis of group composition', *Social Networks*, **24**(2), 135–60.

Ruef, M. (2009), 'Economic inequality among entrepreneurs', *Research in the Sociology of Work*, **18**, 57–87.

Ruef, M. (2010), *The Entrepreneurial Group: Social Identities, Networks, and Collective Action*, Princeton, NJ: Princeton University Press.

Ruef, M. and M. Lounsbury (eds) (2007), *The Sociology of Entrepreneurship*, Oxford, UK: Elsevier.

Ruef, M., H. Aldrich and N. Carter (2003), 'The structure of founding teams: homophily, strong ties, and isolation among US entrepreneurs', *American Sociological Review*, **68**(2), 195–222.

Salisbury, R. (1969), 'An exchange theory of interest groups', *Midwest Journal of Political Science*, **13**(1), 1–32.

Sanders, J. and V. Nee (1987), 'Limits of ethnic solidarity in the enclave economy', *American Sociological Review*, **52**(6), 745–73.

Saxenian, A. (2006), *The New Argonauts: Regional Advantage in a Global Economy*, Cambridge, MA: Harvard University Press.

Schneider, M. and P. Teske (1992), 'Toward a theory of the political entrepreneur: evidence from local government', *American Political Science Review*, **86**(3), 737–47.

Simmel, G. (1908a/1950), *Sociology, Studies of the Forms of Societalization*, Leipzig: Duncker and Humblot, translation in K. Wolff (1950), *The Sociology of Georg Simmel*, New York: Free Press.

Simmel, G. (1908b), 'Note on the stranger', translation in K. Wolff (1950), *The Sociology of Georg Simmel*, New York: Free Press.

Simmel, G. (1917), *Fundamental Problems of Sociology (Individual and Society)*, Berlin: Walter de Gruyter, translation in K. Wolff (1950), *The Sociology of Georg Simmel*, New York: Free Press.

Stinchcombe, A. (1965), 'Social structure and organizations', in J. March (ed.), *Handbook of Organizations*, Chicago: Rand McNally, pp. 142–93.

Swedberg, R. and M. Granovetter (eds) (2001), *The Sociology of Economic Life*, Boulder, CO: Westview Press.

Tajfel, H. and J. Turner (1979), 'An integrative theory of intergroup conflict', in W. Austin and S. Worchel (eds), *The Social Psychology of Intergroup Relations*, Monterey, CA: Brooks-Cole, pp. 94–109.

Taylor, G. (1963), 'Some business partnerships at Lyon, 1785–1793', *Journal of Economic History*, **23**(1), 46–70.

Timmons, J. (1975), 'The entrepreneurial team: an American dream or nightmare?', *Journal of Small Business Management*, **13**(4), 33–38.

Timmons, J. (1979), 'Careful self-analysis and team assessment can aid entrepreneurs', *Harvard Business Review*, **57**(6), 189–96.

Wasserman, S. and K. Faust (1994), *Social Network Analysis: Methods and Applications*, Cambridge, UK: Cambridge University Press.

Weber, M. (1889/2003), *The History of Commercial Partnerships in the Middle Ages*, translated by L. Kaelber, Lanham, MD: Rowman and Littlefield.

Williamson, O. (1975), *Markets and Hierarchies: Analysis and Antitrust Implications*, New York: Free Press.

Williamson, O. (1985), *The Economic Institutions of Capitalism: Firms, Markets, and Relational Contracting*, New York: Free Press.

Williamson, O. and S. Winter (eds) (1993), *The Nature of the Firm: Origins, Evolution, and Development*, New York: Oxford University Press.

Zimmer, C. and H. Aldrich (1987), 'Resource mobilization through ethnic networks: kinship and friendship ties of shopkeepers in England', *Sociological Perspectives*, **30**(4), 422–45.

11. Governance theory: origins and implications for researching boards and governance in entrepreneurial firms

Jonas Gabrielsson and Morten Huse

INTRODUCTION

All firms, small as well as large, new as well as old, can be described as having two complementary systems: a production system and a governance system. The production system consists of the business activities used by the firm to facilitate the transformation of input resources into the output that is offered on the market. Activities organized and carried out in most firms include procurement, operations, logistics, marketing and sales, and interaction with suppliers and customers. The overall focus is to manage the firm and its input resources to efficiently and effectively design, produce and distribute its output. The governance system, on the other hand, allocates rights and responsibilities among the various providers of input resources in and around the firm and gives some of them – generally the providers of financial resources – the power to make decisions and exercise control to influence the direction and performance of the enterprise (Huse, 2007). The overall focus is on determining how critical resources will be acquired, controlled and deployed so as to increase the wealth of the business, and how to deal with conflicts between various coalitions of resource providers who have potentially divergent goals.

The governance system in a firm includes both external and internal mechanisms that direct, administer and control the firm and its operations (O'Sullivan and Diacon, 1999; Collin, 2003). Examples of external governance mechanisms include competition on product markets, state legislation and regulations, managerial labor markets, and pressure from the media. Examples of internal governance mechanisms include the board of directors, auditing, and compensation systems for firm managers. The various external and internal mechanisms making up the governance system of the firm thus form a complex web of institutional arrangements that influence its direction and performance through particular features of incentives, supervision, best practices, 'rules of the game', links to external sources of knowledge, and internal channels to diffuse knowledge.

Entrepreneurial Firms

In this chapter we address the issue of governance in entrepreneurial firms as opposed to the large and mature corporations that most often have been studied in academic research (Gabrielsson and Huse, 2004). However, there is no accepted or consistent way of defining an entrepreneurial firm.[1] We refer in our discussion to firms that are in the early or 'entrepreneurial' stage of the organizational life cycle (Greiner, 1972; Quinn and Cameron, 1983). At this stage, firms are generally involved in building up their resource base, entering new or established markets, and searching for additional capital and allies. Entrepreneurial firms can in this respect – in an 'ideal typical' way (Weber, 1947) – be characterized as operating in one or a few product markets, with small managerial hierarchies, close relationships between owners and managers, and management of the organization in a largely personalized way. These characteristics provide a strong contrast to larger and more diversified corporations which have structurally complex organizations, distant and invisible shareholders, and multiple layers of management. The small entrepreneurial firm thus provides a fundamentally different context when it comes to issues and problems of governance.

We think that our focus on governance in entrepreneurial firms can be of interest for at least two reasons. First, entrepreneurial firms account for a relatively large share of the total amount of organized economic activity in most developed market economies. Second, these firms are considered as the most important for creating value in society, and they are often associated with positive outcomes such as job creation, innovation and economic growth (Birch, 1979; Kirchoff, 1994). Their significance, in terms of sheer numbers as well as their potential for wealth creation, makes the understanding of principles for 'good' governance highly relevant for a wide range of stakeholders in and around the entrepreneurial firm, including founders, investors, and employees.

As noted above, governance refers to a broad range of mechanisms that direct, administer and control the firm and its operations. In this chapter we specifically focus on the governance provided by the 'board of directors', since this internal governance mechanism has been the most widely examined and reported in main entrepreneurship journals (e.g. Ford, 1988; Rosenstein, 1988; Daily and Dalton, 1992; Borch and Huse, 1993; Daily and Dalton, 1993; Rosenstein et al., 1993; Huse, 1994; Finkle, 1998; Fiegener et al., 2000a; 2000b; Fiegener, 2005; Gabrielsson and Winlund, 2000; Johannisson and Huse, 2000; Bennett and Robson, 2004; Gabrielsson, 2007a; 2007b; Voordeckers et al., 2007; Brunninge et al., 2007; Clarysse et al., 2007). We want to emphasize at this point that past studies do not focus solely on entrepreneurial firms (as we define these). Rather, many of them discuss boards of directors in small, often privately held firms. However, most studies include entrepreneurial firms in their samples and often address theoretical issues that are relevant to consider when studying this subset of small firms.

A widely held assumption in research on boards and governance is that the characteristics of entrepreneurial firms generally speak against active boards, as CEOs often have the authority to overrule boardroom decisions and also to directly remove board members. However, empirical studies also suggest that boards of directors in entrepreneurial firms can – and sometimes do – play an active role in shaping strategies and influencing organizational performance in this setting (e.g. George et al., 2001; Daily et al., 2002). Several theories have been employed in past research to explain the conditions under which a board of directors may take action and assert power over the direction and performance of a firm (Zahra and Pearce, 1989; Hung, 1998). Two theoretical perspectives, however, stand out when reviewing research that has addressed the issue of boards and governance in entrepreneurship research, namely 'resource dependence theory' and 'agency theory' (Huse, 2000; Gabrielsson and Huse, 2005).[2] Consequently, we focus on these two theories in the remainder of the chapter.

Aim of the Chapter

In this chapter, we aim to give an overview of the historical and intellectual roots of both resource dependence theory and agency theory with a particular focus on how they have been applied in studies of boards and governance. The underlying motivation for this endeavor is that we believe scholars interested in issues of board governance in entrepreneurial firms could benefit from such an overview for at least two reasons. First, we think that an increased understanding of the origins and history of resource dependence theory and agency theory would contribute positively to continued knowledge accumulation within the field. For example, the two theories are often seen as largely complementary perspectives that are used to justify board tasks such as resource provision and monitoring (e.g. Gabrielsson and Winlund, 2000; Voordeckers et al., 2007). There is, however, often very little reflection and discussion about the assumptions underlying each theory. Both, for example, emphasize the value in adopting outside board members[3] but the underlying reasons for this recommendation as well as the characteristics that outside board members should have to add value differ in the two theories.

Moreover, there may be some potential problems in the joint application of resource dependence theory and agency theory when researching boards and governance in entrepreneurship research. For example, resource dependence theory focuses on how the management team can control actors external to the firm so that the latter will provide or give access to critical resources. In agency theory the focus is on the very opposite – how actors external to the firm can control the management team. Thus, at first glance they seem to provide rather different implications for the design of effective board governance. An overview of the origins of resource dependence theory and agency theory and the problems each theory seeks to address may, therefore, help entrepreneurship scholars to better understand to what extent the two theories can be used together and what might be required to make them more compatible.

Second, we think that both resource dependence theory and agency theory provide interesting implications for researching behavioral aspects of boards and governance in entrepreneurial firms. Research on boards and governance has in recent years increasingly emphasized the need to more closely study behavioral processes and relational dynamics in and around the boardroom (Forbes and Milliken, 1999; Finkelstein and Mooney, 2003; Huse, 2005; Huse and Zattoni, 2008). There has, however, been an excessive bias in past entrepreneurship research towards studying only compositional aspects of boards. Actual board behavior has on the other hand been treated largely as a 'black box' (Huse, 1998) where the behavior or conduct of boards is inferred from their demographic characteristics. As a result, there has been very little attention to how boards in entrepreneurial firms actually work and how board members in this context may improve their behavior to contribute to value creation, despite the importance of such knowledge for further theory-building as well as the development of best-practice recommendations for entrepreneurial firms.

In addition to the reasons stated above, we think that an overview of the historical and intellectual roots of resource dependence theory and agency theory can be of interest for a wider audience of entrepreneurship scholars. Both theoretical perspectives have, for example, been employed in research areas within the entrepreneurship field such as franchising (Dant, 2008), family firms (Schulze et al., 2003; Lester and Cannella, 2006) and strategic alliances in small firms (Das and Teng, 2000). Although we do not specifically address the application of resource dependence theory and agency theory in these contexts, our review and discussion may be relevant for these research areas as well.

The rest of the chapter is structured as follows. The next section briefly introduces the issue of governance in entrepreneurial firms. Thereafter, we examine the historical roots of resource dependence theory followed by a similar examination of agency theory. The chapter then compares the two theories. We also address the implications for the joint application of the theories, and make suggestions for future research that seeks to better understand behavioral processes and relational dynamics in and around the boardroom in entrepreneurial firms.

GOVERNANCE IN ENTREPRENEURIAL FIRMS

Governance has traditionally not been seen as much of an issue in entrepreneurial firms, because they are characterized as relatively non-complex organizations with ownership and control consolidated in one individual (i.e. the owner-manager) where coordination is effected largely by direct supervision. This simplified view, however, has in recent years been increasingly challenged for a variety of reasons. For example, in entrepreneurial firms that start to experience growth there is eventually a need for functional managers to take on duties currently performed by the owner[4] (Greiner, 1972; Churchill and Lewis, 1983). The governance literature identifies this transition as a critical step in the development from a founder-managed to a more professionally managed firm (e.g. Whisler, 1988; Daily and Dalton, 1992; Gedajlovic et al., 2004; Gabrielsson, 2007a). This transition means that job assignments become more specialized, and the increasing complexity in the organization calls for more sophisticated control systems to coordinate major elements of the growing firm. It also means that planning procedures become more formalized and that an effective compensation and reward system has to be developed. Among other things, this marks an emerging need to separate strategic and operational responsibilities and to start contemplating questions about how the firm is governed rather than just managed.

Moreover, some entrepreneurial firms may already, in their early years of operations, seek additional equity from external owners (De Clercq and Manigart, 2007). Firm managers may in this respect have access to superior information regarding the resources and performance of the enterprise and can consequently take advantage of this information asymmetry for their own purposes, which in turn can cut back the returns of other investors (Markman et al., 2001). These potential problems could in turn lead to external owners demanding increased board oversight in the entrepreneurial firm. The pressure from external owners is also something which has been found both in empirical studies of the post-involvement activities of venture capitalists (Gabrielsson and Huse, 2002) and in more general studies of boards and governance in small firms (Westhead, 1999; Fiegener et al., 2000b; Gabrielsson, 2007b).

Furthermore, contemporary literature on governance tends to emphasize contractual and incentive structures in the governance process while neglecting other important tasks, such as assisting the management team in building a wider set of relationships to deal with business risks in the firm's competitive domain and extracting critical resources that are vital to firm performance (Borch and Huse, 1993; George et al., 2001). Entrepreneurial firms are in this respect often coping with liabilities of newness (Stinchcombe, 1965; Shepherd et al., 2000) and smallness (Aldrich and Auster, 1986), which create difficulties in building and maintaining stable relationships with important stakeholders and generating economies of scale. Having access to an active board of directors that can provide the firm with timely resources may, therefore, be a crucial ingredient for improving its chances of long-term survival. A governing board could identify critical strategic issues, increase the legitimacy of the firm, and provide timely access to resources that otherwise would not be accessible (Borch and Huse, 1993; Rosa and Scott, 1999; Deutsch and Ross, 2003).

The arguments above suggest that entrepreneurial firms can benefit from the support that a governing board can offer. As indicated earlier, the two theories most commonly employed for understanding principles for effective board governance in small firms are resource dependence theory and agency theory. We now continue with an overview of the history and intellectual roots of each theory.

RESOURCE DEPENDENCE THEORY

Resource dependence theory seeks to explain organizational and inter-organizational behavior in terms of the critical resources that an organization depends on. The theory posits that an organization must interact with its environment either to purchase resources or to distribute its finished products, where the key to organizational survival is the ability to acquire and maintain resources critical for its operations (Pfeffer and Salancik, 1978, p. 2). A basic premise in the theory is that organizations to a large extent are in permanent interaction with other entities in the environment where resource exchange relationships take place (e.g. Thompson, 1967), thereby creating resource dependencies. The theory predicts that the survival and success of a firm are dependent on its abilities to link the firm with its external environment. As such, the theory posits that the firm should seek to initiate and maintain control over scarce and valued resources essential to organizational survival, in order to achieve organizational effectiveness, defined as 'the ability to create acceptable outcomes and actions' (Pfeffer and Salancik, 1978, p. 7).

Organizations as Open Systems

The general thinking underlying resource dependence theory originates from open system theory, a perspective conceiving the organization as a system that is influenced by and interacts with the environment in which it operates (Katz and Kahn, 1966; Thompson, 1967). Katz and Kahn (1966, p. 16) describe the system perspective as '. . . basically concerned with problems of relationships, of structure, and of interdependence rather than with the constant attributes of objects'. Open system theory was initially developed by the biologist Ludwig von Bertanlanffy in his essay 'The theory of open systems in physics and biology' (1950). In the opening remarks of his essay he states that 'a system is closed if no material enters or leaves it; it is open if there is import and export and, therefore, change of the components' (1950, p. 23). Thus, von Bertanlanffy emphasized the idea that real systems[5] are open to their environment and interact with the environment, which results in continual change and evolution.

Before open system theory, organizations were largely seen as closed and self-contained entities which operated autonomously within relatively fixed boundaries, and studies dealt with issues such as internal operations, motivation, communication, task design, etc. (e.g. Taylor 1911; Barnard, 1938; Fayol, 1949). It should perhaps be pointed out that the idea of using a system perspective to understand organizations was not entirely novel. For example, although dealing mainly with internal operations, Chester Barnard (1938) emphasized the importance of understanding the social character of cooperation in *The Functions of the Executive.* In his book he argues that human organisms function in mutual conjunction with other organisms, with their interdependence evolving over time (p. 11). He also describes the organization as a system composed of the activities of human beings (p. 77). Hence, even if open system theory provided a fresh perspective in the study of organizations when it was introduced in the 1950s, the general idea of applying systems thinking for understanding organizations already existed. The introduction of open system theory, however, raised the idea that organizations are open to and interact in close association with what is construed to be their external environment, and the perspective introduced theoretical concepts such as input, throughput, output, system boundaries and interdependence. These concepts were then increasingly adopted and implemented by scientists across a range of different disciplines, including the study of organizations (e.g. Rhenman, 1964; Emery and Trist, 1965; Katz and Kahn, 1966).

The Organization and the External Environment

By the end of the 1960s the open system perspective was more or less mainstream thinking in organization theory. The external environment is described in this perspective as consisting of other organizations and individuals that exert economic, political and social influence on the focal organization (Katz and Kahn, 1966; Yuchtman and Seashore, 1967). Another feature of the external environment is that it provides resources that enable the organization to persist and evolve over time but also makes the organization dependent on others in order to obtain these resources (Thompson, 1967). Both these features are expected to have a critical impact on the structure and behavior of organizations. However, even if resource dependence theory conceives organizations as open systems (Pfeffer and Salancik, 1978, p. 1), it is also emphasized that the relationship between the environment and organizational structures and decisions is not perfect (Pfeffer and Salancik, 1978, p. 227). Rather, organizations are seen as 'loosely coupled' (e.g. Weick, 1976) with their environments, something which makes external relationships important but, at the same time, indeterminate. These indeterminate relationships allow potential variations in how organizations are able to manage constraints in their resource environments, by maintaining external linkages to organizations on which they depend for critical resources. These potential variations are moreover a key trigger for the analysis of resource dependence, as they point to the value of understanding how the distribution of power in and around the organization influences its behavior and design.

Two fundamental questions addressed in resource dependence theory are: who controls the organization, and how do such distributions of power and influence arise? The interest in these two questions connects resource dependence theory with early literature and research in sociology that analyze power in and around organizations. An important source for this stream of research is Philip Selznick who, in his book *TVA and the*

Grass Roots (1949), uses power-based arguments to study inter-organizational relations. Organizations are described in Selznick's study as adaptive social structures affected by their environments where external groups fight for control of them, which, in turn, constrains organizational action and behaviors. An important part of his study is the analysis of co-optation as a mechanism to cope with the tensions and dilemmas caused by structural arrangements and environmental constraints. Co-optation in this context means inviting a representative of the source of constraint into the internal decision-making or advisory structure of the organization with the aim of averting threats to its stability or existence, thus trading some of the organization's autonomy for support (Selznick, 1949, p. 13).

Another important source for the development of what came to be resource dependence theory is the early work conducted by social exchange theorists such as Blau (1964) and Emerson (1962). These theorists focus on power as a function of social relations and emphasize that some form of interdependence is a necessary condition for exerting influence. Power is, moreover, not zero-sum, as two actors can have power over each other and, thus, be interdependent. The connection between social structure and the use of power is, therefore, central in this stream of research, where power is seen as the mechanics that can explain the relations of the actors in a network. There is however an important difference. Whereas social exchange theorists focus on individual actors, the attention in resource dependence theory was recast towards describing the actions of organizations.

The External Control of Organizations

There are several studies from the late 1960s until the mid-1970s that more or less explicitly build on the general idea underlying resource dependence theory, that organizational behavior is determined by external social constraints and resource interdependence (e.g. Thompson, 1967; Yuchtman and Seashore, 1967; Zald, 1970; Pfeffer, 1972a; 1972b; 1972c; Walmsley and Zald, 1973; Aldrich and Pfeffer, 1976; Pfeffer and Nowak, 1976).[6] However, the most definite reference to resource dependence theory is the book *The External Control of Organizations* by Jeffrey Pfeffer and Gerald R. Salancik, published in 1978. They develop ideas about conflicts of interest in and around organizations, and how power influences structures and patterns of behavior aimed at acquiring and maintaining necessary external resources. The result is a highly political theory that identifies and analyzes the ways in which firms become constrained by their environment and the strategies managers can employ to cope with these dependences. A basic assumption in the theory is that of political struggle, where different coalitions of actors try in a highly self-interested manner to influence each other to their own advantage, and where conflicting demands are described as largely incompatible (Pfeffer and Salancik, 1978, p. 27). In this vein, the theory posits that resource exchange and power relations in and around organizations influence the behavior and design of organizations. Moreover, organizations are seen as unable to internally generate all the resources required to maintain themselves, resulting in dependence on transactions and relations with external actors and organizations in their environment for their survival (Aldrich and Pfeffer, 1976, p. 83). This dependence on external resources constrains organizational action, and managers must effectively manage resource dependences if the organization is to survive and function. As such, organizations are involved in a constant struggle for autonomy and discretion while also being confronted with constraints and external control (Pfeffer and Salancik, 1978, p. 257).

Resource dependence theory focuses on the flow or exchange of resources between organizations (or units within the organization) and the resulting dependences and power differentials that are created. It is these dependences that provide the basis for external control over an organization. These arguments can be directly related back to the pioneering work of the social-exchange theorist Richard Emerson and his essay 'Power-dependence relations' (1962), where he developed the idea that power is the property of a social exchange relationship and not of an actor, because it 'resides implicitly in the other's dependency' (p. 32). Moreover, it is stated that 'the power of A over B is equal to and based upon the dependence of B upon A' (p. 33). Thus, in the analysis Emerson (1962) asserted that dependence and power are a function of the value that one actor places on resources controlled by another and the relative availability of alternative resources. Power is hence seen as deriving from resource connections, and those individuals, subunits or other organizations that exclusively provide the most needed resources will have the most power over or within the focal organization.

Building on these ideas, Pfeffer and Salancik (1978) apply power-dependence concepts to analyze and understand how interactions, with external actors and organizations in the environment where resource exchange relationships take place, affect and constrain an organization. A way of alleviating sources of external constraint is to strengthen the relationship with the particular sources of dependence, something that follows Selznick's (1949) insights regarding organizational co-optation. Pfeffer and Salancik (1978) thus suggest that a main task of the management is to establish 'negotiated environments' (e.g. Cyert and March, 1963, p. 119) that are favorable to the organization (Pfeffer and Salancik, 1978, p. 263). This means that the organization, instead of having to anticipate future reactions in the environment, avoids uncertainty in resource acquisition by entering and negotiating exchange relationships with other organizations. They also present a detailed analysis of specific sets of strategies and tactics that can be employed to manage these external constraints and dependences in the external environment, and they discuss the conditions under which the measures are appropriate. Strategies to manage resource dependences include mergers and acquisitions, diversification, board interlocks and co-optations, joint ventures, and direct political action (Pfeffer and Salancik, 1978, chapters 5–8).

Resource Dependence Theory and the Board of Directors

Researchers interested in issues of boards and governance have used resource dependence theory to provide a conceptual basis for how board members can assist the firm in its attempt to acquire and maintain resources critical for its operations (Zahra and Pearce, 1989; Johnson et al., 1996; Huse, 2005). As indicated above, resource dependence theory identifies the board of directors as playing a crucial role in linking the organization to its environment by co-opting representatives from important external organizations with which it is interdependent (Zald, 1969; Pfeffer, 1972c; 1973; Pfeffer and Salancik, 1978, p. 167). Board members are selected to maximize the provision of critical resources, and board members are seen as important boundary-spanners who provide timely information and convey critical resources to firm managers (Zald, 1967; Pfeffer, 1972c).

An important qualification for board members' ability to link the organization with its external environment is their personal legitimacy and reputation. Pfeffer and Salancik for example argue that 'prestigious or legitimate persons or organizations represented on the focal organization's board provide confirmation to the rest of the world of the value and worth of the organization' (1978, p. 145). The composition of the board can in this respect be seen as an important mechanism for managing resource dependencies. The emphasis on board members as boundary-spanners in resource dependence theory has moreover led to a focus on the value of having large boards composed of experienced and reputable 'outsiders' (Zahra and Pearce, 1989; Johnson et al., 1996). Through their positions and networks of relationships, these outside board members are seen as important in contributing with advice and counsel, facilitating inter-firm commitments and providing access to critical resources.

With its emphasis on mechanisms for acquiring and maintaining resources critical for business operations, resource dependence theory seems particularly applicable to the study of boards and governance in entrepreneurial firms. Entrepreneurial firms often face an uncertain environment and they may also lack both economic and political power (Pfeffer and Salancik, 1978), something which may call for the adoption of board members that can link the organization with its external environment and assist the firm in providing access to critical resources. Entrepreneurial firms may furthermore lack a sense of 'historical legitimacy' (Selznick, 1949, p. 259) and may thus benefit from using co-optation as a means to recruit representatives from important external organizations on the board, to represent the organization and become a basis for its legitimacy claims. An active board of directors can in this respect be expected to be involved in reducing dependency between the entrepreneurial firm and external contingencies and by that ultimately aid in the survival of the firm.

There are studies in the entrepreneurship field that seem to largely support the expectations derived from resource dependence theory. In a study of successful entrepreneurial firms, Daily and Dalton (1992) for example find that the number and proportion of outside board members were positively associated with higher financial performance. In another study of small corporations, Daily and Dalton (1993) report a positive association between the number and proportion of outside board members, board size and financial performance. In both cases, they interpret their findings as consistent with the resource dependence theory assumption that larger boards and more outside board members are associated with higher board involvement in service and resource provision roles, which in turn influence firm performance. There are also empirical studies presenting evidence that resource provision and networking tasks performed by board members are related to performance advantages. Borch and Huse (1993) identify the informal networks mediated by the board of directors in small firms as very important for improved environmental exchange power and in uncertainty reduction, and they find that the members of the board have to be seriously examined in order to match the firm's need for service. Consistent with the idea that interlocks are a mechanism to access scarce resources, George et al. (2001) report in a study of small and medium-sized enterprises (SMEs) that firms with a board networking strategy performed better than those firms that did not actively pursue the development of networks. Furthermore, Gabrielsson and Politis (2007) find that a higher involvement in networking activities by board members improves the competitive performance of small technology based firms by encouraging a more entrepreneurial and proactive strategic orientation. Thus, to conclude, it seems fair to argue that resource dependence theory is a viable approach for researching issues of boards and governance in entrepreneurial firms.

AGENCY THEORY

Agency theory is about the problem of divergent interests between two opportunistic and self-serving parties in a contractual relationship. An agency relationship is a contract where one or more principals hire one or more agents to perform some service, and then delegate decision-making authority to these agents (Ross, 1973; Jensen and Meckling, 1976). The theory identifies that agents are subject to moral hazard[7] when they do not bear the full economic consequences of their decisions. Moreover, delegation of decision-making authority imposes problems of information asymmetry, where the principal cannot perfectly and costlessly monitor the actions of the agent. Consequently, principals face the risk that opportunistic agents will take advantage of the situation for their own benefit by engaging in activities and behavior that harm welfare and induce unwanted costs for principals, such as free riding or shirking.

Conflict of Interests between Shareholders and Managers

Agency theory is a general theory of principal–agent relationships that has been applied to a broad range of substantive contexts. However, the specific problem that agency theory deals with in research on boards and governance is the conflict of interests between shareholders and managers.[8] The identification of this potential conflict is relatively old in the study of business enterprise and can be found in the writings of well-known economists. In *The Wealth of Nations*, Adam Smith (1776 [2000], p. 276) argued that managers could not be expected to watch over other people's money as if it were their own. For this reason, he expected that both 'carelessness and excess' would exist in these types of companies. Alfred Marshall (1920, p. 212) made a similar analysis in his book *Industry and Trade*, where he suggested that salaried managers were seeking the greatest comfort and the least risk for themselves. As a result, they could not be expected to strive very energetically for improvement.

Although addressed by economists such as Smith and Marshall, among others, the potential problem of the conflict of interests between shareholders and managers was brought to a wider audience by Berle and Means (1932) in their book *The Modern Corporation and Private Property*. Their concerns were aimed at ensuring that the accumulated surplus of the organization was given to shareholders, rather than staying in the hands of the emerging powerful class of professional managers. These managers were seen as having interests that were not necessarily in line with those of the shareholders and, given the enormous freedom and power that was delegated to them, Berle and Means (1932) concluded that some kind of control mechanism had to be instituted to see that profits were properly distributed back to the rightful owners. Hence, there was a need for a system of checks and balances to align the actions and behavior of managers with the desires and preferences of shareholders.

　The problem of the separation of ownership from control in the modern corporation that was raised by Berle and Means (1932) led to the subsequent development of managerial theories of the firm, in which the works of Baumol (1959), Marris (1964) and Williamson (1964) are among the most acknowledged. Managerial theories of the firm make the assumption that owners seek to maximize shareholder wealth, while managers maximize a utility function that includes remuneration, power, job security, and status. These theories moreover assume that managers have a certain level of discretion and freedom to alter the goals and objectives of the firm they are managing. It is thus suggested that managers seek to stabilize or improve their own position by maximizing, for example, revenue from sales (e.g. Baumol, 1959) or growth (e.g. Marris, 1964) at the expense of shareholders.

The Emergence of Agency Theory

Even though the problem of the separation of ownership from control has long been recognized and discussed in the economic literature, it was not until the 1970s that a common framework started to emerge for analyzing the problems associated with the separation of ownership from control. The theoretical foundations of these efforts can be traced back to the analysis of labor contracts in agrarian economies, whereby a landowner allows a tenant to use land in return for a share of the crop that is produced – something which is generally called 'sharecropping' (Otsuka et al., 1992; Casadesus-Masanell and Spulber, 2007). Dating back almost 200 years,[9] the sharecropping literature analyzes the alternative contractual arrangements that may exist between a landowner and a tenant farmer, for example the incentive effects of fixed rents compared to rent paid as a share of output produced from the rented land. According to Casadesus-Masanell and Spulber (2007), it is this origin that explains why economists primarily view agents as workers performing production tasks.

An important landmark in the development of agency theory as we know it today is Marvin Berhold who, in the essay 'A theory of linear profit-sharing incentives' (1971), develops a general model for the analysis of incentive contracts between principals and agents. In his analysis, Berhold (1971, p. 461) describes the incentive function as the relationship between the monetary reward and the characteristics of the agent's performance. If the incentive function is acceptable to the agent, then an optimal incentive function (from the viewpoint of the principal) can be selected in terms of a sharing ratio and a fixed reward. The interaction between risk-sharing and performance incentives for the agent is central in his analysis of the optimal sharing ratio. Here, Berhold (1971, p. 481) shows that the optimal sharing ratio decreases when the agent's risk increases, thus shifting the risk to the principal. Similarly, the optimal sharing ratio increases when the principal's risk increases, thus shifting the risk to the agent. As such, the model developed by Berhold (1971) can be considered an early version of agency theory as it emphasizes the provision of appropriate incentives so that agents act in the way principals wish.

Another important landmark for the development of agency theory is Ross's (1973) influential essay 'The economic theory of agency: the principal's problem', which reformulated agency problems and incentive contracts as embedded in agency relationships. Ross defines an agency relationship as 'when one, designated as the agent, acts for, on behalf of, or as representative for the other, designated the principal, in a particular domain of decision problems' (1973, p. 134), thus suggesting that the agency problem is generic in society. The 'principal's problem', according to Ross, is to design an incentive compensation package with fixed and performance-based pay that optimizes the expected utility of both principals and agents. As such, the problem is one of selecting an appropriate compensation system that will produce behavior by the agent consistent with the preferences of the principal.

Agency Theory and the Theory of the Firm

Both Berhold (1971) and Ross (1973) discuss the general problem of agency in relation to incentives and compensation contracting. The problem of agency was then subsequently developed and applied to the theory of the firm by Jensen and Meckling (1976) in their essay 'Theory of the firm: managerial behavior, agency costs and ownership structure'. They recognize the general nature of the agency problem, suggesting that it 'exist[s] in all organizations and in all cooperative efforts – at every level of management in firms' (Jensen and Meckling, 1976, p. 309), but they focus on the control problems that arise in firms as a result of a separation of ownership from the direct control of decision-making in the firm. Based on the ideas of Alchian and Demsetz (1972), they conceptualize the firm as a set of contracts among factors of production (owners, managers, employees, suppliers etc.) where each factor is motivated by its self-interest.[10] Owners, in this nexus-of-contracts view of the firm, are depicted as the rightful residual claimants, because they are the only group of contracting stakeholders that bears the risk of not getting any returns on their investments. All other stakeholders (employees, suppliers, etc.) who provide factor inputs needed for production are, due to the assumption of efficient markets,[11] expected to receive an appropriate compensation for their provision of resources, which is adjusted depending on the market price for each input. Managers have a unique position in the firm as they enter into contractual relationships with other stakeholders, make strategic decisions and allocate resources.

Jensen and Meckling (1976, p. 312) state that a wholly-owned firm managed by its owner will operate decisions that maximize his or her utility. However, they go on to argue that when the owner-manager's fraction of equity falls this will encourage him or her to appropriate larger amounts of corporate resources in the form of perquisites. Thus, the separation of ownership from control induces agency problems in the entrepreneurial firm as owners will bear the costs of managerial decisions that do not maximize shareholder wealth. Opportunistic and self-serving managers can thus be expected to be involved in non-profit-maximizing activities and maximize their own pay and benefits at the expense of firm resources when they do not bear the wealth effects of their decisions. These non-profit-maximizing activities mean that the economic residual created by the firm (the owner's claim) will be reduced. These circumstances imply that owners have proper incentives to monitor the behavior and decisions of managers. To secure their best interests, agency theory thus suggests that principals should resolve potential agency problems through bonding and monitoring mechanisms.[12]

Later, Fama (1980) further developed the analysis in his essay 'Agency problems and the theory of the firm' by arguing that the two tasks usually attributed to the entrepreneur – management and risk-bearing – should be treated as naturally separate factors within the set of contracts that constitutes the firm. From this perspective, he contends that 'ownership of the firm is an irrelevant concept' (Fama, 1980, p. 290) and argues that separation of ownership[13] and control is an efficient form of economic organization as the firm is disciplined through competition from other firms. This competition forces firms to develop devices for efficiently monitoring the performance of the firm as of its individual members (in particular its managers). Moreover, he places particular emphasis on the monitoring and discipline provided by efficient markets, both within and outside the firm. As such, Fama (1980) develops the perspective on management and risk-bearing as separate factors of production where each is faced with an alternative market for its services. These markets also provide them with opportunities, where owners can take their capital elsewhere if they wish and where managers, through the managerial labour market, are motivated toward performance so that they can get promoted (internal labour market) or recruited in the future (external labour market). In sum, Fama (1980) argues that the evolution of devices for monitoring the firm is determined by market forces and that these devices have efficiency properties.

Agency Theory and the Board of Directors

In addition to the market mechanism, agency theory identifies the board of directors as a cornerstone in the governance system of a firm. In the oft-cited essay 'Separation of ownership and control', Fama and Jensen (1983) suggest that the separation of management and risk-bearing functions survives partly due to the benefits of specialization, but also because of an effective common approach to control the agency problems that arise. Here, they emphasize that the contract structures of firms separate the initiation and implementation of the decisions (i.e. decision management) from the ratification and monitoring of decisions (i.e. decision control). The latter is provided by a board of directors who are responsible for hiring, compensating, and firing the CEO and for monitoring managerial and firm performance to shield the invested stakes of shareholders from potential managerial self-interest. The board of directors, consequently, functions as an important information system that can reduce agency problems and maximize shareholder value.

The most important qualification for board members in agency theory is independence, which generally means that they should have no personal or professional relationship to the firm or firm management (Zahra and Pearce, 1989). Board members who are not independent are expected to have fewer incentives to monitor the CEO and other firm managers. An issue that could compromise the board's ability to be independent and set its own agenda is the dual leadership structure (often referred to as CEO duality), and agency theory thus recommends a separation of the CEO and board chairperson roles. Another qualification that can influence the board's ability to be independent is board members' equity compensation, as ownership aligns their own interests with those of shareholders (Jensen and Meckling, 1976). A majority of independent outside board members with an equity stake in the business is then, in turn, expected to make boards actively involved in strategic decision-making and in monitoring managerial and firm performance, thereby enabling them to take independent action and assert power (Fama and Jensen, 1983).

Agency theory is most often connected with the analysis of boards and governance in large publicly held corporations, but it can very well be applied to any firm context when the two functions of decision-making and residual risk-bearing are separated. The analytical focus of agency theory makes it applicable to use when studying effects of the separation of these two functions in the entrepreneurial firm. Agency theory would, for example, suggest that external owners exert pressure to implement independent govern-ance structures in order to protect them from potential managerial opportunism (Jensen and Meckling, 1976). The theory would also posit that small but growing entrepreneurial firms can gain performance benefits from the external oversight an independent board can offer when the organization faces problems of asymmetric information due to increasing delegation and functional specialization (Fama and Jensen, 1983). An active board of directors in entrepreneurial firms can, in this respect, be expected to be involved in reducing the risk of potential managerial misbehavior by instituting proper incentives (for example, performance-based pay) and by closely monitoring managerial and firm performance.

There are some studies in the entrepreneurship field that seem to support expecta-tions derived from agency theory. For example, both Rosenstein (1988) and Gabrielsson and Huse (2002) find in their studies of firms where venture capitalists (VCs) have invested alongside management that VC-backed firms have a larger number of board seats and with outside VC-appointed board members rather than the CEO in power. Moreover, Fried et al., (1998) find that boards in VC-backed firms are more involved in both strategy formulation and evaluation compared to boards where board members do not have large ownership stakes. The findings are in line with agency theoretic expectations that outside ownership significantly changes the governance structure of small firms. This pattern is also found in more general studies of boards of directors in small firms, where influential external stakeholders, such as outside owners, often seek to avoid centralized leadership authority and the domination of the CEO in strategic decision-making by adopting outsiders on the board (e.g. Westhead, 1999; Fiegener et al., 2000b; Gabrielsson, 2007b). The adoption of independent board members seems thus to be a response to satisfy the demands from owners not directly involved in man-aging the company.

There are also some studies that support the idea that external monitoring by inde-pendent boards can provide proper incentives for managers to promote long-term and potentially risky strategies aimed at innovation and change. Brunninge et al. (2007), for example, find that although closely held SMEs in general exhibit less strategic change (compared to SMEs with more widespread ownership structures), they can overcome this potential weakness and achieve strategic change by adopting independent board members on the board. In a study of medium-sized corporations Gabrielsson (2007a) finds that board involvement in the ratifying and monitoring stages of strategic decision-making is positively associated with CEOs' commitment to take a more entrepreneurial strategic posture. In another study of small technology based firms Gabrielsson and Politis (2008) make a distinction between boards' involvement in strategic and financial controls,[14] and they find that boards' involvement in strategic control is positively associ-ated with process innovation, while boards' involvement in financial control is positively associated with organizational innovation. To conclude, there consequently seems to be general support for the use of an agency theory approach when researching issues of boards and governance in entrepreneurship research.

COMPARING THE TWO THEORIES

From our review, it is evident that the two theories have similarities, complementarities, and differences. As the objective of this chapter is to give an overview of the historical and intellectual roots of resource dependence theory and agency theory with a particular focus on how they have been applied in studies of boards and governance, we want to emphasize that the characteristics and assumptions identified are not fully comprehensive, nor do we present a detailed account of all possible relevant comparative aspects. Instead, our aim has been to illustrate those similarities, complementarities and differences that may garner interest among scholars working with issues of board governance in the entrepreneurship field.

With respect to similarities, both theories have assumptions of managerial behavior guided by self-interest. Agency theory is explicit about this assumption, for example in the discussion of utility maximization in agency relationships (Jensen and Meckling, 1976, p. 308). Resource dependence theory, however, also posits that managers treat outside constituencies in a self-interested manner to suit the interests of the organization (Pfeffer and Salancik, 1978, p. 263). Thus, both theories have a self-interested position with respect to the behavior of managers. Moreover, both identify the board of directors as a cornerstone in the governance system of the firm and note especially the value of outside board members. Resource dependence theory, for example, suggests that resource-constrained firms have a considerable lack of economic and political power, which in turn creates a need to be flexible in establishing effective linkages with the external environment through outside board members (Pfeffer and Salancik, 1978). Agency theory, on the other hand, stresses the need to have a vigilant board with a majority of outside (independent) board members that can shield the invested stakes of shareholders from potential managerial self-interest (Fama and Jensen, 1983). Thus, both theories identify outside board members as key contributors in the governance process.

With respect to complementarities, each theory has a different focus. Resource dependence theory, through its attention to interorganizational relationships and power dependences between the firm and various constituencies, primarily focuses on the external environment. On the other hand, agency theory, through its attention to potential managerial self-interest, focuses on the internal environment of the firm, and, in particular, board–management relationships. The two theories are also complementary in the sense that scholars have used them to provide theoretical justifications for both a resource provisioning and monitoring role for the board (Hillman and Dalziel, 2003). Resource dependence theory emphasizes aspects of a board's resource provisioning role, encompassing tasks such as securing critical resources, providing external legitimacy, and networking. Agency theory emphasizes the board's monitoring role, which encompasses tasks such as monitoring managerial and firm performance and being involved in decision control to protect the rights of residual claimants (i.e. shareholders).

There are also some notable differences between the two theories. First, resource dependence theory acknowledges the existence of market inefficiencies and power differentials, and board members are seen as resources (or as resource providers) supporting the dominant coalition in the achievement of corporate goals. As such, the theory has no a priori definition of which stakeholder group belongs to the dominant coalition, and corporate goals and objectives are seen as the result of negotiation and political bargaining among the different coalitions of stakeholders in and around the firm. Agency theory, on the other hand, assumes that stakeholders operate in a context where markets are efficient and relatively quickly adjust to new circumstances. The contracts between all stakeholders, except shareholders, are also assumed to be made ex ante, which means that there is no room for ex post bargaining. If stakeholders do not like the terms of a contract, they can always seek a better alternative. Agency theory consequently identifies shareholders as the rightful dominant coalition, and boards are elected in their service to maximize their wealth by protecting them from opportunistic and self-serving managers.

In addition, there are differences between the two theories when it comes to their view on the rationality of decision-makers. With its close association with concepts and thinking from Cyert and March (1963), resource dependence theory more or less implicitly adopts the assumption that decision-makers in and around the firms are boundedly rational, which means that they experience limits in their ability to process information and solve complex problems (e.g. Simon, 1957). The different modes or strategies of adaptation that are delineated in resource dependence theory can, in this respect, be seen as different kinds of satisficing behavior in an environment of uncertainty. Agency theory, however, assumes that decision-makers are fully rational. This means that they are assumed to search for optimal solutions with the objective of maximizing their own benefits (Jensen and Meckling, 1976, p. 307). Assuming full rationality implies that managerial discretion becomes a potential problem, as it allows greater space for managers to serve their own rather than shareholder objectives. If not constrained or in some way controlled, for example by a vigilant board of directors, increased managerial discretion may lead to agency costs which influence firm performance negatively. This can be put in contrast to resource dependence theory, which posits that managerial discretion is dictated and constrained by environmental conditions, which reduce the organization's ability to take independent action and pursue its objectives and goals. The boundary-spanning activities of the board of directors are, in this respect, an important means for coping in an environment of uncertainty and by that increasing managers' freedom to make decisions and choices. As such, the different views on rationality in the theories mean that they provide contradictory normative implications as to whether managerial discretion should be increased or constrained. The identified similarities, complementarities and differences are summarized in Table 11.1

IMPLICATIONS FOR THE JOINT APPLICATION OF THE THEORIES IN ENTREPRENEURSHIP RESEARCH

Both resource dependence theory and agency theory provide rich and widely acknowledged conceptual foundations that can be used to address issues of governance in entrepreneurship research. Resource dependence theory, for example, fits well to the entrepreneurial context as new and small firms need to build and maintain favorable and stable relationships with key stakeholders to survive and prosper. Their limited influence and bargaining power may, in this respect, call for the importance of gaining access to resources, influence and legitimacy through the networks of their board members (Borch and Huse, 1993). Also, agency theory can be seen as a highly relevant perspective for understanding the risk of conflicting goals between contracting parties in entrepreneurial

Table 11.1   Resource dependence theory and agency theory compared

Similarities	Complementarities	Differences
Managers are assumed to be driven largely by self-interest	Resource dependence theory is externally focused – agency theory is internally focused	Resource dependence assumes incomplete contracting setups among all stakeholders – agency theory assumes ex ante contracting between all stakeholders except between shareholders and managers
The board of directors is identified as a cornerstone in the governance system of the firm, especially outside board members	Resource dependence theory identifies a resource provision role for the board – agency theory identifies a monitoring role for the board	Resource dependence theory identifies need for boards to increase managerial discretion – agency theory identifies need for boards to constrain or control managerial discretion

firms. Conflicts can in this respect arise between owners and managers, as well as between part-owners, for example in the division of the value created by the firm as well as in the struggle for power and control rights (Gabrielsson and Huse, 2005). This, in turn, calls for the need to implement governance mechanisms such as a vigilant and independent board of directors in order to reduce potential agency problems (Gedajlovic et al., 2004).

Although each theoretical perspective can be used in its own right, neither of them seems to be able to independently provide a full explanation of the complexities of governance issues in entrepreneurial firms (Daily et al., 2002). Resource dependence theory, for example, with its emphasis on the ways in which firms become constrained by their environment, has a relatively narrow focus on what goes on inside the organization. The environmental context, on the other hand, is often insufficiently examined in agency theory due to the overemphasis on the problems of agency. The joint application of both resource dependence theory and agency theory may in this respect provide a more holistic and balanced view on board governance in the entrepreneurial firm, whereby the different theories provide complementary perspectives. This combinatory approach is well in line with the growing consensus in studies of boards and governance concerning the need for theoretical pluralism (e.g. Hung, 1998; Daily et al., 2003) and where the behavior of boards can be related to the distinctive organizational characteristics and task environment of the firm (Huse, 1998; Lynall et al., 2003; Huse and Zattoni, 2008) as well as to the personal attributes of the CEO and individual board members (Hillman and Dalziel, 2003; Shen, 2003).

This joint application of resource dependence theory and agency theory in studies of boards and governance in entrepreneurial firms, however, also calls for a need to understand the basic assumptions underlying the two theories. As is evident from our overview of each theory's historical roots, they originate from different intellectual traditions and, thus, also partly rely on different assumptions. Resource dependence theory, with its roots in organizational sociology, adopts a perspective that emphasizes power differentials, market inefficiencies and political struggle to explain organizational action. Agency theory, with its roots in the financial economics discipline, on the other hand, assumes rational actors who contract for profit in efficient markets. Thus, whereas resource dependence theory acknowledges the ongoing struggle for power and influence over organizational resource-allocation decisions among different coalitions of stakeholders, the theoretical assumptions in agency theory completely overlook this possibility. Perhaps the easiest way to deal with this situation when combining the two theories is to relax at least two basic assumptions in agency theory. Relaxing these assumptions does not invalidate either the existence of agency relationships or the potential agency problems that arise from them, but it prompts consideration of some features not treated in the theory's standard version.

The first assumption to be relaxed is that of efficient markets, which means that stakeholders may not have freedom of entry into and exit from contractual relationships (Hill and Jones, 1992). Relaxing this assumption would open up the possibility for power differentials between parties in an exchange. This, in turn, rejects the idea of complete contracting ex ante for all stakeholders except between shareholders and managers (Huse et al., forthcoming). Acknowledging the existence of incomplete contracts for all stakeholders involved in resource exchange would open up the possibility for more ex post negotiation (Rajan and Zingales, 1998) while rejecting the idea that shareholders have all the bargaining power. The second assumption to be relaxed is that of fully rational economic actors.[15] The incomplete contracting between stakeholders can in this respect be explained not only by the existence of information asymmetries but also by bounded rationality. In fact, bounded rationality makes all contracts unavoidably incomplete.

The result of the two relaxations above is a slightly modified version of agency theory which – much in line with resource dependence theory thinking – acknowledges the existence of more or less temporary market inefficiencies and unequal resource dependences and power differentials between managers and stakeholders (for similar reasoning in previous studies, see Hill and Jones, 1992). These market inefficiencies create potential agency conflicts, not only between managers and shareholders, but also between managers and a wider set of stakeholders who cannot receive payments with reference to the market price as their investments have limited or no value outside the context of the firm (Blair, 1998). The board of directors is then primarily functioning as an impartial mediator that balances and interprets the sometimes conflicting interests of the value-adding stakeholders who embody the core capabilities of the firm (i.e. the dominant coalition). Moreover, incompleteness of contracts results in an increased need for ex post negotiation and bargaining among the contracting stakeholders about how to distribute the surplus (Rajan and Zingales, 1998). This creates the need for a mechanism, such as a board of directors, which can coordinate resource allocations and reduce costly and potentially value-destroying bargaining processes.[16] Furthermore, accepting that all economic actors are constrained by bounded rationality suggests that the divergence between the desires of principals and the actions of agents is not necessarily due only to agents' self-serving behavior, which is one-sidedly emphasized in standard agency theory (Jensen and Meckling, 1976), but also to the inability of agents to reliably and competently deliver what is expected (Hendry, 2002).[17] This would mean that, in addition to the risk of opportunism, there can also be agency problems related to the limited information they have, the cognitive limitations of their minds, and the finite amount of time they have to make decisions.

To conclude this section, we think the above-mentioned modifications[18] will bring the two theories closer to each other in terms of basic assumptions without violating the basic premise in agency theory that there is a need to protect the interests of principals (shareholders/stakeholders) from potential misbehavior by agents (managers) through bonding or monitoring activities. In line with resource dependence theory thinking, the changes also suggest that board members can be used to assist managers in dealing with the complexity and uncertainty of strategic decision-making by collecting and utilizing relevant and timely information, knowledge and other resources from various stakeholders in and around the firm. Moreover, we believe that the suggested changes are closer to what is already widely assumed in entrepreneurship research, for example markets in disequilibrium (Knight, 1921; Schumpeter, 1942; Kirzner, 1973), power differentials due to variations in the access to resources (Penrose, 1959; Aldrich and Auster, 1986) and decision-makers as boundedly rational economic actors (Sarasvathy, 2008).

SUGGESTIONS FOR FUTURE RESEARCH ON BOARDS AND GOVERNANCE IN ENTREPRENEURIAL FIRMS

In the introduction of this chapter we suggested that both resource dependence theory and agency theory provide implications for researching behavioral aspects of board governance in entrepreneurial firms. We have also argued in the chapter for bringing the theories closer together. In this section, we summarize a number of areas where we think further research is highly warranted to promote the accumulation of knowledge in these areas.

Researching Behavioral Aspects of Board Governance

An interest in behavioral aspects of board governance calls for closer study of how boards actually work and how board members may improve their behavior to contribute to value creation. A highly interesting area of research within a resource dependence framework is to study the motivations, intentions and behaviors of co-opted individuals on the board of directors in entrepreneurial firms. Co-opted board members, in resource dependence theory, are expected to become involved in helping the focal organization to control its environment by influencing their constituencies. Indeed, Pfeffer and Salancik suggest that, 'when an organization appoints an individual to a board, it expects the individual will come to support the organization, will concern himself with its problems, will variably present it to others, and will try to aid it' (1978, p. 167). However, there is a need to scrutinize this largely untested behavioral assumption that co-opted board members would change their loyalty so that they mainly pursue the interests of the entrepreneurial firm, instead of the organization which until recently has been their main home institution (for a more extensive critique of this assumption, see Donaldson, 1995, p. 154). It could for example be just as likely that they join the board for other reasons, for example, to monitor the focal firm to benefit their home institution.[19]

An interesting area of research from an agency theory point of view is the issue of independence in relation to board members in entrepreneurial firms. Independence is seen in agency theory as a key feature of effective boards (Fama and Jensen, 1983), and this feature has been associated with outside (or non-executive) board members. Past studies, however, have suggested a general need to distinguish between outside and independent board members (see, for example, Gabrielsson and Winlund, 2000). The adoption of outside board members and the separation of the CEO and board chairperson roles, for example, are not necessarily found to be associated with greater board involvement in shaping strategy, reviewing management policies, or contributing professional advice (Ford, 1988). Consequently, an outside board member should not, by definition, be expected to behave independently, even if he or she brings considerable competence and experience into the boardroom. Moreover, conceptualizing independence as a behavioral rather than a structural feature raises interesting questions about to what extent and under what conditions outside board members in entrepreneurial firms are acting 'independently' in the way agency theory prescribes. It also connects to recent discussions about the need to examine whether there is a trade-off between independence and the presence of firm-specific knowledge required to understand and evaluate complex firm decisions (e.g. Huse et al., 2009).

Joint Application of Resource Dependence Theory and Agency Theory

When jointly applying resource dependence and agency theory in entrepreneurial firms, there are also some areas where we think research is highly warranted. The first is how various outside board members contribute with different kinds of value-adding benefits in entrepreneurial firms. Resource dependence theory suggests that outside board members contribute added value by bringing different linkages and resources to a board. Agency theory suggests that outside board members contribute added value by introducing checks and balances to correct potential harmful managerial behavior and protect the assets of the firm. Past research, however, has primarily relied on relatively rough distinctions between inside and outside board members (Gabrielsson, 2007b), whereas a more fine-grained analysis of different categories of outside (and perhaps also inside) board members could provide a much more detailed understanding of what kind of value-added contributions a given type of board member is likely to bring to the board (Hillman et al., 2000).

Another interesting area of research when jointly applying resource dependence and agency theory is the extent to which the entrepreneurial firm is able to effectively implement and use the value-added contributions provided by outside board members. Such attempts may need to distinguish between 'potential' contributions and 'realized' contributions. Potential contributions would here refer to the set of potential benefits that the entrepreneurial firm can receive from its outside board members. The realized contributions, on the other hand, would refer to the successful implementation and incorporation of such resource contributions into the venture's operations with the hope of improving its performance. This conceptual distinction suggests that entrepreneurial firms can vary significantly in their ability to effectively implement and utilize the value-adding contributions that outside board members can bring. Making such a distinction would also allow researchers to abandon viewing the value-adding benefits from outside board members as a simple transferring process, and instead turn more attention towards the study of why some attempts to contribute resources fail while others thrive.

A third area of research when jointly applying resource dependence and agency theory is to study how board members' involvement in monitoring versus resource provision tasks evolves and changes as the entrepreneurial firm develops and moves through the organizational life cycle (e.g. Lynall et al., 2003; Bonn and Pettigrew, 2009). This may also include studies of how boards in entrepreneurial firms balance (or fail to balance) the speed and flexibility in decision-making that often are seen as critical features for competitiveness in small firms (e.g. O'Gorman, 2000) against the need to formalize rules, reporting procedures and job descriptions as the firm grows. Such endeavors would not only contribute to our scholarly knowledge of how processes of board governance emerge and develop over time, but would also go beyond the fundamentally static conceptions of boards of directors that often dominate research on corporate governance (Gabrielsson and Huse, 2004).

CONCLUSIONS

Studies of boards and governance have a long history in business research. Although these studies traditionally have focused on large firms (Gabrielsson and Huse, 2004) this interest has also spilled over to include firms that are in the entrepreneurial stages of the organizational life cycle. In this chapter we have provided an overview of the historical and intellectual roots of resource dependence theory and agency theory with a particular focus on how they have been applied in studies of boards and governance. Despite the frequent use of these theories by scholars addressing issues of governance in entrepreneurial firms, they also tend to be used in a largely metaphorical sense to justify the need for board members to perform resource provision and monitoring tasks. Thus, our underlying motivation for the review has been that a better understanding of the origins and thinking behind the theories should contribute positively to knowledge accumulation within the field.

In short, our review suggests that both resource dependence theory and agency theory provide powerful conceptual foundations that can be used to address issues of board governance in entrepreneurship research. Based on this, we also discuss some similarities, complementarities, and differences between the two theories that may have implications when combining arguments from resource dependence theory and agency theory. With regard to similarities and complementarities, there seems to be enough common ground for their joint application in studies of boards and governance. With regard to differences, however, we identify a need to relax some of the assumptions in agency theory to bring the two theories closer together. This, we hope, will stimulate further research on how board members, through their performance of resource provision and monitoring tasks, can contribute to the creation of wealth, value and satisfaction for the range of stakeholders in and around the entrepreneurial firm.

ACKNOWLEDGMENTS

We are indebted to Franz Lohrke and Hans Landström, the editors of this book, for their valuable comments on earlier drafts of this chapter. We are also grateful for the comments given by Diamanto Politis in the course of developing this work.

NOTES

1. 'Entrepreneurial' can refer to such different firm characteristics as being young (Daily et al., 2002), innovative (Covin and Slevin, 1988), fast-growing (Daily and Dalton, 1993) or owner-controlled (Carland et al., 1984).
2. The dominance of resource dependence theory and agency theory is the case also in studies of boards of directors in general. For an overview, see for example Gabrielsson and Huse (2004).
3. Outside directors have in entrepreneurship research often been defined as directors who are not executive managers or relatives of the CEO (whether employed by the firm or not) (Fiegener et al., 2000b; Gabrielsson, 2007b).
4. Research on small firm growth indicates that managerial appointments are usually made when a firm reaches a size between 10 to 20 employees (Storey, 1994, p. 10).
5. von Bertanlanffy discussed living organisms as open systems in his article, hence the term 'real systems'.
6. Please note that the terminology varies. Yuchtman and Seashore (1967) refer to the systems-resource approach, Zald (1970) and Walmsley and Zald (1973) refer to the political economy model, and Thompson (1967) refers to the power-dependency model.
7. Moral hazard means that people act less carefully when they are protected from some (or all) risk than when they are fully exposed to risk. The moral hazard problem originates from the analysis of insurance market contracts where an individual may influence the probability of the insured event to his advantage (e.g. Spence and Zeckhauser, 1971).
8. A distinction is sometimes made between two different types or versions of agency theory in the literature: the 'positivist' approach and the 'principal–agent' approach. The positivist approach is most often used in corporate governance research. It is more empirical, largely verbal and concentrates on the problem of separation of ownership from control (e.g. Fama and Jensen, 1983). The 'principal–agent' approach is used to analyse all principal/agent relationships. It is more normative, much more mathematical and concentrates on the design of specific ex ante contract specifications (e.g. Holmström, 1979). In this chapter we are referring to the positivist approach in our discussion. However, even if there are some differences in focus and style between the two approaches, we want to emphasize that the background and analytical core is pretty much the same.
9. Early contributors to the economic analysis of labor contracts in sharecropping include for example both Smith (1776) and Marshall (1890).
10. Antecedents of this perspective can be found in Coase (1937) and Coase (1960).
11. Agency theory assumes that markets are in or near an efficient equilibrium (e.g. Fama, 1980; Jensen, 1983).
12. Bonding mechanisms – such as compensation packages – reward agents when they achieve the goals of the principals and penalize them when they violate the interests of principals. Monitoring mechanisms – such as a vigilant board of directors – observe the behavior and performance of the agents.
13. Ownership of capital (risk bearing) should here not be confused with ownership of the firm.
14. The distinction is based on Hoskisson and Hitt (1988) and Baysinger and Hoskisson (1990). Financial controls are clear and unambiguous and based on objective decision areas such as the organizational budget, equity, liquidity and finance. Strategic controls recognize the more long-term dimensions of business enterprise and are based on strategically relevant decision criteria that are more subjective, for example decisions related to external market and user needs and new products.
15. This relaxed assumption is not very controversial as it appears in Eisenhardt's (1989) widely cited article.
16. These resource allocations may of course not lead to a fair return on investments as unequal resource dependencies may make ex post surplus and ex ante investments sharing unrelated.
17. Accepting bounded rationality also suggests that principals cannot always express exactly what they want, but this is another problem not dealt with here. See for example Hendry (2005).
18. These modifications also open the way for the application of new theoretical approaches, such as team production theory, in studies of boards and governance in entrepreneurial firms (Huse et al., 2008).
19. We want to point out that this possibility is far from ignored in resource dependence theory. On the contrary, it was discussed by Selznick (1949) and also in later work by Palmer (1983) and Mizruchi and Stearns (1988). However, we are not aware of any attempts that examine the loyalty of co-opted board members in the entrepreneurship literature.

REFERENCES

Alchian, A.A. and H. Demsetz (1972), 'Production, information costs, and economic organization', *American Economic Review*, **62**, 777–95.

Aldrich, H.E. and E. Auster (1986), 'Even dwarfs started small: liabilities of age and size and their strategic implications', *Research in Organizational Behavior*, **8**, 165–98.

Aldrich, H.E. and J. Pfeffer (1976), 'Environments of organizations', *Annual Review of Sociology*, **2**, 79–105.

Barnard, C.I. (1938), *The Functions of the Executive*, Cambridge, MA: Harvard University Press.

Baumol, W.J. (1959), *Business Behavior, Value and Growth*, New York: Macmillan.

Baysinger, B.D. and R.E. Hoskisson (1990), 'The composition of boards of directors and strategic control: effects on corporate strategy', *Academy of Management Review*, **15**, 72–80.

Bennett R.J. and P.J.A. Robson (2004), 'The role of boards of directors in small and medium-sized firms', *Journal of Small Business and Enterprise Development*, **11**(1), 95–113.

Berhold, M. (1971), 'A theory of linear profit-sharing incentives', *Quarterly Journal of Economics*, **85**(3), 460–82.

Berle, A.A. and G.C. Means (1932), *The Modern Corporation and Private Property*, New York: Macmillan.

Bertanlanffly, L. von (1950), 'The theory of open systems in physics and biology', *Science*, **3**, 23–29.

Birch, D.L. (1979), *The Job Generating Process*, Cambridge, MA: MIT Press.

Blair, M.M. (1998), 'For whom should corporations be run? An economic rationale for stakeholder management', *Long Range Planning*, **31**(2), 195–200.

Blau, P.M. (1964), *Exchange and Power in Social Life*, New York: John Wiley and Sons.

Bonn, I. and A. Pettigrew (2009), 'Towards a dynamic theory of boards: an organisational life cycle approach', *Journal of Management and Organization*, **15**(1), 2–16.

Borch, O.J. and M. Huse (1993), 'Informal strategic networks and the board of directors', *Entrepreneurship Theory and Practice*, **18**(1), 23–37.

Brunninge, O., M. Nordqvist and J. Wiklund (2007), 'Corporate governance and strategic change in SMEs: the effects of ownership, board composition and top management teams', *Small Business Economics*, **29**(3), 295–308.

Carland, J.W., F. Hoy, W.R. Boulton and J.C. Carland (1984), 'Differentiating entrepreneurs from small business owners: a conceptualization', *Academy of Management Review*, **9**(3), 354–59.

Casadesus-Masanell, R. and D.F. Spulber (2007), 'Agency revisited', Northwestern University Working Paper, Boston, MA: Northwestern University.

Churchill, N.C. and V.L. Lewis (1983), 'The five stages of small business growth', *Harvard Business Review*, **61**(3), 30–50.

Clarysse, B., M. Knockaert and A. Lockett (2007), 'Outside board members in high tech start-ups', *Small Business Economics*, **29**(3), 243–59.

Coase, R.H. (1937), 'The nature of the firm', *Economica*, **4**(16), 386–405.

Coase, R.H. (1960), 'The problem of social cost', *Journal of Law and Economics*, **3**, 1–44.

Collin, S.-O. (2003), 'The mastering of the corporation: an integrated model of corporate governance', unpublished manuscript, Department of Business Studies, Kristianstad University College, Sweden.

Covin, J.G. and D.P. Slevin (1988), 'The influence of organization structure on the utility of an entrepreneurial top management style', *Journal of Management Studies*, **25**(3), 217–35.

Cyert, R.M. and J.G. March (1963), *A Behavioral Theory of the Firm*, Englewood Cliffs, NJ: Prentice Hall.

Daily, C.M. and D.R. Dalton (1992), 'The relationship between governance structure and corporate performance in entrepreneurial firms', *Journal of Business Venturing*, **7**, 375–86.

Daily, C.M. and D.R. Dalton (1993), 'Board of directors leadership and structure: control and performance implications', *Entrepreneurship Theory and Practice*, **17**(3), 65–81.

Daily, C.M., D.R. Dalton and A.A. Cannella (2003), 'Corporate governance: decades of dialogue and data', *Academy of Management Review*, **28**, 371–82.

Daily, C.M., P.P. McDougall, J.G. Covin and D.R. Dalton (2002), 'Governance and strategic leadership in entrepreneurial firms', *Journal of Management*, **28**(3), 387–412.

Dant, R.P. (2008), 'A futuristic research agenda for the field of franchising', *Journal of Small Business Management*, **46**, 91–98.

Das, T.K. and B.-S. Teng (2000), 'Instabilities of strategic alliances: an internal tensions perspective', *Organization Science*, **11**(1), 77–101.

De Clercq, D. and S. Manigart (2007), 'The venture capital post investment phase: opening up the black box of involvement', in H. Landström (ed.), *Handbook of Research on Venture Capital*, Cheltenham, UK and Northampton, MA, USA: Edward Elgar, pp. 193–218.

Deutsch, Y. and T.W. Ross (2003), 'You are known by the directors you keep: reputable directors as a signaling mechanism for young firms', *Management Science*, **49**(8), 1003–17.

Donaldson, L. (1995), *American Anti-Management Theories of Organization*, Cambridge, MA: Cambridge University Press.

Eisenhardt, K.M. (1989), 'Agency theory: an assessment and review', *Academy of Management Review*, **14**, 57–74.

Emerson, R.M. (1962), 'Power-dependence relations', *American Sociological Review*, **27**, 31–40.

Emery, F.E. and E.L. Trist (1965), 'The causal texture of organizational environments', *Human Relations*, **18**(1), 21–32.

Fama, E.F. (1980), 'Agency problems and the theory of the firm', *Journal of Political Economy*, **88**(2), 288–307.

Fama, E.F. and M.C. Jensen (1983), 'Separation of ownership and control', *Journal of Law and Economics*, **26**, 301–25.

Fayol, H. (1949), *General and Industrial Management*, Pitman: London.

Fiegener, M.K. (2005), 'Determinants of board participation in the strategic decisions of small corporations', *Entrepreneurship Theory and Practice*, **29**(5), 627–50.

Fiegener, M.K., B.M. Brown, D.R. Dreux and W.J. Dennis Jr (2000a), 'CEO stakes and board composition in small private firms', *Entrepreneurship Theory and Practice*, **24**(4), 5–24.

Fiegener, M.K., B.M. Brown, D.R. Dreux and W.J. Dennis Jr (2000b), 'The adoption of outside boards by small private US firms', *Entrepreneurship and Regional Development*, **12**(4), 291–310.

Finkelstein, S. and A.C. Mooney (2003), 'Not the usual suspects: how to use board process to make boards better', *Academy of Management Executive*, **17**(2), 101–13.

Finkle, T.A. (1998), 'The relationship between boards of directors and initial public offering in the biotechnology industry', *Entrepreneurship Theory and Practice*, **22**(3), 5–29

Forbes, D.P. and F.J. Milliken (1999), 'Cognition and corporate governance: understanding boards of directors as strategic decision making groups', *Academy of Management Review*, **24**(3), 489–505.

Ford, R.H. (1988), 'Outside directors and the privately-owned firm: are they necessary?', *Entrepreneurship Theory and Practice*, **13**(1), 49–57.

Fried, V.H., G.D. Bruton and R.D. Hisrich (1998), 'Strategy and the board of directors in venture capital-backed firms', *Journal of Business Venturing*, **13**, 493–503.

Gabrielsson, J. (2007a), 'Boards of directors and entrepreneurial posture in medium-size companies: putting the board demography approach to a test', *International Small Business Journal*, **25**(5), 511–37.

Gabrielsson, J. (2007b), 'Correlates of board empowerment in small companies', *Entrepreneurship Theory and Practice*, **31**(5), 687–711.

Gabrielsson, J. and M. Huse (2002), 'The venture capitalist and the board of directors in SMEs: roles and processes', *Venture Capital*, **4**(2), 125–46.

Gabrielsson, J. and M. Huse (2004), 'Context, behavior and evolution – challenges in research on boards and governance', *International Studies in Management and Organization*, **34**(2), 11–36.

Gabrielsson, J. and M. Huse (2005), 'Outside directors in SME boards: a call for theoretical reflections', *Corporate Board: Roles, Duties and Composition*, **1**(1), 28–37.

Gabrielsson, J. and D. Politis (2007), 'The impact of ownership and board governance on firm-level entrepreneurship in small technology-based firms', *Icfai Journal of Corporate Governance*, **6**(3), 43–60.

Gabrielsson, J. and D. Politis (2008), 'Board control and innovation: an empirical study of small technology-based firms', in M. Huse. (ed.), *The Value Creating Board: Corporate Governance and Organizational Behaviour*, London: Routledge, pp. 505–19.

Gabrielsson, J. and H. Winlund (2000), 'Boards of directors in small and medium-sized industrial firms: examining the effects of the board's working style on board task performance', *Entrepreneurship and Regional Development*, **12**(4), 311–30.

Gedajlovic, E., M.H. Lubatkin and W.S. Schulze (2004), 'Crossing the threshold from founder management to professional management: a governance perspective', *Journal of Management Studies*, **41**(5), 899–912.

George, G., D.R. Wood and R. Khan (2001), 'Networking strategy of boards: implications for small and medium-sized enterprises', *Entrepreneurship and Regional Development*, **13**(3), 269–85.

Greiner, L.E. (1972), 'Evolution and revolution as organizations grow', *Harvard Business Review*, **50**(4), 37–46.

Hendry, J. (2002), 'The principals' other problems: honest incompetence and management contracts', *Academy of Management Review*, **27**, 98–113.

Hendry, J. (2005), 'Beyond self-interest: agency theory and the board in a satisficing world', *British Journal of Management*, **16** (special issue), 55–64.

Hill, C.W. and T.M. Jones (1992), 'Stakeholder-agency theory', *Journal of Management Studies*, **29**(2), 132–54.

Hillman, A.J. and T. Dalziel (2003), 'Boards of directors and firm performance: integrating agency and resource dependence perspectives', *Academy of Management Review*, **28**(3), 383–96.

Hillman, A.J., A.A. Cannella and R.L. Paetzold (2000), 'The resource dependence role of corporate directors: strategic adaptation of board composition in response to environmental change', *Journal of Management Studies*, **37**(2), 235–55.

Holmström, B. (1979), 'Moral hazard and observability', *Bell Journal of Economics*, **10**, 74–91.

Hoskisson, R.E. and M.A. Hitt (1988), 'Strategic control systems and relative R&D investment in large multiproduct firms', *Strategic Management Journal*, **9**, 605–21.

Hung, H. (1998), 'A typology of the theories of the roles of governing boards', *Corporate Governance: An International Review*, **6**, 101–11.

Huse, M. (1994), 'Board–management relations in small firms: the paradox of simultaneous independence and interdependence', *Small Business Economics*, **6**(1), 55–73.

Huse, M. (1998), 'Researching the dynamics of board–stakeholder relations', *Long Range Planning*, **31**, 218–26.

Huse, M. (2000), 'Boards in SMEs: a review and research agenda', *Entrepreneurship and Regional Development*, **12**(4), 271–90.

Huse, M. (2005), 'Accountability and creating accountability: a framework for exploring behavioural perspectives of corporate governance', *British Journal of Management*, **16** (special issue), 65–80.

Huse, M. (2007), *Boards, Governance and Value Creation*, Cambridge: Cambridge University Press.

Huse, M. and A. Zattoni (2008), 'Trust, firm life cycle, and actual board behavior: evidence from "one of the lads" in the board of three small firms', *International Studies of Management and Organization*, **38**(3), 71–97.

Huse, M., J. Gabrielsson and A. Minichilli (2009), 'Knowledge and accountability: outside directors' contribution in the corporate value chain', in P.-Y. Pierre-Yves Gomez and R. Moore (eds), *Board Members and Management Consultants: Redefining the Boundaries of Consulting and Corporate Governance*, Information Age Publishing, pp. 137–53.

Huse, M., R. Hoskisson, J. Gabrielsson and R. White (2008), 'Governance in small and medium-sized entrepreneurial firms: the case for team production theory', paper presented at the 28th Annual International Conference of the Strategic Management Society, Cologne, Germany.

Huse, M., R. Hoskisson, A. Zattoni and R. Vigano (forthcoming), 'New perspectives on board research: changing the research agenda', paper to appear in *Journal of Management and Governance*, DOI: 10.1007/s10997-009-9122-9.

Jensen, M.C. (1983), 'Organization theory and methodology', *Accounting Review*, **50**, 319–39.

Jensen M.C. and W.H. Meckling (1976), 'Theory of the firm: managerial behavior, agency costs and ownership structure', *Journal of Financial Economics*, **2**, 305–60.

Johannisson, B. and M. Huse (2000), 'Recruiting outside board members in the small family business: an ideological challenge', *Entrepreneurship and Regional Development*, **12**(4), 353–78.

Johnson J.L., C.M. Daily and A.E. Ellstrand (1996), 'Boards of directors: a review and research agenda', *Journal of Management*, **22**(3), 409–38.

Katz, D. and R.L. Kahn (1966), *The Social Psychology of Organizations*, New York: Wiley.

Kirchoff, B. (1994), *Entrepreneurship and Dynamic Capitalism*, London: Praeger.

Kirzner, I.M. (1973), *Competition and Entrepreneurship*, Chicago, IL: University of Chicago Press.

Knight, F.H. (1921), *Risk, Uncertainty and Profit*, Chicago: University of Chicago Press.

Lester, R.H. and A.A. Cannella (2006), 'Interorganizational familiness: how family firms use interlocking directorates to build community-level social capital', *Entrepreneurship Theory and Practice*, **30**(6), 755–75.

Lynall, M.D., B.R. Goldenand A.J. Hillman (2003), 'Board composition from adolescence to maturity: a multi-theoretical view', *Academy of Management Review*, **28**, 416–31.

Markman, G.D., D.B. Balkin and L. Schjoedt (2001), 'Governing the innovation process in entrepreneurial firms', *Journal of High Technology Management Research*, **12**, 273–93.

Marris, R. (1964), *Economic Theory and 'Managerial' Capitalism*, New York: Free Press.

Marshall, A. (1890), *Principles of Economics: An Introductory Volume*, London: Macmillan and Co.

Marshall, A. (1920), *Industry and Trade: A Study of Industrial Technique and Business Organization; and of Their Influence on the Conditions of Various Classes and Nations*, 3rd edition, London: Publisher's green cloth.

Mizruchi, M.S. and L.B. Stearns (1988), 'A longitudinal study of the formation of interlocking directorates', *Administrative Science Quarterly*, **33**, 194–210.

O'Gorman, C. (2000), 'Strategy and the small firm', in S. Carter and D. Jones-Evans (eds), *Enterprise and Small Business: Principles, Practice and Policy*, Harlow: Financial Times, pp. 283–99.

O'Sullivan, N. and S. Diacon (1999), 'Internal and external governance mechanisms: evidence from the UK insurance industry', *Corporate Governance: An International Review*, **7**(4), 363–73.

Otsuka, K., H. Chuma, and Y. Hayami (1992), 'Land and labor contracts in agrarian economies: theories and facts', *Journal of Economic Literature*, **30**(4), 1965–2019.

Palmer, D. (1983), 'Broken ties: interlocking directorates and intercorporate coordination', *Administrative Science Quarterly*, **28**, 40–55.

Penrose, E. (1959), *The Theory of the Growth of the Firm*, Oxford: Oxford University Press.

Pfeffer, J. (1972a), 'Interorganizational influence and managerial attitudes', *Academy of Management Journal*, **15**, 317–30.

Pfeffer, J. (1972b), 'Merger as a response to organizational interdependence', *Administrative Science Quarterly*, **17**, 382–94.

Pfeffer, J. (1972c), 'Size and composition of corporate boards of directors: the organization and its environment', *Administrative Science Quarterly*, **17**, 218–28.

Pfeffer, J. (1973), 'Size, composition and function of hospital boards of directorates', *Administrative Science Quarterly*, **18**(3), 349–64.

Pfeffer, J. and P. Nowak (1976), 'Joint ventures and interorganizational interdependence', *Administrative Science Quarterly*, **21**(3), 398–418.

Pfeffer, J. and G. Salancik (1978), *The External Control of Organizations: A Resource Dependence Perspective*, New York: Harper and Row.

Quinn, R.E. and K. Cameron (1983), 'Organizational life cycles and shifting criteria of effectiveness: some preliminary evidence', *Management Science*, **29**, 33–51.

Rajan, R.G. and L. Zingales (1998), 'Power in a theory of the firm', *Quarterly Journal of Economics*, **113**, 387–432.

Rhenman, E. (1964), *Företaget som ett styrt system*, Stockholm: Nordstedts.

Rosa, P. and M. Scott (1999), 'The prevalence of multiple owners and directors in the SME sector: implications for our understanding of start-up and growth', *Entrepreneurship and Regional Development*, **11**(1), 21–37.

Rosenstein, J. (1988), 'The board and strategy: venture capital and high technology', *Journal of Business Venturing*, **3**, 159–70.

Rosenstein, J., A.V. Bruno, W.D. Bygrave and N.T. Taylor (1993), 'The CEO, venture capitalists, and the board', *Journal of Business Venturing*, **8**, 99–113.

Ross, S. (1973), 'The economic theory of agency: the principal's problem', *American Economic Review*, **63**(2), 134–39.

Sarasvathy, S.D. (2008), *Effectuation: Elements of Entrepreneurial Expertise*, Cheltenham, UK and Northampton, MA, USA: Edward Elgar.

Schulze, W.S., M.H. Lubatkin and R.N. Dino (2003), 'Exploring the agency consequences of ownership dispersion among the directors of private family firms', *Academy of Management Journal*, **46**(2), 179–94.

Schumpeter, J.A. (1942), *Capitalism, Socialism, and Democracy*, New York: Harper and Row.

Selznick, P. (1949), *TVA and the Grass Roots: A Study in the Sociology of Formal Organization*, New York: Harper and Row.

Shen, W. (2003), 'The dynamics of the CEO–board relationships: an evolutionary perspective', *Academy of Management Review*, **28**, 466–76.

Shepherd, D.A., E.J. Douglas and M. Shanley (2000), 'New venture survival: ignorance, external shocks, and risk reduction strategies', *Journal of Business Venturing*, **15**(5–6), 393–410.

Simon, H.A. (1957), *Models of Man: Social and Rational*, New York: John Wiley and Sons.

Smith, A. (1776 [2000]), *An Inquiry into the Nature and Causes of the Wealth of Nations*, New York: Random House International.

Spence, M. and R. Zeckhauser (1971), 'Insurance, information, and individual action', *American Economic Review*, **61**(2), 380–87.

Stinchcombe, A.L. (1965), 'Social structure and organizations', in J. March (ed.), *Handbook of Organizations*, Chicago: Rand McNally, pp. 142–93.

Storey, D.J. (1994), *Understanding the Small Business Sector*, London: Routledge.

Taylor, F.W. (1911), *The Principles of Scientific Management*, New York: Harper and Brothers Publishers.

Thompson, J.D. (1967), *Organizations in Action*, New York: McGraw Hill.

Voordeckers, W., A. Van Gils and J. Van den Heuvel (2007), 'Board composition in small and medium-sized family firms', *Journal of Small Business Management*, **45**(1), 137–56.

Walmsley, G. and M. Zald (1973), *The Political Economy of Public Organizations*, Lexington, MA: Lexington Books.

Weber, M. (1947), *The Theory of Social and Economic Organization*, New York: The Free Press.

Weick, K.E. (1976), 'Educational organizations as loosely coupled systems', *Administrative Science Quarterly*, **21**, 1–19.

Westhead, P. (1999), 'Factors associated with the employment of non-executive directors by unquoted companies', *Journal of Management and Governance*, **3**, 81–111.

Whisler, T.L. (1998), 'The role of the board in the threshold firm', *Family Business Review*, **1**, 309–21.

Williamson, O.E. (1964), *The Economics of Discretionary Behavior: Managerial Objectives in a Theory of the Firm*, Englewood Cliffs, NJ: Prentice-Hall.

Yuchtman, E. and S.E. Seashore (1967), 'A system resource approach to organizational effectiveness', *American Sociological Review*, **32**, 891–903.

Zahra, S.A. and J.A. Pearce (1989), 'Boards of directors and corporate financial performance: a review and integrative model', *Journal of Management*, **15**, 291–334.

Zald, M.N. (1967), 'Urban differentiation, characteristics of boards of directors, and organizational effectiveness', *American Journal of Sociology*, **73**, 261–72.

Zald, M.N. (1969), 'The power and functions of boards of directors: a theoretical synthesis', *American Journal of Sociology*, **75**, 97–111.

Zald, M.N. (1970), 'Political economy: a framework for analysis', in M.N. Zald (ed.), *Power in Organizations*, Nashville: Vanderbilt University Press, pp. 221–61.

12. The historical roots of socio network theory in entrepreneurship research

Sarah Jack and Mary Rose

INTRODUCTION

The field of entrepreneurship has seen a dramatic increase in studies focusing on networks and social relations. This is particularly evident amongst European scholars where network research has emerged as a popular theme since the turn of the century (Uhlaner, 2002). Such interest can partly be attributed to scholars moving away from dealing with the entrepreneur in isolation and instead looking to the consequences of embeddedness and the impact, implications and relevance of networks for entrepreneurship (Hoang and Antoncic, 2003). This line of enquiry has possibly come about as a reaction against the view that the entrepreneur is an atomistic, isolated economic actor, undersocialised and immersed in a process quite different from other social phenomena (Araujo and Easton, 1996; Hoang and Antoncic, 2003). Instead, current thinking seems to be that social relations and the social context cannot only influence entrepreneurship but, because economic action is embedded, social networks can impact economic performance and, consequently, the shape and form of entrepreneurial outcomes (Granovetter, 1992; Ring and Van de Ven, 1992; Snow et al., 1992; Jones, Hesterly and Borgatti, 1997; Arrow, 2000; Jack and Anderson, 2002). It has even been said that within the entrepreneurial context, entrepreneurs are actually a product of their social environment, and how they perceive opportunities is influenced by social interaction and social background (Anderson and Miller, 2002). Some have gone so far as to argue that entrepreneurship is actually a social undertaking which is carried out in – and so should be understood within the context of – social systems (Sarason et al., 2006). This not only raises the importance of social context but also highlights the significance of social relations.

As the view that the entrepreneur is intimately tied through the social relations in which s/he is embedded to a broader network of actors has gained popularity, so has network research (Hoang and Antoncic, 2003; Kim and Aldrich, 2005). Recent reviews demonstrate growth in published articles over time in key academic journals. For example, between 1995 and 2005, 71 articles appeared in key academic journals. Yet, throughout this time there seems to be continued interest in a number of core themes, with embeddedness, evolution, growth and performance, opportunity perception and recognition, ties and social capital remaining very much in vogue (Jack, 2010). This growth in interest demonstrates that networks are becoming more widely acknowledged as one way to explain entrepreneurial success (Elfring and Hulsink, 2003).

Social network theory has been used to demonstrate the nature and effect of the interaction and exchange that takes place between individuals (Harland, 1995; Maguire,

1983). It perceives individuals as being related to each other by sets of transactions which have implications for the actors wider than the exchange itself (Mitchell, 1973). A social network has been defined as 'the actual set of links of all kinds amongst a set of individuals' (Mitchell, 1973) and 'sets of ties linking several actors' (Nelson, 1988, p. 40). The general understanding is that links such as friends of friends (Boissevain, 1974), group obligations (Bourdieu, 1986) and strong and weak ties (Granovetter, 1973) provide those who are party to a particular network with privileged information and access to opportunities, and enable individuals to obtain resources that might be difficult to access otherwise (Jack, 2005). Accordingly, a network perspective illustrates that people are dependent on others and that the individual is an interacting social being able to manipulate others and be manipulated by others (Boissevain, 1973). According to Banck (1973) there are also three notions about a social network that are perceived to be important: (1) an individual has social relations with other individuals, who in turn have social relations with others, either directly or indirectly, (2) an individual is entangled in a network of social relations, the structure of which influences the behaviour of the individual and (3) the individual is supposed to be able to manipulate to a certain measure the social network for his/her own ends (Banck, 1973).

The purpose of this chapter is to demonstrate the historical and intellectual roots of social network theory within entrepreneurship research. In doing so, this chapter highlights the theoretical origins of the entrepreneurial network perspective. We begin by exploring the origins of social network theory. The discussion then demonstrates how the term and key concepts have been applied within entrepreneurship research and used to try and understand the entrepreneur and process in which s/he is immersed. Thereafter we examine the way in which interdisciplinary approaches linked to history enhance our understanding of the networked innovating entrepreneur. Following on from this we explore the ways in which networks may act as a constraint to entrepreneurship. Finally, we consider potential future directions for research. By combining the discussion of social network theory, entrepreneurship, innovation and history, this chapter explores how such combinations enrich our understanding of entrepreneurship and entrepreneurial processes. This approach also helps support a concern raised in the literature that there is a need to view networks using spatial and temporal perspectives (Schutjens and Stam, 2003). We would argue that this can be achieved by drawing on history and historically based theories and turning to historians to help us with this task. This seems to make sense considering 'historians have always assumed that to understand and interpret personal relations was their main business' (Cooley, 1956, p. 122).

THEORETICAL ORIGINS

It is difficult to identify when the term 'social network' was first adopted. The social network approach seems to have emerged from dissatisfaction with a strictly structural approach, offering a deeper understanding of human behaviour (Boissevain and Mitchell, 1973). Historically the term 'a network of social relations' 'was used to represent a complex set of inter-relationships in a social system' but prior to the 1950s it tended to be used as a metaphorical way of looking at things rather than as an analytical concept (Mitchell, 1969, p. 1). Early writings suggest that network theory was seen as key

Table 12.1   Historical foundations of socio perspectives in entrepreneurship network research (adapted from Tichy et al., 1979)

School of thought	Perspective	Key theorist(s)	Key emphasis/focus
Sociology	Process outlook	Park (1924) Cooley (1956) Simmel (1950)	Patterns of interaction and communication as being key to understanding social life
	Functionalism	Parsons (1960) Mitchell (1969)	The need to focus on underlying determinants of recurring social relations
Anthropology	Exchange theories	Levi-Strauss (1969) Malinowski (1922) Frazer (1919) Homans (1961) Blau (1964) Ekeh (1974)	The content of the relationships joining individuals, the conditions under which they would exist and the evolution of such bonds
Social psychology	Role theory – organizations are 'fish nets' of interrelated offices	Katz and Kahn (1966) Kadushin (1968) Gross, Mason and McEachern (1958)	Implies network concepts but has been limited to first order role sets (i.e. individuals directly linked to the focal person) and evidences an individual bias

to bridging sociological analysis of human behaviour and personal/motivational aspects (Noble, 1973). Studies defined networks as 'the set of persons who can get in touch with each other' and contacts as 'the individuals who comprise a network' (Katz, 1966, p. 203). However, others have said it is better to think of a network as 'the set of linkages among persons and contacts as the set of persons connected by these linkages' (Mitchell, 1969, p. 4).

Theoretical origins of network research can be traced to three broad schools of thought: sociology, anthropology and social psychology, especially role theory (Tichy et al., 1979; Nohria and Eccles, 1992). These are represented in Table 12.1 which draws on Tichy et al.'s (1979) work to demonstrate historical foundations of socio perspectives of network research. In Table 12.1 some of the key theorists who, according to Tichy et al. (1979), are considered to have laid the foundations on which network research was built are presented along with their perspectives.

What is interesting about the material presented in Table 12.1 is the key role that anthropology and sociology have played in developing thinking about networks. From sociology and anthropology perspectives, we really begin to be introduced to the aspects of interaction, communication, social relations and the 'bonding' of individuals. However, what stands out from Table 12.1 are elements which are really seen to be quite significant within social network theory but which have been driven by sociology. These elements are (1) exchange and the actual nature of exchange and (2) the need to take a process outlook and consider patterns in behaviour, and this is perhaps why sociological perspectives have really dominated social network research (see also Parkhe et al., 2006). In terms of social psychology and role theory much of the work within this area seems to have considered the relationship between the individual and his/her role in the organization (Katz and Khan, 1966). For instance, Katz and Khan (1966) argue that organizations consist of patterned behaviour, and if members are perceived to misunderstand the boundary of the organization or misbehave, they are seen to be threatening the life of the organization. Such work has helped us to understand the types of roles individuals take on, group norms and conformity. However, this perspective has perhaps been less influential in entrepreneurship, possibly due to the nature of entrepreneurship and entrepreneurial networks, because aspects of social psychology and role theory take more of a group view rather than an individual one. And, 'networks have to do with (social) individuals, rather than with groups' (Banck, 1973). Also, role theory discussions have much more of an intra- rather than inter-firm perspective and thus could be argued to be less applicable for entrepreneurship research. As a consequence, the use of social psychology and role theory will not be elaborated on further here.

A More Sociological Perspective on Social Networks

In tracing the routes of network theory we are introduced to the ideas of the sociologist Park (1924; 1926). According to Park, society exists through communication and, by communicating with other individuals, experiences are shared and life is maintained. Park's (1926) ideas were based on the concept of social distance:

> The individual who is not concerned about his status in some society is a hermit, even when his seclusion is a city crowd. The individual whose conception of himself is not at all determined by the conceptions that other persons have of him is probably insane . . . A person is simply an individual who has somewhere, in some society, social status; but status turns out finally to be a matter of distance – social distance. (p. 10)

In developing his point Park (1926) goes on to argue that in all our personal relationships we are clearly conscious of the degree of intimacy with others. Park (1926) pointed out that while it is the relations that individuals have with and to others that are important, social interaction is an aspect of social phenomena that comes about as a result of changing attitude, the social experiences of the individual and the inhibiting effect of self-consciousness. Moreover, Park (1926) described social relations as far from homogeneous and subject to change.

This notion of interaction runs through much of the early writings regarded as being core to the foundations of social network theory. Simmel (1950), for instance, when writing about society, talks about interaction and how society is the name for a number of individuals connected by interaction. Simmel (1950) continues by saying that interactions produce society and that it is through linking together and coming together that people are tied to others. Thus, it is not purely interaction which is important but the ties which people have to others and how these ties might impact on individuals, affect and influence the way they live their lives. Cooley (1956) introduces us more directly to the idea of individuals contributing to social life and that it is the process of how they choose and the choices that they make in terms of interaction which are interesting aspects. Cooley (1956) also discusses how in order to have society it is necessary that people get together somewhere, but any study of society must be supported by a good understanding of personal ideas. So, while these early writings introduce us to the idea of the social element in people's lives, they do not lose sight of the individual. Instead they perceive the individual as a social animal immersed in a social process.

These themes of interaction and process are continued in later writings. However, here we are also introduced to the recurring nature of social relations and their practical application. The 1950s saw quite a dramatic increase in the number of studies looking at links, exchange and reciprocity in terms of social behaviour and more use of the actual term social network itself. Initial work using the notion of social networks tended to concentrate on the nature of links among people as this was perceived as the most significant feature (Barnes refers to this as 'mesh' and Bott as 'connectedness') (Mitchell, 1969). Early studies include Barnes (1954), who drew on Fortes's (1949) notion of 'the Web of Kinship' to develop the idea of using a social network to describe and consider social behaviour of individuals and their behaviour with others with whom he/she may not necessarily be in touch with directly. Barnes (1954) is certainly one of the first to use the term 'social network' in a more systematic way (Noble, 1973). However, Bott (1955; 1956; 1957) is considered one of the first to actually apply the term 'social network' in a more analytical way (Noble, 1973). Bott's (1955; 1956; 1957) work on conjugal roles and the patterns of relationships in London families began to develop the idea of close knit/ loose knit networks more extensively. Mayer (1961; 1962; 1964) and Pauw (1963) used the idea of a social network to consider the behaviour of types of migrants in London and concentrated specifically on a point drawn out in Bott's work that 'the behaviour of people who are members of a "close knit" group of friends is likely to be considerably influenced by the wishes and expectations of these friends as a whole, while those whose acquaintances do not know one another may behave inconsistently from time to time without involving themselves in embarrassment' (Mitchell, 1969).

Epstein (1961) was probably one of the first to begin to question variation in different parts of a network and relate this more specifically to interaction (Noble, 1973). T. Parsons (1960) refers to the relevance of the interaction processes and the significance of the structures of relationships among actors, the recurring nature of these relations and the systems of norms and expectations that exist within and between relations but also in society as a whole. These aspects are also evident from other studies written around the area. So, for example, Bott's (1955; 1957) work on families and kinship, Granovetter's (1973) work on strong and weak ties and the labor market, and Padgett and Ansell's (1993) work on political parties and elite networks would all claim to be concerned with what actually takes place in people's lives, the relations in which individuals are embedded and how relations might impact on behaviour. Moreover, such studies do not lose sight of the individual but also take the perspective that s/he is immersed in social relations that can have an impact.

A More Anthropological Perspective on Social Networks

The theory of social exchange originated in social anthropology with scholars such as Frazer (1919), Malinowski (1922), Levi-Strauss (1969) and Bohannan (1955) (Ekeh,

1974). Certain unit ideas of social exchange theory are evident throughout sociological writings and really demonstrate the significance of exchange (Ekeh, 1974). Although they might receive varying emphasis and approval or disapproval from social exchange theorists, the following seem to be regarded as being central to social exchange theory: (1) the relationship between economic exchange and social exchange; (2) the structure of reciprocity; (3) restricted exchange and generalized exchange; (4) exploitation and power; and (5) the contribution of social exchange processes to social solidarity (Ekeh, 1974).

Examples of scholarly writing about social exchange theory include Homans (1961) and Levi-Strauss (1969). For example, Homans (1961) talks about interaction and social contacts and describes social behaviour as representing an 'exchange of activity, tangible or intangible, and more or less rewarding or costly, between at least two persons' (p. 13). Homans (1961) also describes how one individual might change (even influence) the behaviour of others. Central to Levi-Strauss's (1969) theory of social exchange is the idea and principle of reciprocity, a social usage consisting of what he refers to as univocal or directional reciprocity. Blau (1964) argues that social exchange is an underlying factor in relations between individuals and groups. He argues that the basic idea of social exchange is based on reciprocity and social reward so the mutual exchange that occurs over time creates a social bond between individuals. Blau (1964) also argues that individuals associate with one another because they can profit from the other and through being associated with the other. Certainly aspects of exchange and reciprocity really lie at the very heart of social network theory. Malinowski's (1922) ethnographical account of life as a native in the South Sea Islands demonstrates the nature of exchange, sociological relations, especially family and group members, and the mechanisms used for exchange between individuals. This work also shows that ties exist between individuals and demonstrates the importance of give and take to the social fabric of a society.

Conclusions from Early Studies on Social Networks

What is clear from this fairly brief historical review is that early work within both sociology and anthropology identified elements which appear to be relevant to network theory. Specifically, the human being is a social being embedded within a social context, a being that is immersed in a network of relationships with whom reciprocal exchange is expected and anticipated to take place. Moreover, these relationships can be manipulated by all parties involved so that if and when made manifest, they can impact on the individuals involved in many different ways and with varying consequences.

SOCIAL NETWORK THEORY AND ENTREPRENEURSHIP

It is on these foundations that entrepreneurial social network theory has and is being built. In doing so, entrepreneurship scholars have drawn on and built upon many of the concepts presented and associated with these foundations of social network theory. Within entrepreneurship, the social network perspective can really be regarded as the primary focus of the majority of research. It is also the most prolific in terms of the development of data analysis tools and their application to a range of social science topics (Araujo and Easton, 1996). The definitions of a network presented earlier in the introductory section emphasize the notion of actors and links between actors. Within the field of entrepreneurship, the personal network perspective is based on the principle that entrepreneurship is a social role (Brüderl and Preisendörfer, 1998, p.214) and that the relationship between the entrepreneur and the social context is perceived to be important. According to Aldrich et al. (1987), the social network perspective rests on two fundamental premises. Firstly, entrepreneurs succeed because they are able to identify opportunities and obtain scarce resources (e.g. money, social support, product ideas, markets, and information) from their environments to start and build businesses. Secondly, resources are obtained through exchange relationships between the entrepreneur and his/her social networks (e.g. relatives' loan money; husbands or wives grant permission to use family resources; colleagues or business contacts become partners or customers; and acquaintances give advice about lawyers, accountants and bankers). This being the case, it would seem fairly certain that an entrepreneur's networks are likely to be based on experience, which not only determines the range of contacts, but may also influence perceptions of opportunities and courses of action (Birley, 1985; Aldrich and Zimmer, 1986; Dubini and Aldrich, 1991; Johannison 1998; Chell and Baines, 2000; Johannison et al., 2002; Lechner and Dowling, 2003).

Networks are important because entrepreneurship can be facilitated or constrained by an entrepreneur's position in a social network (Aldrich and Zimmer, 1986). Studies carried out have demonstrated the importance of building relationships for entrepreneurship (Johannisson and Peterson, 1984; Birley, 1985; Aldrich and Zimmer, 1986; Carsrud and Johnson, 1989; Johannisson et al., 1994; Bloodgood et al., 1995). However, what is especially interesting about networks and entrepreneurship is that although entrepreneurs are generally associated with independence and innovation, entrepreneurship seems to emerge at the junctions of social and professional information networks that supply entrepreneurs with ideas, exchange opportunities and access to valued resources (Araujo and Easton, 1996). According to Johannisson (2000, p.368), whilst management needs structure, entrepreneurship thrives on process, ambiguity and action. This leads entrepreneurs to continuously network as they pursue and react to new realities. So, although some might perceive entrepreneurship as being an individual role, it is actually a social undertaking with individuals being immersed in a social process. According to MacMillan (1983), building contacts and networks is a critical factor in determining the success of a firm. Moreover, it is now recognized that 'organizations are strongly embedded in environments and environmental influences penetrate organizations in many ways' (Aldrich, 1999, p.5).

Networks represent the 'collaborative' relationships formed by individuals within firms, with other firms and with other organizations. Networking itself involves a social process which takes place over time involving identifying common interests, gaining knowledge and experience of other individuals, and building trust, a crucial element of networks (Jack, 2005). The actual activity of networking has been described as a 'system by which entrepreneurs can tap resources that are external to them, i.e. that they do not control' (Jarillo, 1989, p.133). As a consequence, 'entrepreneurs can, in theory, take advantage of the wider social network in which their ties are embedded' (Kim and Aldrich, 2005, p.2). Networks involve links with and to the social structure with such links providing information, creating opportunities and enabling resource access (Uzzi, 1997; Premaratne, 2001; Florin et al., 2003; Hite, 2005). Moreover, links to the social structure and the level/extent to which an individual is embedded can influence, affect and impact on the shape and form of economic outcomes (Uzzi, 1997; Chell and Baines, 2000; McDade and Spring, 2005). Given the emphasis placed on networks, it is not too surprising that we are seeing an increasing number of studies focusing on networks and entrepreneurship.

As highlighted previously, the number of studies focusing on networks and relations in and between individuals has increased dramatically (Hoang and Antoncic, 2003; Parkhe et al., 2006). The actual extent of the popularity of network research is evident from a review of key academic journals between 1995 and 2005 which illustrates that a total of 71 articles relating to a range of themes and aspects and using a variety of contexts were published (Jack, 2010).[1] These studies all claim to be focused on understanding entrepreneurial networks at some level and in some way. And while all might not claim to be using social network theory specifically, by dealing with entrepreneurship and an aspect of networks they are all contributing to our understanding of the whole in some way.

Table 12.2 shows clearly the popularity of network research within entrepreneurship. It also elaborates on the themes that have been studied and the key findings from the various work carried out. What is interesting is the breadth and number of themes that have been considered. However, key themes seem to have been returned to often during the period considered, especially embeddedness, evolution, growth and performance, opportunity perception and recognition, particular ties and social capital. Another interesting point raised from Table 12.2 is that within each theme identified there does not always appear to be agreement in relation to networks. Take, for instance, the strong and weak tie debate as an area where contradictory evidence has emerged.

What studies have shown is that networks not only influence individuals but can also impact significantly on the ways in which organizations are managed, developed, maintained and sustained (Halinen et al., 1999; Ahuja, 2000; Nelson, 2001; Karamanos, 2003). Some claim that networks are even 'reshaping the global business architecture' (Parkhe et al., 2006, p. 560). Assuming this is the case, then understanding networks has important theoretical and practical consequences, particularly in grasping how entrepreneurs and their organizations operate and function (Jack, 2010). What is also clear from Table 12.2 is that while there is a wide body of literature forming and consensus about the significance of networks for entrepreneurship, much less is known about why they may go wrong and what the consequences might be, how they may change in configuration and capability through time, and the differences in networking behaviour among different categories of entrepreneurs in different cultures (Anderson et al., 2009).

Table 12.2 also shows that network research can involve the study of a wide range of features and aspects such as size, structure, interactional processes, influences, behaviours and skills (Coviello, 2005, p. 39). While this breadth might be seen to be problematic by some, it is what also makes network research so interesting.

A criticism of extant work is that rather than focusing on process related issues, as earlier sociological work did, studies have tended to be more concerned with looking at structural aspects of networks, particular elements related to structure and outcomes such as network ties. Although network research has been criticised for this, process related issues have started to become more popular (Jack, 2010; Slotte-Kock and Coviello, 2010) since Hoang and Antoncic's (2003) critique of the network literature and 'cry' for more process work. However, to date structural aspects of entrepreneurial networks have received more attention than processual issues (O'Donnell et al., 2001; Hoang

Table 12.2   Themes and findings of network research 1995–2005 (adapted from Jack, 2010)

Themes	Author(s)	Key finding
Embeddedness	Uzzi (1997)	Explains link between social structure and economic performance
	Johannisson et al. (2002)	Shows supplementarity of layers/orders of embeddedness
	Jack and Anderson (2002)	Key role in shaping, and sustaining environment, creates opportunities, and improves performance
	Uzzi and Gillespie (2002)	Social embeddedness affects financial performance of firm
Evolution	Hansen (1995)	Social resources active ingredient in entrepreneurial networking
	Johannisson (1998)	Knowledge-based entrepreneurs more concerned with networking than traditional entrepreneurs, both include social ties
	Minguzzi and Passaro (2001)	Influenced by relationships established with economic environment
	Schutjens and Stam (2003)	Need for young firm networks to be seen in spatial and temporal context
	Greve and Salaff (2003)	Entrepreneurs build networks that vary by phase of entrepreneurship
	Hite (2005)	Emerging firms tap into external network to discover opportunities and mobilize necessary resources
Gender	Lerner et al. (1997)	Network affiliations (particularly single) important for female entrepreneurs in Israel
	Katz and Williams (1997)	Weak tie network efforts are less than those of managers, female entrepreneurs engage in weak-tie networking less than salaried male managers
Growth and performance	Donckels and Lambrecht (1995)	Need to invest in network formation for growth
	Donckels and Lambrecht (1997)	Importance of forming networks for small business growth
	Lee and Tsang (2001)	Entrepreneurs industrial and management experience affects growth
	Havnes and Senneseth (2001)	Networking sustains long-term objectives of firms
	Lee et al. (2001)	External links to VCs predict start-up performance
	Rodan and Galunic (2004)	Importance of access to heterogeneous knowledge
	Peng (2004)	Strength of kinship networks important for workforce size of rural enterprises
	McDade and Spring (2005)	Able to develop networks that strengthen economic growth in Africa

Table 12.2   (continued)

Themes	Author(s)	Key finding
Human and social capital	Dakhli and De Clercq (2004)	Positive for human capital and innovation but partial for trust and associational activity
Interfirm/alliances	Franke (1999)	Proposes adaptation of net-broker concept to manage virtual web and overcome implications of evolution
	Huggins (2000)	Formal groups potent but initially facilitated through informal network
	Soh (2003)	Performance improves as becomes more central in technology collaboration network
Internationalization	Keeble et al. (1998)	Internationalization embedded in successful local networking, research and technology collaboration
National differences	Drakopolou Dodd and Patra (2002)	National differences in networking exist
Network incubator	Bøllingtoft and Ulhøi (2005)	Mechanisms facilitating or hindering networking in incubators can be divided into two categories
	Clarysse et al. (2005)	Three distinct incubation models relating to network contacts
Opportunity perception/ recognition	Krackhardt (1995)	Predictions about networking conditional on larger structure in which ties are embedded
	Arenius and De Clercq (2005)	Residential area influences perception of entrepreneurial opportunities
Particular ties/ characteristics	Özcan (1995)	Networks strengthen the innovative flexibility and competitiveness of small firms
	Brüderl and Preisendörfer (1998)	Support from strong ties more important than weak ties
	Chell and Baines (2000)	Different ties useful for different purposes, association between networking and business performance
	Elfring and Hulsink (2003)	Strong ties secure crucial information
	Grandi and Grimaldi (2003)	Need to look at team composition when deciding to invest/support new venture
	Kingsley and Malecki (2004)	Geographically and socially mixed, used to gather information
	Julien et al. (2004)	Importance of weak tie networks
	Jack (2005)	Importance of strong tie networks
Raising finance/ venture capital/ BANs	Fiet (1995)	VCs consult formal network more than BANs who distinguish between informants
	Mason and Harrison (1997)	Majority investments via not-for-profit networks, private sector used for different type

Table 12.2   (continued)

Themes	Author(s)	Key finding
	Steier and Greenwood (2000)	Development of supportive network helps survival
	Shane and Cable (2002)	Mechanism for information for investors
	Florin, Lubatkin and Schuze (2003)	Social resources leverage productivity of ventures resource base
	Baron and Markman (2003)	Need to look at particular aspects of social behaviour to understand entrepreneurial success
Resources	Premaratne (2001)	In Sri Lanka entrepreneurial networks provide important resources
Relationship with environment	Yli-Renko and Autio (1998)	Need for systematic research approach for new technology firms
	Littunen (2000)	Need to match growth ambitions with entrepreneurial resources
	Kodithuwakku and Rosa (2002)	Importance of social networks for resource mobilization
Spinouts/spinoffs	Nicolaou and Birley (2003)	Strong non-redundant ties in instrumental networks and strong supportive ties in expressive relationships are important antecedents of entrepreneurial behaviour
Social capital	Cooke and Wills (1999)	Social capital building associated with enhanced business, knowledge and innovation performance
	Batjargal and Liu (2004)	Social capital and strong ties affect investment process
	Yli-Renko et al. (2001)	Knowledge acquisition plays mediating role between social capital and knowledge exploitation
	Shane and Stuart (2002)	Founder's social capital represents important endowment for early stage organizations
	Anderson and Jack (2002)	Social capital is a process with structural and relational aspects
	Liao and Welsch (2005)	No significant differences in various dimensions of social capital between nascent entrepreneurs and general public. Patterns of association differentiate, not amount of social capital
	Davidsson and Honig (2003)	Bridging and bonding social capital (strong and weak ties) predictor for nascent entrepreneurs
Social interaction	Lechler (2001)	Social interaction important in teams but not only success factor
Structure and outcomes	Human and Provan (1997)	Involvement in manufacturing network advantageous, has transactional and transformational outcomes

and Antoncic, 2003; Jack, 2010; Slotte-Kock and Coviello, 2010). As a consequence, we realize and recognize structural features associated with the constitution of networks. We know networks (1) are formed on the basis of relationships that tie relational homogeneity, diversity, density, (2) that the extent to which individuals within a network know each other are relevant issues (3) that ties vary in terms of strength, and (4) that there are different measures of centrality and reachability (see Kim and Aldrich, 2005). We also know that networks enable individuals to access resources and social support (Renzulli and Aldrich, 2005). However, we know much less about the downside of networks.

CONCEPTUAL ROOTS OF SOCIAL NETWORKS

In tracing the roots of social network research there are some concepts which have been used and applied to the study of entrepreneurial networks. In the following section, we highlight a selection to illustrate how current understanding has been shaped.

Strength of Weak Ties

Most network studies looking at ties are characterized by the use and application of Granovetter's strong and weak tie hypothesis (for examples, see Aldrich et al., 1987; Hills et al., 1997). Granovetter (1973), and subsequently Burt (1992a; 1992b), argued that a network should consist of both strong and weak ties because the nature of these ties influences the operation and structure of networks (Jack, 2005). Weak ties represent heterogeneous ties and are perceived to be a critical element of social structure, enabling information to flow into other social clusters and the broader society (Burt, 1992a), and, in turn, creating the possibility of connections to other social systems (Ibarra, 1993). Contrastingly, strong ties are perceived as less beneficial than weak ties: they are likely to provide redundant information because they can be anticipated to move in similar, if not the same, social circles (Granovetter, 1985; Burt, 1992b). Thus, the homogeneity of strong ties is thought to be less effective, breeding local cohesion but also leading to overall fragmentation (Granovetter, 1973; Ibarra, 1993; Maguire, 1983). However, cumulating evidence that emphasizes the importance of weak ties has fuelled the debate on the relative value of strong versus weak ties (Hoang and Antoncic, 2003; Jack, 2005). So, whilst the strong and weak tie hypothesis has become an established paradigm, questions arise over its applicability, particularly within the context of entrepreneurship (Brüderl and Preisendörfer, 1998; Elfring and Hulsink, 2003; Jack, 2005). Network ties, particularly for emerging firms, provide the 'conduits, bridges and pathways' to opportunities and resources but the characteristics of these ties influence how they are 'identified, accessed, mobilized and exploited' (Hite, 2005, p. 113). So, the ties that form a network can have a significant impact on the type and extent of resources acquired (Jack, 2005).

Embeddedness

Granovetter (1985) also argued that actors are embedded in concrete, ongoing systems of social relations and that behaviour is so constrained by ongoing social relations that to construe them as independent is a misunderstanding. According to Uzzi (1997, p. 35), research into embeddedness can help to advance understanding of how social structure affects economic life. He referred to embeddedness as 'a puzzle that, once understood, can furnish tools for explicating not only organizational puzzles but market processes' (Uzzi, 1997, p. 64). As Carsrud and Johnson (1989) note, the new business development process is strongly affected by social contacts or linkages, which in fact form the patterns of social interaction. Burt (1992a) describes this as bridging 'structural holes'. Social embeddedness is relevant to entrepreneurship because it helps the entrepreneur identify social resources, an essential step to founding organizations (Hansen, 1995). Furthermore, being embedded within the social context means access to more support during the entrepreneurial process but also a likelihood of increased entrepreneurial activity (Schell and Davig, 1981).

Embeddedness, however, can also act as a constraint. Whittington (1992, p. 697) pointed out that agency is constrained by an environment that is made up of socio-economic features. Uzzi (1997, p. 57) identified conditions when embeddedness can be turned into a liability, for example: the unforeseeable exit of a core network player; institutional forces rationalizing markets; even over-embeddedness. Embeddedness can also influence the way in which value is and can be extracted – affecting resource availability, opportunity perception and shaping the entrepreneurial event. Steier and Greenwood (1995, p. 349) provided an account of the problems encountered when venture capitalists withdraw funding from an enterprise: 'the entrepreneurs had become their friends'. Anderson and Jack (2000) illustrated that the social stigma attached to failure in small, close communities where everybody knows each other, can have tragic consequences. Even Schumpeter (1934, p. 87) provided an account of how those within the social context can react against someone who wishes to do something new by condemning it, simply because it is an unfamiliar procedure:

> Even a deviation from social custom in such things as dress or manners arouses opposition . . . this opposition is stronger in primitive stages of culture than others, but is never absent. Even mere astonishment at the deviation, even merely noticing it, exercises a pressure on the individual. The manifestation of condemnation may at once bring noticeable consequences in its train. It may even come to social ostracism and finally to physical prevention or to direct attack. (Schumpeter, 1934, p. 87)

So, the fear of social exclusion could prevent any individual activity which would not be acceptable to the group (Schumpeter, 1934). Similarly, Johannisson (1990) argued that individual entrepreneurs take both economic and social risks which may lead to social exclusion while Anderson and Jack (2000) illustrated that social embeddedness can also have negative effects because of group expectations.

Structural Holes

Burt's (1992a, p. 28) structural holes thesis deals with the hole, or gap, which is spanned between non-redundant contacts; 'whether a relationship is strong or weak it generates information benefits when it is a bridge over a structural hole'. Network contacts are redundant if they lead to the same people and hence provide the same information benefits, i.e. each person knows what the other people know (Burt, 1992a; 1992b). Therefore, it is the number of non-redundant contacts that becomes important. Non-redundant contacts are disconnected in some way – 'either directly in the sense of no direct contact or indirectly in the sense of one having contacts that exclude others' (Burt, 1992b, p. 65). Burt (1992a) demonstrated this by explaining that two contacts are redundant to the extent that they are connected by a strong relationship, for instance father and son, which provides easy access but leads to the same information. Where contacts have no direct ties with one another, they are non-redundant because each can lead to different information and resources. Therefore, the structural holes argument is linked to the strength of ties and homogeneity. Burt's (1992a; 1992b) thesis deals with the hole spanned between non-redundant contacts since it is this (structural) hole which he argues is important in generating information benefits.

Although in Burt's (1992a; 1992b) view it is the space between the links (in a network) which is effective and important, the real value of the structural holes argument is in helping to understand the size of the hole and what is actually going on within that hole, particularly if a network is visualized as a grid of mutuality, where people with some commonality are brought together for a variety of reasons. Where contacts have no direct ties with one another, they are non-redundant because each can lead to different information and resources. Accordingly, network positions associated with the highest economic return lie, between, not within, dense regions of relationships, i.e. structural holes (Walker et al., 1997). In the context of entrepreneurship this is relevant because it infers that structural holes may present opportunities for brokering information flows among firms and, consequently, this offers the possibility of greater economic payoffs as potentials are created (Walker et al., 1997).

Social Capital

In the literature of political science, sociology and anthropology, the idea of social capital has been used to refer to the set of norms, networks and organizations through which people gain access to power and resources that are instrumental in enabling decision-making and policy formulation (Serageldin and Grootaert, 2000, p. 45). Social capital is partly the social glue that produces cohesion; it may be thought of as a collection of networks, i.e. the 'social group' into which one is socialized or aspires to be socialized; it is an aggregation of reputations and a way to sort out reputations; and it includes the organizational capital that managers develop through their management style (Stiglitz, 2000, p. 60). Relations within and beyond the firm have also been referred to as social capital (Burt, 1992b, p. 58). It is a feature of social networks that facilitates coordination and cooperation for mutual benefit (Flora, 1998, p. 488), so it can also be viewed as sets of resources embedded in relationships (Burt, 1992a; 1992b). Social capital includes many aspects of the social context which involve social interaction, such as social ties, trusting relationships and value systems which facilitate the actions of individuals located in a particular social context (Nahapiet and Ghoshal, 1998; Tsai and Ghoshal, 1998). According to Anderson et al. (2007) social capital can be considered a productive asset, making possible certain ends which, in the absence of social capital, would not be possible, or would be more difficult (Coleman, 2000).

An actor's embeddedness in social structures endows them with social capital (Portes and Sensenbrenner, 1993; Oinas, 1999). Hence social capital is created within the embedding process; an end (a product of networks) as well as a means (of enabling) (Anderson and Jack, 2002; Jack and Anderson, 2002). According to Walker et al. (1997), in the entrepreneurial context firms with less social capital are more vulnerable to opportunistic behaviour, are less able to build an enduring history of effective cooperative behaviour with partners over time, and have to spend more time and effort monitoring the relationship. In contrast, the more social capital available to a firm, the fewer resources it needs to manage existing relationships and the more resources it can use to establish new ones (Walker et al., 1997).

NEW COMBINATIONS

The above discussion has demonstrated the extent to which the study of entrepreneurial networks has been enriched by the application of theories based on sociology and social anthropology. In this section, we broaden the discussion about the disciplinary roots and demonstrate how links to history enhance our knowledge. Taking the discussion forward in this way is interesting because it helps broaden understanding about the networked innovating entrepreneur.

If interdisciplinarity is a crucial feature of the study of networks, academic boundaries still remain surprisingly acute even in closely related areas:

> Given the inherent interrelatedness of entrepreneurship, innovation and creativity, one would expect there to have been a natural conscious blending of research interests, results, methodologies and diverse applications; yet each field is neatly compartmentalised with little cross pollination. For example, creativity is rooted firmly in psychology and innovation has primarily been examined in fields of technology and engineering. (Brazeal and Herbert, 1999)

This view was echoed in a Harvard Business School interview with Geoffrey Jones, co-editor of *The Oxford Handbook of Business History* (2008). He observed that despite having much to offer the study of entrepreneurship and management, business history has developed in a separate silo, which has 'resulted in the spread of influential theories based on ill-informed understandings of the past' (Silverthorne, 2008). In this context, Schumpeter's (1947) emphasis on the potential for co-evolution of knowledge by economists and economic historians is especially apposite. The creative impact of 'new combinations' on the economic system is equally applicable to academic research, where innovation takes place at the boundaries of disciplines drawing together complementary approaches. In this section we explore both the origins and evolution of theories informed by history and show how they can be combined to develop understanding of the relationship between entrepreneurship, networks and innovation.

Schumpeter, Entrepreneurship, History and Path Dependency

This chapter has already traced the development of sociologically based theories on entrepreneurship. Understanding the relationship between innovation, entrepreneurship, history and networks adds a dimension generally lacking from studies based on social theory, and involves examining both macro and micro perspectives. It inevitably takes us back to Joseph Schumpeter, for whom innovation and entrepreneurship were the dynamic engines of change at the heart of capitalist growth and were inseparable from historical context (Schumpeter, 1934; 1947). Some recent research has integrated historical methodology with analysis of the innovative enterprise (O'Sullivan, 2000; Lazonick, 2003). Lazonick observed that the 'innovative process is cumulative because the possibilities for transforming technological and market conditions today and tomorrow depend on the development of those conditions in the past' (2003, p. 35).

Scholars have challenged the role of Schumpeter's 'hero entrepreneur' at the heart of economic development (Cassis and Minoglou, 2005, p. 10). However, embedding the entrepreneur within a shifting set of networks, implied by Schumpeter's 'new combinations,' provides a dynamic landscape for understanding the innovative entrepreneur and the impact which he or she may have on economies, on regions and on firms. History then is not just about the past. It can be used to understand the present and the future. The links between past and future and the cumulative nature of innovation, are the result of the social learning processes associated with it (Lazonick, 2003).

Path Dependency

Historical analysis and several theories underpinned by history, including path dependency and communities of practice, help us make sense of networking behaviour by entrepreneurs. Path dependency, or the influence of past events and knowledge on the future, was originated by the economist Paul David, who was one of the pioneers of the 'new economic history' combining economics, cliometrics and history to make sense of the economic growth process (David, 1975). His interest in path dependency grew out of this work, and he argued that the solution of comparatively small problems in the past provides the foundation for the choices of the future. The long term impact of 'learning by doing' on human behaviour potentially leads to 'lock in', as in the case of the QWERTY keyboard, which was originally developed for mechanical typewriters to reduce jamming of keys. Its survival through the transition first to electric typewriters and then to the personal computer reflects the way habit and familiarity increase the costs of change (David, 1985). He likened the impact of path dependency to the 'deepening of wheel ruts by each successive vehicle' (David, 1997, p. 123). The idea lies at the heart of evolutionary theories of economic change (Nelson and Winter, 1982) and underpins innovation theories on the emergence of dominant design (Utterback, 1996).

Path dependency has been largely overlooked by scholars of entrepreneurship, (Jones and Wadhwani, 2005). At first glance the 'locking in' of behaviours and activities seems the very antithesis of entrepreneurship, innovation and change. But, if we are to move from generic theories of entrepreneurship to those which explain regional and international differences in behaviour, it is vital to appreciate the forces shaping choices. The application of institutional and evolutionary theories – which themselves draw on both Schumpeter and path dependency theory – help to explain such differences (Nelson and Winter, 1982; North, 1990). 'Institutions are the rules of the game in a society or, more formally, are the humanly-devised constraints that shape human interaction' (North, 1990). They may be either the formal laws created by governments or the informal codes of practice and of behaviour found in organizations, communities, regions or countries. They help to create order and form the basis for cooperation in an uncertain world. For example, formal laws and regulations are the basis of property rights, whilst informal codes underpin trust and shape expectations of the likely behaviour of associates.

The idea that 'institutions matter' and that understanding the rules of the game is crucial to an appreciation of economic behaviour underpins the 'new institutional theory' of North, Williamson, Hodgson and Casson (Williamson, 1985; 2000; Hodgson, 1988; Casson, 1991). Yet, Williamson does not explain the international diversity of experience and has been strongly criticized by sociologists and some economists for his neglect of networks. Starting with the assumption that firms are embedded within the society of which they are part, it has been demonstrated that in East Asia, for example, firms are inseparable from their socially based networks. In this context, networks are not an intermediate stage between firm and market as Williamson implies, but constitute the norm (Redding, 1990; Biggart and Hamilton, 1992). Additionally, drawing on evolutionary theory, some economists have pointed to the path dependency of innovation, showing the impact of firm-specific routines on the choice of technology, which helps to explain divergent as opposed to convergent business behaviour (Langlois and Robertson, 1995).

Entrepreneurs never, therefore, innovate in isolation, so links to investors, competitors, suppliers, customer and governmental organizations need to be considered when studying innovation (Lundvall, 1992; Edquist, 1997). By setting innovation behaviour against the formal and informal rules of the game, business historians and economists have explored the potential of the 'new institutionalism' for international comparisons (Zysman, 1994; Casson and Rose, 1997; Knutsen et al., 1999).

During the 1990s, a number of business historians demonstrated that entrepreneurial, and indeed family, firms were embedded within distinctive regional and sometimes international networks, from which they derived competitive advantage. Scranton demonstrated the development of innovative, specialized networked forms as the basis for Philadelphia's competitive advantage, while Rose, in comparing business values between the United States and Britain, found regionally distinctive behaviours, underpinned by varying types of networks (Scranton, 1997; Rose, 2000). In this work networks were a dynamic phenomenon and acted as a bridge between past and future. The growing interest in social capital, identified earlier in this chapter, is also reflected in business history and, by looking at the benefits of 'connectedness', builds on the historical analysis of networks. In particular this has led to a special issue of the journal *Business History* edited by Pamela Laird, who concluded that building 'social capital mattered most where there were few other assurances of predictability, reliability, authority or reciprocity' (Laird, 2008, p.692). In other words, reliance on social capital building has historically been an important antidote to uncertainty.

Schumpeter saw innovation as evolutionary. But it is by moving beyond the individual entrepreneur to the embedded entrepreneur that the combination of theory and history becomes especially powerful, because innovation is a knowledge-based process, where the entrepreneur combines bodies of skill and expertise. Because innovation occurs most readily at the interstices of areas of expertise, it is enhanced by entrepreneurial networks, which facilitate boundary crossing. Entrepreneurial networks have increasingly been identified as crucial to innovation. Much has been written identifying the importance of networks to combinations of knowledge in the supply chain. As Powell and Grodal observe, '[E]xisting knowledge within a network is recombined in novel ways. Indeed novelty is often the unanticipated result of configuring existing knowledge, problems and solutions. As a consequence of such collisions or transpositions, firms can generate something they were unable to generate on their own' (Powell and Grodal, 2005, p. 75).

Yet networks are not just crucial for vertical collaboration within the supply chain, they are significant when boundary crossing involves mixing old and new knowledge and the avoidance of path dependent 'lock in.' Work that draws on Schumpeter emphasizes how the majority of designs and innovations represent 'new combinations of old and new' – old product and new process, old product and new material, old skills and new products (Abernathy and Clark, 1985). Historical experience demonstrates how important combining old and new knowledge and skills has been for radical innovations such as the automobile (Hounshell, 1984).

Schumpeter believed the trajectory of any innovation was intimately related to its historical context, and argued that creativity involves not necessarily developing something new, but having the imagination to see old things in new ways and move 'outside the ruts of established practice' (Schumpeter, 1947). Creativity alone does not lead to commercialized innovations, and it is here that the link with entrepreneurship and entrepreneurial networks becomes crucial. Entrepreneurship involves the recognition and assessment of opportunities and is often the bridge between creativity and innovation. Innovation is, by implication, an evolutionary process with the discontinuities typically coming from boundary crossing, which leads to new combinations. It is entrepreneurial imagination that transforms the shadow of the past into an inspiration for the future. The entrepreneur is involved in what can be described as the dance of two questions – 'what is needed?' and 'what is possible?' – and the interplay of these two questions is an ongoing process. Responses to the two questions are shaped by changing knowledge of the external environment, by social and business networks, by changes in the legal system, changes in the competitive environment and by market forces (Stefik and Stefik, 2004). Viewed in this light, networks underpin development and change in economies, sectors and firms. Based upon knowledge, they are inseparable from a dynamic approach to the co-evolution of innovation in industries (Malerba, 2006).

Rather than staying trapped by their past, networked entrepreneurs may engage in 'mindful deviation' and in so doing create new innovative pathways. Theorists setting out to develop beyond path dependency to path creation have shown that this can be achieved by a combination of external and internal awareness or receptivity to the unfamiliar, combined with an understanding of the need to convince hearts and minds of the benefits of change (Garud and Karnøe, 2001, p. 6; Bessant et al., 2004, pp. 32–3). All this implies that the dynamic dance of the two questions 'what is needed?' and 'what is possible?' will not be conducted in isolation, but will be embedded in and underpinned by social networks within and outside firms. The innovative entrepreneur is then engaged in a social process and 'those who attempt to create new paths have to realise that they are part of an emerging collective and that core ideas and objects will modify as they progress from hand to hand and mind to mind' (Garud and Karnøe, 2001, p. 20).

It has, for example, been shown how new combinations of knowledge from the industrial past of a region could provide the foundation for competitive advantage in the future. This was the case in the North West of England when networking relationships, underpinned by the social capital of entrepreneurs, combined with the skills of ancillary sectors (that were the legacy of industrialization) contributed to innovation in one of the

UK's more dynamic consumer goods sectors, from the 1960s to the 1990s (M. Parsons and Rose, 2003; 2005; Rose et al., 2007).

This chapter has traced the evolution of thinking on social processes, highlighting how understanding of embeddedness and trust has shaped our understanding of entrepreneurship. A historical perspective highlights the complexity of the innovation process in which entrepreneurs are engaged and demonstrates the importance of a networked approach to innovation.

Communities of Practice

This chapter has already revealed the importance of anthropology in shaping thinking on networks, social change and social capital. The impact extends to innovation through the development of the concept of communities of practice. The communities of practice literature provides an exciting bridge between entrepreneurship, innovation and networks and one which is underpinned by historical path dependency models of 'learning by doing' already discussed. Although informal communities of practice have always existed, the term was first used by anthropologist Jean Lave and educationalist Etienne Wenger in 1987 as part of their analysis of apprenticeship (Wenger and Snyder, 2000). Formalized and developed by Lave and Wenger during the 1990s, this social learning theory is based on the experiential learning achieved within groups united by the shared passion for and practice of particular activities. Sharing history and experience brings with it free flowing communication which in turn fosters a creative and innovative solution to problems (Lave and Wenger, 1991; Lave, 1993; Lave and Chaikin, 1993; Wenger, 1998).

Communities of practice theory has been applied to explain diffusion of innovation, or the barriers to it in large scale companies (Brown and Duguid, 1991) and the entrepreneurial process within family firms (Aldrich and Cliff, 2003). Although largely neglected in small firms, it has found applications in the context of local and regional entrepreneurial networks. Applied to the innovation process, this theory helps to explain the evolution of experience, knowledge and practices especially within industrial clusters. The analysis of Silicon Valley has revealed that the clustering of the same and related industries has created overlapping communities of practice which mean that entrepreneurial knowledge is 'in the air' (Brown and Duguid, 2002). Proximity to competitors reinforces awareness of the implications of their innovations and fine tunes opportunity recognition. In addition, there has developed a breed of venture capitalists experienced in hi-tech start ups, while in universities such as Berkeley and Stanford, academics are habitual entrepreneurs, which reinforces and feeds the environment (Brown and Duguid, 2002; Kenney and Goe, 2004). The lived and shared experience of entrepreneurs, venture capitalists and technologists in Silicon Valley is not based on long lasting relationships. Instead, it is based on the building of tacit knowledge of what makes the region function, a shared knowledge which influences innovation and entrepreneurship. The distinctive history of the region has therefore shaped and continues to shape the communities of practice which are themselves long in the making.

This analysis highlights why history matters to the understanding of the distinctiveness of different industrial clusters and the potential dangers of 'top down' government policies to promote industrial clusters (Brown and Duguid, 2002). It helps us understand the entrepreneurial process and how, through operating within overlapping communities of practice, entrepreneurs may develop innovative ideas – through new combinations. In addition communities of practice can be used to explain the diffusion of innovation and, especially differing patterns of diffusion within different societies.

The importance of communities of practice theory in entrepreneurial networks and innovation is not confined to industrial clusters, however; it is also linked to the role of lead-users in innovation identified by von Hippel. Lead-user innovators are those who innovate for use rather than sale and are consequently typically embedded within a community of practice (von Hippel, 1988; 2005). The development of this theory around both industrial users and consumers has important implications for our understanding of the role of entrepreneurial networks in innovation. It shifts the focus of innovation from the R&D department of the large scale company to networks of users and has been identified in hi tech and low tech sectors and especially in sporting goods, strongly influencing designs and design processes. The majority of lead-users do not, however, become entrepreneurs and those that do are often lifestyle entrepreneurs. However where entrepreneurs are themselves users, and hence part of overlapping communities of practice, this can significantly enhance the quality of dialogue with their customers (von Hippel, 2005; Lüthje et al., 2005; Baldwin et al., 2006; Rose et al., 2007)

NETWORKS AS A CONSTRAINING FORCE AND THE DOWNSIDE OF NETWORKS

The network concept is certainly useful in examining many types of social situations and to interpret a variety of social behaviour (Barnes, 1969; Mitchell, 1969). From work carried out on social networks several interactional characteristics and criteria have been identified as being significant: anchorage, reachability, density, range, content, directedness, durability, intensity and frequency (see Mitchell, 1969, pp. 12–29). But, because of the diversity of contexts in which the term social network has been used and applied, confusion does appear in the literature as researchers have their own interpretations and introduce refinements to the meaning of the term to suit thier own particular problems (Barnes, 1969).

Criticisms have also been made concerning the use of social network theory as an analytical framework, primarily based on the point that a social network perspective often takes social structures as a given (Aldrich, 1982; Granovetter, 1985; Jones et al., 1997), raising concerns about the perception and interpretation of structure and agency in terms of influencing behaviour and how the initiation, reproduction and change of structures are brought about (Emirbayer and Goodwin, 1994; Mizruchi, 1994; Araujo and Easton, 1996). Moreover, those using the term 'network' have been accused of loosely applying it to describe any type of interaction between persons or groups (Shaw, 1997; Havnes and Senneseth, 2001). Yet, despite these criticisms, there does seem to be widespread consensus that networks are a useful mechanism for interpreting social behaviour. However, the study of personal networks requires 'meticulous and systematic detailed recording of social interaction' (Mitchell, 1969, p. 11) and Cooley (1956) would argue that in order to understand social life one should study it through observation.

In addition, much of the network literature demonstrates an almost evangelical faith in the power of networks to improve the environment faced by entrepreneurs. Collaborators, however, may cheat or free-ride on goodwill, leading to a breach of trust and a breakdown in relations, and entrepreneurs may choose to destroy as well as build social capital. Some concerns were raised earlier but here we take a broader perspective.

Successful collaborations are based upon mutual trust and mutual benefit. However, misplaced or misjudged expectations, as the relationship develops, can undermine fragile trust and reverse any potential gains (Bowey and Easton, 2007). In their discussions about network development Smith and Lohrke (2008) point out that even though trust is a core element of networks, trust might also constrain network development and work against the entrepreneurial process. These authors raise the issues that (1) trust levels can change as a result of a negative outcome and that this can impact on how an entrepreneur is perceived and (2) overembeddedness and 'over trust' can lead to distrust. Anderson and Jack (2000) raise concerns about embeddedness and group expectations. They argued that the pressure these aspects can place on the entrepreneur can lead to loss of face and can have tragic consequences, arguments echoed by Schumpter (1934) and Johannisson (1990).

Another concern is that networks are by no means always inclusive and may exclude ethnic groups or those whose backgrounds or life experiences differ from established groupings and the 'accepted' social norm. Successful entrepreneurs from ethnic minorities have been found often to feel there is a need to join predominantly white clubs to build their social capital (Mulholland, 1997). However, social exclusion among socially disadvantaged groups can lead them to develop their own institutional base better tailored to their needs and aspirations.

There is also the 'threat' from technological change and the rise of the internet as these have altered the capabilities of networks and modes of communication. Globalization and flexible organizations are some of the consequences of such technological changes. Recent research has demonstrated, however, that there are barriers to the effective functioning and building of virtual teams and that far from ceasing to be important, geography and locality do still matter (Kimble et al., 2000; Brown and Duguid, 2002; Asheim and Gertler, 2005).

CONCLUSION: THE FUTURE FOR SOCIAL NETWORKS IN ENTREPRENEURSHIP RESEARCH

So, while network research within entrepreneurship has increased in popularity in recent years, the network approach itself is not new and has been used in organizational research since the 1930s and at least the 1950s in sociology and anthropology (Nohria, 1992). Although its use and popularity by social science researchers has without doubt intensified in recent years, much is owed to its founding disciplines which are often overlooked (Parkhe et al., 2006). A perspective that has not been fully explored here, for reasons mentioned earlier, is that of social psychology and especially role theory. Yet, such a perspective might be appropriate when looking at corporate entrepreneurship, the 'building' of teams for entrepreneurship and family business research, especially if it were to build on the work of Bott (1955; 1956; 1957).

Undoubtedly, a substantial body of work has accumulated over the years that devotes considerable attention to the analysis of networks within the entrepreneurial context.

However, network analysts need to be cautious as they have been criticized for being casual, even careless, in their prescriptions of how entrepreneurs can easily achieve optimal network positions when in reality entrepreneurs suffer from barriers of homophily, social boundaries and bounded rationality (Kim and Aldrich, 2005). Table 12.2 highlights popular and relevant research themes such as the structure and patterning of relationships, causes and effects and input-output relationships, and the development of predictive, often sophisticated, models that not only demonstrate that individuals use networks but also that networks have structures with key features. Although this might seem selective, a similar pattern can be found in inter-organizational network research. Here Oliver and Ebers (1998) point that out researchers have dealt with the vast, complex and fragmented field by means of a selective approach, concentrating on particular theoretical issues or literatures.

The productive information and resources gathered through social networks can compensate for constraints and the use of social networks can counteract many difficulties (Jack, 2005). However, as highlighted in our discussion, the use of social networks can also be problematic. Yet, it is through social networks that entrepreneurial action can convert 'limited' resources into a 'rich environment' (Jack, 2005), although for the entrepreneur this can involve taking both economic and social risks. Despite considerable empirical and theoretical development (Hoang and Antoncic, 2003), a need exists to further understanding about particular network aspects, including the embeddedness and impact of social mechanisms (Jones et al., 1997), what really goes on within a network over time by taking a process perspective (Hoang and Antoncic, 2003; Jack, 2010; Slotte-Kocke and Coviello, 2010), and issues surrounding the downside of networks.

There is a perspective that in terms of theory development, network research is at the 'cusp of an exciting new phase of advances', anticipated to 'remain vibrant far into the future' (Parkhe et al., 2006, p. 567). It might even be the case that it is through relations, interactions and networks that entrepreneurship is really carried out (Anderson et al., 2005). So, by continuing to consider networks, by thinking about the networked innovating entrepreneur and by taking a historical perspective, our understanding can only be enhanced.

NOTE

1. *Academy of Management Journal, Academy of Management Review, Administrative Science Quarterly, American Journal of Sociology, Entrepreneurship and Regional Development, Entrepreneurship Theory and Practice, Journal of Business Venturing, Journal of Management, Journal of Management Studies, Journal of Small Business Management, Management Science, Organisation Studies, Organization Science, Small Business Economics*, and the *Strategic Management Journal*.

REFERENCES

Abernathy, W. and K.B. Clark (1985), 'Innovation: mapping the winds of creative destruction', *Research Policy*, **14**(1), 3–22.
Ahuja, G. (2000), 'Collaboration networks, structural holes and innovation: a longitudinal study', *Administrative Science Quarterly*, **45**(3), 425–55.

Aldrich, H.E. (1982), 'The origins and persistence of networks: a comment', in P. Marsden and N. Lin (eds), *Social Structure and Network Analysis*, Beverly Hills, CA: Sage, pp. 281–93.

Aldrich, H.E. (1999), *Organizations Evolving*, London: Sage Publications.

Aldrich, H.E. and J.E. Cliff (2003), 'The pervasive effects of family on entrepreneurship: toward a family embeddedness approach', *Journal of Business Venturing*, **18**(5), 573–96.

Aldrich, H.E. and C. Zimmer (1986), 'Entrepreneurship through social networks', in D. Sexton and R. Smilor (eds), *The Art and Science of Entrepreneurship*, New York: Ballinger Publishing Company, pp. 3–23.

Aldrich, H., B. Rosen and W. Woodward (1987), 'The impact of social networks on business foundings and profit: a longitudinal study', in N.C. Churchill, J.A. Hornaday, B.A. Kirchhoff, O.J. Krasner and K.H. Vesper (eds), *Frontiers of Entrepreneurship Research*, Wellesley, MA: Babson College, pp. 154–68.

Anderson, A. and S. Jack (2000), 'The production of prestige: an entrepreneurial viagra', *International Journal of Entrepreneurship and Innovation*, **1**(1), 45–56.

Anderson, A.R. and S. Jack (2002), 'The articulation of social capital in entrepreneurial networks: a glue or a lubricant?', *Entrepreneurship and Regional Development*, **14**(3), 193–210.

Anderson, A.R. and C. Miller (2002), 'Class matters: human and social capital in the entrepreneurial process', *Journal of Socio-Economics*, **32**, 17–36.

Anderson, A., S. Drakopoulou Dodd and S. Jack (2009), 'Aggressors, winners, victims and outsiders: European schools' social construction of the entreprenuer', *International Small Business Journal*, **27**(1), 126–36.

Anderson, A., S. Jack and S. Dodd (2005), 'The role of family members in entrepreneurial networks: beyond the boundaries of the family firm', *Family Business Review*, **18**(2), 135–54.

Anderson, A., J. Park and S. Jack (2007), 'Entrepreneurial social capital: conceptualising social capital in new high-tech firms', *International Small Business Journal*, **25**(3) 243–67.

Araujo, L. and G. Easton (1996), 'Networks in socio-economic systems: a critical review', in D. Iacobucci (ed.), *Networks in Marketing*, Thousand Oaks, CA: Sage, pp. 63–107.

Arenius, P. and D. De Clercq (2005), 'A network-based approach on opportunity recognition', *Small Business Economics*, **24**(3), 249–65.

Arrow, K.J. (2000), 'Observations in social capital', in P. Dasgupta and I. Serageldin (eds), *Social Capital: A Multifaceted Perspective*, Washington DC: The World Bank, pp. 3–5

Asheim, B. and M.S. Gertler (2005), 'The geography of innovation: regional innovation systems', in J. Fagerberg, J. David, C. Mowery and R.R. Nelson (eds), *The Oxford Handbook of Innovation*, Oxford: Oxford University Press, pp. 291–317.

Baldwin, C., C. Hienerth and E. von Hippel (2006), 'How user innovations become commercial products: a theoretical investigation and case study', *Research Policy*, **35**(9), 1291–313.

Banck, G.A. (1973), 'Network analysis and social theory', in J. Boissevain and J.C. Mitchell (eds), *Network Analysis Studies in Human Interaction*, Netherlands: Mouton, pp. 37–44.

Barnes, J.A. (1954), 'Class and committees in a Norwegian island parish', *Human Relations*, **VII**, 39–58.

Barnes, J.A. (1969), 'Networks and political process', in J.C. Mitchell (ed.), *Social Networks in Urban Situations*, Manchester: University Press, pp. 51–74.

Baron, R.A. and G.D. Markman (2003), 'Beyond social capital: the role of entrepreneurs' social competence in their financial success', *Journal of Business Venturing*, **18**(1), 41–60.

Batjargal, B. and M. Liu (2004), 'Entrepreneurs' access to private equity in China: the role of social capital', *Organization Science*, **15**(2), 159–72.

Bessant, J., J. Birkinshaw and R. Delbridge (2004), 'Innovation as unusual', *Business Strategy Review*, **15**, 32–35.

Biggart, N.W. and G.G. Hamilton (1992), 'On the limits of a firm based theory to explain business networks: the Western bias of neo-classical economics', in N. Nohria and R.G. Eccles (eds), *Networks and Organisations: Structure, Form and Action*, Cambridge, MA: Harvard University Press, pp. 471–90.

Birley, S. (1985), 'The role of networks in the entrepreneurial process', *Journal of Business Venturing*, **1**(1), 107–17.

Blau, P.M. (1964), *Exchange and Power in Social Life*, New York: Wiley.

Bloodgood, J., H. Sapienza and A. Carsrud (1995), 'The dynamics of new business start-ups: person, context and process', in J. Katz and S. Brockhaus (eds), *Advances in Entrepreneurship, Firm Emergence and Growth*, Vol. 2, Greenwich, CT: JAI Press, pp. 123–44.

Bohannan, P. (1955), 'Some principles of exchange and investment among the Tiv', *American Anthropologist*, **57**, 60–70.

Boissevain, J. (1973), 'Preface', in J. Boissevain and J.C. Mitchell (eds), *Network Analysis: Studies in Human Interaction*, Netherlands: Mouton, pp. vii–xiii.

Boissevain, J. (1974), *Friends of Friends, Networks, Manipulators and Coalitions*, Oxford: Basil Blackwell.

Boissevain, J. and J.C. Mitchell (eds) (1973), *Network Analysis: Studies in Human Interaction*, Netherlands: Mouton.

Bøllingtoft, A. and J. Ulhøi (2005), 'The networked business incubator: leveraging entrepreneurial agency?', *Journal of Business Venturing*, **20**(2), 265–90.

Bott, E. (1955), 'Urban families: conjugal roles and social networks', *Human Relations*, **VIII**, 345–85.

Bott, E. (1956), 'Urban families: the norms of conjugal roles', *Human Relations*, **IX**, 325–41.

Bott, E. (1957), *Family and Social Networks*, London: Tavistock Publications.

Bourdieu, P. (1986), 'The forms of capital', in J.G. Richardson (ed.), *Handbook of Theory and Research for the Sociology of Education*, New York: Greenwood, pp. 241–58.

Bowey, J. and G. Easton (2007), 'Entrepreneurial social capital unplugged: an activity based analysis', *International Small Business Journal*, **25**, 273–306.

Brazeal, D.V. and T.T. Herbert (1999), 'The genesis of entrepreneurship', *Entrepreneurship Theory and Practice*, **23**(3).

Brown, J.S. and P. Duguid (1991), 'Organisational learning and communities of practice: toward a unified view of working, learning and innovation', *Organizational Science*, **2**(1), 40–57.

Brown, J.S. and P. Duguid (2002), 'Local knowledge: innovation in a networked age', *Management Learning*, **33**(4), 427–38.

Brüderl, J. and P. Preisendörfer (1998), 'Network support and the success of newly founded businesses', *Small Business Economics*, **10**, 213–225.

Burt, R.S. (1992a), *Structural Holes,* Cambridge, MA: Harvard University Press.

Burt, R.S. (1992b), 'The social structure of competition', in N. Nohria and R.G. Eccles (eds), *Networks and Organizations: Structure, Form and Action*, Boston, MA: Harvard Business School Press, pp. 57–91.

Carsrud, A.L. and R.W. Johnson (1989), 'Entrepreneurship: a social psychological perspective', *Entrepreneurship and Regional Development*, **1**, 21–31.

Cassis, Y. and I. Minoglou (2005), 'Entrepreneurship in theory and history', in Y. Cassis and I. Minoglou (eds), *Entrepreneurship in Theory and History*, London: Palgrave, Macmillan, pp. 3–21.

Casson, M. (1991), *The Economics and Business Culture: Game Theory, Transaction Costs and Economic Performance*, Oxford: Oxford University Press.

Casson, M. and M.B. Rose (eds) (1997), *Institutions and the Evolution of Modern Business*, London: Cass.

Chell, E. and S. Baines (2000), 'Networking, entrepreneurship and microbusiness behaviour', *Entrepreneurship and Regional Development*, **12**(3), 195–215.

Clarysse, B., M. Wright., A. Locket, E. van de Velde and A. Vohora (2005), 'Spinning out new ventures: a typology of incubation strategies from European research institutions', *Journal of Business Venturing*, **20**(2), 183–216.

Coleman, J. (2000), 'Social capital in the creation of human capital', in P. Dasgupta and J. Serageldin (eds), *Social Capital: A Multifaceted Perspective*, Washington DC: World Bank, pp. 13–39.

Cooke, P. and D. Wills (1999), 'Small firms, social capital and the enhancement of business performance through innovation programmes', *Small Business Economics*, **13**(3), 219–34.

Cooley, C.H. (1956), *Human Nature and the Social Order*, Glencoe, IL: Free Press.

Coviello, N.E. (2005), 'Integrating qualitative and quantitative techniques in network analysis', *Qualitative Market Research*, **8**(1), 39–60.

Dakhli, M. and D. De Clercq (2004), 'Human capital, social capital and innovation: a multi-country study', *Entrepreneurship and Regional Development*, **16**(2), 107–28.

David, P. (1975), *Technical Choice, Innovation and Economic Growth*, Cambridge: Cambridge University Press.

David, P. (1985), 'Clio and the economics of QWERTY', *American Economic Review*, 332–37.

David, P. (1997), 'Path dependence: putting the past into the future of economics', in L. Magnusson and J. Ottosson (eds), *Evolutionary Economics and Path Dependence*, Cheltenham, UK and Lyme, USA: Edward Elgar, pp. 51–79.

Davidsson, P. and B. Honig (2003), 'The role of human and social capital among nascent entrepreneurs', *Journal of Business Venturing*, **18**(3), 301–31.

Donckels, R. and J. Lambrecht (1995), 'Networks and small business growth: an explanatory model', *Small Business Economics*, **7**, 273–89.

Donckels, R. and J. Lambrecht (1997), 'The network position of small businesses: an explanatory model', *Journal of Small Business Management*, **35**(2), 13–25.

Drakopoulou Dodd, S. and E. Patra (2002), 'National differences in entrepreneurial networking', *Entrepreneurship and Regional Development*, **14**(2), 117–34.

Dubini, P. and H. Aldrich (1991), 'Personal and extended networks are central to the entrepreneurial process', *Journal of Business Venturing*, **6**, 305–13.

Edquist, C. (1997), *Systems of Innovation: Technologies, Institutions and Organizations*, London: Pinter.

Ekeh, P. (1974), *Social Exchange Theory: The Two Traditions*, Cambridge, MA: Harvard University Press.

Elfring, T. and W. Hulsink (2003), 'Networks in entrepreneurship: the case of high-technology firms', *Small Business Economics*, **21**(4), 409–22.

Emirbayer, M. and J. Goodwin (1994), 'Network analysis, culture and the problem of agency', *American Journal of Sociology*, **99**(6), 1411–54.

Epstein, A.L. (1961), 'The network and urban social organization', *Rhodes-Livingstone Journal*, **29**, 29–62.

Fiet, J.O. (1995), 'Reliance upon informants in the venture capital industry', *Journal of Business Venturing*, **10**(3), 195–223.

Flora, J. (1998), 'Social capital and communities of place', *Rural Sociology*, **63**(4), 481–506.

Florin, J., M. Lubatkin and W. Schulze (2003), 'A social capital model of high growth ventures', *Academy of Management Journal*, **46**(3), 374–84.

Fortes, M. (1949), *The Web of Kinship among the Tallensi*, London: Oxford University Press.

Franke, U.J. (1999), 'The virtual web as a new entrepreneurial approach to network organizations', *Entrepreneurship and Regional Development*, **11**(3), 203–29.

Frazer, J.G. (1919), *Folklore in the Old Testament*, Vol. 2, London: Macmillan.

Garud, R. and P. Karnøe (2001), 'Path creation and the process of mindful deviation' in R. Garud and P. Karnøe (eds), *Path Dependence and Creation*, London: Laurence Erlbaum, pp. 1–37.

Grandi, A. and R. Grimaldi (2003), 'Exploring the networking characteristics of new venture founding teams: a study of Italian academic spin-off', *Small Business Economics*, **21**(4), 329–41.

Granovetter, M. (1973), 'The strength of weak ties', *American Journal of Sociology*, **78**(6), 1360–80.

Granovetter, M. (1985), 'Economic action and social structure: the problem of embeddedness', *American Journal of Sociology*, **91**(3), 481–510.

Granovetter, M. (1992), 'Problems of explanation in economic sociology', in N. Nohria and R. Eccles (eds), *Networks and Organizations: Structure, Form and Action*, Harvard, MA: Harvard Business School Press, pp. 25–56.

Greve, A. and J. Salaff (2003), 'Social networks and entrepreneurship', *Entrepreneurship Theory and Practice*, **28**(1), 1–22.

Gross, N., W. Mason and A. McEachern (1958), *Explorations in Role Analysis: Studies of the School Superintendency Role*, New York: Wiley.

Halinen, A., A. Salmi and V. Havila (1999), 'From dyadic change to changing business networks: an analytical framework', *Journal of Management Studies*, **36**(6), 779–95.

Hansen, E. (1995), 'Entrepreneurial networks and new organization growth', *Entrepreneurship Theory and Practice*, **19**(4), 7–21.

Harland, C.M. (1995), 'Networks and globalisation – a review of research', EPSRC Final Report, Grant No. GRK53178.

Havnes, P. and K. Senneseth (2001), 'A panel study of firm growth among SMEs in networks', *Small Business Economics*, **16**(4), 293–310.

Hills, G.E., G.T. Lumpkin and R.P. Singh (1997), 'Opportunity recognition: perceptions and behaviours of entrepreneurs', in P.D. Reynolds et al. (eds), *Frontiers of Entrepreneurship Research*, Wellesley, MA: Babson College, pp. 168–82.

Hitc, J.M. (2005), 'Evolutionary processes and paths of relationally embedded network ties in emerging entrepreneurial firms', *Entrepreneurship Theory and Practice*, **29**(1), 113–44.

Hoang, H. and B. Antoncic (2003), 'Network-based research in entrepreneurship: a critical review', *Journal of Business Venturing*, **18**(2), 495–527.

Hodgson, G.M. (1988), *Economics and Institutions*, Cambridge: Polity Press.

Homans, G.C. (1961), *Social Behaviour: Its Elementary Forms*, New York: Harcourt, Brace.

Hounshell, D.A. (1984), *From the American System to Mass Production, 1800–1932*, Baltimore: Johns Hopkins University Press.

Huggins, R. (2000), 'The success and failure of policy-implanted inter-firm network initiatives: motivations, processes and structure', *Entrepreneurship and Regional Development*, **12**(2), 11–35.

Human, S. and K. Provan (1997), 'An emergent theory of structure and outcomes in small-firm strategic manufacturing networks', *Academy of Management Journal*, **40**(2), 368–403.

Ibarra, H. (1993), 'Personal networks of women and minorities in management: a conceptual framework', *Academy of Management Review*, **18**(1), 56–88.

Jack, S. (2005), 'The role, use and activation of strong and weak ties: a qualitative analysis', *Journal of Management Studies*, **42**(6), 1233–59.

Jack, S. (2010), 'Approaches to studying networks: implications and outcomes', *Journal of Business Venturing*, **25**(1), 120–37.

Jack, S. and A. Anderson (2002), 'The effects of embeddedness on the entrepreneurial process', *Journal of Business Venturing*, **17**(5), 467–87.

Jarillo, J.C. (1989), 'Entrepreneurship and growth: the strategic use of external resources', *Journal of Business Venturing*, **4**(2), 133–47.

Johannisson, B. (1990), 'Community entrepreneurship: cases and conceptualization', *Entrepreneurship and Regional Development*, **2**, 71–88.

Johannisson, B. (1998), 'Personal networks in emerging knowledge based firms: spatial and functional patterns', *Entrepreneurship and Regional Development*, **10**(4), 297–312.

Johannisson, B. (2000), 'Networking and entrepreneurial growth', in D.L. Sexton and H. Landström (eds), *The Blackwell Handbook of Entrepreneurship*, Oxford: Blackwell, pp. 368–86.

Johannisson, B. and R. Peterson (1984), 'The personal networks of entrepreneurs', paper presented to the ICSB World Conference, Ryerson Polytechnic Institute, Toronto.

Johannisson, B., O. Alexanderson, K. Nowicki and K. Senneseth (1994), 'Beyond anarchy and organization: entrepreneurs in contextual networks', *Entrepreneurship and Regional Development*, **6**(3), 329–56.

Johannisson, B., M. Ramirez-Pasillas and G. Karlsson (2002), 'The institutional embeddedness of local inter-firm networks: a leverage for business creation', *Entrepreneurship and Regional Development*, **14**, 297–315.

Jones, C., W. Hesterly and S. Borgatti (1997), 'A general theory of network governance: exchange conditions and social mechanisms', *Academy of Management Review*, **22**(4), 911–46.

Jones, G. and J. Zeitlin (eds) (2008), *Oxford Handbook of Business History*, Oxford: Oxford University Press.

Jones, G. and R.D. Wadhwani (2005), 'Schumpeter's plea: rediscovering history and relevance in the study of entrepreneurship', Harvard Business School Working Paper, Cambridge, MA: Harvard Business School.

Julien, P., E. Andriambeloson and C. Ramangalahy (2004), 'Networks, weak signals and technological innovations among SMEs in the land-based transportation equipment sector', *Entrepreneurship and Regional Development*, **16**(4), 251–69.

Kadushin, C. (1968), 'Power, influence, and social circles: a new methodology for studying opinion makers', *American Sociological Review*, **33**, 685–99.

Karamanos, K.G. (2003), 'Complexity, identity and the value of knowledge-intensive exchanges', *Journal of Management Studies*, **40**, 1871–90.

Katz, D. and R. Kahn (1966), *The Social Psychology of Organizations*, New York: Wiley.

Katz, F.E. (1966), 'Social participation and social structure', *Social Forces*, **XLV**, 199–210.

Katz, J. and P. Williams (1997), 'Gender, self-employment and weak-tie networking through formal organizations', *Entrepreneurship and Regional Development*, **9**, 183–97.

Keeble, D., C. Lawson, H. Lawton Smith, B. Moore and F. Wilkinson (1998), 'Internationalisation processes, networking and local embeddedness in technology-intensive small firms', *Small Business Economics*, **11**(4), 327–42.

Kenney, M. and W.R. Goe (2004), 'The role of social embeddedness in professorial entrepreneurs: a comparison of electrical engineering and computer science at Berkeley and Stanford Universities', *Research Policy*, **33**(5), 691–707.

Kim, P.H. and H.E. Aldrich (2005), 'Social capital and entrepreneurship', *Foundations and Trends in Entrepreneurship*, **1**(2), 1–52.

Kimble, C., L. Feng and A. Barlow (2000), 'Effective virtual teams through communities of practice', Strathclyde Business School, Research Paper no. 2000/9.

Kingsley, G. and E. Malecki (2004), 'Networking for competitiveness', *Small Business Economics*, **23**(1), 71–84.

Knutsen, H., M.B. Rose and H. Sjögren (1999), 'Introduction to Special Issue', *Scandinavian Economic History Review*, **47**(1) 5–9.

Kodithuwakku, S.S. and P. Rosa (2002), 'The entrepreneurial process and economic success in a constrained environment', *Journal of Business Venturing*, **17**(5), 431–65.

Krackhardt, D. (1995), 'Entrepreneurial opportunities in an entrepreneurial firm: a structural approach', *Entrepreneurship Theory and Practice*, **19**(3), 53–70.

Laird, P. (2008), 'Putting social capital to work', *Business History*, **50**(6), 685–94.

Langlois, R.N and P.L. Robertson (1995), *Firms, Markets and Economic Change*, London: Routledge.

Lave, J. (1993), 'The practice of learning', in S. Chaiklin and J. Lave (eds), *Understanding Practice: Perspectives on Activity and Context*, Cambridge: Cambridge University Press, pp. 3–34.

Lave, J. and S. Chaikin (eds) (1993), *Understanding Practice: Perspectives on Activity and Context*, Cambridge: Cambridge University Press.

Lave, J. and E. Wenger (1991), *Situated Learning: Legitimate Peripheral Participation*, Cambridge: Cambridge University Press.

Lazonick, W. (2003), 'Understanding innovative enterprise: towards the integration of economic theory and business history', in F. Amatori and G. Jones (eds), *Business History around the World*, Cambridge: Cambridge University Press, pp. 31–61.

Lechler, T. (2001), 'Social interaction: a determinant of entrepreneurial team venture success', *Small Business Economics*, **16**(4), 263–78.

Lechner, C. and M. Dowling (2003), 'Firm networks: external relationships as sources for the growth and competitiveness of entrepreneurial firms', *Entrepreneurship and Regional Development*, **15**, 1–26.

Lee, C., L. Kyungmook and J.M. Pennings (2001), 'Internal capabilities, external networks and performance: a study on technology-based ventures', *Strategic Management Journal*, **22**(6/7), 615–40.

Lee, D. and E. Tsang (2001), 'The effects of entrepreneurial personality, background and network activities on venture growth', *Journal of Management Studies*, **38**(4), 584–602.

Lerner, M., C. Brush and B. Hisrich (1997), 'Israeli women entrepreneurs: an examination of factors affecting performance', *Journal of Business Venturing*, **12**(4), 315–39.

Levi-Strauss, C. (1969), *The Elementary Structures of Kinship*, Boston, MA: Beacon Press.

Liao, J. and H. Welsch (2005), 'Roles of social capital in venture creation: key dimensions and research implications', *Journal of Small Business Management*, **43**(4), 354–62.

Littunen, H. (2000), 'Networks and local environmental characteristics in the survival of new firms', *Small Business Economics*, **10**(3), 213–25.

Lundvall, B. (1992), *National Systems of Innovation: Towards a Theory of Innovation and Interactive Learning*, London: Pinter.

Lüthje, C., C. Herstatt and E. von Hippel (2005), 'User innovators and local information: the case of mountain biking', *Research Policy*, **34**, 951–65.

MacMillan, I.C. (1983), 'The politics of new venture management', *Harvard Business Review*, **61**(6), 8–16.

Maguire, L. (1983), *Understanding Social Networks*, London: Sage.

Malerba, F. (2006), 'Innovation and the evolution of industries', *Journal of Evolutionary Economics*, **16**, 3–26.

Malinowski, B. (1922), *Argonauts of the Western Pacific*, New York: Dutton.

Mason, C.M. and R.T. Harrison (1997), 'Business angel networks and the development of the informal venture capital market in the UK: is there still a role for the public sector', *Small Business Economics*, **9**(2), 111–23.

Mayer, P. (1961), *Tribesmen or Townsmen: Conservatism and the Process of Urbanization in a South African City*, Cape Town: Oxford University Press.

Mayer, P. (1962), 'Migrancy and the study of Africans in town', *American Anthropology*, **LXIV**, 576–92.

Mayer, P. (1964), 'Labour migrancy and the social network', in J.F. Holleman et al. (eds) *Problems of Transition*, Proceedings of the Social Sciences Research Conference, University of Natal, Durban, South Africa, July, pp. 21–34.

McDade, B.E. and A. Spring (2005), 'The new generation of African entrepreneurs: networking to change the climate for business and private sector-led development', *Entrepreneurship and Regional Development*, **17**(1), 17–42.

Minguzzi, A. and R. Passaro (2001), 'The network of relationships between the economic and the entrepreneurial culture in small firms', *Journal of Business Venturing*, **16**(2), 181–207.

Mitchell, J.C. (1969), 'The concept and use of social networks', in J.C. Mitchell (ed.), *Social Networks in Urban Situations*, Manchester, UK: University of Manchester Press, pp. 1–50.

Mitchell, J.C. (1973), 'Networks, norms and institutions', in J. Boissevain and J.C. Mitchell (eds), *Network Analysis Studies in Human Interaction*, Netherlands: Mouton, pp. 15–36.

Mizruchi, M. (1994), 'Social network analysis: recent achievements and current controversies', *Acta Sociologica*, **37**, 329–43.

Mulholland, K. (1997), 'The family enterprise and business strategies', *Work, Employment and Society*, **11**(4), 685–711.

Nahapiet, J. and S. Ghoshal (1998), 'Social capital, intellectual capital and the organizational advantage', *Academy of Management Review*, **23**(2), 242–66.

Nelson, R. (1988), 'Social network analysis as an intervention tool', *Group and Organization Studies*, **13**(1), 39–58.

Nelson, R. (2001), 'On the shape of verbal networks in organizations', *Organization Studies*, **22**(5), 797–823.

Nelson, R. and S. Winter (1982), *An Evolutionary Theory of Economic Change*, Cambridge, MA: Harvard University Press.

Nicolaou, N. and S. Birley (2003), 'Academic networks in a trichotomous categorisation of university spinouts', *Journal of Business Venturing*, **18**(3), 333–59.

Noble, M. (1973), 'Social network: its use as a conceptual framework in family analysis', in J. Boissevain and J.C. Mitchell (eds), *Network Analysis Studies in Human Interaction*, Netherlands: Mouton, pp. 3–14.

Nohria, N. (1992), 'Is a network perspective a useful way of studying organisations?', in N. Nohria and R. Eccles (eds), *Networks and Organizations: Structure, Form and Action*, Cambridge, MA: Harvard Business School Press, pp. 1–23.

Nohria, N. and R. Eccles (1992), *Networks and Organizations: Structure, Form and Action*, Cambridge, MA: Harvard Business School Press.

North, D. (1990), *Institutions, Institutional Change and Economic Performance*, Cambridge, UK: Cambridge University Press.

O'Donnell, A., A. Gilmore, D. Cummins and D. Carson (2001), 'The network construct in entrepreneurship research: a review and critique', *Management Decision*, **39**(9), 749–60.

Oinas, P. (1999), 'Voices and silences: the problem of access to embeddedness', *Geoforum*, **30**, 351–61.

Oliver, A. and M. Ebers (1998), 'Networking network studies: an analysis of conceptual configurations in the study of inter-organizational relationships', *Organization Studies*, **19**(4), 549–83.
O'Sullivan, M. (2000), *Contests for Corporate Control and Economic Performance*, Oxford, UK: Oxford University Press.
Özcan, G.B. (1995), 'Small business networks and local ties in Turkey', *Entrepreneurship and Regional Development*, **7**, 265–82.
Padgett, J.F and C.K. Ansell (1993), 'Robust action and the rise of the Medici', *American Journal of Sociology*, **98**(6), 1259–319.
Park, R.E. (1924), 'The concept of social distance', *Journal of Applied Sociology*, **8**, 339–44.
Park, R.E. (1926), 'The concept of position in sociology', papers and proceedings of the American Sociological Society, **20**, 1–14.
Parkhe, A., S. Wasserman and D. Ralston (2006), 'New frontiers in network theory development', *Academy of Management Review*, **31**(3), 560–68.
Parsons, M. and M.B. Rose (2003), *Invisible on Everest: Innovation and the Gearmakers*, Philadelphia: Old City Publishing.
Parsons, M. and M.B. Rose (2005), 'The neglected legacy of Lancashire cotton: industrial clusters and the UK outdoor trade, 1960–1990', *Enterprise and Society*, **6**(4), 682–709.
Parsons, T. (1960), *Structure and Process in Modern Society*, New York: Free Press.
Pauw, B.A. (1963), *The Second Generation*, Cape Town: Oxford University Press.
Peng, Y. (2004), 'Kinship networks and entrepreneurs in China's transitional economy', *American Journal of Sociology*, **109**(5), 1045–74.
Portes, A. and J. Sensenbrenner (1993), 'Embeddedness and immigration: notes on the social determinants', *American Journal of Sociology*, **98**(6), 1320–50.
Powell, W.W. and S. Grodal (2005), 'Networks of innovators', in J. Fagerberg, D.C. Mowery and R.R. Nelson (eds), *The Oxford Handbook of Innovation*, Oxford, UK: Oxford University Press, pp. 56–85.
Premaratne, S.P. (2001), 'Networks, resources and small business growth: the experience in Sri Lanka', *Journal of Small Business Management*, **39**(4), 363–71.
Redding, S.G. (1990), *The Spirit of Chinese Capitalism*, Berlin: de Gruyter.
Renzulli, L. and H.E. Aldrich (2005), 'Who can you turn to: tie activation within core business discussion networks', *Social Forces*, **84**, 323–42.
Ring, P.S. and A.H. Van de Ven (1992), 'Structuring cooperative relationships between organizations', *Strategic Management Journal*, **13**, 483–98.
Rodan, S. and C. Galunic (2004), 'More than network structure: how knowledge heterogeneity influences managerial performance and innovativeness', *Strategic Management Journal*, **25**(6), 541–62.
Rose, M.B. (2000), *Firms, Networks and Business Values: The British and American Cotton Industries since 1750*, Cambridge, UK: Cambridge University Press.
Rose, M.B., T. Love and M. Parsons (2007), 'Path dependent foundation of global design-driven outdoor trade in NW of England', *International Journal of Design*, **1**(3), 57–68.
Sarason, Y., T. Dean and J. Dillard (2006), 'Entrepreneurship as the nexus of individual and opportunity: a structuration view', *Journal of Business Venturing*, **21**, 286–305.
Schell, D.W. and W. Davig (1981), 'The community infrastructure of entrepreneurship: a sociopolitical analysis', in K.H. Vesper (ed.), *Frontiers of Entrepreneurship Research*, Wellesley, MA: Babson College, pp. 563–90.
Schumpeter, J. (1934), *The Theory of Economic Development*, Cambridge, MA: Harvard University Press.
Schumpeter, J. (1947), 'The creative response and entrepreneurial history', *Journal of Economic History*, **7**, 149–59.
Schutjens, V. and E. Stam (2003), 'The evolution and nature of young firm networks: a longitudinal perspective', *Small Business Economics*, **21**, 115–34.
Scranton, P. (1997), *Endless Novelty: Specialty Production and American Industrialization, 1865–1925*, Cambridge, UK: Cambridge University Press.
Serageldin, I. and C. Grootaert (2000), 'Defining social capital: an integrating view', in P. Dasgupta

and I. Serageldin (eds), *Social Capital: A Multifaceted Perspective*, Washington DC: World Bank, pp. 40–58.

Shane, S. and D. Cable (2002), 'Network ties, reputation and the financing of new ventures', *Management Science*, **48**(3), 364–81.

Shane, S. and T. Stuart (2002), 'Organizational endowments and the performance of university start-ups', *Management Science*, **48**(1), 154–70.

Shaw, E. (1997), 'The real networks of small firms', in D. Deakins, P. Jennings and C. Mason (eds), *Small Firms: Entrepreneurship in the 1990s*, London: Paul Chapman, pp. 7–17.

Silverthorne, S. (2008), 'The lessons of business history: a handbook', Harvard Business School Working Knowledge, http://hbswk.hbs.edu/item/5849.html.

Simmel, G. (1950), *The Sociology of Georg Simmel*, translation K. Wolff, Glencoe, IL: Free Press.

Slotte-Kock, S. and N. Coviello (2010), 'Entrepreneurship research on network processes: a review and ways forward', *Entrepreneurship Theory and Practice*, **34**(1), 31–57.

Smith, D.A. and F.T. Lohrke (2008), 'Entrepreneurial network development: trusting in the process', *Journal of Business Research*, **61**, 315–22.

Snow, C., R. Miles and H. Coleman (1992), 'Managing 21st century network organizations', *Organizational Dynamics*, **20**(3), 5–20.

Soh, P. (2003), 'The role of networking alliances in information acquisition and its implications for new product performance', *Journal of Business Venturing*, **18**(6), 727–44.

Stefik, M. and B. Stefik (2004), *Breakthrough Stories and Strategies of Radical Innovation*, Cambridge, UK: Cambridge University Press.

Steier, L. and R. Greenwood (1995), 'Venture capitalist relationships in the deal structuring and post-investment stages of new firm creation', *Journal of Management Studies*, **32**(3), 337–57.

Steier, L. and R. Greenwood (2000), 'Entrepreneurship and the evolution of angel financial networks', *Organization Studies*, **21**(1), 163–93.

Stiglitz, J. (2000), 'Creating and harnessing social capital', in P. Dasgupta and I. Serageldin (eds), *Social Capital: A Multifaceted Perspective*, Washington DC: World Bank, pp. 59–68.

Tichy, N., M. Tushman and C. Fombrun (1979), 'Social network analysis for organizations', *Academy of Management Review*, **4**(4), 507–19.

Tsai, W. and S. Ghoshal (1998), 'Social capital and value creation: the role of intrafirm networks', *Academy of Management Journal*, **4**, 464–77.

Uhlaner, L. (2002), 'Trends in European research at the turn of the century', *Small Business Economics*, **21**(4), 321–28.

Utterback, J.M. (1996), *Mastering the Dynamics of Innovation*, Cambridge, MA: Harvard Business School Press.

Uzzi, B. (1997), 'Social structure and competition: the paradox of embeddedness', *Administrative Science Quarterly*, **42**, 35–67.

Uzzi, B. and J. Gillespie (2002), 'Knowledge spillover in corporate financing networks: embeddedness and the firm's debt performance', *Strategic Management Journal*, **23**(7), 595–618.

von Hippel, E. (1988), *The Sources of Innovation*, New York: OUP.

von Hippel, E. (2005), *Democratising Innovation*, Cambridge, MA: MIT press.

Walker, G., B. Kogut and W. Shan (1997), 'Social capital, structural holes and the formation of an industry network', *Organization Science*, **8**(2), 109–25.

Wenger, E. (1998), *Communities of Practice: Learning, Meaning and Identity*, Cambridge, UK: Cambridge University Press.

Wenger, E.C. and W. Snyder (2000), 'Communities of practice: the organizational frontier', *Harvard Business Review*, Jan–Feb, 139–45.

Whittington, R. (1992), 'Putting Giddens into action: social systems and managerial agency', *Journal of Management Studies*, **29**(6), 693–712.

Williamson, O.E. (1985), *The Institutions of Capitalism: Firms, Markets and Relational Contracting*, New York: The Free Press.

Williamson, O.E. (2000), 'The new institutional economics: taking stock, looking ahead', *Journal of Economic Literature*, **XXXVIII**(4), 595–613.

Yli-Renko, H. and E. Autio (1998), 'The network embeddedness of new, technology-based firms: developing a systemic evolution model', *Small Business Economics*, **11**(3), 253–67.
Yli-Renko, H., E. Autio and H. Sapienza (2001), 'Social capital, knowledge acquisitions and knowledge exploitation in young technology-based firms', *Strategic Management Journal*, **22**(6/7), 587–613.
Zysman, J. (1994), 'How institutions create historically rooted trajectories of growth', *Industrial and Corporate Change*, **3**(2), 243–83.

Section II.4

Integrative Works

13. The psychology of entrepreneurs: a self-regulation perspective

Alan R. Johnson and Frédéric Delmar

INTRODUCTION

In this chapter, we suggest theoretical and integrative links between previous and future research into the psychology and, more specifically, the motivation of entrepreneurs using a self-regulation perspective. Recent research in work motivation has shifted from focusing on the single concept of 'goal setting' and 'intentions' towards a broader understanding of self-regulation processes (Diefendorff and Lord, 2008). Self-regulation is the capacity of individuals to guide their activities over time and across changing circumstances (Kanfer, 1990). We aim to incorporate this broader understanding into entrepreneurship research as we believe it allows for a better understanding of the function and form of the entrepreneurial mindset. In addition, a self-regulation perspective permits integration of empirical findings about the dynamic nature of the entrepreneurial process, while keeping goal-directed individuals as the central actors in that process.

We review psychological research in entrepreneurship for the following reasons. First, self-regulation theories – such as the Theory of Planned Behavior (Ajzen, 1991), through its core concept of behavioral intentions, and Social Cognitive Theory (Bandura, 1991), through its core concept of self-efficacy – are among the most popular motivation theories used in entrepreneurship research. However, it is not well known among entrepreneurship scholars that the foregoing work motivation theories may be integrated within a self-regulation framework, together with more recently emerging research streams, including but not limited to cognitive and learning styles (Sadler-Smith and Badger, 1998) as well as goal generating and goal striving. Thus, we show how these theories may be brought together. We do this by offering a historical review of the literature on entrepreneurship and motivation. Although we also review the earliest research done in this field, our main emphasis is on research done after 1990. We hope our review clearly points towards the common denominator of self-regulation and that it can lead to clearer interpretation and integration of both theoretical and empirical findings.

Second, the foregoing work motivation theories, as they have been applied in entrepreneurship research, have mostly emphasized differences in individuals' characteristics (e.g. perceived behavioral control or self-efficacy) in a relatively static way, while often ignoring individuals' processes and dynamic situational influences in the entrepreneurial context. In addition, entrepreneurship is dynamic because people move in and out from it. Individuals are theorized to evolve under uncertainty and adapt in response to changes in the environment based on their own information processing abilities and their established goals, which may be revised from time to time, perhaps, in the face of performance feedback from interim outcomes in their task environment. Recent methodological developments for working with longitudinal data, brought together in our self-regulation framework, allow scholars to hypothesize and test models that integrate both between-individual and within-individual differences in their dynamic processes, and disturbances from the entrepreneurial context, that is to say, both between and within individual variance on various characteristic and process determinants of entrepreneurial behavior, and subsequent outcomes, with boundary conditions. Multilevel analysis is also made possible by moving between individual and team levels. We believe that our self-regulation framework and empirical agenda can help entrepreneurship scholars to move forward toward more complex models that allow for fuller explanations of how the entrepreneurial mindset is constructed and how it translates over time into both entrepreneurial behaviors, and interim outcomes.

We conceptualize individuals in a time sensitive, episodic, entrepreneurial process in which their characteristics, their self-regulation processes, and their situational influences all contribute to determining their interim outcomes. This view is consistent with the temporal perspective adopted in both previous organizational behavior process theory (Marks et al., 2001) and entrepreneurship process theory (Baron, 2007). Of the two, our framework more closely resembles Marks and her coauthors' episodic perspective, rather than Baron's process composed of a pre-launch phase, a launch-phase, and a post-launch phase, because it is finer-grained than previous entrepreneurial process contributions. It is more fine-grained because individuals' self-regulation processes may repeat within the phases identified in previous entrepreneurship theorizing, that is to say, pre-launch, etc. We refer to this cyclical feature of our framework as 'episodic' to denote our theorizing that individuals do not employ self-regulation processes (e.g. goal establishment and revision) just once, but rather they repeat these processes over and over again. The specific regularity and frequency of individuals' repetitions of self-regulatory processes in entrepreneurship and other contexts, however, is still an open empirical question to be explored in future research (Ployhart, 2008).

In organizational contexts, self-regulation has been used to understand how goals are set, the processes through which goals influence behavior, explanations for goal achievement or non-achievement, and how goals either get revised or new goals are adopted in their place (Vancouver, 2000). From a practical perspective, the importance of self-regulation has grown as a result of changes in most work settings that place more responsibility on employees (Wood, 2005), which is also likely to be the case for entrepreneurs and nascent new venture teams. Flatter organizational structures, because of reduced layers of middle-management, are associated with more worker participation and empowerment initiatives, often combined with virtual and remote work practices, which taken together place more burden on individuals to self-manage their behavior at work. Research on self-regulation can help identify specific strategies that can be taught to both employees and entrepreneurs alike so that they may better manage their work activities (Frayne and Geringer, 2000; Keith and Frese, 2005).

This chapter is divided into three main sections and a discussion, and aims to review and extend cognitive theories used to explain entrepreneurial behavior. Our work is based on current developments in both industrial and organizational (I/O) psychology and organizational behavior where research has converged on a self-regulation perspective to explain the complexity of human behavior, in general, and work motivation, in particular. A self-regulation view in an entrepreneurial context is useful because it allows for the inclusion of both individuals' characteristics and processes in the explanation of their behaviors, and then subsequent outcomes. In the first section, we propose a theoretical framework to guide entrepreneurship scholars who want to integrate a self-regulation perspective into their research. In the second section, we review the research done in entrepreneurship. This review is divided in two parts. The first section reviews research done up until 1990, which can be considered to be research conducted during the emergence of entrepreneurship as a research field. The second part focuses on research after 1990 when entrepreneurship and research journals such as *Journal of Business Venturing*, *Entrepreneurship Theory and Practice*, *Small Business Economics* and others became more established. In the third section, we link our self-regulation model and research in entrepreneurship to the current developments in the I/O literature. Thereby, we trace the historical roots of both entrepreneurship research and I/O psychology and organizational behavior, emphasizing the need for a convergence on a self-regulation perspective to explain the complexity of human behavior, in general, and entrepreneurship, in particular.

A PROPOSED THEORETICAL FRAMEWORK

Self-regulation is the capacity of individuals to guide their activities over time and across changing circumstances (Kanfer, 1990). Regulation implies the modulation of thought, affect, behavior, or attention via deliberate or automated use of specific mechanisms and supportive skills (Karoly, 1993). Vancouver and Day agreed that self-regulation refers to processes involved in attaining and maintaining goals, but take a more private psychological view, where goals represent inherently desired states (Vancouver and Day, 2005). The foregoing definitions of self-regulation suggest that it is central to understanding the self and many aspects of both social and psychological human functioning (Vohs and Baumeister, 2004), and its definitions also suggest that it is typically a conscious, willful process. An alternative view with growing empirical evidence also suggests, however, that self-regulation may also occur without awareness in an automatic fashion (Lord and Levy, 1994).

Self-regulation theories are a subset of cognitive theories that posit psychological constructs (e.g. goal establishment) and social constructs (e.g. shared goal establishment in teams) serve as important determinants of both individuals' behavior and their interim outcomes. Cognitive theories try to explain these behaviors and outcomes based on how individuals perceive and interpret information around them over time (Kanfer, 1990). Entrepreneurship researchers are now turning their attention towards cognitive theories that help to explain how individuals perceive and understand the world around them, and furthermore, in combination with individuals' characteristics, show how over time, their interactions with their environments influence their behaviors, and their subsequent outcomes (Baron, 1998; Delmar, 2006; Frese, 2007). As we mentioned above, cognitive theories assume that individuals do not possess perfect knowledge of the world because there is simply too much information out there to handle. As a consequence, individuals have to select some information and interpret it, and thus, based on information processing from their previous experiences, individuals tend to see and know the world differently

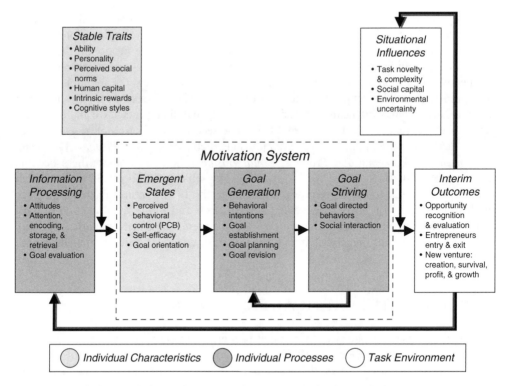

Figure 13.1　The psychology of entrepreneurs: an episodic framework

(Taylor, 1998). In short, just like other individuals, entrepreneurs are actively involved in the construction of their own realities.

In Figure 13.1, we illustrate our episodic self-regulation framework, which we offer to explain some of our foregoing observations about entrepreneurs' behavior and interim outcomes, based on previous research and theory in entrepreneurship. It is based on an integrative self-regulation perspective that has been emerging from I/O, educational, and clinical branches of psychology. This integrative self-regulation perspective has brought together different strands in cognitive theory that deal with human behavior, in general, and more specifically for I/O psychologists, theories that deal with work motivation. Our hope is that the framework may allow entrepreneurship scholars to address some weaknesses and limitations in previous research identified and discussed in the next section. Current research using cognitive theory can be perceived as fragmented because no overarching perspective, or framework, has been proposed to organize accumulating empirical results. It is not obvious how work on, for example, cognitive styles (Brigham et al., 2007), formation of intention (Thompson, 2009), and self-efficacy (Kickul et al., 2009) can be understood relative to each other. A self-regulation framework allows us to make such integrations from previous work, and in addition, it allows us to identify important research areas that yet need to be investigated in order to better explain how entrepreneurs think and behave.

In short, our framework is intended to allow scholars to better integrate various types of characteristics and processes, feedback loops, and boundary conditions for the many aspects of entrepreneurial behavior and interim outcomes to be investigated. All-inclusive models, however, are generally discouraged in our field, primarily because of the absence of overarching theoretical clarity and parsimony. With that in mind, our framework may be more useful to scholars who want to organize several constructs, which have been taken from two or more sub-systems of our framework, into a putative model. For models of this moderate scope, using longitudinal research designs and analysis tools available through structural equation modeling, researchers can test relatively sophisticated hypotheses that combine (a) mediated or indirect relations between three or more variables and (b) control for unobserved heterogeneity of time-invariant characteristics.

Our framework tries to integrate the following features of previous motivation research in an entrepreneurial context:

- *Stable Traits* Individual differences are defined across people (between-individual variations). Differences between individuals tend to be stable, or slowly changing, in an entrepreneurial context and include variables like perceived social norms, ability, personality, and experience. The effects of individual differences on the motivational system tend to be mediated through intra-individual processes (see below).

- *Information Processing* Intra-individual processes and behaviors are all defined within individuals (within-individual variations). These differences within individuals may change over time, often in response to feedback from their task environment. For example, intra-individual processes include variables that operationalize the extent to which people process information but that are not part of the motivation system.

- *Motivation System* is composed of three sub-systems: 'Emergent States', 'Goal Generation' and 'Goal Striving'. The motivation system is also constituted by intra-individual states, processes and behaviors (Chen and Kanfer, 2006).

- *Situational Influences* Context, or situational characteristics, include variables like task novelty, uncertainty, complexity, and stage in the venture creation process that are likely to moderate the effects of intra-individual processes and the motivational system on interim outcomes. In the language of control theory, these are disturbances to the relation between behavior and outcomes.

- *Interim Outcomes* Response variables relevant to entrepreneurship include opportunity identification and evaluation, labor status change, firm creation, financial or strategic performance, and firm growth. All of the foregoing systems in the framework are posited to explain interim outcomes, in some combination, in an episodic, iterative, view of individuals' engagement with the entrepreneurial process. For example, Ozgen and Baron (2007) show how social sources of information facilitate opportunity recognition.

By integrating the foregoing features from previous work motivation our framework allows for:

- A longitudinal perspective and the incorporation of a more dynamic theoretical approach to entrepreneurship as an episodic process with feedback loops. Feedback loops from interim outcomes at a particular time to antecedent systems at a later time are a condition *sine qua non* of a dynamic and episodic framework in the behavioral sciences (Kluger and DeNisi, 1996). In addition, there may be several reciprocal loops operating between other constructs from one time to another, which may not involve interim outcomes. A longitudinal perspective brings in time-varying explanatory factors for entrepreneurial behaviors and outcomes in individuals' lives and facilitates the incorporation of construct valid variables (e.g. self-efficacy) that change in value for particular individuals over time (Austin and Vancouver, 1996).
- Multiple levels of analysis – aggregation to a team level of analysis is often required by the empirical context. Chen and Kanfer (2006) argued that an analogous self-regulation model may be applied at a team level of analysis, which may become relevant as entrepreneurs recruit other individuals into nascent new venture teams.

Figure 13.1 illustrates the more stable psychological characteristics of entrepreneurs towards the left-hand side, which are relatively distal predictors of their behaviors and outcomes. Some examples of entrepreneurs' characteristics from the literature are listed under the broad heading of 'stable traits', which are relatively slow-changing or time-invariant aspects of individuals. As one looks towards the right-hand side of the figure, the characteristics and processes associated with entrepreneurs are progressively more proximal and time-varying predictors of their behaviors and outcomes (Baron et al., 2007; Delmar, 2006; Kanfer, 1992). Some examples of entrepreneurs' characteristics, processes, behaviors, and interim outcomes of interest are listed under each (sub-) system of the work motivation framework.

We next explain the elements of Figure 13.1 in more detail. Firstly, the more stable traits of entrepreneurs are distal influences on outcomes, that is to say, their influence is argued to be indirect, and thus, their affect is argued to be transmitted through several more proximal constructs. The stable traits of entrepreneurs include cognitive ability, personality traits, and human capital. Human capital is taken to include entrepreneurs' previous experience and various knowledge, skills, and abilities (KSAs) that may be relevant to a nascent new venture (Delmar, 2006; Rauch and Frese, 2007). In addition, entrepreneurs' stable traits may contribute to what is fed through from information processing to their motivational sub-systems. Analytically, these influences may be manifested through interactions between stable traits and information processing constructs before feeding through to influence motivational sub-systems and interim outcomes (Simons et al., 1999).

Secondly, information processing is how entrepreneurs are able to make sense of what is happening, both from psychological sources, inside themselves, and from social sources, coming from the task environment that is around them (Hinsz et al., 1997). Information processing is then argued to feed into the self-regulation system (Vancouver, 2000). Perhaps information comes into one or more of individuals' motivation sub-systems in parallel, or perhaps, information enters through one sub-system and passes to the others in series. Vancouver (2000) suggests the former, and this is what is illustrated in Figure 13.1, by the arrow connecting information processing with the dashed rectangle that contains the three motivation sub-systems – emergent states, goal generation, and goal striving.

Thirdly, emergent states, goal generation, and goal striving, have the strongest influence on individuals' interim outcomes, and most other distal influences, with the possible exception of ability, are argued to pass through these motivation sub-systems (Chen and Kanfer, 2006). As we mentioned above, Chen and Kanfer's framework encompasses both individual and team levels of analysis, and many cross-level relations, but our framework for entrepreneurs' self-regulation is restricted to an individual level of analysis. The framework at an individual level may be more relevant during the pre-launch phase (Baron, 2007), but following Chen and Kanfer's framework, it can be extended by adding a team level of analysis if and when entrepreneurs develop their opportunity to include other individuals, to form nascent teams in their new ventures.

Fourthly, situational influences contain many elements that are likely to moderate the influence of the entrepreneurs' characteristics, processes, and behaviors on their interim outcomes. Situational influences include, for example, novel and complex opportunities (e.g. innovation) and the entrepreneurs' social capital (e.g. access to social networks and other facets of the environment). We argue, however, that over time entrepreneurs may reduce their situational constraints (Aldrich and Fiol, 1994) through feedback loops from their interim outcomes. For example, entrepreneurs' social capital can be argued to strengthen their social competence in order to secure necessary funding to create new ventures (situational influences can positively moderate the relation between goal striving and interim outcomes), but once created, new ventures can attract key customers, who may commit to a burgeoning product or service, and such commitments, in turn, are argued to increase the social capital available to entrepreneurs (interim outcome at time (t-1) affects situational influences at time (t), through a feedback relation).

Fifthly, entrepreneurs' interim outcomes include various iterations of milestones in the creation of a new enterprise. Interim outcomes are typically operationalized through a variety of response variables depending on the focal development phase (Baron, 2007), which include opportunity recognition and evaluation, and production of business plans (pre-launch phase), new venture creation, securing of venture funding and survival (launch phase), and preparing the developing firm for initial public offering, growth and profitability (post-launch phase). Many of these outcomes are correlated, but their connections to each other and their antecedents are left unclear from previous research, because researchers are inclined to consider only one or two of these outcomes in a particular study (Delmar, 1997).

Sixthly, and finally, several feedback loops are posited to exist between interim outcomes at time (t-1) and predictors at time (t). From a psychological perspective, we posit that the feedback loop from interim outcomes at time (t-1) to information processing at time (t) may be the most important, because this is the one that allows entrepreneurs to make sense of feedback from their task environment, before going back into the motivation system and revising their goals and planning a new strategy for what to do next (Frese, 2007; Gollwitzer, 1990; Vancouver, 2000). In addition, there is also occasionally a feedback loop posited from goal generating at time t to goal striving also at time t, before any interim outcome feedback. This loop equates to the notion that sometimes individuals realize, in advance of any external feedback, that their established goals and/or implementation plans are unsustainable and need to be revised immediately (Gollwitzer, 1990).

To sum up, we argue that research examining entrepreneurs' profiles in terms of psychological characteristics and processes should take into account task environment complexity and entrepreneurs' responses to that complexity over time. Therefore, research has evolved towards more proximal explanations where entrepreneurial behavior and business performance are explained through cognitive theories and where some situational factors are modeled explicitly. As we see in the next section, previous research in entrepreneurship has focused heavily on individuals' traits (cognitive styles), information processing (attitudes), emergent states (perceived behavioral control and self-efficacy), but also more recently on the fit between context and person (Dimov, 2007). It is still rare to see entrepreneurship studies, however, that take into account goal establishment, goal implementation, goal striving and goal evaluation/revision processes, including the role of feedback from the task environment. In the next section we dig deeper into the strengths and weaknesses of contemporary research.

PREVIOUS USE OF COGNITIVE THEORIES

We use our self-regulation as an umbrella term, or super-ordinate theory, for a set of work motivation theories, which include the most popular cognitive theories that have been used in entrepreneurship research. Current research in entrepreneurship behavior includes cognitive styles of various sorts (e.g. Sadler-Smith and Badger, 1998) and continuing work on behavioral intentions.

Since 1990, entrepreneurship scholars have applied both the theory of planned behavior (perceived behavioral control and behavioral intentions) and social cognitive theory (self-efficacy) extensively, but as we mentioned above, it is not well known that these theories can be integrated in a self-regulation framework. Both the foregoing theories can be described generically as expectancy-valance theories (Pittman, 1998; Vroom, 1964), that is to say, they are based on the assumption that individuals' behaviors are determined by their cognitive evaluation of the information available to them about the positive and negative outcomes of that behavior or object. They were already coupled in Locke's (1991a) special edition of *Organizational Behavior and Human Decision Processes,* which was devoted to cognitive self-regulation theories. These and other contributions from influential scholars have been consolidated during more recent years in two handbooks of self-regulation (Baumeister and Vohs, 2004; Boekaerts et al., 2000), special issues in leading journals (e.g. Boekaerts et al., 2005; Locke, 1991a), and several chapters in edited volumes (e.g. Kanfer et al., 2008).

We structure this section in the following way. First, we discuss the history of psychological research in entrepreneurship up until 1990, focusing specifically on the early work evoking motivation. In the second and major part, we review specific studies made after 1990, starting with a more general overview of strengths and weaknesses of previous research in the field. 1990 serves as an important milestone because the complexity of entrepreneurial behavior became an integral part of the research agenda (Gartner, 1988; Shaver and Scott, 1991) and more sophisticated statistical methods (e.g. structural equation models) became more easily available, permitting the empirical test of more complex models (Davidsson, 1989).

Understanding the Historical Roots of Motivation Research in Entrepreneurship

Most of the early research on the entrepreneur's psychology focused on personality traits. Despite recent advances, however, personality is not likely to explain more than a minor share of entrepreneurial behavior. Personality is often loosely defined in terms of regularities in action, feelings, and thoughts that are stable characteristics of the individual across situation and time (Snyder and Cantor, 1998). The lack of results can be explained by theoretical as well as methodological problems characterizing the perspective (Carsrud and Johnson, 1989; Chell et al., 1991; Delmar, 1996; Gartner, 1988; Herron and Robinson, 1993; Sexton and Bowman, 1985) but even if these problems are mitigated, personality traits remain distal to outcomes as specified in Figure 13.1. It is probably too simplistic to relate a trait to the state of being an entrepreneur or the outcome of the firm. Entrepreneurs are not, to a large degree, different from people in general.

Some trait research, however, is of particular interest to scholars working on the motivation and self-regulation of entrepreneurs. One of the best-known characteristics associated with entrepreneurs is McClelland's 'need for achievement' (McClelland, 1961; McClelland and Winter, 1969), another is 'locus of control' (Rotter, 1966), and these are combined in several motivation theories (Weiner, 1985).

Need for achievement
This trait is also closely related to risk taking as it takes into account the perceived risk of the situation as well as the perceived level of competence. According to McClelland, entrepreneurs are individuals that have a high need for achievement, and this makes them especially suitable to create ventures. McClelland's theory identifies the situations preferred by individuals high in need for achievement, and which situations arouse the achievement motivation. Individuals who are high achievers will choose a situation defined by: individual responsibility, moderate risk-taking as a function of skill, knowledge of results of decisions, novel instrumental activity, and anticipation of future possibilities.

Thus, it is the prospect of achievement satisfaction, not money, which drives the entrepreneur. Money is important primarily as a measure of how well one is doing in business. McClelland's theory has received fairly consistent empirical support, suggesting that there is a relationship between entrepreneurship and achievement motivation (Begley and Boyd, 1987; Bellu, 1988; Davidsson, 1989; Delmar, 1996; Johnson, 1990; McClelland, 1961; Perry et al. 1986). The basic features of self-regulation are present in need for achievement motivation as feedback from interim outcomes is an integral part of the theory.

More recently Miner and his associates have developed McClelland's achievement motivation theory by developing five motive patterns instead of the single achievement motive. This task motivation theory suggests that it is not possible to predict behavior or performance on the basis of a single value, as is the case of need for achievement, but that performance can be predicted by a complex set of values or motive patterns. Miner's five motive patterns form an overall index of task motivation. They are: self-achievement; risk-taking; feedback of results; personal innovation; and planning for the future. Results show consistent validity for the scale, especially the total score on all scales combined correlate significantly with entrepreneurial performance, particularly growth (Bellu, 1993; Bellu and Sherman, 1995; Miner et al., 1989; 1992; Miner et al., 1994).

Locus of control
The concept of 'locus of control' first appeared in Rotter's social learning theory (Rotter, 1966) of how individuals' perceptions of control affect their behavior. The theory assumes that individuals categorize events and situations based on their underlying, shared properties. One such category concerns whether a potential end or goal can be attained through one's actions or follows from luck or other uncontrolled external factors. A person believing that the achievement of a goal is dependent on his or her own behavior or individual characteristics believes in internal control. If, on the other hand, a person believes that an achievement is the result of luck and external factors, she believes in external control. Therefore, locus of control is conceived as one determinant of the expectancy of success (Weiner, 1992).

Empirical results indicate a low to moderate positive correlation between internal control and entrepreneurs, and there is a weak tendency that a high internal orientation is associated with better performance (Brockhaus, 1982; Miller and Toulouse, 1986). A number of studies, however, have reported no significant differences between entrepreneurs and managers with respect to locus of control (Sexton and Bowman, 1985). In psychology, the concept and measurement of locus of control has been heavily criticized (Furnham and Steele, 1993), and the concept has been more or less abandoned in favor of attribution theory which has a more complex view on causality orientation (Anderson and Strigel, 1981; Weiner, 1985) as well as by Bandura's social cognitive theory which was formulated prior to Rotter's locus of control theory. As a result, locus of control is a concept which should probably not be included in future empirical research on entrepreneurial behavior. 'Need for achievement' can still be seen in research on entrepreneurship as a part of more complex efforts and represents probably one of the best-validated traits related to entrepreneurship. In the next section, we look at more recent advances in research.

An Overview of the Strengths and Weaknesses in Present Research

Since the beginning of the 1990s, entrepreneurship research has moved from trait theories towards cognitive theories, which are better able to explain the complexity inherent in entrepreneurs' behavior and subsequent outcomes. Empirical studies are, for example, relying more and more heavily on mediation and moderation analyses (Brigham et al., 2007; Lee et al., 2009; Liñán and Chen, 2009) and structural equation models (Baum et al., 1998; Baum et al., 2001).

The use of cognitive theories allows for a better understanding of why people engage in entrepreneurial behaviors. The contribution of these theories is that they enable us to better understand the interaction between entrepreneurs' characteristics and processes and their situations. Stated differently, there is a movement away from studying entrepreneurs' traits and states, and towards studying their traits, states, and processes in combination with situations, which are posited to lead to entrepreneurial behavior, and subsequent outcomes (Baron, 1998; Carsrud and Johnson, 1989; Shaver and Scott, 1991). Behavior is theorized to be heavily influenced both by how individuals perceive their environment or context (e.g. novelty, munificence, complexity and uncertainty) and how it is mediated through their perceptions. Thus, researchers should, but do not always, acknowledge context as an important boundary condition to their hypothesized relations between entrepreneurs' characteristics and processes and their behaviors and outcomes.

Cognitive theories from a self-regulation perspective provide a basis for understanding the choices made by entrepreneurs and why they persist in doing what they are doing. They have some important advantages. First, they are easy to operationalize. Second, they have demonstrated validity. Third, frameworks such as the one presented here have considerable advantages over personality trait-based models. Instead of talking about a set of non-changeable characteristics, scholars are able to discuss cognitive processes that may alter over time. Cognitive models have both (a) greater power to explain entrepreneurial behavior and (b) more practical advice to offer on how to train and educate future entrepreneurs.

Recent applications of cognitive models in entrepreneurship research, however, have had several important limitations. The first is a tendency to focus on single individual entrepreneurs, as opposed to entrepreneurial teams. Teams are an increasingly popular unit of analysis among scholars and an increasingly relevant real world phenomenon. The second limitation is a tendency to see entrepreneurs' decisions as being static, as opposed to dynamic. This leads to a number of errors: (a) differences between individuals on various characteristic and process variables are overly stressed, as opposed to differences within individuals on these variables over time; (b) the importance of feedback from the task environment, and other variables at earlier time periods, is suppressed or ignored; and (c) important contextual contingencies that moderate relations between individual characteristic and process variables and behavior and/or outcome variables, are often not modeled. The third limitation is that intra-individual processes that indirectly transmit the effects of individual differences and information processing variables to behavioral and outcome variables are poorly integrated. Taken together, these limitations lead to a restricted understanding of what is popularly known as the entrepreneurial mindset and its effects on new venture creation and growth. Actually, our call for a more complex and dynamic view of entrepreneurs' behavior and outcomes is not the first; Shaver and Scott (1991) in their seminal article made some very similar arguments.

In sum, there is a need for an individual level understanding of the characteristics and processes leading to entrepreneurial behavior and outcomes, which has the possibility to include a team level of analysis. Research is evolving towards more integrated and complex models that take into account not only the psychological and non-psychological, for example, age and sex (Gupta et al., 2009), characteristics and processes of entrepreneurs, but also situational variables. Several important pieces, however, are missing as we have pointed out when we presented our framework. Perhaps this is because of an overemphasis on some motivation theories.

Cognitive and Learning Styles

There have been several recent contributions on cognitive styles (Brigham et al., 2007; Dutta and Thornhill, 2008; Haynie and Shepherd, 2009; Kickul et al., 2009) and learning styles (Dimov, 2007). Cognitive style is a type of heuristic that individuals employ when they approach, frame, and solve problems. It can be defined as an individual's preferred or habitual approach to organizing, representing, and processing information (Streufert and Nogami, 1989). It is built-in and automatic (Riding and Rayner, 1998), and it differs among individuals (Messick, 1984). It is someone's preferred way of learning or solving problems. According to Brigham et al. (2007, p. 31), research has shown that: (1) cognitive styles are pervasive dimensions that can be assessed using psychometric techniques; (2) they are stable over time; (3) they are bipolar; and (4) they describe different rather than better thinking processes. In the terms of our framework, cognitive styles would be construed as a characteristic of individuals.

In entrepreneurship research, cognitive styles have been used in several ways. Brigham et al. (2007) use cognitive styles as a moderator of relations between organizational structure and both individuals' job satisfaction and intention to exit. These mediate the effect of cognitive styles on firm turnover. Dimov (2007) and Kickul and her co-authors (2009) looked at how cognitive styles affect individuals' progression from opportunity recognition behaviors to opportunity exploitation behaviors. Dutta and Thornhill (2008) used individuals' cognitive styles as a mediator between competitive pressure and growth intention in a qualitative study of 30 Canadian entrepreneurs.

Haynie and Shepherd (2009) developed a scale for cognitive adaptability based on a meta-cognitive theory that addresses the issue of self-regulation and offers a bridge between cognitive styles and our view of self-regulation. They define cognitive adaptability as 'the ability to be dynamic, flexible, and self regulating in oneís cognitions given dynamic and uncertain task environment' (p. 695). Their approach to self-regulation is from an information processing point of view (i.e. how sense making is achieved) as opposed to our approach from a more motivational point of view, but again in our opinion, these approaches are consistent. According to them, cognitive adaptability is the aggregate of five dimensions: goal orientation, meta-cognitive knowledge, meta-cognitive experience, meta-cognitive control, and monitoring. Their concept is still one of a stable individual trait, but speaks closely to our view of individuals as self-regulating actors, and their dimensions could be redistributed to cover most sub-systems of our framework.

Attitudes and the Theory of Planned Behavior

Taking our review of cognitive theories that scholars have applied to entrepreneurship a little further back in time, two models are of principal interest to us, the theory of planned behavior (TPB) and social cognitive theory (SCT), because they have both been used extensively in entrepreneurship research and integrated under a self-regulation perspective. TPB and SCT address different parts of the motivation system. Attitude-based models such as TPB (Ajzen, 1991; 1995) deal with how individuals' intentions are formed. Conversely, the SCT model, with its self-efficacy concept, focuses on the importance of individuals' perceived domain knowledge and how their motivation is formed in achievement contexts. Self-efficacy is an important complement to intention models because it helps adapt them to achievement contexts and to explain how individuals' perceived competence affects their intentions. The two may be tested within the same framework (Wilson et al., 2007).

Attitudes are a major concept in motivation theory. An attitude is an evaluation of an object or a concept, that is to say, the extent to which someone judges an object or concept to be good or bad (Eagly and Chaiken, 1993). In psychological language, individuals' traits such as 'locus of control' or 'over-optimism' are weak determinants of specific behaviors. Attitudes are more specific and therefore considered to be more proximal to individuals' behavioral intentions, and, thus, attitudes are more important determinants of behavior. In addition, attitudes are interesting because of their applied relevance. If attitudes are believed to have an impact on behavioral intentions, then it is potentially important to understand how attitudes can be changed. Thus, the impact of attitudes on entrepreneurial behavior is worthy of close examination, because (a) they are supposed to have a directive influence on behavior and (b) they are much easier to change than personality and other stable traits. The possibility of changing attitudes suggests that if attitudes characterizing entrepreneurs who start new businesses were known, then other people could be influenced to adopt those same attitudes and, as a result, the number of people starting new businesses could be increased (Davidsson, 1995; Kolvereid, 1996a; 1996b; Krueger, 1993).

One limitation to the foregoing summary of relations between individuals' attitudes and intentions and their behaviors concerns how well individuals' attitudes and intentions actually predict behaviors and how precisely they explain when or why they engage in specific actions (Bagozzi and Warshaw, 1992; Doll and Ajzen, 1992; Kim and Hunter, 1993). Intentions are tendencies or dispositions to behave in a generally favorable or unfavorable way towards the object of an attitude. This means, for example, that it is difficult to predict if someone will start a business because they have positive attitudes towards starting businesses. It is only known that people will act in accordance with their attitudes. This means that people with positive attitudes towards starting businesses will behave favorably to things connected to business start-ups, for example, (a) encourage a friend or relative to start a business, (b) help to finance a start-up effort, or even (c) establish their own business. Thus, a shortcoming of attitude theories is that they don't give much information about how individuals' evaluations of a concept are translated into behavioral intentions, behaviors, actions, and subsequent outcomes. In other words, attitude theories help us understand how and why individuals make choices, but they do not give much guidance about the degree of effort and persistence that individuals will engage in when striving to achieve their chosen goals (Locke, 1991b). Empirical work shows only moderate correlations between intentions and behavior: individuals' intentions explain only around 30 per cent of the variance in their behavior. For example, Kolvereid and Isaksen (2006) found in their longitudinal study of Norwegian entrepreneurs that their intentions predicted 39.7 per cent of the variance in their behavior (Kolvereid and Isaksen, 2006). The development of better-validated instruments of entrepreneurial intentions is now addressing these moderate correlations somewhat (Liñán and Chen, 2009; Thompson, 2009).

Nevertheless, the advantages of attitude research override many of the disadvantages. The possibility to examine attitudes towards different facets of entrepreneurship, across a wide variety of populations, and the possibility to easily communicate the results to a wider audience (e.g. policy makers) remains compelling. Furthermore, even if attitudes are not perfect predictors of individuals' behavior, they are still much better predictors than personality characteristics. Thus, attitude theories have received considerable attention within the field of entrepreneurship. Two attitude concepts have been predominantly researched, namely attitudes towards becoming self-employed, or starting a business, and attitudes towards new business growth. The research on these concepts has been based either on formal attitude theory or on finding simple relationships among attitudes and the concept.

The most prevalent model is Ajzen's (1991) theory of planned behavior (TPB), or theories derived from it. TPB argues that behavioral intentions are predicted by three factors: attitudes, social norms, and perceived behavioral control. TPB is important because models of individuals' attitudes provide understanding about their beliefs and feelings towards entrepreneurship and how they play out in behavioral intentions and actions, and consequently, allow policy makers to create a more supportive environment for new venture creation. Thus, many entrepreneurship researchers have invoked TPB, but few have fully tested the model. Most researchers only test the hypothesized relations between the three predictor factors (i.e. attitudes, subjective norms, and perceived behavioral control) and behavioral intentions, leaving the link between behavioral intentions and either goal striving behaviors or interim outcomes unexamined. More precisely, it is likely that the coefficients among the factors and their relative weights vary across contexts, cultures, age and sex. Nevertheless, some worthwhile results have been achieved by scholars investigating new venture creation (Davidsson, 1995; Kolvereid, 1996a; Kolvereid, 1996b; Kolvereid and Isaksen, 2006; Krueger and Brazeal, 1994; Krueger and Carsrud, 1993; Krueger and Dickson, 1993; Shepherd and Krueger, 2002), new venture growth (Davidsson, 1989; Kolvereid, 1992; Kolvereid and Bullvag, 1996; Wiklund, 1998; Wiklund et al., 2003), and the effect of entrepreneurship education (Athayde, 2009; Peterman and Kennedy, 2003; Souitaris et al., 2007; Wilson et al., 2007).

Irrespective of which of these topics scholars are investigating, they tend to arrive at similar results. First, attitudes do not predict, by themselves, individuals' intentions to start or expand a business. Second, subjective norms have even weaker predictive power than attitudes, which suggests that what others believe or feel is important does not overtly affect entrepreneurs' intentions. Perceived behavioral control, however, is important and stands out as the strongest predictor of behavioral intentions for entrepreneurs; it is also affected by education in the subject. In other words, someone will try to start a business if they believe that they can do it, in terms of, (a) having the ability, and (b) having the knowledge required to carry out the behavior. Thus, perceived behavioral control, or perceived feasibility, is a key component in the prediction of someone engaging in entrepreneurial behavior.

To sum up, research on attitudes and entrepreneurship has yielded consistent findings. A number of studies have found that perceived behavioral control was the single most important predictor of intentions. Both attitudes and subjective norms have been found to play a relatively minor role. Attitude models such as TPB, however, offer little information in explaining how and why a certain behavior is chosen by an individual. Specifically, intentions are far from perfect predictors of subsequent behavior, let alone interim outcomes, and it is not clear what the exact nature of the relation between intention and behavior is.

Social Cognitive Theory

The common denominator between attitude-based models and achievement context models is the search for control. That is, individuals try to organize their lives in ways that give them some perceived control. As we explained above, TPB is concerned with preferences (i.e. what is and what is not important). Achievement context models deal with both behavior and outcomes (i.e. actual performance). The aim of social cognitive theory (SCT) is to explain individuals' goal directed behaviors (Bandura, 1986; 1991; Wood and Bandura, 1989). The theory assumes that most individual behaviors have a purpose, which is regulated, at least tacitly, by some of their own forethought. More precisely, individuals tend to form beliefs about what they can do, they anticipate the likely consequences of their prospective actions, they set goals for themselves, and they plan courses of action that are likely to produce a desired outcome. In SCT, perceived self-efficacy is the central mechanism and is the key to understanding how individuals function during their setting up goals and their carrying out actions needed to fulfill them. In comparison to TPB, which focuses on predicting behavior, SCT is more relevant for explaining the function of perceived behavioral control and its effect on both individuals' behaviors and outcomes (i.e. performance).

Self-efficacy is a concept concerned with individuals' beliefs about their capabilities to produce performances that influence events affecting their lives (Bandura, 1995). In other words, it is about individuals' beliefs in their capacity to mobilize motivation, cognitive resources, and courses of action needed to control events that affect them. Someone's belief in their efficacy influences: (a) the decisions that they make, (b) their degree of aspiration, (c) how much effort they mobilize in a given situation, (d) how long they persist at a task in the face of difficulties and setbacks, and (e) whether their thought patterns are self-hindering or self-aiding. Feedback on individuals' degree of achievement is central to the theory, as individuals' negative or positive achievement spirals affect their perceived self-efficacy, and in turn, their negative and positive achievement spirals affect their perceived self-efficacy. Nevertheless, SCT also posits that negative spirals of achievement can be broken through individuals' engagement with appropriate self-efficacy training.

Scholars have posited individuals' perceived self-efficacy to be a key explanatory factor for entrepreneurial behavior (Boyd and Vozikis, 1994) because, in business settings, it has been associated with individuals' initiating and persisting with achievement oriented behaviors (Wood and Bandura, 1989). Westerberg (1998) has shown that entrepreneurs' perceived self-efficacy has significant effects on their businesses' strategies and performance. In general, the firms of entrepreneurs with high perceived self-efficacy have higher performance (i.e. profitability, customer satisfaction, and firm survival) than the firms of entrepreneurs with low perceived self-efficacy. Forbes (2005), however, turned around the causality implying that the firm's strategic decision making was influencing the entrepreneurs' self-efficacy. Perceived self-efficacy has also been shown to be positively related to someone's intention to start their own business and their exploration of new opportunities (Chen et al., 1998; Kickul et al., 2009; Krueger and Dickson, 1993). It is also an important outcome of entrepreneurship education (Peterman and Kennedy, 2003), especially for women (Wilson et al., 2007).

Although the roots of self-efficacy can be traced back to the classic individual trait concept of locus of control (Rotter, 1966) there is an important difference: individuals' self-efficacy depends on the situation, whereas locus of control is generally stable across situations. Thus, someone can have high self-efficacy in one situation, and simultaneously, they may have low self-efficacy in another. For example, individuals may perceive themselves as capable rock climbers, but poor in business matters, even though the two situations involve considerable risk taking.

It has actually been proposed that the two concepts ('self-efficacy' and 'perceived behavioral control') affecting motivation and behavior are synonymous. However, Ajzen's (1991) own description of the relationship between perceived behavioral control and behavior would suggest that perceived behavioral control may be divided into (a) a reflection of skills and ability and (b) a proxy of actual control. Hence, the first is related to Bandura's (1991) self-efficacy and the second to perceived controllability over behavior (Rotter, 1966). Empirical research supports the theoretical distinction between self-efficacy and perceived behavioral control (Armitage and Conner, 1999; Manstead and Eekelen, 1998), suggesting that perceived self-efficacy (i.e. perceived ability) is a better predictor of intention and behavior than is perceived control. These findings, however, only concern specific types of behavior (e.g. dieting or school achievement), and we do not know if they apply to other behaviors in different domains. Hence, there is still a need to keep both concepts when trying to explain entrepreneurial motivation and behavior.

Summing Up Cognitive Models in Entrepreneurship

This section has reviewed three different cognitive models that are argued to converge towards self-regulation theory, that is to say, cognitive styles, attitude-based models (e.g. theory of planned behavior) and achievement-context models (e.g. social cognitive theory). Various applications of these models have already greatly enhanced scholars' understanding of entrepreneurial behavior. The theoretical value of cognitive models is that they offer a sophisticated theoretical frame of reference which incorporates more of the complexity in entrepreneurs' behavior, and still allows scholars to actually test hypothesized models. The models are, in the configuration of their component constructs, closer to individuals' actual behavior. In addition, cognitive models allow variation both within and between individuals. Taken together, the foregoing features lead to more explanatory power than previous formulations of predictors for entrepreneurial behavior.

To illustrate some of the increased explanatory sophistication available to scholars from using cognitive models to guide their entrepreneurship research, consider, for example, Baron and Markman's (2003) study of entrepreneurs' social competence. Their results illustrate the importance to scholars' understanding that (a) situational constraints can act as boundary conditions on relations between predictors of entrepreneurial behaviors and their response variables of interest, (b) entrepreneurs' skills may develop over time, and (c) more time-varying and proximal concepts are likely to generate important results for understanding the psychology of entrepreneurs. Finally, scholars may offer better explanations for how entrepreneurs behave by focusing on entrepreneurs' cognition, that is to say, how entrepreneurs come to understand the information around them and process that information in order to organize themselves to behave accordingly. However, present research focuses heavily on single individuals and many core motivation theories leave much to be explored.

MORE RECENT APPLICATION OF COGNITIVE THEORIES

In the previous sections, we have first shown a general framework to organize current cognitive theories. We then moved into a review of empirical findings. In this section, based on current discussion in the I/O psychology and organizational behavior literatures, we show how these theories may be brought together and what the advantages of doing so are (Diefendorff and Lord, 2008). In this way we hope to better motivate the acceptance of our framework. It might also help researchers in entrepreneurship to discover new types of theories to explore in an entrepreneurship setting.

Self-regulation addresses not only individuals' willpower to work hard on achieving their goals, but also their flexibility to work smart by approaching their goals pragmatically. Diefendorff and Lord (2008) expanded on these potentially opposing aspects of self-regulation by saying that sometimes self-regulation involves individuals in persisting on a task until they have completed it, but other times individuals need to disengage from a task when even their best efforts are doomed to failure. In the case of entrepreneurs, self-regulation may involve individuals initiating action to take advantage of some opportunity in the environment, but it may also involve them in being cautious and delaying commitments until conditions are right or more important goals have been achieved. Finally, self-regulation may involve individuals' flexibility in allocating attention between two or more goals or focusing on just one goal and ignoring all others. Thus, the key to effective self-regulation is the individual's ability to act in multiple goal environments while responding to internal conditions in a flexible and context-sensitive manner (Mitchell et al., 2008).

Interest in self-regulation has sources across several behavioral science disciplines. In clinical work, early conceptions emphasized psychological processes that were posited to mediate between individuals and their own functioning (Karoly and Kanfer, 1982). Findings in goal setting research seemed to fit this view of psychological processes mediating between individuals and their behavior, and subsequent outcomes, and thus, suggest that a self-regulation perspective might also be useful for understanding the effectiveness of goal setting in organizational settings (Locke and Latham, 1990). In addition, applications of self-regulation theory have incorporated developments in scholars' understanding of both individuals' self structures (Mischel and Ayduk, 2004) and dynamic systems in general (Carver and Scheier, 1998), which bring in emotion as well as cognition (Lord et al., 2002).

Taxonomy of Theories within Self-regulation

In the following sections, we describe a three-way taxonomy of theoretical approaches that can be described as focusing to a greater or lesser extent on 'structure', 'phase', and 'content' of individuals' self-regulation theories (Diefendorff and Lord, 2008; Grant and Dweck, 1999). We further develop this taxonomy by examining the implications of these theoretical approaches for research design and then use these ideas to develop some principles that may help future entrepreneurship researchers to integrate structure, phase, and content perspectives in their empirical work.

Grant and Dweck (1999) observed that most theories have something to say about each aspect of self-regulation; nevertheless, each tends to emphasize one of the three approaches over the others. 'Structural theories' of self-regulation endeavor to formulate general principles that apply to goal directed behavior across an extensive range of individuals, places, and times. Specifically, they describe individuals' self-regulation constructs and relations between constructs (Bandura, 1991; Carver and Scheier, 1998), for example, individuals' goals, behaviors, and some relations between the two, and probably, one or more moderating, or mediating, variables. 'Phase theories' of self-regulation focus on the sequence of goal oriented activities, which typically start with individuals' goal establishment and end with goal attainment, or sometimes, goal revision (Gollwitzer, 1990). These theories break individuals' self-regulation into steps and describe the tasks that individuals try to accomplish in each step, along with their accompanying cognitive, emotional, and behavioral resource requirements. 'Content theories' of self-regulation describe how individuals' differences on one or more characteristics can affect their approach to goals and self-regulation processes (Grant and Dweck, 1999). Table 13.1 summarizes how the foregoing taxonomy of existing theories can be integrated in the self-regulation framework that we illustrated in Figure 13.1 and outlined in the first part of the chapter. The left hand column in Table 13.1 is a re-arrangement of the (sub-) systems and relations posited in our integrative framework, illustrated in Figure 13.1. The three columns to the right of the first column list analogous features from structural, phase, and content theories of self-regulation, respectively. The structural theories column mostly contains features from a control theory (CT) negative feedback loop (Carver and Scheier, 1998). The phase theories column contains mostly features from Gollwitzer's (1990) theory of action phases and mindsets. Finally, the content theory column contains contributions from several authors that conceptualize particular dimensions on which individuals differ. The idea behind Table 13.1 is to show how research can move forward by integrating original source theories, while trying to do not too much violence to the source theory, and to illustrate the value of doing so. An alternative table, for example, might substitute TPB for CT.

Structural Theories

Structural theories of self-regulation identify general systems and relations between those systems and sub-systems that apply to goal directed behavior across a range of individuals, places, and times. According to Kanfer (2005), structural theories, including CT and SCT, have been the most commonly investigated self-regulation theories by organizational researchers, and she includes goal setting theory (Locke and Latham, 1990) with SCT for these purposes (Kanfer, 2005). Diefendorff and Lord (2008) noted the disagreements in the literature about the relative merits of CT and SCT (Bandura and Locke, 2003; Vancouver and Day, 2005; Vancouver et al., 2001), but following their lead, we choose to combine the two approaches and describe their basic tenets, as follows.

Social cognitive theory (SCT) has many similarities to CT. SCT views self-regulation as a cyclical process where individuals receive performance feedback with respect to progress towards their goals, which leads them to make adjustments to their current behaviors in order to reduce discrepancies between their interim outcomes and their goals (Zimmerman, 2000). SCT assumes that individuals structure their goals hierarchically (Bandura and Locke, 2003). Control theory (CT) also assumes that individuals maintain a hierarchy of goals, with short-term concrete goals lower down in the hierarchy, and longer term, more abstract goals higher up. Lower-level goals are conceived as strategies for attaining higher-level goals (Lord and Levy, 1994). Thus, individuals devise lower-level action goals in order to reduce goal-to-performance feedback discrepancies further up in their goal hierarchy.

Table 13.1 Integration of existing theories: (sub-)systems (■) and relations (→)

Integrative framework	Structural theories	Phase theories	Content theories
■ Stable traits	–	–	■ Intrinsic rewards ■ Cognitive styles
■ Information processing	■ Input (Perception of variable)	■ Goal evaluation (Evaluative mindset)	–
Stable traits → Information processing			
Outcomes (t-1) → Information processing	Stimuli	Action conclusion	

■ Motivation system

Integrative framework	Structural theories	Phase theories	Content theories
Information processing → Motivation system	Perceptual signal		
■ Emergent states	–	–	■ Goal orientation
Information processing → Emergent states			
■ Goal generation	■ Standard (Goal)	■ Goal establishment (Deliberative mindset) ■ Goal revision (Evaluative mindset)	–
Information processing → Goal generation	Goal error signal	Goal choice	
		■ Goal planning (Implemental mindset)	
Goal striving (t) → Goal generation (t)		Revise strategy	
■ Goal striving	■ Output (Changes in behavior)	■ Goal striving (Actional mindset)	–
Information processing → Goal striving	Output error signal	Action intension	

Integrative framework	Structural theories	Phase theories	Content theories
■ Situational influences	■ Disturbances	–	–
Outcomes (t) → Situational influences (t+1)			
■ Interim outcomes	■ Effect on environment (Variable)	–	–
Goal striving → Outcomes	behavior		
Situational influences x Motivation → Outcomes	External contingencies		

Bandura and Locke (2003) claim, however, that SCT emphasizes discrepancy pro-duction, that is to say, individuals setting new goals that are higher than their previous interim outcomes. The SCT argument rests on an assumption that motivation resides in individuals engaging effort by their generating challenging goals, specifically, producing discrepancies between their goals and their previous interim outcomes by generating new and even higher goals. The alternative view, attributed to CT, is that individuals engage effort by their striving to achieve their chosen goals, specifically reducing discrepancies between their goals and their previous interim outcomes by putting their plans to achieve their chosen goals into action. These apparently opposing positions on producing and reducing discrepancies between individuals goals and their interim outcomes is, at least partly, reconcilable through the phase approach to self-regulation (e.g. Gollwitzer, 1990), which we discuss in the next section.

Phase Theories

Phase theories of self-regulation describe distinguishable steps that individuals make when conceiving and pursuing goals. Lewin et al. (1944) described the motivation process as consisting of two phases: goal generating and goal striving (Lewin et al., 1944). 'Goal generating' involves individuals weighing the reasons for pursuing their activities to determine what goal will 'emerge or become dominant' (p. 376), for example, to engage in a new venture or not. 'Goal striving' involves individuals performing behaviors in the service of goal attainment, such as initiating action, putting forth effort, trying different task strategies, and persisting in the face of obstacles or setbacks. For example, entrepreneurs may initiate the set-up of a new venture by doing some preliminary activities. Goal setting refers to individuals' selecting goals, whereas goal striving refers to their behaviors directed towards existing goals.

Other researchers have adopted the distinction between goal generating and goal striving, and some have added steps to further explicate the process (Karoly, 1993; Zimmerman, 2000). According to Diefendorff and Lord (2008), Gollwitzer's (1990) four-phase approach to goal setting within a self-regulation perspective is particularly well articulated, has received the most research attention, and is the most widely adopted (p. 158).

The four phases in Gollwitzer's (1990) conceptualization of self-regulation are as follows: (1) goal establishment; (2) goal planning; (3) goal striving; and (4) goal evaluation/revision. Gollwitzer (1990) argued that each self-regulation phase has a spe-cific task to be accomplished and they are each separated by boundary events, specifically, goal choice, action initiation, and action conclusion. In addition, he argues that the task in each phase is facilitated by particular mindsets, which prepare individuals to act in ways that enable them to accomplish the task. The mindsets influence what individuals pay attention to through the contents of their thoughts, and thus help them accomplish phase specific tasks.

The goal establishment phase is accompanied by a 'deliberative' mindset, which helps individuals to be open to information and to attempt to evaluate the feasibility and desirability of competing goals. This phase ends when goals have been selected and individuals move on to the planning phase. The goal planning phase is facilitated by an 'implemental' mindset, which is characterized by cognitive tuning of individuals' goals towards action-related information and an incomplete and optimistic analysis of the desirability and feasibility of their goals. This phase, and goal generation phases more generally, ends when action begins, and at that point individuals enter the goal striving phase. This phase is accompanied by an 'actional' mindset, which helps individuals immerse themselves in their tasks and not be distracted by unrelated information. Once individuals have completed their actions, they enter the evaluation phase, characterized by a similarly named 'evaluative' mindset, which enables individuals to revisit their goals' feasibility and desirability. Individuals carry forward any revisions to their goals, which arise during the evaluation phase, into the next iteration of their self-regulatory goal setting phases.

To sum up, phase models of self-regulation offer a detailed description of how individuals perform tasks in an iterative sequence of goal directed behaviors, and how their accompanying cognitions and thought contents change accordingly through time (Diefendorff and Lord, 2008). However, phase theories do not explain how self-regulation constructs are related to interim outcomes over time (i.e. structural theories), nor do they address the more specific details of what individuals are pursuing (i.e. content theories). In the next section we address content theories.

Content Theories

Content theories of self-regulation focus on specifying the nature and origin of individuals' goals and how individual differences impact on their goals within self-regulation (Ryan and Deci, 2000). Content theories often invoke individuals' characteristics (e.g. basic needs or personality constructs) as determinants of their goals or how individuals' goal content is reflected in their goals. Diefendorff and Lord (2008) include the following examples in their review of the content category of self-regulation theories: self determination (Ryan and Deci, 2000), regulatory focus (Higgins, 1997), and goal orientation (Dweck, 1986). Here we restrict ourselves to Grant and Dweck's (2003) goal orientation theory, which we believe to be most relevant to entrepreneurial context.

Goal orientation focuses on individuals having different types of goal in particular situations (Dweck, 1986), and thus, it is more context sensitive, and more like an emergent state from our framework, than either of the other content theories mentioned, which are more like individual traits. Individuals may adopt either a learning-goal orientation (LGO) or performance-goal orientation (PGO). Individuals adopting an LGO exert effort in order to build up their knowledge, skills, and competences on activities and tend to believe that their abilities can be developed. Individuals adopting a PGO exert effort in order to show off their knowledge, skills, and competences to others and tend to believe that their abilities are fixed. This is an important development from and difference from 'need for achievement'. VandeWalle et al. (2001) further subdivided individuals adopting a PGO, into those with 'approach' and those with 'avoidance' performance goal orientations. Individuals adopting the approach variant of PGO still exert effort in order to show off their knowledge, skills, and competences to others, but those adopting the avoidance variant of PGO exert effort in order to steer clear of displaying any incompetence to others. It is likely that entrepreneurs who adopt different goal orientations might perform differently. The choice of goal orientation might depend on previous entrepreneurial experience.

Summary of the Theory Taxonomy

Structural theories of self-regulation explain how individuals set, pursue, and revise goals over time, without describing any details about what individuals are pursuing. These theories of individual self-regulation posit connections between abstract concepts (e.g. direction, effort, persistence, and strategy development), which are theoretically important to researchers and are practically useful to managers, but are formulated independent from goal phases or goal content. Researchers' empirical testing of structural theories of self-regulation has focused on research questions about individuals' goal attainment, response to discrepancies, and goal revisions. This is still an open and promising field for research by entrepreneurship scholars.

Phase models of self-regulation (e.g. Gollwitzer, 1990) focus on breaking down individuals' phases into discrete, sequenced steps, each with distinctive tasks for them to accomplish, and characteristic cognitive mindsets. Researchers' empirical testing of phase theories has focused on the differences between various cognitive processes that facilitate the unfolding of two or more phases of self-regulation.

Content theories of self-regulation describe the types of goals that individuals pursue and how goal content and goal framing can influence individuals' self-regulation. Researchers' empirical testing of content theories has tended to measure or manipulate the types of goals individuals pursue and examine the influence of goal content on individuals' performance, affect, and well-being, among other response variables.

According to Diefendorff and Lord (2008), although structural, phase, and content theories provide insight into individuals' self-regulation, there have been relatively few attempts to integrate the three approaches. They further suggest that the most important future developments in self-regulation research will come from integrations of two or more of these approaches as researchers attempt to develop more nuanced understandings of goal oriented behaviors. They also express concern that not many studies have addressed these integrative research questions, and furthermore, they worry about the focus on between-person (e.g. goal orientation) rather than within-person variation that would be consistent with extant structural theories of self-regulation (Vancouver et al., 2001). Once more, most of these issues remain to be researched in an entrepreneurship context.

DISCUSSION

We have presented a general self-regulation framework of entrepreneurial behavior that can be used to organize current and future empirical research. It is in line with current developments in I/O psychology and organizational behavior where models are being developed to accommodate more of the subtleties in human behavior, and their subsequent outcomes. In this concluding section, we explore how our framework is similar to other dynamic models such as effectuation theory, and how it can be used to better identify causal effects in an entrepreneurial context. We believe that our framework in combination with modern longitudinal research design and data analysis techniques can serve scholars who will be able to improve the conduct of future research into entrepreneurial behavior and interim outcomes, while at the same time building on the considerable body of knowledge that already exists. We also argue that there is both much to be done and much to be optimistic about.

First, as we have seen above, although entrepreneurship researchers have made significant progress, both substantively and methodologically, there is still only limited knowledge about many of the causal mechanisms that we are interested in. Second, entrepreneurship scholars are likely to rely mostly on observational data, and we need tools to infer causality under these circumstances. Entrepreneurship research, however, is regularly criticized for not paying sufficient attention to problems related to endogeneity and unobserved heterogeneity (Shane, 2006). Third, nevertheless, modern longitudinal designs and analysis techniques offer scholars some important advantages for testing complex models. Fourth, important practical implications arise from cognitive theories that better account for the complexity of entrepreneurial behavior.

How is this framework different from others such as effectuation theory? Effectuation theory (Sarasvathy, 2001) could be argued to be another self-regulation framework, but its direct roots are traced to decision making theories and research on expertise. Sarasvathy and her coauthors (Dew et al., 2004; Sarasvathy and Dew, 2005) developed a self-regulating theory to address how entrepreneurs behave in uncertain situations to make decisions on how to implement new ventures. It was developed to show how expert entrepreneurs go about constructing new ventures and markets. It explains how they think, act, and solve problems. In effectuation theory, expert entrepreneurs also rely heavily on feedback from their environments. However, the objectives of effectuation theory are different from our objectives, as they focus on why some individuals achieve a particular outcome, that is to say, construct new venture(s) and market(s), whereas we focus on how entrepreneurs' behaviors and outcomes are explained by an integration of various self-regulation theories. Nevertheless, the two approaches are consistent, while our framework could be adapted to 'why' research questions about differences between experts and novices, we are focusing on 'how' questions about the combination of various human characteristics, processes, and behaviors as they are applied in entrepreneurial settings.

Counterfactual argumentation or the potential outcome model is an increasingly popular way to generate theory and research designs that are better able to establish causality (Pearl, 2000). Counterfactual argumentation becomes especially important when scholars can no longer rely on experimental research designs. This is likely to be the case in research on entrepreneurial behavior and interim outcomes, even though there have been some very interesting experimental studies recently. The balance between internal and external validity, however, remains a particular challenge for entrepreneurship researchers. Therefore, experimental designs cannot be the only methodology for scholars interested in explaining entrepreneurial behavior. We believe that our framework can help researchers to better identify which models to test and still achieve high internal validity.

Moving scholars interested in entrepreneurial behavior into a longitudinal research design realm offers many exciting possibilities to expand their empirical contexts and extend their potential theoretical contributions. Persistence is a principal element in most definitions of motivation, and thus, serious consideration of persistence requires some longitudinal element to the research design (Ployhart, 2008). However, the most pressing questions associated with entrepreneurial behavior research are not about the operation of self-regulatory mechanisms within a single or short-term cycle, but rather, they are about how person and contextual factors influence the development, use, and maintenance of different self-regulation patterns over time. Examples of practical questions include: how are members of a founding team influenced not only by their own characteristics and processes, but also the characteristics and processes of the emerging new venture team? How do individual differences in self-regulatory skills affect individual suitability for entrepreneurship? What goals and forms of self-regulatory activity increase new venture success? Which aspects or forms of self-regulatory processing promote personal initiative and interpersonal competence? How does the novelty and complexity of the opportunity affect self-regulation processes? Current entrepreneurship research and theories focused on specific characteristics and processes are generally not designed to answer such questions. Longitudinal, multilevel research designs are needed to investigate goal and self-regulatory patterns as a function of individual, context and time (Kanfer, 2005).

ACKNOWLEDGEMENT

The authors contributed to this article equally and order was determined by the toss of a coin. The authors would also like to thank the editors and Kelly Shaver for many helpful comments on an earlier draft of this chapter.

REFERENCES

Ajzen, I. (1991), 'The theory of planned behavior', *Organizational Behavior and Human Decision Processes*, **50**(2), 179–211.

Ajzen, I. (1995), 'Attitudes and behavior', in A.S.R. Manstead and M. Hewstone (eds), *Encyclopedia of Social Psychology*, Oxford, UK: Blackwell, pp. 52–7.

Aldrich, H.E. and C.M. Fiol (1994), 'Fools rush in? The institutional context of industry creation', *Academy of Management Review*, **19**(4), 645–70.

Anderson, O. and W.H. Strigel (1981), 'Business surveys and economic research: a review of significant developments', in H. Laumer and M. Ziegler (eds), *International Research on Business Cycle Surveys*, Munich, Germany: Springer, pp. 25–54.

Armitage, C.J. and M. Conner (1999), 'The theory of planned behaviour: assessment of predictive validity and perceived control', *British Journal of Social Psychology*, **38**, 35–54.

Athayde, R. (2009), 'Measuring enterprise potential in young people', *Entrepreneurship Theory and Practice*, **33**(2), 481–500.

Austin, J.T. and J.B. Vancouver (1996), 'Goal constructs in psychology: structure, process, and content', *Psychological Bulletin*, **120**, 338–75.

Bagozzi, R.P. and P.R. Warshaw (1992), 'An examination of the etiology of the attitude-behavior relation for goal-directed behaviors', *Multivariate Behavioral Research*, **27**(4), 601–34.

Bandura, A. (1986), *Social Foundations of Thought and Action: A Social Cognitive Theory*, Englewood Cliffs, NJ: Prentice-Hall.

Bandura, A. (1991), 'Social cognitive theory of self-regulation', *Organizational Behavior and Human Decision Processes*, **50**(2), 248–87.

Bandura, A. (1995), 'Perceived self-efficacy', in A.S.R. Manstead and M. Hewstone (eds), *The Blackwell Encyclopedia of Social Psychology*, Oxford, UK: Blackwell, pp. 434–6.

Bandura, A. and E.A. Locke (2003), 'Negative self-efficacy and goal effects revisited', *Journal of Applied Psychology*, **88**(1), 87–99.

Baron, R.A. (1998), 'Cognitive mechanisms in entrepreneurship: why and when entrepreneurs think differently than other people', *Journal of Business Venturing*, **13**, 275–94.

Baron, R.A. (2007), 'Entrepreneurship: a process perspective', in J.R. Baum, M. Frese and R.A. Baron (eds), *The Psychology of Entrepreneurship*, Mahwah, NJ: Lawrence Erlbaum, pp. 19–39.

Baron, R.A. and G.D. Markman (2003), 'Beyond social capital: the role of entrepreneurs' social competence in their financial success', *Journal of Business Venturing*, **18**(1), 41–60.

Baron, R.A., M. Frese and J.R. Baum (2007), 'Research gains: benefits of closer links between I/O psychology and entrepreneurship', in J.R. Baum, M. Frese and R.A. Baron (eds), *The Psychology of Entrepreneurship*, Mahwah, NJ: Lawrence Erlbaum, pp. 347–73.

Baum, J.R., E.A. Locke and S.A. Kirkpatrick (1998), 'A longitudinal study of the relation of vision and vision communication to venture growth in entrepreneurial firms', *Journal of Applied Psychology*, **83**(1), 43–54.

Baum, J.R., E.A. Locke and K.G. Smith (2001), 'A multidimensional model of venture growth', *Academy of Management Journal*, **44**(2), 292–303.

Baumeister, R.F. and K.D. Vohs (eds) (2004), *Handbook of Self-regulation: Research, Theory, and Applications*, New York: Guilford.

Begley, T.M. and D.P. Boyd (1987), 'Psychological characteristics associated with performance in entrepreneurial firms and smaller businesses', *Journal of Business Venturing*, **2**(1), 79–93.

Bellu, R.R. (1988), 'Entrepreneurs and managers: are they different?', *Frontiers of Entrepreneurship Research*, Wellesley, MA: Babson College, pp. 16–30.

Bellu, R.R. (1993), 'Task role motivation and attributional style as predictors of entrepreneurial performance: female sample findings', *Entrepreneurship and Regional Development*, **5**(4), 331–34.

Bellu, R.R. and H. Sherman (1995), 'Predicting firm success from task motivation and attributional style: a longitudinal study', *Entrepreneurship and Regional Development*, **7**(4), 349–64.

Boekaerts, M., S. Maes and P. Karoly (2005), 'Self-regulation across domains of applied psychology: is there an emerging consensus?', *Applied Psychology*, **54**(2), 149–54.

Boekaerts, M., P.R. Pintrich and M. Zeidner (eds) (2000), *Handbook of Self-regulation*, San Diego, CA: Academic.

Boyd, N.G. and G.S. Vozikis (1994), 'The influence of self-efficacy on the development of entrepreneurial intentions and actions', *Entrepreneurship Theory and Practice*, **18**(4), 63–77.

Brigham, K.H., J.O. De Castro and D.A. Shepherd (2007), 'A person-organization fit model of owner-managers cognitive style and organizational demands', *Entrepreneurship Theory and Practice*, **31**(1), 29–51.

Brockhaus, R.H.S. (1982), 'The psychology of the entrepreneur', in C.A. Kent, D.L. Sexton and K.L. Vesper (eds), *Encyclopedia of Entrepreneurship*, Englewood Cliffs, NJ: Prentice-Hall, pp. 39–71.

Carsrud, A.L. and R.W. Johnson (1989), 'Entrepreneurship: a social psychological perspective', *Entrepreneurship and Regional Development*, **1**, 1–21.

Carver, C.S. and M.F. Scheier (1998), *On the Self Regulation of Behavior*, New York: Cambridge University.

Chell, E., J.M. Haworth and S. Brearley (1991), *The Entrepreneurial Personality: Concepts, Cases, and Categories*, London, UK: Routledge.

Chen, C., P.G. Greene and A. Crick (1998), 'Does entrepreneurial self-efficacy distinguish entrepreneurs from managers?', *Journal of Business Venturing*, **13**(4), 295–316.

Chen, G. and R. Kanfer (2006), 'Toward a systems theory of motivated behavior in work teams', *Research in Organizational Behavior*, **27**, 223–67.

Davidsson, P. (1989), *Continued Entrepreneurship and Small Firm Growth*, Doctoral Dissertation, Stockholm School of Economics, Stockholm: Economic Research Institute.

Davidsson, P. (1995), 'Determinants of entrepreneurial intentions', paper presented at RENT IX Workshop, Piacenza, Italy.

Delmar, F. (1996), *Entrepreneurial Behavior and Business Performance: A Study of the Impact of Individual Differences and Environmental Characteristics on Business Growth and Efficiency*, Doctoral Dissertation, Stockholm: Stockholm School of Economics.

Delmar, F. (1997), 'Measuring growth: methodological considerations and empirical results', in

R. Donkels and A. Miettinen (eds), *Entrepreneurship and SME research: on its way to the next millennium*, Aldershot, UK: Ashgate, pp. 199–216.

Delmar, F. (2006), 'The psychology of the entrepreneur', in S. Carter and D. Jones-Evans (eds), *Enterprise and Small Business*, Harlow, UK: Prentice Hall, pp. 152–75.

Dew, N., S.D. Sarasvathy and S. Venkataraman (2004), 'The economic implications of exaptation', *Journal of Evolutionary Economics*, **14**(1), 69–84.

Diefendorff, J.M. and R.G. Lord (2008), 'Goal-striving and self-regulation processes', in R. Kanfer, G. Chen and R.D. Pritchard (eds), *Work Motivation: Past, Present, and Future*, New York: Routledge, pp. 151–96.

Dimov, D.P. (2007), 'From opportunity insight to opportunity intention: the importance of person-situation learning match', *Entrepreneurship Theory and Practice*, **31**(4), 561–83.

Doll, J. and I. Ajzen (1992), 'Accessibility and stability of predictors in the theory of planned behavior', *Journal of Personality and Social Psychology*, **63**(5), 754–65.

Dutta, D.K. and S. Thornhill (2008), 'The evolution of growth intentions: toward a cognition-based model', *Journal of Business Venturing*, **23**(3), 307–32.

Dweck, C.S. (1986), 'Motivational processes affecting learning', *American Psychologist*, **41**, 1040–48.

Eagly, A.H. and S. Chaiken (1993), *The Psychology of Attitudes*, Orlando, FL: Harcourt Brace.

Forbes, D.P. (2005), 'Are some entrepreneurs more overconfident than others?', *Journal of Business Venturing*, **20**(5), 623–40.

Frayne, C.A. and J.M. Geringer (2000), 'Self-management training for improving job performance: a field experiment involving salespeople', *Journal of Applied Psychology*, **85**(3), 361–72.

Frese, M. (2007), 'The psychological actions and entrepreneurial success: an action theory approach', in J.R. Baum, M. Frese and R.A. Baron (eds), *The Psychology of Entrepreneurship*, Mahwah, NJ: Lawrence Erlbaum, pp. 151–88.

Furnham, A. and H. Steele (1993) 'Measuring locus of control: a critique of general, children's, health- and work-related locus of control questionnaires', *British Journal of Psychology*, **84**, 443–79.

Gartner, W.B. (1988). '"Who is an entrepreneur?" is the wrong question', *American Journal of Small Business*, **12**(4), 11–32.

Gollwitzer, P.M. (1990), 'Action phases and mind-sets', in E.T. Higgins and R.M. Sorrentino (eds), *Handbook of Motivation and Cognition: Foundations of Social Behavior*, New York: Guilford, pp. 53–92

Grant, H. and C.S. Dweck (1999), 'Content versus structure in motivation and self-regulation', *Perspectives on Behavioral Self Regulation*, **12**, 161–74.

Grant, H. and C.S. Dweck (2003), 'Clarifying achievement goals and their impact', *Journal of Personality and Social Psychology*, **85**(3), 541–53.

Gupta, V.K., D.B. Turban, S.A. Wasti and A. Sikdar (2009), 'The role of gender stereotypes in perceptions of entrepreneurs and intentions to become an entrepreneur', *Entrepreneurship Theory and Practice*, **33**(2), 397–417.

Haynie, J.M. and D.A. Shepherd (2009), 'A measure of adaptive cognition for entrepreneurship research', *Entrepreneurship Theory and Practice*, **33**(3), 695–714.

Herron, L. and R.B. Robinson (1993), 'A structural model of the effects of entrepreneurial characteristics on venture performance', *Journal of Business Venturing*, **8**(3), 281–94.

Higgins, E.T. (1997), 'Beyond pleasure and pain', *American Psychologist*, **52**, 1280–1300.

Hinsz, V.B., R.S. Tindale and D.A. Vollrath (1997), 'The emerging conceptualization of groups as information processes', *Psychological Bulletin*, **121**, 43–64.

Johnson, B.R. (1990), 'Toward a multidimensional model of entrepreneurship: the case of achievement motivation and the entrepreneur', *Entrepreneurship Theory and Practice*, **14**(3), 39–54.

Kanfer, R. (1990), 'Motivation theory and industrial and organizational psychology', in M.D. Dunnette and L.M. Hough (eds), *Handbook of Industrial and Organizational Psychology*, Palo Alto, CA: Consulting Psychologists, pp. 75–170.

Kanfer, R. (1992). 'Work motivation: new directions in theory and research', in C.L. Cooper and L.T. Robertson (eds), *International Review of Industrial and Organizational Psychology*, vol. 7, London: John Wiley & Sons, pp. 1–53.

Kanfer, R. (2005), 'Self-regulation research in work and I/O psychology', *Applied Psychology*, **54**, 186–91.

Kanfer, R., G. Chen and R.D. Pritchard (eds) (2008), *Work Motivation: Past, Present, and Future*, New York: Routledge.

Karoly, P. (1993), 'Mechanisms of self-regulation: a systems view', *Annual Review of Psychology*, **44**, 23–52.

Karoly, P. and F.H. Kanfer (1982), *Self-management and Behavior Change: From Theory to Practice*, New York: Pergamon.

Keith, N. and M. Frese (2005), 'Self-regulation in error management training: emotion control and metacognition as mediators of performance effects', *Journal of Applied Psychology*, **90**(4), 677–91.

Kickul, J., L.K. Gundry, S.D. Barbosa and L. Whitcanack (2009), 'Intuition versus analysis? Testing differential models of cognitive style on entrepreneurial self-efficacy and the new venture creation process', *Entrepreneurship Theory and Practice*, **33**(2), 439–53.

Kim, M. and J.E. Hunter (1993), 'Attitude-behavior relations: a meta-analysis of attitudinal relevance and topic', *Journal of Communication*, **43**(1), 101–42.

Kluger, A.N. and A.S. DeNisi (1996), 'The effects of feedback interventions on performance: a historical review, a meta-analysis and a preliminary feedback intervention theory', *Psychological Bulletin*, **119**, 254–84.

Kolvereid, L. (1992), 'Growth aspirations among Norwegian entrepreneurs', *Journal of Business Venturing*, **7**(3), 209–22.

Kolvereid, L. (1996a), 'Organizational employment versus self-employment: reasons for career choice intentions', *Entrepreneurship Theory and Practice*, **20**(3), 23–31.

Kolvereid, L. (1996b), 'Prediction of employment status choice intentions', *Entrepreneurship Theory and Practice*, **21**(1), 47–57.

Kolvereid, L. and E. Bullvag (1996), 'Growth intentions and actual growth: the impact of entrepreneurial choice', *Journal of Enterprising Culture*, **4**(1), 1–17.

Kolvereid, L. and E. Isaksen (2006), 'New business start-up and subsequent entry into self-employment', *Journal of Business Venturing*, **21**(6), 866–85.

Krueger, N.F. (1993), 'The impact of prior entrepreneurial exposure on perceptions of new venture feasibility and desirability', *Entrepreneurship Theory and Practice*, **18**(1), 5–21.

Krueger, N.F. and D.V. Brazeal (1994), 'Entrepreneurial potential and potential entrepreneurs', *Entrepreneurship Theory and Practice*, **18**(3), 91–104.

Krueger, N.F. and A.L. Carsrud (1993), 'Entrepreneurial intentions: applying the theory of planned behavior', *Entrepreneurship and Regional Development*, **5**(4), 315–30.

Krueger, N.F. and P.R. Dickson (1993), 'Perceived self-efficacy and perceptions of opportunity and threat', *Psychological Reports*, **72**, 1235–40.

Lee, L., P.K. Wong, M.D. Foo and A. Leung (2009), 'Entrepreneurial intentions: the influence of organizational and individual factors', *Journal of Business Venturing* (in press).

Lewin, K., T. Dembo, L.A. Festinger and P.S. Sears (1944), 'Level of aspiration', in J.M. Hunt (ed.), *Personality and Behavior Disorders*, New York: Ronald, pp. 333–78.

Liñán, F. and Y. Chen (2009), 'Development and cross-cultural application of a specific instrument to measure entrepreneurial intentions', *Entrepreneurship Theory and Practice*, **33**(3), 593–617.

Locke, E.A. (1991a), 'Introduction to special issue', *Organizational Behavior and Human Decision Processes*, **50**(2), 151–53.

Locke, E.A. (1991b), 'The motivation sequence, the motivation hub, and the motivation core', *Organizational Behavior and Human Decision Processes*, **50**(2), 288–99.

Locke, E.A. and G.P. Latham (1990), *A Theory of Goal Setting and Task Performance*, Englewood Cliffs, NJ: Prentice Hall.

Lord, R.G. and P.E. Levy (1994), 'Moving from cognition to action: a control theory perspective', *Applied Psychology: An International Review*, **43**(3), 335–67.

Lord, R.G., R.J. Klimoski and R. Kanfer (eds) (2002), *Emotions in the Workplace: Understanding the Structure and Role of Emotions in Organizational Behavior*, San Francisco, CA: Jossey Bass.

Manstead, A.S.R. and S.A.M. Eekelen (1998), 'Distinguishing between perceived behavioral control and self-efficacy in the domain of academic achievement intentions and behaviors', *Journal of Applied Social Psychology*, **28**(15), 1375–92.

Marks, M.A., J.E. Mathieu and S.J. Zaccaro (2001), 'A temporally based framework and taxonomy of team processes', *Academy of Management Review*, **26**(3), 356–76.

McClelland, D.C. (1961), *The Achieving Society*, Princeton, NJ: Van Nostrand.

McClelland, D.C. and D.G. Winter (1969), *Motivating Economic Achievement*, New York: Free Press.

Messick, S. (1984), 'The nature of cognitive styles: problems and promise in educational practice', *Educational Psychologist*, **19**, 59–74.

Miller, D. and J. Toulouse (1986), 'Chief executive personality and corporate strategy and structure in small firms', *Management Science*, **32**, 1389–409.

Miner, J.B., D.P. Crane and R.J. Vandenberg (1994), 'Congruence and fit in professional role motivation theory', *Organization Science*, **5**(1), 86–97.

Miner, J.B., N.R. Smith and J.S. Bracker (1989), 'Role of entrepreneurial task motivation in the growth of technologically innovative firms', *Journal of Applied Psychology*, **74**(4), 554–60.

Miner, J.B., N.R. Smith and J.S. Bracker (1992), 'Defining the inventor-entrepreneur in the context of established typologies', *Journal of Business Venturing*, **7**(2), 103–13.

Mischel, W. and O. Ayduk (2004), 'Willpower in a cognitive-affective processing system: the dynamics of delay of gratification', in R.F. Baumeister and K.D. Vohs (eds), *Handbook of self-Regulation: Research, Theory, and Applications*, New York: Guilford, pp. 99–129.

Mitchell, T.R., W.S. Harman, W.T. Lee and D. Lee (2008), 'Self-regulation and multiple deadline goals', in R. Kanfer, G. Chen and R.D. Pritchard (eds), *Work Motivation: Past, Present, and Future*, New York: Routledge, pp. 197–231.

Ozgen, E. and R.A. Baron (2007), 'Social sources of information in opportunity recognition: effects of mentors, industry networks, and professional forums', *Journal of Business Venturing*, **22**(2), 174–92.

Pearl, J. (2000), *Causality: Models, Reasoning, and Inference*, Cambridge, UK: University Press.

Perry, C., R. MacArthur, G. Meredith and B. Cunnington (1986), 'Need for achievement and locus of control of Australian small business owner-managers and super-entrepreneurs', *International Small Business Journal*, **4**, 55–64.

Peterman, N.E. and J. Kennedy (2003), 'Enterprise education: influencing students' perceptions of entrepreneurship', *Entrepreneurship Theory and Practice*, **28**(2), 129–44.

Pittman, T.S. (1998), 'Motivation', in D.T. Gilbert, S.T. Fiske and G. Lindzey (eds), *The Handbook of Social Psychology*, Boston, MA: McGraw Hill, pp. 549–90.

Ployhart, R.E. (2008), 'The measurement and analysis of motivation', in R. Kanfer, G. Chen and R.D. Pritchard (eds), *Work Motivation: Past, Present, and Future*, New York: Routledge, pp. 17–61.

Rauch, A. and M. Frese (2007), 'Born to be an entrepreneur? Revisiting the personality approach to entrepreneursip', in J.R. Baum, M. Frese and R.A. Baron (eds), *The Psychology of Entrepreneurship*, Mahwah, NJ: Lawrence Erlbaum, pp. 41–65.

Riding, R. and S. Rayner (1998), *Cognitive Styles and Learning Strategies*, London: David Fulton Publishers.

Rotter, J.B. (1966), 'Generalized expectancies for internal versus external control of reinforcement', *Psychological Monographs*, **80**, 1–28.

Ryan, R.M. and E.L. Deci (2000), 'The determination theory and the facilitation of intrinsic motivation, social development, and well-being', *American Psychologist*, **55**, 68–78.

Sadler-Smith, E. and B. Badger (1998), 'Cognitive style, learning and innovation', *Technology Analysis and Strategic Management*, **10**(2), 247–65.

Sarasvathy, S.D. (2001), 'Causation and effectuation: toward a theoretical shift from economic inevitability to entrepreneurial contingency', *Academy of Management Review*, **26**(2), 243–63.

Sarasvathy, S.D. and N. Dew (2005), 'New market creation through transformation', *Journal of Evolutionary Economics*, **15**(5), 533–65.

Sexton, D.L. and N. Bowman (1985), 'The entrepreneur: a capable executive and more', *Journal of Business Venturing*, **1**(1), 129–40.

Shane, S. (2006), 'Introduction to the focused issue on entrepreneurship', *Management Science*, **52**(2), 155–59.

Shaver, K.G. and L.R. Scott (1991), 'Person, process, choice: the psychology of new venture creation', *Entrepreneurship Theory and Practice*, **16**(2), 23–45.

Shepherd, D.A. and N.F. Krueger (2002), 'An intentions-based model of entrepreneurial teams' social cognition', *Entrepreneurship Theory and Practice*, **27**(2), 167–85.

Simons, T., L.H. Pelled and K.A. Smith (1999), 'Making use of difference: diversity, debate, and decision comprehensiveness in top management teams', *Academy of Management Journal*, **42**(6), 662–73.

Snyder, M. and N. Cantor (1998), 'Understanding personality and social behavior: a functionalist strategy', in D.T. Gilbert, S.T. Fiske and G. Lindzey (eds), *The Handbook of Social Psychology*, Boston, MA: McGraw-Hill, pp. 635–79.

Souitaris, V., S. Zerbinati and A. Al-Laham (2007), 'Do entrepreneurship programmes raise entrepreneurial intention of science and engineering students? The effect of learning, inspiration and resources', *Journal of Business Venturing*, **22**(4), 566–91.

Streufert, S.C. and G.Y. Nogami (1989), 'Cognitive style and complexity: implications for I/O psychology', in C.L. Cooper and I.T. Robinson (eds), *International Review of Industrial and Organizational Psychology*, vol. 4, London: John Wiley & Sons, 93–143.

Taylor, S.E. (1998), 'The social being in social psychology', in D.T. Gilbert, S.T. Fiske and G. Lindzey (eds), *The Handbook of Social Psychology*, Boston, MA: McGraw Hill, pp. 58–95.

Thompson, E.R. (2009), 'Individual entrepreneurial intent: construct clarification and development of an internationally reliable metric', *Entrepreneurship Theory and Practice*, **33**(3), 669–94.

Vancouver, J.B. (2000), 'Self-regulation in organizational settings: a tale of two paradigms', in M. Boekaerts, P.R. Pintrich and M. Zeidner (eds), *Handbook of Self-regulation*, San Diego, CA: Academic, pp. 303–36.

Vancouver, J.B. and D.V. Day (2005), 'Industrial and organizational research on self-regulation: from constructs to applications', *Applied Psychology: An International Review*, **54**, 155–85.

Vancouver, J.B., C.M. Thompson and A.A. Williams (2001), 'The changing signs in the relationships among self-efficacy, personal goals, and performance', *Journal of Applied Psychology*, **86**(4), 605–20.

VandeWalle, D., W.L. Cron and J.W. Slocum (2001), 'The role of goal orientation following performance feedback', *Journal of Applied Psychology*, **86**(4), 629–40.

Vohs, K.D. and R.F. Baumeister (2004), 'Understanding self-regulation', in R. Baumeister and K.D. Vohs (eds), *Handbook of Self-regulation: Research, Theory, and Applications*, New York: Guilford, pp. 1–9.

Vroom, V.H. (1964), *Work and Motivation*, New York: Wiley.

Weiner, B. (1985), 'An attributional theory of achievement motivation and emotion', *Psychological Review*, **92**, 548–73.

Weiner, B. (1992), *Human Motivation: Metaphors, Theories, and Research*, Thousand Oaks, CA: Sage.

Westerberg, M. (1998), *Managing in Turbulence: An Empirical Study on Small Firms Operating in a Turbulent Environment*, Doctoral Dissertation, Luleå, Sweden: Luleå Technological University.

Wiklund, J. (1998), *Small Firm Growth and Performance*, Doctoral Dissertation, Jönköping, Sweden: Jönköping International Business School.

Wiklund, J., P. Davidsson and F. Delmar (2003), 'What do they think and feel about growth? An expectancy-value approach to small business managers' attitudes toward growth', *Entrepreneurship Theory and Practice*, **27**(3), 247–70.

Wilson, F., J. Kickul and D. Marlino (2007), 'Gender, entrepreneurial self-efficacy, and entrepreneurial career intentions: implications for entrepreneurship education', *Entrepreneurship Theory and Practice*, **31**(3), 387–406.

Wood, R.E. (2005), 'New frontiers for self-regulation research in I/O psychology', *Applied Psychology*, **54**, 192–98.

Wood, R.E. and A. Bandura (1989), 'Social cognitive theory of organizational management', *Academy of Management Review*, **14**(3), 361–84.

Zimmerman, B.J. (2000), 'Attaining self-regulation: a social cognitive perspective', in M. Boekaerts, P.R. Pintrich and M. Zeidner (eds), *Handbook of Self Regulation*, San Diego, CA: Academic, pp. 13–39.

14. Social entrepreneurship: a historical review and research agenda

Todd W. Moss, G.T. Lumpkin and Jeremy C. Short

INTRODUCTION

Social entrepreneurship (SE) research is currently in a nascent state, yet recent reviews of this stream project a future marked by a variety of contexts and theoretical foundations to describe and explain the SE phenomenon (Short et al., 2009). From its beginnings in the public policy sphere, SE research has grown to include research in nonprofit and for-profit contexts (e.g. Harjula, 2006; Haugh, 2007; Waddock and Post, 1991). Additionally, SE research has expanded from samples in the United States to a variety of countries such as the United Kingdom (Spear, 2006), Canada (Anderson et al., 2006), China (Ma and Parish, 2006), Kenya (Ndemo, 2006), Ukraine (Phillips, 2005), and New Zealand (Luke and Verreynne, 2006), as well as multinational samples (Spear and Bidet, 2005). SE research initially focused on individual 'heroes' and anecdotal evidence, yet today it is becoming more theory-driven and research is gaining a foothold in top management and entrepreneurship outlets (Short et al., 2009). For example, current SE research draws from diverse perspectives such as institutional theory, Austrian economics, and agency theory (e.g. Chamlee-Wright, 2008; Townsend and Hart, 2008; Tracey and Jarvis, 2007). Given the broad spectrum of SE research, in this chapter we espouse a broad definition of social entrepreneurship as a process whereby resources are combined in new ways to explore and exploit opportunities for social value creation by meeting social needs, stimulating social change, or creating new organizations (Mair and Marti, 2006).

To shed light on the development of SE as a field of research, we provide a unique analysis of SE based on historical perspective (Lawrence, 1984). In historical perspective, information from the past is used to interpret current knowledge and to predict future developments. Historical perspective is one method to fruitfully examine advancements in research streams. For example, over the past century, strategic leadership scholars have identified distinct leadership behaviors that were effective in a given time period, only to find that these same behaviors may be ineffective in later periods as circumstances change (Pajunen, 2006). However, historical perspective reveals that a leader's ability to (1) absorb, utilize, and apply external knowledge, (2) understand social relationships, and (3) take the right action at the appropriate time, were the basis of effective strategic leadership in the early 1900s much like they are today (Pajunen, 2006).

To highlight the development of important themes in the salient literature that may hold insights for SE research, we content analyze Special Issue themes from academic journals from the time that SE research first appeared in the literature. The appearance of a particular theme in a Special Issue grants that theme a form of legitimacy; consequently, these themes may be viewed by researchers as increasingly desirable, proper, or appropriate within scholarly domains (c.f. Suchman, 1995). The history of Special Issues thus serves as a framework in which the development of more specific phenomena may be studied. Consequently, developments in SE research may be better described by comparing them with themes in Special Issues found in the greater academic literature. We provide a chronological review of the SE literature to highlight the historical development of the SE field. We show that initial work in SE centered on change processes in the public policy sphere, moving to value creation in the nonprofit sector, and currently focuses on theory-driven research in multiple sectors.

A second contribution of our chapter is to explain how SE research has been influenced by academic thinking in management, entrepreneurship, and other fields publishing SE research over time, as manifest in journal Special Issues. We find that in 62 per cent of the cases, the increase or decrease of themes in Special Issues in one time period is followed by similar changes in later time periods in the same themes in SE articles. This suggests that SE researchers are responsive to contemporary issues in the broader literature.

As a third contribution to research on SE, we use historical perspective to identify research opportunities that may predict future conceptual and empirical efforts examining SE and help frame a SE research agenda. Highlighting key themes of interest in management, entrepreneurship, and research in other fields will provide SE scholars with a glimpse into how to make their research more interesting and attractive to a wider audience, and potentially provide insights for scholars aspiring to publish SE research in top-tier journals. Consequently, we conclude with a proposal for future research based on current trends in journal Special Issues, aimed at increasing the exposure and legitimacy of SE research.

Taken as a whole, we use a unique methodology to *describe* the history of SE research, *explain* its development and *predict* its future, thus addressing the three main goals for organizational research (cf. Kerlinger, 1986). Basing our analysis on historical perspective thus provides researchers with a rich context within which to frame their own SE contributions. By mapping the historical roots of SE research in this fashion, we provide an aid to SE researchers who aspire to set forth in new directions rather than follow the trails of the past. In the sections that follow we describe our methodology, report our results, discuss how SE research has developed in 1991–2008, and close with suggestions for future research.

METHODOLOGY

Historical perspective is defined as 'the study of a subject in light of its earliest phases and subsequent evolution,' with the objective of sharpening one's vision of the present, rather than of the past as traditional studies of history seek to accomplish (Lawrence, 1984, p. 307). One example of the difference between historical research and historical perspective is exemplified by studies of the Great Depression in the United States during the 1930s. 'Historical research' involves studying documents and artifacts of the Depression to reach a better understanding of people's attitudes during that time, while 'historical perspective' is using the same information to explain people's attitudes today (Lawrence,

1984). Placing phenomena in different historical settings is useful for revealing contrasts and discovering unexpected insights (Ancona et al., 2001).

Historical perspective research requires that scholars go beyond the use of cross-sectional data, thus enabling them to generalize findings about changes over time and to examine the stability or variance of these findings. In the case of the Great Depression, for example, research based on historical perspective could examine the stability of people's attitudes regarding employment, spending and investing during the 1930s with their attitudes during the global recession of 2008–10. Such a study could allow scholars to uncover those factors that are generalizable over time. We adopt Lawrence's (1984) historical perspective approach to the specific case of the history of academic thought in management, entrepreneurship, and other fields on the development of SE research. Our rationale for applying historical perspective to SE research is to explore how SE research has evolved over time, and to examine how key areas of academic importance, manifest in Special Issues of top management and entrepreneurship journals, may have influenced the current state of research in SE. Results from our analysis are then used to inform future research opportunities and directions in SE research.

Sample

In order to ascertain the historical development of the SE body of research, we looked for SE articles in peer-reviewed journals in business and other fields using the EBSCO, ABI/INFORM, Web of Knowledge, and Science Direct databases for peer-reviewed scholarly articles. Within these databases, we searched the article title, abstract, and keywords provided by the authors for the phrases 'social entrepreneurship,' 'social entrepreneur,' 'social enterprise,' or 'social venture.' Our search yielded 183 relevant articles, representing the sample used for our coding scheme and content analysis. We had no initial starting date for our sample time frame in order to capture all possible SE articles. The first SE article appeared in 1991, and the growth in the number of SE articles from that time until 2008 is shown in Figure 14.1. Of particular significance in Figure 14.1 is the rapid growth in the number of SE articles. This recent growth in SE research compares favorably with entrepreneurship research more broadly, as highlighted by Ireland and Webb (2007), suggesting that SE research is increasing in the academic consciousness.

Potential reasons for the growth of SE research could be the result of a number of factors. First is the rise of foundations like the Skoll Foundation for Social Entrepreneurship, founded in 1999 by eBay's first president Jeff Skoll, and Ashoka, the global association of the world's leading social entrepreneurs, which tripled in size from 1999 to 2002 (Ashoka, n. d.). Second is the publication of mass-media books by social entrepreneurs such as Mohammad Yunus in 2000 and 2003, and Bill Drayton in 2004. These books highlight the impact of SE around the globe. Finally, social entrepreneurs have been the recipients of national and international awards. Muhammad Yunus is perhaps the best-known example, receiving the Nobel Peace Prize in 2006.

For our comparison sample of Special Issues, we drew from two sets of journals. First, we looked at top management and entrepreneurship journals in order to gauge the impact of these areas on SE research. We examined journals selected by Tahi and Meyer (1999) and Busenitz et al. (2003), who used top journals to gauge the progress and impact of management and entrepreneurship research, respectively. Second, we included Special

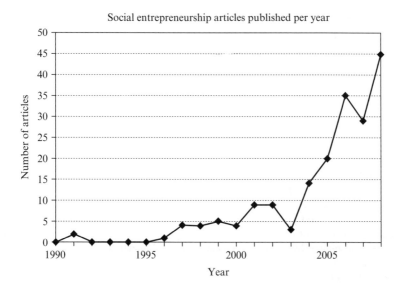

Social entrepreneurship articles published per year

Figure 14.1 Growth of articles on social entrepreneurship over time, 1991–2008

Issues in other social science journals, such as public policy and nonprofit management journals, in which SE research from our sample of articles appeared at least three times. The time period for our search of Special Issues in both sets of journals was 1991–2008, consistent with our sample of SE articles. In our count of Special Issues, we included only those Issues with concrete themes, and not those that published general conference proceedings without an identifiable theme. Our search yielded 400 Special Issues representing 23 journals. Table 14.1 lists each journal, the number of articles about SE that the journal published, and the number of Special Issues in the journal. For example, *Nonprofit Management and Leadership* published five SE articles between 1991 and 2008, and had seven Special Issues during the same time period.

Journal Special Issues highlight areas of research in which growing numbers of scholars are interested (Jermier, 1998), where more attention is warranted (Cohen and Sproull, 1991), and where growth of the phenomenon in question has major implications for research and practice (Schendel, 1991). Additionally, journal Special Issues have significantly higher citation rates than regular issue articles, and therefore have greater impact on knowledge development (Olk and Griffith, 2004). In essence, Special Issues are a key indicator of which themes are considered to be legitimate in a given field at a given time because inclusion of the theme in a Special Issue implies that research in that theme is desirable, proper, and appropriate. As these themes become legitimized, Special Issues may be reasonably expected to steer future thought and research in the direction of these themes. In a general sense, history supplies the raw materials required for historical perspective (Lawrence, 1984). Examining the history of academic thought in SE research, as well as in Special Issues in management, entrepreneurship, and other fields, provides one explanation for how SE research has developed in the way that it has. This explanation may then be extended to predict future directions and opportunities for SE scholars.

Table 14.1   Number of social entrepreneurship articles and Special Issues, 1991–2008

Journal	Social entrepreneurship articles published	Special Issues
Top management and entrepreneurship journals		
Academy of Management Journal	1	25
Academy of Management Review	1	19
Administrative Science Quarterly	–	2
Journal of Management	–	6
Organization Science	–	18
Strategic Management Journal	–	17
Entrepreneurship Theory and Practice	4	28
Journal of Business Venturing	–	10
Strategic Entrepreneurship Journal	2	–
Other journals publishing at least three social entrepreneurship articles		
Journal of World Business	6*	11
International Journal of Social Economics	6*	26
Voluntas: International Journal of Voluntary and Nonprofit Organizations	6	7
Journal of Nonprofit and Public Sector Marketing	6*	9
Harvard Business Review	5	7
Business Strategy Review	5	1
Nonprofit Management and Leadership	5	7
Journal of Business Ethics	5	54
International Journal of Entrepreneurial Behaviour and Research	5*	7
Journal of Developmental Entrepreneurship	4	2
Stanford Social Innovation Review	4	–
Public Administration Review	4	13
Nonprofit and Voluntary Sector Quarterly	4	8
International Journal of Public Administration	3	123
Total	76	400

Note: Asterisk (*) indicates journal published a Special Issue on social entrepreneurship.

Analysis

To start our historical perspective analysis, we coded the titles of the 400 Special Issues into specific dimensions based on research area. In instances where the Special Issue titles were unclear, we referred to the introductory article and titles of the remaining articles in the Special Issue to guide the coding process. Some Special Issue titles were explicit, such as 'Capital Budgeting' in the *International Journal of Public Administration.* Yet the same journal published a Special Issue titled 'Developments of State Audit in Israel in the Memory of Prof. Asher Friedberg,' which required us to search the introductory article to deduce its dimensions of National Culture and Public Sector Management. Two of the authors of this chapter independently categorized the dimensions into broader themes using a modified Delphi procedure (Dalkey, 1969; Reger and Palmer, 1996; Short and Palmer, 2003). During the first round of analysis, the raters classified dimensions for the Special Issues as they saw fit. In subsequent rounds, themes and dimensions that the two raters agreed upon were retained. Each rater then independently reassessed themes and dimensions for which there was not complete agreement. Raters then added dimensions to themes, created new themes, or judged dimensions to be idiosyncratic, but did not alter the theme labels or move dimensions to other themes that were agreed upon in previous rounds. The modified Delphi procedure was continued until the raters were satisfied that further convergence was unlikely. Maintaining rater independence in the coding of dimensions and themes avoided potential biasing that may have occurred due to interpersonal or political processes that could have contaminated independent judgments (Reger and Palmer, 1996). In total, our coding of the 400 Special Issues resulted in 66 specific dimensions, categorized into 13 broader themes. The final step was to code our sample of 183 SE articles according to these dimensions and themes, based on title, abstract, and article introduction, after which we recorded appearance counts of each dimension and theme. The Appendix (Table 14A.1) contains the details of the Special Issues organized by theme.

The coding process allowed for Special Issues and SE articles to be coded into either one dimension or two dimensions, depending on content. For example, *Entrepreneurship Theory and Practice* published a Special Issue on 'Financing and Entrepreneurship' (Entrepreneurial Financing dimension) and another on 'Corporate entrepreneurship in a Global economy' (Corporate Entrepreneurship and Global dimensions). As for SE articles, *Nonprofit Management and Leadership* published an article by Dart (2004) titled 'The legitimacy of social enterprise' (Institutional Theory dimension) and one by Mancino and Thomas (2005) titled 'An Italian pattern of social enterprise: the social cooperative' (Community Enterprises and Co-ops, and National Culture dimensions).

Finally, we sorted the themes in Special Issues and SE articles into three time periods of six years each over the 18 years of our sample: 1991–96, 1997–2002, and 2003–08. Splitting the sample into multiple periods of time, rather than aggregating the sample as a single period (cf. Busenitz et al., 2003), changes cross-sectional data to longitudinal data and consequently enables application of historical information to inform current developments and future possibilities (Lawrence, 1984). In using three time periods, we are able to view curvilinear trends in the data, as well as draw explanatory and predictive conclusions about how changes from one time period to another may influence subsequent time periods. Scholars in previous studies examining change in strategy and entrepreneurship research over time have likewise grouped their samples into three time periods (Dean et al., 2007; Shook et al., 2003).

RESULTS

Table 14.2 shows how the mix of Special Issue and SE article topics has been changing over time. As the number of SE articles has been increasing over time in every theme, basing our conclusions simply on growth in the number of articles would not be very informative. We therefore examined changes in the percentage of Special Issues and SE

Table 14.2   Themes of journal special issues and social entrepreneurship articles

Theme and dimension	Special Issues (number and change in percentage, N = 400)			Social entrepreneurship articles (number and change in percentage, N = 183)		
	1991–96	1997–2002	2003–08	1991–96	1997–2002	2003–08
Change Processes	12	24 (23%)	12 (−54%)	2	2 (−89%)	11 (15%)
Change processes	1	14	7	2	1	8
Role of time	8	7	–	–	–	–
Role of technology	3	3	5	–	1	3
Human Capital	13	14 (−34%)	16 (5%)	–	4[a]	14 (−27%)
Cognition research	–	1	3	–	–	1
Diversity issues	1	2	1	–	–	–
HRM	7	4	2	–	–	1
Individual differences	2	1	2	–	–	6
Leadership	1	3	3	–	3	5
Trust	–	1	2	–	1	–
Women in management	2	2	3	–	–	1
International and Global	17	32 (16%)	29 (−17%)	–	2[a]	17 (78%)
Emerging economies	2	5	7	–	1	6
Global	10	15	16	–	–	1
National culture	5	12	6	–	1	10
Management Practice	10	12 (−26%)	10 (−23%)	–	2[a]	15 (57%)
Decision making	1	3	2	–	–	1
Governance – internal	4	3	5	–	1	4
Management practices	4	6	2	–	–	6
Marketing practices	1	–	1	–	1	4
Management Theory	9	4 (−73%)	8 (84%)	–	1[a]	30 (529%)
Entrepreneurship as a field	1	–	2	–	–	8
Institutional theory	–	1	–	–	–	8
Organizational ecology	2	–	–	–	–	1
Organizational identity	–	1	1	–	1	–
Organizational behavior	3	–	4	–	–	2
Organizational theory	3	2	1	–	–	9
Sociology	–	–	–	–	–	2
Networking and Collaboration	1	8 (392%)	8 (−8%)	1	7 (−25%)	13 (−61%)
Alliances	–	2	1	–	1	–
Collaboration	–	3	3	–	–	5
Cooperation	1	–	–	–	–	1
Networks	–	2	3	–	2	5
Partnerships	–	1	1	1	4	2
Nonprofits	3	11 (126%)	10 (−16%)	–	9[a]	21 (−51%)
Nonprofit management	–	4	5	–	6	9
Nonprofit marketing	–	1	1	–	2	2
Philanthropy	1	2	1	–	1	9
Volunteerism	2	4	3	–	–	1

Table 14.2   (continued)

Theme and dimension	Special Issues (number and change in percentage, N = 400)			Social entrepreneurship articles (number and change in percentage, N = 183)		
	1991–96	1997–2002	2003–08	1991–96	1997–2002	2003–08
Public Policy	24	37 (−5%)	51 (27%)	2	3 (−84%)	14 (−2%)
Civic engagement	–	1	3	–	–	–
Human services	3	5	8	–	–	4
Governance – regulatory environment	1	1	2	–	1	3
Public policy	4	17	15	1	1	4
Public sector management	15	13	23	1	1	2
Public sector marketing	1	–	–	–	–	1
Scholarship and Learning	13	18 (−15%)	21 (7%)	–	3[a]	22 (54%)
Learning/knowledge transfer	–	6	7	–	1	6
Research methods	3	3	5	–	–	4
Role of university	2	3	2	–	1	3
Theory/theory building	8	6	7	–	1	9
Social Responsibility and Ethics	11	23 (29%)	35 (40%)	–	3[a]	19 (33%)
CSR/Social performance	2	4	11	–	2	13
Environmental sustainability	2	3	2	–	1	3
Equity/justice	–	1	1	–	–	2
Ethics	7	15	21	–	–	1
Strategy and Economics	11	14 (−22%)	10 (−34%)	–	4[a]	7 (−63%)
Capabilities	1	3	–	–	–	1
Competition	2	1	1	–	4	–
Corporate strategy	1	2	1	–	–	–
Economics	3	4	6	–	–	3
Resource-based view	1	1	1	–	–	1
Strategic processes	2	2	1	–	–	–
Strategy	1	1	–	–	–	2
Type of Enterprise	1	4 (146%)	9 (107%)	–	1[a]	12 (152%)
Cultural industries	–	1	–	–	–	1
Community enterprises and Co-ops	–	–	1	–	1	9
Family business	1	–	6	–	–	–
Franchises	–	2	–	–	–	2
SMEs	–	1	2	–	–	–
Value Creation	11	20 (12%)	21 (−3%)	1	15 (61%)	72 (1%)
Corporate entrepreneurship	0	3	–	–	–	–

Table 14.2   (continued)

Theme and dimension	Special Issues (number and change in percentage, N = 400)			Social entrepreneurship articles (number and change in percentage, N = 183)		
	1991–96	1997–2002	2003–08	1991–96	1997–2002	2003–08
Economic development	1	3	3	–	2	4
Entrepreneurial financing	1	–	–	–	–	4
Entrepreneurship	–	5	1–	–	4	26
Innovation	3	2	1	1	3	11
Performance	6	4	5	–	1	8
Value creation	–	3	2	–	5	19
Total[b]	136	221	240	6	56	267

Notes:
[a] Change in percentage is undefined; the initial period had no articles in this particular theme.
[b] Special issues and articles were coded into one or two dimensions; total is therefore not the total sample of special issues or social entrepreneurship articles.

articles in each theme over time. For example, in 1991–96 there were 12 Special Issues about Change Processes out of 136 total Special Issue themes (8.8 per cent). In 1997–2002 there were 24 Special Issues regarding Change Processes out of 221 Special Issue themes (10.6 per cent), which increased the percentage of this theme in Special Issues by 24 per cent. During the third period, 2003–08, there was a decrease in the percentage of Change Processes in Special Issues by 54 per cent. Thus, Table 14.2 indicates that the percentage of Special Issues with themes on Change Processes in 1991–2008 is shaped like an inverted U, with an increase from period one to period two and a decrease from period two to period three. In contrast, SE articles about Change Processes displayed the opposite trend. From period one to period two there was a decrease in the percentage articles regarding Change Processes by 89 per cent, but from period two to period three that percentage increased by 15 per cent. SE articles about Change Processes thus show a U-shaped trend. In addition to U-shaped and inverted U-shaped trends, Table 14.2 also indicates that some themes displayed strictly decreasing and strictly increasing trends. For example, the percentage of Special Issues in Management Practice was strictly decreasing, while the percentage of SE articles in the same theme was strictly increasing. In short, Table 14.2 shows that themes in five of thirteen Special Issues were inverted U-shaped (38 per cent), four were U-shaped (32 per cent), two were strictly increasing (15 per cent), and two were strictly decreasing (15 per cent). Trends were quite different for our sample of SE articles, in which three of thirteen were inverted U-shaped (23 per cent), one was U-shaped (8 per cent), seven were strictly increasing (54 per cent), and two were strictly decreasing (15 per cent).

These figures reveal some noteworthy trends in Special Issues and SE research. First, 53 per cent of themes in Special Issues were increasing from periods one to two, while 77 per cent of the themes in SE articles experienced the same trend. This finding makes sense because, as Table 14.2 indicates, the dearth of SE articles in period one means that most themes could only increase in period two. In contrast, the number of increasing and decreasing themes in Special Issues was much more evenly divided. Second, from period two to period three, 47 per cent of themes in Special Issues were increasing, compared with 62 per cent for SE articles. The greater increase in SE themes indicates that research in SE continues to cover a greater diversity of themes over time. Again, the number of increasing and decreasing themes in Special Issues is more evenly split. Overall, these findings suggest that the relative growth or decline of themes in Special Issues from 1991–2008 seems to resemble a random distribution, much like a coin toss. Over the same time period, the growth of themes in SE articles has continually expanded. We next review the implications of these changes.

DISCUSSION

In our discussion, we first describe how SE research developed in 1991–2008 by examining articles published during three time periods. We propose that SE research during each time period is characterized by a number of overarching themes taken from our analysis of Special Issues, and that 'popular' themes in one time period tend to decline in subsequent time periods. Next, we concentrate on how the current developments in SE research may be explained by past developments in Special Issues, finishing with how the current state of research manifest in Special Issues may hold clues into future research opportunities in the emerging research domain of SE.

Period One (1991–96): Public Policy and Change

Bill Drayton organized Ashoka in 1980 to promote positive social change, yet it was not until the early 1990s that SE became the subject of academic research. Only three articles were published during period one. Recall that we coded articles in up to two themes; thus, while only three articles were published during period one, there are a total of six themes as shown in Table 14.2: Change Processes (2), Public Policy (2), Value Creation (1), and Networking and Collaboration (1). These early works do not explicitly extend and build theory; rather, they examine the phenomenon of SE as found in the public and nonprofit sectors.

Waddock and Post first defined social entrepreneurs as 'private sector citizens who play critical roles in bringing about "catalytic changes" in the public sector agenda and the perception of certain social issues' (1991, p. 393). These private sector citizens tried to initiate change processes to improve policy making and implementation, rather than being directly involved in the solutions to solve the social problems; examples of such entrepreneurs include those responsible for Hands Across America (an organization that raised money to fight hunger and homelessness in 1986) and the Partnership for a Drug-Free America. The authors focus on the leadership characteristics necessary for social entrepreneurs, such as the ability to bound complex problems into a single vision; significant personal credibility to create networks and gain resources; and the generation of follower commitment based on social values that creates a collective purpose (Waddock and Post, 1991). While not explicitly stated, SE in this context seems to relate to charismatic and transformational leadership. In these theories, leaders articulate an appealing vision, and induce followers to rise above their own self-interest for the benefit of the team or organization (Yukl, 2005).

At the same time, Roberts and King provided a similar definition for 'policy entrepreneurs' as those who, 'from outside the formal positions of government, introduce, translate, and help implement new ideas into public practice' thus becoming, in effect, public innovators (1991, p. 147). They extend the work of scholars in the public policy domain such as Lewis (1980) and Kingdon (1984), who examined entrepreneurship strictly within governmental organizations. Drawing loosely on innovation theory, Roberts and King (1991) suggest that public policy innovations pass through four stages: creation of the idea; design of the idea into a bill and then a law; implementation of the idea as a new program; and institutionalization of the idea as an established practice. Policy entrepreneurs are therefore involved in the first three of these four stages.

Finally, Garrett (1996) presents a case study of SE in the context of his and others' efforts to create a novel charter school. Project Chrysalis was initially started as a partnership between a local school and a nonprofit organization. These two groups created a service-learning summer program for the largely minority student body in the Houston Independent School District to offer rapid development in an atmosphere free from drugs, gangs, violence, and poverty. The program's success convinced the program directors that the curriculum should be expanded and developed to create a charter school, which required a physical site, school board approval, and additional students. After meeting these requirements, the school opened its doors for the 1995–96 school year.

While not explicitly mentioning theory, Garrett's (1996) case study could serve as an exemplar for a number of theories related to entrepreneurship. For example, opportunity discovery theory suggests that exogenous competitive imperfections arise from contextual changes within an industry or market (Alvarez and Barney, 2007; Kirzner, 1973). The Project Chrysalis experience is suggestive of an opportunity discovery process stemming from such conditions. When Garrett and his colleague graduated from their universities and entered the Teach for America program in Houston, they were disappointed when students who had progressed in their classes struggled and regressed in later years. That is, the teachers noticed a 'competitive imperfection' in the current school system that led to an opportunity to improve student learning by creating a new context for learning.

As these examples show, the pioneering roots of SE were initiated in nonprofit and government entities to promote innovation and change.

Period Two (1997–2002): Nonprofits and Value Creation

Period two contained 31 SE articles, and was characterized by growth in four main themes: Value Creation, Nonprofits, Strategy and Economics, and Human Capital (see Table 14.3). Value creation in an SE context refers chiefly to social value creation through entrepreneurial processes. Social entrepreneurs see where an unmet need exists that the state cannot or will not meet, and then gather resources to make a difference and build organizations for broad social benefit (Emerson, 1999; Thompson et al., 2000). They have also learned how business principles can empower them to more effectively fulfill their social missions (Sagawa and Segal, 2000). In addition to creating social value, social entrepreneurs may also improve economic value creation through efforts in job training and self-employment programs in community revitalization efforts (Wallace, 1999). While

Table 14.3   *Key historical trends in social entrepreneurship research over three time*
periods

	Period 1 (1991–96)	Period 2 (1997–2002)		Period 3 (2003–08)	
	Theme	Theme	Change (%)	Theme	Change (%)
Relative Growth	Public Policy	Value Creation	61	Management Theory	529
	Change Processes	Nonprofits	–[a]	Type of Enterprise	152
	Networking and Collaboration	Strategy and Economics	–[a]	International and Global	78
	Value Creation	Human Capital	–[a]	Scholarship and Learning	54
Relative Decline		Change Processes	−89	Strategy and Economics	−63
		Public Policy	−84	Networking and Collaboration	−61
		Networking and Collaboration	−25	Nonprofits	−51

Note: [a] Change in percentage is undefined; the initial period had no articles in this particular theme.

SE articles in period one tended to focus on changing existing processes, economic and social value creation seems to imply effort on a more grand scale with widespread implications for organizations.

The Nonprofits theme was also an area of key growth during period two. Nonprofit (NFP) organizations are recognized as organizations that increase the general welfare of a citizenry. To improve the performance of NFPs, managers in these organizations are frequently taught entrepreneurship principles (Badelt, 1997). Dees (1998) presents NFPs in a similar manner, as organizations seeking to grow their funding base through integration of for-profit operations to complement their mainstream activities. While SE research in period two contained articles targeting public policy, scholars generally shifted to studying how to improve the entrepreneurial nature of NFP organizations. Finally, there were a moderate number of articles that addressed Strategy and Economics, and Human Capital. Articles in the Strategy theme centered exclusively on competition, with most of the articles describing interactions of NFPs and for-profits battling in the same market space (e.g. Dees, 1998; Ryan, 1999), while Human Capital articles were generally about leadership in an SE context (e.g. Barman, 2002).

Our historical analysis uncovered an interesting trend in SE research during period two. We found that each theme in the first period was found to decline in later time periods. For example, Change Processes and Public Policy were both key themes during period one. However, in period two both of these themes drastically declined relative to other themes in SE. While this change may simply reflect a cyclical research pattern (e.g. Mahoney, 1999), a comparison with those themes that experienced high growth reveals another potential explanation. It appears that the sector of interest during period two shifts from the public to the nonprofit arena, while the key phenomena of interest is value creation rather than change processes. Additionally, if this trend continues, we expect that the key themes in period two (Value Creation, Nonprofits, Strategy and Economics, and Human Capital) will decline in period three. The consensus of scholars in 1997–2002 thus seems to be that SE is principally a phenomenon of social value creation that takes place in the NFP sector, rather than how to bring about change in the public sector.

Period Three (2003–08): Theory-driven across Multiple Sectors

The final period of SE research in our study contained 145 articles, and saw high levels of relative growth in four key themes: Management Theory, Type of Enterprise, International and Global, and Scholarship and Learning (Table 14.3). While research into SE as a NFP phenomenon continues (cf. Foster and Bradach, 2005; Seelos and Mair, 2005), the explosive growth of the Management Theory theme is reflected by the inclusion of different perspectives and greater acceptance into top-tier management and entrepreneurship journals. Part of the expansion may be attributable to the greater use of theory-driven research, as several articles mentioned specific theories that provided the lens through which to study SE. For example, Young (2006) examined social enterprises in light of organizational theory to explain the various structures adopted by these enterprises. Other scholars present conceptual evidence to delineate how social ventures and commercial ventures may be similar and different based on a prevailing model of entrepreneurship (Austin et al., 2006). Maguire et al. (2004) explore SE through the lens of institutional theory to inform institutional entrepreneurship, which strengthens the legitimacy of SE research in the broader academic domain. Their theory-driven work also delineates formal propositions to clearly guide future scholars.

Scholarship and Learning is a second and related theme that has experienced relative growth in period three. Articles in Scholarship and Learning principally aim to add clarity and boundaries to the concept of SE. Some of the work in this theme is concerned with clarifying definitions of SE (e.g. Martin and Osberg, 2007), while others propose models of SE based on their case studies and grounded theory (e.g. Spear, 2006; Tracey and Jarvis, 2007). Work in both Management Theory and Theory and Theory Building is distinct from earlier work in periods one and two in that scholars move from strictly anecdotal evidence to increased qualitative and quantitative analyses.

Third, there is growing consensus that SE is a multi-contextual construct that has more to do with the aim of creating social value rather than a particular sector or organization. In the introduction to a Special Issue of *Journal of World Business* dedicated to SE, Christie and Honig (2006) observe that SE has been reported in entrepreneurial firms, as well as NFP and the public sector. While providing economic benefits, community-based enterprises are examples of SE in that they provide social benefits to community members (e.g. Peredo and Chrisman, 2006; Tracey et al., 2005). Another growing area of SE research involves social cooperative organizations characterized by democratic participation by all members and limited distribution of profits (e.g. Lindsay and Hems, 2004;

Mancino and Thomas, 2005; Thomas, 2004). These types of organizations are officially recognized entities that are separate and distinct from other types of social ventures.

Finally, SE research in period three is marked by a distinct increase in the number of articles in the International and Global theme. The role of national culture is prominent in this theme, as exemplified by a study of indigenous peoples in Canada. There is an inseparable link between the economic and social improvements to individuals, families, communities, and nations that are available through entrepreneurial activity among indigenous peoples (Anderson et al., 2006). Other scholars examine social enterprise in emerging economies, such as in Ukraine (Phillips, 2005), Kenya (Ndemo, 2006), Nigeria (Nwankwo et al., 2007), and India (Rego and Bhandary, 2006). SE scholars increasingly realize that these phenomena are pervasive worldwide and not limited to developed countries such as the UK or the USA.

As with the changes from period one to period two, we found that key themes of relative growth in period two became themes of relative decline in period three (Table 14.3). While a focus on NFP contexts in period two may have been novel, more recent SE research seems to have moved away from defining social ventures by purely NFP status to include a wide variety of sectors and organizations united by a common goal of meeting social needs. Additionally, the relative growth of the Management Theory, and Scholarship and Learning themes in period three could suggest that scholars have recognized the need for improved theory-driven research, to the detriment of other themes that may have been more popular in the past. If key themes in one time period continue to decline in future time periods, we would expect to see the Management Theory, Scholarship and Learning, Type of Enterprise, and International and Global themes to be supplanted by different themes in 2009–14.

Having identified themes that experienced relative growth or decline over the course of the history of SE research in the academic literature, we next use historical perspective to show how themes in journal Special Issues may have impacted the way that SE research has developed and what the future may hold.

Current Developments in Social Entrepreneurship Research

Applying historical perspective provides one explanation for the current developments of SE research in light of past Special Issue themes. We thus explored how changes from 1991–96 (period one) to 1997–2002 (period two) in Special Issue themes compared with developments in SE articles from period two (1997–2002) to period three (2003–08). Our rationale was that the appearance of a specific theme in a Special Issue is an indication that the theme is timely and important, and therefore a legitimate area on which scholars may focus. Accordingly, given that the themes in Special Issues are legitimate research areas, scholars in the emerging field of SE would gravitate toward these themes in their studies of the SE phenomenon to increase the likelihood of their work being published. Increasing scholarly output based on legitimate research themes would thus increase the legitimacy of SE research as a whole in the eyes of the greater academic community. As the legitimacy of SE research increases, SE scholars would consequently increase their chances for promotion, tenure, and merit-pay increases (e.g. Pfeffer, 1993). In short, SE scholars may have incentive to use Special Issue themes as the basis for their own research efforts.

Table 14.2 shows that in eight out of thirteen themes (62 per cent), increases or decreases in themes of Special Issues from period one to period two were followed by respective increases or decreases in the same themes in SE articles from period two to period three. Those themes that increased include Change Processes, International and Global, Social Responsibility and Ethics, Type of Enterprise, and Value Creation. Themes that decreased in both Special Issues and SE articles include Human Capital, Public Policy, and Strategy and Economics. Additionally, in 30 per cent of the themes, or four out of thirteen (Human Capital, Public Sector and Policy, Social Responsibility and Ethics, and Type of Enterprise), the magnitudes of these trends in both Special Issues and SE articles were strikingly similar. For example, the percentage of Special Issues on Social Responsibility and Ethics grew by 29 per cent in period one, followed by a percentage increase in SE articles of 33 per cent in period two. Another example is the Type of Enterprise theme, which showed a percentage growth of 146 per cent for Special Issues followed by a percentage growth of 152 per cent in SE articles. These results suggest that in many themes, historical perspective provides a compelling rationale as to why research in SE has developed in the way that it has.

It is also instructive to look at the five themes where changes in Special Issue trends from period one to period two actually ran counter to later changes in SE articles (Management Practice, Management Theory, Networking and Collaboration, Nonprofits, and Scholarship and Learning). For example, the Management Theory theme displayed the largest percentage decrease of all Special Issue themes from period one to period two (−73 per cent). However, the same theme in SE articles showed by far the largest increase in percentage for the SE themes from period two to period three (529 per cent). Historical perspective provides possible explanations for the discrepancies in the development of Special Issues and SE research by using historical events to interpret findings. In the case of Management Theory, the decrease in Special Issues could be the result of a research cycle within a scholarly community (e.g. Mahoney, 1999). A particular emphasis on Management Theory in Special Issues of social science journals could be highlighted in one period, only to decrease in a subsequent period as other themes become a higher priority to journal editors. However, with SE research in its infancy, Management Theory plays an increasingly important role as scholars explore new theoretical foundations that explain the SE phenomenon and progress the field beyond only anecdotal evidence. Historical factors that are unique to either Special Issues as a manifestation of broader academe, or to SE research in particular, may therefore account for the ways in which specific themes have differentially developed in each area.

Themes in Future Social Entrepreneurship Research

While scholars cannot know the future, an analysis based on historical perspective can provide clues into what the future may bring (Lawrence, 1984). Following the same legitimacy logic used to explain recent SE research, current developments in Special Issues may also provide insights into SE studies yet to come. Next, we examine the potential impact of the growth or decline of Special Issues over the period 2003–08 on the relative growth or decline of themes in SE research for perhaps the next six year-year period. Table 14.4 displays those themes which were decreasing or increasing in both Special Issues and SE

Table 14.4 *Increasing and decreasing themes in Special Issues and social entrepreneurship articles, from period two (1997–2002) to period three (2003–2008)*

Special Issues (SI)	Social Entrepreneurship (SE) Articles					
	Increasing			Decreasing		
	Theme	SI%	SE%	Theme	SI%	SE%
Increasing	Management Theory	84	529	Human Capital	5	−27
	Scholarship and Learning	7	54	Public Policy	27	−2
	Social Responsibility and Ethics	40	33			
	Type of Enterprise	107	152			
Decreasing	Change Processes	−54	15	Networking and Collaboration	−8	−61
	International and Global	−17	78	Nonprofits	−16	−51
	Management Practice	−23	57	Strategy and Economics	−34	−63
	Value Creation	−3	1			

articles, and provides a starting point for our discussion on possible future directions and research opportunities in SE.

Themes growing in 2003–08 in Special Issues include Human Capital, Management Theory, Public Policy, Scholarship and Learning, Social Responsibility and Ethics, and Type of Enterprise. While these themes are on the rise in Special Issues, in SE research the same themes are either decreasing or increasing. Human Capital and Public Policy are currently in decline, but there are a number of opportunities that scholars could explore that would result in an increase in SE research in these themes over 2009–14, consistent with current trends in Special Issues. In the Human Capital theme, there is a paucity of work in the dimensions of Cognition Research, Diversity Issues, Trust, and Women in Management. For example, seven Special Issues focused on Women in Management, three of which were from entrepreneurship journals. Yet only one SE article focuses on women as social entrepreneurs, a study in which Phillips (2005) examines women non-governmental organization (NGO) activists in Ukraine. That only one article focuses on women as social entrepreneurs is all the more intriguing given that the 2004 Global Entrepreneurship Monitor (GEM) study in the UK found that women are far more likely to be social entrepreneurs than mainstream entrepreneurs (Harding, 2004), suggesting that a SE context may be a more fruitful research setting in which to study female entrepreneurship.

The themes of Management Theory, Scholarship and Learning, Type of Enterprise, and Social Responsibility and Ethics are on the rise in both Special Issues and SE articles. Recall that trends identified over multiple time periods suggest that the first three of these themes should decline in 2009–14. However, for these themes to continue to increase, scholars should focus on some of the untapped dimensions for future SE research. For example, the Management Theory theme includes Organizational Identity. There have been two Special Issues on Organizational Identity and only one SE article, in which Young (2001) uses it to propose structural and strategic implications for social enterprises. Yet organizations may have multiple identities that may be in conflict when the needs of one identity are detrimental to the needs of another (Foreman and Whetten, 2002; Golden-Biddle and Rao, 1997). Social ventures must balance competing demands of fiscal health and business savvy while also fulfilling their social missions (McDonald, 2007; Vega and Kidwell, 2007), and these demands may be reflections of dual identities. Additional research in organizational identity is needed and would contribute to additional growth in this theme.

Historical perspective also suggests how themes in Special Issues that are presently in decline may impact the future of SE research. These themes include Change Processes, International and Global, Management Practice, Networking and Collaboration, Nonprofits, Strategy and Economics, and Value Creation. Of these seven themes, three (Networking and Collaboration, Nonprofits, and Strategy and Economics) decline from 1997–2002 to 2003–08 in SE research as well and may continue the downward trend. Research focusing on various aspects of nonprofits is one example. Scholars increasingly recognize that SE may be found in multiple sectors, and not just the nonprofit sector (e.g. Christie and Honig, 2006). As the number of SE publications continues to grow, there could also be a corresponding increase in the diversity of contexts in which SE is studied, as well as studies that compare SE across sectors.

The four themes of Change Processes, International and Global, Management Practice, and Value Creation increase from period two to period three in SE research, while decreasing in Special Issues. Applying a historical perspective to the Management Practice theme provides some clues as to why these trends may continue. The peak number of Special Issues on Management Practice – which includes dimensions on decision making, internal governance, and management and marketing practices – occurred in 1997–2002, the latter part of which happens to correspond with governance scandals such as Enron. The Enron tragedy provided an unfortunate opportunity for academics to address topics related to control, risk, and governance in organizations. It should therefore come as no surprise that Special Issues during period two addressed topics such as critical perspectives on organizational control; risk, management, and options in organizations; and corporate governance reforms in developing economies. In 2003–08, Special Issues focused less on these areas. Over the same time period, SE research on Management Practice has grown relative to other themes. Historical perspective analysis based on a legitimacy logic, however, suggests that 2009–14 will see a decrease in SE research regarding Management Practice that corresponds with the trends seen in Special Issues.

The above suggestions for future developments in SE research in 2009–14 are but one possibility. As the SE field matures and becomes more established in the scholarly community, the degree of variance or change in topics may decrease as 'tribes' of SE scholars coalesce to identify key issues for research that match their common interests. Similarly, there are diverse theoretical perspectives, contexts, and questions regarding SE research, such as those regarding nonprofit, government, and for-profit organizations in a variety of countries. Such diversity suggests that the state of SE research may mirror Gartner's (2001) sentiments about the proverbial theoretical 'elephant' in entrepreneurship studies, in which 'blind' scholars attempt to describe a whole phenomenon when they in fact describe only a small part of it. It may be impossible for scholars to develop a comprehensive theory of SE given the diversity of topics and theories used to study SE. Rather, it may make more sense for communities of SE researchers to systematically engage in the creation of a body of information (Gartner, 2001). These tribes or communities of scholars would therefore develop knowledge about SE based on 'tribal affiliation', independent of topics of interest in the broader management community.

CONCLUSION

The present study is an apt use of historical perspective in a number of ways suggested by Lawrence (1984) that contribute to our knowledge of the historical development of SE research. First, the design of the study was based on the assumption that generalizable findings about changes in the themes of Special Issues and SE articles can only be made using longitudinal data. Second, by comparing Special Issues to SE articles over time, the study provides an explanation for how developments in SE research may have been influenced by themes in Special Issues. Finally, the longitudinal nature of the study allows us to make predictions into how the future of SE research may be shaped by current trends in themes of Special Issues.

While our study presents a novel application of historical perspective to the history of SE research, it is not without limitations. First, our study does not account for other historical phenomena that may influence SE research and research in other academic fields that would be reflected in Special Issues. For example, in our discussion we mention the impact of the Enron disaster on Special Issues. This impact appears to have decreased as time has progressed, and SE research may be expected to follow the same trend. However, a crisis in a prominent nonprofit organization may influence SE research greatly while only producing a mild impact on the broader academic literature as manifested in Special Issues. Alternately, a resurgence in Special Issues in the Corporate Strategy theme would not be expected to impact SE research, as no social ventures of which we are aware are publicly traded or act as holding companies. The nascency of SE research also seems to pre-empt studies on mergers and acquisitions of social ventures.

Second, due to our selection criteria for Special Issues, i.e. journals that have published three or more SE articles, we found that some journals had a greater impact on our findings than others. For example, the *International Journal of Public Administration* published only three SE articles, yet it published 123 Special Issues in 1991–2008, or over 30 per cent of the total Special Issues we coded. Despite these limitations, we believe that historical perspective using journal Special Issues may still be realistically used to make tentative explanations and predictions about SE research.

Historical perspective is a useful tool that provides explanations for phenomena that would be otherwise unavailable if purely cross-sectional data were used. In this chapter, we used a novel methodology to examine nearly two decades of data about the themes of Special Issues in top management and entrepreneurship journals, and in journals that are actively publishing SE research. We used the analysis to provide explanations for developments in SE research based on a legitimacy logic. We found that 62 per cent of the theme changes from our sample of Special Issues from periods one to two corresponded with changes in SE articles from period two to period three, providing exploratory evidence that themes in journal Special Issues influence themes selected by SE scholars.

Additionally, we suggested a few possibilities as to what the future of SE research may hold over the next six years. The legitimacy logic used in this chapter supports the idea that distinct themes in SE research will grow or decline relative to other themes. Alternatively, communities of scholars with interest in distinct SE topics may form as the field matures, independent of developments in the broader management and entrepreneurship fields. We expect the number of SE articles to continue to grow, and to increase in top management and entrepreneurship journals as well. Such growth will serve to strengthen the legitimacy of SE research in the broader academic community. We therefore invite scholars and doctoral students with an interest in SE to target high-impact journals and to embrace topics of current relevance in management and entrepreneurship.

REFERENCES

Alvarez, S.A. and J.B. Barney (2007), 'Discovery and creation: alternative theories of entrepreneurial action', *Strategic Entrepreneurship Journal*, **1**, 11–26.
Ancona, D.G., P.S. Goodman, B.S. Lawrence and M.L. Tushman (2001), 'Time: a new research lens', *Academy of Management Review*, **26**, 645–63.
Anderson, R., L. Dana and T. Dana (2006), 'Indigenous land rights, entrepreneurship, and economic development in Canada: "Opting-in" to the global economy', *Journal of World Business*, **41**(1), 45–55.
Ashoka (n.d.) *About Us*, retrieved 28 July 2009 from http://www.ashoka.org/about.
Austin, J., H. Stevenson and J. Wei-Skillern (2006), 'Social and commercial entrepreneurship: same, different, or both?', *Entrepreneurship Theory and Practice*, **30**, 1–22.
Badelt, C. (1997), 'Entrepreneurship theories of the non-profit sector', *Voluntas: International Journal of Voluntary and Nonprofit Organizations*, **8**(2), 162–78.
Barman, E. (2002), 'Asserting difference: the strategic response of nonprofit organisations to competition', *Social Forces*, **80**(4), 1191–223.
Busenitz, L.W., G.P. West, D. Sheperd, T. Nelson, G.N. Chandler and A. Zacharakis (2003), 'Entrepreneurship research in emergence: past trends and future directions', *Journal of Management*, **29**, 285–308.
Chamlee-Wright, E. (2008), 'The structure of social capital: an Austrian perspective on its nature and development', *Review of Political Economy*, **20**, 41–58.
Christie, M. and B. Honig (2006), 'Social entrepreneurship: new research findings', *Journal of World Business*, **41**(1), 1–5.
Cohen, M.D. and L.S. Sproull (1991), 'Editor's introduction', *Organization Science,* **2**(1).
Dalkey, N.C. (1969), *The Delphi Method: An Experimental Study of Group Opinion*, Santa Monica, CA: The Rand Corporation.
Dart, R. (2004), 'The legitimacy of social enterprise', *Nonprofit Management and Leadership*, **14**(4), 411–24.
Dean, M.A., C.L. Shook and G.T. Payne (2007), 'The past, present, and future of entrepreneurship research: data analytic trends and training', *Entrepreneurship Theory and Practice*, **32**(4), 601–18.
Dees, J.G. (1998), 'Enterprising nonprofits', *Harvard Business Review*, **76**, 54–67.
Emerson, J. (1999), 'Leadership of the whole: the emerging power of social entrepreneurship', *Leader to Leader*, **13**, 12–14.
Foreman, P. and D.A. Whetten (2002), 'Members' identification with multiple-identity organizations', *Organization Science*, **13**(6), 618–35.
Foster, W. and J. Bradach (2005), 'Should nonprofits seek profits?', *Harvard Business Review*, **83**(2), 92–100.
Garrett, K. (1996), 'Project Chrysalis: the evolution of a community school', *MultiCultural Review*, **5**(4), 26–33.

Gartner, W. (2001), 'Is there an elephant in the room? Blind assumptions in theory development', *Entrepreneurship Theory and Practice*, **25**(4), 27–39.

Golden-Biddle, K. and H. Rao (1997), 'Breaches in the boardroom: organizational identity and conflicts of commitment in a nonprofit organization', *Organization Science*, **8**(6), 593–611.

Harding, R. (2004), 'Social enterprise: the new economic engine?', *Business Strategy Review*, **15**(4), 39–43.

Harjula, L. (2006), 'Tensions between venture capitalists' and business-social entrepreneurs' goals', *Greener Management International*, **51**, 79–87.

Haugh, H. (2007), 'Community-led social venture creation', *Entrepreneurship Theory and Practice*, **31**, 161–82.

Ireland, R.D. and J.W. Webb (2007), 'A cross-disciplinary exploration of entrepreneurship research', *Journal of Management*, **33**(6), 891–927.

Jermier, J.M. (1998), 'Introduction: critical perspectives on organizational control', *Administrative Science Quarterly*, **43**(2), 235–56.

Kerlinger, F.N. (1986), *Foundations of Behavioral Research*, 3rd edn, New York: Harcourt Brace College Publishers.

Kingdon, J.W. (1984), *Agendas, Alternatives, and Public Policies*, Boston, MA: Little, Brown.

Kirzner, I. (1973), *Competition and Entrepreneurship*, Chicago, IL and London: University of Chicago Press.

Lawrence, B.S. (1984), 'Historical perspective: using the past to study the present', *Academy of Management Review*, **9**(2), 307–12.

Lewis, E. (1980), *Public Entrepreneurship: Toward a Theory of Bureaucratic Political Power*, Bloomington, IN: Indiana University Press.

Lindsay, G. and L. Hems (2004), 'Sociétés coopératives d'intérêt collectif: the arrival of social enterprise within the French social economy', *Voluntas: International Journal of Voluntary and Nonprofit Organizations*, **15**(3), 265–86.

Luke, B. and M.-L. Verreynne (2006), 'Social enterprise in the public sector. MetService: thinking beyond the weather', *International Journal of Social Economics*, **33**, 432–45.

Ma, D. and W.L. Parish (2006), 'Tocquevillian moments: charitable contributions by Chinese private entrepreneurs', *Social Forces*, **85**, 943–64.

Maguire, S., C. Hardy and T.B. Lawrence (2004), 'Institutional entrepreneurship in emerging fields: HIV/AIDS treatment advocacy in Canada', *Academy of Management Journal*, **47**(5), 657–79.

Mahoney, J. (1999), 'Nominal, ordinal, and narrative appraisal in macrocausal analysis', *American Journal of Sociology*, **104**(4), 1154–96.

Mair, J. and I. Marti (2006), 'Social entrepreneurship research: a source of explanation, prediction, and delight', *Journal of World Business*, **41**(1), 36–44.

Mancino, A. and A. Thomas (2005), 'An Italian pattern of social enterprise: the social cooperative', *Nonprofit Management and Leadership*, **15**(3), 357–69.

Martin, R.L. and S. Osberg (2007), 'Social entrepreneurship: the case for definition', *Stanford Social Innovation Review*, **5**(2), 28–39.

McDonald, R. (2007), 'An investigation of innovation in nonprofit organizations: the role of organizational mission', *Nonprofit and Voluntary Sector Quarterly*, **36**(2), 256–81.

Ndemo, E.B. (2006), 'Assessing sustainability of faith-based enterprises in Kenya', *International Journal of Social Economics*, **33**(5/6), 446–62.

Nwankwo, E., N. Phillips and P. Tracey (2007), 'Social investment through community enterprise: the case of multinational corporations' involvement in the development of Nigerian water resources', *Journal of Business Ethics*, **73**(1), 91–101.

Olk, P. and T.L. Griffith (2004), 'Creating and disseminating knowledge among organizational scholars: the role of special issues', *Organization Science*, **15**(1), 120–29.

Pajunen, K. (2006), 'The more things change, the more they remain the same? Evaluating strategic leadership in organizational transformations', *Leadership*, **2**, 341–66.

Peredo, A.M. and J.J. Chrisman (2006), 'Toward a theory of community-based enterprise', *Academy of Management Review*, **31**(2), 309–28.

Pfeffer, J. (1993), 'Barriers to the advance of organizational science: paradigm development as a dependent variable', *Academy of Management Review*, **18**, 599–620.

Phillips, S.D. (2005), 'Will the market set them free? Women, NGOs, and social enterprise in Ukraine', *Human Organization*, **64**(3), 251–64.

Reger, R.K. and T.B. Palmer (1996), 'Managerial categorization of competitors: using old maps to navigate new environments', *Organization Science*, **7**, 22–39.

Rego, L. and A. Bhandary (2006), 'New model: a social entrepreneur changes the landscape', *Leadership in Action*, **26**(1), 8–11.

Roberts, N.C. and P.J. King (1991), 'Policy entrepreneurs: their activity structure and function in the policy process', *Journal of Public Administration Research and Theory*, **1**(2), 147–75.

Ryan, W. (1999), 'The new landscape for nonprofits', *Harvard Business Review*, **77**(1), 127–36.

Sagawa, S. and E. Segal (2000), 'Common interest, common good: creating value through business and social sector partnerships', *California Management Review*, **42**(2), 105–22.

Schendel, D. (1991), 'Introduction to the special issue on global strategy', *Strategic Management Journal*, **12** (Summer), 1–3.

Seelos, C. and J. Mair (2005), 'Social entrepreneurship: creating new business models to serve the poor', *Business Horizons*, **48**, 241–46.

Shook, C.L., D.J. Ketchen, C.S. Cycyota and D. Crockett (2003), 'Data analytic trends in strategic management research', *Strategic Management Journal*, **24**, 1231–37.

Short, J.C. and T.B. Palmer (2003), 'Organizational performance referents: an empirical examination of their content and influences', *Organizational Behavior and Human Decision Processes*, **90**, 209–24.

Short, J.C., T.W. Moss and G.T. Lumpkin (2009), 'Research in social entrepreneurship: past contributions and future opportunities', *Strategic Entrepreneurship Journal*, **3**, 161–94.

Spear, R. (2006), 'Social entrepreneurship: a different model?', *International Journal of Social Economics*, **33**(5/6), 399–410.

Spear, R. and E. Bidet (2005), 'Social enterprise for work integration in 12 European countries: a descriptive analysis', *Annals of Public and Cooperative Economics*, **76**, 195–231.

Suchman, M.C. (1995), 'Managing legitimacy: strategic and institutional approaches', *Academy of Management Review*, **20**, 571–610.

Tahi, A. and M.J. Meyer (1999), 'A revealed preference study of management journals' direct influences', *Strategic Management Journal*, **20**, 279–96.

Thomas, A. (2004), 'The rise of social cooperatives in Italy', *Voluntas: International Journal of Voluntary and Nonprofit Organizations*, **15**(3), 243–63.

Thompson, J.L., G. Alvy and A. Lees (2000), 'Social entrepreneurship: a new look at the people and the potential', *Management Decision*, **38**, 328–38.

Townsend, D.M. and T.A. Hart (2008), 'Perceived institutional ambiguity and the choice of organizational form in social entrepreneurial ventures', *Entrepreneurship Theory and Practice*, **32**, 685–700.

Tracey, P. and O. Jarvis (2007), 'Toward a theory of social venture franchising', *Entrepreneurship Theory and Practice*, **31**(5), 667–85.

Tracey, P., N. Phillips and H. Haugh (2005), 'Beyond philanthropy: community enterprise as a basis for corporate citizenship', *Journal of Business Ethics*, **58**, 327–44.

Vega, G. and R.E. Kidwell (2007), 'Toward a typology of new venture creators: similarities and contrasts between business and social entrepreneurs', *New England Journal of Entrepreneurship*, **10**(2), 15–28.

Waddock, S.A. and J.E. Post (1991), 'Social entrepreneurs and catalytic change', *Public Administration Review*, **51**, 393–401.

Wallace, S.L. (1999), 'Social entrepreneurship: the role of social purpose enterprises in facilitating community economic development', *Journal of Developmental Entrepreneurship*, **4**, 153–74.

Young, D.R. (2001), 'Organizational identity in nonprofit organizations: strategic and structural implications', *Nonprofit Management and Leadership*, **12**(2), 139–58.

Young, D.R. (2006), 'Social enterprise in community and economic development in the USA: theory, corporate form and purpose', *International Journal of Entrepreneurship and Innovation Management*, **6**(3), 241–55.

Yukl, G. (2005), *Leadership in organizations*, 6th edn, Upper Saddle Creek, NJ: Prentice Hall.

APPENDIX

Table 14A.1   Journal Special Issues organized according to theme[b]

Journal	1	2	3	4	5	6	7	8	9	10	11	12	13	14
Top Management and Entrepreneurship Journals														
Academy of Management Journal	2	2	3	2	4	4	–	1	7	2	–	–	5	32
Academy of Management Review	4	3	1	2	2	1	–	2	5	2	–	–	2	24
Administrative Science Quarterly	–	1	–	1	–	–	–	–	–	–	–	–	–	2
Strategic Management Journal	3	–	2	1	2	1	–	–	2	–	10	–	2	23
Organization Science	2	1	1	5	5	2	–	–	3	–	3	1	–	23
Journal of Management	1	–	–	1	1	–	–	–	3	–	1	–	–	7
Entrepreneurship Theory and Practice	1	11	1	–	2	1	–	–	4	–	1	6	8	35
Journal of Business Venturing	1	1	–	–	–	1	–	–	4	–	1	3	–	11
Strategic Entrepreneurship Journal	–	–	–	–	–	–	–	–	–	–	–	–	–	–
Other Journals														
Journal of World Business	–	2	13	1	–	–	–	1	–	1	2	–	1	21
International Journal of Social Economics	–	–	4	–	–	–	2	2	–	2	5	–	1	16
Voluntas: International Journal of Voluntary and Nonprofit Organizations	–	1	4	–	–	–	6	2	1	–	–	–	–	14
Journal of Nonprofit and Public Sector Marketing	–	–	1	–	–	1	3	4	2	1	–	–	–	12
Harvard Business Review	–	4	–	1	–	–	–	–	–	–	–	–	3	8

Table 14A.1　　(continued)

Journal	1	2	3	4	5	6	7	8	9	10	11	12	13	14
Business Strategy Review	–	1	1	–	–	–	–	–	–	–	–	–	–	2
Nonprofit Management and Leadership	–	–	–	2	–	1	3	–	1	2	1	–	–	10
Journal of Business Ethics	1	4	16	6	–	–	–	–	3	49	2	2	1	84
International Journal of Entrepreneurial Behaviour and Research	1	2	–	–	–	–	–	–	1	1	1	1	7	14
Journal of Developmental Entrepreneurship	–	–	2	–	–	–	–	–	–	–	–	–	2	4
Stanford Social Innovation Review	–	–	–	–	–	–	–	–	–	–	–	–	–	–
Public Administration Review	1	2	–	–	–	2	2	11	1	–	–	–	2	21
Nonprofit and Voluntary Sector Quarterly	–	–	2	–	–	–	7	3	2	–	1	1	–	16
International Journal of Public Administration	31	8	27	10	5	3	1	86	13	9	7	–	18	218
Total journals per theme[a]	48	43	78	32	21	17	24	112	52	69	35	14	52	597

Notes:
[a] Special Issues were coded into one or two dimensions; total is not the Special Issue total.
[b] 1: Change Processes; 2: Human Capital; 3: International and Global; 4: Management Practice; 5: Management Theory; 6: Networking and Collaboration; 7: Nonprofits; 8: Public Policy; 9: Scholarship and Learning; 10: Social Responsibility and Ethics; 11: Strategy and Economics; 12: Type of Enterprise; 13: Value Creation; 14: Total themes per journal.

PART III

Economic History and Entrepreneurship Research

15. Historical reasoning and the development of entrepreneurship theory

R. Daniel Wadhwani

INTRODUCTION

To many, history may seem irrelevant to the study of entrepreneurship today. The pace, nature, and forms of entrepreneurial activity in our time make the phenomenon appear new and unique, with few relevant comparisons in the past (Dana et al., 2004). Historical evidence on entrepreneurship is fragmentary, messy, and difficult to analyze using conventional social scientific methods. Moreover, researchers often label the field itself 'new' or 'young' (Cooper, 2003). History, one could conclude from much of today's scholarship, is at best marginal to our understanding of entrepreneurship.

Yet historical reasoning has played a more profound role in the development of modern conceptions of entrepreneurship than most researchers in the field recognize. Many of the premises that shape the field today originate from historical reasoning and research. Historicism has been especially important in understanding the links in the entrepreneurial process between the actions of individuals or firms and change within industries, economies, and societies.

Not surprisingly, understanding the role of historicism in the development of theories of entrepreneurship requires a deeper historical perspective than is typically offered in conventional accounts that date the emergence of the field to the 1970s and 1980s. This chapter takes that deeper perspective in order to examine the role of historical reasoning and research in the development of entrepreneurship as a field of thought and investigation. The chapter not only establishes that entrepreneurship research and reasoning has a much deeper tradition than is commonly recognized, but also argues that historicism – the analytical tradition of contextualizing behavior and cognition in time and place – has shaped the development of the conceptions of entrepreneurship we use today.

The first section of the chapter examines the role of historicism in the development of entrepreneurship as a field of reasoning and research. I show that historical reasoning has been essential to the development of modern conceptions of entrepreneurship, particularly those that emphasize the role of the entrepreneurial process in explaining evolution within industries and economies. Historicism's assumptions about the agency of economic actors and the evolution of economies have been essential to the emergence of entrepreneurship as an area of research. In the second section, I examine how historicism has been used by a number of key entrepreneurship theorists and researchers. Though historicism does not prescribe a unitary methodology or theory, I show that these scholars share an approach to exploring the past in their research on entrepreneurship that recognizes the uniqueness of historical reasoning. I conclude by considering the role of historical research and reasoning in the future of the field.

THE HISTORICAL TRADITION IN ENTREPRENEURSHIP RESEARCH

Entrepreneurship researchers today famously disagree over the definition of the phenomenon they study. Some have defined it as a type of organizational process, such as starting up a company or entering a new market (Gartner, 1985; 1988), whereas others have offered behavioral and cognitive definitions, particularly focusing on how individuals recognize opportunities (Stevenson and Jarillo, 1990; Kirzner, 1973). One particularly important line of thought, however, conceives of entrepreneurship as a dynamic, disequilibrating process that occurs through the interaction between enterprising individuals and potentially lucrative opportunities (Shane and Venkataraman, 2000; Eckhardt and Shane, 2003). The entrepreneur, in this line of thought, is an innovative economic agent, who pursues new business opportunities that hold the potential to change the way a market or industry functions, and hence acts as an endogenous source of dynamism in market economies (Schumpeter, 1928; 1934; 1942; Gunther McGrath, 2003). Unlike definitions that focus solely on individual behavior or organizational forms, this conceptualization reflects the dynamic and disruptive connotations that we typically associate with entrepreneurship today.

Conceived in this way, the modern concept of entrepreneurship owes much to the historical tradition in economic thought. This section outlines the development of historical reasoning in economic thought and its relationship to the dynamic understanding of entrepreneurship we have today. The first sub-section briefly outlines how and why historical reasoning about economics, markets, and business shaped the origins of the modern view of entrepreneurship. The next sub-section examines how this view influenced the social scientific study of entrepreneurship during most of the twentieth century and assesses the contributions of this research. The final sub-section considers the reasons for the relative decline of historicism in research on entrepreneurship in the last quarter century and its impact on the mix of scholarship being produced today.

Historicism and the Origins of Modern Entrepreneurial Thought

Historicism in economics traces its roots to the 'historical schools' of economic thought that developed in nineteenth-century England and Germany. Historicists were critical of the abstract theories of classical economics (Hodgson, 2001). They often charged that economists – particularly after Ricardo – had developed a body of theory that was largely divorced from the realities of economic life. Classical theory, historicists pointed out, ignored the socio-cultural institutions in which economic exchange was embedded, overlooked the dynamic transformations that the Industrial Revolution was creating in the economy, and ignored the creative agency of entrepreneurs (or 'undertakers', as they were more often called) in using their insight and will to pursue projects that fundamentally changed the economy. In looking at the historical record, for instance, Gustav

Schmoller insisted that the 'enterprising spirit' was crucial to a wide range of real economic activities that involved the creation of new organizational projects and innovation (Herbert and Link, 2006). Hence, as a modern intellectual construct, entrepreneurship grew out of a critique of classical economics' failure to deal with the will and capabilities of economic agents to pursue endeavors that fundamentally changed systems of production within the economy.

Historicism provided fertile intellectual ground for the development of concepts and theories of entrepreneurship for several reasons. First, unlike the classical economists, the historical economists rejected abstract economic reasoning in favor of embedded, inductive research about businesses and industries. Schmoller, in particular, emphasized the production of historical monographs on business and economic topics as the path to progress in economics (Ebner, 2000; Herbst, 1965). In these inductive studies, the historical economists often documented and commented on the role of entrepreneurs as distinct agents within the economy as well as the role of economic mindsets, topics that had largely been ignored by the classical economists (Ebner, 2000). Second, unlike the classical economists, the historical economists did not accept materialist ontology or purely hedonistic motives as the basis for economic behavior. Rather, they included the will and the mind as essential factors in the study of economics. Questions of what shaped entrepreneurial will and mindset were, thus, at the forefront of their study of economic topics. Finally, unlike the classical economists, the historical economists' studies made them keenly aware of the ways in which the Industrial Revolution was transforming industries and economies. They, therefore, embraced a much more dynamic and evolutionary approach to the study of economics than the classical economists (Ebner, 2000). These three characteristics of nineteenth-century historicism – inductive historical methods, the inclusion of will and mind as economic subjects, and an evolutionary perspective on the economy – would fundamentally shape the development of entrepreneurship thought and research over the next century.

The most significant way in which historicism maintained its influence on entrepreneurship theory and research was through the work of early economic sociologists, particularly Werner Sombart and Max Weber. Both embraced the tenets of historicism, often engaged in reasoning about entrepreneurship from historical evidence, and are referred to as members of the 'Youngest Historical School' (Schumpeter, 1954). Unlike the older historians, however, Sombart (1911; 1915) and Weber (1904; 1923) sought not just to produce detailed historical studies about their subjects but also to use inductive reasoning to theorize about 'ideal types' and patterns in entrepreneurial behavior and economic change.

Sombart, for instance, began to conceive of entrepreneurs as essential agents of change within capitalist societies and explored the socio-cultural and religious backgrounds of entrepreneurs and the circumstances that shaped their propensity to create and innovate in methods of economic production. Indeed, Reinert (2002) has suggested that Sombart – not Schumpeter – was the first to introduce the concept of 'creative destruction' to economic research, in his grand synthesis *Modern Capitalism*.

Weber (1904; 1923), too, engaged historical reasoning to induce his contentions about an entrepreneurial spirit in modern capitalism – a mentality that differentiated the market economy as an economic system from earlier forms of economic organization. Though his ideas on the origins of the 'spirit of capitalism' are most often associated with *The*

Protestant Ethic (1904), it is in his less commonly read *General Economic History* (1923, see also Swedberg, 1998) that he most extensively explains his ideas on the origins of modern capitalism. In *General Economic History* Weber explains the mix of economic, political, and cognitive changes that he associates with the development of modern enterprise and the entrepreneurial approach to economic opportunities that distinguish it from traditional economies, in which entrepreneurial attitudes and pursuits were viewed with suspicion.

The younger historicists, thus, theorized that an entrepreneurial spirit or drive underlay the historical shift from what were considered static, 'traditional' economies to dynamic, modern ones. In pursuing economic opportunities in a new way and with new vigor, entrepreneurs undermined the deferential ties that limited economic change in traditional societies and unleashed a new set of expectations and attitudes about economic exchange, productivity, and economic accumulation that defined modern capitalism. In this sense, historicists conceived the entrepreneur as a distinct agent of economic and historical change – a perspective that differentiated them from the materialist dialectics of Marxist views of history as well as the ahistoricism of the classical economists (Swedberg, 1998).

While the historical economists and sociologists embraced the study of entrepreneurship and change in their studies, classical and neoclassical economists continued to largely ignore it. There were a few exceptions to this generalization, and these exceptions typically arose when economists engaged historical evidence. Marshall, for instance, developed the notion of 'industrial districts' – what we now might call entrepreneurial clusters – in work in which he took a much more inductive and historical approach to examining economic phenomena. In *Industry and Trade,* for instance, Marshall (1919, pp. 7–8) admits that 'the more I knew of the work of [the English historicist] Sir W.J. Ashley and the late Professor Schmoller, the warmer became my regard for them.' However, with few exceptions (Knight, 1921), entrepreneurial topics remained marginal in neoclassical economics.

The more significant competing line of reasoning on entrepreneurship to emerge at the time was that of Carl Menger (1871) and the Austrian school of economics. Menger and other Austrian economists shared with the historicists an understanding of the importance of the subjectivity and cognition of economic agents, a line of thought on the nature of entrepreneurship that has been most fully developed by Kirzner (1973), with whom many entrepreneurship scholars are familiar (Koppl and Minniti, 2003). However, unlike the historicists, the Austrian economists gave far less attention to the evolutionary nature of entrepreneurial processes. Austrian economists also remained highly committed to deductive reasoning and to strict methodological individualism, stances that precluded the kind of engagement with examining embedded entrepreneurial phenomena in temporal contexts that historians considered essential to scholarly progress.

In sum, more than other traditions of economic reasoning, historicism embraced a dynamic view of economic processes that sought to understand the origins of the endemic change that seemed to characterize modern economies. It also emphasized the cognitive outlook and social contexts shaping economic agents and the impact of these on the pursuit of entrepreneurial opportunities. In doing so, it laid the foundations for modern conceptions of entrepreneurship and the entrepreneur and for grounded research on the economic agency of these actors that flourished across the social sciences in the twentieth century.

Entrepreneurship and the Study of Modern Economic Growth in the Twentieth Century

Over the course of the twentieth century, the historicist conception of entrepreneurship became a focus of research across a wide range of social scientific disciplines. Scholarly attention turned to entrepreneurship because of its theorized link to economic growth. Social scientists sought to take the early historians' impressionistic notions of the relationship between entrepreneurial spirit and economic change and to engage in more systematic theory and research into the sources of entrepreneurial supply and its impact on economic development. In doing so, social scientists embraced not only the historicist conception of entrepreneurship but also a wide range of historical evidence in their search for the roots of modern economic growth.

More than any other twentieth-century scholar, Joseph Schumpeter shaped the development of historically oriented research on entrepreneurship and economic growth. He did so by bringing together the tools and theories of neoclassical economics and the entrepreneurship-focused, evolutionary view of the economy found among the historical economists. Schumpeter's views on entrepreneurship and economic growth were fundamentally shaped by the historical school (Macdonald, 1965; Ebner, 2000), as well as those of the Austrian economists (McCraw, 2007). But while the young Schumpeter embraced the entrepreneurial dynamism of the historical school, he initially rejected its methods and searched to apply the quantitative tools of the neoclassical school to evolutionary economics. Over time, however, Schumpeter increasingly embraced sociological and historical methods as the way to understand entrepreneurship and the dynamics of capitalist economies. In *Business Cycles* (1939), he immersed himself in the study of the histories of five industries in the United States, Great Britain and Germany – an experience that fundamentally shaped his thinking during the last decade and half of his life. As Thomas McCraw (2006; 2007) has shown, Schumpeter's engagement with business history fundamentally shaped how he came to think about the process of 'creative destruction' in *Capitalism, Socialism, and Democracy*. Looking back at his own career in *History of Economic Analysis* (1954), Schumpeter himself admitted history's influence on his thinking. In another article, he discussed the value of moving back and forth between theory and history in understanding entrepreneurship: 'Personally, I believe that there is an incessant give and take between historical and theoretical analysis and that, though for the investigation of individual questions it may be necessary to sail for a time on one tack only, yet on principle the two should never lose sight of each other' (Schumpeter, 1949, p. 75).

Schumpeter's originality derived from taking the historical economists' ideas about entrepreneurship and embedding them within a theory of endogenous change and growth within capitalist societies (Freeman and Louca, 2001; Herbert and Link, 2006). By doing so he hoped to bring together neoclassical economics' traditional focus on equilibrium economics and the notion of innovative entrepreneurship found in the research of the historical school. His embrace of historical methods and research in turn reshaped how he thought about the process of innovation and entrepreneurship within economies. Despite his early emphasis on the individual heroic entrepreneur, Schumpeter came to argue – especially after his historical work in *Business Cycles* – that large, monopolistic firms could, in fact, innovate and act entrepreneurially. Increasingly he emphasized the many forms that entrepreneurship could take within an economy, a conclusion he drew from the historical record. History also allowed Schumpeter to examine the process of creative destruction over time and to see how innovations disrupted existing business models and transformed industries – a process that was difficult to study using other methodologies.

In fact, one might argue that Schumpeter's contribution to entrepreneurship research was not just theoretical but also methodological. His embrace of historical methods as essential to the study of entrepreneurial processes contributed significantly to the flowering of research in the field following World War II. Schumpeter (along with economic historian Arthur Cole) played an important role in promoting this research agenda by establishing the Center for Entrepreneurial History at Harvard in 1948. The Center drew a number of well-known historians, economists, sociologists, and psychologists, all of whom conducted historically oriented research on entrepreneurship. The Center's publication – *Explorations in Entrepreneurial History* – was the first academic journal dedicated to empirical research in the field and included famously lively debates and forums that engaged both the history and theory of entrepreneurship. Especially in the early years of the Center, entrepreneurial history was embraced as a broad and interdisciplinary social scientific endeavor that sought to build on theories of entrepreneurship through empirical research in the historical tradition (Jones and Wadhwani, 2008). Although the burgeoning interest in research on entrepreneurship and economic growth was centered in the United States, the Schumpeterian research agenda also took root in scholarship being produced in Europe and Asia on the historical origins of modern economies (Jones and Wadhwani, 2007).

The most robust stream of entrepreneurship research to emerge during these years focused on the historical effects of socio-cultural institutions on entrepreneurial behavior. A number of the scholars associated with the Center for Entrepreneurial History – most notably sociologist Leland Jenks (1949) and historians Thomas Cochran (1950; 1960) and David Landes (1949) – drew on and adapted Talcott Parsons's (Parsons and Smelser, 1956; Parsons, 1960) structural functional theories of social roles and norms to examine entrepreneurship in a wide array of historical settings. The fundamental tenet of most of the research was that socio-cultural norms and institutions regulated the permissibility and acceptance of innovative and disruptive entrepreneurship and that studying these norms and role structures historically could lead to a better understanding of their effects on entrepreneurial activity and economic change over time. While the post-war historical scholarship on entrepreneurship eschewed Sombart and Weber's sweeping generalizations about 'ideal types', it nevertheless worked within the Weberian tradition of blending economic and sociological study in historical contexts to examine patterns in how beliefs and norms had affected entrepreneurial behavior (Jones and Wadhwani, 2007; 2008).

The wave of Cold War era scholarship engaged psychologists, political scientists, and economists in addition to historians and sociologists in historical evidence on the cultural and institutional roots of modern entrepreneurial behavior and significantly widened the scope of research to include developing countries as well as developed. Thomas Cochran (1965, p. 25) noted, 'The more economists labored with the exotic cultures of Asia, Africa, and Latin America the more impressed they became with the force and intricacy of social factors' in shaping entrepreneurial behavior and decision making. Identifying which 'social factors' mattered and precisely how they shaped entrepreneurial behavior and economic growth, however, was no simple matter. Although dozens of publications explored the non-economic roots of entrepreneurial behavior in traditional and modern economies, they differed significantly in their stands on which psychological (McClelland, 1961; Hagen, 1962; 1963) and sociological (Cochran, 1960; 1965) determinants mattered. Modern entrepreneurial attitudes and behaviors were, thus, found to depend on a wide variety of factors: the prevalence of achievement orientation in a society (McClelland, 1961), the extent of technological creativity (Hagen, 1962; 1963), the existence of cultural norms that accepted disruptive entrepreneurs (Cochran, 1965; Hirschmeier, 1977), and the ease of status mobility, among other factors. In each case, the cultural, psychological, or social factor under consideration was reported to be critical to the transition from a static, traditional economy to a modern entrepreneurial one.

While welcoming the comparative and historical scope of the research, critics complained about the lack of clarity in the claimed causal relationships and the rigid, often over deterministic view of the influence of culture and society on business. Peter Kilby (1971), an economist who studied entrepreneurship in Africa, noted that the range of activities and skills that entrepreneurship required varied significantly by time and place, while most research treated entrepreneurship as a single variable that fitted neatly into a modernization framework. For instance, institution creation and political processes typically played a major role in new business creation and innovation in these contexts, a historical pattern that most modernization theories ignored. Economic historian Alexander Gerschenkron (1962; 1966) was even more critical of the use of linear modernization models to explain entrepreneurship and economic change. Gerschenkron acknowledged that the development of cultural and institutional norms in some settings may have affected the development of modern entrepreneurship but warned that we 'must be very wary of generalizing such findings and regarding them in a way as necessary prerequisites.' He lamented (1966, p. 252) that '[i]t is precisely this [determinism] that is done by several sociologists and psychologists who are trying to develop general theories of modern industrialization with particular stress on the entrepreneurial element therein.' Gerschenkron's point (discussed more fully later in this chapter) was that the paths to modern industrialization could vary fundamentally and that the value of history was in being able to see such patterns rather than to impose a single linear model on historical development.

By the 1970s, the appeal of broadly conceived studies that made sweeping claims about the historical roots of modern entrepreneurship had begun to decline among social scientists. In part this was because, as Kilby and Gerschenkron pointed out, the historical evidence on entrepreneurship could not be fitted into a neatly linear model of economic modernization. Modernization theory came under attack on multiple fronts as scholars questioned its assumptions about the distinctions between traditional and modern societies and its lack of attention to the role of international power (Leff, 1979; Wallerstein, 1974) in shaping the paths to economic growth available to local entrepreneurs. Interest in entrepreneurship research also waned as historical social scientists, influenced by the interest in the systematic application of quantitative methods to social scientific phenomena, turned to examining topics where such methods could more readily be applied. For instance, *Explorations in Entrepreneurial History* was renamed *Explorations in Economic*

History, a publication dedicated to the application of quantitative methods to the study of the past. Influenced by the work of Alfred D. Chandler (1962), business historians once dedicated to examining the entrepreneur, began instead to focus on organizational innovations in the firm more narrowly as a way of more rigorously studying economic change (Jones and Wadhwani, 2008). Each of these developments undermined the style of the broad synthetic studies that put forth general historical models of entrepreneurial development.

In retrospect, the many weaknesses of the wave of mid-twentieth century scholarship on entrepreneurial history are apparent. It too often relied on a general, linear model of historical development that failed to deal with the wide variations in historical experience it encountered. It often lacked clear specifications about the nature of the entrepreneurial behavior it was studying. It could also often be blind to the issues of power and politics and how these shaped the historical experience of entrepreneurship and the existence of entrepreneurial opportunity around the world. In addition, as a body of research, it failed to build a set of lasting generalizations about the nature of entrepreneurship and its impact on economic change.

Yet, despite its many limitations, its influence on subsequent developments in social scientific and historical work on entrepreneurship and economic change should not be underestimated. The limitations of a grand historical synthesis on entrepreneurship and its relation to economic development led subsequent generations of researchers in the historical social sciences to disaggregate entrepreneurial phenomena and to engage in more focused studies of the elements of the entrepreneurial process. Many of these streams of research have roots in the entrepreneurial history of the earlier era. Much of the current work on institutions and entrepreneurial activity grew directly out of the research of this era and the ideas of many of its most important scholars (North, 1990; Baumol, 1990) were shaped by the entrepreneurial history of this era. Likewise, the discovery of the wide variations in the organizational form of entrepreneurship led to a sustained stream of studies on innovation in organizations (Cuff, 2002; Graham and Shuldiner, 2001; Hounshell and Kenly Smith, 1988). Other streams of research have emphasized the great variety of entrepreneurial paths and trajectories that define modern economies. Still other elements of the earlier scholarship – such as Arthur Cole's (1959) work on the importance of information and spillovers of useful knowledge and opportunities in the entrepreneurial process – are being rediscovered by scholars (Audretsch and Keilback, 2006). Space limitations prevent a full account of the many streams of historical research into which historical work on entrepreneurship fragmented. (For an overview of this work, see Jones and Wadhwani, 2008.) Yet their common roots and assumptions lie in the historical tradition of entrepreneurship research that flourished in the mid-twentieth century.

Rise of the Behavioral Approach and the Marginalization of History

Today, historicism continues to be an influential form of reasoning in the social sciences (North, 1990; Pierson and Skocpol, 2002; Thelen and Steinmo, 1992), but ironically it has been marginalized in mainstream entrepreneurship research, especially in the United States. The reasons for the decline of historicism are complex but largely pertain to the origins of the current wave of work.

The recent stream of entrepreneurship research based in business schools emerged in the 1970s and 1980s just as social scientific interest in applying entrepreneurship to modernization theory was waning. Unlike the earlier research, the recent wave of scholarship has associated entrepreneurship with small businesses and start ups. This inclination was the product of concurrent historical developments, particularly the competitive challenges that large diversified firms in mature industries began to face in the last third of the twentieth century (Landström, 2005). In contrast, small business researchers were finding that start ups and SMEs were an important source of job creation (Birch, 1979) and innovation (Acs, 1984; Acs and Audretsch, 1990) in the economy. The economic vitality (and political legitimacy) of the small business and start up sector – particularly in high technology industries – was seen in sharp contrast to the antiquated administrative rigidity and sluggish performance of large, professionally managed firms. Policymakers in the Reagan–Thatcher years quickly picked up on the shift and promoted entrepreneurship and small business in both policies and rhetoric. Demand for entrepreneurship education – in terms of small business start up and administration classes – began to soar in business schools as students perceived the shift in career opportunities. Interest in entrepreneurship education and research hence grew out of the contemporary concern with small business and job creation, rather than the broader concern with explaining economic change that had motivated earlier researchers (Landström, 2005).

Emerging out of this milieu, the scholarship in this area embraced a behavioral and organizational approach to the study of entrepreneurship. Stevenson and Jarillo (1990), for instance, argued that understanding entrepreneurial behaviors and their efficacy in relationship to the existence of an opportunity was more appropriate for business schools than the broad functional and historical studies of the past, while Gartner (1985; 1988) argued that the key lay in the organizing of a new firm. The scholarship hence tended to focus on narrow, discrete categories of behaviors and cognitive acts, such as firm founding, team building, and financing. Thus, in studying individual and firm-level patterns of entrepreneurship – such as opportunity identification, resource acquisition or team creation – the recent wave of scholarship far surpasses older work. (Details on these contributions can be found in many of the other chapters of this book.)

However, the broader links between these entrepreneurial behaviors and processes of economic change within industries, societies, and economies was almost completely sidelined. In theoretical pieces and in surveys, entrepreneurship researchers repeatedly called for more studies that linked entrepreneurial behaviors at the level of the individual and the firm to processes of change and development at the levels of the industry and economy. Low and MacMillan (1988), for instance, argued that entrepreneurship research needed to address the links between firm and individual level phenomena and processes of change and development at the industry and economy levels, a plea that was later echoed by Davidsson and Wiklund (2001). On the whole, however, very little effort has been made on this front in mainstream entrepreneurship research and the key journals have remained committed to focused studies of entrepreneurial behavior and firm founding. Chandler and Lyon (2001), for instance, found a declining attention in mainstream entrepreneurship journals to the industry, regional, and economy levels of analysis and identified a mere 7 per cent of studies as including multi-year analysis of any sort.

There were a number of notable exceptions to this general pattern of intellectual development. In Europe (and especially in the UK) historicism continued to be more extensively integrated into entrepreneurship research. Casson (1990; 1995; 2010; Casson and Godley, 2005), for instance, continued to take historicism seriously in developing theory, and business historians often engaged entrepreneurial theory systematically in their research (Bergoff and Moller, 1994; Godley, 2001; Nicholas, 1999; 2000). Likewise, European and American researchers who examined entrepreneurial clusters and industrial districts more consistently linked individual and firm behavior to industries, regions, and economies, and engaged the historical record in doing so (Zeitlin, 2008b). A few economists also began to expand the scope of their research to engage in work on information and knowledge spillovers (Audretsch and Keilback, 2006; Rajshree et al., 2008). On the whole, however, until recently mainstream entrepreneurship research showed little interest in the broader relation of entrepreneurship to historical context and economic change.

In recent years, however, entrepreneurship scholars have begun once again to consider more critically the role of change and history in their field. Baumol and Strom (2007) have suggested that mainstream entrepreneurship research ought to take historical evidence more seriously, and Rita Gunther McGrath (2003, p. 521) reminded us that '[t]he study of entrepreneurship is fundamentally about the process of economic change.' Historians, too, have called for a re-engagement with entrepreneurship theory (Cassis and Minoglou 2005; Jones and Wadhwani, 2007; 2008). A return to the use of historical reasoning and the study of change in entrepreneurship necessarily begins with a fuller understanding of the role of historicism in the development of the field. As this section has shown, historical reasoning has played a formative role in the development of the field over the last century and a half. In contrast to the abstraction and historically static approach of classical and neoclassical economics, historicism provided fertile ground for the theoretical development of entrepreneurship, especially as it relates to the central issues of innovation, change and development within the economy. Historicism will likely again be crucial if entrepreneurship research is to re-engage the vital issues of industrial change and development. The next section hence explores historicism from a different angle by considering its role in the thinking of a number of major theorists of entrepreneurship.

HISTORICISM AS A MODE OF INVESTIGATION

What exactly is historicism, and why has it, as a way of reasoning, been important to the development of entrepreneurship as a field? One way to look at history – perhaps the more common way in the mainstream social sciences these days – is to think of it as the cumulative sequence of events that took place in the past. History, in this sense, is simply the evidentiary record from the past. Interpreted in this way, history provides a vast store of evidence and information against which to test and modify theory. Social scientists working in this tradition, including entrepreneurship scholars, have typically used historical evidence to test hypotheses prevalent in their fields. Nicholas (2008), for instance, has used data from the early twentieth century to test the impact of innovation on stock prices, and Foreman-Peck (2005) has elaborated on methods for testing entrepreneurial activity in historical contexts. Sometimes history is also used in this way to modify the basic social scientific theory, but the real value in this first approach is the richness of evidence it provides for testing theory.

The first approach to history is an important and legitimate tradition in the historically oriented social sciences, but it is not the historical tradition that has yielded the most significant insights into the entrepreneurial process. The more significant line of historical inquiry from the point of view of the development of entrepreneurship as a concept is one that approaches the past not simply as a body of empirical evidence to be tested but rather one that approaches *reasoning* about the past as inherently different from social scientific reasoning about the present. The *Oxford English Dictionary* defines this form of historicism as 'the attempt, found especially among German historians since about 1850, to view all social and cultural phenomena, all categories, truths, and values, as relative and historically determined, and in consequence to be understood only by examining their historical context.' History, in this sense, offers insights into the variation of human experience and the origins of phenomena that are not readily apparent by examining the present alone. The point of this approach to historical reasoning is not simply to test existing theory, but rather to expand understanding of the origins or development of a phenomenon or its relationship to other phenomena that are not perceptible through current experience alone and hence often lie outside contemporary theory. It is this approach to the fundamental uniqueness of historical reasoning (and not just history as a body of evidence) that has been the more fruitful one in the development of modern conceptions of entrepreneurship and its place in economic change.

Historical reasoning of this type does not prescribe a unitary methodology or approach to understanding or identifying the differences of the past and how they inform theory and evidence. It would, therefore, be artificial and misleading to describe or prescribe '*the* historical theory or method' for studying entrepreneurship. Rather it is more fruitful to examine the work of a variety of notably successful entrepreneurship theorists and scholars to see how their engagement with historicism shaped their conclusions about entrepreneurship. The rest of this section hence looks at the role of historical reasoning in the work of three notable entrepreneurship theorists: William Baumol, Joseph Schumpeter, and Alexander Gerschenkron.

William Baumol and Historical Institutionalism

Baumol recently wrote in the *Strategic Entrepreneurship Journal* that 'we need to see the great value of history as a source of evidence on the workings of entrepreneurship and its strategic orientations. Because of the inherent heterogeneity of entrepreneurial activities, considerable difficulty besets the analytical study of entrepreneurship via a body of internally compatible and directly comparable statistics' (Baumol and Strom, 2007, p. 237). It is a methodological theme that Baumol has repeated several times during his long career exploring the determinants of the supply of entrepreneurship and its effects on economic growth (Baumol, 1968). Baumol's approach emphasizes the limits of conventional social scientific methods in studying entrepreneurship not simply because the heterogeneity of entrepreneurship makes statistical comparisons difficult, but also because the very heterogeneity of the historical record on entrepreneurship provides a key to understanding entrepreneurial behavior and how it is shaped by its context. Historicism, in Baumol's approach, provides us with an important way to understand entrepreneurship (particularly its supply) because it allows us to examine a richer variety of contexts than is available in the present.

The great variety of entrepreneurship found over historical time allows us to better induce theories of entrepreneurial behavior and how it is shaped by context.

Baumol's approach to historicism is perhaps most clearly apparent in 'Entrepreneurship: productive, unproductive, and destructive' (1990), an article that has often been reprinted and cited as a seminal piece on the relationship between institutions and entrepreneurial behavior. Drawing on secondary source research on business and enterprise from Ancient Rome to the Renaissance, Baumol induces the proposition that social institutions fundamentally shape the allocation of entrepreneurial efforts to productive, unproductive, and even destructive activities by 'influencing the relative payoffs society offers to such activities' (1990, p. 893). In discussing his historicist methodology, Baumol explicitly notes that the differences of the past provide a foundation for examining the effects of institutions on entrepreneurship that conventional social science research on entrepreneurship could not address. 'Given the inescapable problems for empirical as well as theoretical study of entrepreneurship, what sort of evidence can one hope to provide?' asked Baumol (1990, p. 895). 'Since the rules of the game change very slowly, a case study approach to investigation of my hypotheses drives me unavoidably to examples spanning considerable periods of history and encompassing widely different cultures and geographic locations.'

Baumol's approach to the value of historicism in studying entrepreneurship has been long echoed by others examining the relationship between institutions and entrepreneurship. Indeed much of the post-World War II wave of scholarship on entrepreneurial history was motivated by a similar view of the role of historicism in studying entrepreneurship (Jones and Wadhwani, 2008). In that case, the primary research question concerned the sociocultural norms that promoted or inhibited innovative entrepreneurship, but the Baumol approach is broadly applicable to any investigation of the relationship between institutions and entrepreneurial behavior. (For a broader discussion of the applicability of historical institutionalism in the social sciences see Braudel, 1958.)

Schumpeter and the Path Dependence of Entrepreneurial Processes

Though Schumpeter, too, was interested in the relationship between institutions and entrepreneurship and believed the topic to be an important area of study (Schumpeter, 1947), his theoretical concerns and his approach to historicism were different. Schumpeter embraced historicism based on its ability to account for change over time. Unlike methodologies that allowed the researcher to isolate specific causes and effects or that allowed researchers to grapple with the equilibrating nature of markets, historicism's value for Schumpeter lay in establishing and documenting the directionality of economic change in real historical time and context. From a theoretical perspective, history showed that disruptive innovations and changes rippled through industries, economies and societies in sometimes unpredictable ways that fundamentally changed how these industries and economies worked. Entrepreneurship 'shapes the whole course of subsequent events and their "long-run" outcomes', Schumpeter pointed out. It 'changes social and economic situations for good, or, to put it differently, it creates situations from which there is no bridge to those situations that might have emerged in its absence. This is why creative response is an essential element in the historical process; no deterministic credo avails against this' (Schumpeter, 1947, p. 150). In studying such phenomena and their impact, there was little point in trying to isolate Newtonian cause and effect; real value came with studying it as an embedded process taking place in real historical time to examine how exactly an innovation unseated existing businesses and business models and spilled over into a wide array of related areas. There was no real methodological substitute for examining such historical processes.

Like Baumol, Schumpeter came to his conclusion about the value of historicism not based on aprioristic methodological assumptions, but by actually engaging in the historical evidence. As Thomas McCraw (2007) has shown, Schumpeter's studies in business history within his massive *Business Cycles* (1939) laid the foundation for both his methodological turn toward history as well as the evolution of his own theories of the nature of entrepreneurship. Much of *Business Cycles* is in fact an extensive historical account of the development of five industries – textiles, railroads, steel, automobiles, and electricity – in the United States, Great Britain, and Germany. 'With *Business Cycles*, Schumpeter's entrepreneurs cease to be ideal types – as they tended to be in earlier works – and become flesh-and-blood people who did specific things at specific times and places,' explains McCraw (2006, p. 260). The engagement with history, in particular, shaped Schumpeter's accounts of 'creative destruction' and the wider social and economic impact of innovation discussed in *Capitalism, Socialism and Democracy* (1942).

One particularly vivid example for Schumpeter of history's ability to reveal the broader, path-dependent impact of innovation was the railroad. 'Railroadization', as he called it, became his 'stand example'. Railroads were not only innovative businesses in their own right that upended incumbent transportation firms in canals and turnpikes; they also drove down the costs and time involved in transportation in ways that created turmoil and change in the standard business models of a host of industries. The creation of a national railway system transformed production, distribution and marketing businesses in many industries as national competition increasingly replaced local competition. Its growth also stimulated innovation in a host of related industries including fuels, metals, and machinery. History demonstrated how railroads, as entrepreneurial innovations, fundamentally transformed the economy and the nature of many businesses in a way that static models or simplified cause-and-effect studies could not explain (Schumpeter, 1939; McCraw, 2006; see also Jenks, 1944). The notion of path-dependent technological and innovative spillover continues to hold promise in entrepreneurship research (Cole, 1959; 1968; Audretsch and Keilback, 2006).

Schumpeter's engagement with history affected his ideas in a number of ways. He increasingly emphasized the diverse types of organizational forms that entrepreneurship could take, including not just the new firm but also larger corporations and even government agencies. His sense of historicism led him to ponder in *Capitalism, Socialism, and Democracy* (1942) how entrepreneurship was changing the structure and nature of capitalism itself. It was history's unique ability to reveal the process of change that ultimately attracted Schumpeter and was echoed by others who elaborated on the concept of entrepreneurship as a process of continuing change within capitalism.

Schumpeter also gained from history a keen sense of unevenness and lack of linearity in the process of change. It was partly this that led him to look at historical change comparatively in *Business Cycles* and consider how entrepreneurial processes did not usually unfold predictably because of variations in time and circumstance. But it was his contemporary at Harvard, Alexander Gerschenkron, who more fully laid out the contention that the historical record suggested the process of entrepreneurial change or creative destruction could proceed along widely varying paths and forms depending on time and context.

Gerschenkron and the Contingency of Entrepreneurial Processes

Among entrepreneurship scholars, Gerschenkron is probably the least well known of the three figures examined here. However, his influence as an economic historian who theorized about the timing and character of the process of entrepreneurial change is widespread. He is best known for his work on how the timing and context of a country's industrialization affected the character of economic change and industrialization. Gerschenkron (1962) argued that although individual entrepreneurs played a crucial role in the innovation and economic development process of early developers such as Great Britain, countries that followed this industrial leader – such as Germany and Russia – experienced very different entrepreneurial processes in their progress toward industrialization. Late developing countries may have lacked the stock of entrepreneurial talent of early developers but they had the precedent and knowledge of early developers on which they could build. In such a late developing context, other actors and institutions could and did coordinate the entrepreneurial process as a legitimate substitute for individual actors and firms. In Germany, Gerschenkron argued, banks played this crucial role in making entrepreneurial decisions that propelled the creation of industrial concentration and the creation of comparative advantages in heavy industry. In Russia, it was the state.

Gerschenkron's basic position was that the historical record refuted linear or unitary theories of the role of entrepreneurship in historical change; whereas the individual entrepreneur and the start up firm were certainly historically important in some contexts, other actors and organizations acted as 'alternatives' in other contexts. 'There is a deep-seated yearning in the social sciences for the discovery of one general approach, one general law valid for all times and all climes,' Gerschenkron (1962, p.67) noted, '[b]ut these attitudes must be outgrown.' To Gerschenkron history suggested that there were in fact alternative processes of entrepreneurial change and varying paths to industrial development. Careful historical research and reasoning could not and would not reveal any single 'law' of entrepreneurial change but it could allow us to identify and theorize alternative entrepreneurial paths and patterns, and the conditions that gave rise to these.

> What is suggested here, therefore, is that a serious effort should be made to try to establish through empirical research the spatial and temporal limitations within which the use of such an approach is reasonable and defensible. The discovery of these limits will itself push the research work into discovery of other sets of propositions and hypotheses, which may be more promising in treating situations, and historical sequences which differ widely from those for which the conceptual framework originally was designed. (Gerschenkron, 1962, pp.69–70)

Some of the details of Gerschenkron's assertions about the role of banks and the state in late developing countries have been challenged by other scholars, but the central thesis that timing and context affect the character and direction of entrepreneurial change has not really been refuted. In some cases, neo-Gerschenkronians have used the concept to explain the rise of high technology industries in small late developing countries like Israel, Ireland, and Taiwan (Breznitz, 2007). More generally, the notion that history illuminates not general law but alternative strategic choices available to actors has become common in the historical social sciences (Zeitlin, 2008a).

The approaches to historicism taken by Baumol, Schumpeter, and Gerschenkron share a common understanding that history can render insights into concepts, processes and theories that are difficult or impossible to deduce through traditional social scientific methods. Although different in their approach to historicism, they each embrace the assumption that history is not just a body of evidence but a mode of reasoning about the past for which there is no simple substitute in conventional social scientific methods. The extensive record of conceptual contributions from entrepreneurship theorists from Sombart to Baumol suggests the vitality of historicism as a mode of reasoning about entrepreneurial phenomena and the contributions that historicism has made to the modern understanding of entrepreneurship.

CONCLUDING THOUGHTS

Historicism has played a long and formative role in the development of entrepreneurship as an intellectual field. The premises underlying historical schools of thought on economics – such as the evolutionary nature of industries and economies and the role of economic agents as creative actors – lay the foundations for the emergence of entrepreneurship as an area of scholarly inquiry. As we have seen in this chapter, despite its current marginalization, historicism and historical investigation has shaped the development of a number of important areas of entrepreneurship research, and many of the most notable entrepreneurship theorists of the twentieth century explicitly discussed the importance of historical reasoning for progress in the field.

If research in the area is once again to investigate seriously the entrepreneurial process at levels of the industry, region, economy, and society (and not just at the levels of the individual and the firm), then a re-engagement with historicism will almost certainly be necessary because this approach is crucial for contextualizing entrepreneurial behavior at multiple levels and for examining the relationship between entrepreneurship and economic change. Historical perspective, in fact, fundamentally reshapes the questions we ask and the conclusions we draw. Rather than concluding, in a timeless way, that small business and start ups are entrepreneurial and innovative, it demands that we ask why these organizational forms have been especially innovative in a particular time and place (our own). Rather than simply relating entrepreneurship with quantities of innovation and growth, it forces us to ask what paths of development and directions of change particular clusters of entrepreneurial activity opened up and which alternative paths were in turn foreclosed. In short, it demands that we consider critically the dynamic relationship between entrepreneurship and its place in time.

One important step toward re-historicizing research on entrepreneurship is to reconsider how the intellectual history of the field is currently framed. Many researchers in the area think of the field as emerging in the 1970s and 1980s and conceive of its intellectual agenda as relatively new. This self-conception is reinforced by the fact that much of the older scholarship is not easily available in the online databases and guides to research in the field that entrepreneurship scholars typically use to review literature. Though it may take more effort by researchers to ferret out the older scholarship, re-engaging the rich and long intellectual history of the field is important for multiple reasons. It reinforces the legitimacy and gravity of entrepreneurship as a field of social scientific investigation and as a tradition of thought that extends back to at least the nineteenth century. It also offers researchers access to a broader set of theoretical concepts and studies than is available by examining the current literature alone. In addition, it is especially important to examine historicist modes of research that consider the entrepreneurial process at the regional, industry, social and economic levels through time.

Another crucial step toward re-historicizing the field would require expanding the range of methodologies available to researchers, especially as they ask multi-level questions about entrepreneurial processes. Too often, mainstream entrepreneurship researchers today envision the field as making progress and gaining legitimacy only through hypothesis testing using quantitative data and *ceteris paribus* methods that focus on the individual and sometimes the firm. Such research clearly has an important and central place in the field and is capable of addressing a particular (but limited) range of research questions. The effort to study consistent units of behavior or organizational types allows a certain analytical rigor, but its conclusions must be ultimately understood to be specific to a time and place. As historicists recognized, the form and nature of entrepreneurship evolved with the economic system. Methods sensitive to exploring the variation in entrepreneurial behavior and form are hence a crucial complement to conventional social scientific approaches when studying the phenomenon over time, especially in addressing some of the 'bigger' questions about entrepreneurship that conventional social scientific methods and assumptions are poor at addressing. Such issues as the role of entrepreneurship in shaping industrial and economic change, the variety of entrepreneurial behavior and organizational forms, and the relationship between entrepreneurship and other facets of economic institutions and behaviors are often best and most expansively addressed through historical methods that examine entrepreneurship as a complex, socially and historically embedded phenomenon.

Indeed, the long intellectual history of the field illustrates that entrepreneurship itself emerged as a heterodox concept in part because no single school or method seemed to adequately capture the creative role of entrepreneurship in the economy. Entrepreneurial thought and research has in turn flourished most when the field embraced not unitary methodological or theoretical strictures but when it engaged a thoughtful eclecticism in considering the nature of entrepreneurship and its place in the economic world. Historicism has been a crucial element of that eclecticism and will once again play a critical role if entrepreneurship research re-engages the questions of the links between individual behavior and broader processes of change and development within the economy.

ACKNOWLEDGEMENT

The author would like to thank Hans Landström, Franz Lohrke, Geoff Jones, Jeff Fear and audiences at the Academy of Management and Babson Entrepreneurship Research Conference for insightful comments on earlier drafts of this chapter.

REFERENCES

Acs, Z. (1984), *The Changing Structure of the US Economy: Lessons from the Steel Industry*, New York: Praeger.

Acs, Z. and D. Audretsch (1990), *Innovation and Small Firms*, Cambridge, MA: MIT Press.

Audretsch, D. and M. Keilback (2006), 'Entrepreneurship, growth and restructuring', in M. Casson, B. Yeung, A. Basu and N. Wadeson (eds), *The Oxford Handbook of Entrepreneurship*, New York: Oxford, pp. 281–310.

Baumol, W.J. (1968), 'Entrepreneurship in economic theory', *American Economic Review*, **58**, 64–71.

Baumol, W.J. (1990), 'Entrepreneurship: productive, unproductive, and destructive', *Journal of Political Economy*, **98**, 893–921.

Baumol, W.J. and R.J. Strom (2007), 'Entrepreneurship and economic growth', *Strategic Entrepreneurship Journal*, **1**, 233–37.

Bergoff, H. and R. Moller (1994), 'Tired pioneers and dynamic newcomers? A comparative essay on English and German entrepreneurial history, 1870–1914', *Economic History Review*, **47**, 262–87.

Birch, D.L. (1979), *The Job Generation Process*, Cambridge, MA: MIT Program on Neighborhood and Regional Change.

Braudel, F. (1958), 'Histoire et sciences sociales: la longue durée', *Annales*, **13**, 725–53.

Breznitz, D. (2007), *Innovation and the State: Political Choice and Strategies for Growth in Israel, Taiwan, and Ireland*, New Haven: Yale University Press.

Cassis, Y. and I. Minoglou (eds) (2005), *Entrepreneurship in Theory and History*, New York: Palgrave.

Casson, M. (1990), *Enterprise and Competitiveness: A Systems View of International Business*, New York: Oxford.

Casson, M. (1995), *Entrepreneurship and Business Culture*, Aldershot, UK, and Brookfield, VT, USA: Edward Elgar.

Casson, M. (2010), *Entrepreneurship: Theory, Networks, History*, Cheltenham, UK and Northampton, MA, USA: Edward Elgar.

Casson, M. and A. Godley (2005), 'Entrepreneurship and historical explanation', in Y. Cassis and I. Minoglou (eds), *Entrepreneurship in Theory and History*, London: Palgrave, pp. 25–60.

Chandler, A. (1962), *Strategy and Structure: Chapters in the History of the Industrial Enterprise*, Cambridge, MA: MIT.

Chandler, G. and D. Lyon (2001), 'Issues of research design and construct measurement in entrepreneurship research: the past decade', *Entrepreneurship Theory and Practice*, **24**(4), 101–16.

Cochran, T. (1950), 'Entrepreneurial behavior and motivation', *Explorations in Entrepreneurial History*, **2**, 304–7.

Cochran, T. (1960), 'Cultural factors in economic growth', *Journal of Economic History*, 20, 515–30.

Cochran, T.C. (1965), 'The entrepreneur in economic change', *Explorations in Entrepreneurial History*, 2nd series, **3**, 25–37.

Cole, A.H. (1959), *Business Enterprise in Its Social Setting*, Cambridge, MA: Harvard University Press.

Cole, A.H. (1968), 'Meso-economics: a contribution from entrepreneurial history', *Explorations in Entrepreneurial History*, 2nd series, **6**(1), 3–33.

Cooper, A. (2003), 'Entrepreneurship: the past, the present, the future', in Z. Acs and D. Audretsch (eds), *Handbook of Entrepreneurship Research: An Interdisciplinary Survey and Introduction*, Boston, MA: Kluwer Academic Publishers, pp. 21–36.

Cuff, R. (2002), 'Notes for a panel on entrepreneurship in business history', *Business History Review*, **76**, 123–32.

Dana, L.P., H. Etemad and R.W. Wright (2004), 'Back to the future: international entrepreneurship in the new economy', in M.V. Jones and P. Dimitratos (eds), *Emerging Paradigms in International Entrepreneurship*, Cheltenham, UK and Northampton, MA, USA: Edward Elgar, pp. 19–36.

Davidsson, P. and J. Wiklund (2001), 'Levels of analysis in entrepreneurship research: current research practice and suggestions for the future', *Entrepreneurship Theory and Practice*, **24**(4), 81–99.

Ebner, A. (2000), 'Schumpeter and the "Schmoller program": integrating theory and history in the analysis of economic development', *Journal of Evolutionary Economics*, **10**, 355–72.

Eckhardt, J. and S. Shane (2003), 'The individual-opportunity nexus: a new perspective on entrepreneurship', in Z. Acs and D. Audretsch (eds), *Handbook of Entrepreneurship Research: An Interdisciplinary Survey and Introduction*, Boston, MA: Kluwer Academic Publishers, pp. 161–94.

Foreman-Peck, J. (2005), 'Measuring historical entrepreneurship', in Y. Cassis and I. Minoglou (eds), *Entrepreneurship in Theory and History*, London: Palgrave, pp. 77–110.

Freeman, C. and F. Louca (2001), *As Time Goes By: From the Industrial Revolutions to the Information Revolution*, New York: Oxford.

Gartner, W. (1985), 'A conceptual framework for describing the phenomenon of new venture creation', *Academy of Management Review*, **10**, 696–706.

Gartner, W. (1988), 'Who is the entrepreneur? is the wrong question', *American Journal of Small Business*, **13**, 11–32.

Gerschenkron, A. (1962), *Economic Backwardness in Historical Perspective*, Cambridge, MA: Belknap Press of Harvard University.

Gerschenkron, A. (1966), 'The modernization of entrepreneurship', in M. Weiner (ed.), *Modernization: The Dynamics of Growth*, New York: Basic Books, pp. 246–57.

Godley, A. (2001), *Jewish Immigrant Entrepreneurship in New York and London*, Basingstoke: Palgrave.

Graham, M. and A. Shuldiner (2001), *Corning and the Craft of Innovation*, Oxford: Oxford University Press.

Gunther McGrath, R. (2003), 'Connecting the study of entrepreneurship and theories of capitalist progress: an epilogue', in Z. Acs and D. Audretsch (eds), *Handbook of Entrepreneurship Research: An Interdisciplinary Survey and Introduction*, Boston, MA: Kluwer Academic Publishers, pp. 515–32.

Hagen, E. (1962), *On the Theory of Social Change: How Economic Growth Begins*, Homewood: Dorsey Press.

Hagen, E. (1963), 'How economic growth begins: a theory of social change', *Journal of Social Issues*, **19**, 20–34.

Herbert, R. and A. Link (2006), 'Historical perspectives on the entrepreneur', *Foundations and Trends in Entrepreneurship*, **2**, 261–408.

Herbst, J. (1965), *The German Historical School in American Scholarship: A Study in the Transfer of Culture*, Ithaca: Cornell University Press.

Hirschmeier, J. (1977), 'Entrepreneurs and the social order: America, Germany, and Japan, 1870–1900', in K. Nakagawa (ed.), *Social Order and Entrepreneurship: Proceedings of the Second Fuji Conference*, Tokyo: University of Tokyo Press, pp. 3–41.

Hodgson, G. (2001), *How Economics Forgot History*, New York: Routledge.

Hounshell, D. and J. Kenly Smith (1988), *Science and Corporate Strategy: DuPont R&D, 1902–1980*, Cambridge: Cambridge University Press.

Jenks, L.H. (1944), 'Railroads as an economic force in American development', *Journal of Economic History*, **4**, 18–20.

Jenks, L.H. (1949), 'Role structure of entrepreneurial personality', in A. Cole (ed.), *Change and the Entrepreneur: Postulates and the Patterns for Entrepreneurial History*, Harvard University Research Center in Entrepreneurial History, Cambridge, MA: Harvard University Press, pp. 108–52.

Jones, G. and R.D. Wadhwani (2007), *Entrepreneurship and Global Capitalism*, Cheltenham UK and Northampton, MA, USA: Edward Elgar.

Jones, G. and R.D. Wadhwani (2008), 'Entrepreneurship', in G. Jones and J. Zeitlin (eds), *Oxford Handbook of Business History*, New York: Oxford University Press, pp. 501–28.

Kilby, P. (ed.) (1971), *Entrepreneurship and Economic Development*, New York: Free Press.

Kirzner, I. (1973), *Competition and Entrepreneurship*, Chicago: University of Chicago Press.

Knight, F. (1921), *Risk, Uncertainty, and Profit*, Chicago, IL: University of Chicago Press.

Koppl, R. and M. Minniti (2003), 'Market processes and entrepreneurial studies', in Z. Acs and D. Audretsch (eds), *Handbook of Entrepreneurship Research: An Interdisciplinary Survey and Introduction*, Boston, MA: Kluwer Academic Publishers, pp. 81–102.

Landes, D. (1949), 'French entrepreneurship and industrial growth in the nineteenth century', *Journal of Economic History*, **9**, 45–61.

Landström, H. (2005), *Pioneers in Entrepreneurship and Small Business Research*, New York: Springer.

Leff, N.H. (1979), 'Entrepreneurship and economic development: the problem revisited', *Journal of Economic Literature*, **17**, 46–64.

Low, M. and I.C. MacMillan (1988), 'Entrepreneurship: past research and future challenges', *Journal of Management*, **14**, 139–61.

Macdonald, R. (1965), 'Schumpeter and Max Weber: central visions and social theories', *Quarterly Journal of Economics*, **79**(3), 373–96.

Marshall, A. (1919), *Industry and Trade: A Study of Industrial Technique and Business Organization*, London: MacMillan and Co.

McClelland, D. (1961), *The Achieving Society*, Princeton, NJ: Van Nostrand.

McCraw, T. (2006), 'Schumpeter's *Business Cycles* as business history', *Business History Review*, **80**, 231–61.

McCraw, T. (2007), *Prophet of Innovation*, Cambridge: Belknap Press.

Menger, C. (1871/1985), *Principles of Economics*, New York: New York University Press.

Nicholas, T. (1999), 'Wealth making in nineteenth and early twentieth century Britain: industry v. commerce and finance', *Business History*, **41**, 16–36.

Nicholas, T. (2000), 'Wealth making in nineteenth and early twentieth century Britain: the Rubinstein hypothesis revisited', *Business History*, **42**, 155–68.

Nicholas, T. (2008), 'Does innovation cause stock market runups? Evidence from the Great Crash', *American Economic Review*, **98**, 1370–96.

North, D. (1990), *Institutions, Institutional Change and Economic Performances*, Cambridge: Cambridge University Press.

Parsons, T. (1960), *Structure and Process in Modern Societies*, Glencoe, IL: Free Press.

Parsons, T. and N. Smelser (1956), *Economy and Society*, New York: Free Press.

Pierson, P. and T. Skocpol (2002), 'Historical institutionalism in contemporary political science', in I. Katznelson and H.V. Milner (eds), *Political Science: State of the Discipline*, New York: W.W. Norton, pp. 693–721.

Rajshree, A., D. Audretsch and M.B. Sarkar (2008), 'The process of creative construction: knowledge spillovers, entrepreneurship, and economic growth', *Strategic Entrepreneurship Journal*, **3**(4), 263–86.

Reinert, E. (2002), 'Schumpeter in the context of two cannons of economic thought', *Industry and Innovation*, **9**, 23–39.

Schumpeter, J. (1928), 'The instability of capitalism', *Economic Journal*, **38**, 361–86.

Schumpeter, J. (1934), *The Theory of Economic Development*, Cambridge: Harvard University Press. First published in German 1911.

Schumpeter, J. (1939), *Business Cycles: A Theoretical, Historical, and Statistical Analysis of the Capitalist Process*, New York: McGraw-Hill.

Schumpeter, J. (1942), *Capitalism, Socialism and Democracy*, New York: Harper and Brothers (Harper Edition 1976).

Schumpeter, J. (1947), 'The creative response in economic history', *Journal of Economic History*, **7**, 149–59.

Schumpeter, J. (1949), 'Economic theory and entrepreneurial history', in A. Cole (ed.), *Change and the Entrepreneur*, Cambridge: Harvard University Press, pp. 63–84.

Schumpeter, J. (1954), *History of Economic Analysis*, New York: Oxford University Press.

Shane, S. (2003), *A General Theory of Entrepreneurship: The Individual-Opportunity Nexus*, Cheltenham, UK and Northampton, MA, USA: Edward Elgar.

Shane, S. and S. Venkataraman (2000), 'The promise of entrepreneurship as a field of research', *Academy of Management Review*, **25**, 217–26.

Sombart, W. (1911/1982), *The Jews and Modern Capitalism*, English translation, New Brunswick, NJ: Translation Books.

Sombart, W. (1915/1967), *The Quintessence of Capitalism: A Study of the History and Psychology of the Modern Businessman*, English translation, New York: H. Fertig.

Stevenson, H. and J.C. Jarillo (1990), 'A paradigm of entrepreneurship: entrepreneurial management', *Strategic Management Journal*, **11**, 17–27.

Swedberg, R. (1998), *Max Weber and the Idea of Economic Sociology*, Princeton: Princeton University Press.

Thelen, K. and S. Steinmo (1992), 'Historical institutionalism in comparative politics', in S. Steinmo, K. Thelen and F. Longstreth (eds), *Historical Institutionalism in Comparative Politics: State, Society, and Economy*, New York: Cambridge University Press, pp. 1–32.

Wallerstein, I. (1974), *The Modern World System: Capitalist Agriculture and the Origins of the Modern World Economy in the Sixteenth Century*, New York: Academic Press.

Weber, M. (1904/1930), *The Protestant Ethic and the Spirit of Capitalism*, English translation, New York: Scribner.

Weber, M. (1923/1927), *General Economic History*, translation by Frank Knight, New York: Greenberg.

Weiner, M. (ed.) (1966), *Modernization: The Dynamics of Growth*, New York: Basic Books.

Zeitlin, J. (2008a), 'The historical alternatives approach', in G. Jones and J. Zeitlin (eds), *Handbook of Business History*, New York: Oxford University Press, pp. 120–40.

Zeitlin, J. (2008b), 'Industrial districts and regional clusters', in G. Jones and J. Zeitlin (eds), *Handbook of Business History*, New York: Oxford University Press, pp. 219–43.

16. Culture, opportunity and entrepreneurship in economic history: the case of Britain in the twentieth century

Andrew Godley

INTRODUCTION

For much of the twentieth century, Britain was thought to be imbued with an anti-entrepreneurial culture (Aldcroft, 1964). From the aftermath of the First World War until the late 1990s, economic performance was viewed as disappointing and entrepreneurial inadequacies were first to be blamed. The concerns were exaggerated because of the legacy of being the first industrial nation. It is this remarkable juxtaposition of both exceptional entrepreneurial success and subsequent entrepreneurial failure that makes the case of British entrepreneurial culture in the twentieth century so important to any wider understanding of the relationship between culture and entrepreneurship today.

In 1900 British firms enjoyed a 35 per cent share of the global trade in manufactured products, when Britain had less than 2 per cent of the world's population. This economic success was the foundation of global political power. Power brought rewards for Britons in the early twentieth century, most obviously among the entrepreneurial and capitalist classes. In 1913 the richest 0.1 per cent of Britons received over 12 per cent of the nation's income! Economic success had emerged through Britain's early dominance of world textiles markets – cotton and woollen – and then the iron and steel industry, coal, shipbuilding and other pre-mass production forms of mechanical engineering, the so-called the 'staple' industries. But by the beginning of the twentieth century, British economic success was increasingly tied to investments in overseas markets (Matthews et al., 1982; Atkinson 2002). It is these two themes – of specialization in the staple industries and overseas investments – that must be emphasized in order to understand the economic and cultural contexts of entrepreneurship in Britain in the twentieth century.

By 2000 Britain enjoyed only a 6 per cent share of world trade in manufactures, barely one-sixth the share at the century's beginning (*Economist*, 2005). With the disappearance of the staple industries, Britain, the country of the world's first industrial revolution and the global superpower of 1900, had been relegated to the second division of national economies. In what was seen as a great indignity in the UK, Italians celebrated *Il Sorpasso* in 1990, as the GDP of Italy overtook that of the UK for the first time since the days of the Medici. The 1992 ejection from the European Exchange Rate Mechanism seemed to be the culmination of almost a century of economic weakening. Of course, British households were many times richer than they had been at the century's beginning, but such was the deterioration of Britain's rank in the world order, that the overwhelming consensus was that the country had somehow failed during the twentieth century.

Influential commentators penned titles like *The British Disease* (Allen, 1976), *How British is the British Sickness?* (Brittan, 1978), and 'The slide of Britain' (Porter, 1990, pp. 482ff.). But then in the final few years of the century an economic renaissance appeared to take place, as British economic growth accelerated. Suddenly the entire framework for interpreting Britain's twentieth-century economic experience was transformed. What was it all about, after all, if not a story of decline? Although its determinants still remain subject to considerable debate, this very recent transformation in British economic fortunes demands that economic historians begin to reinvestigate the traditional interpretation of relatively poor British twentieth-century performance, the alleged failure of its entrepreneurs, and their apparently anti-entrepreneurial culture.

So, free from having to account for inexorable relative economic failure and its inferred entrepreneurial deficiencies, this survey departs from the conventional treatments of the topic. Instead we begin with a discussion of British entrepreneurship and culture, before rehearsing core themes from widely accepted theories of entrepreneurship, and then proceed to surveying the areas of significant entrepreneurial activity in a more or less chronological fashion. The conclusion then offers some thoughts on the implications of new theory for historical research on entrepreneurship, and on the increasing need for entrepreneurship scholars to embrace more historical research.

BRITISH ENTREPRENEURS AND ENTREPRENEURIAL CULTURE

A summary of the traditional explanation of British industrial lethargy throughout the twentieth century would underline that Britain's entrepreneurs have been an obvious and persistent target. Over the course of the century, the focus of blame has moved from a fairly general concern with their allegedly poor leadership in what were the emerging industries of the second industrial revolution, to specific criticisms of apparent failure by entrepreneurs to invest in new technology, or to adopt improved management techniques. Explanations of why British entrepreneurs failed to invest in new equipment, techniques, or organization (and so apparently to forego profits so willingly) often revolved around allegedly anti-entrepreneurial qualities in British culture. David Landes famously quipped that British enterprise reflected a:

> . . . combination of amateurism and complacency. . . . The British manufacturer was notorious for his indifference to style, his conservatism in the face of new techniques, his reluctance to abandon the individuality of tradition for the conformity implicit in mass production. (Landes, 1969, p. 337)

Despite fierce criticism from scholarly historians, Martin Wiener's claim that Britain possessed an 'anti-industrial spirit' (1981) resonated with politicians and public alike; it has had a powerful impact on public policy, providing the moral underpinning of 25 years of the promotion of the 'enterprise culture'. In fact, and despite the criticism, much evidence has emerged to support one or other of the culturalists' hypotheses. Although sadly for Wiener, his elegant pitch for the influential but effete elite as the principal retardant has been exposed as somewhat shallow.

Landes and Wiener see this British anti-entrepreneurial culture as essentially non-rational in the material world studied by economic historians (Landes, 1997). But despite being the focus of an enormous volume of scholarly research, little economic history has focused systematically at understanding culture itself. This is partly the result of the intellectual heritage of economics in the subject. Even Doug North's Nobel Prize-winning account of how key institutions led to the economic superiority of the West gave little attention to the interaction of national cultures and national institutional structures (North, 1990). Indeed, there are few studies that even exploit typologies and models of culture with anything like the sophistication seen in management scholarship (Hofstede, 2001; Hampden-Turner and Trompenaars, 1993). Outside a few studies exploring the association between entrepreneurship (or more widely defined economic development) and religion, or regional values, there remains a reluctance within the subject to embrace culture as an explanatory variable.

The important conclusion of these few studies is that the differences between British and other nations' entrepreneurs ought not to be overstressed. Recent comparative studies mostly highlight similarities. Where variations are observed, they rarely support the notion of 'failure'. Cassis (1997) and Wardley (1999), for instance, warn against judgments of inferiority among British big business. Berghoff discovered that the entrepreneurs in British provincial towns closely matched German entrepreneurs across a range of parameters (Berghoff and Möller, 1994; Berghoff 1995). Although Nicholas (1999), Rose (1986) and others have debated the relative merits of the persistence of family control, it was only in the United States that family control ever stopped being the norm. And even then recent research suggests that family control in the US remains far more pervasive than generally thought. The implication remains that the most developed nations had broadly similar familial, regional and corporate norms during the process of industrialization and growth.

But this relegation of the cultural explanation for British entrepreneurial failure in the twentieth century to an ever-diminishing residual factor by most economic history research has been challenged by Godley's (2001) analysis of the inter-relationships between culture, immigration and social rigidities, and entrepreneurial aspiration. Godley compares British and US society at the outset of the twentieth century. British society had already matured and stabilized by 1900, with powerful social rigidities set in place. There were fundamental barriers to the supply of entrepreneurs able to bring about 'creative destruction'. As Kindleberger noted, by 1900 the supply of outsider entrepreneurs, with their distinctive cultures, had diminished (Kindleberger, 1964). A wave of European immigrants during the early and middle decades of the nineteenth century had contributed many important figures to the Industrial Revolution and was succeeded by a far larger population of immigrants from 1880 to 1914, but this one was dominated by East Europeans, who lacked both skills and capital to make any immediate impact on the British economy – although, as explained below, their role was to be profound indeed by mid-century.

Moreover, in the early decades of the century, there were relatively few self-made entrepreneurs in Britain. To be sure, there weren't many anywhere else. Even in the United States, the Horatio Alger ideal was exposed as a myth. Senior executives and the leading business owners were disproportionately drawn from the elite. But the sheer extent of the rigidity between the main social classes has been a feature of successive studies of social mobility in Britain. Not only did such immobility retard competitive entry from below, but without any credible prospect for social ascent, it influenced expectations and values among the dispossessed. This was to influence persistently low educational attainment among the working classes, which later became important in explaining low levels of labour productivity growth. But Godley's comparison of East European Jews in both the United States and in Britain showed that as Jewish immigrants assimilated host country cultural values, their preference for entrepreneurship altered. Those in Britain began increasingly to opt for craft employment rather than business careers for any given wage and profit level. With no options for self-advancement, British working class culture reinforced its strong and conservative craft values, erecting an additional barrier to pursuing self-employment. And so with fewer competitive challenges from either immigrants or from aspirant men from below, Britain's entrepreneurial incumbents remained in place. Such relative frigidity among the entrepreneurial class was underpinned by the move to protectionism from the Import Duties Act of 1932 onwards until the 1970s. Cultural and regulatory protection allowed the incumbent business-owning families to serve much of the British market however they wished and with relative impunity for the middle decades of the century.

ENTREPRENEURSHIP THEORY AND ENTREPRENEURIAL OPPORTUNITIES

The relationship between culture and entrepreneurship has been fraught with scholarly contention for over forty years. But the mechanism between entrepreneurship and cultural values can be better understood once the economic function of entrepreneurship is clarified. After all, it is widely acknowledged that there is much more to being an entrepreneur than being self-employed. One of the main reasons why entrepreneurship is valued, and usually commands respect in successful economies, is that entrepreneurship is a scarce ability. The value of entrepreneurship is reflected in the above-average profits earned by firms controlled by successful entrepreneurs. Entrepreneurs can appropriate their personal rewards either through ownership of a firm, or as managers whose success is recognized by promotion, bonuses, stock options, or other forms of performance-related pay.

But what is it that entrepreneurs do with this scarce ability? According to Schumpeter (1939), innovation is the key function of the entrepreneur. Without the entrepreneur, the rate of innovation would be lower, productivity growth would be smaller, and the economy would fail to develop as it should (Baumol, 1990). But why is the capacity to innovate so scarce? According to Schumpeter, innovation requires vision and commitment – vision to imagine an alternative world in which the innovation has taken place, and commitment to mobilize resources to realize the vision rather than to just to sit back and fantasize about it. Only a few people with heroic temperament have these qualities, according to Schumpeter.

Kirzner (1973; 1979) takes a different approach: he argues that entrepreneurs discover opportunities that could easily be missed. Although not every one has an opportunity to innovate, many people have an opportunity to arbitrage. In a volatile economy markets are always in disequilibrium, and people who are alert can always find opportunities to buy cheap and sell dear. Unlike Schumpeter, Kirzner believes that almost everyone has the potential to be an entrepreneur. Recognizing opportunities is a function common to both these writers. From the perspective of the economic theory of entrepreneurship, the emphasis on the various opportunities acknowledges that the demand for entrepreneurship, as for any factor of production, can vary. While conceptualizing entrepreneurship as subject to market forces simplifies our understanding of the topic, Eckhardt and Shane (2003) have underlined that this is a market that rarely settles into any stable equilibrium.

This is an important observation for our reinterpretation of the role of entrepreneurship in British twentieth-century economic history, because if the market for entrepreneurship is assumed to function more or less effectively, for price information to signal where entrepreneurial endeavour is best allocated, a reasonable interpretation of Britain's comparatively disappointing performance is that British entrepreneurs err by acting irrationally: that British culture was indeed somehow disadvantaging entrepreneurs in profit-seeking activities. As noted above, this has been the over-arching meta-narrative in recent decades among British economic historians. If however the assumption of equilibrium-type behaviour in the market for entrepreneurship is relaxed, then very different potential explanations arise, explanations focusing on comparative differences in opportunities facing British and American or German or French or other entrepreneurs.

Explanations of relative entrepreneurial performance that depend solely on access to entrepreneurial opportunities, however, are also insufficient. In a world characterized by disequilibria, market information is unreliable and uncertainty abounds. Not all opportunities are, therefore, what they seem. Some may be traps for the unwary. Knight (1921) emphasizes the risks that are taken by the entrepreneur. No-one can be certain that an opportunity will turn out well. Risks are subjective, so that different people perceive different degrees of risk in the same opportunity (Casson, 1982). This subjectivity (or 'cognitive differences' to adopt the term preferred in the management literature) highlights the difference between being an entrepreneur and being a successful entrepreneur. Entrepreneurs innovate and take risks, but successful entrepreneurs discriminate between good risks and bad risks. They do not need to discriminate perfectly; they simply need to do it better than competitors in the same industry.

The decisions of entrepreneurs, when taken collectively, affect the aggregate performance of the economy. It is sometimes supposed that from a social perspective, more entrepreneurship is always desirable, but this depends upon how entrepreneurship is defined. If defined as innovation, then it is certainly possible to 'have too much of a good thing' because excessive innovation can artificially reduce the supply of traditional products, and subject working lives to unnecessary change. It is also obviously possible to have too much risk. Whilst some risk is unavoidable in any innovation, successful entrepreneurs do not incur avoidable risks, however bold and charismatic they may appear as a result.

The one thing that it is impossible to have too much of is good judgment. Casson, like Schumpeter and Kirzner, assumes that market volatility creates entrepreneurial opportunities. While Eckhardt and Shane (2003) have recently used the term 'discovery' to account for the perception and valuation of entrepreneurial opportunities, Casson used the term 'judgment' (Casson, 1982). Judgment has to be involved whenever a decision is made without access to any generally agreed rule derived from publicly available, validated information (Casson and Godley, 2007). Good judgment trades off the risks of missing good opportunities through failure to innovate against the risk of making mistakes by making the wrong sort of innovation. A successful entrepreneur with good judgment takes only the opportunities that are really profitable. Provided that social incentives are properly aligned by a competitive market system, private profit will be associated with enhanced social welfare and higher performance. The market for corporate control allocates the best entrepreneurs to the most responsible jobs, by recruiting the most reputable entrepreneurs to run the biggest firms in their field. Badly performing entrepreneurs who have lost reputation are replaced; if the board of directors does not dismiss them then the firm will be taken over as shareholders sell out to the highest bidder. The essence of entrepreneurship, therefore, is the exercise of entrepreneurial judgment.

Consider what happens when relevant information is pervasive and cheap. Then firms are able to establish reliable algorithms of how to manage a set of functions, and the business activity represents the classic small firm in perfectly competitive markets. But should some exogenous event cause turbulence in the economy, information may no longer be either cheap or easily available. Any transaction then becomes risky, because, in the absence of credible price information, no single entrepreneur can know what other market participants are doing.

This approach shares many similarities with Eckhardt and Shane's view that entrepreneurial opportunities derive from two generic sources: exogenous shocks (such as changes in policy, societal shifts on the creation of new knowledge) and information asymmetries. Casson's approach, in fact, is less concerned with separating differences in their sources, but more with examining the implications for entrepreneurial behaviour of these two determinants of entrepreneurial opportunities. Thus exogenous events create market disequilibria, leading to the rapid depreciation in the value of the existing stock of knowledge and market institutions.

But the judgment-intensive entrepreneur minimizes risk through a twofold response to increased information asymmetries – first, by developing a framework to interpret the impact of the exogenous shock, and, second, by investing in gaining additional, relevant information. Superior frameworks lead to superior outcomes for any given investment, of course, but developing such a judgment-intensive framework depends on testing the self-perception of complex and inchoate commercial situations, and so requires efficient information acquisition. The acquisition of additional information at times of great uncertainty, therefore, is important not only to reduce asymmetric information in and of itself, but also to assist with the developing and testing of new interpretative frameworks. Both the need to acquire specialist information and the need to refine interpretive frameworks lead entrepreneurs to seek out the opinions of other information gathering specialists. Thus, Casson and Godley have recently emphasized that one of the most striking features of entrepreneurial behaviour, the strength and persistence of entrepreneurial networks, is a response to the need to refine and test interpretative frameworks as well as to ensure privileged access to sources of information (Godley and Casson, 2010). These specialized groups, expert in particular fields, with access to privileged sources of information, are also more likely to find that they can command privileged access to funding, as investors follow their trails.

Entrepreneurship then, certainly in a larger historical context, is about far more than firm formation and venture capital funding (the two features so beloved of management scholars today) and can be most frequently located in those environments that call for the greatest intensity of judgment. Judgment is of course not an observable variable. But given the reasonable assumption that entrepreneurs need other entrepreneurs for privileged access to information, testing and validating their interpretative frameworks, as well as for specialized sources of venture financing, the presence of entrepreneurial networks is likely to be positively correlated with entrepreneurial judgment.

For this summary of history, culture, opportunities and entrepreneurship, the focus is on the case of Britain in the twentieth century (albeit with extensive international comparison). It fashions an explanation for entrepreneurship's apparent long-term secular decline and then sudden re-emergence at the century's end. Posing the entrepreneurial function as a series of investments in information acquisition and developing a level of expertise at interpreting complex commercial situations suggests that entrepreneurs and entrepreneurial networks have high sunk costs. It would be rare for an expertise developed in one sector to be relevant when transferred to another. This may be construed as an entrepreneurial 'failure', but only in the sense that distinguished physicists, say, might be castigated for being flawed violinists. The extent to which British entrepreneurial networks were able to diversify their expertise bases into higher value areas also depended on external circumstances. This approach, with an explicit assumption that the market for entrepreneurship is typically characterized by disequilibrium, therefore follows Eckhardt and Shane in emphasizing the importance of opportunities in explaining the disappointing British entrepreneurial outcomes, rather than the traditional economic historians' emphasis on some as yet not well described cultural norms. But this approach far from ignores the role of culture. Networks loom large in this explanation. Network membership is strongly correlated with some significant (although non-suffocating) level of cultural homogeneity (Granovetter's famous 'weak ties', 1973). Over historical time and space, these culturally specific networks are observable. As the chapter outlines, British entrepreneurs throughout the first three-quarters of the twentieth century found themselves both facing situations where the value of the stock of their entrepreneurial expertise suddenly depreciated because of a series of exogenous events, and yet (with rare exceptions) where their cultural capital, sunk in pre-existing networks, was insufficient to allow successful diversification until the century's end.

ENTREPRENEURSHIP, NETWORKS AND BRITISH CULTURE IN THE TWENTIETH CENTURY

When Royal Dutch Shell acquired Weetman Pearson's oil major, Mexican Eagle, in 1919, the Shell Group had engineered control of Britain's most valuable company (Bud-Frierman et al., 2010). It was one of the most dramatic corporate events in the new century. It also highlights where so much British entrepreneurial activity was located.

British overseas investment had attained wholly unprecedented levels by the First World War. Never before nor since has any nation committed such a large part of its economic resources to activities overseas (Edelstein, 2004). The link between domestic consumption and overseas investment was abundantly clear, for it was such prodigious levels of British investment in foreign economies that led to the creation of transport networks and infrastructure necessary for integrating far flung places into the world trading system, enabling the world's resources to be productively deployed. It was investment in railways, ports and harbours, in tramways and electric utilities, in plantations of tea, coffee, cotton, rubber and cocoa, in mines and oil wells, all around the world, within and outside the Empire, that created the supply lines, the institutional framework for market exchange, as well as the principal economic activities themselves that led to a level of global economic integration that has only very recently been recaptured.

In 1913 British domestic industry remained especially focused on the traditional staple industries; 60 per cent of British exports still came from the cotton and woollen textiles, coal, iron and steel and machinery sectors (Magee, 2004). But these were all sectors that depended upon a high labour content of production. They were all sectors that were vulnerable, therefore, to either cheaper labour or substitution through mechanization. Moreover the sectors that were growing in prominence in the world economy were sectors that relied on both a much higher scientific content of production and far more sophisticated managerial practices – most obviously in electrical engineering, chemicals and advanced mechanical engineering sectors.

The world's leading producers of electric power generation equipment, of synthetic dyestuffs and automobiles depended upon a qualitatively superior level of engineering knowledge in product and process design. Compared with Britain's leading firms in the staples, the technological content of production at Siemens' vast factory site in Berlin, or the move to systematic research and development at Bayer or BASF in the chemicals and pharmaceuticals industries, or the intensity of the flow of production at Ford's Highland Park manufacturing plant, revealed a level of inferiority that shocked British commentators of the day. Britain's share of exports from vehicles and electrical goods was barely 1 per cent in 1913. And while British chemicals output and export share was higher, British chemicals firms were largely focused on increasingly outdated products and processes (Lindert and Trace, 1971).

In these technologically advanced sectors, first movers pursued vertical integration strategies and developed strong managerial capabilities in order to compensate for the absence of specialist market-making intermediaries in what were novel markets. Given the British specialization in older, more labour intensive industries, it is unsurprising that overall British labour productivity had been overtaken by the new technological leaders of the United States and Germany by 1913 (Broadberry, 1998). But it was also the case that with intermediaries already established in these sectors, British entrepreneurs were not forced to develop managerial capabilities in the same way as US and German technologically advanced firms were. Thus, the prevailing theme of British twentieth-century economic history was set. As other nations specialized in the more technologically intensive sectors of the second industrial revolution, British firms and entrepreneurs appeared unable to make the transition from their specialization in the lower productivity staples into the higher productivity new sectors. When British entrepreneurs emerged in these sectors, they typically were able to enjoy success only when protected from the full force of competition. As levels of protection began to disappear in the 1970s and 1980s, so British weaknesses here were exposed, and these firms failed (Godley and Casson, 2010).

ENTREPRENEURSHIP, CULTURE AND OPPORTUNITIES: 1900 TO 1930

British entrepreneurship has largely been criticized because of the relatively poor performance of the British domestic economy, especially during the 1960s and 1970s when other economies began to overtake Britain with great regularity. But at the outset of the period perhaps the greatest concentration of entrepreneurial activity was not to be found in the domestic economy at all, but rather overseas. This was not simply the exploitation of privileged access to the Empire, although, of course, British firms were actively engaged in Imperial markets (Hannah, 1980, pp. 61–3), but rather the concentration on ever more sophisticated business operations throughout the entire globe, notably, like Weetman Pearson, in Latin America.

Of course Britain's entrepreneurs, like their American and German equivalents, were active and successful in the domestic economy as well. Broadberry's study of comparative productivity reveals that British firms held comparative advantages in several staple industries, most notably in cotton textiles in 1913 (Broadberry, 1998). As already noted, however, these sectors tended to be more labour intensive than the newer industries. With British labour comparatively expensive, and with mechanization reducing the advantages of skill, British comparative advantage leached away – to Germany in coal mining as early as 1911, for example. Other countries found their natural resource endowments lent themselves for more efficient use. In iron and steel, for example, it was apparent by 1900 that British ores were located in relatively expensive areas. In a world of scarce entrepreneurial talent, British home-based entrepreneurs were concentrated in what were, at the time, sunset industries. Their routes to increasing profitability were not always obvious or sustainable.

In the past economic historians have criticized what was comparatively poor investment by British entrepreneurs in the newer industries of mechanical engineering and automobiles, the industries of the second industrial revolution (Alford, 1988). These were sectors where competitiveness depended on creating and exploiting new knowledge, and the new knowledge was emerging first in the US and Germany, not Britain. Even worse from the perspective of critics, British entrepreneurs were not even notably successful in gaining second-mover advantages, compared with French, Italian and Japanese entrepreneurs later in the century.

From the perspective of the entrepreneurs themselves, however, it is easier to understand why there was reluctance to embark on wholly new ventures in these sectors, where their existing stock of expertise carried little value and where their traditional networks of information gathering carried little relevance. Given such high sunk costs by entrepreneurs in information acquisition, the costs associated with embarking on ventures in the newer industries may have seemed prohibitive. In particular, in the face of declining profits at home, British entrepreneurs were faced with a very obvious alternative in investing in more profitable opportunities overseas (Jones, 1994). The judgment-intensive, decision making entrepreneur in Britain before 1930 was faced with a far greater range of opportunities from internationalizing than competitors elsewhere, and a far greater likelihood of profitable activities there than by trying to compete with established first-mover German chemicals and electricals or US automobiles and mechanical engineering firms.

By 1914 the range of industries British entrepreneurs were investing in around the globe had increased markedly. Late nineteenth-century foreign direct investment was very much concentrated in railways, land ownership and mining. Although these three sectors still loomed large by 1914, other sectors had together increased their share of British foreign direct investment markedly. Corley's (1994) sectoral breakdown of British overseas firms shows that oil companies represented over 5 per cent of the total by 1914. Overseas banking and insurance companies were 4 per cent of the total. Various utilities companies, from tramways and electric power station builders, to gas and water work producers, together accounted for nearly one-tenth of the total. These newer investments in higher value adding sectors were together at least as significant as the more traditional entrepreneurial ventures by then.

Collectively this role of overseas entrepreneurship was enormously important. The stock of British foreign direct investment was 45 per cent of total global foreign direct investment in 1913. British overseas investments were, in other words, the key entrepreneurial route for integrating resources into the global economy at the time, not the world's emerging giants in automobiles, chemicals and electricals.

These British entrepreneurial teams would, therefore, move from one overseas venture to the next, reconstituting themselves as appropriate, bringing in new experts, dropping those whose expertise was now less relevant. During the early decades of the twentieth century they became ever more global in focus, not only in the regions of the world they operated in, but also in the individuals brought in, with American and European specialists recruited into the teams where necessary. Much of this overseas activity was property-based entrepreneurship, and much required high sunk costs in location-specific, indivisible assets. These were typically large, complex projects that required specialist expertise and access to sophisticated sources of venture capital.

As a new opportunity emerged, an entrepreneurial team formed and then sought first tier financing by selling equity stakes on the London Stock Exchange. Despite the obvious high risk associated with placing new ventures, there was evidently sufficient demand from investors. Companies would then return to the market for any subsequent round of financing. Compared with what is overwhelmingly a private market for venture capital today, the venture capital market in the early decades of the twentieth century appears to have been both more sophisticated and transparent as well as successful in raising what were very large amounts (Corley, 1994).

These entrepreneurial networks of (mostly) British businessmen remained highly active during and after the First World War right through to the 1970s (Jones and Wale, 1999; Jones, 2000). As the world economy developed, so British foreign direct investment switched increasingly from older ventures (building and managing overseas railways, for example) to new (Corley, 1997). They proved to be an optimal organizational response to the worldwide demand for complex project management skills exercised over long distances in an era when relatively poor communications meant corporate head offices were unable to monitor such investments.

Such flexibility and loose and efficient organizational structures, however, depended on a relatively stable institutional structure for their viability. These entrepreneurial ventures were knowledge-transferring, market-creating organizations. But once projects were up-and-running, dedicated operators and specialist intermediaries took control of the resulting revenue flows. The geographically dispersed resources easily became integrated into the existing world economy and its institutions supporting international trade. They remained dependent on what was a sophisticated institutional structure supporting contractual rights. But when the turmoil of the First World War was followed by the greater turbulence of the 1930s global crisis, they were unable to internalize markets. As transaction costs became too high, they had no alternatives and were forced to withdraw. The existing stock of information and institutional structures were unable easily to adapt to the changing global environment, and the number of genuine opportunities declined.

Initially, in fact, the British response to regional shocks was to search for alternative entrepreneurial opportunities and to relocate as market activity was foreclosed. For instance, from 1917 to 1922, first Russia, then the Ottoman Empire, Ireland and Mexico all plunged into civil war and conditions for international trade deteriorated. British entrepreneurs responded by moving to newer regions of the globe and pursuing emerging opportunities. They were responsible for much of the development of the eastern seaboard of China during the 1910s and 1920s, and the rapid economic growth in the short-lived boom in the Middle East in the 1920s, for example (Plüss, 2004; Jones, 2000). But during the 1930s profits plummeted. Although income from British foreign direct investment remained broadly stable in real terms between 1907 and 1927, it fell from then to 1938 (Corley, 1997). After the Second World War, large swathes of the globe put up the shutters again. South East Asia, China, Africa and the Middle East all declared their own *intifas* against the previously ubiquitous British entrepreneur.

Thus, focusing on overseas investments suggests that there was no failure in British entrepreneurial culture during the twentieth century. Rather there was something of a bifurcation in activities. Previously successful areas like the staple industries found the competitive environment increasingly harsh and increasingly sought government protection (Bamberg, 1988). But before the 1930s, opportunities overseas increased. British entrepreneurs with long histories and vast accumulated expertise (notably of course through developing global markets for the staple industries) developed an institutional structure for their entrepreneurial ventures overseas. Their great contribution to the world economy was not especially in the realm of new technology, but in drawing together skills and finance to initiate and complete complex projects far away from the centres of financial power. These were novel solutions to the dilemmas posed by the risks of such long distance trades suffering from opportunistic behaviour by agents in far flung places. The longstanding criticism of the British entrepreneurs in the twentieth century, that they failed to invest in the new industries of automobiles, chemicals and electricals, is, in other words, a simple misinterpretation of the situation. Why should they have ventured into areas where they were particularly at a disadvantage compared with American and German technological leaders and when British entrepreneurial networks were enjoying such striking success at developing and exploiting overseas ventures?

ENTREPRENEURSHIP, CULTURE AND OPPORTUNITIES: 1930S TO 1970S

As far as the wider picture of British entrepreneurship is concerned, the epoch-making events occurred elsewhere. The global economic crisis of the 1930s and the subsequent war and decolonization meant that British outward direct investment was threatened. Overseas assets were sold, often at a loss, and funds repatriated into a stagnant British economy. The Pearson Group, for example, switched focus from being one of the world's most entrepreneurial oil majors, to becoming a London-based investment trust. No doubt the directors' lunches improved, but Pearson's entrepreneurial dynamism fizzled out (Bud-Frierman et al., 2010). Other overseas groups with fewer opportunities to cash out also mutated.

The twin strike on British entrepreneurship of an uncompetitive currency after 1926 and then the global economic crisis of the 1930s simply undermined the ability of entrepreneurs to act in the two core areas of comparative advantage: the traditional staple industries at home and the newer overseas focused entrepreneurial ventures. The expertise so carefully acquired by the key entrepreneurs and their networks over so many years had suddenly lost its value. New entrepreneurs and new networks needed to emerge. And, in what was an unprecedentedly difficult international environment during the 1930s, those new networks began to prosper at home because after the passing of the 1932 Import Duties Act, Britain became a highly protected market.

The conventional treatment of the 1930s in economic history textbooks is to emphasize the emergence of important new firms and sectors in the British economy. Although unemployment still reached almost 30 per cent at the worst moments, the British economy seemed to weather the 1930s crisis better than elsewhere, with entrepreneurs like Morris and Austin in the automobile industry and the successful merger of the Nobel and Brunner Mond chemicals firms to form ICI (in 1926). Although this reflects important shifts in economic activity, we should be cautious, however, in embracing such an interpretation wholeheartedly. By 1939, the staple industries still dominated British output and exports, and the combined output of the much vaunted British motor car industry and the electrical engineering industry amounted to less than 5 per cent of total manufacturing output. The new infant industries remained protected but relatively insignificant. What can be stated is that the impact of rising real living standards from 1933 onwards created new demands, and many British entrepreneurs were not slow in meeting them.

The entrepreneurial response to the growth in consumer demand in Britain continued a long trend. Earlier innovations in branded consumer goods saw the rise of the powerful British tobacco industry, in particular W.D. and H.O. Wills, which amalgamated with others to form Imperial Tobacco (Alford, 1973; Hannah, 2006). Other companies developed strong brands in foodstuffs and confectionery, beverages and branded medicines in the first half of the twentieth century. Rank, Huntley and Palmers, Horlicks, Colman, Cadbury and Rowntree in foodstuffs, Guinness in beverages, and Beecham in household products all embraced novel marketing campaigns and built up strong brands. But, perhaps tellingly, all of these family firms were managed by second, third or even later generations as early as the first decades of the twentieth century.

More pertinently for new entrepreneurial networks, increasing consumer demand meant increasing entrepreneurial opportunities to meet this growing demand for new services. Here the trend was for genuine new entrants – in catering and retailing, in transport and in entertainment. Nevertheless the genuine entrepreneurial entrants in these sectors, like their counterparts in automobiles, electricals and chemicals, were unable to build firms and industries with significant productivity advantages over German and American rivals (Broadberry, 1998; 2006). During the protected 1930s, 1940s and 1950s this largely did not matter. The British market had become a largely domestic concern and British entrepreneurs were able to enjoy success in meeting domestic needs. As tariff barriers began to fall from the 1960s and international competition re-emerged, however, British frailties in the tradable sectors became exposed.

The outbreak of war in September 1939 heralded necessary encroachment of government control over ever greater swathes of the British economy. Along with the entire private sector, entrepreneurship was squeezed. The post-war period began in Britain with a *leitmotiv* that was antipathetic to free market activity. The continuing problems of coal and steel prompted the Labour Government to nationalize the industries to both protect remaining jobs and improve the management. Similarly the continually underperforming railway companies were forced to come under Government ownership. With the creation of the Welfare State, very much higher marginal tax rates, and the adverse effect on planning from the 'stop-go' demand management policies, the post-war environment for entrepreneurs was very different.

Other economies in Europe also pursued the model of extensive state involvement in the economy and experienced successful growth records. The French most notably enjoyed *les trente glorieuses* from the late 1950s as State-led restructuring brought managerial advantages and additional investment to its preferred sectors. But while the British economy grew at an unprecedented rate during the late 1950s and early 1960s, the British experiment with central planning was less successful. The Golden Age, characterized by Big Government, Big Business and Big Unions, began to sour in the British economy during the 1960s and 1970s.

Yet within this standard treatment of faltering post-war economic maturity, entrepreneurial inertia and a relative decline in living standards, there remained an active entrepreneurial hinterland. With annual economic growth at 3–4 per cent, such was the rate of change that entrepreneurial opportunities inevitably emerged. Gerald Ronson, one of Britain's leading property entrepreneurs since the 1960s, suggested it was an easy time to be an entrepreneur because there was so little competition.

Ronson was one of 70 to 80 Jewish property millionaires identified in Oliver Marriott's *The Property Boom* (1967), who collectively transformed much of the British commercial property landscape during the 1950s through to the 1970s. They were the most dynamic entrepreneurial presence in an otherwise sluggish private sector. The most spectacularly successful of all was Charles Clore, whose search for new property deals brought him to realize that traditional and conservatively managed retail chains were sitting on enormously undervalued property portfolios and were reluctant to allow their asset base to be realized. Clore decided that they should be forced to and so pioneered competitive takeovers in Britain with his hostile acquisition of the large, integrated shoe company J. Sears.

Sears in 1953 could be described as a stereotype of the conservatively managed, third or fourth generation British family firm; its entrepreneurial phase had finished several decades before (Jefferys, 1954). It was one of Britain's largest firms and dominated shoe manufacturing, with the largest shoe factory in Britain. Its undervalued property portfolio of 920 shoe stores (in High Streets throughout the land) was the attraction to Clore (Clutterbuck and Devine, 1987, p. 64). The 1948 Companies Act provided the legal structure for transfers of share ownership, but until Clore, no one had tested the legitimacy of contested takeovers. The culture and tradition of the City was that if the target company's board did not agree to the takeover, minority shareholders would not accept an offer. By appealing directly to shareholders and offering them an attractive price, Clore introduced the market for corporate control into Britain, after having become aware of the idea while in the United States. He went on to repeat the trick several times and so indirectly became Britain's leading retailer during the 1960s. Moreover, the demonstration effect prompted others to hunt for publicly listed firms, where management seemed chronically unable to generate any reasonable profit from their asset bases. The ultimate knock-on effect of Clore's innovation on the British economy was enormously significant. Clore's reward was a huge personal fortune but popular infamy. By the early 1970s, the property entrepreneurs appeared to be the only group in society (apart from pop stars and football players) with the Midas touch. But unlike Ringo Starr or George Best, entrepreneurs plumbed new depths of unpopularity.

Much of British productivity growth from the 1950s through to the 1980s came from the substantial invasion of American multinationals (Godley, 1999; 2003; 2006; Godley and Williams, 2009a; 2009b). This mostly caused indigenous British business to lose out, as British entrepreneurs were unable to compete with US manufacturing and service standards. Elsewhere, however, British entrepreneurship gained, though in a wholly unanticipated manner. The creation of the Eurobond market was the catalyst that enabled London to recapture its position as the world's leading centre of international finance and the role of American multinational subsidiaries was crucial. Siegmund Warburg had pioneered the concept of firms issuing dollar-denoted bonds as an innovative use of the pool of offshore dollars. But President Kennedy's Interest Equalization Tax (1963) along with the Foreign Direct Investment Program (1968) required US corporations to finance overseas investment by overseas borrowings. Eurobond issues rose dramatically in consequence from $348m in 1963 to £5,508m in 1972 (Ferguson, 2009; Roberts, 2001).

The City of London had stagnated in the years since 1930. Investment banking had diminished in importance and British positions in international trade had deteriorated, so there was relatively little to do. Banking had also become heavily regulated. Where innovation was occurring, with Clore's property-related activities, or with Warburg's creation of the Eurobond market, participation was restricted to a small group of insiders – the entrepreneurial networks. The London Stock Exchange, formerly the locus of so much dynamic venture capital funding for overseas investments before the 1930s, had sacrificed competitive behaviour for comfort. Overseas ventures had collapsed. In Michie's history of the London Stock Exchange, the chapter covering the 1950s is entitled 'Drifting towards oblivion' (Michie, 1999). The Eurodollar and Eurobond markets lifted the City out of its torpor.

This was too late for British entrepreneurship to benefit from any of the technology bubbles in the American stock markets during the 1950s and 1960s. Without any equivalent of the active US Over-the-Counter securities trading market, there were almost no Initial Public Offerings in electricals in Britain during the late 1950s and early 1960s. New issues to young electrical companies in the US peaked at $135m and $140m in 1959 and 1960 respectively (O'Sullivan, 2006). In Britain there were successful diversifications by the dominant and long established electricals companies into consumer appliances (AEI developed their 'Hotpoint' brand), but the entrepreneurial developments met with only short-lived success. A.J. Flatley gained some prominence for novel clothes drying machines and John Bloom some notoriety for his electric washing machines, but neither entrepreneur could match the market power of the large incumbents and so they withdrew in 1962 and 1964, respectively (Corley, 1966, pp. 55–61). The dead hand of protectionism short-circuited competitive entry and there was simply no equivalent of the American electronics revolution that ultimately led to the modern computer industry there.

Outside the stultifying effect of government control, entrepreneurs remained active in the postwar 'Golden Age', most spectacularly in property, but also in transforming British retailing and pharmaceuticals. Entrepreneurs in Britain's traditional overseas markets struggled against the forces of decolonization and nationalist economic policies. One who kicked against this trend was Tiny Rowland, who built up Lonrho, but so aggressive was his approach in sub-Saharan Africa that Conservative leader Edward Heath described him as the 'unacceptable face of capitalism' and was widely lauded for doing so. No doubt Rowland deserved vilification. But the reputation of entrepreneurship was at a low ebb. For as the economic fortunes of most began to stagnate in the 1970s, the politics of envy dictated that the successful few were vilified. There was no one to champion the entrepreneurs' cause. That such a high proportion of the successful few at this time were second or third generation Jewish immigrants prompted them to adopt low profiles. In obituaries in the British press, Jewish magnates were described principally for their philanthropic work. Even then anti-entrepreneurialism meant Britain lost out. These Jewish tycoons endowed more university chairs in Israel than Britain. Elsewhere the dynamic, innovative few left in the 'Brain Drain', especially for the former dominions, the United States, and, increasingly, mainland Europe. Emigration's corollary was the unprecedented rate of immigration, especially of Asians from the Indian subcontinent and East Africa, many of whom would become important British entrepreneurs by the century's end.

ENTREPRENEURIAL CULTURE AND OPPORTUNITIES IN THE 1980S AND 1990S

In very recent years the role of the state in the British economy has been peeled away through successive reforms in the Thatcher, Major and Blair governments. The privatization programme was supposed to release entrepreneurial dynamism into older and mature industries. In fact, more important to the British economy has been the impact of the resumption of globalization in the 1980s and 1990s. As the South East Asian 'tiger' economies and then China became more fully integrated into the world economy, many British businesses found themselves unable to compete. As the floor on world unskilled wages fell, so British clothing manufacturing virtually ceased, for example. But British entrepreneurs were quick to spot the opportunities of managing long-distance trading relationships with the low-cost producers in these low-wage economies. Indeed, as China has grown to become the factory of the world, the value adding activity is in the market-making, not the manufacturing. Suddenly the long dormant British business skills of international negotiation and managing cross-cultural relationships flourished, as did the much diminished but never extinguished networks of expertise. The leading retailers Philip Green and Tom Hunter both rose to prominence through managing their Asian supply chain, for instance. The continued British presence in Hong Kong provided an important bridge for business links into China and longstanding connections with India have powered the 'offshoring' move there.

Firm formation continued to rise throughout the 1990s. But in contrast to the 1970s entrepreneurship was increasingly seen as a desirable option. Close examination of entrepreneurial attitudes (e.g. Global Entrepreneurship Monitor, 2008) show that in the heady days of the 'dot.com bubble', entrepreneurship became seen increasingly as an attractive career route. As so often in the past, it was outsiders that represented the driving force, with many Asian immigrants (especially those expelled from East Africa after 1972) creating successful businesses.

CONCLUSION

The conventional survey of British economic performance over the twentieth century has prompted considerable gloom among economists and economic historians and, in consequence, a persistent search for scapegoats. The entrepreneur has never been far away as a favourite target, and some sort of cultural failing has been a repeated accusation. But the theory advanced here of entrepreneurship existing outside a stable market equilibrium, and so the entrepreneurial function as a series of lumpy investments in information acquisition and in collective framework validation efforts can help entrepreneurship researchers both to better understand the British experience in the twentieth century (for so long thought to be the classic case of 'entrepreneurial failure'), and to extend such an analysis to other countries' historical experiences.

First, it changes our understanding of British entrepreneurship. This survey began by giving belated but nevertheless due emphasis to Britain's role as provider of entrepreneurial services to the world in the first half of the twentieth century. This specialization in transferring knowledge-intensive project management skills into complex infrastructure or resource-focused investments has been neglected by historians for too long. It was this entrepreneurial endeavour that powered global economic integration from the 1880s through to the 1920s, not the firms of the second industrial revolution. British entrepreneurs had developed specialized skills, specific institutional structures and sophisticated and culturally specific entrepreneurial networks to engage in these activities. As the profitability of the staple industries in the world's most advanced economy began to slacken in the 1900s, British entrepreneurs naturally gravitated toward overseas opportunities.

Yet fortune was not on their side. The international crisis of the 1930s, the Second World War, slow post-war restructuring, and then the traumas of decolonization reduced the value of much of the stock of painfully acquired entrepreneurial expertise. Growth in the world economy from the 1930s on was increasingly based on high technology manufacturing, where British entrepreneurial expertise was relatively thin. Without much use, these entrepreneurial networks slowly dispersed, or entered sectors where their expertise carried little favour. Only with the resumption of rapid global economic integration in the 1980s, and especially in the 1990s did British comparative advantage in managing long-distance international trade reassert itself.

At home the competitive environment deteriorated, partly because of direct effects of government policy in promoting protectionism and encouraging the cartelization of British business, but also because of restrictions on immigration and the long acceptance of grave social divides in British culture. Free from competitive rivalry after 1932, British incumbent entrepreneurial families and business owners responded predictably and settled for a comfortable life. Unsurprisingly British relative productivity fell alarmingly after World War Two and innovative, entrepreneurial types emigrated in droves.

The most significant new group of entrepreneurs to emerge in the middle decades of the century were a group of East European Jewish immigrants, who largely enjoyed their career success through exploiting the property market. This was closely bound up with retailing, and many proved to be exceptional retailers also. As the reversal of protectionism continued from the 1980s onward, so entrepreneurship slowly began to renew itself in Britain: first, in overseas trading and multinational investments, and then finally in the embrace of new technology at the century's end.

This chapter has, therefore, sought to demonstrate how entrepreneurial opportunities ebbed and flowed, prompting appropriate responses from British entrepreneurs at different times. Given Britain's striking preference for international trade and investment already by the early decades of the century, its entrepreneurs were acutely vulnerable to the exogenous shocks that circumscribed globalization during the century's middle decades.

This chapter has also emphasized the importance of information asymmetries and the varying institutional responses to them, with a focus on collective information acquisition and framework validation. Developed further this ought to produce much richer descriptions and more robust interpretations of other entrepreneurial behaviour in the twentieth century; of the divergent outcomes of different ethnic groups in their entrepreneurial endeavours in the US, for example, or of the remarkably persistent strength among German entrepreneurs in engineering-intensive sectors, or of Italian entrepreneurs in fashion-intensive sectors, for instance.

Entrepreneurship researchers ought to go beyond simply writing better history, however. As Eckhardt and Shane (2003) have clearly indicated, one important methodological consequence of explicitly recognizing the limits to assuming any form of equilibrium in the market for entrepreneurship is that conventional cross-sectional analyses will provide misleading results. Far more appropriate methods, they contend, for understanding and analysing entrepreneurial behaviour must instead be those that embrace longitudinal analysis. Detailed reconstruction of historical entrepreneurial activity ought therefore to become ever more important not only for better economic history, but for our quest to better understand entrepreneurship itself.

ACKNOWLEDGEMENT

This chapter draws on material contained in 'Britain, 1900–2000', in D.S. Landes, J. Mokyr and W.J. Baumol (eds) (2010), *The Invention of Enterprise: Entrepreneurship from Ancient Mesopotamia to Modern Times*, New York: Princeton University Press, pp. 243–72.

REFERENCES

Aldcroft, D. (1964), 'The entrepreneur and the British economy, 1870–1914', *Economic History Review*, **17**, 113–24.

Alford, B.W.E. (1973), *W.D. & H.O. Wills and the Development of the U.K. tobacco Industry, 1786–1965*, London: Methuen.
Alford, B.W.E. (1988), *British Economic Performance, 1945–1975*, Basingstoke: Macmillan.
Allen, G.C. (1976), *British Disease: A Short Essay on the Nature and Causes of the Nation's Lagging Wealth*, London: Institute of Economic Affairs.
Atkinson, A.B. (2002), 'Top incomes in the United Kingdom over the twentieth century', University of Oxford Discussion Papers in Economic and Social History, No 43, Oxford.
Bamberg, J. (1988), 'The rationalization of the cotton industry in the interwar years', *Textile History*, **19**, 83–102.
Baumol, W. (1990), 'Entrepreneurship: productive, unproductive and destructive', *Journal of Political Economy*, **98**, 893–921.
Berghoff, H. (1995), 'Regional variations in provincial business biography: the case of Birmingham, Bristol and Manchester, 1870–1914', *Business History*, **37**, 64–85.
Berghoff, H. and R. Möller (1994), 'Tired pioneers and dynamic newcomers? A comparative essay on English and German entrepreneurial history, 1870–1914', *Economic History Review*, **47**, 262–87.
Brittan, S. (1978), 'How British is the British sickness?', *Journal of Law and Economics*, **21**, 21–32.
Broadberry, S. (1998), *The Productivity Race*, Cambridge: Cambridge University Press.
Broadberry, S. (2006), *Market Services and the Productivity Race, 1850–2000: Britain in International Perspective*, Cambridge: Cambridge University Press.
Bud-Frierman, L., A. Godley and J. Wale (2010), 'Weetman Pearson in Mexico and the emergence of a British oil major, 1901–1919', *Business History Review*, **83** (Summer), 275–99.
Cassis, Y. (1997), *Big Business: The European Experience in the Twentieth Century*, Oxford: Oxford University Press.
Casson, M. (1982), *The Entrepreneur: An Economic Theory*, Oxford: Martin Robertson.
Casson, M. and A. Godley (2007), 'Revisiting the emergence of the modern business enterprise: entrepreneurship and the Singer global distribution system', *Journal of Management Studies*, **44**, 1064–77.
Clutterbuck, D. and M. Devine (1987), *Clore: The Man and his Millions*, London: Weidenfeld and Nicolson.
Corley, T.A.B. (1966), *Domestic Electrical Appliances*, London: Cape.
Corley, T.A.B. (1994), 'Britain's overseas investments in 1914 revisited', *Business History*, **36**, 71–85.
Corley, T.A.B. (1997), 'Competitive advantage and foreign direct investment: Britain, 1913–1938', *Business and Economic History*, **26**, 21–36.
Eckhardt, J. and S. Shane (2003), 'Opportunities and entrepreneurship', *Journal of Management*, **23**(3), 333–49.
Economist (2005), *The World in 2005*, London: The Economist.
Edelstein, M. (2004), 'Foreign investment, accumulation and empire, 1860–1914', in R. Floud and P. Johnson (eds), *The Cambridge Economic History of Modern Britain*, Cambridge: Cambridge University Press, pp. 190–226.
Ferguson, N. (2009), 'Sigismund Warburg and the creation of the Eurobond market', *Business History*, **51**, 364–82.
Global Entrepreneurship Monitor (2008), http://www.gemconsortium.org/.
Godley, A. (1999), 'Pioneering foreign direct investment in British manufacturing', *Business History Review*, **73**, 394–429.
Godley, A. (2001), *Jewish Immigrant Entrepreneurship in New York and London, 1880–1914: Enterprise and Culture*, Basingstoke: Palgrave.
Godley, A. (2003), 'Foreign multinationals and innovation in British retailing: 1850–1962', *Business History*, **45**, 80–100.
Godley, A. (2006), 'Selling the sewing machine around the world: Singer's international marketing strategies, 1850–1920', *Enterprise and Society*, **7**, 266–314.
Godley, A. and M. Casson (2010), 'Britain, 1900–2000', in D.S. Landes, J. Mokyr and W.J. Baumol (eds), *The Invention of Enterprise: Entrepreneurship from Ancient Mesopotamia to Modern Times*, New York: Princeton University Press, pp. 243–72.

Godley, A. and B. Williams (2009a), 'The chicken, the factory farm, and the supermarket: the industrialization of poultry farming in Britain and the United States, 1950–1980', in R. Horowitz and W. Belasco (eds), *Food Chains*, Philadelphia: University of Pennsylvania Press, pp. 47–61.

Godley, A. and B. Williams (2009b), 'Democratizing luxury and the contentious "invention of the technological chicken" in Britain', *Business History Review*, **83**(2), 267–90.

Granovetter, M.S. (1973), 'The strength of weak ties', *American Journal of Sociology*, **78**(6), 1360–80.

Hampden-Turner, C. and F. Trompenaars (1993), *The Seven Cultures of Capitalism: Value Systems for Creating Wealth in the United States, Britain, Japan, Germany, France, Sweden and the Netherlands*, New York: Doubleday.

Hannah, L. (1980), 'Visible and invisible hands in Great Britain', in A. Chandler and H. Daems (eds), *Managerial Hierarchies: Comparative Perspectives on the Rise of the Modern Industrial Enterprise*, Cambridge, MA: Harvard University Press, pp. 41–76.

Hannah, L. (2006), 'The Whig fable of American tobacco', *Journal of Economic History*, **66**, 42–72.

Hofstede, G. (2001), *Culture's Consequences: Comparing Values, Behaviours, Institutions, and Organizations across Nations*, 2nd edition, Thousand Oaks, CA: SAGE.

Jefferys, J. (1954), *Retail Trading in Britain 1850–1950*, Cambridge, UK: Cambridge University Press.

Jones, G. (1994), 'British multinationals and British business since 1850', in M. Kirby and M. Rose (eds), *Business Enterprise in Modern Britain*, London: Routledge, pp. 172–206.

Jones, G. (2000), *From Merchants to Multinationals*, Oxford, UK: Oxford University Press.

Jones, G. and J. Wale (1999), 'Diversification strategies of British trading companies: Harrisons and Crosfield, c.1900–c.1980', *Business History*, **41**, 69–101.

Kindleberger, C.P. (1964), *Economic Growth in France and Britain, 1851–1950*, Oxford, UK: Oxford University Press.

Kirzner, I.M. (1973), *Competition and Entrepreneurship*, Chicago: University of Chicago Press.

Kirzner, I.M. (1979), *Perception, Opportunity and Profit*, Chicago: University of Chicago Press.

Knight, F.H. (1921), *Risk, Uncertainty and Profit*, Boston: Houghton Mifflin.

Landes, D. (1969), *Unbound Prometheus: Technological Change and Industrial Development in Western Europe from 1750 to the Present*, Cambridge, UK: Cambridge University Press.

Landes, D. (1997), *The Wealth and Poverty of Nations*, New York: Norton.

Lindert, P. and K. Trace (1971), 'Yardsticks for Victorian entrepreneurs', in D. McCloskey (ed.), *Essays on a Mature Economy: Britain after 1840*, London: Methuen, pp. 121–40.

Magee, G. (2004), 'Manufacturing and technological change', in R. Floud and P. Johnson (eds), *The Cambridge Economic History of Modern Britain*, Cambridge, UK: Cambridge University Press, pp. 74–98.

Marriott, O. (1967), *The Property Boom*, London: Hamish Hamilton.

Matthews, R.C.O., C.H. Feinstein and J.C. Odling Smee (1982), *British Economic Growth, 1856–1973*, Oxford, UK: Oxford University Press.

Michie, R. (1999), *The London Stock Exchange: A History*, Oxford, UK: Oxford University Press.

Nicholas, T. (1999), 'Clogs to clogs in three generations? Explaining entrepreneurial performance in Britain since 1850', *Journal of Economic History*, **59**, 688–713.

North, D. (1990), *Institutions, Institutional Change and Economic Performance*, Cambridge: Cambridge University Press.

O'Sullivan, M. (2006), 'Riding the wave: the US financial markets and the postwar electronics boom', paper presented to the Business History Conference, Toronto, 8–10 June.

Porter, M. (1990), 'The slide of Britain', in *Competitive Advantage of Nations*, Basingstoke: Palgrave Macmillan, pp. 482–506.

Plüss, C. (2004), 'Globalizing ethnicity with multi-local identifications: the Parsee, Indian Muslim and Sephardic trade diasporas in Hong Kong', in I. Baghdiantz, G. McCabe, G. Harlaftis and I. Minoglou (eds), *Diaspora Entrepreneurial Networks*, Oxford: Berg, pp. 200–220.

Roberts, R. (2001), *Take Your Partners. Orion, the Consortium Banks and the Transformation of the Euromarkets*, London: Palgrave.

Rose, M. (1986), *The Gregs of Quarry Bank Mill: The Rise and Decline of a Family Firm*, Cambridge, UK: Cambridge University Press.

Schumpeter, J.A. (1939), *Business Cycles*, New York: McGraw-Hill.

Wardley, P. (1999), 'The emergence of big business: the largest corporate employers of labour in the United Kingdom, Germany and the United States c. 1907', *Business History*, **41**, 88–116.

Wiener, M. (1981), *English Culture and the Decline of the Industrial Spirit*, Cambridge, UK: Cambridge University Press.

17. Industrial renewal and entrepreneurship in Sweden: a structural cycle explanation

Hans Landström and Lennart Schön

INDUSTRIAL RENEWAL AND ENTREPRENEURSHIP OVER TIME

It has been known for many years that the level of entrepreneurship in a society differs strongly over time. For example, in his historical exposé including ancient Rome, early China, and, in particular, the Middle Ages and Renaissance Europe, William Baumol (1990) demonstrated that entrepreneurship behavior in terms of innovative activities and business development differs significantly from one time period to another. However, he argued that it is not the supply of entrepreneurs in a society that changes over time, but the variety of roles to which the entrepreneur's efforts can be allocated. Some of these roles can be regarded as productive in the sense of promoting innovation and business development, whereas others can be considered more or less destructive and damaging to the economy (e.g. rent seeking and organized crime). The 'rules of the game', i.e. the relative rewards for different kinds of entrepreneurial activities in a society, in turn, have a profound effect on entrepreneurial behavior in different periods and societies.

It can also be argued that there is a strong relationship between the growth and dynamics in a society and the level and characteristics of entrepreneurship. For example, Kyrö (2006) stated that entrepreneurship is a phenomenon that gains in importance in periods when society experiences some form of 'transition', i.e. when ideas of freedom and the need for a new kind of reality are especially vital for growth. In this respect the dynamics in society seem to have cyclical variations. For example, the evolution of entrepreneurship, innovation and industrial dynamics during the transition that took place at the beginning of industrialization in the eighteenth and nineteenth centuries was followed by an era during which modern society was built on the large corporations and mass production that emerged and dominated the western world.

The idea that society follows such long-term cycles or long waves originated in the nineteenth century (cf. Juglar, 1862; Jevons, 1884), but attracted more attention among scholars in economics and economic history in the interwar period following the publication of the observations of the Russian economist Nikolai Kondratiev in the 1920s. The interest in long cycles vanished during the post-war boom, but reappeared in the 1970s and 1980s. With the crisis in the 1970s, evidence of long fluctuations increased, notably due to the work of Christopher Freeman and Carlota Perez (Freeman and Perez, 1988). Their interest, however, was very much directed toward the appearance of technical innovations and the political framework of the economy. In this respect, the Lund School of

Structural Analysis has developed the economics of innovation, from entrepreneurial activity to structural change at macro level.

In this chapter we follow this vein of thought – society undergoes some form of long-term cycles, and the characteristics of innovation and entrepreneurial behavior change over the course of these long waves. Thus, the first aim of the chapter is to explain the characteristics of innovation and entrepreneurship over time using an intellectual framework of long-term cycles in society.

The theory of long-term cycles follows an intellectual tradition in economic history based on Schumpeter's ideas about 'business cycles' and the Swedish economist and economic historian Erik Dahmén's theory on 'development blocs'. We place these theories in a framework of long structural cycles elaborated by a group of economic historians attached to the Lund School of Structural Analysis at Lund University in Sweden. As Schumpeter's and Dahmén's reasoning is extremely important for our understanding, the second aim of the chapter is to present the 'business cycles' and 'development bloc' theories in greater detail, and in this sense the chapter traces the intellectual roots of the idea of long structural cycles.

The contributions of the chapter are:

- A detailed elaboration of the theories behind the reasoning of long structural cycles in society, including Schumpeter's theory of 'business cycles' and Dahmén's argumentation in his theory of 'business cycles'.
- On the basis of these theories to discuss the long structural cycles identified in the Swedish economy since the mid nineteenth century, in which industrial society exhibits a pattern with periods of positive transformation pressure followed by rationalization and negative pressure ending in a structural crisis.
- An explanation of cyclical variations in innovative and entrepreneurial activities in 'transformation' and 'rationalization' periods.

The chapter is divided into six sections. After this introduction, the next two sections elaborate on the life and contributions of Joseph Schumpeter, and discuss in detailed his book *Business Cycles*, published in 1939. A presentation of Erik Dahmén's 'development bloc' theory follows. The next section provides a detailed description of how the Lund School of Structural Analysis has used the 'development bloc' theory in the context of long-term cycles and empirically developed it in a Swedish context. Finally, the chapter ends with some remarks on the relationship between cyclical variation, and innovative and entrepreneurial activities in society.

JOSEPH SCHUMPETER – LIFE AND CONTRIBUTIONS

The end of the nineteenth century was characterized by the emergence of new industries and the building of modern enterprises, and many authors claimed to foresee the death struggle of small firms in the economy. However, despite the prevailing beliefs, Joseph Schumpeter was convinced that a unique and central factor existed in economic activity – the entrepreneur – who was the key figure in economic development and dynamics due to her/his ability to introduce innovations and initiate new activities, i.e. there was an 'energy' within the economic system that created disequilibrium in the market. Thus, similarly to the way in which Adam Smith defined of land, labor and capital as the key input factors of the economy in *An Inquiry into the Nature and Causes of the Wealth of Nations* (1776/1976), Schumpeter added innovation as a driver of economic growth and prosperity in society. Thus, the concept of innovation plays a central role in Schumpeter's writing. In general, Schumpeter's scientific work can be regarded as rather fragmented, but throughout his career there is a clear line of thought – to construct a new economic theory built on newness and disequilibrium, which complemented Walras's theory of a static (and stationary) economy (Swedberg, 1994). In this section we summarize Schumpeter's contributions, but also provide a picture of the individual behind them.

The Life of Joseph Schumpeter

Joseph Alois Schumpeter was born on 8 February 1883, in the small town of Triesch, at that time part of the Austro-Hungarian Empire (presently Trest in the Republic of Slovakia). The family was Catholic and had for several generations belonged to the elite of the town. His father, who was a textile manufacturer, died when Joseph was only four years old. At the beginning of the 1890s the family moved to Vienna. The ten-year-old Schumpeter was sent to a very exclusive private school, and in 1901 he graduated with top grades. He immediately enrolled at the law department of the University of Vienna (economics was at that time taught at the law department). At the turn of the century several of the world's most famous economists such as Carl Menger, Eugen von Böhm-Bawerk and Friedrich von Wieser were active at the Department of Law. In 1906 at the age of 23, Schumpeter obtained his doctoral degree in economics (formally law). After graduation, Schumpeter's career could be regarded as changeable and did not always follow a clear path; for example, despite his obvious genius, he was never offered an academic position at the University of Vienna. Schumpeter's career is summarized in the Box 17.1 (Swedberg, 1994; Reisman, 2004).

Schumpeter experienced a great deal of misfortune in the mid 1920s. His financial problems as a consequence of too risky investments and the bankruptcy of the Biedermann Bank of Vienna, in addition to the fact that his mother died in 1926, followed a couple of months later by his wife and son (Josef) in childbirth, made him very pessimistic and melancholic and to some extent self-destructive. His wife and mother became a personal cult, and he immersed himself in work and travel (Swedberg, 1994; Reisman, 2004).

In terms of his professional career, Schumpeter is often regarded as difficult to understand. He wanted to learn how to teach, but communication was not his strength: his arguments were not always easy to follow, his meaning was not always clear, and his literary style often obstructed his message, as he wrote in a rather complex way, characterized by long sentences, numerous qualifying phrases, careful definitions of terms, and so on (Reisman, 2004).

To some extent Schumpeter's ideas and arguments about the innovative entrepreneur who generated 'creative destruction' in the economy did not become incorporated into mainstream economics or economic policy-making and were more or less erased by Keynes and his *General Theory of Employment, Interest and Money* (1936/73). In

---

BOX 17.1   THE CAREER OF JOSEPH SCHUMPETER

1906	Post-doctorate degree at the London School of Economics
1907–08	Practiced law at the International Mixed Tribunal in Cairo
1909	'Habilitation' degree (associate professor) at the University of Vienna
1909–11	Teacher of economics at the University of Chervotsky (a town then in the east of the Austro-Hungarian Empire but today in Ukraine)
1911–21	Professor of Economics at the University of Graz
1919	Finance minister in a Social Democratic government in Austria
1921–24	President of the Biedermann Bank of Vienna (during the economic crisis of 1924 in Austria, the bank failed and Schumpeter became bankrupt)
1925–32	Professor of Economics at the University of Bonn
1927–28, 30	Visiting Professor at Harvard University
1931	Visiting Professor at Tokyo College of Commerce
1932–50	Professor of Economics at Harvard University (Schumpeter became an American citizen in 1939)

Joseph Schumpeter died of a cerebral hemorrhage on the night of 7–8 January 1950, at the age of 66.

---

comparison with Schumpeter, Keynes's reasoning had a much more profound effect on the economic debate, which may be due to the fact that he was more normative and emphasized, to a greater degree, the state's opportunities to influence economic development. In addition, the Great Depression in the 1930s made Schumpeter's theories appear irrelevant and even wrong. Thus, Keynes received far more attention, while Schumpeter's works only attracted a small minority of scholars in economics, as well as other social scientists, particularly sociologists.

The lack of interest among mainstream economists is reflected in the citation patterns. From 1956 until roughly the mid 1990s, Keynes received a great many more citations by mainstream economists. However, an interesting fact is that since the world economic slowdown in the 1970s, there has been a major revival of Schumpeter's ideas and works, and as a consequence since the mid 1990s he has received more citations in general compared to Keynes and has just caught up with the latter in terms of citations in economics journals. From the mid 1990s, Schumpeter's book *Capitalism, Socialism and Democracy* (1942) appears to have become more influential, and there is growing acceptance of his central messages, not only by scholars in general but also among economists (Diamond, 2008). As politicians have not always been successful in dealing with the occasional occurrences of serious economic difficulties and fairly low economic growth in industrial countries, Schumpeter's reasoning has become the subject of more and more interest and attention.

The Contributions of Schumpeter

Schumpeter was a highly productive researcher and during his career he wrote nine major books, more than 200 papers and over 90 book reviews. His most influential books are *The Theory of Economic Development* (1934), *Business Cycles* (1939), *Capitalism, Socialism and Democracy* (1942), and *History of Economic Analysis*, which was published posthumously in 1954. Short summaries of the books are provided in Table 17.1.

Some comments can be made regarding Schumpeter's main contributions. Firstly, the first edition of *Theorie der Wirtschaftlichen Entwicklung* appeared in 1911 but was officially published in 1912, while the second edition of the book was published in German in 1926. The English edition entitled *The Theory of Economic Development* (which is the most frequently cited) was based on the second edition of the German version and published in 1934. However, the first and second German editions are quite different. The main changes made by Schumpeter in the second edition were that he rewrote large sections of Chapter 2 ('The fundamental phenomenon of economic development') and Chapter 6 ('The business cycle'), and completely omitted his original Chapter 7 ('The economic system seen as a whole') (Reisman, 2004). The first edition of the book (1912) is considered more eccentric, whereas in the more streamlined 1926 and 1934 editions Schumpeter tries to relate more strongly to the mainstream discussion in economics at that point in time (Swedberg, 1994).

Secondly, it should be noted that Schumpeter's work and view on entrepreneurship underwent a change over time (see Table 17.2). Up to the 1930s he was mainly interested in developing his mode of reasoning about entrepreneurship and in integrating these trains of thought into his new economic theory based on innovation and change. However, during the interwar period in the US he had encountered a different corporate world to that of the Austria of his youth. In the US, the corporate scene was dominated not by small firms with clearly distinguishable entrepreneurs but by large corporations with advanced research departments engaged in planned research, which inspired Schumpeter's interest in innovative activities in existing organizations. This change in focus finds expression in his book *Capitalism, Socialism and Democracy* (1942).

SCHUMPETER'S 'BUSINESS CYCLES' (1939)

In his book *Business Cycles* (1939) Schumpeter elucidated his arguments on long cycles, which had been already introduced in his theory of economic development (Schumpeter, 1912/1934). In this section we present Schumpeter's theory of business cycles as well as the intellectual tradition on which it is based.

The Intellectual Roots of 'Long Cycles'

The idea that economies and societies move in long cycles has attracted researchers for a long time (see reviews in Freeman, 1984; Reijnders, 1990; Tylecote, 1992). The nineteenth century produced pioneering contributions by Juglar (1862) and Jevons (1884), while Marx (1893/1971) also stressed the importance of 'industrial cycles', arguing that the cycle is a manifestation of the limitation of the capitalist mode of production and

Table 17.1   The major works of Joseph Schumpeter

The Theory of Economic Development (1934)	Business Cycles (1939)	Capitalism, Socialism and Democracy (1942)	History of Economic Analysis (1954)
The book is regarded as Schumpeter's principal work on economic theory, in which he first presented his famous theory of entrepreneurship. Schumpeter focused on the forces that change the equilibrium in the economic system, through the introduction of innovations. The entrepreneur is the central actor in this development toward disequilibrium – in the 'hunt' for profit s/he breaks traditions and habits by introducing innovations. Another central actor is the bank. As changes take time, someone needs to assume the risks before the innovation has reached the market, and in this respect, the banks are central, as they lend money to the entrepreneur.	In the *Theory of Economic Development* (1934) Schumpeter introduced his theory of business cycles, but it was in *Business Cycles* (1939) that he elucidated his arguments and explained the cyclical nature of the creation of new businesses – swarms – during different periods of time. The book contains an extremely detailed exposition of different phases of the business cycles in Germany, England and the USA since the mid 18th century. In addition, *Business Cycles* contains an interesting methodological discussion. In contrast to the focus on aggregated analysis in neo-classical economics, Schumpeter argued in favor of more disaggregated and historical analysis.	*Capitalism, Socialism and Democracy* constitutes without doubt Schumpeter's most popular work. In this book he focused on the institutional structure of society and raised the question as to whether capitalism as an economic system would be able to survive. Schumpeter argued that increased rationality in society weakens entrepreneurship and leads to the stagnation of capitalism. Due to economies of scale, large corporations have an innovative advantage over small firms, and the economic landscape is dominated by giant corporations. In the book he viewed capitalist society as an evolutionary process, and it is the innovations created by companies that initiate this process by destroying the old and creating the new, i.e. 'creative destruction' –which is the core of capitalist society.	The book was edited by Schumpeter's widow from an uncompleted manuscript and published posthumously in 1954. It contains a very detailed historical analysis of the development of economics (and closely related sciences) – from the Greeks to modern times. *History of Economic Analysis* – which is about 1200 pages long – is regarded as one of the best works ever written about the history of economics.

Sources: Swedberg (1994); Pålsson-Syll (1998); Reisman (2004).

Table 17.2   Schumpeter Mark I and Mark II

	Schumpeter Mark I regime	Schumpeter Mark II regime
	The Theory of Economic Development (1934; 1912)	*Capitalism, Socialism and Democracy* (1942)
Industry characteristics	Less concentrated markets. Low entry barriers. Large number of small firms.	More oligopolistic and monopolistic markets. High entry barriers. Economies of scale.
Similarities	Innovations are central to economic development. Entrepreneurship is a function that is delimited in time. The capitalist assumes the risk.	
Differences	Focus on the individual. Only 'first degree' innovations are counted.	Focus on the function. A lower requirement on the innovation level.

Table 17.3   Kondratiev's long cycles

	Rise	Decline	
Cycle I	1787–93	1810–17	1844–51
Cycle II	1844–51	1870–75	1890–96
Cycle III	1890–96	1914–20	

that its periodical recurrence would put the entire bourgeois society on trial (Reijnders, 1990). However, it was the Russian Nikolai Kondratiev, who worked in Moscow in the 1920s and founded the Moscow Business Conditions Institute (Koniunkturnyi Institut), who received the most attention and is regarded as the 'father' of long waves, despite the fact that it has been questioned whether he was really the originator of the idea, which had been outlined by the Dutch economist J. van Gelderen in 1913 (Tinbergen, 1984).

Kondratiev argued that economic cycles or long waves of 45 to 60 years occur in society (Kondratiev, 1925/1979) and identified three long waves in the economy, the approximate timing of which can be seen in Table 17.3.

Some comments can be made on the three long waves identified by Kondratiev and later accepted by Schumpeter. First, they were allied in the most simplified form to the dissemination of steam power, the railway boom, and the joint effects of the motor car and electricity. Second, according to Kondratiev, the long waves are international in character, i.e. their periods coincide especially in European countries. Finally, in his original paper Kondratiev observed that during the downswing of long waves there was an increase in the rate of discovery and invention of production and communication techniques, which were then applied on a large scale in the subsequent upswing, i.e. the diffusion of innovations in the capital goods sector of the economy was associated with the upswing (Kondratiev, 1925/1979, p. 536). At that point in the development of his ideas he did not formulate an explanatory theory of the relationship between these phenomena. Later, however, he developed his position toward a fuller model of the process (Kondratiev, 1935).

An interest in Kondratiev's works emerged among Western economists during the depression of the 1930s, because unlike these economists, he had predicted not only the economy's decline, but also that it would end and be followed by a new boom (Tylecote, 1992).

Business Cycles (1939)

The argument that inventions and innovations were important for economic develop-ment was picked up by Joseph Schumpeter, who had been thinking along similar lines in his 1934 book, and formed the basis for his own long wave theory. Schumpeter stressed the role of technical progress and tried to explain how basic innovations (e.g. the steam engine and the railway) and the 'swarming' of smaller, secondary innovations which fol-lowed, created a long wave, but also how the initial impulse gradually dissipated, thus leading to a downswing (Tylecote, 1992).

The book *Business Cycles*, published in 1939, is a massive and impressive two volume work of almost 1100 pages. Schumpeter was ambitious in his approach to the study of the cyclical process of the economy. The ultimate goal of his study was to develop a 'conceptually clarified history, not of crises only, nor of cycles or waves, but of the economic process in all its aspects and bearings to which theory merely supplies some tools and schemata, and statistics are merely a part of the material' (Schumpeter, 1939, p. 220). Schumpeter differs from Kondratiev in that the latter clearly exhibits the traits of an inductive approach, i.e. Kondratiev stressed the importance of empirical observations and developed his theory by generalizing from observations to the economy as a whole, whereas Schumpeter was more or less deductive – starting with an abstract general level of argumentation and subsequently filling in more details that corresponded more closely with reality (Reijnders, 1990).

According to Schumpeter, innovations are the vehicle of economic change, and he considered innovation a distinct internal factor of change. Innovation intrudes into the system and gives rise to a cumulative process of growth. However, innovations do not remain isolated events and are never randomly distributed over the whole economic system, but tend to cluster in certain sectors and their surroundings, occuring in bunches, simply because a pronounced burst of basic innovations is followed by a growing swarm of imitators (Schumpeter, 1939, p. 75). Once the application of the original innovation has become general, recuperative forces take over and establish a new equilibrium (of the same nature as the former equilibrium but situated at a higher level).

The entrepreneur becomes important in the innovation process as s/he is an individual who has the ability to decide in favor of untried possibilities because her/his horizon is wider and her/his propensity to resist change is lower than that of other individuals. If the entrepreneur becomes successful s/he will make a profit during a period, but her/his success will also help others to overcome their original inhibition, because it is easier to make similar things or improve it in similar lines. There will be many imitations that will spread the innovation over a larger part of the economy (Reijnders, 1990).

Schumpeter's theory of business cycles is based on the general idea that innovation is a strong vehicle for economic change that forces the economy to move from one equilibrium to another and that innovations tend to cluster in time. According to Schumpeter, business cycles comprise two phases, a primary and a secondary movement (see Schumpeter, 1939, p. 145; see also Reijnders, 1990, pp. 31–5):

- A 'primary movement' occurs when the entrepreneur intervenes in a market in equilibrium by buying plant and equipment in order to fulfill her/his innovative work. S/he can only obtain the necessary resources by diverting them from their previous use, which immediately disrupts the existing market equilibrium. But the real changes occur when the new firms are up and running, as they gradually challenge the market position of the 'old' firms and strengthen the disequilibrium process that had already started. The 'old' firms face competition from firms that are superior in productive capacity and cost structure, causing some to disappear and forcing others into a painful process of modernization. The disappearance of 'old' firms does not necessarily imply a recession as long as new firms continue to emerge, and in this respect the recession threat may be overcompensated. However, the turning point comes when the entrepreneurial activity vanishes, and (1) production takes place at the minimum cost that equals price, and profit disappears, i.e. the shift from monopolistic to pure competition, and/or (2) the entrepreneurial activity creates a dynamic that makes it very difficult to plan new ventures and calculate the risk of failure, which further hampers other entrepreneurial activities. Thus, Schumpeter's 'primary movement' includes two phases: 'prosperity' and 'recession'.
- A 'secondary movement' is initiated and based on the first. The prosperity created by the upturn of the primary movement creates a reaction from the 'old' firms that tend to respond to the new situation in a speculative way – cyclical clusters of errors occur, especially when a recession is on the way, and behavior is governed by pessimism, creating a spiraling negative effect that results in a depression. The depression may continue indefinitely, although Schumpeter expected it to be hampered by the fact that not all elements in the chain break down – the healthy elements of the economy function as a buffer and contribute to a weakening of the contractive forces. Revival occurs when the economy starts 'feeling' its way back to equilibrium. Thus, Schumpeter's introduction of a secondary movement leads to a representation of a cycle consisting of four phases: 'prosperity' (growth); 'recession' (maturity); 'depression' (decline); and 'revival' (introduction).

Schumpeter argued that different cycles appear simultaneously (1939, pp. 166–8), and their length can vary widely, although he expected the duration of the different cycles to cluster around certain average values. In this respect, Schumpeter suggested a three-cycle scheme including a 'long cycle' of approximately 60 years (similar to the Kondratiev cycles), an 'intermediate cycle' of about ten years, and a 'short cycle' of approximately 40 months (pp. 170–74). Schumpeter also indicated that the different cycles are interrelated, and he assumed that each higher order cycle constitutes what he termed the 'neighborhood of equilibrium' for the cycle of the next lower order, i.e. the longer waves present a movement that is perceived as normal business conditions in cycles of the next lower level (Reijnders, 1990).

In order to demonstrate the existence of long waves, Schumpeter rejected a strict use of rigid statistical methods and argued that the method used should always be based on a thorough historical analysis. In *Business Cycles* Schumpeter placed a great deal of emphasis on the historical development of business cycles in Great Britain, France, Germany, and the United States. More than two-thirds of the book is devoted to this historical analysis, in which Schumpeter used only time-series data for the purpose of illustrating his arguments as opposed to testing his theory.

Criticism of Schumpeter's Theory of 'Business Cycles'

Even though Schumpeter's book and thesis did not receive as much attention as Kondratiev's initial ideas, it did not escape criticism (Kuznets, 1940; Tylecote, 1992) on the following grounds: (1) Schumpeter's theory is based on the relationship between the distribution of entrepreneurial ability in a society and the development of innovations. But given an infinite supply of possible innovations there is no reason why the entrepreneur should wait for the next pioneering step, and in this respect the 'rhythm' of Schumpeter's cycles can be questioned. (2) Schumpeter left a crucial gap in his theory by his failure to explain the creation of basic innovations and why they appear in clusters every fifty years or so, i.e. he was unclear about why such clusters occur every 45 to 60 years. (3) Schumpeter applied an historical method to the analysis of his long waves of economic development; the problem is that he was unsuccessful in linking his cycles to clearly observed statistical realities.

ERIK DAHMÉN AND 'DEVELOPMENT BLOCS'

Erik Dahmén (1916–2005) became one of the leading Swedish economists and is regarded as the main proponent of the so-called Swedish School of Growth. Over the years, Dahmén's thinking influenced many Swedish economic historians and economists, but outside Scandinavia he seems to be more or less neglected. Dahmén wrote mainly in Swedish, and as is the case with many other pioneering works (cf. Schumpeter), his concepts are not always distinct, and his ideas were overshadowed by Schumpeter's.

Early Contributions of Erik Dahmén's Thinking

Dahmén began his studies in economics at Lund University in Sweden in 1935 under the guidance of the Swedish economist Johan Åkerman. At that time Åkerman was greatly influenced by Thorstein Veblen and his evolutionary (Darwinist) theory of society (Erixon, 2007). Åkerman devoted a great deal of attention to the work of Friedrich von Hayek and his discussion on capital misallocation. Against this background, Åkerman suggested that Dahmén should focus his studies on the problem of capital misallocation, thus capital misallocation by firms became the point of departure in Dahmén's bachelor thesis, presented in 1939, but also the basis of his theory development throughout the rest of his career (Henriksson, 2002).

In his bachelor thesis (1939) Dahmén elaborated on the role of capital misallocation in the structural transformation process. One important observation that Dahmén made in his bachelor thesis was that capital misallocation tended to 'clump' together. He demonstrated that misallocation within one area of the economy was usually followed by additional misallocations in other areas, indicating that capital misallocations are connected and interdependent (Westberg, 2007), thus creating 'clusters'. This clustering process can be explained in different ways, but one important reason was that investments were dependent on each other, which can also be regarded as an important factor explaining the long-term business cycles in the economic system. In later works, Dahmén used the concept 'development blocs' to describe this clustering process and argued that the process is valid in expansion situations as well as in the contraction of the economy (Henriksson, 2002).

In his subsequent PhD studies Dahmén was soon introduced to the works of Schumpeter. The second edition of Schumpeter's *Theorie der Wirtschaftlichen Entwicklung* (1926) was included in Åkerman's course in economics at Lund University, but it was not until Dahmén read Schumpeter's book *Business Cycles* (1939) that he more seriously started to immerse himself in Schumpeterian thinking. Schumpeter's reasoning allowed Dahmén to better articulate his own conceptual contributions, and it was probably through the influence of Schumpeter's writings that in spring 1941 he coined the concept 'development blocs', despite the fact that it was more or less a renaming of the clusters of capital misallocations that he had identified in his bachelor thesis (Henriksson, 2002). In this respect, 1941 can be considered the year in which a shift took place in Dahmén's way of thinking, from a depressive Hayekian view to a more open and creative Schumpeterian perspective.

This change is expressed in his licentiate thesis (1942) 'Ekonomisk strukturanalys. Begreppet felinvestering som konjunkturteoretiskt instrument' (Economic structural analysis. The concept of capital misallocation as a business cycle instrument), in which he elaborated further on his view of economic development and change and especially on the importance of capital misallocations for business cycles and long-term economic development. In addition, in his licentiate thesis Dahmén formulated a broad research program for his subsequent research that included four general structures (or analytical areas): production structure; economic-political structure; monetary structure; and social structure. His idea was that these four structures constituted an integrated theory of economic transformation. Dahmén was unable to carry out this plan for various reasons and instead focused on the development of a conceptual formation around the analysis of the production structure (Westberg, 2007).

Dahmén always regarded himself as Schumpeterian, although these early contributions reveal that he presented some of his ideas ahead of his master and that in many respects they are characterized by a stronger theoretical coherence and greater originality than those of Schumpeter. For example, it is worth mentioning that as early as 1939 Dahmén formulated a basic theoretical view on the role of capital misallocation in the structural transformation process that he later presented in his licentiate thesis (1942). Thus, Dahmén was ahead of Schumpeter in developing a theory about the process that Schumpeter later called 'creative destruction' in *Capitalism, Socialism and Democracy* (1942), but for which he, in contrast to Dahmén, provided no theoretical foundation (Westberg, 2007). In addition, Dahmén studied two aspects of the transformation process – one positive and one negative – which implies that his model was in many respects better-developed than his source of inspiration. Finally, not only did Dahmén present his thoughts earlier than Schumpeter and produce a better-developed transformation process model, but he also succeeded in creating a methodological tool for historical causal analysis – something Schumpeter failed to achieve. Dahmén presented this contribution in his PhD thesis, which subsequently achieved the most attention all of his work internationally.

Dahmén's Thesis 'Entrepreneurial Activity and the Development of Swedish Industry, 1919–1939' (1950)

After presenting his licentiate thesis in 1942, Erik Dahmén moved to Stockholm where he had obtained a position at the Research Institute of Industrial Economics (Industrins Utredningsinstitut, IUI), a private research institute founded in 1939 by the Federation of Swedish Industries and the Swedish Employers' Confederation 'to conduct research on economic and social issues with relevance for industrial development'. It was at the Institute that Dahmén wrote his major work *Svensk industriell företagarverksamhet: kausalanalys av den industriella utrecklingen 1919–1939* (*Entrepreneurial Activity and the Development of Swedish Industry, 1919–1939*) (1950; 1970), which was presented as his PhD thesis at Lund University in 1951. Dahmén became professor of economics at the Stockholm School of Economics in 1958. It is significant that for a long time Dahmén was also closely connected to one of the major banks in Sweden, Stockholms Enskilda Bank (later a part of SEB), and the sphere around the Wallenberg family – long one of the leading families in Swedish industry.

Development blocs and complementarities

Dahmén's thesis was based on detailed empirical studies of several industries in Sweden and built on the ideas in his licentiate thesis (1942). In the thesis he introduced a large number of new concepts that he elaborated on at a later stage of his career. The most important one was that growth and economic development occur in the context of development blocs. The basic idea was that in many cases economic transformation originates from synergies and complementarities between different technologies, investments, companies and industries. In order to fully utilize industrial opportunities it is often necessary to make investments that complement each other in various industries and product areas, and when this occurs a development bloc has been created. In other words: development blocs are a form of cluster (or network) of integrated physical production and distribution that creates powerful synergy effects in time and space.

Thus, in order to understand the dynamics of development blocs, the concept of *complementarities* became important: that is, different parts of a combination could affect each other in a positive way. In simple terms, one example of complementarities is egg and bacon (at least in some civilizations), the opposite being substitutions, where one factor compensates for another. For example, tea and coffee are usually regarded as substitutes for each other (Schön, 2007). Neoclassical economic theory is mainly based on substitutions, where the problems are focused around the question of how to distribute scarce resources between competing aims. In contrast, Dahmén's reasoning is based on complementarities. Development blocs are formed around innovations that change these complementarities, which in turn require a transformation of the economy. Thus, renewal and growth within one area of the economy create a need and an opportunity to increase capacity, thus leading to renewal within other, complementary areas of the economy. For example, the extension of the railroads and railroad system in the nineteenth century became a strong force that made trade in society more extensive and efficient, i.e. a development bloc was created around transportation in general and railroads in particular that implied a far-reaching transformation in society. A development bloc works as a breeding ground for other (sequential) innovations, i.e. chain reactions occur, leading to pressure to make changes within the development bloc as new forms of dependencies arise between different areas of society (Westberg, 2007).

Development blocs can be more or less extensive, ranging from individual activities to far-reaching transformation processes in society. Thus they can occur in different ranges, from small scale to large changes that involve a large part of society. In this respect, the most important are those innovations that have a far-reaching influence on the production and infrastructure of society (Schön, 2007) – what was later called 'General Purpose Technologies' (Bresnahan and Trajtenberg, 1995). The concept of the development bloc is, however, more dynamic and open than the taxonomic concept of a general purpose technology. In particular, the development bloc concentrates on the innovative transformation of complementary links in the economy, which is a strategic characteristic of economic growth.

The positive and negative sides of the transformation process
At an early stage Dahmén realized that the transformation process comprised two aspects, one positive and one negative. In his 1942 licentiate thesis Dahmén analyzed different mechanisms that could be considered central for understanding how the positive side laid the foundation for the negative side of the transformation process. In contrast to Schumpeter, Dahmén devoted a great deal of time and thought to understanding both aspects of the transformation process and developing a comprehensive model of the total transformation (whereas Schumpeter talked more generally about 'the logic of creative destruction'). In a similar way to that by which innovations are created, some existing phenomena become obsolete, as they are subject to competition from growing development blocs. Phenomena on the negative side of the development bloc are characterized by a need to change or wind up activities in favor of those situated on the positive side. This also makes it possible to release resources (e.g. labor and capital) and transfer them to the positive side of the development bloc or to other sectors of the economy. During his final years Dahmén devoted a great deal of effort to elaborating on the concept of 'transformation push' to describe the dynamics between the positive and negative side of the transformation process (Westberg, 2007).

Methodological considerations
Throughout his career, Dahmén argued that in order to understand economic development and growth it is necessary to be in close contact with the economic reality under study (something that Dahmén himself experienced through his long and close relationship with the Swedish industrialists Marcus and Jacob Wallenberg), as opposed to building abstract models based on sophisticated mathematical methods. In this respect Dahmén was highly critical of the development of mainstream economics. In addition, the interest among economists must, according to Dahmén, be directed toward the behavior of individual companies and the market processes created by those companies, as an understanding of economic development on an aggregated level demands that one

understands micro level (firm level) behavior. The analysis must also include institutional conditions of importance for the companies' behavior and the interplay between the companies and their markets (Karlson et al., 2007).

In order to achieve this understanding of the relationship between the micro and macro level of analysis, Dahmén used a causal analysis, in which the point of departure is the changes that occur at company level, especially among the firms leading (pioneering) the development. It is not possible to explain the transformation processes on more aggregated levels until such changes are analyzed (Westberg, 2007). In addition, one main thesis in the causal analysis developed by Dahmén is that industrial transformation cannot be separated from the historical circumstances, and therefore it is necessary to make a historical reconstruction and analysis of the circumstances in which the transformation processes are embedded (Carlsson, 2007).

According to Dahmén, there is a constant struggle between new and old in the economy – new innovations drive old combinations of production factors out of the market – and in this respect entrepreneurship and technical development are driving forces in the transformation. For both Dahmén and Schumpeter, the entrepreneur is the real source of change, as s/he introduces innovations to the market and thus becomes the driving force behind the transformation processes. The entrepreneur identifies new market possibilities and needs and is the actor behind the changes and growth in society due to taking initiatives and commercializing the business opportunities created by the innovations (Schön, 2007).

The Swedish School of Growth

For a long time Erik Dahmén was an active researcher at IUI in Stockholm. Bo Carlsson and Gunnar Eliasson were also active at the Institute and can be considered the successors of Dahmén as well as central contributors to the research tradition known as the Swedish School of Growth.

The Swedish School of Growth emphasizes economic growth as an evolutionary process in which entrepreneurship and innovations play an essential role – the 'new' challenges the 'old' in a process of creative destruction that generates economic development. Growth becomes the combined consequences of individual firm formations, expansions, contractions, and liquidations. In addition, the design of institutions ('the rules of the game') that influence entrepreneurship and innovations is considered of crucial importance for growth in the economy (Johansson and Karlsson, 2002).

Bo Carlsson, attached since the 1980s to the Case Western Reserve University in Ohio, USA, is probably the best-known researcher among Dahmén's successors. Carlsson has particularly emphasized the importance of technology innovations in industrial development with a technological systems theory (Carlsson and Stankiewics, 1991; Carlsson, 2002). According to Bo Carlsson, technological systems refer to 'networks of agents interacting in a given area of technology, operating within a particular infrastructure, to generate, exploit and diffuse technology' (Carlsson and Stankiewics, 1991, p. 111) and, thus, it is the emergence and uses of a generic technology in various applications that are focused upon, for example, the use of biotechnology in many different industrial applications. In this respect, Carlsson emphasizes the flow of knowledge that keeps the technology system together rather than the flow of products and services.

Gunnar Eliasson, Professor Emeritus in Industrial Economics at the Royal Institute of Technology in Stockholm, and for a long time CEO at IUI, developed a theory about 'competence blocs' in which he emphasized non-physical and non-technical aspects of production and argued that technical as well as economic competencies are required in order to create and utilize business opportunities, i.e. it is necessary to develop a comprehensive competence bloc with distinct but supplementary competencies (Eliasson, 1996; Eliasson and Eliasson, 1996). A competence bloc can be regarded as the total supply of competencies that are necessary to create, choose, and identify profitable products and services and to develop them for industrial production. The competence bloc includes advanced customers, inventors and innovators, entrepreneurs, industrialists, venture capitalists, and actors on the secondary markets, as well as skilled workers. The actors within the competence bloc represent different functions, and in order to create an efficient industrial process it is necessary to have a competence bloc that is complete, where each function includes a critical mass of actors (Henrekson and Stenkula, 2007).

As indicated by this short discussion, the various contributions by the pioneers within the Swedish School of Growth complement each other in the sense that, in his theory of development blocs, Dahmén emphasized the physical dimension of industrial development, whereas the technological system approach by Carlsson was focused on the importance of the technology, while Eliasson's reasoning highlighted the importance of competence and human capital for the creation of a dynamic economy and growth. A common framework for all three contributions is the central importance of the institutions, in the form of, for example, laws, rules, and norms, in industrial development and growth (Johansson and Karlsson, 2002).

DEVELOPMENT BLOCS IN STRUCTURAL CYCLES

Erik Dahmén's idea about development blocs has received a great deal of attention, especially among the group of researchers associated with the Swedish School of Growth. Dahmén has also inspired structural economics researchers at the Department of Economic History at Lund University, Sweden – the university where Dahmén started his academic career in the 1930s. Over a long period, a group of economic historians in Lund have tried to empirically develop the theory and concepts initially created by Erik Dahmén, who never formulated a theory on structural cycles – he only made the observation that the economy follows some form of long-term cyclical waves. However, based on the 'development bloc' concept, one main argument among economic historians at Lund University has been that since the mid 19th century, industrial society has exhibited a pattern of structural renewal and positive transformation pressure followed by periods of rationalization and negative pressure that end in a structural crisis. Thus, Dahmén's initial finding that there was a shift from negative transformation pressure in the Swedish economy during the 1920s to positive pressure after the crisis of the 1930s has been extended into a long-term cyclical pattern. There are also indications that behavior at the micro level interacts with these shifts in trends at the macro level. In this way the research group at Lund University links Dahmén's reasoning on development blocs with Schumpeter's theory on structural cycles.

Long-term Structural Cycles: The Development of the Swedish Economy

Studies on Swedish economic development since the mid nineteenth century reveal a pattern of structural change that has been modeled within a framework of a structural cycle linked to the industrial and social dynamics expressed by the development bloc concept.

The investment ratio in Swedish industry, defined as fixed capital investments in relation to value added in industry in fixed prices, over the period 1850 to 2005 (Figure 17.1), is a major indicator of shifts in behavior. The ratio exhibits a strong cyclical pattern – with low points in the early 1890s, early 1930s, and late 1970s or early 1980s. These low points coincide with international crises, after which followed roughly 25–30 years characterized by a rising investment ratio that culminated in the mid-1870s, the late 1910s,

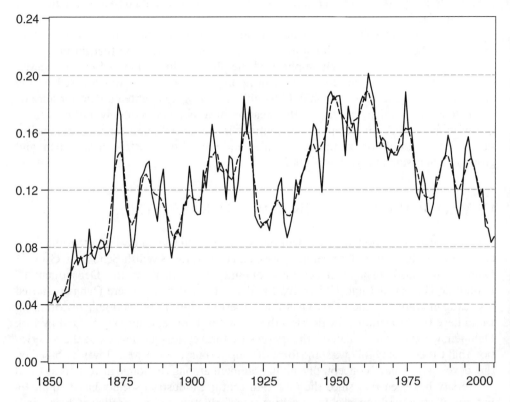

Note: Investments include only material investments (buildings and equipment), about which information is available dating back to the nineteenth century. Since there was a shift to more immaterial investments from the mid 1970s onwards, the level of the curve is lower from the 1980s.

Source: Schön (1994), Swedish National Accounts.

Figure 17.1   *The ratio of investments to value added in Swedish industry, 1850–2005 (fixed prices with annual and five-year moving averages)*

the early 1960s and around 2000, and subsequently 10–15 years of a falling ratio to the troughs in the years of crisis (Schön, 1998).

The investment ratio shown in Figure 17.1 indicates a periodization of Swedish industrial development in cycles of 40 to 50 years running from one crisis to another, with the troughs in the years 1845/50, 1890/95, 1930/35, and 1975/80. The investment pattern has its counterpart in the periodization of labor productivity increases in Swedish industry from 1890 onwards. In the subsequent decades leading up to the crises, development had the opposite characteristics – while the contribution from the reallocation of resources was negligible, productivity growth within branches accelerated, due to the fact that, on the one hand, new productivity-raising techniques became more diffused and adapted to all branches, making the industrial structure more homogeneous, and, on the other, that growth branches experienced a relative fall in prices, which reduced or eliminated their lead in value added per worker, thus contributing to an increased homogenization of the industrial structure (Schön, 1998).

It can be debated as to whether it is possible to generalize this pattern to other countries. As Sweden is a small and industrially specialized country that has been highly dependent upon the world market, it can be assumed that the patterns identified in Sweden accurately reflect important patterns in countries around the world and thus without doubt correspond strongly to international trends (Schön, 1998). However, some particularities in timing and characteristics can be found. For example, in the 1930s, Sweden was mainly on the positive side of the worldwide crisis and performed better than most other countries – industry moved quite rapidly from a crisis to new expansion. On the other hand, the international crisis that occurred with the downswing in 1973/74 was delayed and prolonged by a few years in Sweden, and we can date the crisis and the turning-point in the Swedish economy to the period 1975/1980 (ibid.)

Long-term Structural Cycles: Transformation, Rationalization and Crisis

According to our analysis in the previous subsection, evidence from Sweden indicates that the economy has followed long-term structural cycles of about 40–50 years and that each structural cycle has been initiated and shaped by some international economic crisis. The creative destruction of a structural crisis opens the way for the expansion of new development blocs that have been formed during the preceding periods. Within each long-term structural cycle there has been a shift between two fundamentally different behaviors that we can term *transformation* and *rationalization*, characterized by (Schön, 1991; 2001):

- A transformation period, i.e. a period dominated by the transformation of industrial structures in which resources are reallocated between industries and by the diffusion of basic innovations in the economy, thus providing new bases for such reallocation. During these periods, investment is generally long term and directed toward increasing capacity in new areas of production, as well as *development power* of industry. At the same time, a large number of new ventures as well as new combinations of old ones are funded during this period, which stimulates the supply of risk capital on the market. These characteristics indicate a diffusion of new development blocs with innovative activities in production with relatively

Table 17.4　Long term cycles

Transformation	Rationalization	Crisis (turning point)
1850	1875	1890
1890	1920	1930
1930	1960	1975
1975	2000	(2010)

small-scale innovative activities related to production and directed to markets close at hand. New development blocs turn expansion inwards, i.e. innovative production mostly takes place on a fairly small scale and is directed toward the familiar local markets. The end of the transformation period is characterized by a series of structural tensions, for example, renewal in similar directions in many industrial countries and incipient industrial development in new countries add both to development perspectives and to uncertainty; and

- A rationalization period, i.e. a period dominated by the concentration of resources in the most productive units within the industry and by measures to increase efficiency in the different lines of production – aimed at enhancing the efficiency of existing structures and operations and decreased resource utilization. Thus, rationalization leads to more rapid growth in productivity and to higher growth rates of real income as well as to stagnation in the ratio of investments to income. Investments, which are short-term in character, are directed toward reducing costs in existing structures and operations, as well as increasing the *competitive power* of industry. Specialization and widening of markets become more important, i.e. international competition increases with the weakening of domestic markets and international integration measures are intensified.

Although transformation and rationalization are processes that to a large extent take place simultaneously in an economy, historically there have been shifts in emphasis between periods of transformation and rationalization. These shifts occur with considerable regularity within a long structural cycle, for example, 25 years of emphasis on transformation, followed by some 15 years of emphasis on rationalization. Thus, we can find a pattern of long cycles characterized by crisis – transformation – rationalization and, starting from the mid nineteenth century, the following long cycles can be identified (Table 17.4).

The model of long-term structural cycles can be regarded as deterministic, but it should not be exaggerated – the cycles tell us about a way to move, due to a systematic play of forces, but they do not tell us where to go. The model emphasizes crises as a period of comparatively open-ended choice between paths to follow in the decades to come (Schön, 1998).

Long-term Structural Cycles and Development Blocs

According to our argument, an economic crisis represents a fundamental turning point in the long-term economic development in society and creates changes in terms of growth that appear after the crisis. In the new transformation period we can find not only an increase in the investment ratio and a shift to long-term investments, but also the appearance of new growth branches and development blocs. In the development of long-term structural cycles in Sweden we can find different development blocs centered round basic innovations, particularly in the field of power and communication (Schön, 1991; 1998).

The upswing in the long-term structural cycle from the 1850s onwards was mainly linked to the breakthrough of mechanized factories in Sweden, the modernization of steel processes, and the construction of railways, as well as a period of increased utilization of Swedish natural resources for an expanding export trade.

The structural cycle at the end of the nineteenth century witnessed the breakthrough of modern industrial society and increased the sophistication of urban industry in terms of machinery and new consumer goods. This development was based on the diffusion of new motor, electrical, or combustion engines, with a widening scope for mechanization within industry. Due to the importance of energy-intensive industries in Sweden, electricity gained a particularly important position during the structural cycle around the turn of the century.

From the 1930s, and especially after the Second World War, new development blocs were created around the expansion of electrification and the diffusion of automobiles. There was a wave of investments around the development of an infrastructure linked to basic innovations of the preceding cycle. For example, it created a much broader spectrum of applications for electrical applications and small motors in handicraft and household.

In the cycle initiated in the 1970s, the appearance of the microprocessor became the centre of new development blocs, i.e. the use of knowledge and information in the production of goods and services created new directions of growth. However, the importance of innovative activities during periods of transformation should not be emphasized too strongly. It could be argued that the basic innovations forming the structural cycle had appeared long before the start of the cycle. But the appearance of an innovation is of minor importance in this context – it is the diffusion that counts. An extensive diffusion requires that a new technology becomes competitive within a wide range of applications and that complementary activities sustain the diffusion of the development bloc.

CYCLICAL VARIATIONS IN RELATION TO INNOVATION AND ENTREPRENEURSHIP

In this concluding section we link our discussion on development blocs and long structural cycles, on the one hand, and innovative and entrepreneurial activities on the other.

First, we elaborate on the connection between structural changes and innovative activities. As indicated above, a close connection between innovative activities and structural crises can be questioned due to the fact that the basic innovations often appeared decades before the start of the crisis. When innovations first appear they are generally expensive to implement, have a narrow range of applications, are fairly small scale and directed toward familiar markets. In order to form new development blocs around the innovation, it is necessary to acquire efficient capital equipment at a reasonable price.

Thus, in order to create a broad impact and extensive diffusion, new technologies must become competitive within a wide range of areas. The diffusion of innovations is facilitated by a continuing adaptation of new technology to different areas and conditions, accomplished in a dual process of standardization and specialization, which is further strengthened through geographical expansion. The diffusion of the innovation will widen markets and strengthen consumer demand, but also increase competition on the market.

Second, we elaborate further on the relationship between structural cycles and entrepreneurship. In the upswing after a structural crisis, entrepreneurial activity has flourished in new growth branches with a pronounced increase in the number of new firms. Such was the case in the 1850s, 1890s, 1930s, and 1980s. However, the radical innovations at the center of new development blocs usually appeared some decades earlier. Early start-ups have taken the lead in transformation after the crises, while further entrepreneurial initiatives have spurred the growth of the new development blocks. Some decades later – as in the 1880s, 1920s, and 1960s – concentration into larger units has been part and parcel of rationalization.

In transformation, long-term investments in new ventures, knowledge, ideas and firms provide greater scope for visions of the future. Visionary leaders come to the fore and set the agenda. Transformation pressure is positive, which is in line with Dahmén's terminology, and investments are made to provide new opportunities. At an early stage of development, there is close interaction between the innovating entrepreneur and the market, which increases the importance of local or regional economies. That is particularly the case with innovations that generate spillovers. Standardization and specialization lead to the widening of markets and diffusion of knowledge. During rationalization, however, technology becomes more standardized and competition is fiercer. Transformation pressure is negative toward cost-reducing investments. Rational leaders with a short-term perspective of efficiency-increasing measures take over the steering wheel.

The relation between structural cycles and the characteristics of innovative and entrepreneurial behavior in the economy is summarized in Table 17.5.

Table 17.5 shows that innovative activities in transformation periods are characterized by product innovation, initially on a relatively small scale and directed to markets close at hand. Entrepreneurial activities increase and many new independent ventures (start-ups) appear in the economy, often based on visionary entrepreneurs making long-term investments in new areas of production. There is also knowledge diffusion, both in new technological areas and geographically. The driving forces behind the development include a high degree of variation and uncertainty in society. The transformation and diffusion of new technologies are further stimulated by deregulation and an expanding risk capital market.

In rationalization periods innovations become more process oriented in order to increase the efficiency of production, and entrepreneurship decreases in terms of the number of start-ups, while there is an increase in mergers and corporate entrepreneurship. Managers who make short-term investments directed toward reducing costs dominate the economy, the markets become wider and international competition increases. The driving forces in rationalization periods include homogeneity and stabilization of the economy, whereas economics of scale dominate the development of the industrial structure (larger corporations).

Table 17.5 Innovative and entrepreneurial activities during transformation and rationalization periods

	Transformation periods	Rationalization periods
Innovative activities	Product innovations – on a fairly small scale, directed toward a familiar market close at hand	Process innovations – in order to increase the efficiency of production
Entrepreneurial activities	Increase of independent new ventures (start-ups) Increase of innovative new ventures Visionary entrepreneurs who set the agenda and make long-term investments directed toward new areas of production Diffusion of technologies in different areas and geographical contexts	Decrease of independent new ventures (start-ups) Increase in mergers, outsourcing, and corporate entrepreneurship Rational managers, who make short-term investments directed toward reducing costs Specialization and widening of markets, increased international competition, and more intense international integration
Driving forces	Variation and uncertainty Spill-over effects and knowledge diffusion Deregulation An expanding risk capital market	Homogeneity and stability Economies of scale Regulation A contracting risk capital market

REFERENCES

Baumol, W.J. (1990), 'Entrepreneurship: productive, unproductive, and destructive', *Journal of Political Economy*, **98**(5), 893–920.

Bresnahan, T.F. and M. Trajtenberg (1995), 'General purpose technologies: engines of growth?', *Journal of Econometrics*, **LXV**, 83–108.

Carlsson, B. (ed.) (2002), *Technological Systems in the Bio Industries: An International Study*, Dordrecht: Kluwer Academic Publishers.

Carlsson, B. (2007), 'IVA:s storprojekt: en tillämpning av den Dahménska ansatsen', in N. Karlson, P. Storm, D. Johansson and B. Mölleryd (eds), *Erik Dahmén och det industriella företagandet*, Stockholm: Ratio, pp. 99–122.

Carlsson, B. and R. Stankiewics (1991), 'On the nature, function, and competition of technological systems', *Journal of Evolutionary Economics*, **1**(2), 93–118.

Dahmén, E. (1939), 'Begreppet felinvestering som konjunkturteoretiskt instrument', Bachelor Thesis in Economics, Lund University, Sweden, and presentation at the Nordic Seminar for Young Scholars in Socio-Economics, Copenhagen, 27–30 May.

Dahmén, E. (1942), 'Ekonomisk strukturanalys. Begreppet felinvestering som konjunkturteoretiskt instrument', Licentiate Thesis in Economics, Lund University, Sweden.

Dahmén, E. (1950), *Svensk industriell företagarverksamhet: kausalanalys av den industriella utvecklingen 1919–1939*, Stockholm: IUI.

Dahmén, E. (1970), *Entrepreneurial Activity and the Development of Swedish Industry, 1919–1939*, Homewood: Irwin Inc.

Diamond Jr, A.M. (2008), 'Schumpeter vs. Keynes: in the long run not all of us are dead', paper, Department of Economics, University of Nebraska, Omaha.
Eliasson, G. (1996), *Firm Objectives, Controls and Organization*, Dordretcht: Kluwer Academic Publishers.
Eliasson, G. and Å. Eliasson (1996), 'The biotechnical competence bloc', *Revue d'Economic Industrielle*, **78**(40), 7–26.
Erixon, L. (2007), 'En skördetid för Dahmén? Den svenska tillväxtskolan i dagens national-ekonomi', in N. Karlson, P. Storm, D. Johansson and B. Mölleryd (eds), *Erik Dahmén och det industriella företagandet*, Stockholm: Ratio, pp. 151–90.
Freeman, C. (1984), *Long Waves in the World Economy*, London: Frances Pinter.
Freeman, C. and C. Perez (1988), 'Structural crises of adjustment, business cycles and investment behaviour', in G. Dosi, C. Freeman, R. Nelson, G. Silverberg and L. Soete (eds), *Technical Change and Economic Theory*, London: Pinter, pp. 38–68.
Henrekson, M. and M. Stenkula (2007), *Entreprenörskap*, Stockholm: SNS Förlag.
Henriksson, R. (2002), 'Den dahménska ansatsens tillkomst och dess ställning i den schumpeteri-anska traditionen', in D. Johansson and N. Karlsson (eds), *Den svenska tillväxtskolan. Om den ekonomiska utvecklingens kreativa förstörelse*, Stockholm: Ratio, pp. 65–94.
Jevons, W.S. (1884), *Investigations in Currency and Finance*, London: Macmillan.
Johansson, D. and N. Karlsson (2002), 'Den svenska tillväxtskolan', in D. Johansson and N. Karlsson (eds), *Den svenska tillväxtskolan. Om den ekonomiska utvecklingens kreativa förstörelse*, Stockholm: Ratio, pp. 17–42.
Juglar, C. (1862), *Des crises commerciales et leur retour periodique en France*, Paris: Guillaumin.
Karlson, N., P. Storm, D. Johansson and B. Mölleryd (2007), 'Introduktion', in N. Karlson, P. Storm, D. Johansson and B. Mölleryd (eds), *Erik Dahmén och det industriella företagandet*, Stockholm: Ratio, pp. 9–21.
Keynes, J.M. (1936/1973), *General Theory of Employment, Interest and Money*, New York: Harcourt Brace.
Kondratiev, N.D. (1925/1979), 'The major economic cycles', translation (first published in Voprosy Koniunktury, 1925), *Review*, **11**(4), 519–62.
Kondratiev, N.D. (1935), 'The long waves in economic life', *Review of Economic Statistics*, **17**, 105–15.
Kuznets, S. (1940), 'Schumpeter's business cycles', *American Economic Review*, **30**, 257–71.
Kyrö, P. (2006), 'The transitional development of entrepreneurship – dialogue between new economic activity, work and freedom', *Estudios de Economia Aplicada*, **24**(2), 105–26.
Marx, K. (1893/1971), *Das Kapital*, Volume II, Berlin: Dietz Forlag.
Pålsson-Syll, L. (1998), *De ekonomiska teoriernas historia*, Lund: Studentlitteratur.
Reijnders, J. (1990), *Long Waves in Economic Development*, Aldershot, UK and Brookfield, VT, USA: Edward Elgar.
Reisman, D. (2004), *Schumpeter's Market. Enterprise and Evolution*, Cheltenham, UK and Northampton, MA, USA: Edward Elgar.
Schön, L. (1991), 'Development blocks and transformation pressure in a macro-economic perspective – a model of long-term cyclical change', *Skandinaviska Enskilda Banken Quarterly Review*, **3–4**, 67–76.
Schön, L. (1994), *Omvandling och obalans. Mönster i svensk ekonomisk utveckling* (*Transformation and Imbalance. Patterns in Swedish Economic Development*), Stockholm: Långtidsutredningen (Swedish National Accounts).
Schön, L. (1998), 'Industrial crises in a model of long cycles: Sweden in an international perspective', in T. Myllyntaus (ed.), *Economic Crises and Restructuring in History. Experiences of Small Countries*, St. Katharinen, Germany: Scripta Mercaturae Verlag, pp. 397–413.
Schön, L. (2001), 'Swedish industrial growth and crises in the 20th century', paper at the workshop Growth, Crises and Regulation in the European Economies, University of Helsinki, 1–4 March.
Schön, L. (2007), 'Utvecklingsblock i den globala ekonomin: några framtidsperspektiv', in N. Karlson, P. Storm, D. Johansson and B. Mölleryd (eds), *Erik Dahmén och det industriella företagandet*, Stockholm: Ratio, pp. 22–47.

Schumpeter, J.A. (1934), *The Theory of Economic Development*, Cambridge, MA: Harvard University Press.

Schumpeter, J.A. (1939), *Business Cycles*, New York: McGraw-Hill.

Schumpeter, J.A. (1942), *Capitalism, Socialism and Democracy*, New York: Harper & Row.

Schumpeter, J.A. (1954), *History of Economic Analysis*, London: Allen & Unwin.

Smith, A. (1776/1976), *An Inquiry into the Nature and Causes of the Wealth of Nations*, Oxford: Clarendon.

Swedberg, R. (1994), *Schumpeter. Om skapande förstörelse och entreprenörskap*, Stockholm: Ratio.

Tinbergen, J. (1984), 'Kondratiev cycles and so-called long waves', in C. Freeman (ed.), *Long Waves in the World Economy*, London: Frances Pinter, pp. 13–18.

Tylecote, A. (1992), *The Long Wave in the World Economy*, London: Routledge.

van Gelderen, J. (1913), 'Springvloed: beschouwingen over industrieële ontwikkeling en prijsbeweging', *De Nieuwe Tijd*, **18**(April–June), 4–6.

Westberg, K. (2007), 'Den Dahménska ansatsens aktualitet', in N. Karlson, P. Storm, D. Johansson and B. Mölleryd (eds), *Erik Dahmén och det industriella företagandet*, Stockholm: Ratio, pp. 48–71.

18. Entrepreneurial capitalism in East Asia: how history matters

David Ahlstrom and Linda C. Wang

INTRODUCTION

The rise of East Asian economies from Japan to China and Southeast Asia has motivated much study of how these economies grew so quickly and inspired a model for economies in the developing world (Berger and Hsiao, 1988; Fallows, 1995; Johnson, 1982; Rowher, 1995; Vogel, 1979). This has encouraged further inquiry on specific East Asian business systems including what has come to be called Chinese entrepreneurial capitalism or more generally 'Confucian capitalism' (Baumol et al., 2007; Bond and Hofstede, 1990; Hamilton, 2006; Kotkin, 1992; Redding, 1990; Whitley, 1992).[1] Confucian capitalism is thought by many to be a key mode of economic organization in East Asia not only because of its economic significance to local economies, but also because of its complex network organization and compatibility with the modern virtual organization (Ahlstrom et al., 2004; Chen, 2001; Redding, 1990; Whitley, 1992). Researchers have stressed the importance of Chinese culture, in general, and Confucianism, in particular, as a key explanation for this putatively unique business system in East Asia much in the way Max Weber's (1951) 'Protestant work ethic' has been used to explain economic growth in the West (e.g. Kao, 1993; Redding, 1990; Seagrave, 1995; Weidenbaum and Hughes, 1996; Whitley, 1992).

Indeed, the economies that have developed the most rapidly during the twentieth century are mainly Confucian-influenced East Asian ones, most notably those of Japan, South Korea, Hong Kong, Singapore, Taiwan, and Mainland China.[2] Limited evidence asserts an association between (primarily Confucian) cultural values and economic growth over time in these economies (e.g. Bond and Hofstede, 1990). That Confucian system is thought to include harmonious and tolerant Chinese management style, thrift and self-sacrifice, loyalty to top management and reciprocal loyalty to valued employees and suppliers. In addition, at the strategic level, Confucianism places an emphasis on social capital and networking, which is of particular importance in a globalizing world (De Bary, 1988; Chen, 2001).

Can it be concluded that Chinese cultural influence, in general, and Confucianism, in particular, have played a major, largely unambiguous role in the emergence of entrepreneurial capitalism and growth in these East Asian economies as its proponents suggest (Bond and Hofstede, 1990; Kotkin, 1992; Weidenbaum and Hughes, 1996)? This view is perhaps best summarized by economic historian David Landes (2000, p. 2) who wrote: 'If we learn anything from the history of economic development, it is that culture makes almost all the difference.' Yet does culture really make almost all the difference? Or is culture's role a lot more ambiguous and mixed in with institutions and various traditions that are more proximate contributors to entrepreneurial and economic development? If the latter is the case, then how might the historical background and context of the region and its institutions help to explain entrepreneurial capitalism in East Asia? Research that addresses historical context (Van de Ven, 2007; Zald, 1996) is beneficial to theory development, because it does not allow complex phenomena such as entrepreneurial development to be automatically attributed to culture or some other latent variable with little further explanation (Singh, 2007).

In keeping with that spirit of inquiry, this chapter explores historical evidence regarding entrepreneurial capitalism in East Asia, particularly investigating the culturist explanation to entrepreneurial growth there.[3] Culture has been cited as an important explanatory factor in many studies by sociologists and economic historians going back to Max Weber (1951), David Landes (1998) and other theorists (Cochran, 1960; Harrison, 2006; Shane, 1995; Hayton et al., 2002). Given the commercial primacy of the largest migrant group in the region, the Chinese, it is easy to see how economic data promote ideas of the exceptionalism of Chinese entrepreneurialism through Confucian influence. The share of listed equity in Southeast Asian stock markets controlled by Chinese firms has been estimated at between 50 per cent and 80 per cent, depending on the country in question. This compares with an ethnic Chinese share of population of 10 per cent in Thailand, 29 per cent in Malaysia and 77 per cent in Singapore and single digits elsewhere in Southeast Asia. Researchers in the 1990s estimated that ethnic Chinese interests controlled 45 per cent of major firms in the Philippines, and a majority or near-majority of the largest corporations in Indonesia, Thailand, and Malaysia (Eklof, 2002, p. 223; Rivera, 1991; Studwell, 2007, p. xv). More recent research holds that small numbers of ethnic Chinese families dominate economies from Hong Kong to Southeast Asia (*Economist*, 2009). It seems obvious to some that culture must be the explanation, especially given the other successful economies in East Asia such as Japan and Korea have strong Confucian influence.

But does culture really make almost all the difference as David Landes says? History seems to tell a different, more ambiguous story about culture's contribution to the development of entrepreneurial capitalism in East Asia. In spite of limited correlational evidence (e.g. Bond and Hofstede, 1990), there actually is little research that shows culture's direct, positive influence on entrepreneurship or other firm performance outcomes in East Asia in spite of much theorizing on culture's effects (Singh, 2007). This is not to say that culture does not matter, but researchers and other observers must be careful in rushing to cultural explanations before examining historical context, path dependencies, institutions, firm development and other key processes that are largely distinct from culture values (Krugman, 1994; Van de Ven, 2007).

To examine questions about what history can add to the understanding of entrepreneurial capitalism in East Asia, the arguments about the development of firms in this region and culture's impact must be investigated. Accordingly, in this chapter we examine the culturist argument and how it has been used to explain economic development in East Asia. Next, we consider the limits of the cultural explanation, and raise four key problems, each of which is examined in historical context to build an understanding of entrepreneurial capitalism in East Asia. Finally, we assess this chapter's contribution in employing a history-based, organizationally oriented level of analysis for future research into the effects of history, path dependencies, and culture on the development of entrepreneurial capitalism in East Asia.

CULTURE AND OTHER FORCES IN EAST ASIA

Research in this area can be broadly categorized into the culturist and culture-skeptic (Yeung 2007) views on East Asian development, and is summarized in Table 18.1.

The culturist argument as a basis for entrepreneurial and economic development goes back to Weber's (1951) well-known hypothesis that the Protestant work ethic lay behind the development of capitalist society. Similarly, Weber argued that Confucianism could hinder the establishment of capitalism, though not its development. Interestingly, a number of analysts up to the 1970s concurred with Weber's argument that Confucian values, particularly conservatism and antagonism to commercial activity (merchants occupy a very low position in the Confucian firmament), actually impeded rather than aided East Asian development.[4]

By the end of the 1970s, with East Asian growth in full swing, this belief turned sharply. Well-known Rand strategic analyst Herman Kahn (1979) wrote about a distinctive capitalism rising in East Asia influenced primarily by Confucianism. Kahn's work was picked up by a number of journalists (e.g. Fallows, 1995; Kotkin, 1992; Rowher, 1995; Seagrave, 1995) and social scientists coming from a range of disciplines from business to sociology to history (e.g. Pan, 1990; Redding, 1990; Weidenbaum and Hughes, 1996; Whitley, 1992). Gordon Redding's (1990) account was among the most influential. Though expressing some doubt, it articulated a particularistic cultural style of Chinese entrepreneurial capitalism and how it led to entrepreneurial development and economic growth. Others were more specific in stressing that culture can lower transaction costs and improve organizational and government coordination from which other firms and economies should learn (Chen, 2001; Fallows, 1995; Gibney, 1992).

Such culturist theories reached their apex during Asia's boom years of the 1990s as a number of books about the powerhouse economies of East Asia appeared. Though some were cursory journalistic accounts (e.g. Rowher, 1995), many were more serious academic studies. Among the more influential were the pioneering work of Thomas Sowell's (1997) *Migrations and Cultures* and Joel Kotkin's (1992) *Tribes: How Race, Religion and Identity Determine Success in the New Global Economy*, which showed how ethnic ties and culture promote economic prosperity. Other works included *The Lords of the Rim* (Seagrave, 1995), Murray Weidenbaum and Samuel Hughes's *The Bamboo Network: How Expatriate Chinese Entrepreneurs Are Creating a New Economic Superpower in Asia*, Chris Jenks's (1993) *Culture: Key Ideas*, and historian David Landes's (1998) landmark *The Wealth and Poverty of Nations*. Others, wanting to avoid too close an association with Confucianism or Chinese culture, utilized the purposely vaguer term 'Asian values' in assessing and promoting economic systems, particularly in countries with smaller ethnic Chinese minorities (e.g. Fallows, 1995; Mahathir, 1999; Mahbubani, 2008). Still others focused more on the Chinese diaspora's impact on business in the region and its key role utilizing essentially culturist arguments as well (Lever-Tracy, 2002; Ong and Nonini, 1997; Seagrave, 1995).

Yet at the same time, a small but steady stream of economists and other social scientists

Table 18.1   Key authors on culture and entrepreneurial development in East Asia

Main influences on entrepreneurial system	Key author	Key citations on entrepreneurship and development in East Asia
Culturist		
Culture	Frank Gibney	Gibney, F. (1992), *The Pacific Century: America and Asia in a Changing World*, New York: Scribners.
	Joel Kotkin	Kotkin, J. (1992), *Tribes: How Race, Religion and Identity Determine Success in the New Global Economy*, New York: Random House.
	Chris Jenks	Jenks, C. (1993), *Culture: Key Ideas*, London: Routledge.
	David Landes	Landes, D. (1998), *The Wealth and Poverty of Nations*, New York: W.W. Norton.
	Gordon Redding	Redding, S.G. (1990), *The Spirit of Chinese Capitalism*, Berlin and New York: W. de Gruyter.
	Thomas Sowell	Sowell, T. (1997), *Migrations and Cultures: A World View*, New York: Basic Books.
	Murray Weidenbaum	Weidenbaum, M. and S. Hughes (1996), *The Bamboo Network*, New York: Free Press.
Chinese diaspora	Constance Lever-Tracy	Lever-Tracy, C. (2002), 'The impact of the Asian crisis on diaspora Chinese tycoons', *Geoforum*, **33**(3), 509–23.
		Lever-Tracy, C., D. Ip and N. Tracy (1996), *The Chinese Diaspora and Mainland China*, London: Macmillan.
	Donald Nonini	Ong, A. and D. Nonini (1997), 'Toward a cultural politics of diaspora and transnationalism', in A. Ong and D.M. Nonini (eds), *Ungrounded Empires*, London: Routledge, pp. 323–32.
Business systems	Victor Limlingan	Limlingan, V.S. (1986), *The Overseas Chinese in ASEAN*, Manila: Vita Development Co.
	Victor Mallet	Mallet, V. (2000), *The Trouble With Tigers: The Rise and Fall of South-east Asia*, London: HarperCollins.
	Richard Whitley	Whitley, R. (1992), *Business Systems in East Asia*, London: Sage.
Culture skeptics		
Institutions and path dependency	Arif Dirlik	Dirlik, A. (1992), 'The Asia-Pacific idea', *Journal of World History*, **3**(1), 55–79.
		Dirlik, A. (ed.) (1998), *What is in a Rim? Critical Perspectives on the Pacific Region Idea*, Lanham, MD: Rowman and Littlefield.

Table 18.1   (continued)

Main influences on entrepreneurial system	Key author	Key citations on entrepreneurship and development in East Asia
	Linda Lim	Lim, L.Y.C. (1996), 'The evolution of Southeast Asian business systems', *Journal of Southeast Asia Business*, **12**(1), 51–74.
	Henry Yeung	Yeung, H.W.C. and K. Olds (eds) (2000), *Globalization of Chinese Firms*, New York: Macmillan, pp. 1–28. Yeung, H.W.C. (2004), *Chinese Capitalism in a Global Era: Towards Hybrid Capitalism*, London, UK: Routledge
	Kunio Yoshihara	Yoshihara, K. (1988), *The Rise of Ersatz Capitalism in South East Asia*, Singapore: Oxford University Press.
Entrepreneurship	Thomas Menkhoff	Menkhoff, T. and S. Gerke (eds) (2002), *Chinese Entrepreneurship and Asian Business Networks*, Richmond, UK: Curzon.
	Siu-lun Wong	Wong, S. (1988), *Emigrant Entrepreneurs*, Hong Kong: Oxford University Press.
	Shaker Zahra	Hayton, J.C., G. George and S. Zahra (2002), 'National culture and entrepreneurship: a review of behavioral research', *Entrepreneurship Theory and Practice*, **26**(2), 33–53.
History	Wellington Chan	Chan, W.K.K. and A. McElderry (eds) (1998), 'Historical patterns of Chinese business', *Journal of Asian Business*, Special Issue, **14**(1), 1–69.
	Edmund Gomez	Gomez, E.T. and H.H.M. Hsiao (eds) (2001), *Chinese Business in South-East Asia*, Richmond, UK: Curzon.
	Lynn Pan	Pan, L. (1990), *Sons of the Yellow Emperor: The Story of the Overseas Chinese*, Boston: Little, Brown & Co.
	Joe Studwell	Studwell, J. (2007), *Asian Godfathers*, London: Profile Books.

more skeptical of culturist argument started to emerge (L.Y.C. Lim, 1996; 2000; Mallet, 2000; Sachs, 2000; Yeung, 2004; 2006; Yoshihara, 1988). Led by Japanese and Southeast Asian scholars, their ranks broadened in the run-up to and aftermath of the Asian financial crisis in 1997–98 (Studwell, 2007). These commentators questioned the robustness and resilience of East Asian firms, particularly expressing skepticism with the argument that Confucian culture (or some other vague notion of 'Asian values') was the reason for East Asian economic growth (Yoshihara 1988). Other commentators in trying to explain the impressive growth of entrepreneurial capitalism in East Asia commended other forces such as the unique business structures and varieties of capitalism not necessarily linked directly to culture (Menkhoff and Gerke, 2002; Whitley, 1992). Some researchers stressed the importance of historical context and development (Chan and McElderry, 1998; Gomez and Hsiao, 2001; Pan, 1990), whereas others saw the development through a lens of business groupings (Limlingan, 1986), institutions (Peng, 2003; Carney et al., 2009), and collaborative rentier arrangements with East Asian governments (Lim, 1996; Mallet, 2000; Studwell, 2007).[5] All, however, shared skepticism about culturist arguments.

To many of the culturist school, however, links between ethnic Chinese around the region and the success of Confucian-influenced societies seem obvious in that the economic dynamism of the system is based on cooperation, long-term contracts and reduced transaction costs (Gibney, 1992). The culture-skeptic school counters that although the DaVinci Code-like aura of the sprawling 'Confucian conglomerates' does make for stirring stories, the culturist view fails to distinguish important institutional forces and historical processes that could shed more light on the development of entrepreneurial capitalism in East Asia (Studwell, 2007; Wilkinson, 1996).

CHALLENGING THE CULTURIST PERSPECTIVE

How can this debate be resolved? As Gomez and Hsiao (2001) maintain, the historical context is helpful in understanding entrepreneurial capitalism in East Asia and the limits of cultural explanations. Admittedly, national culture is an important influence on the organization of societies, business systems and institutions, and on individual, group and organizational behavior (Fukuyama, 1995; Landes, 1998; Redding, 1990; Westwood, 1997). Culture does matter, and its frequency in social science research reflects this (Huntington and Harrison, 2000; Whitley, 1992). Yet, the culture argument is a thorny one that must be made with care to avoid the critique that it is always possible to find some cultural considerations to explain whatever has happened, particularly when there is a great deal of causal ambiguity in the success of the firms and industries being studied (Barney, 1991).

Although the culturist perspective on the success of East Asian entrepreneurial capitalism is interesting and captures a lot of attention, the account has several key flaws, four of which are illuminated by a better understanding of the historical context and development of the region. First, economic development in East Asia has shown long periods of both growth and stagnation, whereas the culture has been largely invariant, or at least has been treated that way by culturist studies (Singh, 2007). This means it is difficult to attribute recent economic growth to culture without some qualification. Second, the supposedly homogeneous Chinese culture yielded differences in behavior (subcultures) when various Chinese communities migrated to different countries around Southeast Asia. This lack of cultural homogeneity raises further questions about a uniform Confucian culture in East Asia influencing firm organization and performance. Third, the cultural argument has been heavily socially constructed by politicians, researchers, and governments in recent years as a post hoc explanation for entrepreneurial development (Dirlik, 1998). This raises significant validity questions about retrospective explanations for firm success without any process studies tracing firm and industry development. Finally, cultural and institutional factors apart from Confucianism, such as Taoism, Buddhism, Christianity, and varying forms of governance have also played a role in influencing the economic systems in East Asia (Berger and Hsiao, 1988; Studwell, 2007). There are further potential methodological issues with the culturist argument such as the ecological fallacy problem when using population level data to infer behavior of individuals or firms (King et al., 1994), problems with measurement of culture, and, as noted, fallacious assumptions of cultural homogeneity and time-invariance of culture. The methodological dimensions of these problems have been well covered elsewhere and are not addressed at length here (e.g. Gaur, et al., 2007; Singh, 2007).[6]

HISTORICAL CONTEXTS

Asia's Development: Miracle Growth?

Among the many successful East Asian economies, Japan is often cited as the exemplar for the culture and economic success claims (e.g. Johnson, 1982; Landes, 1998; Vogel, 1979). Japan has often been held up as a poor East Asian country that seemed to rise almost overnight to become the second largest economy in the world. Yet those who see the 'overnight' emergence of a powerful Japan only in the 1960s and 1970s overlook that country's relatively early industrialization in the nineteenth century and the military challenge it posed to several European powers and the United States in the first half of the twentieth century, particularly in World War Two. Industrialization in earnest came to the West in the mid-1800s, and Japan began to industrialize with the Meiji Restoration not long after that. Japan was able to accelerate its modernization by being a fast follower in a number of industries (Westney, 1987) and bringing in top foreign experts in numerous fields to help in that endeavor (Jones, 1980). Near the end of the nineteenth century, Japan was able to defeat a much larger and well-armed China in the Sino–Japanese War and a decade later, routed a major European power (Russia) in the Russo–Japanese War of 1904–05. By World War One, Japan was already an industrial power with near-universal education and literacy, a budding Pacific empire, and a powerful military (Andrain, 1994, pp. 31–4; Costello, 1982).

During World War One Japan took advantage of disruptions in the European economies to capture markets for consumer goods and textiles, first in Asia and later in Europe and America. In the 1920s, Japan boasted the world's third largest navy and the largest economy in Asia (Costello, 1982). By the late 1930s, its economy was third in the world; Japan's prewar auto industry was on a par with Europe's (Perkins 2000). Immediately before and during World War Two, Japan produced very impressive military hardware such as super battleships like the Yamato, the Long Lance Torpedo and the Zero fighter, and had designed the long-range six-engine Fugaku bomber, with which the Japanese planned to deliver the world's first smart bombs (and biological weapons that they had already tested) to North America (Costello, 1982; Francillon, 1979; Frank, 1999).[7] Thus, Japan's postwar economic miracle was hardly that; Japan was just returning to the economic prominence it held in the decades before the war.

The underdevelopment of other parts of Asia has also been exaggerated, which in turn can overstate current economic performance. Before the Industrial Revolution transformed the world's economy, the huge agricultural populations of Asia produced a significant share of the world's economic output. For instance, for much of the last millennium, China accounted for nearly a third of world GDP (Chen, 2009). At the time of the reign of Chinese Emperor Qian Long in the latter part of the eighteenth century, the Chinese economy was larger than that of the British Empire. At the end of the eighteenth century, Asia as a whole registered 37 per cent of the world's economic output. Yet by the twentieth century, Asia's share of GDP had dropped considerably, rising slightly back to 31 per cent by the end of the century (Perkins, 2000).

By the late twentieth century, Asian economies had recovered considerably from their weak performance in the previous two centuries, and were achieving growth rates of 8 to 10 per cent annually versus about 3 per cent in the West. Cultural arguments were suddenly back in vogue. The same cultural attributes that had been used by Weber and others to explain Asia's underdevelopment were now being used to explain Asia's rapid growth. Researchers and commentators explored the ways that kinship, racial, and ethnic ties created new international business networks and government–business partnerships, enabling low costs and rapid growth (e.g. Fallows, 1995; Kotkin, 1992; Mahbubani, 2008). If the culturist argument were correct, it would be hard to see how the relatively invariant Confucian cultures in East Asia could engender such sizeable variation in economic performance.

Further problems with the culturist argument are evidenced by the recent history of East Asian entrepreneurial capitalism (Baumol et al., 2007; Huang, 2008; Krugman, 1994). Returns in listed companies in East Asia have been far from impressive, even during the decade and a half boom years of equity markets, before the 2007–08 financial upheavals. In contrast to the tiger economies image, East Asia posted the worst stock market performance of any emerging region in the 1990s and 2000s. For example, from 1993 – when the first significant international investments came into Southeast Asian equity markets – to the end of 2006, total dollar returns with dividends reinvested in Indonesia and Malaysia were worse than for money left in a London bank account. Singapore produced less than half the gain of the New York or London markets, with which only the Hong Kong stock market was comparable. Thailand and the Philippines actually produced negative returns; this all remained generally true in 2009–10 in light of the large drops in equity markets in 2007–08.

East Asian history over the centuries shows other significant swings in economic performance and productive capacity in the region. The fact that several East Asian economies went from being leading economies throughout the Middle Ages, to stagnation for a century or two, then back to dynamic economic growth and again to checkered growth in recent years, challenges the validity of cultural factors as an explanation for entrepreneurial development. Clearly, the essential cultures did not change – at least few argue that they did. This additional scope and historical context alone suggests problems with the culturist argument, which are further evidenced by the lack of homogeneity in Chinese business around East Asia.

Culture and the Heterogeneity of Chinese Business

The large swings in performance of firms and economies in East Asia in the nineteenth and twentieth centuries cast doubt on culture's power to explain the growth of entrepreneurial capitalism. But simply because the performance of firms and economies has been inconsistent does not rule out culture's influence. Firm performance is multifaceted, and culture may be having a significant effect on organizations that is masked somewhat by the sharp ups and downs in world markets. This begs the question: do the firms in East Asia have key commonalties that can be explained by (relatively uniform) cultural variables putatively present in ethnic Chinese firms in Asia? Regionally common structures might suggest isomorphic cultural elements at work and suggest the importance of underlying cultural variables.

The central role of the family in Confucian-influenced society is a good starting place and requires little explanation. The Confucian system establishes clear hierarchical relationships within the family and between the family and higher levels of the government, culminating in the head of government. This system is still a central component of Chinese, Korean, and Japanese society. Yet how similar are the organizations of the region? Do they have some characteristics that have been derived from the same underlying (Confucian) culture or are other ethical philosophies such as Taoist, Buddhist, and Christian teachings, and other institutional factors also exerting influence?

The Chinese emigrants of the era of mass migration from the nineteenth century through the end of China's revolution in 1949 were not especially homogenous to begin with (Pan, 1990). This is evident in the matter of spoken language. China remains a place where one need journey only 100 kilometers from home to encounter a different, largely unintelligible Chinese dialect (DeFrancis, 1984). When migration out of China to Southeast Asia took place, people left home not so much as Chinese, but as members of rather different dialect groups that all happened to be from China, such as the Cantonese, Hainanese or Hakka, who grouped together (and did business together) in their new Southeast Asian domiciles (Pan, 1990). Explorer George Windsor Earl noted in the early 1800s that there was much friction among the various Chinese dialect groups in Southeast Asia, almost as if they were from different countries (Earl, 1837). Victor Purcell, writing just after World War Two, observed that different Chinese dialect groups in Southeast Asia had been brought into a proximity not experienced in China. This led to a great deal of friction, not cooperation, in their adopted homelands. People groups speaking different dialects regarded one another almost as foreigners and conflict was common (Purcell, 1947). Some dialect groups even blamed others (such as the Hakka or Cantonese) for fanning the Taiping Revolution and other uprisings in China (Yu, 2002).

The fragmentation by dialect groups also created significant differences in migrants' behavior (Pan, 1990). For example, the Hakka people often owned Chinese medicine shops, the Hainanese opened coffee shops, and the Shanghai natives ran garment factories. The tendency for the dialect groups to stick together and create their own associations reinforced the diversity among firms and business groups in Southeast Asia (Pan, 1990). In such circumstances, the indistinct association between countries and their cultures limits conclusions to broad generalizations that have little explanatory value. Ethnic Chinese business is not a uniform, self-contained entity, but exhibits a great deal of variation. The assumed Chinese transnational ethnicity and the implied economic relationships among ethnic Chinese entrepreneurs need to be put in the context of production processes centered in foreign direct investment and sophisticated supply chains around Asia (Yeung, 2004).

If the firms in Southeast Asia and Hong Kong are rather diverse, this further calls into question the uniform culturist argument. With such localized identities come parochial and sometimes conflicting values and interests among Chinese businesses, which may bear closer resemblance to a global patchwork of many small enterprises that have little similarity with each other (Kao, 1993; Studwell, 2007; Wilkinson, 1996). East Asian firms and particularly overseas Chinese ones can be quite different and do not work together as the culturists predict (Studwell, 2007). In business dealings, the Taiwanese often distrust their Hong Kong or mainland counterparts, whereas Singaporeans are conscious of deep-seated differences between themselves and the mainland Chinese. It is interesting that when the Singapore government decided to create a major industrial park in China they did not choose a Chinese province in which they would have clan and dialect connections, such as Guangdong or Fujian, but rather they selected a region west of Shanghai, where they perceived the future business prospects to be strongest, contrary to what a culturist argument would predict.

Researchers have often used the major East Asian conglomerates as exemplars of Confucian businesses.[8] Can many East Asian firms be characterized as 'smaller and younger versions' of the most successful conglomerates in the region, such as those run by Hong Kong's Li Ka Shing or Malaysia's Robert Kuok? Are they similar to the nimble billionaires described in business literature such as *Forbes Global* or the hagiographies on Chinese business leaders (Chan, 1996; G.T. Lim, 2004; MacBeth, 2003)? Many must believe this, because a literature review on Chinese enterprise in East Asia shows that the research has been limited to a number of key individuals and conglomerates. Yet recent research has led to doubts as to whether a few conglomerates run by a handful of Asia's leading ethnic Chinese-owned firms can be used as the research site to support the culturist argument. Hong Kong, in spite of its laissez faire image, has rather limited competition in a number of areas from banking to airlines, to cargo handling to retail, all of which benefits the largest regional firms such as Mr Li Ka-Shing's Cheung Kong. Several other regional economies have done the same thing: for example Macau allowed Stanley Ho to enjoy a four-decade monopoly in casino gambling (which ended in 2002). Although much popular literature would argue that there is extensive business cooperation among Chinese entrepreneurs, detailed empirical studies have indicated that such ethnic capital is concentrated in the hands of a small number of family firms, almost Latin America style (Claessens et al., 2000; *Economist*, 2009). The average ethnic Chinese family firm is not a smaller version of the large East Asian conglomerates, and the large conglomerates can hardly be called 'Confucian capitalists', as many of them derived initial success from government concessions and licenses (Studwell, 2007; *Economist*, 2009).

The Social Construction of Confucianism

The recent intellectual history of Confucianism presents a third difficulty with the culturist argument and reinforces the necessity of understanding historical processes.[9] As noted, those determined to find the roots of entrepreneurial success in ethnic Chinese communities in Asia have been aided in their views by a fashionable theory. What the Protestant ethic has done for Europe, it is posited, Confucianism has done for East Asian societies (Chen, 2001). Yet the insistence on Confucianism and its influence on commerce in East Asia is heavily socially constructed, having been presented in recent years to explain the growth of entrepreneurial capitalism in East Asia, particularly in ethnic Chinese communities.

That there might be a Confucian variant of capitalism was an idea that did not originate in China or among Chinese scholars but in recent scholarship in the West, with extensive government support in East Asia (Dirlik, 1998). Though many in the postwar period held that Confucianism and traditional aspects of Chinese culture hindered entrepreneurial development, Japan's rise and China's reforms under Deng Xiao-ping led to a gradual restoration of Confucian ideology (Dirlik, 1998). Neo-Confucian societies, as Hermann Kahn (1979) described them, were thought to register higher growth rates than other cultures because of two related sets of characteristics that included the nurturing of dedicated, responsible, and educated individuals with an enhanced sense of commitment and loyalty to the family and its business. These were thought to be cultural ideals embedded in the Confucian ethic.

Kahn's observations have been echoed and extended by many writers and researchers from the popular press, sociology, management, and history (Kotkin, 1992; MacFarquhar, 1980; Mahbubani, 2008; Pan, 1990; Redding, 1990). Over the years, the research become more detailed and nuanced, attributing further elements of Confucianism to Chinese capitalism while omitting the anti-entrepreneurship elements. Confucian values, as expressed in daily life through strong family structures, commitment to education, and kinship or pseudo-kinship social networks are among the most frequently researched and cited of such Chinese cultural characteristics. The discourse was further broadened through a series of conferences, especially in East Asia and around the Pacific Rim including the University of Hawaii. These conferences produced numerous proceedings and volumes of discussions on Confucianism and its relationship with modernization and entrepreneurship (Dirlik, 1992). Numerous articles have been published in the People's Republic of China – over one thousand on Confucianism in the 1980s alone – only a few years after many Confucian temples and artifacts were destroyed in the Cultural Revolution's effort to root out vestiges of Confucianism. It may be no exaggeration to point to the discussion of Confucianism as one of the most prolific intellectual industries of that decade (Dirlik, 1998).

Singapore was particularly aggressive in its Confucian and Sinification campaigns. In the late 1970s, a movement got under way under the direction of the Singapore government and what was the first Chinese-language university outside China – Nanyang University (now the English language-based Nanyang Technological University). Former Premier Lee Kuan Yew proclaimed to a Chinese New Year's gathering in 1982 the importance of instilling Confucian values in Singapore's citizens, particularly the schoolchildren. Singapore also instituted a very successful 'speak Mandarin' campaign whereby Chinese students in Singapore would learn Mandarin Chinese as a second language, or study in a Chinese language school. The Singapore government introduced Confucianism into the school curriculum and started to fund conferences on Confucianism and entrepreneurship (Dirlik, 1992).

Taiwan similarly built its legitimacy as an alternative form of governance to that of Mainland China upon its faithfulness to a more traditional Chinese culture, emphasizing Confucianism. Mainland China has started funding Confucian institutes, and in early 2009, China funded the first Confucian institute in the Caribbean, at the prestigious University of the West Indies in Jamaica.

This all suggests that what has come to be called 'Confucian capitalism' may be little more than a social construction of a new post-revolutionary discourse on capitalism. This is a phenomenon that British historian Eric Hobsbawn (Hobsbawn and Ranger, 1992) has called 'the invention of tradition'; that is, the reorganization and rearrangement of social, political, and ideological characteristics associated with a particular tradition or value set – in this case Confucian values (transformed to 'Asian Values' in Malaysia and other East Asian countries where Chinese are in the minority) – to achieve certain policy ends. The recent intellectual history of this topic suggests that Confucianism as a belief system is not well specified and may be a recent construction, especially with respect to its impact on commerce. This led one Korean researcher to write that the rapid transformation of scholarly opinion on Confucianism is unmatched in the evaluation and application of a set of traditions (Koh, 1992). The extensive attention given to Confucianism would have been unlikely without the intense activity and sponsorship of the 1980s and early 1990s by East Asian governments (Koh, 1992). Much research remains to be done on the characteristics of Confucian organizations and the implications for their structure and performance.

Other Institutional Factors

A fourth problem with a strict Confucian-culturist view and its impact on entrepreneurial capitalism is that Confucianism is but one of many forces acting on firms and entrepreneurs in East Asia; others include Taoism, Buddhism, and Christianity (Berger and Hsiao, 1988). Taoism, with its balancing forces, plays a big part in the day to day life in Chinese communities (Nisbett, 2004). Yet Confucianism and Taoism have rather different views of urban and rural life, money-making and commercial activity. Indeed, there is an adage that every Chinese is a Confucianist when he is successful and a Taoist when he is a failure (Nisbett, 2004). This is not to say that Confucianism is not important, but it needs to be specified clearly and its effects separated from Taoism, and other nebulous cultural terms such as the ever-present *guanxi*, which is treated like an all-purpose, unique cultural phenomenon, even though it is not.

What can be gathered from Confucian and Taoist influence on Chinese societies? Confucianism traditionally scorned hard work and all forms of physical exertion while idealizing leisure and effortless success. This might be surprising to North Americans raised on rugged individualism or to Japanese familiar with stories extolling the hard work of farmer and reformer Ninomiya Kinjiro. The Confucian gentleman had long fingernails and pale skin, to show that he did not have to work outside doing manual labor. Taoism reinforced this attitude by elevating to the highest philosophical level the principle of *wu-wei*, or non-effort, of accomplishing things with the minimum expenditure of energy. Similarly, in Chinese military thinking, such as the work of Sun Tzu – which is very influential in East Asian business thought – it was best to win battles not by exerting prodigious effort but by compelling the opponent to exhaust himself (Sun, 1963; Graff and Highham, 2002). Writing on Chinese business makes a similar point about how effective strategies will allow opponents to flail away until they are tired or quit (Chen, 2001).

Apart from winning through less effort, Taoist philosophy emphasizes the importance of 'good luck', the likelihood of which can be increased by proper ritual acts (Tu, 1996). Taoism has the concept of the Tao (the Way), or the forces of nature and history, that gives a philosophical foundation to the basic Chinese view that much of life is determined by forces external to the actors involved. In this view, some people are more skilled than others in going with history's ebb and flow and thus receiving good luck. Others take their own lonely path and are destined for bad luck or too much extra effort. Still others foolishly buck the tide altogether and are destined to frustration and defeat (Nisbett, 2004). This stress on good fortune does not, however, produce a fatalistic approach to life as there are always things that can be done to return to good luck. If things turn out badly, it might have only been bad luck, attributable to the individual's failure to appease the correct authorities, which can be corrected in time. Similarly, Chinese culture also stresses the rewards of supplication, or humbling oneself, a psychological orientation that also goes against the grain of the self-reliant individual (Lai et al., 2010).

The paradoxical combination of achievement, conformity, and dependency was central to the traditional Chinese socialization practices, which sought to teach the child early that conformity to the rituals and wishes of others was the best way to good luck and that being 'different' was dangerous. Confucian duties of the sons to the father, and of the younger and older brothers to each other, were lifetime obligations. The tradition was, thus, inward looking, and there was a basic instinct to distrust people outside of the family and close friends, which further illustrates the mixed effect Confucianism has on commerce (Spence, 1990). In contrast, many Japanese primary schools prominently displayed a statue of Ninomiya Kinjiro, the nineteenth-century reformer who used to carry his firewood while at the same time reading a book, to illustrate diligence to the Japanese people. In Japan, however, the tests of achievement in both samurai and merchant families were in terms of competition against outside parties and forces. Moreover, a son or younger brother could set out on his own; if successful, he became a *gosenzo* – the head of a new family line, established through his risk-taking and independence, not unlike the Horatio Alger-style, rugged individualist extolled in the US.

What does the historical record say about the important philosophies of Confucianism, Taoism and their impact on early entrepreneurship in China? The Chinese invented paper, printing by movable type, gunpowder, an early mechanical clock, the magnetic compass, and an early piston bellows. Yet these technological advances were often developed by Taoist monks and scholars, primarily for ritual or ceremony at the behest of the Emperor or Mandarinate and not for commercial purposes (Kennedy, 1987). Property rights did not exist such that these innovations could be protected, developed, and wealth concentrated for further expansion. Many in China and later in Southeast Asia thought entering the Civil Service was the surest way of success and this drew some of the most intelligent and innovative individuals into government bookkeeping and bureaucracy as the most sought after and respected profession (Pan, 1990). Similarly, for every Chinese citizen who prospered from trading, there were hundreds who remained aloof from commercial activities. More recently, higher levels of the Protestant work ethic in Malaysia than in Britain (Furnham and Muhiudeen, 1984) and the existence of high levels of Confucian-style values in the US (Robertson and Hoffman, 2000) raise further doubts about the usefulness of national culture for explaining entrepreneurial capitalism, and emphasize further the importance of the historical context of development in these economies (Dielman, 2010).

The enthusiasm for business is by no means a general Chinese trait. In China itself, the merchant has been disparaged as the lowest of people until the economic reform period, though in some official circles in China the entrepreneur is still not to be trusted, even after decades of economic reform (Huang, 2008). In a society ordered by Confucian values, the ability to profit from trading was never admired, and this likely dampened

Chinese entrepreneurship. Confucian disregard for science and commerce has also at times been a constraint to economic development. If there is such a thing as a tradition of entrepreneurship among the Chinese, it is found more among the coastal Chinese and the diaspora (Scarborough, 1998). The fiercely independent Teochew entrepreneurs and the Hokkien traders who sailed to Southeast Asia were not heirs to some long mercantile, Confucian tradition. Rather, they were people who, by emigrating, were able to leave the local culture and institutions behind and seek out the trading opportunities that allowed them to build their businesses and to keep their wealth.

DISCUSSION

The previous section shows ways in which historical context can help to improve the understanding of culture's impact on entrepreneurial capitalism and development in East Asia, particularly with regard to culture's influence. At the most general level, the relative economic success of East Asian economies and firms suggests that certain factors including cohesive, thrifty families, a focus on prescribed roles, discipline, and filial piety have a cultural basis and are important to entrepreneurship. These factors, however, are also present in important family business systems around the world, which raises the question of whether institutions, particularly the rule of law, and resulting organizational processes and structures, explain more about the industrial systems in East Asia and other developing economies than culture (Peng et al., 2008; Singh, 2007).

Specifically, the more abstract argument about a Confucian value system driving a unique form of Chinese entrepreneurialism does not stand up well to analytical scrutiny. In particular, it fails to distinguish between Confucianism and a roster of vague moral teachings including influences from Taoism, Buddhism and Christianity, and other belief systems that are not always observed in practice by their followers. Nor does it explain the significant differences in entrepreneurial orientation among various dialect groups outside of China. Notions of a cultural imperative downplay historical context. Those who say that Chinese are born entrepreneurs commit the same logical fallacy as those who say European Jews were born to be jewelers and bankers. Such arguments overlook that in pre-nineteenth century Europe, Jews were excluded from guilds and from many areas of trade and farming, while the Christian church proscribed its followers from lending money at interest. Most economic opportunities for European Jews were restricted while those in banking were thus easily available.

Something similar is true of vocations in Southeast Asia. Colonial administrators were drawn from indigenous populations, while many commercial areas associated with trading, gambling, and real estate were left to the ethnic Chinese immigrants. Educated Indians and Sri Lankans in the British Empire tended to be recruited for government and professional positions. Hence an observer outside the high court in downtown Singapore or Kuala Lumpur today could be forgiven for believing that some underlying cultural influence accounts for the large number of lawyers and judges of subcontinental heritage. Yet this proclivity to law is not created by Indian culture, but is based on the legacy of British colonial rule on the Malay Peninsula. When the Chinese arrived in Southeast Asia, they were frequently barred from government service and from many professions, and were often not permitted to own agricultural land or engage in farming; opportunities in trade and commerce, however, were left open to them. When World War Two came, Japan, as an occupying power, turned to established Chinese traders to help run the local economies. This opened further commercial opportunities from banking to rice trading to property management, hotels and gaming which Southeast Asia's Chinese-owned conglomerates effectively exploited (Seagrave, 1995; Studwell, 2007).

But there is Confucianism and neo-Confucianism, and the Confucianism the exponents of this theory are talking about is not that of old imperial China, but a set of values and attitudes common to all the national cultures falling within the orbit of Chinese civilization and Confucian influence (Bell and Chaibong, 2003). They further argue that these attributes – a developed capacity for discipline and delayed gratification, an emphasis on harmony in social relations, and respect for superiors – have given the tiger economies of East Asia a comparative advantage in modern capitalist development. In this view, Chinese managers, who have a widely noted cultural tendency to rely on informal ties and personal connections to achieve organizational goals, fit well within this regional trading economy, and possibly the increasingly global world economy. However, Boisot and Child (1996), Peng (1997), and Peng and Heath (1996) argue that, in addition to cultural influences, institutional imperatives during the transition may further necessitate the extensive reliance on personalized exchange relationships, a (cultural) reliance that should wither over time.

Such an institutional interpretation is borne out by similar findings from developing economies throughout Central and Eastern Europe (e.g. Grabber and Stark, 1997; Buck et al., 1998). In these countries there is little influence of the Chinese (or Asian) culture that places a premium on interpersonal ties. The importance of cooperative relationships or family ties for businesses in Asia and other emerging economies is due to the underdevelopment of institutions and markets rather than to cultural factors (Fukuyama, 1995; Peng and Heath, 1996). Ethnic business networks in Asia can also be explained by inadequate markets, corrupt governments, weak legal systems, poor financial and banking sectors, and the absence of reliable intermediaries, as opposed to culture. Rather than being primarily driven by cultural values such as trust and collectivist tendencies, Fukuyama (1995) argues that these networks operate within low trust cultures driven importantly by inadequate institutions. Chandler's (1990) concept of 'personal capitalism' to explain the overlaps of structure and management of family businesses in Britain has potential for explaining business patterns in Asia, as Carney (1998) illustrates with Chinese family businesses in Hong Kong.

Culture might be a useful latent moderator, but is unable to explain much on its own, apart from the institutional and historical, path-dependent context of its setting (Singh, 2007). Though there is correlational evidence on culture and GDP growth (Bond and Hofstede, 1990), much research remains to be done on culture in general, the prevalence of Confucian and other cultural values among entrepreneurs in East Asia, and the relationship of these values to individual and organizational behavior, and (ultimately) to firm structure and performance.

Implications for Research

To understand entrepreneurship and competitiveness in Southeast Asia is to understand Chinese businesses, how they were started, and how they have developed. Although there has been much recent research on the Chinese family business (e.g. Ahlstrom et al., 2004; Carney, 1998; Yeung, 2002; 2006), researchers have often treated the cases largely ahistorically and have seldom followed the growth and development of these firms over time (Ahlstrom et al., 2004; Roseberry and O'Brien, 1991). Past research has often looked at the contemporary conditions of Chinese firms around Southeast Asia and concluded, from their reported profit margins, and growth rates, and from surveys of competitiveness, that these firms are becoming the next, Sony, Toyota, or Samsung (e.g. *Asia, Inc.*, 1997). Yet building a brand and competing globally is a notoriously complex process and it often takes years if not decades for a firm to build those capabilities. This is reflected in past lists of potential globally competitive firms among Chinese family businesses that failed to become world beaters, often because of internal family dissent (Cushman, 1991; Wong, 1985), or government intervention (*Economist*, 2009; Huang, 2008) – problems which would have been highlighted by historical or process research intended to trace their development.

A very limited amount of research has been conducted that actually follows the development of these firms (Dielman, 2010). Such research is needed to identify the regionally and globally competitive firms as opposed to a cross sectional slice of what may only be today's good performers, benefiting from government concessions or arbitrage opportunities (Yoshihara, 1988; Studwell, 2007). The few studies that have been conducted using historical research examining these firms' development and the impact of local institutions have eschewed cross sectional studies, preferring to follow these firms' life cycles.[10] Wong (1985) conducted one such study, finding that Chinese family businesses in East Asia typically go through four stages of development: emergent, centralized, segmented, and disintegrative.

The disintegrative stage is of particular interest as it calls attention to why Chinese family firms have had a great many problems in growing beyond a certain size or establishing a sustained presence in an industry (Ahlstrom et al., 2004; Carney, 1998; Yoshihara, 1988). For example, one major factor contributing to the disintegration of the family firm is the issue of succession and control of the firm or its divisions. There are several prominent examples, such as the gradual breakup of the Haw Par Group built by Aw Boon Haw (the firm that produces Tiger Balm ointments). At one point, the Haw Par Group was considered a major player in the regional newsprint business, but it has gone the way of many disputed family firms. In order to avoid problems associated with attributing causality to correlations, firms such as these need to be studied over time using process research (Van de Ven, 2007), with the help of archival data such as firm documents, financial data and news reports to ascertain how they started, how they grew and how centrifugal forces may have affected their sustainability. This chapter has challenged the popular notions of a common culture-based form of Chinese entrepreneurial capitalism and suggested ways in which historical study can help to build understanding.

The phenomenon of troubled family firms is by no means unique to Chinese culture or Confucianism, though some commentators have suggested that problems may arise from the purported low trust nature of Chinese societies (Fukuyama, 1995). Goody (1996, pp. 141–8) discovered similar problems among family firms in India, and Rose (1993) found a similar problem with succession and continuity of family firms in the West. Even studies of the old Quaker family firms that were so active in early British and American commerce found some problems with succession, control, and breakup of family firms in spite of strong cultural admonitions to the contrary (Walvin, 1998). A clearer understanding of the entrepreneurial firm and its process of founding and growth (or breakup) will help to identify processes that are common to most family firms or to isolate those unique to entrepreneurial firms in ethnic Chinese communities.

Expanding the scope of analysis beyond cross sectional studies or literature reviews of the past few years shows that the culturist argument for economic development in East Asia is problematic. This chapter concurs with the argument that there is a heterogeneity of styles of business organization and management and influences among members of the Chinese business community (e.g. Hodder, 1996). In addition, even the overseas Chinese in East Asia are not homogeneous and do not have a homogeneous cultural base, apart from an emphasis on family business and connections, which may be a reaction to the institutional structure of the region (Peng, 2003). Research on the development of firms in East Asia and the historical context, as well as the history of the region, would shed much more light on how firms and economies developed, what can be learned from the East Asian experience, and how indispensable (or dispensable) is culture in that developmental experience.

In sum, culture does impact entrepreneurship; it is implausible that a force as prevalent as culture, within which business activities are embedded, can be irrelevant. Culture is a broadly based underlying cognitive factor that affects society in general. Entrepreneurship rests on the argument that the contextualization that will improve strategy theory should primarily focus on the institutional environment and stage of development, not on cultural influences.

Yet little research has been able to establish the direct and specific impact of cultural values on entrepreneurship firm strategy and performance (Singh, 2007). Much research measures culture implicitly at the national level, or uses a single measure for everyone in a given country. This makes it difficult to conclude whether the observed differences between firm samples in two countries are due to cross-cultural or cross-national differences (Lau and Ngo, 2001). In the 1950s and 1960s, social scientists argued that East Asia was not likely to become wealthy because Confucianism, Taoism, and other socio-cultural factors limited the appetite for goods and services and further hindered commercial development. But, as is well known, the last several decades have witnessed the significant economic growth of Japan, Hong Kong, Singapore, South Korea, Taiwan, and Mainland China. As such, the current line of culturist thinking argues that the current success of Asia is culture-driven and based on the emphasis given to study, hard work and harmonious relationships. Yet how did this happen without any major changes in culture? If Asia's workforce is hard-working and harmonious because of culture, it should have also been that way one or two hundred years ago. If culture was not causing economic growth in those economies in past centuries, how did essentially the same culture start causing economic growth recently? To use cultural variables as a direct explanation for the economic growth in East Asia over the past several decades one would have to find some significant and striking changes in those variables in recent years, yet such changes did not occur. As this chapter has argued, culture may moderate commercial activity but it falls short as a direct explanation for entrepreneurship and economic growth.

Future research utilizing a historically based, organizational level of analysis is necessary to better understand entrepreneurial capitalism in East Asia. Research into the dynamics of these economies and their organizations should be undertaken through an inter-disciplinary approach. This could help provide insights into new theoretical perspectives or models that could be developed to explain more cogently the effects of institutions, culture, history and path dependencies on the development of entrepreneurial capitalism in East Asia (Khanna, 2009). This chapter contributes to that effort by suggesting several of the problems and limitations of the culturist argument, and what needs to be better understood about the history of a region so that cogent cultural factors can be grasped and utilized in future study of the development of entrepreneurial capitalism in East Asia.

NOTES

1. The term 'Confucian capitalism' is a heuristic term to describe the historically and geographically specific form of entrepreneurial capitalism that refers to the social organization and political economy of the Confucian-influenced economies. These include the 'overseas Chinese' societies outside mainland China proper, particularly in East and Southeast Asia (Hong Kong, Macau, Taiwan, Singapore, Indonesia, Malaysia, the Philippines, Thailand and Vietnam), as well as Korea and Japan.
2. Malaysia, Thailand, and Vietnam also have sizeable Chinese minorities and have experienced solid economic growth.
3. The culturist explanation (in the East Asian context) stresses learned cultural values such as need for achievement, thrift and other values often linked to Confucianism in explaining the development of entrepreneurial capitalism and economic growth in East Asia (Wilkinson, 1996).
4. Although Weber did not think Confucianism was particularly helpful to capitalism's development, he thought that the Confucian emphasis on hierarchy and order would help to build an economy once capitalism was suitably introduced and nurtured (Pye, 2000).
5. Rentier capitalism refers to a type of capitalism whereby much income is generated from property and received as interest, rents, dividends, or capital gains. In East Asia, rentier capitalism and its gains are thought to be heavily derived from government concessions (such as gaming rights or local rice distribution) given to the favored – often well-connected Chinese businesspeople (Studwell, 2007).
6. There are several other methodological and research design problems related to the way culture is measured and used in many studies. For example, even if culture and related factors influence firm strategy and performance, their impact is likely to be complex and indirect, possibly by influencing organizational structures, processes, authority relationships, and corporate governance. As a result, culture's impact on strategy, entrepreneurship, and individual firm performance is still far from accepted (Gaur et al., 2007; Shane, 2008; Singh, 2007).
7. The Fugaku six-engine bomber was designed to have a range of 20 000 kilometers – sufficient to attack the US West Coast and return to Japan or fly through to German-occupied Europe. Designed in 1942, it never went into production as the project was cancelled not long after the Allied invasion of France in 1944. Japan did continue with the development of smart bomb biological weapons. After successfully testing them in China, Japan had several ready and scheduled for use, to be delivered by light aircraft launched from modified submarines. Only the war's end prevented their deployment against the United States west coast in the autumn of 1945 (Francillon, 1979; Frank, 1999, pp. 324–5).
8. It was not uncommon for culturalist writers to argue that East Asian business leaders such as Thaksin Shinawatra, the embattled former Prime Minister of Thailand, and Indonesia's Bob Hasan are exemplary Confucian business leaders who did not receive significant government concessions in building their business empires. Recent research (and events) in Thailand, Indonesia and elsewhere strongly suggest otherwise (Studwell, 2007).
9. Neither the intellectual history of Confucianism nor the process of entrepreneurial development is meant to be exhaustive here. Rather, they provide an illustration of what must be studied to unpack changing dynamics of Chinese capitalism so that culture's impact can be suitably addressed.
10. It is always interesting to follow up on the lists of 'most competitive' family firms in Southeast Asia a decade later. For example, a fine Asian fast food chain – Jollibee of the Philippines – was supposed to dispose of McDonalds in short order because Jollibee had better 'connections' among the overseas Chinese around the region and understood Asian tastes better than McDonalds (Pritchard, 1998). About a decade later, Jollibee had about 160 restaurants around East Asia, while McDonalds has over a thousand – and that number excludes those in Japan.

REFERENCES

Ahlstrom, D., M.N. Young, E.S. Chan and G.D. Bruton (2004), 'Facing constraints to growth? Overseas Chinese entrepreneurs and traditional business practices in East Asia', *Asia Pacific Journal of Management*, **21**(3), 263–85.

Andrain, C.F. (1994), *Comparative Political Systems: Policy Performance and Social Change*, Armonk, NY: M.E. Sharpe.

Asia, Inc. (1997), 'Aiming high: 50 most competitive companies', 6 June, 34–37.

Barney, J. (1991), 'Firm resources and sustained competitive advantage', *Journal of Management*, **17**(1), 99–120.

Baumol, W.J., R.E. Litan and C.J. Schramm (2007), *Good Capitalism, Bad Capitalism*, New Haven, CT: Yale University Press.

Bell, D.A. and H. Chaibong (eds) (2003), *Confucianism for the Modern World*, Cambridge: Cambridge University Press.

Berger, P.L. and H.M. Hsiao (1988), *In Search of an East Asian Developmental Model*, New Brunswick, NJ: Transaction Publishers.

Boisot, M. and J. Child (1996), 'From fiefs to clans and network capitalism: explaining China's emerging economic order', *Administrative Science Quarterly*, **41**(4), 600–28.

Bond, M.H. and G. Hofstede (1990), 'The cash value of Confucian values', in S.R. Clegg and S.G. Redding (eds), *Capitalism in Contrasting Cultures*, New York: Walter de Gruyter, pp. 383–90.

Buck, T., I. Filatotchev and M. Wright (1998), 'Agents, stakeholders and corporate governance in Russian firms', *Journal of Management Studies*, **35**(1), 81–104.

Carney, M. (1998), 'A management capacity constraint? Obstacles to the development of the overseas Chinese family business', *Asia Pacific Journal of Management*, **15**(2), 137–62.

Carney, M., E. Gedajlovic and X. Yang (2009), 'Varieties of Asian capitalism: toward an institutional theory of Asian enterprise', *Asia Pacific Journal of Management*, **26**(3), 361–80.

Chan, A.B. (1996), *Li Ka-shing: Hong Kong's Elusive Billionaire*, Toronto: Macmillan.

Chan, W.K.K. and A. McElderry (eds) (1998), 'Historical patterns of Chinese business', *Journal of Asian Business*, Special Issue, **14**(1), 1–69.

Chandler, A.D. (1990), *Scale and Scope: The Dynamics of Industrial Capitalism*, Cambridge, MA: Belknap Press.

Chen, M. (2001), *Inside Chinese Business: A Guide for Managers Worldwide*, Boston, MA: Harvard Business School Press.

Chen, M. (2009), 'Competitive dynamics research', *Asia Pacific Journal of Management*, **26**(1), 5–25.

Claessens, S., S. Djankov and L. Lang (2000), 'The separation of ownership and control in East Asian corporations', *Journal of Financial Economics*, **58**, 81–112.

Cochran, T. (1960), 'Cultural factors in economic growth', *Journal of Economic History*, **20**, 515–30.

Costello, J. (1982), *The Pacific War 1941–1945*, New York: Harper Perennial.

Cushman, J.W. (1991), *Family and State: The Formation of a Sino-Thai Tin Mining Dynasty, 1979–1932*, Singapore: Oxford University Press.

De Bary, W.T. (1988), *East Asian Civilizations*, Cambridge, MA: Harvard University Press.

DeFrancis, J. (1984), *The Chinese Language: Fact and Fantasy*, Honolulu: University of Hawaii Press.

Dielman, M. (2010), 'Shock-imprinting: external shocks and ethnic Chinese business groups in Indonesia', *Asia Pacific Journal of Management*, **27**(3), 481–502.

Dirlik, A. (1992), 'The Asia-Pacific idea', *Journal of World History*, **3**(1), 55–79.

Dirlik, A. (ed.) (1998), *What is in a Rim? Critical Perspectives on the Pacific Region Idea*, Lanham, MD: Rowman and Littlefield.

Earl, G.W. (1837), *The Eastern Seas*, London: W.H. Allen.

Economist (2009), 'Pharaoh capitalism', 14 February, p. 82.

Eklof, S. (2002), 'Politics, business and democratization in Indonesia', in E.T. Gomez (ed.), *Political Business in East Asia*, London: Routledge, pp. 216–49.

Enright, M.J. (2005), 'Rethinking China's competitiveness', *Far Eastern Economic Review*, **168**(9), 16–20.

Fallows, J. (1995), *Looking at the Sun: The Rise of the New East Asian Economic and Political Systems*, New York: Vintage.

Francillon, R.J. (1979), *Japanese Aircraft of the Pacific War*, London: Putnam and Co Ltd.

Frank, R.B. (1999), *Downfall: The End of the Imperial Japanese Empire*, New York: Penguin Books.

Fukuyama, F. (1995), *Trust: The Social Virtues and the Creation of Prosperity*, New York: Free Press.

Furnham, A. and C. Muhiudeen (1984), 'The Protestant work ethic in Britain and Malaysia', *Journal of Social Psychology*, **122**(2), 157–61.

Gaur, A.S., A. Delios and K. Singh (2007), 'Institutional environments, staffing strategies, and subsidiary performance', *Journal of Management*, **33**(4), 611–36.

Gibney, F. (1992), *The Pacific Century: America and Asia in a Changing World*, New York: Scribners.

Gomez, E.T. and H.M. Hsiao (eds) (2001), *Chinese Business in Southeast Asia: Contesting Cultural Explanations, Researching Entrepreneurship*, Richmond, UK: Curzon.

Goody, J. (1996), *The East in the West*, Cambridge, UK: Cambridge University Press.

Grabber, G. and D. Stark (1997), 'Organizing diversity: evolutionary theory, network analysis and postsocialism', *Regional Studies*, **31**(5), 533–44.

Graff, D.A. and R. Higham (eds) (2002), *A Military History of China,* Boulder, CO: Westview Press.

Hamilton, G.G. (2006), *Commerce and Capitalism in Chinese Societies*, London: Routledge.

Harrison, L.E. (2006), *The Central Liberal Truth: How Politics Can Change a Culture and Save it from Itself*, Oxford: Oxford University Press.

Hayton, J.C., G. George and S. Zahra (2002), 'National culture and entrepreneurship: a review of behavioral research', *Entrepreneurship Theory and Practice*, **26**(2), 33–53.

Hobsbawm, E. and T. Ranger (eds) (1992), *The Invention of Tradition*, Cambridge, UK: Cambridge University Press.

Hodder, R. (1996), *Merchant Princes of The East: Cultural Delusions, Economic Success, and The Overseas Chinese in Southeast Asia*, Chichester, NY: John Wiley and Sons.

Huang, Y. (2008), *Capitalism with Chinese Characteristics: Entrepreneurship and the State*, Cambridge, UK: Cambridge University Press.

Huntington, S.P. and L.E. Harrison (2000), *Culture Matters: How Values Shape Human Progress*, New York: Basic Books.

Jenks, C. (1993), *Culture: Key Ideas*, London: Routledge.

Johnson, C. (1982), *MITI and the Japanese Miracle: The Growth of Industrial Policy, 1925–1975*, Stanford, CA: Stanford University Press.

Jones, H.J. (1980), *Live Machines: Hired Foreigners and Meiji Japan*, Tenterden, UK: Paul Norbury Publications.

Kahn, H. (1979), *World Economic Development: 1979 and Beyond*, New York: Morrow Quill.

Kao, J. (1993), 'The worldwide web of Chinese business', *Harvard Business Review*, **71**(2), 24–36.

Kennedy, P. (1987), *The Rise and Fall of the Great Powers*, New York: Random House.

Khanna, T. (2009), 'Learning from economic experiments in China and India', *Academy of Management Perspectives*, **23**(2): 36–43.

King, G., R.O. Keohane and S. Verba (1994), *Designing Social Inquiry: Scientific Inference in Qualitative Research*, Princeton, NJ: Princeton University Press.

Koh, B. (1992), 'Confucianism in Asia's modern transformation', *Korea Journal,* **32**(4), 46–64.

Kotkin, J. (1992), *Tribes: How Race, Religion, and Identity Determine Success in the New Global Economy*, New York: Random House.

Krugman, P. (1994), 'The myth of Asia's miracle', *Foreign Affairs*, **73**(6), 62–78.

Lai, J.Y.M., L.W. Lam and Y. Liu (2010), 'Do you really need help? A study of employee supplication and job performance in China', *Asia Pacific Journal of Management*, **27**(3), 541–60.

Landes, D. (1998), *The Wealth and Poverty of Nations*, New York: Norton.
Landes, D. (2000), 'Culture makes almost all the difference', in L.E. Harrison and S.P. Huntington (eds), *Culture Matters: How Human Values Shape Human Progress*, New York: Basic Books, pp. 2–13.
Lau, C.M. and H.Y. Ngo (2001), 'The HR system, organizational culture, and product innovation', *International Business Review*, **13**(6), 685–703.
Lever-Tracy, C. (2002), 'The impact of the Asian crisis on diaspora Chinese tycoons', *Geoforum*, **33**(3), 509–23.
Lever-Tracy, C., D. Ip and N. Tracy (1996), *The Chinese Diaspora and Mainland China*, London: Macmillan.
Lim, G.T. (2004), *My Story: Lim Goh Tong*, Subang Jaya, MY: Pelanduk Publications.
Lim, L.Y.C. (1996), 'The evolution of Southeast Asian business systems', *Journal of Southeast Asia Business*, **12**(1), 51–74.
Lim, L.Y.C. (2000), 'Southeast Asian Chinese business', *Journal of Asian Business*, **16**(1), 1–14.
Limlingan, V.S. (1986), *The Overseas Chinese in ASEAN*, Manila: Vita Development Co.
MacBeth, M. (2003), *Quiet Achiever: The Life and Times of Tan Sri Dr. Tan Chin Tuan*, London: Times.
MacFarquhar, R. (1980), 'The post-Confucian challenge', *Economist*, 9 February, 67–72.
Mahathir, M. (1999), *A New Deal for Asia*, Kuala Lumpur, Malaysia: Pelanduk.
Mahbubani, K. (2008), *The New Asian Hemisphere: The Irresistible Shift of Global Power to the East*, New York: Public Affairs.
Mallet, V. (2000), *The Trouble with Tigers: The Rise and Fall of South-east Asia*, London: HarperCollins.
Menkhoff, T. and S. Gerke (eds) (2002), *Chinese Entrepreneurship and Asian Business Networks*, Richmond, UK: Curzon.
Nisbett, R.E. (2004), *The Geography of Thought: How Asians and Westerners Think Differently . . . and Why*, New York: Free Press.
Ong, A. and D. Nonini (1997), 'Toward a cultural politics of diaspora and transnationalism', in A. Ong and D.M. Nonini (eds), *Ungrounded Empires*, London: Routledge, pp. 323–32.
Pan, L. (1990), *Sons of the Yellow Emperor: The Story of the Overseas Chinese*, Boston: Little, Brown & Co.
Peng, M.W. (1997), 'Firm growth in transition economies: three longitudinal cases from China, 1989–96', *Organization Studies*, **18**(3), 385–413.
Peng, M.W. (2003), 'Institutional transitions and strategic choices', *Academy of Management Review*, **28**(2), 275–96.
Peng, M.W. and P.S. Heath (1996), 'The growth of the firm in planned economies in transition: institutions, organizations, and strategic choice', *Academy of Management Review*, **21**(2), 492–528.
Peng, M.W., D.Y.L. Wang and Y. Jiang (2008), 'An institution-based view of international business strategy: a focus on emerging economies', *Journal of International Business Studies*, **39**(5), 920–36.
Perkins, D. (2000), 'Law, family ties and the East Asian way of business', in L.E. Harrison and S.P. Huntington (eds), *Culture Matters: How Human Values Shape Human Progress*, New York: Basic Books, pp. 232–44.
Pritchard, C. (1998), 'Big Mac rival makes a bee-line for the top', *Business Review Weekly*, 2 March, pp. 41–2.
Purcell, V. (1947), 'Chinese settlement in Melaka', *Journal of the Malayan Branch of the Royal Asiatic Society*, **20**(1), 15–25.
Pye, L.W. (2000), 'Asian values: from dynamos to dominoes?', in L.E. Harrison and S.P. Huntington (eds), *Culture Matters: How Human Values Shape Human Progress*, New York: Basic Books, pp. 244–55.
Redding, S.G. (1990), *The Spirit of Chinese Capitalism*, Berlin and New York: W. de Gruyter.
Rivera, T.C. (1991), *Class, the State and Foreign Capital: The Politics of Philippine Industrialization, 1950–1986*, unpublished PhD dissertation, Madison, WI: University of Wisconsin.
Robertson, C.J. and J.J. Hoffman (2000), 'How different are we? An investigation of confucian values in the US', *Journal of Managerial Issues*, **12**(1), 34–47.

Rose, M.B. (1993), 'Beyond Buddenbrooks: the family firm and the management of succession in nineteenth-century Britain', in J. Brown and M.B. Rose (eds), *Entrepreneurship, Networks and Modern Business*, Manchester: Manchester University Press.

Roseberry, W. and J. O'Brien (1991), 'Introduction', in J. O'Brien and W. Roseberry (eds), *Golden Ages, Dark Ages: Imagining the Past in Anthropology and History*, Berkeley: University of California Press, pp. 1–18.

Rowher, J. (1995), *Asia Rising. How History's Biggest Middle Class will Change the World*, Singapore: Butterworth-Heinemann.

Sachs, J. (2000), 'Notes on a new sociology of economic development', in L.E. Harrison and S.P. Huntington (eds), *Culture Matters: How Human Values Shape Human Progress*, New York: Basic Books, pp. 29–43.

Scarborough, J. (1998), 'Comparing Chinese and Western cultural roots: why East is East and . . .', *Business Horizons*, **41**(6), 15–24.

Seagrave, S. (1995), *Lords of the Rim: The Invisible Empire of the Overseas Chinese*, London: Bantam.

Shane, S. (1995), 'Uncertainty avoidance and the preference for innovation championing roles', *Journal of International Business Studies*, **26**(1), 47–68.

Shane, S. (2008), *The Illusions of Entrepreneurship: The Costly Myths that Entrepreneurs, Investors, and Policy Makers Live By*, New Haven, CT: Yale University Press.

Singh, K. (2007), 'The limited relevance of culture to strategy', *Asia Pacific Journal of Management*, **24**(4), 421–28.

Sowell, T. (1997), *Migrations and Cultures: A World View*, New York: Basic Books.

Spence, J.D. (1990), *The Search For Modern China*, New York: Norton.

Studwell, J. (2007), *Asian Godfathers: Money and Power in Hong Kong and Southeast Asia*, London: Profile Books.

Sun, T. (1963), *The Art of War*, S.B. Griffith (translation), London: Oxford University Press.

Tu, W. (ed.) (1996), *Confucian Traditions in East Asian Modernity: Moral Education and Economic Culture in Japan and the Four Mini-Dragons*, Cambridge, MA: Harvard University Press.

Van de Ven, A. (2007), *Engaged Scholarship*, Oxford: Oxford University Press.

Vogel, E. (1979), *Japan as Number One. Lessons for America*, Cambridge, MA: Harvard University Press.

Walvin, J. (1998), *The Quakers: Money and Morals*, London: John Murray.

Weber, M. (1951), *The Religion of China: Confucianism and Taoism*, New York: Free Press.

Weidenbaum, M. and S. Hughes (1996), *The Bamboo Network: How Expatriate Chinese Entrepreneurs are Creating a New Economic Superpower in Asia*, New York: Free Press.

Westney, D.E. (1987), *Imitation and Innovation: The Transfer of Western Organizational Patterns to Meiji Japan*, Cambridge, MA: Harvard University Press.

Westwood, R.I. (1997), 'Harmony and patriarchy: the cultural basis for "paternalistic headship" among overseas Chinese', *Organization Studies*, **18**(3), 445–80.

Whitley, R. (1992), *Business Systems in East Asia: Firms, Markets and Societies*, London: Sage.

Wilkinson, B. (1996), 'Culture, institutions and business in East Asia', *Organization Studies*, **17**(3), 421–47.

Wong, S. (1988), *Emigrant Entrepreneurs*, Hong Kong: Oxford University Press.

Wong, S.L. (1985), 'The Chinese family firm: a model', *British Journal of Sociology*, **36**(1), 58–72.

Yeung, H.W.C. (2002), *Entrepreneurship and the Internationalisation of Asian Firms: An Institutional Perspective*, Cheltenham, UK and Northampton, MA, USA: Edward Elgar.

Yeung, H.W.C. (2004), *Chinese Capitalism in a Global Era: Towards Hybrid Capitalism*, London, UK: Routledge.

Yeung, H.W.C. (2006), 'Change and continuity in Southeast Asian ethnic Chinese business', *Asia Pacific Journal of Management*, **23**(3), 229–54.

Yeung, H.W.C. (2007), 'The dynamics of Southeast Asian Chinese business', in H.W.C. Yeung (ed.), *Handbook of Research on Asian Business*, Cheltenham, UK and Northampton, MA, USA: Edward Elgar.

Yeung, H.W.C., and K. Olds (eds) (2000), *Globalization of Chinese Firms*, New York: Macmillan.

Yoshihara, K. (1988), *The Rise of Ersatz Capitalism in South East Asia*, Singapore: Oxford University Press.
Yu, M. (2002), 'The Taiping rebellion: a military assessment of revolution and counter revolution', in D.A. Graff and R. Highman (eds), *A Military History of China*, Boulder, CO: Westview Press, pp. 135–52.
Zald, M.N. (1996), 'More fragmentation? Unfinished business in linking the social sciences and the humanities', *Administrative Science Quarterly*, **41**(2), 251–61.

Index